REFERENCE

INTERNATIONAL EDUCATION

VOLUME 1

INTERNATIONAL EDUCATION

AN ENCYCLOPEDIA OF CONTEMPORARY ISSUES AND SYSTEMS

VOLUME 1

EDITED BY

DANIEL NESS
AND CHIA-LING LIN

M.E.Sharpe
Armonk, New York
London, England

Library of Congress Cataloging-in-Publication Data

International education : an encyclopedia of contemporary issues and systems / edited by
Daniel Ness and Chia-ling Lin.
    p. cm.
  Includes bibliographical references and index.
  ISBN 978-0-7656-2049-1 (hardcover : alk. paper) 1. Education—Encyclopedias. I. Ness,
Daniel, 1966– II. Lin, Chia-ling.

LB15.I565 2012   vol.1
370.3—dc23   2012031129

Printed and bound in the United States

The paper used in this publication meets the minimum requirements of
American National Standard for Information Sciences—Permanence of
Paper for Printed Library Materials,
ANSI Z 39.48.1984.

EB (c) 10 9 8 7 6 5 4 3 2 1

CONTENTS

VOLUME 2

Editors

Daniel Ness
CERTA Education Research Corp.

Chia-ling Lin
Nassau Community College

Board of Advisors

Stephen J. Farenga
CERTA Education Research Corp.

Hsiu-Zu Ho
*University of California,
Santa Barbara*

Bonnie Johnson
CERTA Education Research Corp.

Gary Natriello
Columbia University

Keiichi Ogawa
Kobe University, Japan

William F. Pinar
*University of British Columbia,
Canada*

Mie Shigemitsu
*Osaka University of Economics,
Japan*

Contributors

Emad Alfar
Nassau Community College

Lava Deo Awasthi
Ministry of Education, Nepal

Gideon Ben-Dror
*Deputy Director General, Israel
Ministry of Education*

Angela Blaver
Kennesaw State University

Alma S. Boutin-Martinez
*University of California,
Santa Barbara*

James R. Campbell
St. John's University

Chang Jia-chung
Kobe University, Japan

Wei-Wen Chen
University of Macau, China

Chia-Jung Chung
*California State University,
Sacramento*

Velta Clarke
*State University of New York,
The College at Old Westbury*

Mariana Coolican
Kobe University, Japan

Daniel Doerger
Northern Kentucky University

Betty C. Eng
City University of Hong Kong

Miloni Gandhi
University of Southern California

Jaesook Gilbert
Northern Kentucky University

Lynette D. Glasman
*University of California,
Santa Barbara*

Naftaly S. Glasman
*University of California,
Santa Barbara*

Kumi Hashimoto
*University of California,
Santa Barbara*

Vishna A. Herrity
*University of California,
Santa Barbara*

Piljoo Paulin Kang
*California State University,
Northridge*

Yuto Kitamura
Sophia University, Japan

Ravy S. Lao
*University of California,
Santa Barbara*

Isaac Larison
Northern Kentucky University

Emily Thao Tien Le
*University of California,
Los Angeles*

Jin Sook Lee
*University of California,
Santa Barbara*

Jing Lei
Syracuse University

Amy Lewis
The University of Hong Kong

Sun Ah Lim
*University of California,
Santa Barbara*

Charles Lin
Independent Scholar

Roseanne Macias
*University of California,
Santa Barbara*

Annette Mahoney
*Hunter College, The City
University of New York*

Rebeca Mireles-Rios
*University of California,
Santa Barbara*

Mavel Moreno
*University of California,
Santa Barbara*

Julie Thuy Nguyen
*University of California,
Santa Barbara*

Sharon Anne O'Connor-Petruso
*Brooklyn College, The City
University of New York*

Yukari Okamoto
*University of California,
Santa Barbara*

Jessica Phillips
*University of California,
Santa Barbara*

Evelyn M. Plaice
*University of New Brunswick,
Canada*

Yvonne Quintanilla
Northern Kentucky University

Vivian Lee Rhone
*University of California,
Santa Barbara*

Barbara Rosenfeld
*Brooklyn College, The City
University of New York*

Eric Rowley
Northern Kentucky University

Zohra Saed
*Baruch College, The City
University of New York*

Cheri Scripter
*University of California,
Santa Barbara*

Satoko Shao-Kobayashi
*California State University,
Northridge*

Suzanne Soled
Northern Kentucky University

Rassamichanh Souryasack
*University of California,
Santa Barbara*

John Stewart
*University of New Brunswick,
Canada*

Mimi Tao
*University of California,
Santa Barbara*

Charlene Bumanglag Tomas
University of Hawaii

Connie Nguyen Tran
*University of California,
Santa Barbara*

Shivali Tukdeo
*National Institute of Advanced
Studies, Bangalore, India*

Yasuo Uchida
Doshisha University, Japan

Marilyn Verna
Independent Scholar

Mian Wang
*University of California,
Santa Barbara*

Eva Wong
College of William and Mary

Rose Wong
*University of California,
Santa Barbara*

FOREWORD BY GARY NATRIELLO

With the accelerating growth in the production and distribution of knowledge from research in all forms and formats, there has never been a greater need for comprehensive, high-quality reference works that provide the essential orientation to fields of knowledge. So it is that this new *International Education: An Encyclopedia of Contemporary Issues and Systems* arrives at just the right time to sketch out the landscape for the intersection of two very broad fields. The field of international education and the field of human development both represent the work of countless scholars tackling an incredibly wide range of issues. The *Encyclopedia* turns the challenge of covering this extensive territory in each field into an advantage by using each field as a lens through which to view the other.

The editors utilize three strategies in the design of the volume to create a truly international perspective on major themes in the field of education. First, the division of the *Encyclopedia* into two major parts ensures substantial coverage of key topics. Part I provides a set of entries on major topics in education that are particularly salient in an international context. The entries in this section provide a foundational perspective; they might well stand on their own as contributions to an international understanding of key issues in education. Part II includes entries for the nations of the world, organized by major regions. This strategy of including both parts in the same volume makes readily available both essays on key topics in education and essays on the educational policies and practices of the nation-states of the world.

A second strategy evident in the design of the volume further strengthens the international perspective on education. Each part is organized to take advantage of the intersection of educational issues and an international perspective. The eight major sections in Part I are included for their potential to highlight the international dimensions of critical topics in education. The section on sociopolitical and cultural issues hosts entries on topics such as children's rights, physical and mental health, and poverty, all topics that are enriched when placed in an international educational context. The section on gender taps into widely acknowledged gender differences at various developmental stages and how they relate to education in terms of achievement, access, and opportunities. The sections on formal and informal education examine the levels of formal schooling across the globe as well as the state of nonschool educational institutions such as museums, libraries, and the workplace. A section on curriculum considers the interaction between content areas and cultural contexts. Basic areas in intellectual and motor development are covered by entries in a sixth section. The seventh section takes on the topic of technology in education as it operates across the globe. Finally, the eighth section considers institutions with a global reach that provide opportunities for the development, promotion, and support of education. Each of these sections in Part I is defined to highlight international aspects.

While international dimensions are implicit in the organization of sections in Part I, they are explicit in the sections in Part II. The eight sections in Part II represent major regions of the world. Each section provides a set of entries on the nations in the region. This third strategy offers a breadth that would be difficult to realize in any other way as the reader can find an essay on each of the nation-states.

The interweaving of topics in education and international perspectives inherent in the structure of the overall volume, as well as in the organization of the sections in each major part, is further reinforced by the approach taken in each individual entry. The entries in Part I address their topics in an international frame. Conversely, each entry in Part II explicitly discusses the educational environment, policies, and practices currently operating.

The organization of this volume offers readers an intriguing experience that is rare for a standard reference work such as an encyclopedia. Although it is possible to access the material much like any other encyclopedia, one entry at a time, it is also possible to access material as in a database or a matrix of information, with the entries of Part I on one axis and those of Part II on the other axis. With this configuration in mind, a reader can begin with a topic in Part I and then move to an entry for a particular nation-state in Part II to see how it plays out in specific policies and practices. Alternately, a reader can begin with the entry for a nation-state in Part II, identify an element of educational policy, and then turn to a related entry in Part I. The overall effect is to allow the very traditional form of the encyclopedia to be accessed in the thoroughly contemporary style of a database.

ACKNOWLEDGMENTS

International Education: An Encyclopedia of Contemporary Issues and Systems is a timely reference given the turbulent themes—children in poverty, standards, school finance, and high-stakes testing to name only a few—that are jeopardizing educational equality worldwide. This work would have never come to fruition without the support and assistance of numerous individuals.

We thank our professor and mentor, Gary Natriello at Columbia University, who provided us with the nascent ideas for the need of a reference in international education. Gary was the first to demonstrate growing trends in global education, particularly that of the Internet—a trend that has drastically altered the enterprise in terms of curriculum, instruction, assessment, and academic publishing. We are also grateful to William F. Pinar at the University of British Columbia, for his unswerving dedication in challenging the very institutions that stymie educational progress and free thinking in international curriculum. These volumes were organized in a manner that articulates Bill's ideas, which emphasize the need for more democratic approaches to schooling throughout the world. We wish to thank the remaining members of our Advisory Board—Stephen J. Farenga, Hsiu-Zu Ho, Bonnie Johnson, Keiichi Ogawa, and Mie Shigemitsu—for their contributions in making this work a reality. Further, we gratefully acknowledge the expertise of the entry authors and remaining section editors, and especially appreciate their patience in the process of the encyclopedia's publication.

Also, the personnel at M.E. Sharpe are to be commended for their assistance in the progress of the work at each junction. We thank Jim Ciment and Todd Hallman for their encouragement in the project as a whole. We also are grateful to Laurie Lieb for her scrupulous reading of the text, ensuring that every word or phrase suits the prose that fits references of this type. Henrietta Toth was instrumental as the liaison between the authors and editors and Sharpe personnel. Cathy Prisco has played a vital role in the production of these volumes. The contents herein would not nearly be at their level of accuracy, precision, and attention to detail were it not for Cathy's critical and reliable support.

Finally, we wish to thank Eric, a very patient nine-year-old boy, who has been asking for some time when the encyclopedia project would be completed. He can now be assured in knowing that the final product is now in print.

INTRODUCTION

As a global society, to what extent has the world reached education access for all? What is the status of formal instruction in countries that have more than 50 percent of their population living in poverty? How do females compare with males in literacy acquisition and mathematical competency in the context of a particular world region? Why do certain countries place more emphasis on child labor and less emphasis on literacy and other forms of content and technological knowledge? In answering these and other questions, *International Education: An Encyclopedia of Contemporary Issues and Systems* identifies the intersection between education throughout the world and how human initiative and inventiveness influences it.

Correlation vs. Causation: Why Is Education Important to Society?

Humans' overall proclivity for finding access to information and education almost seems inherently natural. People's seemingly organic and intrinsic desire to be formally educated is connected with associations we make with education and access to schooling. To be sure, we associate formal education with success, higher standards of living, greater longevity, sustainability, fame and recognition, and access to greater levels of resources. A premise of this encyclopedia is that, in general, countries with strong educational infrastructures have high levels of success, defined by a high gross national product as well as high numbers of citizens entering the workforce and earning adequate wages to support themselves and their families. But one of the most fascinating outcomes of all these associations is simply that they are just associations. In other words,

education is not causal; it neither influences nor determines one's success, wages, reputation, access to health care, or, for that matter, longevity. There is no causal relationship between education and financial or related success. A strong system of education in a particular country is not a cause for a strong (or weak) economy or financial stability. However, a strong system of education is correlated with a country's overall economy. That is, our premise is based on many interesting correlations; causation is not a factor. Indeed, the more educated a person is, the greater the chances that person will earn more income, have more resources available, and even live longer. In short, education is associated with better lifestyles; it does not cause them.

Due to the putative relationship between education, success, and overall positive outcomes, most, but by no means all, societies, especially within the last two centuries, have generally placed high premiums on formal schooling. This link between education and success has enormous ramifications for the political and economic directions of countries throughout the world. It might be helpful to understand and more importantly appreciate this correlation with an illustrative example: Data suggest that children who live in households that own many books tend to perform better in school than children who live in households with few or no books. This correlation is telling in that a book, by its very nature, cannot change behavior. Books, however, are rather seen as tools within an environment so that individuals can play an active role by reading and understanding the content within the book's covers. By virtue of the fact that books serve as tools that provide content, the strong relationship between books and success provides an analogue for other available contexts, such as technologies (e.g., electronic hardware and software, the Internet, calculators, and the like) and success.

Another important example of the correlation of education to success is the large corpus of research that shows a link between the education of girls and women and the birthrate. In other words, the greater the educational opportunities for the female population of a given country or region, the fewer the number of children born and, hence, the lower the birthrate. More specifically, from the perspective of global education—taking into account the educational systems of developing countries—women who reach higher educational levels tend to bear fewer children. Again, this is a correlation and not a causal relationship. Education is only a predictor of what will happen with the birthrate when more women have access to formal schooling; it does not cause women to have fewer children. We can generalize, then, that educational access is correlated to many positive outcomes. These volumes suggest numerous strong relationships between educational access and overall success and well-being.

Importance of Education for a Global Democracy

Nations in all corners of the globe are quickly transforming from industrial and postindustrial societies to ones with elaborate Information Age–based systems. As a result, the topic of global education has never been as important as it is today.

Most demographers and statisticians argue that income level is the most important variable that demonstrates global social disparity. Income level and demographic data provided by the World Bank help put our world of 7 billion—and growing!—into perspective. There are roughly 1 billion people in the world today whose per capita income is below the equivalent of $995. We refer to this group as "1." The overwhelming majority of the population in "1" live in most countries of sub-Saharan Africa and in a number of countries in South Asia (e.g., Burma, Laos, and Cambodia) and Central Asia (e.g., Afghanistan). This population lives in abject poverty for the most part. Next, approximately 4 billion people, the overwhelming majority of the world's population, have a per capita income between $996 and $3,945. This group is "2." Most people in this income bracket

live in various countries of sub-Saharan Africa, Asia (e.g., Iraq, Syria, India, Indonesia, Vietnam, Thailand, the Philippines, and China), Eastern Europe (e.g., Ukraine, Georgia, and Moldova), and parts of Central and South America. Then there is group "3," about 1 billion people whose income bracket falls between $3,946 and $12,195. These people live primarily in Russia, most countries of Eastern Europe, Western Asia (e.g., Turkey, Jordan, and Lebanon), South Africa, Malaysia, most countries in South America, and Mexico. And finally, there is group "4," also about 1 billion people whose per capita income is $12,196 or more. People in this category live in the United States, Central and Western Europe, Israel, South Korea, Japan, Australia, and New Zealand.

Educational opportunity is an important predictor of income level. It is also highly correlated with quality of health care and both industrial and technological resources. In turn, income level is an accurate predictor of life expectancy throughout the world. Countries in group "1" tend to have the lowest life expectancy, with an average of 59 years, while those of group "2" have the second lowest, about 68 years. Those of group "3" have an average life expectancy of about 72 years, and group "4" countries tend to have the highest life expectancies, about 80 years. Similarly, these levels of income are generally accurate in predicting the number of deaths under age five as well as the number of deaths caused by disease—group "1" countries having the highest number of deaths and group "4" having the least. Finally, income level is an excellent predictor of rates of literacy and the number of years of education in a given country. In these cases, literacy rates are lowest in group "1" countries and highest in group "4" countries. The Figure on page xvii demonstrates how these and other factors are interrelated—most notably, how a high-quality education can make a difference not only in success in the workforce, but also in health and living conditions. Again, the data presented demonstrate numerous correlations between educational access and a better, healthier life.

One possible causal factor that can affect educational access throughout the world is political transition. Political instability generally contributes to a substandard educational system and, therefore, to limited access to formal schooling, especially for women and minority populations. Formal education for an entire nation that involves critical thinking as

Figure: **Global Demographical Data Based on Income Level**

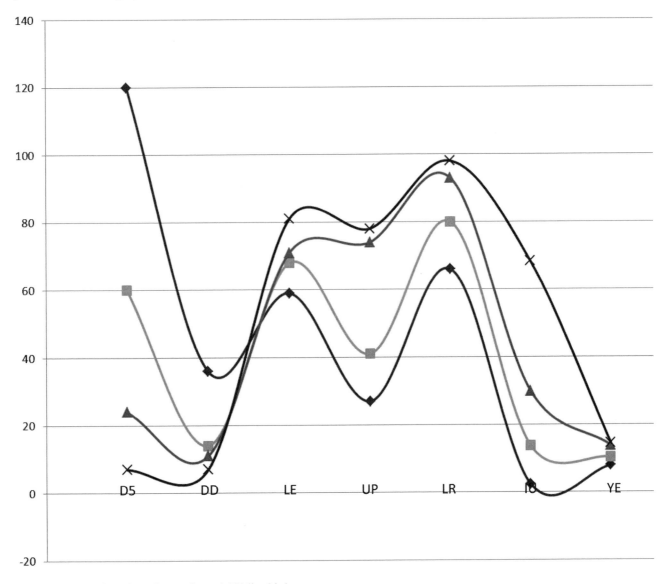

D5 = number of deaths under age 5, per 1,000 live births
DD = percent of deaths caused by disease
LE = life expectancy by age
UP = percent of urban population
LR = literacy rate
IU = Internet use per 100 people
YE = number of years of education

Sources: Population Reference Bureau, www.prb.org; World Bank Education Statistics, www.worldbank.org.

part of the curriculum can have an equalizing effect that can possibly lead to positive outcomes and a successful workforce. It is useful, then, to view education as a means to a successful democratic society. This generalization is based on more than two centuries of events that changed the course of education throughout the world. To be sure, the adverse conditions that led to the overthrow of the French monarchy in 1791 paved the way toward compulsory schooling for both males and females in the 1830s. Likewise, the formation of the fledgling American republic in the 1780s and the movement to abolish slavery in the first half of the nineteenth century served as catalysts for public education in the United States. In fact, since World War II, numerous democratically turned authoritarian regimes in Central and South America, Africa, and parts of Asia modified their education systems, which, in turn, benefited the people of those countries.

Democracy and formal education can be viewed as a symbiotic relationship—not only do democratic movements provide compulsory systems of education that allow an entire population to flourish; education systems, in and of themselves, serve as the lifelines of their countries. Indeed, people who are scientifically literate can question the motives and intentions of politicians and lawmakers. They can decide on the most productive way to solve social inequities. Moreover, a scientifically literate society provides a favorable setting for ongoing research that may lead to new discoveries or uses of new medicines and alternative or renewable energies that can potentially have a positive influence on the environment.

Moreover, there is a rapidly growing emphasis in schools of education and the social sciences in general on the international panorama with regard to teaching, learning, and educational development. To be sure, academic departments that originally focused their attention on issues like English as a Second Language (ESL), formal mathematics teaching methods, sociology of education, and linguistics and education are currently broadening their missions, restructuring in order to examine the role of education from an international and transcultural perspective. Despite the widespread interest in education on the international front, there is no broad chronicled reference work on the state of education from an international perspective for the public at large. All we have with regard to international education are specialized reference works, which emphasize specific educational issues.

Intended Audience

Given the rising attention accorded to international and transcultural education, as well as the rapidly changing climate of international education in today's Information Age, *International Education: An Encyclopedia of Contemporary Issues and Systems* is intended for a wide-ranging readership. In particular, this volume serves as an invaluable reference source for students in high school, college, or the university, not only for general themes in international education,

but as a resource in other social science fields. The encyclopedia will also be valuable to students in master's and doctoral programs as a quick reference tool. As an encyclopedia highlighting the global changes in most academic specializations, personnel associated with departments of education, psychology, sociology, anthropology, political science, geography, linguistics, history, mathematics, and most of the natural sciences will find this book a useful resource. Moreover, this book will serve as an excellent reference tool for educational administrators and practitioners. It will also be a valuable resource for education libraries and university and public libraries throughout the world.

How to Use This Encyclopedia

International Education: An Encyclopedia of Contemporary Issues and Systems is a thorough examination of international education that showcases seminal concepts in education from an international perspective as well as the inner workings of educational systems in 175 countries. The work is divided into two parts. Each part is divided into sections that emphasize important themes of education from a global perspective.

Part I includes eight sections that range in size from five to eleven entries. Section 1, "Sociopolitical and Cultural Issues in Education," emphasizes the importance of diversity as a key component of successful educational systems. Issues include discrimination, children's rights, children's health, parenting, drugs and alcohol, poverty, child labor, violence, and war. Section 2, "Gender and Education," focuses on the role of gender in education worldwide. Issues include achievement, access, and cognitive similarities and differences according to gender. "Formal Education" is the theme of section 3. Entries in this section examine the roles of curriculum, instruction, and assessment in global education, as well as different education levels. Section 3 also includes discussion of international comparisons, accreditation and licensure, and teacher preparation around the world. "Informal Education," the fourth section, follows with a focus on experiential education, expert-novice situations, the role of learning in nontraditional settings (e.g., home, museums, and libraries), and learning at work. The fifth section, "Content, Curriculum, and Resources," discusses the roles of content from various cultural perspectives. Entries in this section focus on the topics of curriculum history, ethnomathematics, ethnoscience, the arts and humanities, and the role of worker education and unions. "Intellectual and Motor Development" is the focus of Section 6. Issues in this section include linguistic development, spatial and quantitative development, psychomotor development, and cognition from an international perspective. Section 7, "Technologies and Global Education," discusses the frequent and all-encompassing changes occurring in global technology. Of primary concern are roles of electronic and asynchronous learning, distance learning, the Internet, technology as it relates to poverty, technology and the curriculum, and the future of technology as a global educational initiative. Section 8, the final section of Part I, concerns the role of educational institutions. Titled "Institutions of Education Throughout the World," the section begins with an overview of global monetary agencies—specifically those that provide educational opportunities for children and adolescent populations in war-torn nations or those with high poverty rates. Other topics in Section 8 include global curriculum organizations, global health and well-being organizations, educational activist organizations, and teachers colleges.

Part II of the encyclopedia covers the history, political role, curriculum, and economic status of the educational systems in almost all of the world's countries. Part II is divided into sections, each containing between four and 50 entries and covering a particular world region. After a brief introduction to each country, each entry discusses the nation's educational system; the curriculum, instruction, and assessment; teacher education; informal education practices; system economics; and future prospects.

1. Introduction. The introduction to each entry consists of a brief history and overview of the country's political and sociological climate, two factors that often serve as indicators of the overall educational values of its citizens.

2. Educational System. Information in this area differs from entry to entry, depending on each country's own system. This section may include an introduction and then go on to discuss precompulsory and compulsory education (including history, development, and current and future prospects) and post-

compulsory education (also including history, development, and current and future prospects). We use "compulsory education" as a general term referring to education as a requirement for citizens between certain ages. For example, in the United States, students are generally (but not always) required to attend school from about five to 17 or 18 years of age. Precompulsory education represents formal or informal educational practice prior to mandatory education. In the United States, this phase is generally designated as "early childhood education." Postcompulsory education represents formal or informal educational practice beyond compulsory education. In most postindustrial countries and a number of developing countries, students who complete their mandatory education may decide to attend the college or university. However, this decision is very often determined by the family's socioeconomic status and not by the student's individual desire or volition.

3. Curriculum, Instruction, and Assessment. Discussion of curriculum, instruction, and assessment generally involves the primary branches of intellectual or health-related inquiry: language, mathematics, science, arts and humanities, health education, and social education. Other branches of inquiry that are unique to a given country are also discussed.

4. Teacher Education. The three primary issues discussed here are the length and type of educational background a teacher candidate of any grade level must have in order to teach in the given country; specified content to be mastered by teacher candidates; and accreditation and licensure (if required in the first place). Other issues unique to a given country are also discussed.

5. Informal Education. Issues having to do with informal education include experiential education; expert/novice situations; home, museums, and libraries; learning at work; learning at play; and situated learning.

6. System Economics. Issues having to do with system economics—that is, the revenue that supports a particular country's educational system—include the annual expenditure on

mandatory education; annual expenditure on postcompulsory (and possibly precompulsory) education; and expenditure on teacher education, accreditation, and licensure. Evidence of graft or corruption—if it can be verified—will also be discussed.

7. Future Prospects. Finally, each entry concludes with a discussion of future prospects—namely, the outlook, progress, and expectations of a country's system of education, based on a synthesis of data that provides a general projection of the educational system and possible suggestions for consideration.

The world is encountering a social and educational crossroads—one-seventh of the earth's population lives comfortably while another seventh lives in abject poverty and horrid conditions. Nearly 5 billion people are struggling to escape poverty or earn higher wages in order to obtain more favorable living conditions. Indeed, formal education and schooling mean different things to different people. Given the sweeping changes in systems of education throughout the world, we hope that, in the short term, this work informs readers of important terms and conditions of contemporary education practice. In the long term,

we hope that readers use this reference as a means to further their studies and research in the exciting field of international education.

Daniel Ness and Chia-ling Lin

REFERENCES

Anderson, Lorin W. *International Encyclopedia of Teaching and Teacher Education* (Resources in Education Series). Oxford, UK: Pergamon, 1996.

English, Leona. *International Encyclopedia of Adult Education.* New York: Macmillan, 2005.

Farenga, Stephen J., and Daniel Ness, eds. *Encyclopedia of Education and Human Development.* Armonk, NY: M.E. Sharpe, 2005.

McCulloch, Gary, and David Crook. *The Routledge International Encyclopedia of Education.* New York: Routledge, 2008.

Peterson, Penelope, Eva Baker, and Barry McGaw. *International Encyclopedia of Education.* Boston: Elsevier Science, 2010.

Postlethwaite, T. Neville. *International Encyclopedia of National Systems of Education* (Resources in Education Series). Oxford, UK: Pergamon.

Rosling, Hans, and Zhongxing Zhang. "Health Advocacy with Gapminder Animated Statistics." *Journal of Epidemiology and Global Health* 1:1 (2011): 11–14.

Saha, Lawrence J. *International Encyclopedia of the Sociology of Education* (Resources in Education Series). Oxford, UK: Pergamon, 1997.

TOPICS IN INTERNATIONAL EDUCATION

TOPICS IN INTERNATIONAL EDUCATION: INTRODUCTION

Part I of *International Education: An Encyclopedia of Contemporary Issues and Systems* consists of eight sections that focus on key constructs and issues in international education. These areas of emphasis are: Sociopolitical and Cultural Issues; Gender; Formal Education; Informal Education; Content, Curriculum, and Resources; Intellectual and Motor Development; Technologies and Global Education; and Institutions of Education Throughout the World.

Sociopolitical and Cultural Issues in Education

Few controversial issues in education are as important today as race, social class, and culture and their impact on achieving educational equity. The problem that society faces, however, is that in everyday discourse, these terms are grossly oversimplified and often painted with a very broad stroke—black and white being one of the most common and distorted of the dichotomies (Adams, Bell, and Griffin 1997). Other distorted sociopolitical and cultural categorizations refer to social class differences (e.g., lower class, working class, middle class, and upper class) and levels of so-called intellect (e.g., learning disabled or learning challenged, mainstream or "average," and "gifted"). Aside from oversimplified categorizations, specific terms—for example, "multiculturalism," "multicultural education," "equity," and "diversity"—themselves are used so frequently that their very meanings become distorted as a result of overuse. In addition, their meanings change depending on how they are used in different contexts. This section addresses sociopolitical and cultural issues and challenges facing both formal and informal educational institutions worldwide.

Gender and Education

Gender and Education begins with a discussion of overall gender disparity in institutions of formal education. The second entry—Globalization, Gender, and Education—discusses the increasingly multifaceted phenomenon and process of globalization in local and global contexts and how it impacts gender and education. The process of globalization can create both opportunities and inequalities for all members of society. Unfortunately, women's access to information and communication technologies (ICT)—powerful tools that can bring about economic, political, and social change on a global level—is limited by factors including illiteracy, inequities in terms of social practice, locale, and excessive costs. Increasing women's participation in ICT can yield a range of benefits such as increasing one's earning power, improving one's educational status, enhancing knowledge of health and reproductive issues, promoting greater awareness and interest in political matters, and providing avenues for empowerment, improved status in society, and ultimately an enhanced quality of life. The entry on "Gender and Achievement" discusses various international programs and initiatives that address gender equity worldwide. For example, the United Nations Commission on the Status of Women (CSW), which was established to promote gender equality and the empowerment of women worldwide, meets annually with the United Nations Economic and Social Council to evaluate progress, reaffirm policies, and identify challenges in specific areas and regions. Also considered are various international studies of achievement in mathematics, science, and reading as well as occupation and career aspirations with respect to gender differences—for example, the Trends in International Mathematics and Science Study (TIMSS), the Programme for International Student Assessment (PISA), and the Progress in International Reading Literacy Study (PIRLS). The entry concludes that despite increases in gender parity, improvement in academic achievement for girls, and increased representation in professional fields and civic leadership, female discrimination and underachievement remain prevalent worldwide.

In Educational Access and Opportunities, it is shown that barriers such as poverty, poor health, and social conflict also undermine efforts toward access and opportunities. Worldwide, girls experience greater health risks and insufficient care, with gender biases that favor boys in nutrition and health care acting as a contributing factor. It is noted that although there have been global efforts to make primary school tuition-free, millions of children and their families find the cost of schooling a deterrent. Many developing countries are challenged by inadequate facilities, textbook shortages, and insufficient instructional time and further impacted by rapid urbanization and the increased spread of certain diseases. The final entry, Gendered Mind, focuses on the research on gender differences in the brain, cognition, intellectual styles, and ways of knowing. The entry discusses recent advances in imaging technologies and provides evidence that shows the anatomical, chemical, and functional differences between the male and female brains and gender differences in brain lateralization as well as in specific areas of the brain affecting abilities, such as navigation and language. The research examining cognitive differences between males and females refines gender differences in spatial differences to specific tasks on mental rotation, spatial perception, and spatial visualization. Such findings vary across nations, with the United States samples yielding some of the greatest gender differences and China yielding some of the least. Despite reliable gender differences found, there is considerable individual variation within the gender groups.

Formal Education

Formal education is the process that takes place when a society undertakes to school its population in organized settings and environments known as schools that practice systematized methods of instruction for delivering knowledge and information, particularly in the form of disciplines—most notably, language and literacy and mathematics. It includes the educational system that is hierarchically structured from elementary school through the university level in general or specialized academic studies and results in the awarding of diplomas. Despite numerous disparities from one country to another, there seems to be a fairly consistent pattern of formal schooling. There is usually a program of compulsory schooling as soon as the child reaches the age of five or six (sometimes older). Depending on the country, this program continues on to secondary education, which is also compulsory in most school systems. Upon graduation, students may have an option to continue in a tertiary education system (college or university education), enter a professional trade, or simply attempt to find employment in an entry-level position.

It is important to note the distinction between the differences among countries in terms of the number of hours per day that students attend school and, perhaps more importantly, the number of hours teachers spend teaching students. In short, only a fraction of the school day in most classroom settings throughout the world is devoted to actual instructional time. For example, in any typical day, there might be seven "instructional" periods, and any two periods will often have a 10-minute interval between each. These intervals total approximately one hour of the entire school day. Moreover, students spend between 15 minutes to an hour each day for lunch, an additional 45 minutes to an hour for study or library time, and perhaps an additional hour for free play, recess, or non-instructional sports and fitness. So, in a seven-hour school day, only half of this time might be allotted to actual instructional time.

Given the diversity of schooling practices in all countries worldwide, there is no standard number of hours of schooling per day for any one country. Nevertheless, it is possible to estimate the number of hours of schooling per day based on samples of schools in different regions within a particular country. The table shows the approximate number of teaching (i.e., instructional) hours when compared to the number of hours of schooling per day and the average number of days per academic year for a list of 20 countries. East Asian countries with advanced economies, such as Japan and Taiwan, average eight to nine hours of schooling per day, yet the average number of hours teachers are instructing their students is less than half that time. Similarly, Israel, where students spend the same approximate number of hours per day in school, provides an average 2.75 hours of actual daily instruction. Indonesia has the lowest approximate number of hours of schooling per day. The number of hours of daily instruction is significantly higher in the United States, Australia, and Argentina when compared with the number of daily instructional hours of other countries on the list. It is also noteworthy to compare the differences among countries in terms of the standard number of days of school per calendar year. Indonesia has the greatest number of school days per calendar year. North and South Korea are not far behind. Among the list, the United States and Turkey each have 180 days of school per academic year, while Russia has the least number of academic school days (171 in total) per year. In addition, it should be noted that the average number of hours of daily instruction seems to be a somewhat convincing indicator of academic success (as indicated by PISA scores in reading, mathematics, and science). Finland, Korea, Germany, Japan, and Taiwan have significantly low average hours of daily instruction and high average scores in reading, mathematics, and science proficiency. However, this is by no means consistent given that numerous countries with relatively few hours of daily instruction show poor standing in terms of scores in language and mathematics ability (see Table on page 6).

The first three entries in this section provide an overview of how formal education is organized according to the necessary tools of formal education: curriculum, instruction, and assessment. The essential question about curriculum has to do with what students of a given demographic will study and learn in order to function and compete in society. Questions considered in this entry are the following: What should students within a particular cultural or societal setting learn? What in particular does this society value? Do these values affect the content that students will be expected to learn? Instruction refers to the medium by which a population receives what it learns. The entry on instruction outlines the essential methods of delivery of content that teachers implement in conducting instruction. Assessment refers to how society will determine the point at which students within this demographic will have achieved the necessary education they need in order to succeed in society.

The next four entries discuss the levels of education that have become more or less standardized over the last century—early childhood education, primary education, secondary education, and higher or tertiary education. The next entry discusses the role of international comparisons—a phenomenon that has begun only recently. It is also important to discuss the role of educational accrediting bodies—institutions that seem to have cast very large webs on schooling institutions throughout the world. Finally, the last entry of the section investigates the role of teacher preparation throughout the world.

It is important to note, however, that education in the new century is becoming increasingly interdisciplinary. In addition, the lines of separation between the notions of primary education, secondary education, and tertiary education are becoming finer and finer, almost to the point that colleges and universities and even private organizations are preparing teachers whose skill sets span content levels and age and grade levels as well. Accordingly, separate departments of study for primary education and secondary education are waning in number while the number of integrative departments that emphasize intergenerational schooling (for both children and adults) and content across age levels is increasing.

Informal Education

Informal education involves the lifelong process of learning that is usually initiated by the learner or acquired spontaneously from daily experiences and educational resources in the environment—from learning at home using the Internet and mass media, from family and community members, from work and play, or from the library and museums. Nonformal education refers to any organized and planned educational activity outside the established formal system that is voluntary, supports individual or social learning, has specific educational objectives, and promotes the development of knowledge, skills, values, and attitudes.

This section is comprised of six entries devoted to the field of informal education. Research on learning suggests that the majority of children ages five to 16 spend only 18 percent of their waking hours in a school setting. While school is seen as the primary site of learning, the reality is that a great deal of learning takes place outside of traditional,

Table: **Topics in International Education: Introduction**

Average Number of Hours of Daily Instruction in Comparison to the Average Number of Hours per School Day and Average Number of Days per Academic Year: 20 Postindustrial Countries

Country	Average hours of daily instruction	Average hours per school day	Average number of days per academic year
Israel	2.8	8	208
Finland[a,b,c]	2.9	6	188
Korea, Republic of[a,b,c]	3.1	8	220
Germany[b,c]	3.2	7	193
Russia	3.3	5	167
Turkey	3.3	7	180
Hungary	3.3	6	181
Indonesia	3.5	4	239
United Kingdom (excluding Scotland)[a]	3.6	7	190
Japan[a,b,c]	3.9	8	200
Republic of China[a,b,c]	4.0	8	200
OECD average	4.175	6.8	184
China[e]	4.3	9	175
Korea, Democratic People's Republic of[d]	4.4	8	225
Spain	4.4	7	174
Scotland[a]	4.5	7	190
Mexico	4.7	6	191
Botswana	5.0	6	189
United States[a]	5.9	6	180
Australia[a,b,c]	6.7	6	196
Argentina	6.7	7	171

[a]Ranks among the top 25 countries with the highest average reading scores conducted by the Programme of International Student Assessment (PISA).

[b]Ranks among the top 25 countries with the highest average mathematics scores conducted by PISA.

[c]Ranks among the top 25 countries with the highest average science scores conducted by PISA.

[d]Country not affiliated with PISA.

[e]Parts of China scored within the top 10 regions of the world in terms of reading, mathematics, and science. These regions are Shanghai, Hong Kong, and Macao.

Sources:
Organization for Economic Cooperation and Development (OECD). *Education at a Glance 2011: OECD Indicators.* Paris: OECD Publishing, 2011.
World Bank Education Statistics, 2011. www.worldbank.org

formal educational institutions in informal social and cultural contexts. While the value of school learning is supported by an extensive body of research and is not to be minimized, Lauren Resnick (1987) posits that in-school learning tends to be solitary, based in symbols and the abstract, and unrelated to real-world experiences. Out-of-school learning in informal education contexts involves the completion of intellectual or physical tasks using real elements, which promotes more meaningful learning. Learners in informal settings are intrinsically motivated to develop personal meaning from the learning experience, which may have more significance in the workplace and for a country's overall economy than memorizing facts or scoring high on assessment instruments. Societies today are being transformed into nations of lifelong learners supported by an extensive network of organizations and media, including museums, science centers, libraries, television, film, books, and the Internet, which promotes free-choice learning—learning based upon an individual's needs and interests in science and technology. These free-choice learning institutions are developing a more prominent role in providing science and other learning opportunities worldwide. With the increased use of the Internet, children and adults spend tremendous amounts of time learning not only in school, but at home, in the library, on the job, and during all hours of the day and night, guided by their personal interests.

Content, Curriculum, and Resources

The section on global content and curriculum is based on curriculum-based themes that occur throughout the world. The opening entry, Curriculum in Education from a Historical Perspective, treats the subject of curriculum through a historical lens. The second entry, Ethnomathematics, identifies numerous mathematical thinking practices from various cultural perspectives. Mathematical discoveries have come about as a result of the social and economic needs of a particular society. In some cases, mathematical discoveries were derived from serendipitous events that led to the discoveries themselves. In other cases, they were the result of the examination of artistic and aesthetic endeavors, as was the case, in part, with *sona* sand drawings from the Kalahari Desert region of southern Africa. The third entry, Ethnoscience, introduces similar strands of scientific understandings through different cultural and historical perspectives. The fourth entry examines the role of arts and humanities from various cultural and worldly perspectives—not simply so-called Western standpoints. The final entry is on informal curriculum and the growing trend of education for emancipation, particularly as it relates to worker education.

Intellectual and Motor Development

In common discourse, it is believed by both education experts and the general public that there are two primary functions of formal schooling: socialization and academic achievement. The present section focuses on the foundations of the second of these functions—namely, the effect of cognition and development on formal schooling. Despite the level of efficacy of any formal schooling system, it is clear that a large subset of academic achievement is based on theoretical frameworks and research programs in the fields of intellectual development—also referred to in this section as cognitive development—and motor development.

Cognitive development is studied so that it is possible to learn more about what people know about the world. This is important for a number of reasons. First, our understanding of cognitive development has the capability to contribute to finding optimal methods for advancing student knowledge in schools—regardless of where they are located in the world. The rationale behind this idea is that the more teachers and researchers know about cognition in infancy, early childhood, childhood, and adolescence, the better prepared schools will be to accommodate student needs in terms of academic achievement. Second, cognitive development research seems to be intertwined with the whole concept of the so-called Information Age, the present period that has been differentiated from earlier periods—such as the Industrial Age—when students went to school primarily to learn skills related to blue-collar occupations. The present Information Age, in contrast, is highlighted by the emphasis on the Internet and technology in the workforce. This emphasis is predicated on the idea that the acquisition of information is privileged and that the primary way to obtaining information is through formal schooling. Thus, one of the key questions for many researchers in the areas of psychology and education has to do with the ways in which humans either possess or acquire knowledge. Accordingly, cognitive science and neuroscience have been important fields of study in education. Finally, cognitive development research is reaching new heights in that the current study of human knowledge intersects with new research on brain function and behavior. In particular, researchers are asking whether mind (i.e., the construct for thinking) and brain (i.e., the organic material that all humans, and nonhumans, possess within the skull cavity) work in tandem or are perhaps one and the same when it comes to cognition. A significant part (but by no means all) of what present-day researchers examine in terms of intellectual development emanates from the theories of Jean Piaget and his four-stage developmental framework. More recently, there has been a good deal of emphasis on the sociocultural theories of Lev Vygotsky, who essentially proposed a Marxist psychological framework for human and cognitive development. Despite the overwhelming impact of Piaget's work in the fields of psychology and education in the United States during the latter half of the twentieth century, specialists in cognitive science since Piaget have made numerous inroads in our understanding of how children and adolescents develop their knowledge of the world. A number of these specialists focus on what Piaget overlooked (e.g., the advanced cognitive abilities of infants), what he possibly overemphasized (such as the strong role that developmental stages played in his work), and also on positions with which Piaget may have disagreed (such as the role of heritability or a nativist perspective in cognitive development). Experts in cognitive science and development have also reconsidered the role of social psychology as well as the brain-based underpinnings of cognition.

One important common thread that links intellectual and cognitive development with motor development is that both domains involve the use of the brain and nervous system. This section is devoted to the ways in which humans develop from an intellectual and motor perspective. The present section is divided into six entries, which examine the topics of intellectual and motor development in light of new findings from a global perspective, not solely from purely Western methodologies.

Technologies and Global Education

Technology and Global Education details the history and development of the Internet, the effects of Web 2.0 and new and emerging technologies, and their transformational impact on how people teach and learn in educational systems worldwide. This section also discusses the plight of individuals lacking access to Information Age technological infrastructures and current international programs designed to bridge the Digital Divide. A repeated theme throughout this section is the chameleonic role of educational technology, the unforeseen power of new and emerging technologies, the changing role of both teachers and learners in all educational systems, and the quest by educational, government, and business leaders worldwide to produce work-ready citizens for the global economy.

The first entry, The History and Development of Technology Education, details the evolution of educational technology from a global perspective over the past 60 years and its symbiotic growth with the second generation of the Internet, Web 2.0. In the second entry, the three developmental perspectives of educational technology and the critical role of each nation's ed tech policies and implementation of information and communication technologies are discussed. Concrete examples of ed tech policies and ICT implementation from the United States of America, the European Commission, and Asia are provided. The entry closes with the current challenges facing educational technology worldwide and future implications.

The third entry, Synchronous and Asynchronous E-Learning, provides a comprehensive description of the various electronic communication tools, classified according to synchronous and asynchronous delivery, which has morphed worldwide into both the onsite and offsite educational systems. The impact of Web 2.0 is discussed and specific examples and projects are provided for each electronic communication tool. The entry closes with the positive and negative aspects of electronic synchronous and asynchronous learning and the crucial components needed for successful e-learning.

The next entry, The Internet, traces the development and history of the Internet in the United States of America from the early 1960s to current electronic learning (e-learning) and usage worldwide. Emphasis is on the changing role of technology education, the inclusion of business and government leaders to foster an internationally competent workforce, and current e-learning international programs and projects.

Next comes the entry titled Technology in Rich and Poor Countries, which traces the powerful and ubiquitous role technology plays in the development of each country's economic, cultural, and political standing and the Global Age. Emphasis is on the manner in which globalization benefits primarily developed countries. Strategies for helping underdeveloped nations transform themselves into globally competitive nations are provided.

The following entry, Technology and the Curriculum, highlights the development and changing role and definitions of computer technology in the classroom. The restructuring of education due to technology, strategies to integrate the computer and technology into the classroom, and the necessity for implementing a technology plan are discussed. Fundamental steps and barriers to technology integration and new technologies are also discussed. This section closes with Future of Technology, which highlights the unprecedented growth of technology, its transformational effect on education and economics worldwide, and current implementations, trends, and challenges faced by a variety of countries. Also described are the needs of both teacher and student in technology-infused learning environments, the need to reduce technology costs, and the necessity to provide a universal design that facilitates web-based language translation tools and makes digital resources available to everyone.

Institutions of Education Throughout the World

This section discusses the roles of educational institutions other than preprimary, primary, secondary, and tertiary establishments. First, global monetary agencies such as the World Bank, the Asia Development Bank, and the International Monetary Fund are considered. These organizations are most often nongovernmental agencies that support educational systems in developing countries, most notably, fledgling educational systems in sub-Saharan African nations, Central and South American nations, and South Asian nations. In addition to providing financial and material support, global monetary agencies interact with the governments of these countries in order to develop educational systems that use best-practice techniques in preparing youth for the workforce.

The next subject discussed in this section is global curriculum organizations. These organizations are essential in developing curricula for a given educational system that adhere to the traditions as well as present-day needs of a particular society. For example, nations that are well-equipped in information and communication technologies may be unable to provide educational access for different population groups. Curriculum organizations tend to the needs of various systems that may lack certain content areas. These organizations emphasize the need for dialogue as the key component for change in methodologies of both formal and informal learning.

The entry that follows concerns the role of education on people's health and well-being. Research suggests that there exists a positive correlation between economic growth and technological advancement, on the one hand, and life expectancy on the other. It has also been shown that global changes have contributed to adverse outcomes—for example, migrations as a result of political instability and epidemics as it relates to the growth of certain diseases. It should be clear, then, that the status of a country's educational system seems to be an indication of both positive and negative outcomes. As indicated in the entry on global health and well-being, a large gap exists between the poorest countries and the most affluent ones. As will be shown, the near elimination of common diseases of the past, such as polio and certain forms of malaria, has been offset by the development of relatively new ones, such as HIV/AIDS.

Following the entry on global health organizations is a discussion of educational activist organizations. The primary goal of these organizations is to advocate for a given demographic in terms of dialogue among policy makers about education and other related social issues. Organizations of this type include teachers' unions, certain philanthropic foundations, nongovernmental organizations, private voluntary organizations, student organizations, and nonprofit organizations. Educational activist organizations have been increasingly assaulted by for-profit and right-wing political groups throughout the world that consider these organizations threatening to their own existence.

The last two entries in this section have to do with teachers colleges and their pivotal role and influence in the development of global education initiatives. The initial role of teachers colleges, particularly in the United States, was to prepare for a future society that educates its entire people and not a privileged few. Although this agenda has shown progress, especially during the twentieth century, it has been stifled in recent years by conservative politicians who have made repeated attempts to usurp financial resources from educational unions in order to serve the interests of for-profit institutions.

Vishna A. Herrity, Hsiu-Zu Ho, Chia-ling Lin, Daniel Ness, Sharon O'Connor-Petruso, and Keiichi Ogawa

REFERENCES

Adams, Maurianne, Lee Anne Bell, and Pat Griffin. *Teaching for Diversity and Social Justice: A Sourcebook.* New York: Routledge, 1997.

Central Intelligence Agency. *The CIA World Factbook.* New York: Skyhorse, 2012. https://www.cia.gov/library/publications/the-world-factbook/index.html.

Organisation for Economic Cooperation and Development (OECD). *Education at a Glance 2011: OECD Indicators.* Paris: OECD Publishing, 2011.

———. Programme for International Student Assessment Results. 2009. http://stats.oecd.org/PISA2009Profiles/#.

Resnick, Lauren B. The 1987 Presidential Address: Learning in and out of school. *Educational Researcher,* 16:9 (1987): 13–19.

UNESCO. *Global Education Digest 2012: Comparing Education Statistics Across the World.* Montreal: UNESCO Institute for Statistics, 2012.

World Bank Education Statistics, 2011. www.worldbank.org.

SOCIOPOLITICAL AND CULTURAL ISSUES IN EDUCATION

TERMS ASSOCIATED WITH RACE AND CULTURE IN EDUCATION

Educators and educational researchers use numerous terms that are associated with the sociopolitical and cultural contexts of the field of education. Many of these terms have to do with cultural differences in relationship to global education. A clearer understanding of these terms' definitions should enable readers to gain a broad conception of both the realities and distortions about various world cultures and how members of these cultures go about their everyday activities both in school settings and at home or in the workplace. In addition, it is important for both beginning and veteran educators to consider the ramifications of these terms in the context of school and the classroom environment. Generally, traditionalist educators—namely, those who espouse the dominant, time-honored formal schooling practices as evident in so-called Western societies—tend to devalue the importance of recognizing the meanings of the terms discussed below, often passing them off as part of a "liberal agenda." In fact, this is not the case at all; a number of conservative politicians align themselves with ideas that are putatively construed as liberal-minded. Aside from political considerations, it is important to consider how schools and classrooms are changing as a result of increasing diversity throughout the world. Here are some questions to consider when contemplating the meaning of the terms below: In what ways do teachers use these terms? Consequently, how do students use these terms? How are the notions of country of origin, ethnicity, heritage, nationality, and citizenship differentiated? Perhaps most impor-

tant, how might it be possible to learn about fellow classmates, students, or teachers while, at the same time, showing appreciation for backgrounds different from one's own?

Affirmative Action

Affirmative action refers to policies that consider race, ethnicity, gender, and, more recently, intellectual level as a means of promoting and fostering equal opportunity—primarily in employment and education. Overt discrimination, which took the form of racism and sanctioned segregation, served as the primary impetus that initiated affirmative action and related laws and policies in the United States and other countries as well. With the famous Supreme Court case *Regents of the University of California v. Allan Bakke* in 1978, affirmative action was tested in the courts. In the final outcome, Bakke won the case. Nevertheless, the court decided, with a final vote of 5 to 4, that affirmative action was constitutional, for it provided greater opportunity for a greater number of candidates who apply for college or graduate school. At the same time the court barred the use of quota systems for college entrance due to their unconstitutionality; the court concluded that quota systems discriminated against nonminority candidates.

"African American" and "Black"

Unfortunately, the pernicious combination of intense racism and hostility toward recently freed slaves in the former Confederate states (after the Thirteenth Amendment of the Constitution banned the institution of slavery in the United States) made it grueling for black Americans in postbellum America to live contentedly. In general, since racism pervaded the North and South, both before and after the American Civil War, many citizens of the so-called majority referred to black Americans with either pejorative or outright derogatory and offensive terms. Since the 1970s, "African American" has been the accepted term associated with black Americans. More recently, this term has gradually decreased in usage as a result of its connections with ancient Rome; originally, the Romans applied the Latin term Africa to the habitable regions of the southern shores of the Mediterranean Sea in the areas of present-day Algeria, Tunisia, Libya, and Egypt. Johannes Leo Africanus, the sixteenth-century, European and Middle Eastern explorer applied the term to the northern part of the continent as well as much of the sub-Saharan region. Given this association with a continent named after a white colonist, the term "black" or "black American" has emerged in place of "African American" as the accepted reference. Still other speakers and writers use none of these descriptions and instead would rather use the term "persons of color."

"Asian" and the "Oriental" Label

The term "Asian" encompasses a broad range of peoples, cultures, and customs. To refer to an inhabitant of Beijing, China or Osaka, Japan, solely as Asian undercuts the meaning and associations with which this term identifies. To begin with, the term "Asian" can apply to locales as far west as Turkey, or perhaps the Ural region of the Russian Federation, as far south as Papua New Guinea and Indonesia, as far north as Siberia, and as far east as Big Diomede Island, off the coast of the Chukchi Peninsula and a short distance from Little Diomede in Alaska.

In recent decades, international comparisons have shown that students from the developed East Asian countries—primarily Japan, Taiwan, South Korea, Singapore, and parts of China (particularly Hong Kong)—outperform students in other countries of other regions. This finding is indicative of comparisons of students who belong to middle- and upper-income households. It also contributes to a stereotype that suggests a link among "Asian," developed countries of the Pacific Rim and the ability to outperform others. Accordingly, global educational comparisons fail to consider the broader socioeconomic and cultural dilemmas that are prevalent and even rampant

in these countries. A closer investigation of the academic achievement levels of low-income Japanese and American students, for example, would yield more similar results than one might expect.

"Oriental" is not only outdated as a term; it is used in a derogatory way; the term "oriental" was constructed by European and American colonists who used it to refer to the peoples whose lands were far away and in an entirely different hemisphere. It was used as a way to describe the physiological characteristics of Asians, their manners, mores, and various cultural habits and values that were considered exotic by a significant segment of the white European and American population. Unlike other derogatory terms, many, but by no means all, Asians often use the term freely and do not seem to draw parallels to its imperialistic associations.

Citizenship

"Citizenship" is a term that is associated with the status of livelihood within a political community—most often, a country. A citizen is a member of a country's political community who benefits from the rights and freedoms that the country offers under the extent of the law. Citizenship plays an important role in the context of education—particularly formal education. For example, in antebellum America, black slaves were considered property rather than citizens under the US Constitution, and therefore were not free nor did they benefit from the rights that were granted to citizens. As a result, all slaves were forbidden an education under the law. In addition, due in part to a growing racist sentiment in the late antebellum years, most free African Americans, in both the North and South, were not given the same educational opportunities as their white peers.

Culture

"Culture" refers to the habits and values of a specific group of people who live together. The term comes from anthropology, where human societies are classified according to social complexity. Accordingly, cultures vary in size—from bands of 25 to 50 individuals and tribes of a few hundred to a few thousand people to chiefdoms of several thousand people and nation-states of millions of people.

At the same time, the word is often used quite

Table: **The Four Levels of Human Society**

Level	Name	Number of people	Description	Example
1	Band	25–50	Bands are always on the move. They are nomadic hunter-gatherers with no institutionalized political structure.	Dobe Ju/'hoansi (Botswana and Namibia)
2	Tribe	Below 100 to several thousand	The population densities of tribes, which are higher than those of bands, are supported by horticultural production. Tribes stay in one location for many years at a time.	Yąnomamö (northern Brazil and southern Venezuela)
3	Chiefdom	Several thousand	The chiefdom is based on hereditary authority. Status differences in chiefdoms are institutionalized.	Trobriand Islanders (New Guinea)
4	Nation-state	Millions	A nation-state's society is marked by its centralized authority and by an army or police force that enforces the rule of law.	Botswana, Canada, China, France, Venezuela

loosely. For example, some people frequently use the terms "culture" and "ethnicity" interchangeably. Culture, however, is not ethnicity. Ethnicities are subcategories of race; culture is specifically the habits, traditions, and ways of knowing the world that a group of people find useful and important as a means of functioning. The word "heritage," too, is often used interchangeably with "culture." Again, these words have different meanings. Heritage refers to an individual's ethnic bloodline. In other words, someone whose ethnic bloodline is Chinese can be culturally Mozambican if the individual was born and raised in Mozambique. From an imperialistic standpoint, culture is frequently used as a means of subordination—particularly by upper-income individuals who use the term as a means of distinguishing themselves from members of lower socioeconomic classes.

Ethnicity

Like the terms "culture" and "race," "ethnicity" is a loaded term that has several meanings depending on the context and nature of verbal discourse. The most generalizable meaning has to do with the subgroups of race. For example, Asian subgroups include Taiwanese, Japanese, Hmong, Tamil, and the like. White subgroups include Macedonian, Frisian, Irish, Hungarian, and the like. On another level, ethnicity is construed by many people as having connection with particular religions. Many individuals, for example, describe themselves as Jewish in terms of ethnicity, but not in the practice of their religion per se. Ethnic-

ity, in this case, refers to historical implications that connect these individuals with the ways in which their ancestors have dealt with moral, intellectual, and everyday matters. In this sense, ethnicity is close in meaning to culture.

Heritage

"Heritage" refers to one's blood lineage and ancestry. Etymologically, the term was defined as something that is inherited, thus implying the genetic origin of one's background. This term contrasts greatly with "culture," which, as described above, indicates one's manners, mores, and making sense of the world. In many cases, heritage and culture are synonymous—as in a person of Han Chinese ancestry who lives on the coast of mainland China. For other people, the terms are different—such as an individual who is Ghanaian by heritage, but moves to Japan at a very young age, learns Japanese, and practices the manners and mores of Japanese society. In the context of education, it is important to avoid overgeneralization of certain terms—such as "culture" or "heritage"—that have possibly entirely different meanings, yet are used almost identically by many educators.

Hispanic, Spanish, Latina, Latino

The term "Spanish" refers to a language. Nevertheless, it is often, and erroneously, used to designate an ethnic group or a combination of many ethnic groups from certain Caribbean islands as well as areas on the North and South American mainland. The term

"Hispanic," in comparison, is also an inaccurate designation. It is also derogatory for at least two reasons. First, the word "Hispanic" can be construed as a paternalistic reference to Spain as a colonizing power. Some cultural historians argue that the term is derived from the male pronoun "his" together with a term for "Spain," even though the term "Hispania" was first used by the ancient Romans in reference to the Iberian Peninsula. Second, "Hispanic" is a census designation used as a means of classifying individuals in the United States and in other countries. As Peter McLaren argues in *Critical Pedagogy and Predatory Culture* (1995), the term's use is a way for a colonizing nation to impose power on colonized ethnic groups. It is true that the terms "Latina" and "Latino" are the preferred terms. Some have argued, however, that the use of a feminine ending emphasizes a gender gap problem. As a solution, some posit that the term "Latino" should be applied to both women and men, while others say that "Latina" should be used. At the same time, it is possible to refer to a large group of people as Latino—people from Cuba, Puerto Rico, or the Dominican Republic, for example. But the term "Latino" or "Latina" is not applicable to someone who comes from Mexico, in which case the terms "Chicana" and "Chicano" have been appropriated.

Indian

The term "Indian" has been historically applied to Native Americans or Native People of the North and South American continents. Most sources seem to suggest that the term was first used by Christopher Columbus and his seamen on his initial voyage in reference to the people who inhabited the island that he named San Salvador. In general, European explorers who sailed westbound at this time believed they were eventually going to land in Asia, or what many referred to as the Indies. Accordingly, Columbus, and subsequent explorers as well, referred to the present-day Caribbean islands as the Indies. The term "Indian," then, was applied to the peoples who inhabited these islands and, eventually, to those who inhabited the continents of North and South America. The term "Indian" is rejected as an applicable designation of Native Americans on two counts: First, it is a product of Spanish colonization and subsequent intrusion and colonization by other European nations; second, the term is based on the false assumption of explorers at

the time that westbound exploration would lead to the Asian continent or nearby islands.

It should be noted also that the use of the term "Native American" has been discouraged by a number of indigenous peoples of the Americas because the term "America," whose etymology, although unclear, seems to emanate from the name of an Italian explorer, Amerigo Vespucci, is disconnected from their traditions and heritages. For this reason, the term "Native People" has been an acceptable alternative. At present, the term "Indian" is often applied to people residing in Western nations who emigrated from the Indian subcontinent, as well as their offspring. The term is frequently, and erroneously, applied to Pakistani residents, primarily those who reside in Europe and North and South America.

From an educational perspective, a number of cultural scholars have argued that the use of the term "Indian" to refer to populations that settled in the Americas prior to European colonization should be eliminated from classroom discourse or, at the very least, phased out.

Minority

The term "minority" is vague. Nevertheless, it is a frequently used term in educational discourse, let alone common discourse, and refers to an individual who is not a member of a so-called dominant class. This dominant class may not necessarily be greater in terms of number. It may be dominant based on other factors, such as race, social class, economic mobility, the ability to vote in local and national elections, and the like. Due to its pejorative use, "minority" is another term that many cultural historians believe should be avoided. With regard to ethnicity, educators are using the term "persons of color" or "people of color" more frequently as a more desired reference.

Nationality

Nationality is often construed to be synonymous with citizenship. In addition, some might argue that there is no difference between ethnicity and nationality or ethnicity and citizenship. In the general sense, however, nationality is commonly believed to refer to the country of birth. Accordingly, it is difficult to discern nationality in many cases. For example, someone who is ethnically Taiwanese might have been born in Taiwan and carry Taiwan citizenship. Another individual can be ethnically from Taiwan, carry Canadian citizenship, but reside in the United Kingdom. As Étienne Balibar notes in an article in *Public Culture* (1996), it is difficult to distinguish between nationality, citizenship, ethnicity, and other aspects of identity.

Persons of Color

The term "persons of color" is the generally accepted way to refer to someone who is not white or not white and of European ethnicity—specifically in the United States. In particular, persons of color include blacks, Native Americans, Latinos, Latinas, and Asians. There are connotations associated with other terms—such as "nonwhite" and "minority"—that many believe to be pejorative. The connotation of "nonwhite" conjures up notions of white as the norm and nonwhite as the negation of white. Similarly, the term "minority" is also construed in a negative light since it suggests belonging to a smaller, weaker, and less important group. It is noteworthy to mention that the term "persons of color" or "people of color" is not novel in the current context; it can be traced back to 1855 in the Worcester, Massachusetts, city council minutes, which are available at the Worcester Historical Museum archives. Given the condescending nature of "minority" and "nonwhite" (which essentially implies "not in the majority"), "persons of color" has become widespread in general discourse as well as in educational circles.

Political Correctness

The concept of political correctness presupposes the use of a universally accepted proper term as a reference to an idea (e.g., "special education" instead of "education for the feebleminded") or ethnic group (e.g., "Asian" instead of "Oriental"), whereby the use of an improper term will result in a pejorative or possibly offensive or abusive meaning. The term "political correctness" and its derivatives (politically correct, etc.) originated from modernist thinkers of the early twentieth century who argued in absolutist terms. In this case, a reference to a particular group or idea was either "correct" or "incorrect." As postmodernism replaced modernism in the twentieth century, the term radically changed in meaning—particularly

after the 1950s and at the onset of the civil rights movement—and has taken on a relativist (and not absolutist) position.

Race

"Race" is a difficult term to define. This is due in part to its overuse and also as a result of centuries of categorizations of peoples throughout the world. In general, the most common factors in creating race classifications are physiological differences, skin color variation, and the geographic location of indigenous people. Nevertheless, these classifications are socially constructed and, more often than not, used as a means of oversimplifying reality. For example, reference to a certain "indigenous people" as a classification of race is difficult to pinpoint because groups vary in terms of historical periods. In a video called *Prejudice: Answering Children's Questions* (1992), Margaret Gillan identifies five different groups that are categorized in terms of race. This categorization is based almost exclusively on geographic location in the world. The groups are Asians (people who are indigenous to eastern Asia, most of central Asia, and southern Asia), blacks (people who are indigenous to Africa), Latinos and Latinas (the Americas), Native People (people who are indigenous to the Americas), and whites (people who are indigenous to Eurasia—present-day Europe, western Asia, and parts of central Asia).

Racism

Racism occurs in numerous forms. It is not culturally bound; in other words, racist ideology is apparent among members of most ethnic or cultural groups, and members of all ethnicities may be subject to racist victimization. It is also important to note that people who practice racism vary in terms of socioeconomic status. They might seem "normal" and even be described by those who know them as "caring" or "compassionate" in terms of how they conform to societal rules. Nevertheless, at various times and places in history, a segment of the population that practiced racist ideology carried out atrocities against others. Examples of these actions are evidenced by historical documentation of numerous genocides throughout history.

Racism has been a factor in education since the beginning of formal schooling. During the antebellum period in American history, it was a crime for anyone to educate either free or enslaved black Americans. Educators in the South who taught black slaves how to read were often jailed or banished from their towns. In contrast, there were few, if any, punitive measures taken against northern educators who taught black Americans or newly arriving immigrants. This is not to say, however, that racism did not exist in the North. After the American Civil War, racism was a dire problem in schools throughout the country. Moreover, the victims of racism expanded beyond black Americans and included virtually all immigrants of various ethnic backgrounds. Jim Crow laws that were established in 1876, toward the end of Reconstruction, mandated de jure segregation of black Americans from white facilities. This included institutions of education. This so-called separate-but-equal practice was indeed separate but in no way equal. Facilities for whites were invariably of better quality than those for blacks. Although Jim Crow laws came to an end in 1965, the *Brown v. Board of Education* ruling in 1954 helped to advance desegregation in public schools.

Racism is common in education throughout the world. In most cases, the victims of racism are members of minority groups of a certain country. In this case, "minority" refers to any racial or ethnic group that consists of fewer members than some other, dominant group. De jure racism—state-sponsored racism—has been a common problem in the history of educational practice. Countries that practiced de jure racism in educational institutions include Germany, Japan, Israel, South Africa, and the United States. De facto racism—racism that is allowed but not ratified legally—is a common practice in the Dominican Republic, where individuals of Haitian background are often victims of racial discrimination.

Daniel Ness and Chia-ling Lin

REFERENCES

Balibar, Étienne. "Is European Citizenship Possible?" *Public Culture* 19 (1996): 355–376.

Bhopal, Kalwant, and Preston, John, eds. *Intersectionality and "Race" in Education*. New York: Routledge, 2011.

Cashmore, Ernest. *Dictionary of Race and Ethnic Relations*. 4th ed. New York: Routledge, 1996.

Gay, Geneva. "Acting on Beliefs in Teacher Education for Cultural Diversity." *Journal of Teacher Education* 61 (2010): 143–152.

Gillan, Margaret. *Prejudice: Answering Children's Questions* [video]. New York: NYNEX Kids Now, 1992.

McLaren, Peter. *Critical Pedagogy and Predatory Culture*. New York: Routledge, 1995.

Regents of the University of California v. Allan Bakke, 438 US 265 (1978).

EDUCATION AND RACIAL DISCRIMINATION

Racial discrimination—the determination of a person or group to act on racial prejudices—has occurred throughout history and has plagued educational systems throughout the world since the beginnings of formal education. It is important to note the difference between racial prejudice and racial discrimination. Racial prejudice is a psychological predisposition whereby the individual with prejudice possesses negative thoughts about someone's race or ethnicity. Prejudice against people can take many forms, such as racial, gender, age, sexual orientation, geographic, and socioeconomic prejudices. Prejudice occurs at the level of thought. Discrimination, on the other hand, occurs at the level of action. From this standpoint, then, laws—that are created and enacted by the legislative branch, enforced by the executive branch, and interpreted by the judicial branch of government—are actions that are carried out so as to treat citizens in ways that affect their everyday lives.

One of the most infamous and extreme examples of racial discrimination in education was the barring of education for black slaves in the United States during the antebellum years, and subsequently the segregation of schools based on race as a result of Jim Crow laws. In antebellum states of the South, it was against state constitutional law to teach black Americans to read and write. Penalties were numerous, including fines and even incarceration of teachers who engaged in teaching reading and writing to free blacks or slaves. During the century between the American Civil War and the civil rights period, these laws led to "separate but equal" schooling for African American children under de jure (literally, according to law) segregation practice. Racial segregation was a major factor in universal discrimination against African Americans and, at the time, other ethnic groups as well. Despite the notion of separate but equal schooling, education for African American students was anything but equal when compared to that of white students. Unfortunately, racial discrimination has occurred in every educational setting up to the present day and has included members of all ethnic backgrounds. Currently, although de jure segregation has been abolished, many areas throughout the world practice de facto segregation—in other words, segregation that actually happens even though it is not law. This characteristic is common in large urban and suburban areas where there is a clear demarcation between affluent and impoverished neighborhoods. Most often, inhabitants of impoverished neighborhoods are persons of color.

Major Cases in Educational Discrimination Worldwide

Racial and ethnic discrimination in education occurs not just in multiethnic countries such as the United States; it occurs on every inhabited continent and in nearly every country. Discrimination is a problem not only in imperialist regimes, certain socialist states, monarchies, and dictatorships, but also in republics and countries that are self-described democracies. As seen in cases involving educational discrimination, discriminatory practices are not monolithic in type. Some types of discrimination occur as a result of non-intent-based practice, whereby students are indirectly subjected to discrimination as a result of practices that separate groups of children based on race and ethnicity from other children and places the minority group in substandard settings. An example of students subject to discrimination indirectly can be seen in numerous settings where affluence and poverty are evident. A household's socioeconomic status often determines residence and neighborhood, school district ranking, emphasis on law enforcement, and adequate upkeep of homes. These settings have been apparent throughout history and even to the present day in most countries throughout the world. Other types of discrimination occur as a result of explicit practices that enforce the separation of two or more groups. In these cases, the legislation does not distinguish between discrimination and equality under the law, even if one group does have poorer conditions than another. This was the case in the United States until the 1950s.

The following four judicial cases demonstrate the pervasiveness of racial and ethnic discrimination in educational settings worldwide. They are indicative of educational practices that have been institutionalized for many years.

Brown v. Board of Education

Prior to the *Brown v. Board of Education* cases (*Brown I*, 347 US 483, 1954; *Brown II*, 349 US 294, 1955), state laws throughout the United States either permitted or required the act of segregating white and black children in public schools. In most cases, schools for African American children were inferior to those of white children in terms of facilities and supplies. Representatives of several black children maintained that legislation enforcing either the permission or requirement of segregation violated the constitutional requirement of equal protection of laws.

The Supreme Court ruled in favor of Brown. According to the court, "separate educational facilities are inherently unequal. Even where physical facilities and other objective factors are equal, a segregated school system denies equal educational opportunities to the minority group." This case is somewhat different from other cases throughout the world—such as those concerning Roma children in Bulgaria and the Czech Republic—in that Roma children were clearly subjected to discrimination, whether or not the educational establishments had intent to discriminate against them. In the Brown case, however, the act of segregation did not necessarily mean that children would receive different treatment in one context or the other—even though facilities were significantly better in all-white schools.

D.H. and Others v. Czech Republic

The Roma are a subgroup of the Romani people, whose origins are from South Central Asia. As gypsies, the Roma have concentrated in many parts of Europe, particularly in central and eastern regions of the continent. There are frequent occurrences of discrimination against Roma in European countries. The European Roma Rights Centre (ERRC) found that school selection processes in the city of Ostrava in the Czech Republic frequently discriminate on the basis of race and ethnicity. Since Roma children constitute the greatest number of non-Czech students, they are severely discriminated against in school settings. According to ERRC, more than half of Romani children are schooled in remedial settings. Moreover, more than half of the population of remedial special schools is composed of Romani children. A Romani child is more than 27 times more likely to be placed in remedial schools or those for learning disabled students than another child who is not of Romani ethnicity. Romani children who do manage to avoid being placed in remedial and learning disabled school settings are often sent to substandard urban schools. Finally, the ERRC found that Czech school and education officials have used mental ability tests that are culturally biased against Czech Roma. The test results contribute to the improper placement procedures, which contribute to increasing racial prejudice.

On November 14, 2007, the European Court of Human Rights concluded, with a vote of 13 to 4, that Roma students were the recipients of unlawful discrimination as a result of their overwhelming enrollment in Czech special schools. This case of discrimination was a breach of Article 14 of the European Convention, which prohibits discrimination in any form, in conjunction with Article 2 of Protocol No. 1, which secures the right to education for children of all ethnic backgrounds. The court awarded €4,000 ($5,279) to each of the applicants in nonpecuniary damage and €10,000 ($13,197) jointly for costs and expenses.

D.H. and Others v. Czech Republic was a watershed case in that it contributed to major changes in the educational systems of European nations in terms of implicit racial segregation in schooling procedures. Nevertheless, racial segregation still exists throughout the Czech Republic and other countries in the region where Roma populations, as well as other minority populations, are large. With discrimination aside, this case makes it clear that legislation used as a means of differential treatment toward a particular ethnic group can be deemed discriminatory, even if there was no intent.

European Roma Rights Centre v. Ministry of Education

School 103 in Sofia, Bulgaria, consisted entirely of Romani children. The facilities and conditions at this school were extremely poor, and students were not expected to perform as well as peers in nearby schools. Teacher quality was also very poor in School 103. Most teachers were unable to work with bilingual children. Moreover, there was no leadership in terms of school attendance. These substandard conditions led to the Bulgaria Case—*European Roma Rights Centre v. Ministry of Education* (2004)—which was subsequently decided on October 25, 2005. The Bulgarian court agreed that the substandard conditions of School 103 were the result of lack of opportunity for Romani children to enroll in other schools and that School 103 was used to segregate Romani children in a neighborhood that consisted of an almost entirely Romani population. Segregation was used in part to prevent Romani children from attending mainstream schools and also in part to avoid racist abuse by non-Romani groups. The court found that the poor material conditions in School 103, the low educational results of the children, and the failure of the school authorities to exert control of truancy were a clear indication of unequal and degrading treatment of the children. The Bulgarian education legislation that led to this situation violated the prohibition of racial segregation that is part of the Protection Against Discrimination Act. Even though the national standard educational requirements were applicable to the school, it was apparent that the Romani children could not meet these requirements to a degree comparable with that of children in other schools. The evidence of this was sufficient to prove a violation of their right to equal and integrated education.

This is an example of indirect discrimination: even though there was no direct legislation that discriminated against the applicants (as in the case above of *D.H. and Others v. Czech Republic*), the state had not done enough to create equality between schools (see the section on direct and indirect discrimination on the Right to Education Project website). Most recently, the ERRC has claimed discrimination against Roma children in the Ukraine. Specifically, Roma children are segregated from other schoolchildren by being placed in separate and inadequate buildings for schooling. According to researchers at the Ukrainian Institute for Social Research (UISR), approximately half of Roma children do not attend school or are regularly absent from class. This problem is most prevalent in densely populated Roma communities, particularly in Zakarpattia and Kharkiv oblasts.

San Antonio Independent School District v. Demetrio P. Rodriguez et al.

San Antonio Independent School District v. Demetrio P. Rodriguez (411 US 1 [1973] United States Supreme Court) was a class action lawsuit on behalf of children whose families—nearly all of whom were Mexican American—resided in a school district with an extremely low property tax base. The plaintiffs argued that the State of Texas was discriminatory in that it violated constitutional law through a narrow approach to equal protection. They challenged the state's dependence on local property taxes to finance schooling, arguing that it specifically did not grant equal protection of the law to all children as required by the Fourteenth Amendment of the Constitution of the United States. The Supreme Court's conclusions were in favor of the San Antonio Independent School District: the justices concluded that the Texas law, similar to those in other states, was constitutional in that the method of financing school systems was consistent with the premise that every child would be assured a basic education. They believed that the Texas law sanctioned, supported, and promoted participation by all members of the district and also gave its residents significant control of the schools. The court found the argument on the part of the plaintiffs vague and without merit. Despite the court's decision in the case, there is indication of a narrow approach to their interpretation of the meaning of "equal protection under the law." There was evidence of disparities in the level of education in the San Antonio Independent School District when compared to those of other districts. The Supreme Court, then, did not strictly examine how school districts were funded and how certain children were being deprived of education depending on the school district to which they belonged.

Daniel Ness and Chia-ling Lin

REFERENCES

Christie, Pam. "The Complexity of Human Rights in Global Times: The Case of a Right to Education in South Africa." *International Journal of Educational Development* 30:1 (2010): 3–11.

Corral, Irma, and Hope Landrine. "Racial Discrimination and Health-Promoting vs. Damaging Behaviors Among African-American Adults." *Journal of Health Psychology,* 17 (2012): 1–7.

La Morte, Michael W. *School Law: Cases and Concepts.* Upper Saddle River, NJ: Pearson, 2005.

O'Higgins, Niall. "'It's not that I'm a racist, it's that they are Roma': Roma Discrimination and Returns to Education in South Eastern Europe." *International Journal of Manpower* 31:2 (2010): 163–187.

Right to Education Project. "Cases on Racial Discrimination." Right to Education: Promoting Mobilization and Legal Accountability. www.right-to-education.org/node/690.

Seheda, Serhiy, and Oleksandr Tatarevskiy. *The Bill "On Protection against Racial, National and Ethnic Discrimination."* Kiev: International Center for Policy Studies, 2005.

Tyack, David. *The One Best System: A History of American Urban Education.* Cambridge, MA: Harvard University Press, 1974.

RACIAL DIVERSITY (MULTICULTURALISM), EDUCATION, AND PROGRESS

Racial and ethnic diversity—also referred to as multiculturalism—is the recognition of groups of different cultural backgrounds contributing to the demography of a given area—whether it be a neighborhood, village, town, city, region, or country. Ethnic diversity can also apply to school settings. Diversity need not be related to a person's ethnicity—it also can be applied to gender, age, educational attainment, cognitive ability, socioeconomic status, and geographical location. The most conventional implication of the terms "diversity" and "multiculturalism," nevertheless, refers to race and ethnicity.

Despite the positive implications of racial and ethnic diversity, many environments and communities do not support this kind of condition. At the same time, political figures often articulate their support in favor of ethnic diversity. This is common in many communities throughout the United States where education is presumed to be better in districts whose administrators and legislators levy high property taxes. In New Jersey, for example, rampant de facto segregation occurs as a result of some districts excluding groups of lower socioeconomic status.

Since the nineteenth century, diversity as it relates to multiculturalism was a de facto paradigm in numerous countries throughout the world. To the present day, multiculturalism exists in both de facto and de jure governments throughout the world. Despite its implications of internationalism and global context, the term "multicultural education" stems from an intellectual perspective that is almost entirely an American phenomenon. In addition, different scholars who specialize in the subfields of diversity and culture in education define multiculturalism in a variety of ways.

James Banks and Cherry Banks

James Banks and Cherry Banks have written on the subject of multiculturalism and multicultural education for several decades. Like most multiculturalists in education, Banks and Banks emphasize the racial and ethnic implications of diversity. Their 1995 book, which bears the title of the subject—*Multicultural Education*—is a popular text in many education courses. Banks and Banks claim that *multicultural education* is "a field of study and an emerging discipline whose major aim is to create equal educational opportunities for students from diverse racial, ethnic, social-class, and cultural groups." More important, perhaps, is their argument that a crucial goal of multicultural education "is to help all students to acquire the knowledge, attitudes, and skills needed to function effectively in a pluralistic democratic society and to interact, negotiate, and communicate with peoples from diverse groups in order to create a civic and moral community that works for the common good."

Banks and Banks state that the subfields of culture studies—such as feminist pedagogy, queer pedagogy, ethnic studies, and the like—are not the only elements that constitute multiculturalism and multicultural education. In addition, multicultural education includes what Banks and Banks refer to as the traditional fields of study—such as mathematics, earth and life sciences, language, and history. As they posit, "Multicultural education not only draws content, concepts, paradigms, and theories from specialized interdisciplinary fields such as ethnic studies and women's studies (and from history and the social and behavioral sciences), it also interrogates, challenges, and reinterprets content, concepts, and paradigms from the established disciplines. Multicultural education applies content from these fields and disciplines to pedagogy and curriculum development in educational settings." Banks and Banks, therefore, define multiculturalism as "a field of study designed to increase educational equity for all students that incorporates, for this purpose, content, concepts, principles, theories, and paradigms from history, the social and behavioral sciences, and particularly from ethnic studies and women's studies."

Lisa Delpit

Multiculturalism and multicultural education can also be defined in a way that distinguishes and differentiates—and does not unite—members of different groups. Lisa Delpit refers to multicultural education in this way. In her well-known text, *Other People's Children* (2006), Delpit contends that students of color are often mislabeled as academic underachievers based on the failure of teachers to understand their students' experiences in and out of school. She maintains that each cultural group has different "codes and rules for discourse." The interaction between people of different cultural groups is often hampered by the differences in these codes and rules. Inversely, at home and in the community, students of various cultures do not gain the wherewithal to communicate with the so-called culture of power that typically controls schools and school systems. This problem is compounded, according to Delpit, as a result of increasing populations of nonwhite students in school systems that hire less than 10 percent nonwhite teachers. The solution to this problem is not through major school or systemic reform; rather it lies, in Delpit's words, "in some basic understandings of who we are and how we are connected and disconnected from one another." One way to ameliorate this problem is to learn how to listen to students' experiences. Likewise, educators need to bring personal experience to bear on ideas that are brought into the classroom.

In addition to educational inequality in the United States, Delpit's book also examines adverse conditions of schooling in non-Western schools throughout the world. Social and cognitive dissonance often occurs when Peace Corps volunteers, most often with good intentions, arrive in a developing country to help students learn. Delpit would argue that it is not the case that these volunteers are unable to help and engage these students, but they need to immerse themselves in the culture to the point that there is a mutual consideration of intercultural awareness between teacher and student. Another example of this dissonance occurs when Western schooling systems that are administered by American and European societies essentially annex and take control of the school systems of developing countries. Consequently, there is an initial lack of mutual understanding between those in control of the system and the children and families within these systems.

Geneva Gay

In her book *A Synthesis of Scholarship in Multicultural Education* (1994), Geneva Gay seems to concur with Delpit in arguing that educators must not treat all students in a monolithic way, because by doing so, they fail to consider the cultural heritage of each individual. As Gay maintains, "When educators claim that their top priority is to treat all children like human beings, regardless of ethnic identity, cultural background, or economic status, they are creating a paradox. A person's humanity cannot be isolated or divorced from his or her culture or ethnicity. One cannot be human without culture and ethnicity, and one cannot have culture and ethnicity without being human."

Sonia Nieto

One common thread among all the individuals mentioned is that each one emphasizes an unswerving commitment to public dialogue regarding racism, sexism, and any form of prejudice. Sonia Nieto's work differs from other authors in that her focus is to identify specific measures that teachers and parents can take in order to address issues regarding racism and all forms of discrimination in schools. As evidenced in her book *Affirming Diversity: The Sociopolitical Context of Multicultural Education* (2003), Nieto's major contributions tackle the problem of language differences among students and the discrimination that ensues.

Nieto and other multiculturalists are major critics of those who contend that poor students or students of color are underachievers because they "fail" to speak in "Standard English"—for example, African American students who speak Black English Vernacular (BEV). She is a critic of Eleanor Wilson Orr, who argues in her book *Twice as Less* (1997) that BEV impedes African American students from succeeding in school because it is inferior to Standard English. These multiculturalists claim that it is not the case that one form of language is inferior to another, but rather that one form, namely, Standard English, might not yet be learned by these students. Most persons of color, according to multiculturalist arguments, must learn Standard English in order to be in equal competition with those who are members of the so-called culture of power.

Christine Sleeter

Christine Sleeter takes a more progressive approach to multiculturalism and multicultural education in arguing that the common school subjects (i.e., language arts, mathematics, social studies, and natural science) should address the struggle against racism and any other form of intolerance toward fellow individuals head on. Sleeter has developed five approaches toward multiculturalism. These approaches are titled Teaching the Culturally Different, Human Relations, Single Group Studies, Multicultural Education, and Social Reconstructionist. Using the Teaching the Culturally Different approach allows the practitioner to tap into culturally relevant curriculum as a means of raising the ability levels of students of color. The Human Relations approach, according to Sleeter, emphasizes social and cultural variations among people of all backgrounds with an attempt to avoid differences having to do with power obtained through racism, force (i.e., war), and economic disparity. The Single Group Studies approach aims at the elimination of exploitation by having students investigate the histories and contemporary issues relating to the oppression of people of color, women, low socioeconomic groups, and gays and lesbians. The Multicultural Education approach is similar to the ways of teaching discussed by the writers above because it emphasizes democracy and pluralism by engaging students with content related to the value of cultural knowledge and differences of members of various cultures other than their own. The fifth approach, known as the Social Reconstructionist approach, is used by teachers to instruct students particularly about the oppression and discrimination of populations throughout the world. Students engage in activities that help them learn about their roles as representatives of social change as a means of participating in, and contributing to, a society that does not oppress and discriminate against its populations.

Additional Authors

Additional contributors who have impacted education in terms of cultural influences and the manners by which current educational standards often oppress and exploit various peoples in the world include William Ayers, Carl Grant, Jonathan Kozol, Dale Johnson and his colleagues, and Peter McLaren. Bill Ayers is an important critic of those who challenge social justice in education. Within the last several decades, he has written on the trials and tribulations of teachers and schoolchildren—specifically those who have not benefited from adequate education and school infrastructures. Grant has mostly been a valuable contributor to anthologies and general texts on the topic of multicultural education for students of education. He has worked extensively with other authors examined here, particularly Christine Sleeter. In the well-known text *Savage Inequalities* (1993), Kozol describes visits to six impoverished neighborhoods where he documented gross inequities of children living in poor, high-crime communities. In doing so, he maintains that the days of segregation are not over, in the sense that more districts are following de facto segregation practices even though segregation is outlawed. Kozol continues this thesis in his more recent book, *The Shame of the Nation* (2006). Dale Johnson and his colleagues have given much attention to the sources of inequality of education, namely, the problems of corruption in education accreditation and high-stakes testing enterprises and collusion with policy makers. Their book *Trivializing Teacher Education* (2005) emphasizes how unjust bureaucratic interests serve the coffers of education policy makers and accrediting agencies, such as the National Council for the Accreditation of Teacher Education (NCATE), but fail to help children receive a satisfactory education. Their other book, *Stop High Stakes Testing* (2008), addresses the problem of educational bureaucracy with respect to the unequal footing of poor children in urban, suburban, and rural areas when compared to their middle-income and affluent peers. McLaren's contribution has furthered the work of educational theorists Paulo Freire and Ivan Illich, whose works on the world's oppressed populations became classic texts in the field of culture and its impact on education. McLaren's primary area of research is critical pedagogy, which investigates methods that students can implement in order to question and challenge domination.

Daniel Ness and Chia-ling Lin

REFERENCES

Anyon, Jean. *Ghetto Schooling: A Political Economy of Urban Education.* New York: Teachers College Press, 1997.

Ayers, William C. *Teaching Toward Freedom: Moral Commitment and Ethical Action in the Classroom.* Boston: Beacon, 2005.

Banks, James A., and Cherry A. McGee Banks. *Multicultural Education: Issues and Perspectives.* 4th ed. New York: John Wiley, 1995.

Delpit, Lisa. "Education in a Multicultural Society: Our Future's Greatest Challenge." *Journal of Negro Education* 61:3 (1992): 237–261.

————. *Other People's Children: Cultural Conflict in the Classroom.* New York: New Press, 2006.

Gay, Geneva. *A Synthesis of Scholarship in Multicultural Education* (Urban Education Monograph Series). Naperville, IL: North Central Regional Educational Laboratory, 1994.

Grant, Carl. *Educating for Diversity: An Anthology of Multicultural Voices.* Boston: Allyn & Bacon, 1995.

Johnson, Dale D., Bonnie Johnson, Stephen J. Farenga, and Daniel Ness. *Stop High-Stakes Testing: An Appeal to America's Conscience.* Lanham, MD: Rowman & Littlefield, 2008.

————. *Trivializing Teacher Education: The Accreditation Squeeze.* Lanham, MD: Rowman & Littlefield, 2005.

Kozol, Jonathan. *Savage Inequalities: Children in America's Schools.* New York: Harper Perennial, 1993.

————. *The Shame of the Nation: The Restoration of Apartheid Schooling in America.* New York: Three Rivers, 2006.

McLaren, Peter. *Life in Schools: An Introduction to Critical Pedagogy in the Foundations of Education.* 5th ed. Upper Saddle River, NJ: Allyn & Bacon, 2006.

Nieto, Sonia. *Affirming Diversity: The Sociopolitical Context of Multicultural Education.* 4th ed. Boston: Allyn & Bacon, 2003.

Orr, Eleanor Wilson. *Twice as Less: Black English and the Performance of Black Students in Mathematics and Science.* New York: Norton, 1997.

Sleeter, Christine E. *Multicultural Education as Social Activism.* Albany: State University of New York Press, 1996.

CHILDREN'S AND ADOLESCENTS' RIGHTS WORLDWIDE

Children's rights are a set of laws designed to ensure the well-being and healthy living conditions of all individuals throughout the world who are traditionally under the age of 18 years. Further, these rights condemn and include provisions that penalize individuals for actions of physical and mental abuse, neglect, and depravity toward children. The term "children's rights" became prevalent during the civil rights movement in the United States during the 1960s and 1970s. At the time of its original use, the term was vague and lacked a precise definition. In her seminal article titled "Children under the Law," Hillary Rodham argued in 1973 that the term "children's rights" was a "slogan in search of a definition." However, since that time, thanks to a variety of media and scholarly research studies, public awareness of children's rights has become increasingly prevalent, particularly among policy makers, lawyers, judges, and journalists. This is especially the case given that the segment of the world's population with the greatest need for counsel and support—namely, children and adolescents—is the most vulnerable of all groups in society. Perhaps the most commonly cited and supported treaty on children's rights in the world is the United Nations Convention on the Rights of the Child (UNCRC), which was established by the United Nations Children's Fund (UNICEF) in 1989. According to UNICEF, the UNCRC is the first legally binding agreement that focuses specifically on the health, welfare, and protection of individuals under 18 years of age.

Despite efforts over the last few centuries that have gradually led to the improvement of the well-being of children throughout the world, problems remain and can potentially worsen. Any dialogue or debate concerning children's rights in the twenty-first century must consider the realities of widespread poverty and misery as well as mortality that characterize the lives of children from developing societies, on the one hand, and the significant progress that children's rights legislation has made, on the other. Current data on child labor and maltreatment of children and adolescents are revealing. To be sure, approximately 215 million children and adolescents are engaged in some form of labor, and although this figure seems to be declining, there is no indication that the pattern can reverse. In addition, more than half of these children and adolescents work in hazardous conditions. With the population of the world past the 7 billion mark, countries with the highest birth rates tend to be those with poor economies and generally high levels of child labor. Moreover, these countries—mostly in central and southern Africa, parts of central, southern, and eastern Asia, and certain areas of South America—tend to be those with the poorest systems of education.

Prior to 1989, essentially no treaty existed that protected children's and adolescents' rights throughout the world. In 1989, the UNCRC was written, ratified, and approved by nearly all members of the UN. The convention was the first legally binding treaty that declared the need to protect all children from oppression, hunger, abuse, and wanton and immoral actions against children and adolescents. These actions include forced labor, prostitution, slavery, and military service. The convention includes 54 articles and two so-called Optional Protocols explaining that children have the same basic human rights as adults. These rights include the right to survival; to develop to the fullest; to protection from harmful influences, abuse, and exploitation; and to participate fully in family, cultural, and social life. The four core principles of the convention are nondiscrimination; devotion to the best interests of the child; the right to life, survival, and development; and respect for the views of the child.

Children's Rights Issues

There are a number of issues that affect the rights of children throughout the world. These issues include child labor, sex trading and slavery, poor living conditions, and lack of education. It is important to note that the overlap among these issues is significant and is shown to be evident throughout the world, particularly in developing nations.

Child Labor and Sex Trading

Child labor affects nearly 212 million of the world's children from five to 14 years of age. Most of these children (127.3 million) live in Asia. Other regions with high numbers of child workers are sub-Saharan Africa (48 million), Latin America and the Caribbean (17.4 million), and the Middle East and North Africa (14.3 million). Even developed and transitioning countries have children at work (approximately 5 million). Child labor takes numerous forms: agriculture, street vending (including the sale of contraband), quarrying, warfare, and the sex trade. Child sex trafficking and child prostitution is a disconcerting characteristic in nearly one-quarter of all the countries in the world. In fact, according to the Human Rights

Watch website, which covers current events concerning the oppression and subjugation of children, the countries that have the most rampant cases of child prostitution and sex trafficking include Thailand, Myanmar, Cambodia, and Brazil. The following list includes other nations where child prostitution is either condoned or on the rise:

Africa: Cameroon, Liberia, Sierra Leone,
                   Zambia
Asia: Afghanistan, Bangladesh, India,
                   Indonesia, Nepal, Philippines,
                   Sri Lanka, Vietnam
Europe: Russia, Ukraine
North America: El Salvador, Mexico, Nicaragua
Oceania: Australia, New Zealand
South America: Argentina, Brazil, Chile,
                   Colombia, Ecuador, Peru

Child prostitution and sex trafficking do not exclusively involve girls; both males and females are forced to work in prostitution. The practice of *bacha bazi*—sexual enslavement and prostitution of prepubescent boys—is especially severe in Afghanistan and nearby central Asian countries.

Poor Living Conditions

Poor living conditions are common in all countries, not just those considered "developing." Children engaged in labor and forced into the sex trade are at risk of contracting disease and other types of health conditions—most often sexually transmitted diseases for those working in the sex industry. Most of these children also end up in poverty. Other forms of maltreatment of children occur in the context of cultural rituals and practices such as child marriage, genital mutilation, and virginal testing. Child marriage is the betrothal of either males or females to others of the same age or older. This practice is particularly abhorrent when the children being betrothed are those who have not yet reached puberty. The custom of child marriage currently exists in parts of Africa, Asia, Oceania, and South America.

Genital mutilation is a cruel and painful custom that is somewhat common among children of certain cultural backgrounds whose elders often force youth to participate in rituals that can have perilous and potentially even life-threatening consequences. These children most often live under adverse conditions. One of these forms of mutilation is female genital mutilation, which is defined by the World Health Organization as having "no health benefits for girls and women." Other forms of poor living conditions that children endure include poverty, disease, homes and schools infested with disease-bearing insects and vermin, and high crime environments.

Lack of Education

A third issue that has adversely affected the rights of children worldwide is the lack of education. Data show that the regions with the highest incidences of child labor and the poorest living conditions are those that also have limited or nonexistent education resources and infrastructures. This is particularly a trenchant situation in India, where the continuation of the caste system has made it extremely difficult for children of lower castes to receive an education. The lack of formal education for many of the world's children is evident in many developing countries, particularly in Africa, Southeast Asia, and parts of Latin America. It should also be noted that although education is compulsory for most children and adolescents of a given country, they often do not attend school for a variety of reasons, such as labor and a family's lack of financial resources.

Children's Rights Throughout the World

Despite international efforts to grapple with maltreatment of children and adolescents throughout the world, various regions have dealt with this issue in more or less culturally or societally specific ways. While children's rights may be an indispensable issue in one area of the world, the topic might be either proscribed or entirely disregarded in others. In addition, although most infringements of children's rights occur in developing societies, a government's or region's approach to the topic of children's rights is not necessarily based on level of poverty or socioeconomic class. For example, South Africa, a country with a rather low gross national product and a high rate of poverty, has attempted in recent years to uphold laws pertaining to international children's rights. The progress of children's rights, especially in poor societies, depends on the elimination of child labor and sex trafficking, the improvement of child welfare and decrease in the number of families in poverty, the eradication of HIV-AIDS and other deadly diseases, the razing of child prisons, the implementation of greater educational opportunity for girls, the abolition of the use of child soldiers, and the eradication of certain cruel and harmful cultural practices, such as genital mutilation, virginity testing, and child marriage.

Africa

Contrary to popular belief, concern for children's rights is a major issue in certain governments and several nongovernmental organizations in Africa. For example, the African Charter on the Rights and Welfare of the Child was approved in 1990 and adopted by the Organization of African Unity. It was in 1999, however, that the African Network for the Prevention of and Protection against Child Abuse and Neglect spearheaded an initiative that led to the African Charter on the Rights and Welfare of the Child as a mandate for all country members. Nevertheless, the violation of international children's rights is perhaps more evident in Africa than in any other continent (parts of Asia are a not-too-distant second). Especially in sub-Saharan Africa, children beyond the age of infancy and under the age of 18 are frequently forced to undergo genital mutilation, a practice that has been condemned by numerous health, political, and social organizations. Many African children are involved in child marriage or prostitution or recruited as soldiers on the battlefield, where they are paid less (if anything at all) than adult soldiers: military leaders believe that children can be forced to obey orders more easily than can adults.

The arguments as to the rate of progress in ending these practices are conflicting. On the one hand, Chirwa (2009) argues that foundations, NGOs, and governments themselves cannot solve the problems of child poverty, child labor, soldiering, and sex trafficking. Instead, there must be a concerted effort at all levels—from the family and community to the top ranks of government. On the other hand, Sloth-Nielsen (2008) argues that since the increase in the number of constitutional democracies in Africa in the 1990s, there has been a much greater committed effort, particularly with regard to law reform, to increase both awareness of children's rights and insti-

tutional and actual change in rectifying the injustices of all forms of child maltreatment. Geraldine Van Bueren, concurring, argues that countries in western and central Africa are beginning, albeit gradually, to establish child parliaments, which are educational and practicing programs under the auspices of various governmental ministries that provide children with knowledge of democracy and political participation. Although education may not necessarily resist adult mistreatment, providing children with knowledge is an initial step that may lead them closer to a freer life.

Asia and Oceania

The continents of Asia and Oceania (Australia, New Zealand, and the Pacific island nations), taken as a whole, comprise some of the most diverse societies in the world in terms of cultural values, religion, economy, language, treatment of women and children, and education. Countries in Asia and Oceania face several challenges with regard to children's rights. The first challenge is ensuring the protection of children from labor, trafficking, and other forms of maltreatment. A second challenge is the formidable task of meeting the United Nations' Millennium Development Goals (MDGs) for Sustainable Development by 2015: (1) eradicating extreme poverty and hunger, (2) achieving universal primary education, (3) promoting gender equality, (4) reducing child mortality, (5) improving the health of mothers, (6) controlling or eliminating deadly diseases, (7) promoting and fostering environmental sustainability, and (8) developing a global partnership. Although children's rights and MDGs are not the same, there is much overlap. It should be clear that the improvement of educational systems and health care—two of the eight MDGs—are essential in improving the rights of children.

In general, central and south Asia are most affected by the lack of children's rights. There are numerous reasons, but poor economies and the number of children living in poverty are two of the most prevalent. A number of these countries have extremely low GDPs, thus showing high poverty levels. Some countries, with both low and moderate GDPs, have religious rituals or values, such as child marriage and virginal testing, which run counter to the rights of children and women. In countering child maltreatment, many developing countries in Asia and the Pacific are engaging in "south-south" cooperation, a form of cooperation by which developing countries share knowledge, skills, technical advancements, and personnel for the purpose of improving the living conditions of children and other vulnerable populations. Triangulation occurs when such countries also get assistance from industrialized countries, such as China, South Korea, Japan, India, Malaysia, Taiwan, and Singapore. Current strengths of south-south cooperation include trade and other forms of economic development. However, the program has not shown improvements in other key components of child rights, such as health, sex trafficking, and food security. Moreover, child marriage continues to be problematic in both economically poor and wealthy countries, particularly India, Indonesia, parts of Pakistan, Papua New Guinea, Saudi Arabia, Sri Lanka, and Yemen. Sex trafficking and prostitution of children, both girls and boys, is common in Afghanistan, Bangladesh, Cambodia, India, Indonesia, Myanmar, Nepal, the Philippines, Sri Lanka, and Thailand. Countries that often force children into other forms of labor, such as labor in agriculture or in quarries, include some of the previously mentioned nations as well as China, Kazakhstan, Kyrgyzstan, Mongolia, North Korea, Tajikistan, Turkmenistan, and Uzbekistan.

Europe

Children's rights in Europe, particularly northern, western, and most of southern Europe, have made great progress since the 1950s. In particular, laws regarding the abolishment of corporal punishment—both in school and at home—have greatly contributed to children's and adolescents' success rates in school and in their communities. Countries that have passed laws banning corporal punishment in school and at home include Austria, Bulgaria, Croatia, Cyprus, Denmark, Finland, Germany, Greece, Hungary, Iceland, Latvia, Luxembourg, Moldova, Netherlands, Norway, Portugal, Romania, Spain, Sweden, Switzerland, and Ukraine. In fact, nearly all remaining countries in Europe, with the exception of France, have banned corporal punishment at least in the school. From a historical standpoint, most regions of northern, western, and southern Europe protect the property rights of orphans after the death of parents. Laws were also passed ensuring that orphans whose parents had no property were placed with relatives

or other families. Despite progress made in defending the rights of children in these regions of Europe, more initiative is needed to address inequality between native-born children and immigrant children, particularly children of southeastern and eastern Europe and children of Middle Eastern families who tend to be at an socioeconomic and educational disadvantage.

Despite the encouraging status of children's rights in northern, western, and most of southern Europe, the status of children in eastern and southeastern Europe is unsatisfactory and disappointing in several instances. One important example of children's rights violations in this region concerns the inequality of Roma children in several eastern European countries. Roma children are generally tracked into poor schools and primarily vocational institutions regardless of their academic achievements. In addition to ethnicity, children who have been diagnosed with physical and intellectual disabilities have been stigmatized in a number of eastern European countries, particularly Moldova. Fortunately, several high-profile individuals, such as the British politician Emma Nicholson and author J.K. Rowling, have led efforts to abolish poor treatment of children in eastern Europe.

North America

As is the case in African and certain Asian countries, the recognition of children's rights in Central America and the Caribbean is relatively new. Homelessness, labor, sex trafficking, and lack of health care and education have been the norm and not the exception for children in many countries in North America. Countries with the most acute child welfare problems in the Caribbean and Central America tend to be those that are the poorest. A combination of social and political strife and natural disasters has contributed to deprivation in children's lives in this region. This is evident in Haiti, economically the poorest country in the Western Hemisphere, even before the devastating earthquake of 2010. Central American and Caribbean countries that are currently moving to establish rights for children include Belize, Dominican Republic, El Salvador, Guatemala, Honduras, Jamaica, Mexico, Nicaragua, and Panama.

Although surprising, violation of children's rights in the United States is not uncommon. As of 2012, twenty state constitutions either condone corporal punishment of children in schools or allow latitude to school districts that decide on their own forms of punishment. Moreover, most of these states—particularly in the South and Midwest—have some of the lowest median incomes in the country. For example, the Louisiana state government has established a highly punitive annual state assessment known as the Louisiana Educational Assessment Program (LEAP) that disproportionately castigates the children of poor families, many of whom attend schools with dilapidated infrastructures and no heat, hot water, or electricity. Many poor rural children in Louisiana and other states in the South, Midwest, and West face much more critical issues than passing tests. These issues include neighborhood violent crime, drug and alcohol abuse, poor health care, and lack of bare necessities to live comfortably. The deck is stacked against many Louisianan children of poor families because they must compete with middle- and upper-class children who attend schools with necessary amenities and who can afford to seek additional help in preparing for the LEAP. Those who fail the LEAP must repeat the previous school year. Moreover, national governmental and educational bodies—such as the US Department of Education and the teacher-accrediting organization known as the National Council for the Accreditation of Teacher Education (NCATE)—have done little, if anything, to hold governors and state legislatures accountable in this regard.

The United States has also been vague regarding rights of children whose parents are undocumented immigrants. Current immigration laws are ambiguous with regard to noncitizen parents of citizen children. This lack of concern on the part of politicians in both the federal government and state governments has contributed to family separations, particularly among immigrants from Central America and the Caribbean nations. In fact, political leaders who often espouse conservative lifestyles and definitions of "family" are often those who censure undocumented parents of citizen children as well as the children themselves. Parents often do not have the right to due process when family separation occurs.

Despite these drawbacks, from a historical standpoint, the landmark case known as *Brown v. Board of Education of Topeka* (1954) contributed to the link between the meanings of civil rights and children's rights, thus positively impacting the landscape for all American children. In short, the *Brown* decision ensured that African American children were given equal protection under the Fourteenth Amendment.

South America

Children's rights in South America have only recently been recognized. Historically, South American societies have grappled with ongoing child homelessness and child labor and other forms of maltreatment of children, especially in Brazil, Peru, and Ecuador. From the end of the 1990s to the present, policy initiatives have helped counter the adverse effects caused by unfavorable, harmful, or oftentimes hostile living environments. To begin with, initiatives in certain countries have been helping children communicate their concerns and ideas to adults through various media, including television, newspapers, the Internet, and child welfare conferences. Next, attempts to resolve problems that children face have typically been undertaken soon after the problems at hand have arisen. Efforts are being made to change from this more or less crisis model to one of anticipated prevention so as to avert a problem from arising altogether. For example, instead of dealing with the harmful effects of violence against children, communities are now initiating programs to thwart the onset of violence in their neighborhoods. Although the situation for children is improving, street children continue to engage in begging, other children work, and yet others continue to live in violent communities. These problems often contribute to health complications in adolescence and adulthood. Government policies to deal with these problems have been enacted in some countries in South America, but not in all.

Children's Rights Organizations

To meet the global need to eradicate all forms of child labor and the abuse and other types of maltreatment of children, a number of children's rights groups have been established since the early 1990s. Some of these institutions are listed and described below.

Africa

Only recently has a conscious effort been made to promote and foster children's rights in Africa. The country that has made the most strides in this effort is South Africa. Spearheading this effort are university centers, institutes, and departments that are indirectly, yet successfully, making appeals to government officials. In particular, the Children's Institute at the University of Cape Town has issued initiatives that have contributed to recent policies and interventions that support child and adolescent equality and the rights of young people in South Africa. The Children's Institute was established in 2001 as a means of generating progressive change in children's lives. The institute engages in research that is combined with practical endeavors for the purpose of reaching a wide audience—policy makers, educators, and families—in order to provide evidence-based knowledge and best-practice techniques in the social sciences and law that will help children and adolescents who are the most vulnerable in any given demographic succeed in society.

The Children's Institute engages in the following initiatives that have helped emphasize the importance of the child in society. The first initiative is the *South African Child Gauge*, an annual publication that tracks both negative and positive conditions of children in South Africa. The second is the Children Count Project. This initiative provides consistent indicators that inform both educators and politicians of children's socioeconomic status as well as health conditions and circumstances in various communities. Third, the Child-Centered Analysis of Government's Budgets monitors the allocation of funding for children in various districts and communities. Fourth, the Healthy Cities Project investigates poverty and health conditions in urban settings. Finally, the Children's Radio Project provides opportunities for children and adolescents to convey their concerns and describe their living conditions on various radio programs throughout the country.

Asia

Despite varying levels of children's rights in Asia, few, if any, governmental agencies or private organizations have initiated effort to control violations of children's rights on the continent. Like Asian countries with high standards of living, those with low standards of living tend to ignore the topic. As in Africa, children's rights movements in Asia have emanated from university settings. In particular, the Centre for Child Development at the Hong Kong Baptist University

emphasizes the need to overcome societal obstacles to children's rights on the continent. Established in 1991, the Center for Child Development supports children and adolescents by improving education, particularly in Chinese-speaking regions, as well as by dismantling obstacles, such as poor health care for youth, child labor, and sex trafficking of children. One of the center's prime objectives is interdisciplinary research and program development in the areas of education, sociology, psychology, social work, art and music, and communications for the improvement of children's lives.

Belgium

The Children's Rights Knowledge Center, headquartered in Ghent, Belgium, has affiliations with the University of Antwerp, the Free University of Brussels, Ghent University, the University College Ghent, and the University of Leuven. Founded in 2010, the institution's major objectives include the collection of both national and international data for research in the field of children's rights, using research findings for practical purposes as a means of improving the lives and well-being of children, and the writing and preparation of policy notes that can potentially affect the outcomes of policies in children's rights.

Italy

The UNICEF Innocenti Research Centre in Florence, Italy, promotes policy analysis and research that can potentially have a strong impact on all facets of children's rights. The primary objective of the Innocenti Research Centre is to provide a forum for international discussion and exchange among key constituents of children's rights initiatives by encouraging, promoting, and disseminating research results through a variety of media. The center is connected with the United Nations Children's Fund and represents one of its several intellectual branches. The center supports the enactment of the Millennium Development Agenda and the Millennium Development Goals. Research projects funded by the Innocenti Research Centre seek to decrease child poverty, implement international children's rights policies, eradicate child trafficking and other practices harmful to children, and end the recruitment of children as soldiers.

Spain

The Catalan Interdisciplinary Research Network on Children's Rights and Children's Quality of Life consists of 12 research initiatives, located in five Catalan universities. In total, these 12 initiatives are directed by 76 researchers who specialize in psychology, journalism and media studies, education, and sociology. Despite its beginnings as a network within the Catalan region of Spain, the Network on Children's Rights has increased its reach and is now present in many other European countries as well as in Africa and Asia. The network's aim is to carry out the mission of the United Nations Convention on the Rights of the Child as a means of promoting the quality of life for children and adolescents throughout the world. Researchers within the network have studied children's rights in regard to parents and schools and have developed audiovisual media for helping communities develop contexts for promoting children's and adolescents' rights. The researchers have also organized efforts to change cultural perceptions and values in numerous communities throughout the world so that children do not have to live in the same manner and poor conditions as that of their ancestors.

United Kingdom

As the first university-affiliated center on international children's and adolescents' rights, the Program on International Rights of the Child (PIRCH) was established in 1991 at the University of London. The main goal of PIRCH is to promote legal support in the children's rights movement by searching for lawyers and other legal advisers who are interested in working in children's rights. PIRCH is also known for conducting research in legal issues related to children's rights as well as disseminating up-to-date findings in all areas of child studies. PIRCH has also become a leader in the area of international standards and best practice within the context of juvenile justice.

Oceania

The Centre for Children and Young People is located at Southern Cross University in New South Wales, Australia. Its aim is to foster the role of researchers and practitioners in improving the lives of children throughout the world. The center's interdisciplin-

ary approach emphasizes research and advocacy of youth as well as partnerships with both the public and private sectors. Committed to improving the lives of children in Australia and abroad, the center focuses in particular on native Australian children, who have historically been alienated and subjugated to Western domination. The Centre for Children also provides a legal perspective as a means of challenging obstacles to children's rights in the region.

Canada

Based in Victoria, British Columbia, in Canada, the International Institute for Child Rights and Development (IICRD) is dedicated to improving the well-being of children and adolescents worldwide. Founded in 1994 as a nonprofit organization, IICRD encourages child-based programs in different countries to follow the mandates of the United Nations Convention on the Rights of the Child as a means of improving the lives of children. One of the organization's initial missions was its attempt to eradicate HIV/AIDS, particularly in Africa, a deadly condition that affected the most vulnerable children. IICRD has also contributed significantly in assisting children of indigenous families in different parts of the world—groups who were particularly alienated by colonial empires. The organization has initiated the establishment of numerous pediatric centers in South America, Central America, and various parts of Africa and Asia.

United States

The Children's Environments Research Group (CERG) is a children's rights research organization affiliated with the City University of New York. Like other children's rights groups, CERG attempts to use research from a variety of disciplines as a means of supporting the development of policies that lead to the improvement of children's and adolescents' lives. Its focus on the link between research and practice has led the group to develop a wide range of programs that support child rights initiatives. CERG has developed assessment systems that enable researchers to identify what UNICEF calls "child friendly communities," communities where government officials work in collaboration with local environments as a means of supporting children's rights. The organization has also established initiatives that develop public space for children to engage in play and other child-related activities. CERG has also initiated programs that evaluate the functions of institutions—such as hospitals, zoos, and schools—that are essential for the growth and development of children.

South America

Like other institutions dedicated to children's rights, the International Center for Research and Policy on Childhood (CIESPI) is a research institute that engages in practical endeavors to improve the lives of children, particularly those in Brazil who live in destitute circumstances. CIESPI seeks to promote education by providing children and adolescents with the knowledge and vocational skills needed for future employment. The organization also aims at educating children and adolescents in understanding their own rights, given the vulnerabilities associated with individuals less than 18 years of age. CIESPI also has developed initiatives that promote art and music education as well as initiatives involving the integration of play and learning.

Daniel Ness and Chia-ling Lin

REFERENCES

Alaimo, Kathleen, and Brian Klug, eds. *Children as Equals: Exploring the Rights of the Child.* Lanham, MD: University Press of America, 2002.

Center for Child Development at Hong Kong Baptist University. http://ccd.hkbu.edu.hk.

Children's Institute at the University of Cape Town. www.health.uct.ac.za/research/groupings/childrensinstitute/about/.

Cohen, Howard. *Equal Rights for Children.* Totowa, NJ: Littlefield, Adams, 1980.

Hindman, Hugh D., ed. *The World of Child Labor.* Armonk, NY: M.E. Sharpe, 2009.

Human Rights Watch. Children's Rights. www.hrw.org/crd.

International Institute for Child Rights and Development. www.iicrd.org.

International Labour Organization. "Facts on Child Labour 2010." www.ilo.org/childlabour.

———, International Programme on the Elimination of Child Labour. *Every Child Counts: New Global Estimates on Child Labour.* Geneva: International Labour Organization, 2011.

———. *Investing in Every Child: An Economic Study of the Costs and Benefits of Eliminating Child Labour.* Geneva: International Labour Organization, 2010.

Johnson, Dale D., and Bonnie Johnson. *High Stakes: Children, Testing, and Poverty in American Schools.* Lanham, MD: Rowman & Littlefield, 2006.

Joint Committee on Human Rights. The United Nations Convention on the Rights of the Child. London: The Stationery Office Limited, House of Lords and House of Commons, 2003.

Pardeck, Jean A. *Children's Rights: Policy and Practice.* New York: Routledge, 2006.

Rodham, Hillary. "Children under the Law." *Harvard Educational Review* 43:4 (November 1973): 487–514.

Ruxton, Sandy. *What About Us? Children's Rights in the European Union: Next Steps.* London: National Society for the Prevention of Cruelty to Children, 2005.

Sloth-Nielsen, Julia. "Domestication of Children's Rights in National Legal Systems in African Context: Progress and Prospects." In *Children's Rights in Africa*, ed. Julia Sloth-Nielsen, 53–72. Burlington, VT: Ashgate, 2008.

UNICEF. *Building a World Fit for Children: The United Nations General Assembly Special Session on Children, 8–10 May 2002.* New York: UNICEF, 2003.

———. Convention on the Rights of the Child, 2011. www.unicef.org/crc/.

———. Monitoring the Situation of Children and Women through the Multiple Indicator Cluster Survey (MICS). 2008. www.childinfo.org/files/childinfo_mics.pdf.

———. *A World Fit for Children: Millennium Development Goals, Special Session on Children Documents, the Convention of the Rights of the Child.* New York: UNICEF, 2002.

United Nations General Assembly. Resolution Adopted by the General Assembly (62/88). "Declaration of the Commemorative High-Level Plenary Meeting Devoted to the Follow-up to the Outcome of the Special Session on Children." December 13, 2007. http://documents.un.org.

United Nations General Assembly Special Session on Children. Resolution Adopted by the General Assembly (S-27/2). "A World Fit for Children." May 10, 2002. www.unicef.org/specialsession/wffc/.

———. Background, Reports, and Documents. www.unicef.org/specialsession/index.html.

US Department of Health and Human Services, Administration for Children and Families. Third Incidence Study of Child Abuse and Neglect. Washington, DC: US Department of Health and Human Services, 1996.

Van Beuren, Geraldine. "Acknowledging Children as International Citizens: A Child-sensitive Communication Mechanism for the Convention on the Rights of the Child." In *The Human Rights of Children: From Visions to Implementation*, ed. Antonella Invernizzi and Jane Williams, 117–132. Burlington, VT: Ashgate, 2011.

World Health Organization. Female Genital Mutilation Fact Sheet. www.who.int/mediacentre/factsheets/en/.

CHILDREN'S PHYSICAL HEALTH ISSUES

Children's physical health issues with regard to education and human development concern the biological well-being of students who are learning in a formal setting. Physical health issues can adversely affect children by placing the quality of work and school related performance at risk. It is important to consider, however, that health problems and concerns are not necessarily linked to individual decision-making outcomes or conditions; indeed, they are linked closely with sociological matters, such as childhood poverty and racial and ethnic discrimination.

Healthcare for low-income children is significantly inferior to that for children from middle- and upper-income families. Poor children are more likely to have low birth weight and problems in growth. In addition, given the poorer quality of living conditions, they are more likely to contract lead poisoning because they often live in dwellings whose walls contain lead-based materials. According to the Children's Law Center, poor children are at a much greater disadvantage than middle- and upper-income children in terms of physical health issues and proper treatment. In contrast to middle- and upper-income children, poor children are 1.6 times as likely to die in infancy; 1.8 times as likely to be born premature; 1.9 times as likely to have a low birth weight; 2.7 times as likely to have no regular source of health care; and 2.8 times as likely to have little, if any, prenatal care. Adequate health care can contribute to improving these risks. Nevertheless, it is not enough. Squalid conditions in the home, homelessness, low income, poor nutrition, domestic abuse, illegal immigration status, inadequate child care, lack of health insurance, and physical disabilities all contribute to adverse health outcomes for children. If children do not have proper nutrition and adequate health care, they are less likely to succeed in formal activities such as schooling. From a humanistic psychological perspective, children and adolescents who live in poverty can focus little, if any, attention on their education if basic needs—such as food, clothing, shelter, health, and safety—are not being met by the community. Therefore, if healthcare is not a major priority in certain segments of society, educational success, let alone the achievement of educational goals, will not be an important goal for children living in these situations.

Common Physical Health Problems in Children

Common physical health problems in children include respiratory conditions, such as asthma; chronic diseases, such as diabetes and HIV/AIDS; orthopedic conditions; and obesity. Although not considered an illness or disease in itself, obesity is a leading risk factor in a number of diseases, including cardiovascular disease and various types of cancer.

Asthma and Other Respiratory Conditions

Many children who suffer from asthma and other respiratory diseases cannot obtain effective treatment because their physical environment causes or exacerbates their medical condition. Approximately 40 percent of childhood asthma is attributable to conditions in the home. Children with respiratory illnesses suffer extraordinary health risks when they are forced to live in substandard homes infested with rodents or containing mold or other allergens.

Chronic Diseases

Serious chronic diseases, including (1) sickle cell anemia, (2) conditions associated with HIV/AIDS, and (3) diabetes, affect many children. Families often need assistance in obtaining quality medical care for such diseases and in asserting children's rights to an appropriate education despite such diseases. Children in fragile medical states may also need assistance in improving housing conditions—such as a broken heater.

According to the National Cancer Institute, the most common types of childhood cancers, especially in developed countries, are leukemias (blood cell cancers) and cancers of the brain and central nervous system. These types of cancer account for more than half of new cancer cases. Approximately one-third of childhood cancers worldwide are leukemias. The most widespread type of leukemia in children, particularly under the age of 15, is acute lymphoblastic leukemia. The most widespread brain tumors are gliomas (brain or spine) and medullablastomas (originating in the cerebellum). Less common solid tumors, but nevertheless prevalent, are neuroblastomas (brain-related cancers occurring outside of the brain), Wilms' tumors (developed in the kidneys), and sarcomas such as rhabdomyosarcoma (tendons) and osteosarcoma (bones).

Orthopedic Impairments

Children often need specific medical devices to treat orthopedic impairments. One example of an orthopedic impairment is congenital vertical talus, which affects the feet in early infancy. Children with orthopedic conditions, no matter what their level of mobility, need their homes and schools to be physically accessible. Children of parents or guardians who are unable to provide for specific orthopedic equipment will be at a strong disadvantage in terms of school and social mobility.

Childhood and Adolescent Obesity

Obesity is frequently listed as one of the most glaring problems in childhood and adolescent health in the twenty-first century. Although obesity, in addition to very poor nutrition, is pandemic, the problem is most severe in areas where people live in squalid conditions—both in urban and rural locales. These areas are characterized by overwhelmingly high levels of poverty. According to researchers, in fact, obesity (as well as poor dental health) is a key indicator of poverty. These markers are particularly evident in the United States, which has the second-highest percentage of obese adults (25 percent) in the world (Australia has 26 percent). In 2008, Mississippi topped the charts as the "most obese state" in the United States as well as the state with the highest level of poverty.

Improving Children's Health

A number of steps can be taken to initially improve the physical health and well-being of children, particularly children who live in poor conditions. For example, children's asthma is exacerbated by unsanitary living conditions that can be alleviated by some simple, fairly inexpensive steps. First, it is important to rid dwellings of vermin (i.e., rats, mice, and other unwanted

rodent populations), mold, and insects (such as cockroaches, beetles, and other insects that are known to carry disease). According to the Centers for Disease Control, vermin, mold, and insect infestations are the cause of repeated emergency room visits for thousands of urban, low-income children. Rural children, unfortunately, are less likely to live near health-care facilities. Nevertheless, people need to insist on local and regional government initiatives to prevent the spread of vermin and insect populations. Given that children living in poverty are twice as likely to have poor health as middle- and upper-income children, institutional change is needed to ameliorate health and societal disparities. Societal and environmental factors, such as unsafe housing, inadequate education, low income, domestic abuse, and lack of health insurance, have adversely affected health outcomes for poor children. Again, government mandates and initiatives are needed to improve living conditions so that all children will have nearly the same advantage when pursuing a formal education.

At the very least, all students' achievement at school can occur only under circumstances in which each member of a country's entire population has equal access to adequate health care. Since various forms of assessment play a major part in the educational outcomes of all students, regardless of nationality, it is imperative that all schoolchildren receive the same benefits of health care as their peers. Nevertheless, a major problem in education is that poor children are held to the same standard as their middle-income and upper-income peers in terms of their performance on high-stakes examinations. Policy makers and education experts can safeguard and fortify the services that are shown to increase educational outcomes for children involved in child welfare systems as well as children whose disabilities or developmental delays have had adverse effects on their education and health. In particular, children's success in education, particularly those with physical disability, depends in part on whether political and educational leaders secure early intervention services, respond to school discipline matters, and maintain children's school stability and school enrollment.

Child Abuse and Neglect

In addition to poverty and the lack of adequate health care, child abuse also contributes to deficiencies in learning and children's lack of motivation in schooling. Child abuse shatters lives, stunts physical, motor, and even cognitive development, is often the cause of long-term mental health problems, and prevents children from growing to their potential at school and at home. Removing children from their abusive families and placing them in foster care may not be an ideal solution because this can often lead to other forms of physical and mental distress, which can further adversely affect educational outcomes. Fortunately, child abuse and neglect can be prevented. Poverty, a family history of physical and mental illness, and a family history of violence are some of the many difficulties that devastate some parents and lead to abuse and neglect.

Research has shown that increases in public benefits provided through several locally and federally based organizations have led to decreases in the frequency of child abuse and neglect. Moreover, given that physically and mentally abused children often move in with grandparents, organizations that provide essential assistance to poor children living with grandparents and other relatives can contribute to successful educational outcomes. In addition, successful preschool programs that provide services and support systems to parents have been shown to protect children from abuse and neglect in the long term.

The identification of and the incentive to resolve problems associated with physical abuse and neglect can be helpful; however, indications of abuse must be addressed early. For example, home visiting programs allow professionals to visit young families to teach parental skills. Substance abuse by parents affects thousands of children and is a leading cause of both physical and mental child abuse and neglect. Effective substance abuse programs, especially residential programs that let young children stay with their parents, can help keep families together.

Mental health problems among both adults and children are the underlying causes of many abuse and neglect incidents. Certain specialized mental health services, such as parent-child interaction therapy and functional family therapy, have been proved to help parents manage their children's most difficult behaviors without resorting to abuse or neglect.

Another factor that puts schoolchildren at risk is the problem of inadequate housing. Family members often need to find new housing quickly in order to flee domestic violence. This scenario is prevalent in families in poverty. Like the previous conditions, inadequate housing is a problem that may be rectified in certain instances through special programs. Two examples in the United States are Rapid Housing, which enables families to overcome housing issues that would otherwise lead to the child's removal from the home, and the Family Unification Program, which provides vouchers—such as the Housing Choice Voucher Program, which issues Section 8 vouchers—to help families afford safe housing. Many physical abuse and neglect programs have been shown to save taxpayer money. As data collected by the Washington State Institute for Public Policy (2008) show, home visiting programs for parents of high-risk young children seemed to curb physical abuse by at least one-half in comparison to no visitation.

All children need advocates for their overall betterment and well-being. A potentially successful model for improving children's health from a legal perspective is a medical and legal collaboration between law firms that advocate for children's issues and local or regional hospitals and medical centers. This form of collaboration between law practice and health-care provider establishes lawyers as part of a multidisciplinary approach for the improvement of childhood health care. Legal advocates and medical experts team together as a means of solving children's medical conditions. In collaboration with medical experts, legal advocates can help children in medical need by challenging existing legal and administrative obstacles that impede the improvement of children's health. This collaboration often works in favor of children's physical health, particularly in the creation of housing initiatives that improve living conditions of children with respiratory illnesses, most commonly, asthma.

Daniel Ness and Chia-ling Lin

REFERENCES

Children's Law Center. "Physical Health." www.childrenslawcenter. org/issues/physical-health.

Johnson, Dale D., B. Johnson, Stephen J. Farenga, and Daniel Ness. *Stop High Stakes Testing: An Appeal to America's Conscience.* Lanham, MD: Rowman & Littlefield, 2008.

Lee, Stephanie, Steve Aos, and Marna Miller. *Evidence-based Programs to Prevent Children from Entering and Remaining in the Child Welfare System: Benefits and Costs for Washington.* Washington State Institute for Public Policy. www.wsipp.wa.gov/ rptfiles/08-07-3901.pdf.

National Cancer Institute. *Childhood Cancers: Questions and Answers.* www.cancer.gov/cancertopics/factsheet/Sites-Types/childhood.

Sered, Susan Starr, and Rushika Fernandopulle. *Uninsured in America: Life and Death in the Land of Opportunity.* Berkeley: University of California Press, 2005.

CHILDREN'S MENTAL HEALTH

A supportive mental health system is an important component of children's overall health, development, and ability to learn and participate in school. Indeed, children and adolescents who have untreated mental health conditions or disorders usually have considerable difficulty in school and future education. Moreover, they are often more involved with the criminal justice system and have fewer stable, long-term placements in the child welfare system than other children.

Mental health concerns are not limited to any one ethnic, social, religious, or gender-related group. It has been documented that numerous low-income children, particularly those involved with the child welfare system, have experienced mental health issues at one point or another. In fact, Rachel Masi and Janice Cooper, in *Children's Mental Health: Facts for Policymakers* (2006), show that nearly half of children in the welfare system have mental health problems. Further, in *Blueprint for Change* (2006), Kathleen Skowyra and Joseph Cocozza show a greater percentage of mental health conditions among children in the child welfare and juvenile justice systems than in children within the rest of the population. Nearly 70 percent of youth involved with the juvenile justice system have a diagnosable mental health condition. Living in poverty, witnessing violence, being the victim of both physical and mental abuse and neglect, and being taken away and disconnected from one's family are all difficult situations that often contribute to a variety of mental health problems in later childhood and adolescence. Children in the child welfare system frequently require interventions for reducing maltreatment from abuse and addressing traumatic situations when they occur. Moreover, poor children with mental health concerns perform less well than their middle-income and affluent peers on similar high-stakes examinations because mental health services are often unavailable in low-income school districts and neighborhoods.

In the United States, approximately one in five children has a diagnosable mental disorder, and one in 10 suffers from a serious mental health problem that impairs how the child functions at home and school. Low-income children have more mental health conditions than other children. The prevalence of serious mental health conditions among poor children of school age on Medicaid is 13.5 percent. In the United States, nearly 70 percent of all children and adolescents in need of treatment, mostly due to poverty, do not receive mental health services. For example, the Children's Law Center of Washington, DC, cites data from the Child and Family Services Agency that indicates that only 35 percent of child clients are receiving mental health services. Moreover, the Department of Mental Health provides mental health services to less than 4 percent of all children whose parents or guardians are enrolled in Medicaid.

The following are some of the commonly diagnosed mental illnesses, as defined in the fourth edition of the *Diagnostic and Statistical Manual of Mental Disorders* (DSM-IV), in schoolchildren throughout the world:

- Adjustment disorder
- Antisocial disorder
- Attachment disorder
- Attention-deficit hyperactivity disorder
- Bipolar disorder
- Borderline intellectual functioning
- Conduct disorder
- Depression
- Mental retardation
- Mood disorder
- Physical or sexual abuse
- Post-traumatic stress disorder

Autism Spectrum Disorders

A group of disorders known as autism spectrum disorders (ASD) characterize the wide range of conditions that affect communication and social interaction—two key components of schooling and classroom environments. ASD includes several conditions, two of which are autism and Asperger's syndrome.

Autism is a neurological and developmental disorder that affects an individual's social interaction with others and abilities to communicate information. Signs of autism occur during infancy and usually, but not always, progress gradually to age two or three, at which time it is possible to diagnose the disorder.

The prevalence of autism worldwide is somewhat unclear. In the United States, however, recent estimates show that one out of every 100 infants will show symptoms of autism. During the last few decades of the twentieth century, most estimates seemed to indicate a less serious picture of one in every 1,000 infants developing the disorder.

It is often difficult to determine the rate of autism in various parts of the world because stable populations—populations in which fertility and mortality are constant—do not exist in certain regions. For example, due to diverse political, ethnic, and social systems, it is difficult to determine the prevalence of autism in Africa at the present time. In addition, stable populations are not prevalent in many countries throughout Africa. Epidemiologists have also found it difficult to determine the prevalence of autism in Australia. In 2008 a study on Australian children between six and 12 years old reported an ASD incidence rate between one and 3.5 children per 1,000. These numbers, however, are inconclusive.

At least two studies have been conducted in the Pacific Rim, one in Hong Kong in 2008 and another in Japan in 2005. The Hong Kong study indicated an ASD rate comparable to that of the United States and Canada. Moreover, the rate was slower than that of most European countries. Overall, the study showed a prevalence of ASD of 1.68 per 1,000 for children below 15 years. In 2005 Japan issued a study of ASD using data collected on 300,000 children in Yokohama. The incidence rate in 1989 in children seven years and younger was one case per 208 children. Four years later, the incidence rate grew to one case per 116 children. Oddly, when the incident rate of 1994 was compared with the previous four-year period, the incidence rate grew drastically from one per 103 children to one per 62 children.

As in Japan, autism seemed to increase in Denmark after 1990, regardless of vaccine use. A study examining children between the ages of two and four showed that in 1990, the autism incidence rate was 0.05 per 1,000, but it jumped to nearly 0.5 per 1,000 after 2000. A similar study eight years later demonstrated a 30 percent increase in autism among children of the same age range between 2000 and 2005. Within these five years, autism among children in Denmark increased dramatically within the first two years and then steadily declined. Overall, incidence of mental disorders for school-age children increased in Denmark after 2000. Due to diverse populations, the incidence of ASD in the United Kingdom is less evident. What is clear is the lack of evidence associating vaccinations to onset of ASD. Nevertheless, general developmental disorders increased from 0.001 per 1,000 to 0.298 per 1,000 between 1988 and 2000.

In 2009 a study reported an increase in Israeli cases of ASD during the 20-year period between 1984 and 2004, namely, from no cases to 0.19 cases per 1,000 children. Improvements in diagnostic treatment may have contributed to the overall increase. Estimates in neighboring countries are rather low. In Saudi Arabia, for example, the incidence rate for autism is 1.8 per 1,000—approximately the same as that of most European countries.

Asperger's syndrome is a neurological disorder that falls within the ASD category. Children affected by Asperger's syndrome are unable to interact with others for a sustained or continued period of time. The titular discoverer of Asperger's syndrome, Hans Asperger, an Austrian pediatrician, noticed the behaviors of certain children who were unable to convey nonverbal messages and whose everyday behavior demonstrated an awkward, clumsy character. Often considered by psychologists and psychiatrists as a condition describing a high-functioning person with autistic tendencies, Asperger's syndrome was added to the DSM-IV in 1994. Asperger's individuals often fail to understand emotional cues and gestures relating to nonverbal communication between various people. Due to onsets of increased stress when addressing obsessive behaviors, such as constant hand or foot tapping or clapping, it is difficult to attempt to modify behavioral tendencies associated with Asperger's syndrome.

Children with Asperger's syndrome may not show any signs of poor speaking and general communication abilities—especially in the home environment. However, when they enter school, they are often subjected to negative reactions from classmates because they cannot express themselves clearly in environments outside the home. Despite having average or above-average cognitive ability, children who suffer from Asperger's syndrome often have difficulty identifying other people's emotions and, at the same time, may not know how to express their own. One major hallmark of children with Asperger's syndrome is the tendency to react to stressful situations rather than thinking rationally. These children tend to lack restraint by engaging in hypersensitive verbal behaviors—that is, behaviors that show the appearance of a lack of sensitivity, though not destructive or detrimental in any way—without thinking about the ramifications of doing so. Examples of these behaviors include the lack of recognizing social cues, avoidance of routine change, avoidance of eye contact, delayed motor development, increased sensitivity toward changes of light, sound, textures, or tastes, and a seeming lack of empathy. Moreover, given that children with Asperger's syndrome often react adversely to changes in the environment, it would be helpful for adults to provide routines for these children's daily activities. It is crucial for parents and teachers to be aware of the symptoms of Asperger's Syndrome, as it may adversely affect social skills in middle school and high school. In many instances, due to isolation from peers during later childhood, these children may experience the onset of depression because, although they understand the importance of friendship, they feel unable to establish bonds with others.

At present, neuroscientific researchers are still unclear about the origins of Asperger's syndrome. However, there is evidence to suggest that its onset is a result of a genetic predisposition, rather than environmental factors. Through longitudinal research, neuroscientists found that children are more likely to have Asperger's syndrome if they have relatives who have the condition. Although there is no cure for the disorder, it is possible to control most, if not all, of the symptoms of Asperger's syndrome through a combination of psychosocial and psychopharmacological interventions. Psychosocial interventions include, but are not limited to, the following: individual psychotherapy, to help children deal with emotions and situations involving social interaction; education and training for adults who work with children who are affected by the condition; behavioral modification, which may involve classical conditioning techniques; and educational intervention—that is, possible modifications associated with pedagogy. Psychopharmacological interventions include, but are not limited to, the following: psychostimulants (such as methyphenidate, dextroamphetamine, metamphetamine, and clonidine), tricyclic antidepressants (such as desipramine and nortriptyline), and strattera (atomoxetine) for hyperactivity, inattention, and im-

pulsive behaviors; mood stabilizers (such as valproate, carbamazepine, and lithium), beta blockers (such as nadolol and propranolol), and neuroleptics (such as risperidone, olanzapine, quetiapine, ziprasidone, and haloperidol) for irritability and aggressive behavior; selective serotonin re-uptake inhibitors (SSRIs) (such as fluvoxamine, fluoxetine, and paroxetine) and tricyclic antidepressants (such as clomipramine) for preoccupations, rituals, and obsessive and compulsive behaviors (see OCD described below); and SSRIs (such as sertraline and fluoxetine) and tricyclic antidepressants (such as imipramine, clomipramine, and nortriptyline) for the control of anxiety.

The education of children with Asperger's syndrome as well as other ASDs should be individualized so that social routines and communication skills are built into the curriculum and aligned with the content. Several support groups have formed on behalf of children and adolescents with ASD and Asperger's syndrome. The organization called More Advanced Individuals with Autism, Asperger's Syndrome, and Pervasive Developmental Disorder (MAAP) has recently collaborated with Online Asperger Syndrome Information and Support (OASIS) to support families with children and adults who have ASD-related conditions. Appropriate curriculum for children with ASD includes procedural techniques that tap into the change of unwanted behaviors. These techniques must be concrete and literal—that is, teachers and caregivers must avoid abstractions when teaching content so that children do not become anxious and overwhelmed with specific content. With proper intervention, children with Asperger's syndrome as well as other ASD-related disorders have the potential to be successful contributors to society as adults.

Attention-Deficit and Hyperactivity Disorder

Attention-deficit hyperactivity disorder (ADHD) is a very common condition among young and school-age children that is repeatedly considered as a leading cause of underachievement in school. The American Psychiatric Association claims that 3 to 5 percent of American schoolchildren are diagnosed with ADHD at any given time. Data on ADHD throughout the world, however, are inconclusive in terms of a consistent number of children, since percentages vary depending on the country in question. The primary symptoms of ADHD are lack of attention, frequent periods of hyperactivity, and impulsive behavior. A specialist will conclude a positive diagnosis of ADHD if these symptoms persist for at least six months. It is important for caregivers to avoid a conclusion of ADHD if a child exhibits some inattention or hyperactivity. These traits are present in most children and even adults as well.

The following symptoms are most commonly used for diagnosis:

Inattention. A child with ADHD shows significant deficits in sustained attention and effort. The child is unable to remain on task and has difficulty paying attention, following directions, and remembering. ADHD children at play often lose attention, thus hampering their social interaction with others. In addition, given that lack of attention, ADHD can indeed adversely affect schoolwork as well as attentiveness to personal health and hygiene.

Hyperactivity. The most visible symptom is hyperactivity because hyperactive behavior can easily be identified by the caregiver. It is exemplified by the inability to control motor activity. Accordingly, an ADHD child often lacks the ability to remain sitting in a stationary position for an extended period of time.

Impulsivity. The symptom of impulsivity may be apparent when a child is unable to control actions within any situation or environment. ADHD children are often unable to delay gratification, and it is often difficult for them to share with their peers or take turns in social situations due to their inability to control their instinctual desires. As a result, others often perceive ADHD children's actions as self-centered and at times hostile.

Most research in ADHD seems to suggest that the condition is the result of neurological deficits that hamper the ability to control impulsive actions and, instead, contribute to the inability to delay gratification through bouts of frustration when interacting with others. Neurological research has shown the existence of a strong biological factor that may be a primary factor of the cause of ADHD. Studies have shown less activity in the frontal lobe regions of the brain, which involve behavioral inhibition, persistence of responding, resistance to distractions, and control of one's activity level. If children with ADHD

are untreated, they run the risk of rejection by others as a result of their disruptive behaviors. Like ASD, although environmental factors, such as negative parental influence or bullying by others, may exacerbate symptoms, they are not the cause of ADHD.

Given that no treatment has been shown to cure ADHD, it is necessary to detect the condition as early as possible. Early detection can limit the severity of ADHD symptoms. A treatment plan should include several components: behavior management, effective school instruction, counseling services, and, if necessary, medication. The most common medications prescribed for ADHD are psychostimulants, such as methylphenidate (Ritalin), dextroamphetamine (Dexedrine), and pemoline (Cylert). Psychostimulants have been proven to control hyperactive tendencies and improve attentiveness. In some situations, antidepressants are used in the event psychostimulants do not curb ADHD symptoms.

Disorders Associated with Neuroses

Disorders related to neurotic conditions affect millions of children throughout the world. These disorders generally impair mood, dispositions, and idiosyncratic behaviors. Heightened anxiety is often a hallmark of neurosis. Common disorders that are categorized as neurotic-related conditions are depression, obsessive-compulsive disorder, personality disorder, and post-traumatic stress disorder. These conditions are by no means categorically defined; in fact, there are numerous subcategories within each condition. Other anxiety-related neuroses include somatoform related conditions, such as heightened illness concern (formerly called hypochondriasis). Two of the common conditions associated with school-age children are depression and obsessive compulsive disorder.

Major depressive disorder, or, simply, depression, is a common disorder in children and young adults. The disorder is characterized by low mood, a lack of interest or pleasure in activities that are considered enjoyable, and a low confidence or sense of worth. Depression can be a result of a combination of both physiological and psychological conditions. It often emerges as a result of a death in the family or of a loved one, a traumatic experience, changes in physiology, or inheritance from family members with the condition. It can also stem from organic imbalances, whereby certain neurotransmitter substances, such as serotonin or norepinephrine, are either limited or in abundant amounts. Depression is most common in the United States, with more than 1,600 per 100,000 people having the condition. Countries with rates close to that of the United States include Canada, Brazil, France, Finland, Pakistan, India, Afghanistan, Bangladesh, and Nepal, with approximately 1,200 to 1,300 per 100,000 people. The lowest rates of depression worldwide seem to be in countries in sub-Saharan Africa. Depression is a serious disorder because it can often lead individuals, even children, to attempt suicide. Although the United States, the country with the highest rate of depression, has a 3.5 percent suicide rate, China, India, and Japan account for approximately 40 percent of the world's suicides. To counter this risk of suicide, numerous world agencies, such as UNICEF and the World Health Organization, are attempting to provide both mental and medical care for a growing number of people, nearly half of whom live in developing countries, with major depressive disorder.

Obsessive-compulsive disorder (OCD) is a condition that prevents functioning in daily activities because the individual who is diagnosed with OCD is unable to control intrusive thoughts (i.e., obsessions) or break repetitive actions (i.e., compulsions). For example, some people believe that they will be infected with a fatal disease if they come into contact with certain objects, people, or animals. Accordingly, they will engage in particular rituals (compulsions), such as frequent hand washing, as a means of eliminating bacteria or other elements they believe to be fatal. It is known that biological factors contribute to between 45 and 65 percent of the symptoms associated with OCD. Individuals with OCD symptoms have deficits of the neurotransmitter substance known as serotonin.

The prevalence of OCD worldwide varies, depending on the country. OCD prevalence is not based on social or economic factors. For example, the greatest prevalence of OCD seems to be in South American countries. With more than 120 cases per 100,000 people, Argentina and Uruguay have the highest rate of OCD. The prevalence of the condition in other South American countries is relatively close—with over 100 per 100,000 population. Similar statistics are evident in most countries of Central America,

Africa, the Middle East, eastern Europe, Central Asia, and Russia. Areas with the lowest levels of OCD—that is, less than 60 per 100,000 people—include East Asia, parts of southern Asia, and Australia. Western European countries, Canada, and the United States seem to fall in the middle with approximately 75 per 100,000 people. Given the lack of medical care in many countries, control of OCD, as well as other neurotic disorders, has become a worldwide problem. Despite some knowledge of worldwide prevalence, the number of children throughout the world who have OCD is unclear.

Psychotic Disorders

Psychotic disorders are those in which individuals suffer from a loss of contact with reality. The most common way to treat individuals with psychoses in the past was through institutionalization. Institutionalizing individuals with schizophrenia and other psychotic disorders greatly waned over the last half century. Individuals with psychoses can be treated today without being institutionalized as a result of the marked improvement of medications used to treat and control—but not cure—psychotic-related conditions.

Schizophrenia is a broad term that refers to conditions whereby individuals suffer from hallucinations, delusions, and thought disorders. There are several types of schizophrenia, including paranoid schizophrenia, hebephrenic schizophrenia (regression to childhood), and catatonic schizophrenia (lack of control of motor skills).

Parents with schizophrenia are likely to have children who have the condition. Identification of childhood schizophrenia includes, but is not limited to, the following: irregular quick and sudden movements, talking to oneself, withdrawal, agitation, and emotional outbursts that do not characterize given situations (e.g., a child who cries after being praised by a peer or an adult).

Bipolar disorder is a condition that affects mood whereby the individual has drastic mood shifts, from mania to severe depressive episodes. Bipolar disorder in children is a prevalent condition, depending on the country or cultural environment.

Current Trends Involving Children's Mental Health

Since the 1970s to the present, the provision of mental health services has changed from a predominance of institutional care, such as mental and residential hospitals and facilities, to systems of care that are designed to provide culturally competent, family-centered, community-based services. The main purpose in this transition is to ensure that each child with a given mental condition has an individualized, coordinated treatment plan that utilizes a variety of treatment models and services to support the child at home and in the community. It is difficult to identify an exhaustive list of support systems. Nevertheless, the common support systems include the following: diagnostic evaluations and psychological testing; crisis stabilization; in-home family stabilization services and parent training services; individual, group, and family therapy; psychiatric treatment and medication management; substance abuse treatment; acute in-patient hospitalization; short- or long-term residential treatment; and a variety of evidence-based specific therapy models, including cognitive behavioral therapy (CBT) and trauma-focused CBT, or functional family therapy.

The child mental health system in large cities is often disjointed, making it very difficult for children to get the mental health treatment they need. Children with mental health problems receive services through a complicated variety of agencies and providers, including public or private health insurance; schools and school systems; special education services, whereby children are diagnosed with some type of emotional disability; and city and state agencies. In addition, mental health services for children and adolescents are often provided through various private agencies, community-based organizations, religious institutions, and networks of individual clinicians and doctors.

Daniel Ness and Chia-ling Lin

REFERENCES

American Psychiatric Association. *Diagnostic and Statistical Manual of Mental Disorders.* 4th ed. Washington, DC: American Psychiatric Association, 1994.

Burns, Barbara, et al. "Mental Health Need and Access to Mental Health Services by Youths Involved with Child Welfare: A National Survey." *Journal of the American Academy of Child and Adolescent Psychiatry* 43:8 (2004): 960–970.

Geller, Barbara, and Melissa P. DelBello. *Bipolar Disorder in Childhood and Early Adolescence.* Westport, CT: Guilford, 2003.

Johnson, Dale, et al. *Stop High-Stakes Testing: An Appeal to America's Conscience.* Lanham, MD: Rowman & Littlefield, 2008.

Masi, Rachel, and Janice L. Cooper. *Children's Mental Health: Facts for Policymakers.* New York: National Center for Children in Poverty, 2006.

Newschaffer, Craig J., et al. "The Epidemiology of Autism Spectrum Disorders." *Annual Review of Public Health* 28 (2006): 235–258.

OASIS @ MAAP. www.aspergersyndrome.org/Home.aspx.

Skowyra, Kathleen R., and Joseph J. Cocozza. *Blueprint for Change: A Comprehensive Model for the Identification and Treatment of Youth with Mental Health Needs in Contact with the Juvenile Justice System.* Delmar, NY: National Center for Mental Health and Juvenile Justice and Policy Research Associates, 2006. www.ncmhjj.com/Blueprint/pdfs/Blueprint.pdf.

PARENTING

Parenting is one of the most important influences that affects a child's educational progress. Nearly all research in parenting and child development agrees that the care-giving environment for the young child dramatically influences cognitive development, social interaction skills, and emotional functioning. Parents and caregivers play an exceptional part in the formation of the child's environment; they provide experiences through which the child constructs a sense of identity and character, as well as beliefs about the world. There is no one answer as to how parents influence young children, or how young children develop and end up in later life as a result of parental effect.

The limitations of parenthood have detrimental effects on children—especially when families are obligated to focus on providing the essential elements of survival, such as health care; basic needs, which include food, clothing, and shelter; and safety both within and outside the home and school. Parents who are required to redirect their focus to basic needs do so at the expense of providing emotional stability, let alone adequate education. Further, it has been shown that disruption in emotional support compromises advancement in various developmental domains. This disruption interferes with the child's achievement of expected landmarks in most areas having to do with cognitive development.

In addition to parental influence on the child, there also seems to be a symbiotic relationship between the child's behavior and the subsequent manner in which a parent provides care. Numerous social psychologists, such as Gerald Patterson and Albert Bandura, argue the existence of a reciprocal relationship in that the child's actions can potentially control how a parent disciplines a child as a result of aggressive behavior.

Parenting Since 1950

Parenting has changed drastically since the 1950s. A number of these changes heightened the level of complexity of parenting and its impact on child development. In developed societies prior to the 1960s, homebound mothers were the norm; within the past several decades, however, the scenario of a stay-at-home mother has become increasingly rare indeed. The increase in the number of mothers working outside the home in the 32-year period between 1975 and 2011 is staggering. According to the Bureau of Labor Statistics in the US Department of Labor (2011), the percentage of mothers in the labor force with children under the age of six increased from 40 percent in 1975 to nearly 64 percent in 2010. Similarly, the percentage of mothers in the labor force with children from age six to age 17 increased from approximately 55 percent in 1975 to nearly 78 percent in 2010. According to data provided by the Children's Defense Fund, over 13 million preschoolers (approximately 60 percent of all children under the age of five in the United States) before 2000 were either enrolled in child-care facilities or needed child care. It is important to note, however, that current research shows a positive correlation between the increase in percentage of working mothers, particularly those engaged in part-time employment, and more successful parenting. This finding contradicts the stereotype that working mothers are less successful in raising their children than are non-working mothers.

The increase in divorce rates (particularly in developed societies), the number of single-parent households (in most countries throughout the world), the number of working mothers, and blended and extended family structures have greatly altered the meaning of the family. Moreover, the family structure in most heterogeneous societies changed in terms of race and ethnicity. In the United States, the widespread societal problem of divorce affects approximately 40 percent of children born to married parents. As research seems to suggest, unlike children who live in two-parent households, nearly one-quarter of all children of divorced parents will demonstrate signs of maladjustment in situations that require social interaction. There are many examples of maladjustments, including problems with school and cognitive development, social behavior, self-control and regulation, and substance abuse. With more divorced parents remarrying, blended families, too, are on the rise, with a concomitant rise in the number of half siblings. Like children of divorced parents, children in blended families experience a greater degree of maladjustment than their peers with two original parents. It is important to note, however, that although these changes are significant and although social and physical dilemmas can arise, many children will not experience any difficulties.

Single-parent households are on the rise throughout the world. Although some working mothers have little, if any, difficulty in providing care for their children, the majority of single mothers do—regardless of whether they are divorced or bear children out of wedlock. These mothers have meager earnings, primarily after divorce. Therefore, for divorced mothers, transitions are more tenuous than for custodial fathers. Divorced mothers often are required to find a second or even a third job in order to make ends meet. This frequently results in job instability, increased stress, and transitions into poor and often unsafe communities.

Throughout the world, many women seek work outside the home even though they are working as mothers, in order to provide for their children and others who might be dependent upon them. Many factors contribute to this need. One factor is the inability of a spouse to find work or to find a stable job. Another factor is divorce or the death of a spouse. In addition, many women want to increase the income of the family. In some cases, women work outside the home because they choose to do so, possibly in order to enhance a career. One major question that researchers have asked in recent decades is the extent to which children are affected by mothers who work shortly before and after childbirth. In general, social and cognitive comparisons of children whose mothers do and do not work after childbirth do not show significant changes. Nevertheless, some studies examining specific tendencies show adverse outcomes for children whose mothers work shortly after childbirth. For example, cognitive outcomes of three-year-old children whose mothers returned to work after they were born were weaker than those of three-year-old children whose mothers waited at least nine months after their children were born before they returned to work.

Latchkey Problem

One of the major problems in developed countries that have experienced a drastic increase in single-parent families is the rise in the number of "latchkey children." The term "latchkey" refers to children who are at home alone either after school or when school is not in session. The lack of parental caregivers and supervision at home may contribute to an increase in social and cognitive problems in late youth and adolescence. As a result, juvenile delinquency, substance abuse, sloth and inactivity, unsupervised peer contact, and sexual contact may emerge. Parents and children must find ways to deal with these adverse circumstances in order to avoid potential problems; for example, parents must find ways to monitor their children. One example of child monitoring is the implementation and use of after-school programs that focus on the avoidance of bad behavior. Latchkey children who are encouraged to attend legitimate after-school programs that promote learning and physical well-being tend to get higher grades in school and achieve better social adjustment with other peers and adults.

Classification Systems of Parenting

The work of Urie Bronfenbrenner investigates parenting practices according to the ecological systems perspective, which emphasizes the interaction of all environmental factors, such as the individual in relationship to culture and the environment. In his book, *The Ecology of Human Development* (1981), Bronfenbrenner developed the ecological systems perspective in which he takes into account an expansive and far-reaching organization of factors that describes how parents interact with others in the family, at school, at work, and in the community at large. It also considers how legislation and policies interact with the daily lives of all those involved. In her article, "Current Patterns in Parental Authority" (1971), Diana Baumrind, a leading figure in the area of child development and parenting, developed a classification of parenting that is used as one possible yardstick in categorizing parenting styles. According to this classification system, there are four main styles of parenting: authoritarian, authoritative, neglectful, and indulgent.

Authoritarian parents are quite punitive and strict in raising their children. They place limits on their children and do not consider verbal interaction as an option of discourse. Authoritarian parents often engage in corporal punishment as a means of coercing their children to do something. This often results in negative consequences. A great deal of social learning theory research, particularly that of Albert Bandura, as described in his *Principles of Behavior Modification* (1969), strongly suggests that authoritarian parenting contributes to an increased amount of aggressive behavior on the part of the child.

Authoritative parents, however, are quite different from their authoritarian counterparts. Rather than parents who impose strict, often corporal, discipline, authoritative parents enforce rules of behavior while, at the same time, providing some leeway for their children depending on their age and development. Unlike authoritarian parents, authoritative parents allow for verbal exchange as one possible mode of discourse for explaining a particular behavior. Parent and caregiver researchers have generally concluded that the authoritative parenting style is the most optimal because it encourages parents to behave in a supportive, affectionate manner with their children while developing rules that govern their functioning.

Unlike authoritarian or authoritative parents, neglectful parents, a third type, do not become involved in the everyday goings-on of their children. An extreme example of a neglectful parent is one who leaves children at home with little or no supervision. When they get older, children of neglectful parents are often inept socially and often lack confidence. It is important to note that, in many cases, there is overlap between the authoritarian parent and the neglectful parent—for example, a parent who corporally punishes the child, but then leaves home without providing supervision. Finally, there are indulgent parents, who overindulge their children and place few if any restrictions on their behaviors. These children often become recalcitrant, and at times rebellious, when they are told by someone to do or say something. They also may find it difficult to maintain relationships with others and will have difficulty regulating their thoughts when speaking or their actions.

Research indicates that authoritative parenting is the most productive type for the physical, social, and intellectual development of children. This is so for a number of reasons. First, this style of parenting provides an environment whereby the children can engage in verbal interaction with parents. This interaction is necessary in order to solve problems that arise in or outside of the home environment. Given the environment, children learn how to express both their opinions and their emotions with the knowledge that their parents are considering their point of view within discussion. Second, and in line with the first reason, authoritative parenting usually allows for two-way communication between parent and child. It is not simply a system whereby the parent does all the speaking while the children remain silent. Third, parent research suggests that this form of parenting, given a set of parameters and limits set by parents, contributes to the child's independence. It develops a sense of autonomy for the child. It is also worth noting that authoritative parenting style contributes to the child's words and actions in a way that demonstrates the child to be attentive to what the parent is saying and doing. The positive relationship between authoritative parenting and increased competence on the part of the child is evident from the standpoint of social class, ethnicity, race, and gender.

Discipline

One important question that must be addressed when considering the role of parenting worldwide is the extent to which parents enforce limits on children's words, actions, and behaviors, and the types of limits they exact. The term "parental discipline" is used when categorizing these limits on children. Martin Hoffman (1970) argues, in his article "Conscience, Personality, and Socialization Techniques," in favor of three types of disciplining styles that parents and other caretakers use with children: love withdrawal, power assertion, and induction. Similar to the clas-

sification of parental types, there are both negative and positive outcomes when exacting discipline, but this depends singularly on which of the three types of Hoffman's disciplining categories is used. The first two categories, love withdrawal and power assertion, are negative, and therefore generally detrimental to children's outcomes.

Love withdrawal, the first of these categories, occurs when a parent knowingly severs interaction with the child and explicitly states a lack of interest in communicating or being with the child. The child, then, intuits a lack of affection from the parent or caregiver. This form of discipline is detrimental because it induces stress and anxiety in the child, which has been shown to contribute to neurological conditions in adolescence and adulthood. Moreover, parents who carry out this form of discipline may often have neurological symptoms of their own, such as passive-aggressive behaviors.

Power assertion, the second of Hoffman's discipline categories, needs greater treatment due to more evidence of its use throughout the world. With power assertion, the parent demonstrates full power and control, causing the child to feel helpless. Power assertion is exhibited most frequently through corporal punishment. Specified types of power assertion in the form of such physical punishment include whipping, spanking, tongue burning, and washing the mouth out with soap. When comparing both love withdrawal and power assertion, it has been shown that outcomes of both are highly detrimental to the well-being of children. Researchers have often labeled the types of parental behaviors as overreaction. Different kinds of overreaction occur when parents use physical aggression, shout, engage in constant blaming or name-calling, and make threats. Constant bombardment with acts of overreaction leads not merely to neurological symptoms in the child later in life, but also antisocial behavior, which will undoubtedly affect school performance. It can also lead to various forms of abuse of the self and others as well as psychotic symptoms in some people.

The sanctioning of corporal punishment has been shown by child development and education researchers to be detrimental not only to the physical, social, and intellectual development of children, but to society in general. Parental corporal punishment is considered legal throughout the United States, in some European countries, and in most countries of

Asia and Africa. In a number of other postindustrial nations, however, corporal punishment by parents, namely, using physical force as a means of punishing children, is outlawed. This is particularly the case in many European countries, Sweden being the first country to adopt this statute in 1979, and in Israel. Other European nations that have passed such laws are Austria, Croatia, Cyprus, Denmark, Finland, Germany, Latvia, and Norway. Since the 1979 law banning corporal punishment was enacted in Sweden, it has been shown that crime rates in general, especially those involving youth populations, have been declining rapidly. In particular, rape, suicide, drug and alcohol abuse, and truancy have been on the decline. However, other statutes related to societal changes, such as a ban on capital punishment, may have contributed to this important decline in crime as well. Despite the fact that corporal punishment generally leads to spontaneous compliance, its adverse effects clearly outweigh any form of advantage. Indeed, research shows that corporal punishment leads to various forms of aggression, lack of interest and respect in others, and a lack of concern for rules and other forms of social parameters and restrictions.

In addition, the sanctioning of corporal punishment by a given country presents the implication, and, at times, the reality, that other individuals than the parents are condoned, or are even given permission by the parents, or even worse, full latitude as defined by the state, to exact corporal punishment on a child. In particular, corporal punishment in schools in the United States is legal in at least 20 states (Ohio passed a statute in 2008 making corporal punishment illegal in schools). Even more egregious, nonprofit, federally funded organizations that are intended to look out for children and students, such as the National Council for the Accreditation of Teacher Education (NCATE), indirectly condone corporal punishment and other forms of physical discipline. For instance, in the book *Stop High-Stakes Testing* (2008), Dale Johnson and his colleagues note that all 20 states that permit corporal punishment are so-called partner states with NCATE, an organization with an anecdote on its website that states its protection of children. Outside of the 20 US states that sanction corporal punishment, countries that either condone or practice this form of discipline include Afghanistan, Botswana, Indonesia, Iran, Malaysia, Nigeria, Pakistan, Saudi Arabia, Singapore, Somalia, Sudan, Tanzania, Yemen, Zimbabwe, and several Caribbean nations.

In short, corporal punishment is a highly devastating form of power assertion. This and other types of power assertion have long histories and are most often associated with religious and cultic practices from antiquity to the present. Corporal punishment is archaic and a very hurtful practice that affects children's mental and physical well-being and, at times, can turn fatal, depending on social and environmental circumstances. The long-term dangers of power assertion include clinical anxiety, depression, addiction to drugs, and alcoholism. Moreover, it has been shown to be linked with the individual's demonstration of rage and other violent actions later in life.

The third and final discipline form is induction, which, unlike the two previous forms, demonstrates positive outcomes for both the parent and the child. Induction is a disciplinary action on the part of parents and other adults who adhere to using reason and logic as a means of teaching children both moral action and behavior that is socially and culturally appropriate in a given situation. Parents and others who engage in induction use supportive techniques as a form of discipline. Children identify with parents and other caregivers by noticing that the adult figure cares about them and that their behaviors would put them in vulnerable or possibly dangerous situations. Induction also considers the roles of two-way interaction in the adult-child dyad and reflection. Children are intended to identify possible repercussions and effects that their actions had on other individuals. Rather than emphasizing fault and poor conduct, induction stresses positive conduct, the act of reasoning through one's actions, and dealing with emotion.

Successful parenting workshops stress induction as a means of disciplining children. In these workshops, parents are taught to adapt to the developmental levels of each child as a rule before using disciplinary techniques. Parents learn how to interact with children by monitoring their own language and making anecdotal records of events as they arise. In addition, workshops that employ induction as a proper method of engaging disciplinary action teach parents how to avoid physical discipline and, at the same time, provide clear and concise language in communicating with children.

Parenting is a difficult task that involves numerous parameters. Many parents are overwhelmed by how much responsibility is involved in raising happy, healthy, and socially and intellectually interactive children. This will especially be a challenge for parents in countries whose educational systems are in the midst of transformation from learning environments containing few if any resources and adverse learning conditions to ones that promote learning and healthy lifestyles. It is important to emphasize that knowledge about parenting in a global context is essential for anyone interested in education because parenting directly influences both social and intellectual outcomes within the schooling environment.

Daniel Ness and Chia-ling Lin

REFERENCES

Bandura, Albert. *Principles of Behavior Modification.* New York: Holt, Rinehart and Winston, 1969.

Baumrind, Diana. "Current Patterns of Parental Authority." *Developmental Psychology* 4:1 (1971): 1–103.

Bronfenbrenner, Urie. *The Ecology of Human Development.* Cambridge, MA: Harvard University Press, 1981.

Brooks-Gunn, Jeanne, Wen-Jui Han, and Jane Waldfogel. "Maternal Employment and Child Cognitive Outcomes in the First Three Years of Life: The NICHD Study of Early Child Care." *Child Development 73, 4* (2002): 1052–1072.

Buehler, Cheryl, and Marion O'Brien. "Mothers' Part-Time Employment: Associations with Mother and Family Well-being." *Journal of Family Psychology 25, 6*(2011): 895–906.

Hoffman, Martin L. "Conscience, Personality, and Socialization Techniques." *Human Development* 13 (1970): 90–126.

Johnson, Dale D., and Bonnie Johnson. *High Stakes: Children, Testing, and Failure in American Schools.* Lanham, MD: Rowman & Littlefield, 2002.

Johnson, Dale D., Bonnie Johnson, Stephen J. Farenga, and Daniel Ness. *Stop High-Stakes Testing: Appealing to America's Conscience.* Lanham, MD: Rowman & Littlefield, 2008.

Patterson, Gerald. *Living with Children: New Methods for Parents and Teachers.* Champaign, IL: Research Press, 1977.

US Department of Health and Human Services, Health Resources and Services Administration, Maternal and Child Health Bureau. *Child Health USA 2010–2011.* Rockville, MD: US Department of Health and Human Services, 2011.

DRUGS AND ALCOHOL

Drug and alcohol abuse among children and young adolescents is a major problem in the educational context. These forms of abuse are the leading cause of unintended deaths not related to disease or old age throughout the world. Drug abuse, which often begins in the early years, can result in overdosing and frequently fatality. Alcohol abuse, too, leads to alcoholism and, if not fatality to oneself, fatality to others in the form of automobile accidents, unintended assault, rape, and other forms of crime. Drug and alcohol abuse is not limited to any particular country. Most country's borders are porous enough to pass illicit drugs into the system and thereby adversely affect society. In the context of education, drug and alcohol abuse is extremely important for a number of reasons. First, regardless of social class, drugs and alcohol become prevalent in secondary school, often after (but sometimes before) the onset of puberty. Second, these substances affect students who would otherwise avoid them through coercion and peer pressure. Third, the illicit drug trade is one of the leading forms of illegal street economies throughout the United States, Canada, and Europe. Since many drugs are illicit, drug trafficking often leads to violence in the form of murder and other forms of violent assault. This activity is often carried into schools, as illegal sales of drugs are not uncommon at the lockers in the school hallways. Young people throughout the world and in various environmental contexts ingest drugs.

Drug Categories

The National Institute on Drug Abuse (NIDA), an offshoot of the National Institutes of Health (NIH), attempts to teach students between the ages of 10 and 15 (approximately grades 5 through 9) about the effects of drug use and abuse and their real potential of adversely affecting the body and mind. NIDA lists several categories of drugs and outlines their general effects on the human body. This list is fairly broad and accounts for drug abuse cases throughout the world.

Anabolic Steroids

Steroids are artificially manufactured substances that add to current levels of hormones. These drugs in general do not produce adverse affects when prescribed by medical practitioners. Anabolic steroids are artificial forms of testosterone, an essential human hormone, that people take to increase muscle mass for a variety of purposes, mostly for aesthetic reasons, and not for health-related purposes. Anabolic steroids are usually ingested through the mouth in the form of a pill or by injection. What makes these steroids harmful is that they can cause chemical changes in the brain affecting mood as well as increasing risks for illness.

Cocaine

Cocaine is a white, powdery drug that is produced from the coca plant, which is common to countries of northwestern South America. Cocaine, usually ingested through nasal inhalation, is often smoked in the form of crack—a mixed form of cocaine that may contain other substances. In parts of Africa, cocaine is often mixed with non-drug-related substances, such as gunpowder, which can be extraordinarily lethal if overdosed.

Hallucinogens

Hallucinogens induce hallucinations. They are divided into three categories of drugs: psychedelics, dissociatives, and deliriants. Psychedelics are perhaps most common among young people. Perhaps the most abused psychedelic drug is lysergic acid diethylamide, or, LSD. In addition to LSD, other abused hallucinogens are the amphetamine MDA, also known as the love drug; the amphetamine MDMA, also known as ecstasy; PCP, more commonly known as angel dust; and mescaline. The major problem with hallucinogens, apart from being potentially fatal, is that they impede brain function by distorting the use of the five senses as well as spatial relationships and notions of time. As a result, this drug type makes it difficult for users to concentrate, communicate with others, and differentiate between what is real and what is mere illusion.

Inhalants

Inhalants are similar to drugs. Although they are not in the form of the typical powdery substance or leaf, they can pose lethal threats to one's health. Inhalants are in the form of gasoline, various chemical sprays, and paints that are inhaled deliberately as a means of addiction. Like tobacco, cocaine, and other substances that are smoked or inhaled, inhalants in the form of aerosol particles travel to the lungs by way of the larynx and trachea. These substances are absorbed by the lungs and eventually enter the bloodstream. When a substance enters the bloodstream, it will affect various parts of the body, often adversely. Most drugs affect thinking processes that emanate from the brain.

Marijuana

Marijuana is the most common term for the drug cannabis, which, according to the United Nations and UNICEF, is the most widely used illicit drug in the world today. Although the adverse effect of marijuana is not unlike that of tobacco, most countries prohibit the sale and use of the drug. The cannabis in marijuana is more potent than the nicotine in tobacco, not because of its addictive properties (which are relatively the same as nicotine's), but because of how quickly it may negatively affect brain behavior. Cannabis inhalation can be helpful in certain medical circumstances; however, even this benefit is under scrutiny in the medical professions.

Methamphetamines

Methamphetamines are harmful because they often induce hallucinations, aggressive behavior, paranoia, and possible obsession. Insomnia is a common condition resulting from methamphetamine abuse. Methamphetamines can be ingested in many ways—nasal ingestion (snorting), swallowing, via injection, or inhaling by smoking. The smoking version of the drug is often called crystal meth or ice because it is in the form of crystals. Other names for methamphetamines are chalk, speed, and glass. Like other forms of drugs, methamphetamines limit the amount of dopamine that is to be transmitted through brain neurons.

Opiates

Opium poppies produce latex, a white milky substance that is found in 10 percent of the world's flowering plants and is one of the key components for producing rubber. Opium is produced when the latex of opium poppies is hardened. Approximately 12 percent of the latex from the opium poppy consists of morphine, an addictive drug that is processed from the opium poppy to produce harmful illicit drugs in the form of opiates, such as heroin. After a short time period, an individual can become dependent on the use of heroin, morphine, and codeine.

Prescription Drug Abuse

Not all drugs that are abused are illicit. In fact, drug abuse is extremely common when people ingest substances that are prescribed by doctors but taken in ways that do not follow the prescription. Prescription drug abuse is also evident when people become dependent on a medication either because they were gradually addicted to it after it was prescribed to them or because they were given the drug (in the form of a medication) by a second party. Prescription drugs are extremely dangerous and can lead to poisoning and even death if an individual is not detoxified immediately.

Tobacco

Tobacco is one of the most lethal substances of drug abuse. This is because nicotine, the drug in tobacco, can be highly addictive when active. Moreover, with the exception of Bhutan, tobacco purchase and use are legal in all countries. So even if laws prevent minors from purchasing tobacco products, few, if any, laws mandate that they cannot use them. These two factors alone—addiction and few legal restrictions against use by minors—contribute to a habit that kills more people throughout the world than many diseases combined. According to the World Health Organization (WHO), tobacco is the leading preventable cause of death in countries throughout the world. Fortunately, tobacco use in developed countries is either waning or, at worst, topping off. Unfortunately, tobacco use in developing countries is increasing—in some cases, rapidly. Tobacco use is addictive and eventually lethal. Essentially, when an individual smokes a tobacco product, the lungs absorb the nicotine, which continues through the bloodstream; eventually, the drug, at least in part, enters and circulates through the brain. Further, the process of absorption of nicotine and other tobacco-related by-products into the lungs, over several years, contributes to numerous, often fatal diseases—most commonly, heart disease, lung- and throat-related cancers, chronic obstructive pulmonary disease, and

stroke. Tobacco, along with other plant-related drugs, can also be chewed by addicts. This form of intake is common in Pacific islands, the Caribbean, and parts of Central and South America, southern Asia, and Africa. Research also confirms that secondhand smoke is equally, if not more, injurious to the health of those involved, not only children, but fetuses as well.

Alcohol

Alcohol is most often in liquid form. When taken moderately, some forms of alcoholic beverage are nontoxic and, in the case of most types of red wine, even good for one's health. But alcohol is often imbibed not for health reasons but for recreational use, even to the point of inebriation. When alcohol is consumed frequently, this form of recreational use eventually leads to alcoholism, which, like other addictions, is detrimental to the body and brain function. Most countries throughout the world have legalized the sale of alcoholic beverages to adults, and some even to minors. With the possible exceptions of Bahrain, Qatar, and Tunisia, alcoholism is illegal for sale or consumption in countries of the Middle East and northern Africa, mostly due to Sharia, the law of Islam. Therefore, these countries have the lowest consumption rates among minors and adults, and few, if any, alcoholism incidents. On the other hand, countries with significantly high and perilous rates of alcohol consumption affecting minors (as well as adults) are mostly in Europe (e.g., Austria, Belgium, Croatia, Czech Republic, Denmark, France, Germany, Hungary, Ireland, Luxembourg, Moldova, Portugal, Russia, Slovakia, Spain, and United Kingdom). Countries outside of Europe with high consumption rates include Nigeria, St. Lucia, and Uganda. A country with a high consumption rate does not necessarily reflect levels of alcohol abuse, however. Countries with high levels of alcohol abuse are Russia, several eastern European nations, and Uganda. Australia and the United States also have considerable problems of alcohol abuse, especially among young people.

Drug Abuse Throughout the World

This section summarizes drug abuse in different parts of the world. Given the global dimensions and complexity of international drug abuse as well as space limitation for issues of international education, a comprehensive discussion of worldwide drug abuse is not possible here. Accordingly, this section draws from specific occurrences of drug use and abuse by minors in various regions of the world with a focus on a particular context.

The context of children and drugs in countries of Africa has to do with drug use in war and labor-related activity. In his book *Children at War* (2006), Peter Warren Singer describes in detail how children are initiated as soldiers through the ingestion of drugs. In order to encourage fearlessness, many warlords in some of the developing nations in sub-Saharan Africa initially force children to take drugs, mostly barbiturates, cocaine, and amphetamines. Children are then told that drugs build confidence and bravery. In Liberia and Sierra Leone, child soldiers often take a substance called "brown-brown," a potent mixture of cocaine or heroin with gunpowder. Khat, a flowering evergreen shrub that is native to countries of East Africa and the Arabian Peninsula, is a stimulant often given to child soldiers of Burundi, parts of Kenya, Rwanda, Somalia, Sudan, and Uganda, as well as Saudi Arabia, Oman, and Yemen. Experts have attributed violence and aggression to the use of khat, a key disposition that warlords encourage in child warriors.

A growing number of Afghans—including children—are resorting to the use of opium in the form of heroin as a means of escaping war and impoverishment. It is an inexpensive habit—approximately one US dollar per day—given the locale of opium poppy fields. According to a United Nations survey (United Nations 2009), approximately one in 12 Afghans, including both children and adults, abuse drugs. This is more than twice the number of people in 2005. The problem is also growing in neighboring countries, such as Pakistan, Tajikistan, Turkmenistan, and Uzbekistan, where poppy is prevalent and the consumption of alcoholic beverages is held to a minimum (with the exception of a few miles of border with China, all neighboring countries follow Islam, which forbids alcohol consumption). The Afghan government is avoiding dealing the problem despite the fact that it is jeopardizing the war effort and stability in the region. This problem adversely affects children because they are the usual recipients of secondhand smoke from heroin and other opium-based drugs. The opium habit among men and women is often indulged in secret. Moreover, children are often the laborers at the poppy farms. This factor increases young Afghans' chances of acquiring the habit.

The context for child drug abuse in Indonesia is the environment for the intake of nicotine and smoking as a general habit. Not only is smoking legal in Indonesia; no laws exist in the country that prohibit young children—even infants—from smoking cigarettes and taking in smoke of other tobacco-related products. This problem poses serious hazards for Indonesian children, particularly the onset of tobacco-related disease and illness well before adulthood. In addition, child smoking contributes to numerous adverse effects related to brain function and school performance. It is evident that the lack of prohibition of child smoking is a national dilemma. Compounding this problem, however, is adult disregard and, in many cases, approbation and amusement in child smoking. As outlined above, smoking tobacco or cannabis is detrimental to school performance and leads to a host of chronic and terminal diseases and physical conditions.

Australia, Europe, and North America are usually not the sources of the drug trade, but are clearly three of its primary destinations. In terms of transport, drugs are usually shipped in bundles that are previously packaged, sometimes in vacuum-packed bricks, and wrapped in plastic bags or banana leaves as a means of retaining moisture and freshness. Next, drugs are smuggled in passenger luggage or baggage, sent by overnight express mail, or shipped as a form of "legal" cargo, oftentimes as vegetables, tea, or coffee. It is also worthy of note that a number of European countries have legalized a number of drugs (such as marijuana, cocaine, heroin, and methamphetamine) that are still illegal in the United States. Drug-related crime is most prevalent in Central and South America, particularly Mexico, Colombia, and Venezuela. In many cases, the drug trade is the primary form of economy among certain people of these regions. As a result, guns and other weaponry are bought and sold, making this environment where drug cartels are in control especially dangerous in terms of crime. In the United States, and to a smaller extent in Canada, the drug trade is particularly problematic in terms of abuse as well as the formation of gangs in inner-city environments. Safer cities in these countries adopted strict gun laws that, to an extent, limit the amount of drugs transported within the city environs. Cities that have not adopted this measure and others restricting transport suffer from high crime rates that not only affect communities but also create internal problems in the schools.

Addressing Drug- and Alcohol-Related Problems

Evidence from successful outcomes suggests that modification of curriculum that includes teaching about drug abuse, alcohol consumption, and sexually transmitted disease in the school context is very helpful in stemming these problems. Despite potential opposition from conservative groups, members of religious communities, and traditionalist politicians, adopting in-school programs that emphasize drug and alcohol abuse has the potential of greatly reducing drug abuse and related problems. If parents do not explain the hazards of drugs to children, teachers can initiate discussion in this regard. School is often the best environment for this interaction because children and older students are often secretive and do not wish to discuss these matters with parents, siblings, or religious personnel. Addressing drug and alcohol problems in the school context is necessary not only in postindustrial societies but also in developing societies.

Daniel Ness and Chia-ling Lin

REFERENCES

Johnson, Dale D., et al. *Stop High-Stakes Testing: An Appeal to America's Conscience*. Lanham, MD: Rowman & Littlefield, 2008.

National Institute on Drug Abuse (NIDA). The Science Behind Drug Abuse. http://teens.drugabuse.gov/mom/index.php.

Nelson, Soraya Sarhaddi. "Drug Addiction, and Misery, Increase in Afghanistan." National Public Radio. April 16, 2009. www.npr.org/templates/story/story.php?storyId=102984398.

Singer, Peter Warren. *Children at War*. Berkeley: University of California Press, 2006.

United Nations Office on Drugs and Crime. "Drug Use in Afghanistan: 2009 Survey." Vienna, Austria: United Nations, 2009.

POVERTY AND EDUCATION

Poverty, a condition characterized by the scarcity of essential resources for livelihood, exists in both the developed and developing countries. It is necessary to note that some of the putatively wealthiest countries, including the United States, Argentina, and Chile, have some of the most abject conditions of poverty. It is therefore important to address the nature of poverty in the world, how poverty adversely affects the education of children, and the kinds of activities in which children engage in order to subsist.

Poverty impedes the advancement of societies throughout the world. Several indicators suggest how a particular country compares with others in terms of human advancement. For the purpose of determining how poverty affects education as it relates to human advancement, both sociologists and educationists have examined indices in the following areas: the percentage of a population earning less than US$1.25 per day; dispersion of income or wealth (as indicated by a country's Gini coefficient); comparisons of countries in terms of human development (i.e., Human Development Index); statistics of hunger, malnutrition, famine, or starvation; life expectancy; level of literacy; and level or amount of educational attainment (i.e., education index). The Table (see page 48) compares 40 countries throughout the world in terms of these indicators.

Poverty Indicators in Forty Countries

A number of interpretations can be gathered from analyzing the data in the table. It is important, however, to avoid oversimplification, for this can dilute the reality of existing education factors and situations of any country's overall population. Brief definitions and descriptions of each of the seven categories are given below, followed by several interpretations of data provided in the table.

Poverty Index

Poverty is a condition in which a given population is not provided an adequate degree of necessities for basic survival, such as proper shelter, food, and clothing. The World Bank identifies an individual in severe poverty as someone who lives on less than $1.25 per day. The indicator presented in the Table represents the percentage of a country's population that lives in conditions of severe poverty. It is necessary to point out, however, that a country with less than 3 percent

Table: **Comparison of Countries Based on Seven Indicators**

Country	Continent	<$1.25/Day (percentage)	Gini Coefficient	Human Development Index	Hunger (percentage)	Life Expectancy	Literacy Index (percentage)	Education Index
Algeria	Africa	6–20	.35–.39	.754	2–4	72.5–75	60–70	.743
Central African Rep.	Africa	>61	>.60	.369	>35	40–45	35–50	.419
Egypt	Africa	<3	.35–.39	.703	2–4	70–72.5	70–80	.731
Gabon	Africa	3–5	.35–.39	.755	5–19	50–55	80–90	.838
Madagascar	Africa	>61	.45–.49	.543	>35	60–65	70–80	.671
Mali	Africa	41–60	.40–.44	.371	20–34	45–50	<35	.300
Morocco	Africa	3–5	.25–.29	.654	5–19	70–72.5	50–60	.563
Mozambique	Africa	>61	.45–.49	.402	>35	40–45	35–50	.474
Nigeria	Africa	>61	.40–.44	.511	5–19	45–50	60–70	.648
Sierra Leone	Africa	41–60	>.60	.365	>35	40–45	<35	.396
South Africa	Africa	21–40	>.60	.683	5–19	45–50	80–90	.840
Zambia	Africa	>61	.50–.54	.481	>35	<40	60–70	.664
Cambodia	Asia	41–60	.40–.44	.593	20–34	60–65	70–80	.700
China	Asia	6–20	.45–.49	.772	5–19	72.5–75	90–97	.849
India	Asia	41–60	.35–.39	.612	20–34	67.5–70	60–70	.638
Iran	Asia	<3	.40–.44	.782	2–4	70–72.5	80–90	.804
Japan	Asia	<3	.35–.39	.960	<2	>80	>97	.949
Kazakhstan	Asia	3–5	.30–.34	.804	5–19	67.5–70	>97	.966
Mongolia	Asia	21–40	.30–.34	.727	20–34	65–67.5	>97	.913
Thailand	Asia	<3	.40–.44	.783	20–34	72.5–75	80–90	.886
Australia	Australia	<3	.30–.34	.970	<2	>80	>97	.993
Austria	Europe	<3	.25–.29	.955	<2	77.5–80	>97	.962
Bosnia&Herzegovina	Europe	<3	.55–.59	.812	5–19	77.5–80	90–97	.874
France	Europe	<3	.30–.34	.961	<2	>80	>97	.978
Latvia	Europe	<3	.35–.39	.866	2–4	70–72.5	>97	.961
Moldova	Europe	6–20	.35–.39	.720	5–19	70–72.5	>97	.900
Norway	Europe	<3	<.25	.971	<2	77.5–80	>97	.989
Russia	Europe	<3	.40–.44	.817	<2	65–67.5	>97	.933
United Kingdom	Europe	<3	.30–.34	.947	<2	77.5–80	>97	.957
Canada	N. America	<3	.30–.34	.966	<2	>80	>97	.991
Haiti	N. America	41–60	.55–.59	.532	>35	55–60	50–60	.578
Honduras	N. America	21–40	.50–.54	.732	20–34	67.5–70	80–90	.800
Mexico	N. America	<3	.45–.49	.854	5–19	75–77.5	90–97	.879
United States	N. America	<3	.45–.49	.956	<2	77.5–80	>97	.968
Argentina	S. America	3–5	.45–.49	.866	<2	75–77.5	>97	.946
Bolivia	S. America	6–20	>.60	.729	20–34	65–67.5	90–97	.885
Brazil	S. America	6–20	.55–.59	.813	5–19	70–72.5	90–97	.888
Colombia	S. America	6–20	.40–.44	.807	5–19	72.5–75	90–97	.875
Peru	S. America	6–20	.50–.54	.806	5–19	70–72.5	80–90	.885
Uruguay	S. America	<3	.40–.44	.865	<2	75–77.5	>97	.955

Sources:
Central Intelligence Agency. *CIA World Fact Book 2011.* Washington, DC: Skyhorse, 2010.
United Nations Development Programme (UNDP). *Human Development Report 2009—Overcoming Barriers: Human Mobility and Development.* New York: UNDP, 2009.
———. International Human Development Indicators. New York: UNDP, 2010. http://hdr.undp.org/en/statistics/.
World Health Organization. World Health Statistics. Geneva: World Health Organization, 2011.

of its population living on less than US$1 per day may not necessarily rate positively in other areas. For example, Thailand is listed as having less than 3 percent of its population living on a daily allowance of less than US$1. At the same time, the country has a rather high Gini coefficient (over .40), indicating that wealth and resources are not equally distributed when compared to other countries. Moreover, with a human development index of .783, Thailand rates lower than other countries in terms of technological advancement.

Gini Coefficient

The Gini coefficient provides information on a country's dispersion of wealth or income among its overall population. It was named after Corrado Gini, an important statistician of the early twentieth century. With modifications over the last several years, the Gini coefficient generally represents inequality of wealth when comparing countries, states, or political municipalities. Countries with lower Gini coefficients tend to have more equality among their people, while those with higher coefficients tend to have more social disparities. For example, Scandinavian and Central European nations tend to have lower Gini coefficients when compared with other regions of the world.

Human Development Index

The Human Development Index is an indicator that helps identify the rate of technological and human advancement of a given country. Therefore, in various country comparisons, the terms "developed," "highly developed," or "underdeveloped" refer to the Human Development Index. Low indices show countries with lower gross domestic products and are developing nations, while those with high indices generally have higher gross domestic products and are labeled as "developed."

Hunger

Hunger refers to the level of malnutrition and illness of a country based on the lack of food, starvation, and occurrences of famine. It is measured by the percentage of a country's population that is malnourished. Hunger can potentially exceed 35 percent in certain countries.

Life Expectancy

Life expectancy refers to the expected number of years remaining for someone at any given age. In order to indicate the average life expectancy, most life expectancy indicators, including that in the Table, use birth as the given "starting" age in order to find the greatest possible age of a given country. Demographical statisticians use e_x as the general mathematical symbol for life expectancy where e represents the expected number of years of life from x, which is one's present age.

Literacy Index

The literacy index is a way of identifying the percentage of a country's population that is able to read fluently and has at least a modicum of aptitude in written communication. UNESCO defines literacy as the "ability to identify, understand, interpret, create, communicate, compute and use printed and written materials associated with varying contexts. Literacy involves a continuum of learning in enabling individuals to achieve their goals, to develop their knowledge and potential, and to participate fully in their community and wider society." The world's literacy rate has dramatically increased within the last 50 years; the rate of illiteracy—lack of reading and writing ability—more than halved from 1970 to 2004.

Education Index

The education index is an indication of the educational attainment of a country's population. It is determined by two-thirds weighting of a country's literacy rate and a one-third weighting of that same country's gross enrollment ratios for primary school (generally, grades 1 through 5 or 6), secondary school (generally, grades 6 or 7 to 12), and tertiary school, which is generally an extension of high school by way of professional specialization or college. The higher the education index value of a given country, the higher the educational attainment of people of that country.

Interpretations of Comparisons

Perhaps the most basic observation about the table is intuitive—that the countries that have a rather high education index are those that score positively in other categories; similarly, the countries that have a poor education index generally score poorly in most of the other six categories. Most of the countries that fare poorly in nearly all categories are countries of Africa. Moreover, most of those that fare well overall are in Europe (New Zealand, which is not included in the list, and Australia also fall into this category). Even more telling is the consistency of countries that appear in the top 10 and the bottom 10 for each of the seven categories. Five countries are consistently listed in the top 10 in each category: Australia, Austria, Canada, France, and Norway. Similarly, five countries consistently record at the bottom of the list: the Central African Republic, Haiti, Mozambique, Sierra Leone, and Zambia. It is clear from this observation that of the top five countries, three are in Europe

(Austria, France, and Norway) and one is in North America (Canada). Likewise, of the poorest faring five countries, four are in Africa (Central African Republic, Mozambique, Sierra Leone, and Zambia) and one is in North America (Haiti).

It is also important to note that countries such as Japan, the United States, and the United Kingdom, which are putatively considered "highly developed" and "wealthy," do not always score in the top 10 countries of certain categories. For example, with a Gini coefficient of nearly .46, the United States scores fairly low in terms of dispersion of wealth among its population.

It is also important to examine each indicator when compared to the education index to determine the existence of relationships. In terms of the poverty index (i.e., percentage of a country's population living on less than $1.25 per day), 11 of the 14 countries with the lowest level of poverty (less than 3 percent of its population) have an education index of .933 or higher. Only Egypt (.731), Mexico (.879), and Thailand (.886) scored lower. Further, of the 10 countries with the highest level of poverty (six of which are in Africa), nine have an education index lower than .800. In examining dispersion of wealth within a country (Gini coefficient), seven of the top nine countries (i.e., countries whose Gini coefficients are .34 or lower) have an education index of .913 or higher. Countries with high Gini coefficients (i.e., lower dispersion of wealth among the population) tend to include both highly developed and developing nations. Perhaps the most telling statistic is the correlation coefficient comparing human development with education (a correlation is a common statistical relationship that shows how frequently one variable occurs with another). There is an extremely strong correlation (.94) between these two indices among the 40 countries in the Table, indicating that countries with a high human development index will more than likely have a high education index.

Although not as highly correlated as the human development index, hunger is somewhat correlated with the education index. All of the 11 countries with less than 2 percent of their population malnourished have an education index of .933 or higher. Of the 11 countries with 20 percent or more of their population suffering from a shortage of food, eight have an education index less than .800. With the possible exceptions of Kazakhstan, Mongolia, Latvia, Moldova,

Russia, Algeria, Egypt, and Morocco, there seems to be a moderate correlation between life expectancy and education attainment. Finally, the literacy category is closely associated with education attainment. In general, the higher the literacy rate, the higher the education index. Indeed, all 15 countries with a literacy index of 97 percent or greater have an education index of .900 or above. Of the nine countries with a literacy index of 70 percent or less, eight have education indices lower than .700.

In sum, poverty is a significant factor when considering both levels of educational attainment and rates of literacy of a given country. In a similar manner, the opposite is also true—namely, that a country's rate of literacy and education index are telling factors in terms of levels of poverty. A future step for any country's administration would be to find ways to improve the education establishment, given the fairly negative correlation between poverty and high-quality education. It is also important to note that a strong educational system is in no way a precondition for the diminution of poverty. Growing economic concerns in so-called developed, postindustrial nations—such as the United States, Italy, Greece, Spain, and certain countries of the Pacific Rim—are evidence of this.

Daniel Ness and Chia-ling Lin

References

Central Intelligence Agency. *CIA World Fact Book 2010*. Washington, DC: Skyhorse, 2009.

UNESCO. *The Plurality of Literacy and Its Implications for Policies and Programs: Position Paper*. Paris: UNESCO, 2004. http://unesdoc.unesco.org/images/0013/001362/136246e.pdf.

United Nations Development Programme (UNDP). *Human Development Report 2009—Overcoming Barriers: Human Mobility and Development*. New York: UNDP, 2009.

———. *International Human Development Indicators*. New York: UNDP, 2010. http://hdr.undp.org/en/statistics/.

World Health Organization. *World Health Statistics*. Geneva: World Health Organization, 2011.

Child Labor and Education

Child labor is an impending problem in the world today. Even 12 years after the commencement of the twenty-first century, child labor is present in nearly every country—both developed and developing—even though the great majority of legislatures throughout the world forbid it. Child labor practices are gross injustices that occur in many nations worldwide. The International Labour Organization places the number of working children at nearly 250 million worldwide. David Parker (2008) puts the number of children under 16 who are working at 320 million, one-fourth (80 million) of whom never get the chance to complete or even attend primary school. Child labor is a worldwide problem.

Few, if any, countries are immune from child labor. Even countries that have putatively been described as "developed" and "Western" and "technologically advanced" have children working in both agriculture and industry. These countries include Canada, France, the United Kingdom, and the United States, among others. The problem is exacerbated because administrative and political bodies in virtually every country throughout the world do not wish to share any data having to do with children at work. This demonstrates not ignorance but negligence on the part of these countries. We do know, however, the countries with egregious levels of child labor. These include, but are by no means limited to, the following countries: Bangladesh, Bolivia, Brazil, Costa Rica, Ecuador, Egypt, El Salvador, Guatemala, Honduras, India, Indonesia, Mexico, Morocco, Nepal, Nicaragua, Pakistan, Peru, Philippines, Thailand, Turkey, and most countries of Africa. Although African countries have similar child labor problems as countries in Central and South America and Asia—namely, alarmingly high rates of child labor in agriculture, industry, mining, brickwork, and street vending—they have abominable problems concerning child sex trafficking and child sex tourism.

The problem of child labor poses a vicious circle because children who are willingly or not willingly engaged in this physically and emotionally destructive practice are members of families who are caught in a whirlwind of intergenerational poverty. As a result, they are victims of social exclusion and receive little to no formal education. It is also the case that children whose parents obtained an education are much more likely to follow their parents' footsteps. Perhaps the most evident predictor is the number of years of education obtained by the mother (not necessarily the father). A woman who obtains an education is more than likely able to get adequate health care, marry, and have a small, healthy family with educated children.

Prior to the end of World War II, child labor was rampant throughout the world. It was not until 1948 when the United Nations General Assembly adopted the Universal Declaration of Human Rights that child labor began to wane. This adoption led to the enactments of numerous laws condemning child labor and application of sanctions toward entities that promoted it. One such enactment was the United Nations' Convention on the Rights of the Child in 1989, which urged that all countries should institute the right of all children to obtain, at the very least, a primary education and should protect children from societal ills—labor, exploitation, and the like—that adversely affect their physical and mental well-being. A second enactment was the Prohibition and Immediate Action for the Elimination of the Worst Forms of Child Labor—also known as Convention 182—put forth by the International Labour Office in 1999. Convention 182 is perhaps the most comprehensive treaty to date in that it identifies all forms of child labor, and even modern-day slave labor, which contribute to unhealthy, unsanitary, and potentially dangerous lifestyles. Unfortunately, however, United Nations treaties, even Convention 182, have not ended or, at the very least, curbed worldwide child labor and bondage. To do so requires political reform on a national scale and more punitive measures toward organizations or industries that harbor or condone these activities. At a more local level, doing so requires individuals to identify the facts of child labor and share them with family, friends, neighbors, colleagues, and younger generations.

Modes of Child Labor

Many international organizations, such as UNICEF, the International Labour Organization (ILO), and Human Rights Watch (HRW), have worked continuously to improve living conditions of children throughout the world. Nevertheless, it has been estimated that nearly 320 million children are forced into labor. Almost half of these children are working in extremely dangerous conditions—for example, in factories with toxic working conditions or as prostitutes associated with the sex trade. One particularly dangerous mode of "labor" in which children are often coerced to participate is as soldiers, combatants, or mercenaries. Given the treacherous lifestyle and adverse conditions associated with this work, both in combat and off the battlefield, child soldiering is yet another tragic and dismal example of child labor.

Agriculture and Animal Husbandry

According to the International Labour Office, more children throughout the world work in agriculture and animal husbandry than in any other industry. Agriculture and animal husbandry pose great danger and health risks to children. Few, if any, countries are immune to the tribulations of child labor associated with agricultural activity. It can be claimed, however, that the types of children's agricultural activities depend on where in the world they live. Many child laborers in Indonesia depend on the fishing industry for their own and their family's survival. Many southern and central Asian countries employ children in animal husbandry—often involving the unsanitary activity of cleaning stables—and rice cultivation. Child laborers in the Middle East and northern Africa are often sent to cotton fields as cotton pickers. Also, children in Central and South America engage in agricultural labor under harsh conditions in mangrove swamps, tobacco fields, and the like. In the United States, farmers occasionally employ migrant workers, often minors, who tend to citrus farming during the winter and sugar beet farming in the northern Midwest during the summer and fall.

Agricultural labor can pose grave health risks to minors. Children attending to tobacco farming or cigar manufacturing, for example, are exposed to nicotine, which is absorbed through the skin as they pick the leaves. Such exposure can lead to stomach illnesses, causing vomiting and chronic nausea.

Mines, Quarries, and Brick Factories

Historically, children as young as seven or eight years have worked as laborers in mines, stone quarries, and brick factories. Those who worked in rock quarries and mines usually resided in countries that were squarely part of the Industrial Revolution— particularly poor children in the United States, the United Kingdom, and Germany. In the United States, miners were often young children who worked nearly 12-hour shifts for six days per week. The notion of

child development was a novelty, one that mostly applied to children of the middle and upper-middle classes. Many of these young laborers did not live beyond the age of 30 or 40 years.

Today, the overwhelming number of child laborers who work in mines and quarries and who mix and fire clay in kilns for brick production live in Asia, particularly India and Nepal, as well as South and Central America, mostly in Bolivia, Nicaragua, and Peru. Like their predecessors, many of these children are as young as seven years of age. Like other manual labor sectors, brick making and mining clearly pose perilous conditions for young workers. Children engaged in mining and quarrying run the risk of respiratory illness due to the inhalation of toxic gases. Those who work in brick mixing and firing run the risk of disease when clay holes fill with water during rainy seasons and mosquitoes and other disease-carrying insects cluster in one location.

Working children make bricks with clay and water that is mixed in a mold. They sprinkle sand to prevent bricks from sticking together. Before being laid to dry, the bricks are stamped with the manufacturer's name. Children then load trucks with the dried bricks, most of which weigh from 5 to 8 pounds (about 2.27 to 3.63 kilograms) apiece. In one day, a young child of eight or nine will load as much as one ton of bricks.

Many child laborers who work in quarries or mines earn extremely meager wages, while others, whether knowingly or not, presently work as slave laborers. Anti-Slavery International has been somewhat successful in preventing the occurrence of child slave labor.

Textiles and Other Manufacturing

Like mining and quarry labor, children have historically composed a large segment of the world population engaged in manufacturing and the textile industry. In the United States, after Massachusetts and other northern states enacted laws limiting the number of hours that children could engage in factory labor, other states, particularly southern states in the decades following the Civil War, lengthened working hours for minors. These states included North Carolina, South Carolina, Tennessee, and Virginia. These children worked in often treacherous conditions. Many of them never received any formal schooling.

Manufacturing requires workers to operate machinery for the production of goods. The use of such machinery can be perilous. Perhaps more than any other industry, textile and clothes manufacturing has come under the greatest scrutiny over the years regarding the employment of children in textile factories. Within the last three decades, many clothing labels were boycotted by consumers throughout the world as a result of their association with factories in various countries on most continents—particularly in Asia—that condone child labor. These labels included Gap, Hanes, Nike, and American Apparel. In addition, other companies, especially Wal-Mart, not only fail to provide adequate wages and benefits for their employees, but have notoriously and implicitly engaged in child labor practices in the production of numerous goods that are sold in the retail market.

Journalists have frequently observed children within the textile industry as a common feature in textile factories throughout the world. The United States is not immune to the adverse conditions of child labor. In several instances, Wal-Mart violated numerous labor laws throughout the country. According to Steven Greenhouse writing in the *New York Times* (2004), an examination of time records for 25,000 employees during one week in July 2000 demonstrated 1,371 cases in which minors (individuals under 18 years) were found to be working too late, working during school hours, or working for more than eight hours in a day. Moreover, evidence demonstrates that minors lost 15,705 mealtimes (i.e., lunch or dinner) and missed 60,767 break times.

The Sex Industry

Child sex tourism is an odious form of exploitation and abuse of children. Individuals who either conduct or promote child sex tourism—whether overseas or in the native country—engage in pedophilia, which is a felony in the United States and a crime in virtually every jurisdiction throughout the world. Despite its universal proscription, child sex tourism is regrettably sanctioned by constituents (business and industry) either outside of jurisprudence or clandestinely associated with it. A number of nonprofit organizations, such as End Child Prostitution, Child Pornography, and the Trafficking of Children (ECPAT), suggest that the number of children who are drawn into the sex trade each year exceeds 1 million worldwide. The

International Labour Office (2011) puts the number of children working for the sex tourist industry at approximately 1.8 million throughout the world.

One of the most unconscionable modes of employment in which children are forced to engage is prostitution and other related work in the child sex industry. The sex industry caters to sex tourism, which can be found throughout the world. The ILO found that sex tourism accounts for up to 14 percent of the gross domestic product of Indonesia, Malaysia, the Philippines, and Thailand. Along with India, these four countries have long been considered primary locations that have contributed to the wealth of the sex industry, particularly in reference to child sex. Unfortunately, the industry has spread beyond Asia to a number of Central American destinations, including Costa Rica, El Salvador, Guatemala, Honduras, and Mexico.

This form of "industry" is a deleterious outgrowth of the international tourist industry that surged exponentially in the 1960s, fueled particularly by American and European males traveling to Central and South America, South Asia, and Africa. By the end of the following decade, child sex or sex with minors (individuals under 18 years) was common—and remains so—in a number of cities in South Asia, including Bangkok in Thailand and in the Svay Pak district of Phnom Penh in Cambodia, and Central and South America, including Recife in Brazil and San José in Costa Rica. In this unconscionable form of child labor, children, most of whom have been sent to work as prostitutes involuntarily, rarely, if ever, have the option of leaving the sex industry or seeking protection from pimps.

According to the Child Exploitation and Obscenity Section (CEOS) of the US Department of Justice website, there are several reasons why child sex tourism has become so prevalent since the 1970s and 1980s. First, it is a result of poverty. Countries where children engage in sex tourism usually have high rates of poverty and illiteracy. Parents or guardians of children of poor families, particularly in those countries mentioned above, either encourage or go as far as coerce their children, both girls and boys, to engage in sexual acts with foreign tourists. To this end, mothers and fathers often sell their children to make ends meet. As David Parker claims, tourists from Australia, Canada, Europe, and the United States spend much money as they "often cross the line between propriety and sexual exploitation." Child sex tourists are predators in that they engage in activities that encourage the exploitation and abuse of children. Although often seen as harmless, these individuals, often from developed nations, travel to foreign countries to engage in sexual activity with children, perhaps because their engagement in sexual activity with minors in their native country would lead to incarceration. Thus, their travel to foreign countries like Thailand or Indonesia to engage in sexual acts with minors will more than likely preclude any possibility of legal intervention or imprisonment.

A second reason that explains the prevalence of child sex tourism has to do with the Internet. Sex trafficking agents use the Internet as a marketing tool. Their websites provide anecdotal accounts of other child sex tourists and describe fees, sex venues, and methods or processes of procuring a child prostitute. These Internet sites also provide brochures and "guides" that provide details on common locations. CEOS states that in 1995, at least 25 business establishments in the United States used the Internet to promote child sex tourism among their employees and potential clients traveling overseas. Given its relatively easy access, the Internet, therefore, provides a virtual venue that has spurred growth of interest in child sex tourism. On a positive note, however, the Internet can be extremely useful in helping international law enforcement agencies to track, arrest, and incarcerate individuals, groups, or businesses that engage in sexual trafficking of minors.

In addition, foreign governments may directly or indirectly influence the growth of sex tourism, even with children. These governments tend to be those located in countries with poor economies. In many instances, tourism is one of the major sources of income for countries with high levels of poverty. In promoting the tourist industry, governments often tacitly condone the sex tourism industry, even at the expense of exploiting children as young as nine or ten years of age.

Children as Street Vendors

Another common venue of child labor is the street, where children attempt to sell various merchandise or edibles. Common street vending services include, but are by no means limited to, exterior painting, shining shoes, repairing automobiles and motorcycles, artistic performances, waiting in restaurants, dock working, prostitution (see above), and selling fruits and vegetables, newspapers and magazines, cigarettes, and fish. Although a number of these activities can teach important skills for future employment, they can be very dangerous for young children and minors. In addition, although some forms of street labor may seem risk-free, children who engage as street vendors are often raped or robbed of their earnings by peers and adults. Children on the street also fall prey to numerous social ills, such as drug trafficking, prostitution, and violence.

Children who perform in public often do so as panhandlers in numerous venues in cities throughout the world. Child performers can be encountered on New York City subways, usually as dancers or singers. This is also common in other large cities where children often live below the poverty line.

Children as Garbage Collectors and Beggars

In addition to the modes of child labor mentioned earlier, many children find work by searching for usable merchandise that has been discarded. Children throughout the world also can be seen begging, either with parents or guardians or on their own. Garbage picking and begging can pose severe health risks, because families that engage in this form of labor—most of whom live on streets, sidewalks, or public areas—are subject to numerous ailments and disease. Families that live near garbage dumps, for example, often live among vermin, birds, and insects that may carry potential contagions that cause maladies.

Children who engage in garbage picking and begging live throughout the world, most notably in Bangladesh, India, Indonesia, Mexico, Nicaragua, and Turkey. India has perhaps one of the largest populations of children who work as garbage pickers. Begging occurs in virtually every country in the world, even in Canada, England, and the United States. Children, for example, often stand with male or female guardians, usually with written posters indicating financial distress, on subway platforms and street corners in several cities throughout the United States and Canada.

According to David Parker, between 3,000 and 5,000 families near Jakarta, Indonesia, engage in garbage collecting for the purpose of selling parts of items that were thrown away. These families earn between US$7 and US$10 per day—well below the poverty line for a family of four. Children primarily in India and Indonesia use gunny bags for the purpose of collecting scraps that can be sold or turned into possibly more valuable items.

Slavery

More than 27 million slaves exist in the world today. Despite this fact, no country in the world has either legalized or condoned this social and economic system. Instead, institutions that further slavery use different terms—mostly euphemisms—as a means to elude and deceive the media, thereby attempting to downplay and minimize the existence of this blatantly nefarious system of human abuse, alienation, humiliation, and exploitation. With the exception of Antarctica, slavery exists on every continent. The most flagrant forms of slavery—specifically child slavery—exist in many African countries, India, and a number of countries in Southeast Asia. In addition, implicit forms of slavery exist in Europe, North America, South America, and, to a lesser extent, Australia. As for the United States, slavery did not end with the Emancipation Proclamation of 1862 or the Thirteenth Amendment to the US Constitution; on the contrary, there are approximately 60,000 slaves in the United States—most of whom are underage and work in the agricultural, textile, and sex trades.

Education is an important factor in the discussion of slavery because those who instituted this social and economic system have historically barred slaves from schools and other institutions of learning.

Grappling with Ending Dependence on Child Labor

It is important to note that most administrators in countries throughout the world fail to provide an accurate number of children who are engaged in labor either to make ends meet for their family or to obtain a modicum of income for subsistence. This failure is due to either a conscious effort to mislead sociologists and education researchers or to outright denial that child labor even exists in the country under investigation. Therefore, it is a difficult task for researchers or philanthropists to find a way to end child labor throughout the world. Some foundations—for ex-

ample, the William J. Clinton Foundation—may help in this regard, given the overwhelming strength of current and former politicians who engage in philanthropic missions.

There are a number of things an individual can do to curb or prevent the spread of child labor. First, it should be clear that financial resources are as important as material resources. Concerned individuals can provide support to a trusted aid organization or charity whose endowments or funds are devoted to the populations in need. A rule of thumb is that 80 percent or more of the funding should be applied directly to the populations in question. A second way to help prevent and possibly stop the ever-troubling spread of child labor and abuse is to volunteer one's skills and expertise in areas in need. For example, trained physicians could consider spending a few days or longer helping children in ravaged areas. Teachers can also put their skills to practice by joining various highly qualified organizations that cater to educating populations that have historically been alienated from formal education. The Peace Corps is one of these organizations. A third way is to support political candidates who stress the importance of children's rights, not only in the United States, but also throughout the world.

Daniel Ness and Chia-ling Lin

REFERENCES

Greenhouse, Steven. "In-House Audit Says Wal-Mart Violated Labor Laws." *New York Times*, January 13, 2004.

International Labour Office. Bitter Harvest: Child Labor in Agriculture. 2002. www.ilo.org/Search3/search.do?searchWhat=bitter+harvest&locale=en_USInternational.

Labour Organization, International Programme on the Elimination of Child Labour. "Every Child Counts: New Global Estimates on Child Labour." Geneva: International Labour Organization, 2002.

Knapp, Derek. "Child Slave Labor in Wal-Mart." IHS Child Slave Labor. 2005. http://ihscslnews.org/view_article.php?id=65.

Parker, David L. "Before Their Time: Child Labor Around the World." *American Educator* 32:1 (2008): 38–43.

———. *Before Their Time: The World of Child Labor.* New York: Quantuck Lane, 2007.

Parker, David L., and Sarah Bachman. "Economic Exploitation and the Health of Children: Towards a Public Health Model." *Health and Human Rights: An International Journal* 5 (2002): 93–119.

US Department of Justice. *Child Exploitation and Obscenity Section: Child Sex Tourism*. Washington, DC: Department of Justice, 2010. www.justice.gov/criminal/ceos/sextour.html.

Violence, War, and Education

Youth violence (i.e., violence committed *against* youth and violence committed *by* youth) and the recruitment of children to fight in wars are two extremely disturbing states of affairs that are prevalent in today's world. Youth violence occurs at a number of levels: at home in the form of child abuse or sibling abuse; at school, which can be the scene of bullying or mass murder; or in the street, as a result of gang affiliation (or lack thereof) or of non-gang-related crimes. Fortunately, both informal and formal education can curb the levels of violence and the initiation of children as participants in war.

Youth Violence

In this section, youth violence is divided into three main categories: violence at home; violence at school; and neighborhood-related violence (outside of home and school). As indicated in the descriptions and explanations, each of these categories tends to influence another. For example, violence in the home often influences children who are witnesses to engage in aggressive behavior in school. Moreover, witnessing or engaging in school aggression works in reverse as well, contributing to violence in the home and in the neighborhood.

Violence at Home

Violence against children in the home occurs when the child is the victim of abuse by adults or older siblings. Causes of violence in the home are numerous. The most prevalent causes include gun violence, parental alcoholism, and sexual abuse of one parent by the other or of another child. A child's witnessing of or victimization by these abuses contributes to the child's false notion that these forms of cruelty and exploitation are acceptable forms of behavior. Research studies conclude a positive correlation between corporal punishment and increased levels of aggression among children. In addition, research demonstrates that there is a consistent relationship between child abuse in the home and social and cognitive skills inside and outside of school.

Violence at School

School violence can be seen in a number of different forms. One common form is bullying. School bullying is widespread, affecting millions of students every year throughout the world. Many victims of bullying report physical injuries inflicted by the bully perpetrators. Schools and districts often overlook the problem of bullying despite its wide range and severity. Nevertheless, bullying constitutes one of the most egregious problems faced by students in formal schooling throughout the world. Bullying seems to be most prevalent during the middle school years, waning in the latter part of secondary school. According to the National Center for Educational Statistics, 19.6 percent of elementary schools, 38.6 percent of middle schools, and 19.8 percent of high schools in the United States issued reports of bullying in the 2009–2010 academic year. The national average for this year was 23.1 percent. Although the 2009–2010 academic year report showed a 1 percent decrease in bullying when compared to the 2005–2006 academic year, the number of cyberbullying incidents increased from 2000 to 2010. Much of this increase has to do with the near exponential rise in popularity of social networking websites, such as Facebook. In some cases, some victims of bullying commit suicide because they see no hope that their persecutors will relent or that school administrators or possibly parents will intervene. The first indication of legal action taken against bullies whose victim committed suicide is a case in western Massachusetts that involved the relentless abuse of an adolescent teenager in 2009 and early 2010. This case has the potential of becoming a legal precedent in future cases involving bullying that leads to the suicide of a victim.

Another type of school violence occurs in the form of a mass murder or killing spree. Although incidents of this type have occurred throughout history, they have become increasingly prevalent in recent decades—both in primary and secondary schools and in tertiary-level institutions. School violence occurrences in the United States include the Columbine

High School massacre in Littleton, Colorado, in 1999; the Westside Middle School incident in Jonesboro, Arkansas, in 1998; and the mass murders at the Virginia Polytechnic Institute and State University in 2007. It is a mistake, however, to assume that school violence is a predominantly American phenomenon; it is not. Perhaps one of the most atrocious incidents of this type of crime was the Beslan School hostage crisis in September of 2004, in which nearly 400 persons were killed—including more than 150 children. Recent atrocities involving schoolchildren outside of the United States are numerous. These include, but are by no means limited to, the following incidents: the Azerbaijan State Oil Academy shootings of 2009, which left 13 dead; the 2007 siege of Lal Masjid in Islamabad, Pakistan, which left over 150 dead; and the 2007 Baghdad Mustansiriya University bombing, which killed over 70 people. In China savage attacks on young children, although rare, are not unknown events; in 2004 numerous children were injured as a result of a series of knife attacks in day-care centers and schools. In the spring of 2010, there was a spate of stabbing incidents in various cities in China, which led to the deaths of 17 children ranging in age from three years to adolescence. The killings began in March, when a man attacked and killed eight students and wounded several other individuals outside an elementary school in Nanping in the province of Fujian. That incident sparked at least four additional copycat attacks within the period of six weeks. The Education and Public Security ministries enforced local school security to ensure higher levels of enforcement throughout the country. The motives of these recent school stabbings are not known. There are indications, however, that the attackers suffered from stock market losses, the loss of their homes, and failures of intimate relationships. More widespread reasons concern not the motives of the individual perpetrators, but social injustices as well as a rapidly changing society that is unable to control problems associated with mental illness.

Despite these horrific incidents of school violence, violent crime in schools has steadily decreased since 1994. According to the US Department of Justice, the annual rate of serious violent crime in 2007 (4 per 100 students) was less than half the rate in 1994 (13 per 100). These data come from the Justice Department's National Crime Victimization Survey, which unlike police reports or school records, provide complete data sets of incidences. Regardless of the seemingly downward trend of incidents, however, school violence is a major problem in the United States.

Other forms of school violence are widespread throughout the world. Sexual assault is rampant in many countries with formal schooling. For example, in South Africa, more than 40 percent of victims of violence maintain that the perpetrators assaulted them in school. Moreover, a large number of these incidents were sexual assaults. In Poland the education ministry issued a law that makes head teachers responsible for identifying students with violent or abusive behaviors. Such students will be discharged from school and required to enter community service or be incarcerated. This statute also applies to the parents of the violent and aggressive children. Other countries in eastern Europe issued similar statutes that give increased power to teachers. School violence is also prevalent in Australia, particularly in Queensland and South Australia. In 2009 Australian authorities addressed this issue through increased security and suspensions. Teachers are also victims of school violence. This is especially the case in Great Britain, where nearly half of a group of teachers in one survey maintained that they were threatened with violence, mostly by students.

Neighborhood-Related Violence

Without question, neighborhoods prone to violence contribute to violent and abusive behavior in other environmental settings. Schools in communities with high crime rates tend to have high rates of violence within the school environs, such as drug related violence and sexual assault. There is also a strong link between high crime neighborhoods and low socioeconomic status. These areas tend to show high rates of poverty; residents generally live in dilapidated buildings and have high rates of malnutrition. Moreover, street gangs often use schools as recruiting grounds for new members, thereby increasing the level of violence. Teachers, too, are more likely to be victims of violence in schools that are located in these communities.

Children in War

The participation of children in war is a terrible and disturbing reality. Although children have served as soldiers for centuries, it seems plausible to assume that child warfare would diminish in the twenty-first century. Unfortunately, as Peter Singer points out in *Children at War* (2006), the exact opposite has occurred—child warfare has escalated greatly in recent years. Numerous reports indicate an upward trend in child warfare. According to Michael Wessells in *Child Soldiers* (2006), there are over 300,000 child soldiers worldwide. Further, more than one-third of those initiated as soldiers are girls—a powerful indication that those who recruit youth as soldiers do not seem to discriminate on the basis of gender. At the same time, "service" in combat is only one of several roles in which child soldiers participate. They also act as porters and messengers, spies, land mine detectors, and sexual slaves for other soldiers. In rare instances, individuals under the age of 18, a number of whom have been allegedly diagnosed with learning or mental disorders, have served as suicide bombers, coerced by others as a result of religious motivation. From 1997 to 2003, there were at least 43 countries throughout the world where child soldiers participated in warfare—nearly one-quarter of the world's nations. Africa has the greatest number of countries with child soldiers, with at least 19 nations that seem to sanction child warfare. Many of these countries' child soldiers fought in wars between 2001 and 2004. In addition to these countries, Wessells includes the following nations that put children on the battlefields or in reconnaissance: Central African Republic, Guinea, Indonesia, Myanmar, Philippines, and Nepal. Although the Philippine constitution upholds laws that bar children under 18 from participating in the military, numerous secessionist groups, many of which desire Islamic rule (e.g., on the island of Mindanao), recruit children into the armed forces and local militias.

Countries recruit children as soldiers, even for purposes of combat, for a number of reasons. First, children are less inclined than adults to demand or ask for wages. Second, attrition is less likely to occur with children than with adults because younger individuals have less reason to rationalize the strengths and weaknesses of engaging in combat. Third, they are often seen as individuals who do as they are told. As one Chadian official said in an interview described in the Human Rights Watch publication *Early to War* (2007), "Child soldiers are ideal because they don't complain, they don't expect to be paid, and if you tell them to kill, they kill."

Finally, unlike wars of the past, those of the last several decades increased the likelihood of the use of assault rifles, such as the AK-47 used by the former Soviet Union and the American M-16. Before World War II, it was unlikely that children would engage in combat because they would be no match for adult soldiers with the same skill in fighting or the use of weaponry. The weapons were too heavy and cumbersome or too difficult to use. In recent times, however, children are seen as excellent recruits for war because it is not difficult to train them to use automatic assault weapons, which are relatively easy to use and not cumbersome to carry.

In war-ravaged societies, some children see the military as a form of sanctuary and protection—especially children who are orphaned or who were violently abused at home. The military, such as the rebel Karen army in Myanmar, often provides decent clothing and regular, balanced meals for children who are recruited for combat or other war-related endeavors. In Liberia, children as young as seven years are recruited by rebel groups and militias, which are often seen as safe havens for them. Children also fight in rebel armies and militias because they see a purpose. They often offer themselves as combatants against armies that may have been involved in the murders of loved ones (parents, friends, siblings). They may enter combat to fight for their religion or culture or to end what they see as (or are told are) social injustices.

Regardless of reason, however, child soldiers are subject to grave abuses, whether recruited willingly or by force. Many are beaten, tortured, or even murdered if they attempt to run away because their superiors label them as traitors. One religious leader from Thailand described the recruitment procedures of children by rebel and separatist militias in the following way: "When the armed groups have got recruited children and youth, they then would *supah* or take an oath. After that, they cannot withdraw. Otherwise, other members would kill them, called 'blood halal' or killing without guilt, because this is an act of betrayal to religion by '*munafiq*.'" Munafiq refers to someone who betrays Islam. A 15-year-old boy who escaped the separatist Lord's Resistance Army in northern Uganda said, "Sometimes in the bush, the rebels would beat us without mercy whether you made a mistake or not. We would also be made to carry heavy loads on our heads for long distances and made to assemble out in the cold each day as early as 5 A.M."

Despite the growing concern about the increase of children's participation in war, there are a large number of child combatants who eventually, through education and family integration, return to civilian life—some of whom serve as exemplars to others who are still involved in war-related endeavors.

Reversing Course: Turning Soldiers and Violent Offenders Back to Children

One of the most difficult tasks is to use education as a means to reverse the course of a child soldier's career and change the child soldier back to the child. Childhood warfare deprives and cheats children of

Table: **Child Soldiers in Countries Throughout the World**

Region and country	Conflict and time period
Africa	
Algeria	Civil war between government forces and antigovernment Islamist rebel groups, 1991–2002
Angola	Struggle for independence in 1961; ensuing wars for party control, 1975–2002
Burundi	Civil war between Hutu and Tutsi tribes, 1993–2005
Chad	Civil war, 2005–present
Côte d'Ivoire	Civil war, 2002–2004
Dem. Rep. of the Congo	Civil war–antigovernment forces, 1996–2003 (yet children still enlist in militias)
Eritrea	Eritrean-Ethiopian War, 1998–2000
Ethiopia	Civil war, 1974–1991; Eritrean-Ethiopian War, 1998–2000; war in Somalia, 2006–2009
Liberia	First and second civil wars, 1989–1996; 1999–2003
Republic of Congo	Civil war between partisans of two presidential candidates, 1997–1999
Rwanda	Civil war resulting in mass genocide (approximately 800,000 dead), 1990–1994
Sierra Leone	Civil war between Civil Defense Force and Revolutionary United Front, 1991–2002
Somalia	War between Somalia and Ethiopia, 2006–2009
Sudan	First and second Sudanese wars, 1955–1972; 1983–2005
Uganda	Wars and skirmishes between Ugandan armies and the Lord's Resistance Army, 1980s–present
Asia—South/East	
East Timor	Indonesian occupation of East Timor, 1975–1999
India	Indo-Pakistani wars and skirmishes, 1947–present
Indonesia	Invasion of East Timor, 1975–1999; Papua skirmishes, 1993–present
Myanmar	Continuous recruitment and use of children in militia groups and army combat
Nepal	Nepalese Civil War, 1996–2006
Papua New Guinea	Secessionist revolts, 1989–1997
Philippines	Islamist and other secessionist groups, 1990s–present
Sri Lanka	Civil war between government and Liberation Tigers of Tamil Eelam, 1983–present
Asia—Central/West	
Afghanistan	War with Soviet Union, 1979–early 1980s; international war with Taliban regime, 2001–present
Iran	Iran-Iraq War, 1980–1988
Iraq	Numerous conflicts, belligerents including United States, European nations, and Iran, 1970s–present; Iraqi-Kurdish civil wars, 1994–1997
Israeli occupied territory	Periodic wars between Palestinian liberation groups and Israel, 1940s–present
Lebanon	Use and recruitment of children for Palestinian-backed groups against Israel, 1970s–present
Pakistan	Indo-Pakistani wars and skirmishes, 1947–present; war with Afghanistan, 2001–present
Russian Federation	Wars with central Asian republics, particularly Afghanistan, 1979–1989
Tajikistan	Civil war, 1992–1997
Turkey	Kurdish civil wars, 1978–present
Uzbekistan	Andijan massacre, 2005
Europe	
Bosnia	Nationalism after fall of Yugoslavia
Kosovo	Nationalism after fall of Yugoslavia
Macedonia	Nationalism after fall of Yugoslavia
Northern Ireland	Centuries of conflict between United Kingdom and Irish nationalists
United Kingdom	Centuries of conflict between United Kingdom and Irish nationalists
Americas	
Colombia	Internal armed conflicts, 1964–present
Ecuador	Wars and skirmishes with Peru
Mexico	Children recruited for drug wars, 2005–present
Peru	Wars and skirmishes with Ecuador

both their physical and psychological development. The task of the educator, then, is to reverse this trend after initiation takes place. It is important to note that of the 42 countries listed in the Table (see page 59), 35 countries (over 83 percent) have education indices below .750. Moreover, in nearly all of the nations in Africa and Asia, 40 percent or more of the population earns less than one dollar per day. Some 20 percent of the people in these countries also experience hunger; these nations also have a shorter average life expectancy (up to 60 years) than those of developed nations and a low human development index (below .600). Given low education indices, these countries also show a pattern of much less than 100 percent literacy rate, some countries even ebbing below 70 percent.

The answer for school systems, education ministries, and governments is not to issue martial law on their people. Instead, leaders and citizens should be vigilant in other, more productive ways that set long-term goals of ending violence and child combat. According to Ron Avi Astor, writing in the *Teachers College Record* (2007), some of the most important lines of defense are students, teachers, and family members. Most vicious attacks are associated with a friend or family member who is likely to know the attacker or group of attackers. Astor also argues that the public needs to be cognizant of the factors that contribute to an attacker's potential violence: suicidal or homicidal thoughts or beliefs, infatuation or obsession with weapons, a specified group to be targeted, and so forth. It is also important to focus on the victims of tragedies and not the perpetrators. Since the perpetrators most often seek fame and glorification, one way to limit these attacks and copycat attacks is to reduce media attention on perpetrators. A similar line of defense is necessary to change the course of child soldiering. United Nations sanctions against countries that engage in child soldiering have often been effective. Nevertheless, more needs to be done on the microlevel—such as intervention on the part of outside government and non-government agencies in which child soldiers, many of whom are orphans,

are given the opportunity to change course. Finally, a number of countries throughout the world require their citizens to engage in precrisis and postcrisis intervention. Astor argues that communities in the United States rely too heavily on police, fire, and ambulance personnel to engage in such intervention; instead, all citizens should be trained in the ability to engage in precrisis and postcrisis planning.

Daniel Ness and Chia-ling Lin

REFERENCES

Astor, Ron A. "Lessons That Should Be Learned from the Virginia Tech Mass Murders." *Teachers College Record.* 2007. www.tcrecord.org/Opinion.asp.

Child Soldiers Global Report. 2008. www.childsoldiersglobalreport.org.

Gershoff, Elizabeth T. "Corporal Punishment by Parents and Associated Child Behaviors and Experiences: A Meta-Analytic and Theoretical Review." *Psychological Bulletin* 128 (2002): 539–579.

Human Rights Watch. *Early to War: Child Soldiers in the Chad Conflict.* New York: Human Rights Watch, 2007.

National Center for Education Statistics, US Department of Education. "Crime, Violence, Discipline, and Safety in U.S. Public Schools: Findings from the School Survey on Crime and Safety: 2009–10." http://nces.ed.gov/pubs2011/2011320.pdf.

———. "Indicators of School Crime and Safety, 2005–06: School Survey on Crime and Safety (SSOCS)." Washington, DC: National Center for Education Statistics, US Department of Education, 2007. http://nces.ed.gov.

Singer, Peter W. *Children at War.* Berkeley: University of California Press, 2006.

Straus, Murray A. "Discipline and Deviance: Physical Punishment of Children and Violence and Other Crime in Adulthood." *Social Problems* 38 (1991): 133–154.

US Department of Justice, Bureau of Justice Statistics. "National Crime Victimization Survey (NCVS)." Washington, DC: National Center for Education Statistics, US Department of Education, 2007. http://bjs.ojp.usdoj.gov/index.cfm?ty=dcdetail&iid=245.

Wessells, Michael. *Child Soldiers: From Violence to Protection.* Cambridge, MA: Harvard University Press, 2006.

GENDER AND EDUCATION

GENDER DISPARITY WORLDWIDE

While progress has been made worldwide in closing the gender gap in education, disparities still exist. The United Nations (UN) Millennium Development Goals (MDGs) of worldwide gender parity in primary and secondary education by 2005 was not met. According to the Millennium Development Goals Report of 2008, while two out of three countries in 2006 had achieved gender parity at the primary school level, girls still accounted for 55 percent of the out-of-school population. The largest gender gap in primary school enrollment is found in the regions of Oceania, sub-Saharan Africa, and western Asia. In the areas of western and central Africa where low retention rates and high repetition in grades are commonly found, girls, in particular, fail to enroll and remain in school. The MDG 2008 report states that in these regions factors such as drought, poverty, food shortages, child labor, armed conflict, and HIV/AIDS contribute to low school enrollment and high dropout rates for all students, but are particularly devastating for girls. While gender parity in primary school enrollment has been reached in the developed regions of the world (i.e., 100 girls per 100 boys), gender parity is still lagging in the developing regions (i.e., 94 girls per 100 boys). In developing countries, little gender difference in primary school enrollment is found for households in urban areas or for the richest households. However, in order to increase the attendance of girls in rural areas and from the poorest households, targeted interventions (such as having satellite schools in remote areas, eliminating school fees, providing school meals, ensuring a safe school environment, and promoting later marriage)

are needed. With respect to the secondary school level, the enrollment rate for girls is higher than that for boys in three regions (eastern Asia, southeastern Asia, and Latin America and the Caribbean). It appears that where gender parity has been achieved at the primary education level, girls generally continue on to secondary school, whereas some boys join the labor force. On the other hand, in regions such as sub-Saharan Africa, western Asia, southern Asia, and Oceania, the gender gap further widens in enrollment at the secondary level. The MDG 2008 report further estimates that of the 113 countries that failed to achieve gender parity in both primary and secondary school enrollment by 2005, only 18 are likely to achieve the goal of gender parity by 2015.

As discussed in the UN's *Gender Achievement and Prospects in Education* (GAP) report, gender disparity has significant implications. Girls who are denied educational access and opportunities are more vulnerable to poverty, hunger, violence, abuse, exploitation, maternal mortality, HIV/AIDS, and other diseases. Educated women are more likely to have healthy babies, send their children to school, protect their children and themselves from sexual exploitation and trafficking, and contribute to political, social, and economic development. Unless significant progress is made in meeting the goals of gender parity and universal quality education, the GAP report concludes that none of the other development goals (such as raising economic productivity, lowering infant and maternal mortality, improving health and nutritional status, reducing poverty, and combating HIV/AIDS and other diseases) are likely to be met.

While international efforts to promote women's education have generally focused on increasing women's participation in schooling and acknowledge the benefits of women's education for society, feminist scholars urge the expansion of the focus to examine how education can improve the lives of the women themselves and become an important avenue toward empowerment.

The subarea of gender research examines cognitive differences between males and females in terms of spatial differences, more specifically, tasks on mental rotation, spatial perception, and spatial visualization. Such findings vary across nations, with the US samples yielding some of the greatest gender differences and China yielding some of the least. The research on gender differences in intellectual styles views this construct as largely subject to socialization and other environmental factors, such that styles should be recognized as states rather than traits that are often construed as innate. International and intercultural differences have been found with respect to the intellectual style of "field dependence/independence," with boys tending to be more "field independent" when compared to girls, who tend to be more "field dependent." Studies in China, Turkey, and other countries, however, reveal mixed or inconsistent results. These cultural variations in gender differences, along with studies that show that, with training, students can improve their test scores in field independence, support the social constructive nature of this particular intellectual style. Much attention has been given to gendered ways of knowing, particular in Western societies. That females and males may tend to utilize different epistemologies, such as separate or connected ways of knowing, can have important implications for classroom curriculum and practices.

Worldwide, girls experience greater health risks and insufficient care, with gender biases that favor boys in nutrition and health care acting as a contributing factor. With respect to disabilities, it appears that disabled girls' education tends to be negatively affected in regard to exclusion and insufficient resources; generally, disabled girls have relatively lower school enrollment than disabled boys. Although there have been global efforts to make primary school tuition free, millions of children and their families find the cost of schooling a deterrent. Many developing countries are hampered by inadequate facilities, textbook shortages, and insufficient instructional time and further challenged by rapid urbanization and the increased spread of HIV/AIDS. Associated with high rates of sexual exploitation and abuse, girls in parts of southern Africa and the Caribbean are estimated to be four to seven times more likely than boys to be infected with HIV/AIDS. Pregnancy and marriage are also other factors that lead to school dropout.

The UN Commission on the Status of Women (CSW), established to promote gender equality and the empowerment of women worldwide, meets annually with the UN Economic and Social Council to evaluate progress, reaffirm policies, and identify challenges in specific regions. In 2007, for example, CSW placed high priority on the elimination of violence against female children, especially girls in Palestine and Afghanistan due to the current instability of those governments. When reviewing various international studies of achievement in mathematics, science, and reading as well as occupation and career aspirations with respect to gender differences (e.g., Trends in International Mathematics and Science Study [TIMSS], Programme for International Student Assessment [PISA], and Progress in International Reading Literacy Study [PIRLS]), the World Values Survey revealed, surprisingly, that both men and women believed that males made more proficient political leaders. While this perspective was more prevalent in socially conservative countries including Bangladesh, China, Iran, and Uganda, one of five women in the United States held the same belief regarding male leaders. Despite increases in gender parity, improvement in academic achievement for girls, and increased representation of women in professional fields and civic leadership, female underachievement and discrimination against women remain prevalent worldwide.

The process of globalization can create both opportunities and inequalities for all segments of society. Unfortunately, women's access to information and communication technologies (ICT)—tools that can be powerful in bringing about economic, political, and social change on a global level—is limited by factors such as literacy, social practice, locale, and costs. Increasing women's participation in ICT could yield a range of benefits such as improving women's earning power, educational status, and status in society; promoting their knowledge of health and reproductive issues and their awareness and interest in political matters; and providing avenues for their empowerment and ultimately an enhanced quality of life.

Hsiu-Zu Ho

REFERENCES

Stromquist, Nelly P. "Women's Education in the Twenty-First Century: Balance and Prospects." In *Comparative Education: The Dialectic of the Global and the Local*, ed. Robert F. Arnove and Carlos Alberto Torres, 176–203. Lanham, MD: Rowman & Littlefield, 2003.

United Nations. *Millennium Development Goals*. 2012. www.un.org/millenniumgoals/.

United Nations Educational, Scientific and Cultural Organization. 2012. www.unesco.org/new/en/unesco/.

United Nations Girls' Education Initiative. "The GAP Report: Gender Achievements and Prospects in Education: Reporter's Notebook." 2012. www.ungei.org/index.php.

GLOBALIZATION, GENDER, AND EDUCATION

Theoretical discussions on the nature and effects of globalization vary. Although the concept of globalization is widely used, the term is often vaguely defined and its usage highly contested. Most people think of globalization as the expansion of technology and communication. For others, the term is associated with a global economy. For some, globalization is seen as a "mixed blessing"; as Madeleine Green and her colleagues note in *The Brave New (and Smaller) World of Higher Education* (2002), on the one hand, the term "connotes the free flow of ideas, capital, people, and goods around the world" and, on the other hand, "implies the hegemony of the capitalist system, the domination of rich nations and corporations, and the loss of national identity and culture." Whatever definition is ascribed to the word, it can be argued that globalization has a huge impact on every aspect of our lives and that it is changing the face and shape of education.

A broad definition of globalization is offered by David Held and colleagues in *Global Transformations* (1999, 2): "the widening, deepening, and speeding up of worldwide interconnectedness in all aspects of contemporary social life." In general, most discussions of globalization fall into three categories: economic, political, and cultural.

In the area of economics, globalization is viewed as the driving force for the creation of an internationally market-driven economy. In today's rapidly changing economic climate, a common rhetoric that most politicians and policy makers use is that a nation's competitiveness will depend on the knowledge and skill of its workers. Thus, the mission is to use the educational system as a tool to prepare students to enter a globally competitive workforce. For example, more and more countries are beginning to place an emphasis on science and information technology curricula, in the hopes of producing more engineers, computer technicians, and scientists.

In terms of politics, with the growing role of international organizations in education, the quality of national educational systems is increasingly compared globally. For instance, policy discussions at the national level are shaped by important studies conducted by prominent organizations, such as the Trends in International Mathematics and Science Study (TIMSS), conducted by The National Center for Educational Statistics, and the Programme for International Student Assessment (PISA), conducted by the Organization for Economic Cooperation and Development. Conclusions drawn from such assessments have significant impacts on educational standards and the ways education is delivered for many countries.

Finally, at the cultural level, there has been much debate whether globalization has a homogenizing effect, thus diminishing cultural diversity around the world, or if globalization has the potential to foster and increase the flows of people, goods, information, and images, thereby increasing cultural diversity. In the realm of education, youth today are increasingly connected through technology that spans thousands of miles. For example, students and educators are beginning to create international collaboration ventures such as the Flat Classroom Project, which connects students in a school in Dhaka, Bangladesh, with a school in the United States in Camilla, Georgia. On the opposite end, critics warn that globalization is turning education into a commodity, with the delivery and experience of education streamlined in cost-efficient, calculable, and predictable ways. This phenomenon is sometimes termed "McDonaldization" or cultural homogeneity. For example, some scholars have observed that the standardization of curriculum in professional courses such as master's of business administration (MBA) programs has resulted in a pool of graduates who have the academic qualifications but lack real-world experience and leadership. The argument is that such emphasis on standardization will diminish diversity, encourage conformity, and produce a narrow range of outcomes for schooling.

Intergovernmental Organizations and Global Educational Initiatives

The growing emphasis on a global perspective on education is best reflected in the development of intergovernmental organizations (IGOs). These IGOs often operate on a model of public-private partnership, working closely with governments, the private sector, and civil society to form global educational initiatives. IGOs have a big role in shaping and influencing educational policy making on a global scale, while on a national level, governments are collaborating with IGOs in order to inform their educational policies. Focusing on the problems of providing equality, access, and equity for all students, most of these IGOs promote the interests of women and girls in education. In this category, the main actors in forging global educational policies are UNESCO, the World Bank, and the Organization for Economic Cooperation and Development (OECD).

UNESCO

The United Nations Educational, Scientific and Cultural Organization (UNESCO) was founded on November 16, 1945. As determined by the Charter of the United Nations, the purpose of the organization is "to contribute to peace and security by promoting collaboration among the nations through education, science and culture." Over the last six decades, UNESCO has paid much attention to the education of girls and women, through conferences, workshops, research, and publications. Currently, the biggest and most ambitious educational project implemented by UNESCO is the Education for All (EFA) initiative. Conceived at a world conference in Thailand, in 1990, and reaffirmed in Senegal in 2000, the key principles of EFA are universal access to learning, a focus on equity, education as a human right, enhancing the environment for learning, and strengthening partnerships. With an implementation plan for reaching most of its targets by 2015, EFA focuses on meeting the learning needs of all children, youth, and adults through six internationally agreed educational goals. One of the goals of EFA is to "achieve gender parity by 2005, and gender equality by 2015." According to UNESCO, to achieve gender parity is to have equal participation of girls and boys in all forms of education, especially in the numbers of girls and boys enrolled in primary and secondary schools. Achieving gender equality means that all girls and boys have the same conditions "to enjoy basic education of high quality, achieve at equal levels and enjoy equal benefits from education." Similar aims are also articulated in the UN's Millennium Development Goals (MDGs). Two of the MDGs specifically address education—achieving universal primary education and promoting gender equality and the empowerment of women. To expand EFA and the MDGs' educational objectives, the United Nations Literacy Decade (UNLD) 2003–2012 was launched. In 2003, the number of illiterate adults in the world surpassed 860 million. Therefore, one of the main missions of UNLD is to achieve a 50 percent improvement in levels of adult literacy by 2015, giving special attention to women. The UNLD sees the importance of improving the literacy rates for women because increased literacy has an impact on mother and child health, fertility rates, and income levels.

World Bank

The World Bank is one of the largest global investors in education. An intergovernmental organization that works with other global organizations, the World Bank was founded in 1944 to rebuild Europe after World War II. Today, it is an institution made up of 185 member countries, providing financial and technical assistance to developing countries around the world. The World Bank lends money to governments and global NGOs to fund diverse educational projects, such as "A Better Managed Education System in Uganda," "Philippines: Introducing Competition to the Benefit of School Children," "India: How 'Bollywood' Music Videos Are Boosting Literacy," "Tunisia: A School System Striving for Its Own Graduation," and "Yemen: Reaching Even the Most Distant Students." Projects that are directly related to gender parity and equality in education include "Bangladesh: School Girls Hold Power and Promise," "Expanding Girls' Education in Turkey," and "More Girls in Pakistan's Schools." In addition, the World Bank has partnerships with other IGOs. For instance, the World Bank is an active member and donor to the United Nations Girls' Education Initiative.

The World Bank also uses educational standards established by other IGOs. Most of the World Bank's educational initiatives, for example, are guided by the goals set out by UNESCO's EFA initiative and the OECD's Development Assistance Committee, particularly in the areas of universal primary education, adult literacy, and gender parity.

OECD

The Organization for Economic Cooperation and Development, founded in 1961, was centered on economic development, but in later years has included a commitment to gender equality issues. OECD's work in the areas of gender and educational equality is conducted primarily through the Network on Gender Equality and the Directorate for Education. The organization sees gender and educational equality as key to the economic growth and financial stability of nation-states around the world. Published yearly since 1992, comparable national statistics on various aspects of educational appropriation and performance are now offered in the publication *Education at a Glance*. The data collected include results of policies for equality of females and males in education, showing whether educational policies are having the desired or intended effect. OECD recently launched the Programme for International Student Assessment (PISA), which measures reading, literacy, mathematics literacy, and science literacy of 15-year-olds (students near the end of compulsory education). PISA also examines gender differences, students' engagement as learners in terms of their motivation and learning strategies, and students' performance in the context of their economic, social, and cultural backgrounds.

Collaborative educational initiatives on a global level are one of the most promising strategies for the promotion of equal educational access and opportunities for both males and females. As shown in the examples above, more and more IGOs are embracing and implementing policies that aim to reduce or eliminate gender inequality at all levels of education. However, the role and effectiveness of these IGOs in addressing such issues have been debatable. For example, in the Mid-Decade Assessment of the UNESCO Education for All initiative, it was found that the goal of achieving gender parity in primary and secondary

education by 2005 was met only by 55 out of 149 countries. Although these numbers do indicate that some countries have managed to achieve relatively equal enrollment ratios between boys and girls, when the data are disaggregated, gender disparities for girls still persist in retention and dropout rates, access to lower secondary education, and overall completion in all levels of education. In some countries, particularly in the Arab states and southern and western Asia, the disparities are large. For example, in Yemen there are 144 girls out-of-school for every 100 boys; in India and Benin, the ratio is 136:100. Moreover, in countries where gender parity has been achieved, there is a concern that governments might take this as a sign that gender inequality issues have also been addressed and that no further reforms are needed. Clearly, questions about the commitment of nations to work toward educational equality for all their students must also take into consideration the matter of sustainability. Many of the countries that have not met or are in danger of not meeting the global aspirations of achieving gender parity and equality are also countries with high debt repayments. While it is true that IGOs like the World Bank and International Monetary Fund are the largest sources of financial assistance to global educational initiatives, educational researchers have also argued that the terms for loans are too restrictive and the repayment conditions imposed on borrower countries are too harsh. Many countries have had to increase their school fees or put a cap on teachers' wages in order to secure loans or pay off debts. Lastly, critical voices are beginning to question whether large-scale, ambitious global educational initiatives such as the Millennium Development Goals (MDGs) and Education for All can be effectively implemented. With such broadly defined objectives, the needs and circumstances of specific communities and countries can be overlooked. Even with monetary contributions from IGOs, it has been estimated that the United Nations would need an additional $50 billion per year to achieve all the MDGs by the target date of 2015.

International studies such as TIMMS and PISA that measure and compare students' achievement levels in various countries are valuable in that they provide useful data that can help governments plan and implement their educational policies. However, there are many limitations in using only quantitative data to address gender inequality issues in education. Researchers and organizations have pointed out that using a measurable outcomes-based approach to comparing boys' and girls' educational performances often disregards the historical and sociocultural factors that create gender inequalities. For example, traditional gender roles in many societies greatly influence the learning outcomes and educational expectations for boys and girls. In many schools, textbooks and curriculum continue to utilize content that is gender-biased. Furthermore, because most global educational initiatives tend to narrowly focus on test indicators, it has been argued that the reliance of the United Nations and other IGOs upon the achievement of numerical "targets" could undermine educational and gender equality programs.

Information Communication and Technology

One of the prevailing features of globalization is the growth and invention of new information and communication technologies (ICT). New technologies offer a powerful tool in bringing change to social, economic, and political life on a global level. Since the beginning of the 1990s, the use of ICT in education has developed rapidly. Such uses include the growing popularity of distance education, online message boards for class discussions, and computer programs such as PowerPoint to supplement teaching. ICT has also been regarded as the entry point for most countries to engage in an internationally market-driven economy. This has propelled many governments to expand the use of ICT in their schools. For example, in Malaysia, 30 percent of the annual education budget is allocated for technological materials and support.

Studies have shown that supporting women's participation in ICT would produce a range of benefits. Simple access to information and improved communications can increase income levels, enhance knowledge in health and reproductive issues, promote greater awareness and interest in political matters, and improve families' welfare and economic security. In India, for example, the number of women working in ICT has been increasing gradually over the past decade. Data from that country shows that women working in ICT are earning higher salaries at rates equivalent to their male counterparts and

have increased their opportunities to work abroad. With higher earning power, many of these women are able to contribute significantly to their families' incomes, providing pathways for empowerment and an improved status in society. Hence, women's access to ICT can substantially improve the quality of their lives.

In the past decade, the world has seen a dramatic increase in the use of the Internet. Between 1995 and 2002, the number of Internet users jumped from 16 million to 580 million. According to 2011 data, there were over 2 billion Internet users worldwide. However, the use and accessibility of the Internet are still confined to a relatively small number of the world's population. For instance, Europe, which has only 5 percent of the world's population, has slightly more than one-quarter of the world's Internet users. In contrast, 14 percent of the world's population resides in Africa, but this region comprises only 3.7 percent of the world's Internet users. This "digital divide" also translates to a gender gap in Internet usage. Although more research is necessary, current available evidence indicates that women's usage of and access to ICT is much lower than that of men. In Asia women make up 22 percent of all Internet users, in Latin American 38 percent, and in the Middle East 6 percent. Currently, there are no comprehensive data on women Internet users for Africa. In some countries, the gender gap in Internet use is quite pronounced. For instance, women's Internet usage is only around 20 percent in Italy and Indonesia.

Many factors limit women's access to ICT, depriving them of the advantages of globalization and the information society. These obstacles include illiteracy and the lack of education, social practices and beliefs, prohibitive cost, and geographical location. According to UNESCO's statistics published in 2003, it is estimated that nearly one in seven of the world's 6 billion people cannot read or write. Although recent figures show that women are gaining access to education and literacy, women and girls still make up two-thirds of illiterate people. Around the world, there are more girls out of school than boys. Lower literacy rates and lower access to basic education restrict many women and girls from gaining the necessary skills and knowledge to use ICT or gain employment in the ICT sector.

Overall, more women than men are excluded from the information society, both as students and users.

Due to cultural norms in many societies, women and girls are perceived to be less capable of understanding scientific and technical concepts. While in many parts of the world, the number of women pursuing higher education is equal to or surpassing the number of men, women are still underrepresented in fields traditionally seen as more suitable for males, such as engineering, sciences, and math. For example, in the United States, women hold only 22 percent of undergraduate degrees in computer science and engineering.

Even when girls and young women are able to enroll in ICT courses, they continue to face obstacles because of gender discrimination in curriculum, teaching methods, and attitudes of teachers and students. In addition, once they complete their schooling, female graduates usually experience more difficulties in finding employment in ICT sectors; when they do secure jobs, their salaries are often lower than their male counterparts'. In a 2007 study conducted by the Association of Professional Engineers, Scientists and Managers Australia, more than 25 percent of the professional women surveyed reported a pay disparity when compared with their male colleagues. For women who held senior management positions, the figure was much higher, with over 40 percent reporting a pay disparity. While some countries, such as India, have shown improvement in the number of women working in ICT sectors, a majority of the women are still concentrated in lower-skilled, lesser-paid, entry-level jobs related to data entry or word processing. Hence, for some women, the rapidly advancing sphere of ICT brings new opportunities, but for others it merely means new patterns of gendered inequalities.

Two of the most important factors in determining an individual's access to ICT are the cost and the geographical location. Users of ICT around the world tend to be the educated elite and those who can afford the cost of buying and maintaining equipment. However, this problem is more common for women because they constitute 70 percent of those living in poverty. To date, most ICT infrastructure and facilities are clustered in urban or industrial areas. Internet access is still relatively sparse in rural areas due to unreliable infrastructure (electricity and phone lines) and the high costs of setting up ICT locations and equipment. Such barriers to access have immense consequences for women's use of ICT because, in general, more women than men live in rural areas. Additionally, with women shouldering most caretaking and domestic responsibilities, they might find it more difficult than men to move or travel to bigger towns or cities.

Globalization is a reality that has become an increasingly penetrating phenomenon in both international and local contexts. As a multifaceted process, the web of globalization cuts through the many threads of society, spanning across the realms of economics, politics, communications, and culture. In the educational arena, globalization has unfolded the need for worldwide educational reforms with particular references to issues of equality, access, and equity for all children, and the wider utilization of information and communication technologies to address such challenges. Today, IGOs such as the United Nations, the World Bank, and OECD are playing pioneering and leading roles in supporting a global approach to educational development and reforms. Through universal frameworks such as the Millennium Development Goals and Education for All, promising work is being done to alleviate poverty, improve human rights, increase the access and quality of education, and promote gender equality and the empowerment of women. Although assessments of such global educational initiatives have shown some gains and successes, equity issues are still critical and acute all over the world. An MDG report released in 2007 estimated that 72 million children of primary school age were not in school, with girls and children from poor countries the least likely to attend school. While the world is becoming more connected through expanding numbers of Internet users and telephone subscribers, ICT is still accessible by a population that is mostly male, educated, and wealthy. Consequently, it is clear that much work still needs to be done in order to develop equitable educational systems for both males and females. This goal can be achieved only through partnerships and commitment at all levels of governance—international, national, regional, and local. International forays into educational reforms must be made in conjunction with the needs and aspirations of each nation, paying close attention to historical and sociocultural influences. In addition, the potential of ICT to transform education should be capitalized to expand participation to all social groups. Lastly, local governments must continue to give priority to public investments in education, followed by adequate financial backing from donor countries and IGOs.

Clearly, the process of globalization can create both opportunities and inequalities for all segments of society. As Nico Cloete and his colleagues (1999) note, "every individual in the world partakes of both the local and the global, albeit highly unevenly," and as a result, many males and females around the world do not share the same social conditions and prospects for equitable education. As the world becomes more connected, it has also become clear that gender and educational inequities are problems that are shared globally and hence must be solved collectively. In the era of globalization, such collective action and commitment are not only inevitable but crucial in forging new visions of educational ideologies and practices that are truly universal, accessible, equitable, and empowering for all individuals around the world.

Eva Wong

REFERENCES

Association of Professional Engineers, Scientists and Managers Australia. *APESMA Women in the Professions Survey Report 2007*. Melbourne, Australia: APESMA, 2007. www.apesma.com.au.

Belawati, Tian. *Malaysia ICT Use in Education*. Paris: UNESCO, 2004. www.unescobkk.org.

Burbules, Nicolas C., and Carlos Alberto Torres. "Globalization and Education: An Introduction." In *Globalization and Education: A Critical Perspective*, ed. Nicolas C. Burbules, and Carlos Alberto Torres. 5–26. New York: Routledge Falmer, 2000.

Cloete, Nico, Michael Cross, Johan Muller, and Sury Pillay. "Culture, Identity and the Role of Higher Education in Building Democracy in South Africa." In *Diversity and Unity: The Role of Higher Education in Building Democracy*, ed. Michael Cross, Nico Cloete, Edgar F. Beckham, Ann Harper, Jayalakshmi Indiresan, and Caryn M. Musil, 20–48. Cape Town, South Africa: Maskew Miller Longman, 1999.

Featherstone, Mike. "Global Culture: An Introduction." In *Global Culture: Nationalism, Globalization and Modernity*, ed. Mike Featherstone, 1–14. Thousand Oaks, CA: Sage, 1990.

Flat Classroom Project. http://flatclassroomproject2006.wikispaces.com.

Goldstein, Harvey. "Education for All: The Globalization of Learning Targets." *Comparative Education* 40 (2004): 7–14.

Green, Madeleine, Peter Eckel, and Andris Barblan. *The Brave New (and Smaller) World of Higher Education: A Transatlantic View*. Washington, DC: American Council on Education, 2002. www.acenet.edu/bookstore.

Hafkin, Nancy, and Nancy Taggart. *Gender, Information Technology, and Developing Countries: An Analytic Study*. LearnLink, 2001. http://learnlink.aed.org.

Held, David, Anthony McGrew, David Goldblatt, and Jonathan Perraton. *Global Transformations: Politics, Economics and Culture*. Cambridge, MA: Polity, 1999.

Heyneman, Stephen P. "The History and Problems of the Making of Education Policy at the World Bank, 1960–2000." In *Global Trends in Educational Policy: International Perspectives on Education and Society*, volume 6, ed. David P. Barker and Alexander W. Wiseman, 23–58. Amsterdam: Elsevier, 2005.

Internet Word Stats. *Usage and Population Statistics*. www.internetworldstats.com/stats.htm.

OECD. www.oecd.org.

Ritzer, George. *The McDonaldization of Society*. Revised ed. Thousand Oaks, CA: Pine Forge, 1996.

Tung, Ko-Chih. EFA *Mid-Decade Assessment Meeting Report: Annual EFA Coordinators Meeting/EFA Mid-Decade Assessment Planning Meeting*. Bangkok, Thailand: UNESCO Asia and Pacific Regional Bureau for Education, 2005.

UCLA World Internet Project. www.newsroom.ucla.edu/portal/ucla/First-Release-of-Findings-From-4849.aspx?RelNum=4849.

UNESCO. *Education for All: Global Monitoring Report 2008*. Paris: UNESCO, 2007.

———. www.unesco.org.

United Nations. *Millennium Development Goals Report*. New York: United Nations, 2007.

———. *United Nations Millennium Development Goals*. 2008. www.un.org/millenniumgoals/.

World Bank. www.worldbank.org.

GENDER AND ACHIEVEMENT

The path toward gender parity in the twenty-first century has been successful, but goals for achieving gender equality in primary and secondary school by 2005 have not been met. In 2007 the United Nations Children's Fund (UNICEF) estimated that 115 million children were without access to basic education; of that number, 62 million were girls. This failure means that girls are still left behind in a world that is increasingly globalizing, modernizing, and readying for competition in a market economy. The hurdles for getting girls into school—poverty, gender roles, cultural traditions, health epidemics, political strife, lack of governmental accountability, and inadequate management—are too high and cannot be readily measured. The bleak reality of female discrimination has led to the establishment of various intergovernmental organizations that work to close the gender gap in education. The following institutions—the United Nations Children Fund, the Gender Achievements and Prospects in Education Program, and the Commission on the Status of Women—have participated in such efforts.

United Nations Children's Fund

The United Nations Children's Fund (UNICEF) advocates for quality compulsory education for all children with an emphasis on gender equity. In 2002 UNICEF designed the "25 by 2005" initiative that targeted 25 nations in most danger of failing to close the gender gap in primary and secondary education by 2005 and also of failing to meet the UN's Millennium Development Goals by 2015. The selection of the 25 nations was based on meeting one or more of the following criteria: (1) female enrollment rate was lower than 70 percent; (2) primary schools in the nation exhibited a gender gap of 10 percent or more; (3) more than 1 million girls in the nation were not attending school; (4) the nation was included in the World Bank's Education for All initiative; and (5) school enrollment and attendance were prevented by national crises (e.g., health epidemics, civil war). Afghanistan, Bangladesh, Chad, Ethiopia, India, Mali, Pakistan, and Turkey were among the chosen 25 nations.

Due to disparate economic, political, and cultural climates in the 25 nations, the initiative has been utilizing different approaches to improve school enrollment rates and quality education for each nation. Working directly with children is one of the strategies implemented, and school-age girls and boys are encouraged to actually participate in the educational research. For example, participants have been asked to identify reasons for low enrollment and attendance rates, as well as to provide suggestions for improvements. According to UNICEF, the incorporation of children's perspectives in the research process has been beneficial on multiple levels, including an increase in youth self-empowerment.

Gender Achievements and Prospects in Education Program

Developed by the United Nations Girls' Education Initiative, the Gender Achievements and Prospects in Education Program (GAP) is a multimedia project that brings together the knowledge and observations of individuals who work in social development and education. The goal of GAP is to assess progress made in gender parity in education through field reports, interviews, dialogues, and collaborations.

A GAP study revealed that in 2003, Afghanistan was one of the nations that required the most improvement in increasing its annual female attendance rate in primary school. Approximately six out of every ten girls in Afghanistan were enrolled in school, yet only about four of the ten girls enrolled actually attended. Bhutan, a landlocked nation in the Himalayas, was the second nation in Asia in need of the most improvement; less than half of all children in Bhutan, boys and girls included, attended primary school.

Other GAP studies revealed that the degree to which goals of gender parity and achievement in education will be met varied from country to country and region to region. In some nations, the quality of education, student retention rates, and achievement levels had often been compromised as governments attempted to enroll large numbers of children in school. For instance, the primary school enrollment rate in Rwanda was high in comparison to other African nations (the Rwandan government provides free basic education), but at the same time, the dropout rate increased from 14 percent to 18 percent in 2004. In spite of increased student enrollment, particularly in Kenya, Rwanda, Tanzania, and Uganda, the number of children in school remained low. The great discrepancy between student enrollment and student attendance can be attributed in part to deleterious effects of poverty, health pandemics, and other national calamities.

As of 2002 the adult literacy rate of 26 percent in Chad resulted in the nation being ranked among the lowest of all "25 by 2005" countries. Mali also ranked poorly: about 39 percent of all girls in the nation were enrolled in school, yet only 33 percent of those enrolled actually attended school. The adult literacy rate in Mali was also disconcerting as only 19 percent of the population could read and write.

Commission on the Status of Women

Other efforts include the United Nations' establishment of the Commission on the Status of Women (CSW). The creation of CSW was directed exclusively toward the promotion of gender equality and empowerment of women worldwide. In regard to educational improvement, CSW collaborates with other UN agencies and affiliates to (1) improve current efforts in eliminating gender inequalities in primary and secondary schools; (2) determine the root cause of school dropout rates among young girls; (3) reassess the relationship between dropout rates, gender, and age; (4) enact legislation that encourages female school enrollment regardless of race, ethnicity, and disability; (5) provide free compulsory education, especially for girls, and to expand their education at all levels and in all academic areas; and (6) encourage women to enter the labor market.

Additionally, the CSW meets with the UN Economic and Social Council annually to evaluate progress, reaffirm policies, and identify challenges. In its fifty-first meeting with the council in 2007, CSW placed high priority on the elimination of discrimination and violence against girls, especially girls in Palestine and Afghanistan due to the current instability of the governments. CSW also urged the UN and international governments to review, amend, and, when appropriate, abolish laws, policies, and cultural customs that discriminate against girls and women in ways that inhibit their access to social mobility and opportunity.

Girls' Schooling and Achievement in the Twenty-First Century

Studies show that access to schooling has increased over time, especially in the last 20 years, due to economic and political expansion. Countries in the twenty-first century need to become more economically competitive in order to improve their per capita income, and one way to achieve this goal is through mass education. Additionally, increasing pressure from the women's movement for empowerment and leadership, and the adoption of positive strategies of gender equity, have been important in the further promotion of successful models of educational equity and achievement.

Attendance Patterns

Even though gender gaps remain and the pace of growth is slow overall, UNICEF states that "the world is technically on track to meet the goal of gender parity in primary education" (2005). The Gender Parity Index (GPI) showed general improvements in primary school attendance rates in 2011 with substantial national variation, even though stark distinctions remain. Among developing countries ($N = 81$) with a GPI measurement, Colombia, Ghana, Peru, São Tomé and Príncipe, Suriname, and Vietnam were the only nations listed to have achieved full gender parity (GPI = 1.0) with equal numbers of boys and girls attending primary school. Of the 81 countries, Chad, Mali, Niger, Pakistan, and Yemen were among the countries exhibiting the greatest gender disparity.

Studies show that gender disparity in primary education begins with first grade enrollment. According to the global average in 2005, 94 girls attended first grade for every 100 boys. Compared to regions such as sub-Saharan Africa and the Middle East, southern and western Asia have made the most significant improvement in first grade enrollment among girls since 1999—the numbers have increased from 83 to 92 girls per 100 boys. On the other end of the spectrum, according to UNESCO, countries that need the most improvement include Afghanistan, the Central African Republic, Chad, Niger, Pakistan, and Yemen, each having an enrollment of 80 girls or less for every 100 boys starting the first grade.

Gender disparities in education tend to increase at higher levels of schooling. The overall number of girls attending secondary school and tertiary education is much lower than girls attending primary school. UNESCO's 2008 figures (2010) show that only 33 percent of nations with available data achieved gender parity in secondary school; however, out of the 130 countries from which data was collected, approximately 5 percent had achieved gender parity in tertiary school. In order to encourage higher secondary school enrollment, stipends were provided, for example, in Bangladesh and Malawi as a way to compensate the family for the loss of income otherwise contributed by the student. Development agencies providing these funds affirm that a larger number of girls have actually enrolled in secondary school as a result.

While gender disparity in primary and secondary

schools favors boys, gender disparities at the tertiary level in most developed countries are in fact disadvantaging boys. That is, according to the 2008 UNESCO report, in developed countries and those in transition, there are 130 women enrolled for every 100 men (i.e., GPI = 1.3). However, in many developing nations, women remain at a major disadvantage. Gender disparity favors men in southern and western Asia (GPI = .76) and sub-Saharan Africa (GPI = .66). In Latin America and the Caribbean (GPI = 1.20), central and eastern Europe (GPI = 1.22), and North America and western Europe (GPI = 1.24), gender disparity favors women.

In many parts of the world, school environments and classroom dynamics also play an important role in children's school attendance rates. In some regions, school classrooms are physically unsafe for both boys and girls due to civil wars and political strife. Gender bias in teachers' attitudes, pedagogy and curricula, and textbooks and other teaching materials continues to be pervasive, and fields of studies and occupational choices still reflect gender ideologies and practices.

Science, Mathematics, and Reading Achievement

In 2009 the Programme for International Student Assessment (PISA), conducted by the Organization for Economic Cooperation and Development (OECD), provided a worldwide assessment of 15-year-olds' scholastic performance in science, mathematics, and reading. The PISA 2009 survey placed greater emphasis on reading achievement. The triennial survey encompassed results from more than 400,000 students from 65 countries and economies (34 OECD countries/economies and 31 partner countries/economies).

PISA 2009 assessed students' cognitive and affective competencies in science. Among OECD countries, those who had a greater majority of students who performed at the highest science proficiency levels included Australia, Finland, Japan, and New Zealand. Compared to assessments of math and reading, gender differences in science were much smaller. The countries with the largest gender differences were Denmark and the United States, where boys outperformed girls. However, in Finland, Greece, Slovenia, and Turkey, girls performed better on the science assessment compared to boys. In rank order,

Shanghai-China, Finland, Hong Kong, Singapore, and Japan, respectively, were the overall top five in science performance ranking; Kyrgyzstan was ranked the lowest.

However, different trends were revealed in a 2003 science achievement study conducted by Trends in International Mathematics and Science Study (TIMSS)—a survey that spanned 51 countries. The study revealed that science achievement levels among boys in the eighth grade were significantly higher than those for girls in the same grade in a majority of the countries surveyed. However, since 1999, overall improvement in science performance has been favoring girls, but still not to the level of boys.

Results of the PISA 2009 survey showed that males achieved higher mathematics achievement than females in 35 out of 65 countries/economies surveyed (inclusive of OECD and partner countries/economies). Belgium, Chile, the United Kingdom, and the United States were the top four nations with the greatest gender disparity. Males exhibited the highest levels of mathematical knowledge in Canada, Finland, Japan, Korea, Netherlands, and Switzerland. However, the overall gender disparity in mathematical achievement was substantially less than the disparity in reading achievement. Without the consideration of gender in achievement levels, Chinese Taipei, Hong Kong-China, Korea, Shanghai-China, and Singapore were the top five highest-performing countries/economies; students in Kyrgyzstan were the lowest performing. The TIMSS 2003 study, however, revealed that gender differences in mathematics achievement were insignificant in many countries.

Gender disparities in achievement were most significant in reading performance. Females outperformed males in all 34 OECD countries/economies. Among OECD countries, Finland, New Zealand, Canada, Japan, and South Korea, respectively, ranked the highest in female achievement, and female students in Mexico and Chile ranked the lowest. Among OECD countries/economies, students in Chile, Netherlands, and the United States showed the least gender disparity in reading achievement. Without the consideration of gender, students in Shanghai-China, followed by South Korea and Finland, respectively, were among the top performers, and students in Kyrgyzstan were the lowest performing. Across OECD countries, on average, girls tended to attain more than half a proficiency level (one year of schooling) compared to boys.

In 2011 the Progress in International Reading Literacy Study (PIRLS)—a five-year-cycle study—conducted its third survey of fourth-graders from 43 countries and their performance in reading compared to that of the United States. In relation to gender and achievement, results revealed a significant difference in the combined reading literacy scale (inclusive of the processes of comprehension, purposes for reading, and reading literacy behavior and attitudes). The average score for girls was higher than the average score for boys throughout all countries, with the exception of Luxembourg and Spain, whereas fourth-grade girls in Kuwait showed the largest difference, ranking this country the highest scorer in female achievement in reading literacy. The PIRLS 2006 study also revealed that, on average, girls read more than boys.

Occupational Aspirations and Leadership

In 2000 a PISA study revealed gender differences with regard to professional occupations and career aspirations of 15-year-old students. While males anticipated careers in mathematics, physics, engineering, and other fields related to machinery, more female students expected professions in health and education. In 2006 UNICEF reported the narrowing gender gap in the labor force, worldwide. With respect to leadership and representation in public office, there has been a higher number of female representatives in public office. For example, in 2006, Chile and Jamaica elected their first female heads of government; the Republic of Korea appointed its first female prime minister; 14 women held top governing positions worldwide.

Conversely, in the same year, the World Values Survey revealed that over 80 percent of men in seven North African and Middle Eastern countries believed that they were more entitled to employment than females, especially when jobs were scarce. A similar proportion of males believed that females were not capable of attaining leadership roles and that males were better political leaders. Female views were equally, if not more discriminatory toward their own gender. A large proportion of female respondents either agreed or strongly agreed that males made more proficient political leaders. This outlook was more prevalent throughout Bangladesh,

China, Iran, and Uganda. In the United States, one out of every five women harbored the same belief that males were better leaders and more entitled to employment.

In 2007 UNICEF reported that a Gallup Poll conducted in five Latin American nations (Argentina, Brazil, Colombia, El Salvador, and Mexico) conveyed further striking statistics on social attitudes relating to gender and job opportunities. The poll revealed that 50 percent of the respondents (women and men) in each of the five nations believed that their society favored males over females; only 20 percent of respondents in Brazil considered that males and females were treated equally; and less than 50 percent of respondents in Argentina and Brazil believed that men and women had the same job opportunities.

Further Challenges

Other forms of gender discrimination contribute to limited access to education among girls, including the oppression of girls and women through the preference for sons over daughters at birth, restriction of women's social mobility and political inclusion, gender-based violence, and poverty. UNICEF affirms that females make up a majority of the world's population living in poverty and that, along with children, females account for 80 percent of civilian casualties due to war and political conflict worldwide (2007). Studies also show that natural disasters and calamities have indelible consequences on educational access. While all children's education is generally affected, when compared to boys, girls generally are ultimately more likely to be out of school because of calamities. UNICEF has assisted in the construction of 41 schools that have helped more than 8,000 children and provided resources to nearly 150 preschools and primary and secondary schools that have benefited over 28,000 children.

Additional studies show further discrepancies in achievement. For example, children whose mothers are not educated are more than twice as likely to be out of school as children whose mothers have acquired some education. UNICEF estimates that 75 percent of the children in developing countries not attending primary school have uneducated mothers (2006). Research reveals that educated women are more likely to send their children to school, while illiteracy among mothers contributes to low rates of school enrollment, attendance, and academic achievement among their daughters.

The Realities of Gender and Education

Although one of the UN's Millennium Development Goals is to eliminate gender disparity in all levels of education by 2015, girls still encounter barriers to accessing primary and secondary education. For example, in 2008, the primary enrollment ratio for girls and boys was 96:100. Regions such as Oceania, western Asia, and sub-Saharan Africa still face challenges in regard to gender parity in primary education. In regard to secondary education, gender differences in enrollment are very prevalent in sub-Saharan Africa, southern Asia, and western Asia; however, in areas such as Latin America and eastern Asia, girls' enrollment in secondary school is greater compared to boys'. Poverty remains a critical factor in school enrollment; for example, primary school–age girls who live in the poorest 60 percent of households are three times more likely not to be in school compared to girls from the wealthiest households. In regard to secondary school, girls in the poorest households are almost twice as likely not to be in school compared to girls from the wealthiest households.

Although developing regions are generally on the path toward gender parity in school enrollment, in reality young girls around the world do not have the same opportunities as boys to attend school, be properly educated, and express their full potential. UNICEF defines the monitoring of learning and achievement as the assessment of knowledge, skills, and values acquired by students; if children cannot attend school or learn to read and write, their learning, educational achievement, and social mobility are hindered. Despite efforts at the local, national, and international levels, women and girls continue to face adversity, and educational access remains a struggle.

Intergovernmental organizations (IGOs) have created both local and global educational initiatives to address gender disparities in education and other domains of society. Yet, despite changing patterns of gender parity, improvement in academic achievement, and increased representation in professional fields

and civil leadership, discrimination against women and female underachievement remain prevalent throughout the global society. In spite of records touting gender equity, an overwhelming proportion of women around the world remain shackled by social expectations, gender roles, and male privilege.

Rose Wong and Hsiu-Zu Ho

REFERENCES

Institute of Education Sciences, National Center for Education Statistics. The Reading Literacy of U.S. Fourth Grade Students in an International Context: Results from the 2001 and 2006 Progress in International Reading Literacy Study (PIRLS). www.nces.ed.gov.

International Association for the Evaluation of Educational Achievement. Trends in International Mathematics and Science Study (TIMSS). 2011. www.iea.nl/timss2003.html.

Organization for Economic Cooperation and Development. Global Education Digest 2010: Comparing Education Statistics Across the World. www.uis.unesco.org.

———. PISA 2006: Science Competencies for Tomorrow's World: Executive Summary. www.oecd.org.

———. PISA 2009 Results: What Students Know and Can Do—Student Performance in Reading, Mathematics and Science (volume 1). www.oecd.org.

United Nations. Commission on the Status of Women: Report on the Fifty-First Session, 26 February–9 March 2007. www.un.org.

———. The Milennium Development Goals Indicators 2011. http://mdgs.un.org/unsd/mdg/SeriesDetail.aspx?srid=611

———. The Millennium Development Goals Report. 2010. www.un.org.

United Nations Children's Fund. The State of the World's Children 2007. www.unicef.org.

———. Tsunami Report, 5 Year Anniversary, December 2009. www.unicef.org.

———. UNICEF'S Emergency Response to the 2004 Tsunami. www.unicef.org/maldives.

United Nations Girls' Education Initiative. Djibouti Newsline. Girls in Rural Villages Missing Out on Education. www.ungei.org.

———. The GAP Report: Gender Achievements and Prospects in Education. www.ungei.org.

———. The GAP Report: Gender Achievements and Prospects in Education: Reporter's Notebook. www.ungei.org.

———. The GAP Report: Gender Achievements and Prospects in Education: 25 by 2005 Country Data. www.ungei.org.

———. Girls Too! Education for All. www.ungei.org.

USAID from the American People. Djibouti. www.usaid.gov.

EDUCATIONAL ACCESS AND OPPORTUNITIES

In the last several decades, equal educational access and opportunities for girls and boys have become an important issue in children's rights agendas. Having access to education increases life chances and has lifelong economic and social benefits for children and their families. Barriers, such as poverty, health, and social conflict, are also crucial components that undermine efforts toward access and opportunities.

As of 2007 over 100 million children worldwide were not enrolled in primary or secondary education programs. Most of these children lived in some of the poorest regions in the world where family incomes were often less than US$1 per day. In 2004 approximately three-quarters of the children not enrolled in school lived in sub-Saharan Africa (50 percent) and southern and western Asia (19 percent). Of children who were enrolled in school, approximately 75 percent did not reach the fifth grade. Additionally, males have an overall higher rate of primary school enrollment and completion than girls, with the exception of Latin America and the Caribbean. On average, for every two boys who are not in school, there are three girls not enrolled in school. The numbers of out-of-school girls are higher than average for the Arab states, the Middle East, and southern and western Asia. Sub-Saharan Africa has the highest number of girls, over 20 million, who are out of school.

Although there are still disparities between the enrollment rates of girls and boys in schools, progress has been made in closing the gender gap. Based on 2006 data available from 176 countries, 59 countries showed gender parity at the primary and secondary education levels—an increase of 20 countries from 1999. However, improvements vary by region. More than half of the countries in sub-Saharan Africa, the Arab states, and southern and western Asia have not achieved gender parity. Worldwide, the status of girls' educational access and enrollment has improved, especially at the primary school level. For example, many countries in Asia show an overall increase in access to education. In India enrollment rates for girls increased from 84 percent to 96 percent between 1998 and 2002. In Vietnam girls and boys achieved comparable enrollment rates in 2006.

Despite a steady decrease in the number of out-of-school children between 1999 and 2004, over 150 million children in developing nations are still not able to complete five years of basic education. Approximately 40 percent of children living in the least developed countries end up dropping out of primary school, while only 14 percent of girls and 25 percent of boys move on to secondary school. These statistics are of great concern. The world community has identified the relationship between education and quality of life and has responded by promoting global education goals. Leaders around the world have come to recognize education as a universal human right.

In 1948 the United Nations (UN) adopted General Assembly Resolution 217A(III), thereby sanctioning the International Bill of Human Rights. This document codifies inalienable rights for all men, women, and children in all parts of the world. These include the human right to an adequate standard of living, the right to equality between men and women, the right to work and receive adequate wages, and the right to participate fully, and with dignity, in one's social, economic, and political environment. The International Bill of Human Rights also entitles every man, woman, and child to a free and compulsory primary education that is then to be followed by accessible forms of secondary and higher education. These rights include freedom from discrimination at all levels of education and access to information pertaining to health, nutrition, reproduction, and family planning.

In 1945, prior to drafting the International Bill of Human Rights, the UN created the United Nations Educational, Scientific and Cultural Organization (UNESCO). After decades of multinational research, implementation, and evaluation, the benefits of education have become clear: education empowers individuals by allowing them to exercise their civil, political, economic, social, cultural, and individual rights. UNESCO, along with national governments and other development partners, is working toward universal free primary education for all by 2015.

However, the obstacles that compromise the growth and development of education are complex and demanding. In 2007 one out of three children worldwide had never been inside a classroom. Communities with high rates of illiteracy, political instability, human rights violations, and extreme poverty are often unable to exercise their universal educational rights. In particular, UNESCO and other international and intergovernmental organizations have recognized an inextricable dependency between human rights violations, acute poverty, and access to education. These problems must be solved simultaneously.

Although poverty can be defined in many ways, most international agencies rely on an absolute poverty line that has been determined by the World Bank. As of 2007 poverty was defined as having an income of US$2 or less a day. Using this definition, one half of the global population is living in poverty. Of these nearly 3 billion people, one-third cannot read or write their names. Seventy percent of the world's poor are women. Furthermore, according to UNICEF, in 2005 some 30,000 children died every day because of poverty.

Of the countries that struggle the most with access to free primary education, many also have the lowest gross domestic product per capita and the largest debt repayments. Although progress has been made in many parts of the world, various countries in sub-Saharan Africa, Southeast Asia, and the Arab states are still struggling to provide free primary education. In these areas, gender parity has also been difficult to achieve. Girls are more likely than boys not to be in school, particularly in areas with social norms and values that limit gender equity and rely on patriarchal frameworks. Girls are often kept at home to take care of family members and perform domestic duties. When financial means are limited, gender discrimination usually takes the form of male preference. In these environments, if money is needed for school supplies and transportation, boys are more likely than girls to receive formal schooling.

Sociocultural norms and attitudes can significantly influence gender-based educational decisions. Prescribed gender roles for girls often exclude them from attending school. Girls in Afghanistan, for example, are systematically prohibited from going to school due to political and religious practices. Female roles typically include domestic and caregiver responsibilities, and expectations for adhering to these cultural directives are high. There is little support for girls who break gender norms; in some cases, girls may be penalized for pursuing educational opportunities. Those who are able to attend school often drop out due to the needs of the household and family. For example, the need to stay home and take care of one's

family is one of the top causes of school dropout among girls in Latin America.

Preferential treatment and higher allocation of resources for boys provide them more opportunities in education and greater resources to ultimately break out of the poverty cycle. Girls, on the other hand, often depend on marriage as a way to secure stability; many girls marry at a very young age. For example, Ethiopian girls as young as seven or eight years old enter into marriages. In India, it is customary for girls to marry in their early teens. Poor families in rural Albania often encourage early marriages for girls in order to ease the family's short-term economic problems. The result of early marriage impedes in girls' educational advancement. Once they are married, girls drop out and rarely return to school.

Health issues pose another threat to gender equality in school enrollment, according to UNESCO. From 2007 estimates, of the 33 million people living with HIV/AIDS, 2 million were children under the age of 15. HIV/AIDS is a prevalent reason for school dropout in many regions of Africa and Asia. Girls and boys are forced to leave school because of infection, to care for sick family members, and to work to support the family. Globally, the 2002 rate of HIV/AIDS infection for women was comparable to or higher than the rate of infection for men. In many parts of southern Africa and the Caribbean, girls are four to seven times more likely than boys to be infected with HIV/AIDS. According to Human Rights Watch (2003), the higher rate of infection in girls is associated with high rates of sexual exploitation and abuse. Many of the abuse cases are related to teachers and schools. A survey by Jewkes and colleagues conducted in South Africa indicated that schoolteachers were the perpetrators in as many as 33 percent of childhood rape cases, thus making schools unsafe for girls. Pregnancy is also a common reason that prevents girls from continuing their schooling. This is particularly relevant for girls in Malawi and Chile. The shame and stigma attached to premarital pregnancy is also prevalent, particularly in developing nations. There is little information on the impact of disability and gender on children's educational experiences. UNESCO's global estimate of the number of children who have disabilities is 150 million, with nearly 80 percent from developing countries. In general, school enrollment is relatively higher for disabled boys than girls. What little data is available reveals that girls' education is negatively impacted by disability in terms of exclusion and insufficient resources. Many disabled girls are hidden in the home and kept out of school. In India, for example, girls often drop out of school due to the negative social stigma attached to disabilities. In addition, their opportunities are further limited because of social marginalization. Worldwide, gender biases in nutrition and health care tend to favor boys and thus contribute to increased risks and inadequate care for girls. Disability often forces children and their families further into poverty, thus slowing educational advancement.

Political conflict and war also serve as barriers to educational access and opportunities. The destruction of schools and loss of teachers during conflict and war pose major problems in the advancement of education. The disruption that conflict and war create in the lives of children extends beyond education. In countries where conflict is a consistent reality of daily life, children cannot go to school because they are displaced, orphaned, disabled, and/or psychologically traumatized. Half of the world's out-of-school population lives in countries that are affected by conflict and war. According to the United Nations, an estimated 300,000 children, some as young as seven years old, have been recruited, coerced, or forced to become child soldiers and actively engage in fighting wars. The problem is most critical in Africa, which has the highest number of children serving as soldiers. The military use of children as combatants affects boys in particular; enforced military activities often result in imprisonment or execution. In addition to performing military and domestic duties, girls are sexually exploited and at times treated as sexual slaves.

Clearly, attaining universal primary education is a complex goal. All children are affected by poverty, illness, disabilities, deep-rooted gender roles, and violent conflicts. Furthermore, since the effects of these issues are often gender-biased, more support is needed to ensure that opportunities for girls in education reach parity with those afforded to boys. It has become apparent that gender equity is an essential component for universal education worldwide.

UNESCO's reports on monitoring its Education for All program measure progress in education, outlined existing challenges in schools, and emphasized the need for worldwide participation and steadfast universal education goals. From 1999 to 2005, primary school enrollment across the globe rose from 647 million to 688 million. Compulsory education now exists for 95 percent of the 203 countries and territories studied. Substantial progress toward universal enrollment and gender parity in countries such as India and Mozambique has proven that partnerships between national governments and international donors can be effective. Furthermore, resources are expanding. Notably, international financial aid for basic education doubled between 2000 and 2004.

Despite global efforts to abolish primary school tuition fees, the cost of schooling is still prohibitive for millions of children and their families. Many developing countries are currently facing textbook shortages, inadequate school facilities, and insufficient amounts of instructional time. International, national, and local assessments are reporting substandard learning outcomes in many developing countries. Rapid urbanization and the violent spread of HIV/AIDS have created fundamental economic challenges. Twenty percent of men and 25 percent of women are still illiterate, and adult literacy rates have continued to decline.

Given these factors, UNESCO has chosen to foster educational policies that focus on inclusion, literacy, quality, capacity development, and finance. Long-term international, national, and local commitments are needed to increase participation, equity, and quality in education, particularly in the most poverty-stricken and marginalized communities. It is estimated that US$11 billion is needed annually for low-income countries to address universal primary education, educational programs, and literacy. Increasing and maintaining consistency in international aid and employing 18 million new teachers worldwide by 2015 have now become essential goals.

UNESCO has also continued to promote gender equity and gender equality in education. In 2005 gender parity at both the primary and secondary levels occurred in only 59 out of 181 participating countries worldwide. Of the remaining 122 countries, 63 percent have achieved gender parity at the primary level, 37 percent at the secondary level, and 3 percent at the tertiary level. These gender disparities are more prevalent among the poorest families and for those who live in poverty-stricken areas. Once educational access has been achieved, girls tend to stay in school longer and outperform boys, particularly at the secondary level. However, severe gender biases still affect girls in places such as Afghanistan, Chad, and Yemen. At the tertiary level, for the first time, more women than men are entering higher education institutions in many parts of the world. However, women are still underrepresented in traditionally "male fields" such as engineering, natural sciences, mathematics, and agriculture.

Achieving equity in education will require continued efforts to address gender disparities in all parts of the world. Local, national, and international leaders must continue to identify and resolve gender-biased practices that have traditionally compromised gender equity. Further research is needed to raise awareness of issues that affect girls and boys in education, particularly in the areas of human rights violations and extreme poverty. In order to make timely progress toward the 2015 deadline for the UN's Millennium Development Goals, stable financial resources will be needed to generate and sustain long-term advancements in education.

Julie Thuy Nguyen and Cheri Scripter

REFERENCES

Human Rights Watch. Human Rights Watch World Report 2003 (Events of 2002). www.hrw.org/wr2k3/.

Jewkes, Rachel, Jonathan Levin, and Loveday Penn-Kekana. "Risk Factors for Domestic Violence: Findings from a South African Cross-Study." *Social Science and Medicine* 55:9 (2002): 1603–1617.

Quisumbing, Agnes R., Jonna P. Estudillo, and Keijiro Otsuka. "Land and Schooling: Transferring Wealth Across Generations." IFPRI Food Policy Statement 41, February 2004. www.ifpri.org.

UNESCO. The Challenge of Achieving Gender Parity in Basic Education: A Statistical Review, 1990–1998. http://unesdoc.unesco.org.

———. Education for All: Global Monitoring Report. http://unesdoc.unesco.org.

———. Education of Girls and Women. Bureau of Public Information, Information Sheet. 2006. www.unesco.org.

———. "Gender Equality in Education." www.unesco.org.

United Nations. International Bill of Human Rights. Paris: United Nations, 1948.

———. Report of the United Nations High Commissioner for Human Rights on the Mid-Term Global Evaluation of the Progress Made Towards the Achievement of the Objectives of the United Nations Decade for Human Rights Education (1995–2004). www.hurights.or.jp/pub/hreas/4/16un_decade.pdf.

———. World Youth Report 2007. Young People's Transition to Adulthood: Progress and Challenges. www.un.org.

United Nations Children's Fund. The State of the World's Children. 2011. www.unicef.org.

World Bank Group. GenderStats. www.worldbank.org.

GENDERED MIND

The gendered mind is based on theories related to gender differences of the brain, cognition, intellectual styles, and ways of knowing. Researchers have focus primarily on psychological differences between men and women. Despite the existence of substantial individual variation between males and females, longitudinal research is used to adequately address developmental changes throughout the lifespan.

The Brain

Until the twenty-first century, scientists understood little about the structural differences between the male and female brain. They observed that females had smaller brains, which also correspondingly weighed less, than male brains. It was also found that there were differences in the hypothalamus and pituitary. At that time, researchers of male and female brain differences focused on differences in hormonal functions, the hypothalamus, and brain size and weight. Unfortunately, this information was sometimes used to explain and justify male superiority over girls and women.

Due to recent technological innovations, our understanding of the brain has increased substantially. Today, scientists are making specific comparisons that allow for more accurate distinctions. For instance, the brain region or structure under examination is compared to the overall volume of the individual brain itself, thus accounting for individual ratios. With the assistance of positron-emission topography (PET) scans, magnetic resonance imaging (MRI), and functional MRI (fMRI), we now know that the male and female brains differ anatomically, chemically, and functionally. There are gender differences in several regions that affect memory, vision, hearing, navigation, language, and emotion.

Anatomical differences, which are present from birth, are thought to be the result of the influence of sex hormones on the developing fetal brain. For instance, females, when compared to males, have, on average, twice as many neurons present in the two layers of the temporal lobe, which is associated with language processing and understanding. Scientists have hypothesized that this brain difference may be one of the underlying reasons why girls outperform boys on language-based measures, such as word fluency tests and Stanford Achievement Tests (SAT-9) scores in reading, language, and spelling.

Brain lateralization is another area of gender differences. Vertebrates have lateralized brains: the two halves are distinct from each other and generally are involved in functions corresponding to a specific side of the brain. This has resulted in a more efficient use of cognitive functions. However, there are differences found in lateralization as a function of gender. For instance, language capabilities were thought to be concentrated in the left hemisphere. The use of MRIs has indicated that females can use both sides of the brain when engaged in language-based cognitive tasks, whereas males typically do not. This argues for a female brain with more dispersed language centers than was previously thought. While these brain differences are measurable, more research needs to be done to determine if and how these various differences impact males and females throughout the human lifespan.

Cognition

The study of cognitive differences between males and females has been pursued for decades. In reviewing this research, several issues have become apparent. As in other genres, positive results are peer reviewed and published, while studies that show no differences, or null results, are published less often. Studies of gender differences in cognition have been limited to findings that are often based on samples of convenience, such as undergraduate students. In addition, there are methodological issues in examining cognitive developmental differences as the studies may be correlational, normative, or meta-analytic. Comprehensive longitudinal studies are needed to more fully examine gender differences in cognitive development.

Over time, cognition has been defined in a variety of ways and from discipline to discipline. In *A Dictionary of Psychology* (1952), James Drever defined cognition as "a general term covering all the various modes of knowing—perceiving, imagining, conceiving, judging, and reasoning." More recently, cognition has been understood as receiving, processing, storing, and retrieving information. This "mind as a computer" metaphor is also known as the information-processing model.

Most psychometric tests involving overall general intelligence show few gender differences, and the effect sizes that have been found are small. However, when analyzing specific subareas, differences do emerge. Initially it was thought that gender differences were concentrated in three general cognitive areas: visual-spatial, mathematical, and verbal. Further studies that have refined this thinking have shown that it is within specific subtypes of these areas that gender differences emerge.

In the visual-spatial arena, the tasks that show the most dramatic differences are in mental rotation, spatial perception, and spatial visualization tasks, all of which favor males. The effect sizes range from small to large depending on the country under study, with the United States showing some of the greatest gender differences and China indicating some of the least. Mental rotation is tested by providing a series of figures (two- or three-dimensional) with the goal of matching the first figure with the correct rotated version. Spatial perception is measured by orientation tasks, such as matching one or more given lines to an array. Spatial visualization is examined by asking the subject to identify embedded figures within a larger design or by imagining how an unfolded shape would look when folded.

In examining mathematical skills in males and females, the results have varied depending on age, subject pool, and methods utilized. For instance, standardized tests of the quantitative Scholastic Aptitude Test (SAT) and Graduate Record Examination (GRE) have revealed gender differences, favoring males, with small to medium effect sizes. Negligible or small differences have been found in computational skills and in the comprehension of mathematical concepts, particularly in several Asian countries and Turkey.

Gender differences in verbal proficiency generally favor girls when examining measures of speech or verbal production and verbal fluency. However, negligible differences have been found in reading comprehension, vocabulary, and the verbal subtest of the SAT.

Overall, while there are some differences in cognition between males and females, it should be noted that there is substantial individual variation within the two groups. Further study is needed, particularly in refining exactly which cognitive subtypes continue to show gender differences during various stages of development and schooling.

Intellectual Styles

It should be noted that several terms (such as cognitive styles, thinking styles, and learning approaches) have been used to discuss stylistic differences in learning, cognition, and intellect; henceforward the term "intellectual styles" will be used. There is evidence that distinct intellectual styles can be measured and do influence performance and behaviors, including learning, teaching, social behaviors, cognitive and psychosocial development, and well-being. While there may be these constructs, the various intellectual styles are largely subject to socialization and other environmental factors.

Threefold Model of Intellectual Styles

Essentially the threefold model of intellectual styles proposed by Li-fang Zhang and Robert Sternberg in *The Nature of Intellectual Styles* (2006) is a compilation of several prominent theories and addresses three commonalities: style malleability, style value, and style overlap. This model holds that styles are considered states, rather than traits, and are relatively less stable. These states are subject to change and socialization, particularly when motivation is a factor. In examining aspects of the three styles (Types I, II, and III) such as autonomy or thinking mode, it appears that some are valued more than others and that this can vary by culture, gender, and age of the student. In addition, the various components of the three intellectual styles may involve similar aspects of one or more of the other categories, such as learning approach. This overlap does not contradict the uniqueness of each intellectual style.

One of the intellectual styles that was used to develop this model was that of field dependence/independence measured by the group embedded figures test. The task is to find and identify the eight simple figures within each of the 25 complex figures. The higher the score, the more field independent the test-taker. Historically, boys in the United States tend to score higher than girls on this test. However, results are mixed or inconsistent for boys and girls in other countries, specifically in Turkey and China. It has been thought that field independence is a socialized construct as studies aimed at increasing scores have yielded positive results.

Multiple Intelligences

In his book *Multiple Intelligences* (2006), Howard Gardner utilized specific criteria to generate his separate intelligence categories, particularly biopsychological information-processing capacity. The intelligences are linguistic, logical mathematical, musical, spatial, bodily kinesthetic, interpersonal, intrapersonal, and naturalist. Gardner believes that these intelligences are present in each human being and that some are preferred or better developed than others. For instance, studies have shown that boys rely more heavily on spatial intelligence than girls. There has been some evidence that this is also the case with logical mathematical reasoning. However, girls tend to score higher on linguistic measures. These results are important for teachers, administrators, and test developers, as most formal assessments tend to center around linguistics and logical mathematical constructs.

This perspective has been embraced within the field of education, both nationally and internationally; however, it is usually applied only to student learning. Further research is needed to examine the interplay of the intelligence styles of the teacher and the students with pedagogy and the teaching curriculum.

If students have a better understanding of the role of multiple intelligences in the development of their learning/intellectual styles, they may be able to adapt their learning environment and communicate more effectively with their teachers. In turn, teachers can diversify their instructional practice and assessments so as to offer multiple pathways to access and measure the content. It would also benefit teachers to become more aware of their own styles and ways of thinking about student performance in order to become more effective for students with diverse learning styles.

Ways of Knowing

Historically, researchers have been increasingly interested in different epistemologies, or ways of knowing, of women and men. Two perspectives have been identified: separate and connected ways of knowing. It has been found that both types of knowing are utilized and should not be considered opposites or dichotomies. Instead, these constructs are much like masculinity and femininity, where both can be present, but to a lesser or greater degree.

Studies utilizing the Knowing Styles Inventory (KSI) have indicated that separate and connected ways of knowing are distinct components. Separate knowing occurs when one distances, or separates, oneself from the ideas of others and prefers to think with detachment. Connected knowing is more involved: the thinker tries to understand the ideas of others by taking their perspective and then explores the idea in a larger context. A common example is hermeneutical debate, whereby an individual is engaged in argumentation with other colleagues for the purpose of presenting multiple positions on a topic and suggestion possible alternatives. This is particularly common when groups are engaged in various forms of analytical thinking.

In general, males tend to engage in more separate knowing, whereas females usually engage in more connected ways of knowing. In fact, women have reported higher levels of discomfort in using separate knowing, as do men when using connected knowing.

It has also been found that connected knowing is associated with social desirability, perspective-taking, empathetic concern, and the femininity factor of the Bem Sex Role Inventory (BSRI). Separate knowing is associated with the masculinity factor of the BSRI and negatively correlated with social desirability.

It should be noted that ways of knowing are not associated with the magnitude of learning, but do affect one's attitude toward knowledge and scholarship because the two ways of knowing use different methods for examining concepts and ideas. Different ways of knowing have implications for the educational arena as traditional secondary schools and universities tend to encourage separate ways of thinking about concepts and ideas, which can be a disadvantage for girls and women. Further research is needed to determine if there are separate ways of knowing that are subject-specific, particularly in science and math, or culture-specific.

While gender gaps have been closing in several cognitive areas, differences do remain. It may be that educational environments need to be tailored differently for girls and boys at various ages, taking into account brain-based research. In addition, a greater understanding of intellectual styles and ways of knowing may benefit not only students, but also parents, educators, and policy makers.

Angela Blaver

REFERENCES

Baxter Magolda, Marcia B. *Knowing and Reasoning in College: Gender-Related Patterns in Students' Intellectual Development.* San Francisco: Jossey-Bass, 1992.

Belenky, Mary F., Blythe M. Clinchy, Nancy R. Goldberger, and Jill M. Tarule. *Women's Ways of Knowing: The Development of Self, Voice, and Mind.* New York: Basic Books, 1986.

Bem, Sandra L. "Theory and Measurement of Androgyny: A Reply to the Pedhazur-Tetenbaum and Locksley-Colten Critiques." *Journal of Personality and Social Psychology* 37 (1979): 1047–1054.

Drever, James. *A Dictionary of Psychology* (rev. H. Wallerstein, 1964). Harmondsworth, UK: Penguin Books, 1952.

Gardner, Howard. *Multiple Intelligences: New Horizons in Theory and Practice.* New York: Basic Books, 2006.

Hines, Melissa. *Brain Gender.* New York: Oxford University Press, 2004.

Knight, Kim H., Morton H. Elfenbein, and Julie A. Messina. "A Preliminary Scale to Measure Connected and Separate Knowing: The Knowing Styles Inventory." *Sex Roles* 33 (1995): 499–513.

Maccoby, Eleanor E., and Carol N. Jacklin. *The Psychology of Sex Differences.* Stanford, CA: Stanford University Press, 1974.

Richardson, John T.E. "Introduction to the Study of Gender Differences in Cognition." In *Gender Differences in Human Cognition,* ed. Paula J. Caplan, Mary Crawford, Janet Shibley Hyde, and John T.E. Richardson, 3–29. New York: Oxford University Press, 1997.

Zhang, Li-fang, and Robert J. Sternberg. *The Nature of Intellectual Styles.* Mahwah, NJ: Lawrence Erlbaum, 2006.

FORMAL EDUCATION

CURRICULUM

Curriculum is a body of knowledge that one deems important for another person or group of people to learn, usually for the betterment of society. It is often considered the program of study in which content is defined, arranged, and emphasized. It is important to note that the definition of "curriculum" is not singular. For many teachers and school personnel, curriculum is taken putatively simply as a set of subjects that students must learn in order to advance to subsequent grade levels. The word "curriculum" is derived from Latin, in which language it referred to the act of running (as in "courier") or the literal course in a chariot race. The term "curriculum" has taken on a figurative meaning when considering a course of study.

By tradition, the foundations of curriculum design were considered a set of educational activities that were organized and evaluated in a parallel manner. Additional elements of curriculum development included students' past and present interests, developmental levels, social outcomes, uses of technology, integration of subject matter, and national and local standards. Curriculum writers emphasized the common features in each of the subject areas. In science, for example, they sought after commonalities, such as the reliance on evidence, investigation, and arrangement of factual knowledge into concepts, theories, principles, and laws. In order to develop a curriculum, the teacher or curriculum specialist needs to identify in advance what is important and how both students and teachers are to go about studying this important content. Only then can the curriculum be discussed and carried out within a particular community. Given this emphasis on community, it should

be evident that what one develops as a curriculum has traditionally been conducted in schools. For our purposes, to this day, curriculum is still developed for schooling students. Teachers use various instructive techniques, often in the form of lessons, to carry out the curriculum. For a more contemporary account of curriculum development, it is also necessary to consider various forms of knowledge dissemination in addition to classroom or school teaching—for example, the Internet or taped courses developed by experts.

Definitions of Curriculum Among Curriculum Theorists

From a Western perspective, we can see that the notion of curriculum, namely, a plan set out to educate the youth of a political state or region, can be found in the work of Aristotle in his *Nicomachean Ethics*. In this text Aristotle writes on the importance of educational curriculum as prescribed by the study of politics. Aristotle believes that the welfare of the polis (in general terms, the city-state) is more important and essential than the welfare of the individual. This notion dictates the hierarchy of the study of politics above every other area of study. Aristotle elaborates on the model of what an exceptional curriculum should be through his classification of knowledge into three categories: theory, praxis, and product. More recent curriculum theorists have used the Aristotelian model as well. In the book *Local Education* (2000), Mark Smith draws from the Aristotelian notion of knowledge by investigating curriculum as a transmission of knowledge; curriculum used as a way to achieve a product for students; curriculum as an ever-changing process; and curriculum for praxis—that is, the use of what we know about something, and applying what we know to the real world. In doing so, Smith categorizes different curriculum thinkers according to their present-day emphases. For example, Smith places Ralph Tyler and Franklin Bobbitt, the well-known curriculum specialists of the early and middle twentieth century, in the category of "scientific curriculum makers" due to their emphasis on a curriculum product that can serve as a practical basis for a society's needs. He justifies this categorization by the influence of psychological behaviorism and social efficiency on Tyler and Bobbitt—in particular, the growing trend of learning theory. It is important to note that Tyler and Bobbitt both emphasize the shaping of schools and their curricula to focus on a set of objectives to meet the needs of society.

In *An Introduction to Curriculum Research and Development* (1975), Lawrence Stenhouse argues that the product metaphor for curriculum, in the tradition of Tyler or Bobbitt, alienates students because content is taught and learned as an end and not as a process or for practical purposes. Unlike Tyler and Bobbitt, Charles Taylor has focused less on modeling curriculum on societal needs and, instead, more on the importance of Western civilization and its values as a necessary element of what students need to know at present as part of a so-called liberal education. G. Stanley Hall finds curriculum important not as a behaviorist model or for its focus on tradition and the preservation of Western values, but for its accommodation to the nature and needs of children based on what is important for them at any given stage of their lives. Accordingly, Hall is a developmentalist in terms of his views of curriculum and curriculum theory. Jean Piaget, too, is important in the arena of developmentalism as he clearly opposes the views of his behaviorist contemporaries. In fact, much of the science curriculum in schools around the world today is based on Piaget's model, particularly the developmental appropriateness of the task at hand. This model emphasizes the developmental pattern of discovery (early childhood and childhood), inquiry (childhood), and experimentation (late childhood and adolescence).

Unlike the previously mentioned theorists, according to Smith, Lester Frank Ward places his attention on curriculum as praxis, not so much in promoting societal efficiency (as behaviorists contend), but on furthering schools as settings for social equality and justice. In this model, curriculum should emphasize the inequalities of race, gender, sexual orientation, and any other forms of bias in society. It aims to address the problems of abuse of power and furthers the role of an essential democracy in helping to resolve societal problems. Other theorists who may fall into this category include John Dewey, Paulo Freire, Ivan Illich, William Pinar, Madeline Grumet, Janet Miller, William Ayers, Peter McClaren, and Kevin Kumashiro.

One of the many provocative arguments that Bill Pinar makes in his book *What Is Curriculum Theory?* (2003) is that for the last 60 (or more) years, students have essentially been held hostage to a curriculum that has emphasized manhood, strength, and masculinity—one that can be traced to the events leading to the Cold War. This Cold War curriculum called attention to what the United States and its NATO allies viewed as an alarming phenomenon—the rapid development of scientific advancements in the Soviet Union and its allies. This curriculum was shaped by a powerful interest on the part of governments to engage students in high levels of scientific knowledge at the expense of an emphasis on equal rights among subordinated populations. The Soviet launching of *Sputnik* in 1957 prompted the United States government to push mathematics and science content in directions that had little if any meaning in the real world. For example, the "new math" movement, which lasted from the late 1950s to the early 1980s, highlighted mathematics content—for example, set theory, modular arithmetic, and arithmetic in bases other than 10—that was void of everyday concerns or even applications in other college or university disciplines.

A Multicultural Curriculum

It is important to consider the debate within the last few decades about reforming the curriculum so that it embraces a multicultural emphasis. Multiculturalism is an offshoot of a number of factors. In the United States, two important factors are an ever-increasing immigrant population from both developing and developed nations (as is also true in many European countries and Canada) and the aftermath of the civil rights movement, which, over time, generated a great deal of debate about the kind of content schools are to provide for the nation's students. By the 1980s, many influential individuals, both liberal and conservative, from both inside and outside the academy, had begun to argue that multicultural components of curricula were creating divisiveness and to call for something of a revival of traditional Western values in the curriculum. These individuals, the so-called traditionalists, included Allan Bloom—whose text *The Closing of the American Mind* (1987) served as a driving force and inspiration for like-minded writers—Dinesh D'Souza, E.D. Hirsch Jr., William J. Bennett, Nathan Glazer, Lynn Cheney, and Arthur M. Schlesinger Jr. Subsequent writers included Harold Bloom, Thomas Sowell, and Richard Bernstein. The multiculturalists, the opponents to the traditionalists, include James A. Banks, Christine Sleeter, Vanessa J. Lawrence, and Michael R. Hillis, educational theorists who emphasize the need for a change in the so-called traditional curriculum.

According to the multiculturalists, there are at least two factors driving this need to modify traditional curricula by including multiculturalism as part of the foundation on which school teachers should base their instruction. One factor is the quickly expanding global economy. The other factor is the need to consider the often neglected contributions of persons of color—both from the United States and from other nations. It is quite difficult, however, to predict how the multicultural changes and inclusions in the so-called traditional curricula will influence future generations of students because it is still premature to identify any form of impact. Moreover, given a great deal of resistance from mostly conservative groups, changes that take place in school curriculum will be quite gradual, possibly taking several years or decades to occur.

Meaning of Curriculum in an International Context

We have seen how the meaning of "curriculum" is modified depending on which definition is used. If we take the notion of curriculum as meaning something important to learn in a particular culture, context, or society, it should be self-evident that what is important to learn in one context may vary in another. It seems clear that since all societies are grappling with social change and attempting to improve the lives of people in both developed and developing nations,

school curricula depend on the nature of problems and situations that affect different areas or regions. What may be an adequate curriculum for students of New York City may not serve in the best interests of students in Dhaka, Maputo, or even Helsinki or Sydney. Engaging in curriculum development for a particular region of the world depends on numerous factors. These include (but are not limited to) the following: geographic area, socioeconomic status disparities, gender, and ethnicity. For example, geographically, curriculum development will take on different structures from a practical standpoint in an area with a dry climate when compared to areas with moderate or wet climates. This might include methods of transporting water for students in dry areas or the accommodation of water storage in wetter regions. Similarly, students near coastal areas have somewhat different needs from those who live further inland, and students living near the Arctic Circle face certain environmental conditions that differ from students who live in tropical areas. These conditions may be due to differences in climate or even differences in daylight from one time of the year to another. These factors may directly affect classroom curriculum through an emphasis of environmental education and methods of resource management. From the perspective of social class, gender, or ethnicity, it is perhaps more important to examine a curriculum that emphasizes praxis for the purpose of social justice and equality of all students, regardless of income, gender, or ethnic background.

Daniel Ness and Chia-ling Lin

REFERENCES

Bloom, Allan. *The Closing of the American Mind*. New York: Simon & Schuster, 1987.

Dewey, John. *The Child and the Curriculum*. Chicago: University of Chicago Press, 1902.

Grundy, Shirley. *Curriculum: Product or Praxis?* East Sussex, UK: Falmer Press, 1987.

Pinar, William F. *What Is Curriculum Theory?* Mahwah, NJ: Lawrence Erlbaum, 2003.

Smith, Mark. *Local Education: Community, Conversation, Praxis*. Philadelphia: Open University Press, 2000.

Stenhouse, Lawrence. *An Introduction to Curriculum Research and Development*. London: Heineman, 1975.

Tyler, Ralph W. *Basic Principles of Curriculum and Instruction*. Chicago: University of Chicago Press, 1949.

INSTRUCTION

Instruction is a form of communication as a means for learning. In the context of education and schooling, instruction is a concept that allows for the facilitation of learning through various channels—most commonly, a teacher. The basis of instruction is to reach particular objectives that are often standardized by a set curriculum. In general, instruction is the conduit through which teachers or other communication modes provide or facilitate factual, conceptual, or procedural knowledge to their students. Traditionally, elements of instruction have included the selection of method and material, and classroom organization and management. Formulated instructional procedures allowed teachers to pursue their objectives while using various pedagogies. Instruction was considered effective when the intended learning outcomes were achieved as reflected through observable behavior. More than assessment or curriculum, instruction is most closely associated with cognitive levels of intellectual ability because level of cognition often predicts the most ideal form of instruction.

Traditional Instructional Forms and Theoretical Positions

In the traditional school setting, the so-called traditional form of instruction is clearly the human teacher, whose job it is to transmit new knowledge to students. One can stretch the number of "traditional forms" to also include books. If an expert in a particular field writes a book, this publication can ostensibly be a form of instruction, assuming that the manner in which it is written "teaches" or uses a method for progressive learning of the subject. At any rate, it is important to emphasize the traditional role of instruction as the communication of knowledge between a living teacher and a living student. Most educational theorists and researchers have based their work on seven primary theoretical positions on instruction. These positions are those of Benjamin Bloom, Robert Gagné, David Ausubel, John Anderson, M. David Merrill, Charles Reigeluth, and Jean Piaget.

Benjamin Bloom

Perhaps one of the most significant sources for instruction in schools is Benjamin Bloom and David Krathwohl's *Taxonomy of Educational Objectives* (1956). This important work has been referenced in most research studies relating to instruction, processes of student learning, and assessment. It is a classical study in most introduction-to-education courses, particularly on the topics of curriculum, instruction, and assessment. Although this source emphasizes learning objectives, the manner in which students acquire knowledge through these objectives is based on the kind of instruction that takes place. The taxonomy is based on three domains that influence the way that students learn: the affective, psychomotor, and cognitive domains.

Affective Domain

We often think of affect in terms of emotion. In terms of education, affect most closely identifies with differences in disposition and attitude toward a particular subject. According to Bloom, there are five levels under the affective domain. Beginning with the lowest level, the names of these levels are: receiving, responding, valuing, organizing, and characterizing.

Receiving. Receiving is the lowest level of the affective domain. Receiving takes place when the student sits passively while instruction from the teacher occurs. It is the lowest level of learning from an affective standpoint because all that is required is for the student to be attentive to what the teacher is saying. In essence, the teacher's instruction is a stimulus for the student's paying attention. The overwhelming majority of time spent on instruction does not go beyond the level of receiving.

Responding. Responding, the second level of the affective domain, requires a slightly more active role from the student. In this case, the teacher-student model is not one-directional, whereby the teacher bestows information, expecting the student to absorb it passively, as is the case in receiving. Instead, there is greater interaction, especially on the student's part. The student responds to the teacher's instruction in such a way that fosters two-way communication. It is important to note that most instruction that occurs rarely exceeds responding.

Valuing. Valuing, rarely achieved by all or most students in a classroom, occurs when the teacher is able to engage students in such a way that allows for the development of strong connections between students and a given topic or phenomenon under discussion. Students, then, find value in a topic within a particular subject or discipline. In other words, the student does not merely respond to the teacher with an answer to a question. Rather, the student demonstrates genuine interest in the given topic.

Organizing. When students engage in organizing, they essentially have a set of values related to various topics in a given subject that they construct and classify in a particular way. They organize what they value in various ways that encourage understanding of various systems of knowledge—to use Piaget's terminology, students accommodate what they value into schema (mental structures). Students identify connections, compare, and contrast what they learn as they organize knowledge.

Characterizing. The organization and internalization of values and ideas that the student possesses can now influence the individual's outlook on a particular topic or phenomenon. Therefore, when students engage in characterizing, they have built perspectives on subjects of knowledge that allow them to communicate this knowledge freely and perhaps cogently.

Psychomotor Domain

The psychomotor domain refers to one's ability to manipulate or change given situations. This is done physically, with one's hand or with a separate object, as a means to an end—acquiring a new behavior or set of skills. In *The Classification of Educational Objectives in the Psychomotor Domain* (1972), Elizabeth Simpson, expounding on Bloom's emphasis on the psychomotor domain, developed seven categories: perception, set, guided response, mechanism, complex overt response, adaptation, and origination.

Perception. In the context of instruction and learning, perception is the ability to utilize sensory cues from the environment as a means of guiding motor activity. For example, when a teacher asks a question, students raise their hands. The perception occurs when students realize a question is being asked.

Set. Set simply refers to the student's readiness to act on something. This is somewhat related to the affective domain in that it involves a degree of interest or motivation. Examples include raising the hand to answer questions and taking an active role in participatory exercises or projects.

Guided response. Guided response involves the ability to engage in complex learning, whereby students follow a model that the teacher presents. Examples of guided response include imitation of the model, trial and error, experimentation, and the like. In sum, the role of practice is essential because it contributes to increased performance.

Mechanism. Mechanism refers to the level of psychomotor ability whereby students are able to maintain a degree of consistency after practice and the period of trial and error. A common non-school-related analogy here is the process of learning how to ride a bicycle. At first, the student must focus on balance. The student might initially fall off the bicycle a few times before being able to maintain balance consistently. Mechanism occurs after the initial difficulties and inconsistencies in the early learning process of a given skill are eradicated.

Complex overt response. Complex overt response occurs when a student becomes skilled in specific motor actions that involve complex patterns of movement. A student engages in complex overt response while showing evidence of being able to perform tasks fluently and with very limited error.

Adaptation. At the point of adaptation, a student's skills are highly developed to the point that the performance of a given task can be applied to virtually any situation that demands it. For example, an individual who uses a computer for word processing demonstrates adaptation when the computer is used for programming and synthesizing new ideas and concepts. The pianist plays the piano not solely for performing someone else's music, but his or her own newly composed music.

Origination. Origination is the last level in the psychomotor domain because it involves motor skills and movement that relate to synthesizing or creating new things. An athlete or dancer who creates a new movement or a student who develops a new theory is examples of origination.

Cognitive Domain

In *Prospects: The Quarterly Review of Comparative Education* (2000), Elliot Eisner argues that Benjamin Bloom's taxonomy is not solely a classification of cognitive levels or a system of categorizing developmental stages. Unlike Piaget's stage theory of cognitive and intellectual development, Bloom's taxonomy is not dependent on developmental stages. In contrast to developmental stage theories, Bloom wanted to demonstrate that reaching any subsequent level is dependent on one's ability to master the preceding levels, and not on distinct intellectual and biological stages of development.

Knowledge. For Bloom, knowledge refers to the ability to identify facts and recognize something or some idea by labeling. Essentially, this is the ability to name various pieces of information. According to Bloom, this is the fundamental first level before any subsequent level can be mastered.

Comprehension. Comprehension is the ability of students to show evidence of mastering conceptual knowledge. An eloquent term that sums up the meaning of comprehension is "understanding." In general, to comprehend is to understand. One major prerequisite for comprehension is the ability to know series of facts and be able to put facts together coherently.

Application. Application refers to students' ability to apply a concept or a practical model to different contexts or situations. According to Bloom, this ability to apply is entirely dependent on their ability to understand an idea or concept that is taught to them. Clearly, adept instructional techniques are essential for students to reach this cognitive level.

Analysis. Analysis is the students' ability to compare and contrast the parts of a given whole concept, idea, or set of data. An analyst is a student who is able to dissect a donated organic specimen and identify the various internal parts, diagram sentences according to their grammatical structure, identify the theoretical structure of a musical composition, or compare and contrast the writings or theories of different people. To be able to do this, students need to know and be able to apply a given concept to a particular context or situation as described under the level of *application* above.

Synthesis. Synthesis is the ability to put things or ideas together—in short, creation. Students who are syn-

thesizers are those, for example, who write essays, create poetry, compose music, and build structures without the use of a predetermined model. For students to reach the level of synthesis, they must gain the ability to analyze concepts, information, theories, laws, and the like.

Evaluation. Evaluation is the highest level in Bloom's taxonomy. At this level, students are able to judge the quality of something. They are capable of making decisions and selecting appropriate ideas or systems of knowledge within a particular area or discipline. Students who reach the level of evaluation must also be able to master the fifth level—synthesis. That is, they create or synthesize disparate concepts, facts, ideas, or semiotic (symbol-related) systems.

Some researchers have argued that a student's ability to evaluate or judge content may be equal to or possibly cognitively lower in level than synthesis because they believe that to create a new object, idea, or phenomenon is more intellectually complex. The Figure (see page 87) shows a visual account of Bloom's categories within the cognitive domain.

Robert Gagné

In addition to Bloom's taxonomy, perhaps the best known of the learning theory and teacher-centered approaches, Robert Gagné, in *The Conditions of Learning* (1985), proposed a taxonomy that focuses on three major criteria: verbal information, intellectual skills, and cognitive strategies. Verbal information refers to content that can be explained by students through verbalizing orally, writing, or even drawing diagrams or pictures. For example, a student might be able to verbalize the following: On a map, if one inch stands for 74 miles, then how many inches would stand for 341 miles? The next cognitive ability level, according to Gagné, is to be able to simplify text in the forms mentioned above through the use of non–textually based symbolic representation. This is called intellectual skills. An example of this level using the previous example would be to simplify the meaning by shortening the verbiage in the text—namely, the use of mathematical symbols:

$$\frac{1}{74} = \frac{n}{341}$$

Figure: **Schematic of Cognitive Domain of Bloom's Taxonomy**

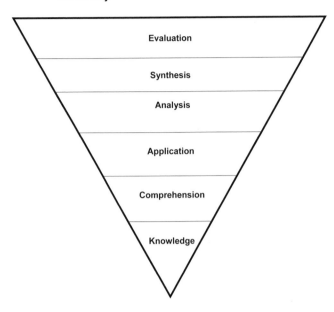

Gagné then argues that a higher level of cognitive functioning in the learning and instruction process would involve cognitive strategies. In this case, the student can operate successfully on the various acquired skills and intellectual abilities that can enable the solving of problems.

David Ausubel

In *The Psychology of Meaningful Verbal Learning* (1968), David Ausubel differentiates between two types of learning that effect instructional technique: rote learning and meaningful learning. Rote learning involves the identification of individual pieces of factual information in a more or less individual manner. This information is generally isolated in nature and does not account for relationships between or among different data. As Ausubel states, in rote learning, "learned materials are discrete and relatively isolated entities" that do not "permit the establishment of relationships." Meaningful learning, on the other hand, is an approach to learning and instruction that involves the student's ability to make connections between and among different pieces of information. Ausubel posits that meaningful learning "takes place if the learning task can be related in a nonarbitrary, substantive fashion to what the learner already knows." Unlike the other taxonomies, Ausubel's work relates to Bloom's taxonomic model

only tangentially and indirectly. Rote learning seems to fit well with Bloom's *knowledge* level; meaningful learning seems to associate with Bloom's *comprehension* level (as seen in the Table on page 89), yet it can also relate with the other levels as well, depending on the outlook of the researcher.

John Anderson

In *Cognitive Skills and Their Acquisition* (1981), John Anderson, like Ausubel, considers two types of knowledge that contribute to instructive methodologies: declarative knowledge and procedural knowledge. Declarative knowledge, according to Anderson, is defined very specifically as a type of knowledge that develops in terms of chunks or cognitive units. A cognitive unit can be a proposition, a spatial representation, or a string of data that consists of elements that are encoded into a particular order or relationship. Due to chunking as a means of breaking up a unit for the purpose of memorizing information, a cognitive unit can have no more than five elements. Declarative knowledge can also be referred to as descriptive knowledge or propositional knowledge. Procedural knowledge, on the other hand, requires the student to determine how to go about a question, problem, or project without the need for direct instruction. Unlike declarative knowledge, procedural knowledge is aimed to facilitate long-term retention.

In general, declarative knowledge lends itself to a strict form of instruction and assessment, while procedural knowledge allows for more open-ended, dialectic (i.e., involving both student and teacher input) form of instruction and assessment. Declarative knowledge often requires instruction to occur in a lecture-oriented format where the teacher is a dispenser of knowledge and the student is an absorber of that knowledge. It discourages creativity and independent problem solving. In contrast, emphasis on procedural knowledge is more tolerant of freethinking, analysis, and creativity on the part of the student. Instruction in this case is a matter of teacher guidance and the facilitation of knowledge.

R. David Merrill

As described in "Component Display Theory" (1983), there are four general categories in Merrill's taxonomy: remembering verbatim, remembering paraphrased information, using a generality, and finding a generality. In sum, a large amount of Merrill's taxonomy has to do with how memory interacts with cognitive processes. To illustrate, remembering verbatim deals with the storage and retrieval of information from memory. In this respect, then, remembering verbatim is somewhat parallel with Bloom's *knowledge* level. Paraphrased remembering is an extension of verbatim in that it requires the student to make associations with various ideas in an integrative manner. In line with Bloom's taxonomy, paraphrased remembering fits comfortably with *comprehension* (Bloom's second level). When using a generality, the student is classifying information based on a previously constructed rule. Essentially, the student is generalizing information that fits an old rule or theory. An example of this level in mathematics would be when a student is able to categorize numbers based on their properties—a classification that has been in existence for centuries. The final level in Merrill's taxonomy is called finding a generality. This occurs when a student—usually a student with experience or a level of expertise in a subject—is able to create a new classification system for a given set of specific information. This final level of Merrill's taxonomy connects quite fittingly with Bloom's last three levels.

Charles Reigeluth

In "Instructional Design" (1983), Charles Reigeluth attempts to clarify earlier taxonomies, particularly that of Bloom, through his identification of four categories for educational instruction: memorizing information, understanding relationships, applying skills, and applying generic skills. In general, memorizing information is somewhat analogous to Bloom's knowledge level, as well as Ausubel's rote learning and Anderson's declarative knowledge. It represents the most basic form of knowledge acquisition—quick factual memorization of basic elements of knowledge. Understanding relationships, Reigeluth's second level, requires students to make connections between the elements mentioned in the first level so as to acquire a further understanding, not solely of factual information, but of more complex forms of knowledge, such as concepts, theories, and laws. This level is aligned fairly closely with Bloom's comprehension level. Applying skills requires students to engage in activities that promote experience in learning. It is slightly more difficult to teach due to its hands-on

approach, but it is not as complex as applying generic skills, Reigeluth's last level. The applying-skills level is comparable to *application* in Bloom's taxonomy and *procedural knowledge* in Anderson's theory. This level is also domain-dependent and is based on concepts that apply to only one field. To apply generic skills takes much longer than the apply-skills level because it is, in Reigeluth's words, "domain-independent"—in other words, this level requires a knowledge base that works across different subjects and disciplines. At this level, the student has the ability to compare and contrast various viewpoints, develop a theory, or create a project that does not depend on an earlier model. Constructs at this level are more original than in the previous level.

As a means of putting these six taxonomies into perspective, the Table (see page 89) shows how the categories from each of the six theorists relate to one another. In essence, lower level skills are shown on the same rows while higher-level skills are shown on related rows.

Piaget

Jean Piaget's approach to instruction of content cannot be applied to the previous six theorists because their theoretical approaches are in line with behaviorist models of learning. Piaget is foremost a cognitivist in his approach and fully supports a developmental or stage model of instruction and learning. During the 1960s, changes to instruction were greatly influenced by the work of Piaget, whose conception of instruction was based on his celebrated stage theory of intellectual development. Piaget argued that learning through instruction was based on a three-phase learning cycle: an exploratory, hands-on phase; a concept development phase; and a concept application phase. In short, Piaget showed that one's stage affects one's intellectual maturity. Therefore, students in the preoperational stage or possibly the concrete operational stage (the second and third stages, respectively) will strongly benefit from experience and opportunities of being immersed in environments that are conducive to intellectual development—that is, exploration and hands-on activities. Next, students in the concrete operational and formal operational stages (the third and final stages, respectively) can benefit from concept development—in other words, opportunities that allow students to classify or cat-

Table: **Six Instructional Taxonomies in Perspective**

Bloom	Gagné	Ausubel	Anderson	Merrill	Reigeluth
Knowledge	Verbal information	Rote learning	Declarative knowledge	Verbatim memory	Memorization of information
Comprehension		Meaningful learning		Paraphrased memory	Understanding relationships
Application	Intellectual skill		Procedural knowledge	Using a generality	Application of skills
Analysis				Finding or developing a generality	Application of generic skills
Synthesis	Cognitive strategy				
Evaluation					

Notes: Arrows indicate that a particular category for one taxonomy comprises categories that are related in other taxonomies. Shaded regions indicate that a particular category does not continue to higher cognitive levels. For example, in Anderson's taxonomy, there is no category that is comparable to Bloom's final three levels—analysis, synthesis, and evaluation.

egorize information so that it can be organized in a way that allows for conceptual development and the storage of concepts in memory. Finally, individuals at the formal operational stage are developmentally at the level where they can apply concepts that they have classified and organized when they are engaged in activities that require complex thinking, such as experimentation, comparative analysis, empirical study, and the like.

The Future of Instructional Forms

It is impossible to consider schooling without teachers—in other words, human engagement in the instructional process. Nevertheless, many novel forms of instruction have already begun in the learning experience. Distance learning is one of the most popular forms of non-face-to-face instruction. Despite the form of instruction, two aspects are certain. First, humans create the curriculum that is to be used for instructional purposes. So whether instruction takes place verbally, in real time within the classroom, as a videotaped or compact disc performance, on line via the Internet, or as a virtual classroom where students are able to interact with instructors and possibly other students over long distances, instruction will always be carried out by people whose lives and

careers are focused on the business of transmitting knowledge to students who ostensibly need to learn new information for their personal edification, betterment, attainment of skills, or the like. And second, the type of instruction provided often influences the cognitive level of individual students. This can be clearly seen from the taxonomies provided above. Lecturing clearly does not influence synthesis or the creation of something new. At the same time, one-on-one interaction might not necessarily be a good form of instruction for students who are learning a topic or concept for the first time.

Daniel Ness and Chia-ling Lin

REFERENCES

Anderson, John R. *Cognitive Skills and Their Acquisition*. Hillsdale, NJ: Lawrence Erlbaum, 1981.

Atkin, J. Myron, and Robert Karplus. "Discovery or Invention?" *The Science Teacher* 29:5 (1962): 45.

Ausubel, David. *The Psychology of Meaningful Verbal Learning*. New York: Grune & Stratton, 1968.

Bloom, Benjamin, and David Krathwohl. *Taxonomy of Educational Objectives: Handbook I, The Cognitive Domain*. New York: David McKay, 1956.

Eisner, Elliot W. "Benjamin Bloom." *Prospects: The Quarterly Review of Comparative Education* 30:3 (2000).

Gagné, Robert M. 4th ed. *The Conditions of Learning* New York: Holt, Rinehart, & Winston, 1985.

Merrill, M. David. "Component Display Theory." In *Instructional-Design Theories and Models: An Overview of Their Current Status*, ed. C.M. Reigeluth, 279–333. Hillsdale, NJ: Lawrence Erlbaum, 1983.

————. *To Understand Is to Invent: The Future of Education.* New York: Viking, 1974.

Reigeluth, Charles M. "Instructional Design: What Is It and Why Is It?" In *Instructional-Design Theories and Models: An Overview of Their Current Status*, ed. C.M. Reigeluth, 3–36. Hillsdale, NJ: Lawrence Erlbaum, 1983.

Simpson, Elizabeth J. *The Classification of Educational Objectives in the Psychomotor Domain.* Washington, DC: Gryphon House, 1972.

ASSESSMENT

Assessment is an essential part of the schooling process. The job of teachers is at least threefold in terms of their everyday professional activities. They are followers of a curriculum. They must adhere to a curriculum in order to meet the requirements of a local, regional, or national educational authority. This adherence in effect follows in accordance with what students of a certain age are expected to have learned at the end of a particular point during the school year. Second, teachers must find a means to achieve the end—adherence to the curriculum. Instruction is the means by which a teacher achieves this objective. There are many forms of instruction, as we saw in the last chapter. The most common form involves the standard method of using verbal communication to teach a particular concept or skill. Third and last is the component of assessment. To be sure, teachers must know how to assess their students in order to determine levels of development and understanding at given points throughout the school year. This section identifies numerous forms of assessment. These forms are classified under two general prototypes: summative assessment and formative assessment.

It is very difficult to categorize different assessments because one type of assessment may overlap with another. For example, a student might be asked to write an essay as a summative assessment. This form of assessment is also subjective in that a grade does not depend on a single answer (as would a multiple-choice question). Subjective forms of assess-

ment might also be examined by a teacher in the form of portfolios. But portfolios are often categorized as formative, not summative, assessments. Thus, it is difficult to compartmentalize various forms of assessment during the process of categorization.

Summative Assessment and Its Various Forms

Summative assessments are those that are evaluative in nature. They usually occur after a period of time—one week, one month, one semester, etc.—during which learning of a particular subject takes place. Other words associated with the term "summative" are "sum" and "summary"—in essence, words that indicate the result or end product of something. As mentioned earlier, these assessments can be both objective and subjective. Examples of an objective summative assessment include multiple-choice examinations, true-false tests, fill-in-the-blank questions, and matching items. Nearly all summative assessments are formal assessments in that they are in the form of written tests that students must submit for a grade.

Norm-referenced tests are assessments that measure a student's academic ability when compared to other students of the same grade or relative age level. Evaluators of norm-referenced tests are not concerned necessarily that the student understands the content being tested. Rather, the evaluator is interested in how the student compares with a larger body of students. Norm-referenced examinations are mostly timed examinations that take on a variety of forms mentioned earlier (e.g., multiple-choice, true-false). Moreover, a norm-referenced test can be administered to students through a variety of platforms. The most common is paper and pencil or pen. Within the last decade, computer-generated exams have become increasingly common. Rather than filling in an oval or filling a blank with a pencil, a student answers a question on a computer screen by a simple click of a mouse. All norm-referenced tests receive some form of grade or level of achievement for teachers, parents, students, and administrators to consider.

People who administer criterion-referenced tests are not so much interested in how a single student compares with others. Instead, they are interested in whether a student is able to answer a particular question (i.e., the criterion) that is typically answered correctly by other students, usually at the same age-level. Criterion-referenced tests are usually administered in a singular fashion—that is, one student at a time. Criterion-referenced tests are important in that they allow teachers to determine individual levels of development of particular students so that they can be placed at the proper educational level.

Since the 1980s, there has been a greater emphasis on performance-based assessment as a means of identifying what students can accomplish when they are actually engaged in the process of problem solving and not merely answering questions through pencil-and-paper testing. An example of a performance-based assessment is a science test that assesses what students are able to do with various scientific devices, such as an electric circuit. They have to test these pieces of equipment in order to determine how electricity functions, or how density works, and so forth. Other forms of performance-based assessment are portfolios, readings and recitations, journals that enable the student to identify personal development in a particular discipline, musical recitals, art exhibitions, and the like. Teachers who institute performance-based assessment practices generally attempt to align the assessment with some kind of national standards or outcome-based education. Unlike the typical multiple-choice format, questions in performance-based assessment are generally in a free-form format, as indicated by the platforms mentioned above. Performance-based assessments also differ from the traditional pencil-and-paper format in that questions and tasks usually involve real-world examples that test students' everyday abilities and skills. Educators have also used the term "authentic assessment" in reference to performance-based assessment because it is viewed as more relevant to everyday life and work than is the standardized pencil-and-paper assessment model.

Generally speaking, summative assessment is often seen as an assessment *of* learning, not an assessment *for* learning, because it is almost entirely about what and how a student can perform at any particular time. The grade that a student receives is an outcome of what the student can do in a given subject. Summative assessment as an assessment of learning is generally given at the conclusion of a topic or chapter or at the end of a course, semester, or academic year.

Summative Assessments and High-Stakes Testing

Perhaps the greatest controversy surrounding the role of summative assessment is high-stakes testing—a term that has dominated the media since 2000, especially when topics in education are aired. High-stakes testing is a form of assessment that uses benchmarks for the purpose of grade promotion or school or college entrance. The problems of high-stakes tests are multifold. First, the decks are stacked against poor children who must take the same or similar high-stakes examinations with their more affluent counterparts. The children of families in poverty face many difficulties. They have higher rates of health problems than children who live in more adequate circumstances. Health problems include extremely poor dental hygiene, asthma (often due to rat and cockroach infestations as well as lead-based paint on the walls), obesity (which often leads to heart disease and diabetes), and various forms of cancer. Poor children's relatives are often incarcerated. They live in substandard housing, often in high-crime neighborhoods with little if any feeling of security. Given these dire circumstances, it is evident that children who live in poverty have more immediate concerns than passing a high-stakes examination.

Second, from the standpoint of students of more affluent households, high-stakes testing is not so much about content as it is about the form of a test—that is, how to take it, not what is on it. This mentality of cracking the code of taking a test is best illustrated through the lens of students whose families are able to afford specialized education, such as the use of a tutoring company or a so-called boutique educator. Like a boutique doctor, who is on call every minute of the day for wealthy families, the boutique educator is an individual, often with a law background, who tutors students in high-stakes testing techniques, usually for exorbitant fees, so that a student can obtain optimal scores on specified high-stakes tests, such as the SAT or ACT. Moreover, affluent families have the wherewithal to expose their children to a variety of learning environments—museums and science centers, national parks, overnight camps, overseas travel, and the like—that prepare them not only to pass examinations, but to continue to college and graduate school. Most children who live in poverty will not have these experiences, because they have more pressing issues to think about—such as a safe place to sleep, enough food to eat, and decent clothes to wear.

Formative Assessment and Its Various Forms

Formative assessments are generally assessments for learning—in other words, assessments that allow for students to build on their current skills without the emphasis on an end product such as a grade. There are many forms of formative assessments. One type is anecdotal record taking. This type of assessment occurs when teachers identify students' abilities by observing how they engage in various cognitive activities, either alone or with other students. Teachers will often take notes on what individual students can do when engaged in different intellectual tasks. Diagnostic assessment, another form of formative assessment, is similar to most forms of criterion-referenced tests in that administrators and teachers using them make an attempt to evaluate students in order to identify an appropriate environment for learning on an individual basis. It is different, however, from both norm- and criterion-referenced tests in that no grades are given. In one popular form of diagnostic assessment, students are given the opportunity to examine their own level of learning at any given time—often referred to as self-assessment. There is also a type of formative assessment known as forward-looking assessment, whereby the student is asked to interpret various hypothetical scenarios—that is, possible future situations—as a means of determining skill levels.

Theoretical Underpinnings of Assessment Practices

There are two overarching philosophical paradigms from which assessment practices originated and developed: empiricism and rationalism. The empiricist paradigm derived from John Locke's emphasis on the senses as the only means by which humans gain knowledge of the world. Locke believed that the mind originated as a *tabula rasa*—a blank slate—and that only through experience through time does the individual gain knowledge. Locke greatly influenced later philosophers, especially the Scottish philosopher

David Hume, whose work demonstrated the processes of causation. Cause-and-effect relationships were essential to the empiricist tradition because it revealed ways in which humans perceive events in terms of space and time. The empiricists, then, maintained that reality is based on what we are able to see, hear, touch, smell, and taste. As a result, the work of numerous assessment specialists is predicated on the empiricist philosophical paradigm, and by the beginning of the twentieth century, their focus was undergirded by psychological behaviorists, psychometricians, and measurement specialists. Assessment experts whose work emphasized the empirical approach include John Anderson, Robert Gagné, and Herbert Simon. In addition to these specialists, psychometricians whose work focused on intelligence testing fall into the so-called empiricist category. These individuals include Charles Spearman, Lewis Terman, L.L. Thurstone, and, more recently, Arthur Jensen. The primary method of assessment used in this paradigm is to identify specific knowledge components as evidenced by mastery and fluency of knowledge. Psychometric evaluations are used to standardize test results. Standardized testing is the principal modus operandi for determining outcomes.

The rationalist paradigm developed from the work of the French philosopher René Descartes, the Swiss philosopher Jean-Jacques Rousseau, and, subsequently, the German philosopher Immanuel Kant. The rationalists agree that sensory perception is part of knowledge, but strongly differ from their empiricist counterparts in that they believe that knowledge is based on mental constructions that presuppose the senses. Unlike the empiricists, rationalists believe that infants and young children's minds are not blank slates, but working minds. Both general and specific knowledge bases are constructed by the mind, and problems based on this knowledge are solved using rationally based criteria. Humans essentially assimilate information that they retrieve and that fits within a particular pattern of inquiry. Knowledge schemes that do not fit a particular norm must be accommodated into the mind. Assessment specialists whose work has emphasized the rationalist approach include Robbie Case, John Flavell, and Jean Piaget. The primary method of assessment used in the cognitive rationalist paradigm is to identify specific knowledge as evidenced by outcomes related to student involvement in particular cognitive tasks. Rather than using psychometric evaluations, cognitive researchers use interviewing procedures and problem-solving devices that enable students to achieve outcomes.

In recent years, a third philosophical approach to assessment emerged out of the need to consider social and contextual influences. This sociocultural paradigm stems from the philosophical perspectives of Johann Fichte, Georg Hegel, and Karl Marx, all of whom emphasized the importance of dialectic (i.e., communication and dialogue) between two or more individuals as a means of solving cognitive problems. The leading theorists, both past and present, who espoused this point of view include Lev Vygotsky, his students Alexei Leontiev and Alexander Luria, Alan Collins, Ann Brown, James Greeno, John Bransford, and Michael Cole. For the socioculturalists, the human mind is unique in that language and symbolism play an important role in communicating ideas. The primary method for achieving an understanding of how students gain knowledge from a sociohistorical and cultural perspective is to assess their participation through inquiry-based and performance-based interactive practices of learning. These methods include performance-based assessment (e.g., student performance at a task), portfolios, and observation techniques. In sum, the technique used should emphasize the importance of both social and environmental factors that affect learning and acquisition of concepts.

Validity and Reliability of Assessment

In order for a form of assessment to be implemented, it must pass two criteria: validity and reliability. It is important to note that a test can be valid but not reliable. Similarly, it can be reliable but not valid. The following discussion on validity and reliability will shed some light on why these two criteria must be considered before implementing any form of assessment.

Validity refers to what a test is intended to measure. Simply, a test is valid if in fact it assesses what it is intended to measure. For example, a valid mathematics assessment for students of the eighth grade will measure what students whose ages fall within the eighth-grade level are able to achieve. Many factors contribute to a test's validity (or lack thereof). The first is content. If that eighth-grade mathematics test includes spurious word problems or content having little to do with mathematics, then the test will lack validity. A second factor is the age appropriateness of the content. Using the same example, if the content for 13- or 14-year-old eighth graders includes mathematics content appropriate for earlier grades (e.g., single-digit subtraction) or later grades (e.g., processes of calculus integration), then validity must be questioned. A third factor has to do with whether a question on the assessment makes sense to both the student and an expert. If not, the validity of the test must be questioned. Fourth, the test must correspond to other important variables. For example, one class of students might perform differently when compared to another class of students.

Valid assessment provides samples of behavior that allow the classroom teacher to observe and evaluate student responses indicating conceptual knowledge or understanding of a topic. These samples of behavior—or observable student responses—are elicited through informal teacher queries during a host of media, such as comprehensive examinations, laboratory experiments, and the like. The content area and the level of behavioral objectives of the assessment techniques range from mastering fundamental building blocks to integrating concepts at a higher level. The critical evidence of valid assessment is the appropriate match between what has been taught and what is being tested. Standardized tests (e.g., national, regional, or statewide) play a major role in educational assessment; however, traditional and alternative classroom-initiated formats—such as journals, group evaluations, teacher observations, well-focused classroom tests, performance assessments, and the like—have also emerged as valuable tools in a comprehensive assessment program.

Reliability refers to the consistency of a test when it is administered to different groups of students and in different contexts. Poor test reliability is the result of a number of factors. These include, but are not limited to, the following: poor data collectors, vague questions, and items that have too many categories from which to choose. In general, a test that has high reliability has several properties. First, the test outcomes are consistent from one administration of the test to another. Second, if an examinee takes multiple forms of the same test (i.e., the content is the same but test questions are modified), the outcomes on all should be very similar. Third, the test should be internally consistent. In other words, a respondent should provide similar answers to similar questions. For example, one test item might read "I enjoy science." A similar item might read "I am always eager to participate when the teacher asks questions about science." A student's answers to these questions should be fairly similar in order for the test to be reliable. A reliability score is between 0 and 1. The closer it is to 0, the less reliable the test. The closer it is to 1, the more reliable the test. In general, reliability indices seldom, if ever, reach 100 percent reliability (i.e., 1). Assessment specialists generally consider a reliability score of 0.8 to be fairly high.

Daniel Ness and Chia-ling Lin

REFERENCES

Anderson, John R., Lynne M. Reder, and Herbert A. Simon. "Situated Learning and Education." *Educational Researcher* 25:4 (1996): 5–11.

Bransford, John D., Ann L. Brown, and Rodney R. Cocking. *How People Earn: Brain, Mind, Experience, and School.* Expanded ed. Washington, DC: National Academy, 2000.

Brown, Ann. L., and Joseph. C. Campione. "Psychological Theory and the Design of Innovative Learning Environments: On Procedures, Principles, and Systems." In *Innovations in Learning: New Environments for Education*, ed. Leona Schauble and Robert Glaser, 289–325. Mahwah, NJ: Lawrence Erlbaum, 1996.

Case, Robbie., at al. "The Role of Central Conceptual Structures in the Development of Children's Thought." *Monographs of the Society for Research in Child Development* 61 (1–2, Serial No. 246, 1996).

Gagné, Robert M. *The Conditions of Learning.* 4th ed. New York: Holt, Rinehart & Winston, 1985.

Johnson, Dale D., Bonnie Johnson, Stephen J. Farenga, and Daniel Ness. *Stop High-Stakes Testing: An Appeal to America's Conscience.* Lanham, MD: Rowman & Littlefield, 2008.

EARLY CHILDHOOD EDUCATION

Early childhood education is a broadly defined term that can include the education of children from shortly after birth to preadolescent ages (12 or 13 years old). In general parlance, however, most discussion of early childhood education points to the education of children between the ages of three and six. Regardless, it is important to note that early childhood education can be entirely different when comparing one area or nation to another. A number of factors contribute to these differences, including children's age, type of curriculum, and compulsion for attendance.

Children's Age

Age is perhaps the most important predictor in determining in which grade level a child should be placed. Most children who enter the first grade—the typical initial grade level for compulsory schooling—are five to seven years of age. This is a fairly good indication for the cutoff between early childhood and primary education. In other words, most early childhood programs accommodate children less than seven years old. It is more difficult, however, to ascertain when early childhood education begins. Nevertheless, in most cases, assuming that strict day care is excluded from the concept of "preschool," most countries seem to indicate a starting age of three or four years.

Early Childhood Curriculum

Traditionally, there were two camps regarding early childhood education curriculum. One camp believed that an early childhood education curriculum should emphasize the role of health and well-being, interactions with adults and peers, and suitable ways in which children should conduct themselves. The other camp emphasized the need for introduction to academic subjects. Two well-known early childhood programs throughout the world, both originating in Italy, are Reggio Emilia and Montessori. The Reggio Emilia approach to early childhood education began shortly after the end of the World War II in Reggio Emilia, the city that the educational philosophy is named after. This approach to early childhood, like Montessori, has spread to nations throughout the world. It particularly emphasizes the importance of a child-centered learning environment. Often referred to as the "child's third teacher," the role of the physical environment is essential for child development. In this context, environment involves the ways in which children establish a relationship between the classroom and the school by remodeling new spaces from old ones. An example of environmental influence include the ways in which children modify the physical arrangement of the classroom to suit their goals and interests as a result of motor and intellectual development. A child at three years of age, for instance, might use blocks to create a large square shaped structure for the goal of pretend play, while a five-year-older will often alter the classroom environment so that the goal of block play is to build and construct objects. A Reggio Emilia classroom is adorned with plants and often includes an open piazza. There is also a strong interaction between a place of learning and home life, as evidenced by the openness of a kitchen and living environment. Children are engaged in long-term projects as means of expression and of learning because such projects prepare students to engage in academic learning with an acute sense of analytical thinking. Moreover, the role of symbolism is stressed in the Reggio Emilia system. Children are encouraged to demonstrate what they have learned through a variety of media, such as drawing, dramatic play, sculpture, writing, and many other forms of communication. The Reggio Emilia method espouses the developmental models presented by cognitive philosophers and practitioners—in particular, John Dewey, Lev Vygotsky, Jean Piaget, and Jerome Bruner. Accordingly, there is a strong connection between Reggio Emilia and constructivist philosophy, which maintains that prior knowledge is an essential ingredient to the solving of problems and cognitive and intellectual development.

Maria Montessori developed schools in the early twentieth century. Her method focused on structured activities that were thought to improve development in all areas of life. Unlike the Reggio Emilia method, which emphasized the child's autonomy within the environment, Montessori was mostly interested in providing structure and organization for children. As such, she and her colleagues created materials for children to use in order to address developmental issues. After an ebbing of interest in her method from the 1920s to the 1940s, the Montessori method and philosophy witnessed several revivals in the United States during the 1960s and 1970s and in other areas around the world, particularly the United Kingdom, Australia, Japan, and Taiwan. The late twentieth-century revivals were most likely in response to the need for alternatives to the typical nursery or elementary school systems, which limited student autonomy and did not seem to serve critical points in early childhood. It was also during these decades that Piagetian

theory became prominent in the United States. And, as indicated above, Montessori's theoretical framework seems to have anticipated the work of Piaget and other developmentalists in early childhood.

Nevertheless, the Montessori school surely has its critics. The approach was seen as radical by a number of behaviorist theorists and advocates who put social development well before cognitive or intellectual development. Thus, Montessori's critics seem to have greatly influenced the educational panorama for the first several decades of the twentieth century, and although her methods are quite popular today, her educational system in the United States and in most other countries favors teacher-centered classrooms, whereby students are directed and instructed and have virtually no free choice at all. Regardless of her shortcomings, Montessori was one of the first theorists and practitioners to put the philosophical perspective of Rousseau into practice. In addition, unlike the famous theorists who succeeded her, Montessori was perhaps the first to recognize the spontaneous capabilities of young children and appreciate the relationship between these capabilities and intellectual development in general.

Comparisons of Early Childhood Programs in Different Countries

In order to gain insight into the topic of early childhood education, it is necessary to identify the goals of early childhood education from the vantage point of ministries of education from a variety of countries. Case synopses of early childhood education programs in Argentina, Canada, Ghana, Italy, Jordan, Kyrgyzstan, the Netherlands, the Philippines, and Romania are provided below.

Argentina. Nearly half of all Argentinean children between the ages of three and five are enrolled in preschool programs. However, despite a putative reputation as a country of wealth, Argentina suffers from chronic poverty both in and outside the metropolitan areas. As a result, most poor children do not have the same access to education as their wealthier counterparts do. Some initiatives, such as the Oscarcito Project, have attempted to counterbalance the situation.

Canada. Canadian preschools place great attention on involving children in activities that foster motor development, social interaction skills, and a modicum of intellectual abilities. A second focus of

Canadian preschools is to acquaint children with a setting that serves as a unique transition between the home environment and the more academically focused environment of primary school. The Canadian Ministry of Education's goal for preschool education is to shape each child's personality development and skills in interacting with others.

Ghana. In Ghana the Department of Social Welfare is responsible for day-care programs for children from birth to two years old. Formal preschool, which is headed by the Ghana Education Service, begins at age three and lasts until age five. Unfortunately, early childhood development programs have been hampered by the lack of coordination between the Department of Social Welfare and the Ghana Education Service. Preschools that are under the auspices of the Ghana Education Service are intended to prepare children for compulsory education at the elementary levels. Despite great interest in expanding programs of preschool education in Ghana, funding, resources, poorly qualified personnel, and dilapidated infrastructure are impeding the initiative.

Italy. Preschools in Italy are unique in that they are time-honored institutions that have long focused on children's intellectual and social development and advancement of knowledge. In Italy, preschool education is appropriated for children between the ages of three and six years. Called *scuola materna* (sometimes called *scuola dell'infanzia*, which refers to nursery school), schooling at this level is noncompulsory, although most parents do enroll their children. The *scuola materna* is free and partially subsidized by the government; however, for private preschools, parents must pay tuition. Evidence of well-known early childhood programs, such as Montessori and Reggio Emilia, can be found in preschools in Italy. Preschools in Italy are not day-care centers where children are merely tended to or watched over. Essentially, preschool programs in Italy focus on the environment as teacher. Early childhood is an explorative period in which children engage in activities that foster and expand upon their intrinsic intellectual propensities.

Jordan. In Jordan education in early childhood is called preprimary education. It is specialized for children beginning at age three years and eight months. Rather than an emphasis on academic knowledge (like nearly all early childhood programs), the essential goal of preprimary education is to develop positive habits related to health, social relationships, and learning school subjects. Preprimary schools focus on developing children's personality and attitude toward learning and interacting with other children. According to Article 8 of the Education Law of 1955, the aim of preprimary education is "to provide [a] suitable atmosphere . . . [to] create a balanced education of the child, including aspects of personal physical, mental, spiritual, and emotional help . . . to build good health habits and the development of social relationships and strengthen the positive trends of school life." The Jordanian preprimary schools also attempt to prepare young children with an easier transition from home to school.

Jordan's Education Ministry also follows the model of other nations' early childhood programs by making preprimary education optional for parents. Enrollment of children between the ages of three and six years is approximately 25 percent. Unlike the ministries of education in other countries, however, the Jordanian ministry oversees and manages all preprimary schools in the country. Therefore, although all preprimary schools are private, they remain under the auspices of the Jordanian Ministry of Education. The average student/teacher ratio at the preprimary level is 21 to 1, although there is an average of 24 students per class. Between 1990 and 2005, the enrollment in Jordanian preprimary schools increased dramatically. In 1990 there were nearly 45,000 preschool students. One decade later, that number increased to nearly 70,000 preschool students. As of 2008 there was an estimated 80,000 to 85,000 preschool students enrolled in preprimary schools in Jordan. Likewise, the number of teachers also increased—from nearly 2,000 in 1990 to approximately 4,000 today.

Kyrgyzstan. After the Soviet era, many state-run industries and farms in Kyrgyzstan could no longer function. This adversely affected education, particularly preschool services. As a result, nearly 70 percent of all schools for early childhood and kindergarten were sold to private companies and organizations. Within the last two decades, the few remaining rural kindergartens that were not purchased by private agencies have suffered from a lack of resources and dilapidated infrastructures, as well as a paucity of curricular materials. Currently, preschool education in Kyrgyzstan is a growing part of the country's educational system. Children who attend are between the ages of three and six; as in other countries, preschool education is not compulsory. In 2004 the Kyrgyzstan Ministry of Education allocated the equivalent of approximately $5.4 million for preschool education. Most of this funding was distributed among three areas: children's well-being and nutrition, salaries of preschool personnel, and public utilities (heat, electricity, water, etc.) for infrastructure.

Netherlands. Compulsory education in the Netherlands begins at the age of four years. However, numerous programs during the early childhood years are provided for the nearly 1.3 million children from birth to six years old. In the Netherlands, children younger than four have ample opportunities to attend preschools. Prior to the 1980s, preschools in the Netherlands served the same function as day-care centers or nursery schools, where children would for the most part be looked after while parents were working. Since 1986 nursery schools and primary schools have been integrated into one institution, whereby the primary component accommodated students from four to 12 years old and the preschool component accommodated children under four. Other countries whose preschools and primary schools are integrated are Austria, France, Ireland, and Portugal. According to Kees Broekhof in *Preschool Education in the Netherlands* (2006), preschool is mainly for children between two and four years old from families of low socioeconomic status, especially those whose parents have low levels of education. Children are prepared for specified playgroups. By age four, children enter primary school where they begin the first grade.

Philippines. Compulsory schooling in the Philippines begins at age six when children enroll in the first grade and ends at age 13 when children finish the seventh grade. Despite compulsory elementary education, only 76 percent of eligible students attend school full-time. Nevertheless, although children under seven years have the opportunity to attend preschool and kindergarten, the number of parents who enroll their children in early childhood education programs is unclear. In general, preschool education in the Philippines is optional and mostly available for parents who can afford it. Some government initiatives, however, provide preschool services for at-risk students—those in poor neighborhoods who suffer from developmental disabilities.

Romania. Preschool and kindergarten in Romania accommodate students between three and six years old. However, compulsory schooling begins at six years, the age for transition to primary school. Preprimary education is free and provided in institutions specifically designed for nursery and kindergarten. Most of these schools are public. In 2006 there was an initiative to repair the infrastructure of preprimary schools and ensure highly qualified educational staff. Part of the initiative also asked for a wider age range for early childhood education, particularly from birth through seven years.

Compulsion for Early Childhood Education Attendance

A number of issues arise when comparing early childhood education policies in different countries. First, it is necessary to consider the educational philosophy of the preschool curriculum. In other words, should academic subjects be emphasized during early childhood? Or is an emphasis on social interaction, personal hygiene, and learning important habits more important? Some education researchers argue that any focus on academics be omitted altogether. The country profiles described above are inconsistent on this topic. It seems as if there is a slight emphasis on social habits in most cases. But this is not apparent in every case.

A second issue concerns the reason why children would be either encouraged or obliged to attend preschool in the first place. In most countries where preschool is not compulsory, parents send their children to preschool for a variety of reasons. Several decades ago, it was common for mothers to work at home while children were attending school. Preschoolers would normally attend school for half a day and could expect their mothers and sometimes fathers to take them home. For most parents, the impetus to send children to preschool rests in the perceived need to have children interact with others and build social character. Few children attend preschool to improve on academic subjects because emphasis in this area usually does not commence until the first grade. Nowadays, children often attend preschool because both mothers and fathers are obliged to earn income by working outside the home. Generally, countries that have compulsory early childhood programs do not consider parental necessity important for the simple reason that all children are compelled to attend school, regardless of the parent's circumstances.

A third factor that is considered in early childhood education when comparing one country to another is whether a country's ministry of education mandates that children between certain ages prior to the first grade attend school. Contrary to popular belief, early childhood education is compulsory in some countries. For example, early childhood school attendance is not mandatory in countries such as Canada, the United States, and France, but it is mandatory in countries such as Cuba. Other countries, such as the Czech Republic, maintain highly developed early childhood programs that encourage, but do not compel, parents to enroll their children.

Numerous studies in early childhood education and sociology suggest that strong investments in early childhood education programs will yield strong returns. According to a recent longitudinal study at Harvard University, children who attend kindergarten could benefit as adults in terms of success and employment. According to Raj Chetty, an economist at Harvard University, "Teachers use basic skills that you might use later in life, like how to study hard, how to focus, patience, manners, things like that, in addition to better academic skills. And all these things have a long-term payoff."

Daniel Ness and Chia-ling Lin

REFERENCES

Broekhof, Kees. *Preschool Education in the Netherlands*. Saint-Ismier Cedex, France: Sardes, 2006.

Chetty, Raj, John N. Friedman, Nathaniel Hilger, Emmanuel Saez, Diane W. Schanzenbach, and Danny Yagan. "How Does Your Kindergarten Classroom Affect Your Earnings? Evidence from Project STAR." National Bureau of Economic Research. Cambridge, MA: Harvard University, 2010.

Jordan Ministry of Education. *Laws and Regulations*. Amman: Jordan Ministry of Education, 2010.

National Public Radio. "Want to Make $1,000 More a Year? Try Kindergarten." 2010. www.npr.org.

UNICEF. *Jordan's Early Childhood Development Initiative: Making Jordan Fit for Children*. UNICEF MENA-RO Learning Series 2 (2010).

PRIMARY EDUCATION

Primary education is the first compulsory education period in nearly all national educational systems throughout the world. In most cases, the entrance to compulsory education is clear; however, the point at which students either graduate or are promoted to the first secondary grade level is less clear. It is a generally regarded as the period of education between the initial year of compulsory schooling, most usually the first grade, and the year of a grade level that almost always precedes adolescence. Primary education programs can end as early as the fourth grade or as late as the eighth grade. In postindustrialized societies, it is at this point in a student's education that free play and creative activities take on a waning role, and typical academic instruction gradually increases in importance. It is essential to consider that in some countries, not all schoolchildren attend compulsory schooling. And if they do, they do not necessarily commence their formal schooling at the age designated by the educational ministry.

Entrance to Formal Primary Education

As stated above, first grade is the overall starting point for most children's formal primary education in countries throughout the world. There are some exceptions to this generalization, however. In Cuba, most states in the United States, and in some countries in Europe, for example, compulsory education commences with kindergarten or preschool. At the other extreme, certain developing nations in Africa and Asia do not make first grade compulsory for all children. At the same time, kindergarten is the generally accepted entrance into formal schooling because this is the time when children generally learn about alphabets and a modicum of numbers (usually 1 to 10 or 1 to 20). Again, since it is difficult to generalize about the compulsory nature of schooling, it is necessary to emphasize that the term "kindergarten" in various societies is broader in meaning than simply one year of schooling for five- or six-year-old children. In China, for example, kindergarten refers to the schooling of children from about age two to age six—a much larger age span than in many other nations.

Sample Representation of Countries

Below is a list describing compulsory primary education in a sample of 14 countries around the world.

This list is based on multiple factors, so that one factor does not outweigh any other factor. In other words, countries selected differ in terms of economic development (i.e., developing or developed), population, and geographic region, among other factors.

Austria. Compulsory schooling in Austria begins for the child at age six and ends most often at age 12. This statute was initiated by Empress Maria Theresa in 1775 for both boys and girls. More recently, the School Law of 1962 has made it mandatory that children attend school for nine years, upon which point they enter tracks—an academic track or a vocational track.

Burkina Faso. Children of Burkina Faso are expected to attend school from ages seven to 14, which comprises mostly primary school grades and some middle-school grades. Although these grades are compulsory, attendance is often not taken and is therefore not enforced by school authorities. One major obstacle for Burkinabé children is a language barrier; French is the official language of the country and, therefore, the general form of communication in Burkinabé primary and secondary schools. It is important to note, however, that different Burkinabé families speak different languages and must therefore attempt to master French as the language of instruction.

Bolivia. Despite the growing rate of literacy in Bolivia, illiteracy remains a major obstacle of advancement. As a result of compulsory education, primary school enrollees jumped from slightly over 70 percent in the early 1970s to nearly 90 percent in the early 1990s. Compulsory schooling in Bolivia generally begins when the child reaches six years and ends after a five-year cycle—at 10 or 11 years of age.

China. Primary education in the People's Republic of China lasts for approximately six years, from ages six to 12. Both primary and intermediate, or middle school, education (approximately three years) in China is compulsory—thus conforming to the so-called nine-year system. This nine-year plan was developed as a means of eradicating illiteracy throughout the country. By 2000 nearly 75 percent of the primary school-age population had completed primary school. By 2010 it is estimated that the percentage increased to nearly 90 percent.

Cuba. Primary education in Cuba begins when children reach age five and lasts for six years until age 11. Based on a Marxist-Leninist educational tradition, Cuban primary school supports and advocates educational inclusion of all Cuban citizens. Likewise, the Cuban government condemns and disapproves of capitalist influence of any kind in primary and secondary grade levels. Primary school students of all ages and both genders are required to dress in school uniforms, which identify grade level based on uniform color. By age 12 primary education students begin their initial three years of secondary education schooling.

Estonia. Primary schooling in Estonia is compulsory and lasts for six years from first grade through sixth. All children must attend school for nine years (grades 1 through 9). Even children of parents who are not citizens are required to attend school during this period. The official language in schools is Estonian (not Russian), and there are approximately 175 days in the Estonian academic year.

Haiti. As the poorest country in the Western Hemisphere, Haiti has had to grapple with a regrettable literacy rate among its children and adults. Prior to the January 2010 earthquake that devastated the lives of nearly all citizens, primary education in Haiti was essentially a privilege and not a right. Therefore, primary education was not compulsory as it is in most other countries. In Haiti current initiatives mandate an extensive overhaul of the Haitian educational system in order to provide free schooling for all its students. At present, over 90 percent of all educational institutions with an infrastructure are privately run. If successful, this large endeavor is projected to be in full operation by 2025 or shortly thereafter.

Jordan. Primary education in Jordan involves 10 years of compulsory schooling. Children begin primary education at age five years, eight months and continue to age 16. The content is broad and comprises general academic areas of study, social interaction, emotional interaction, and physical education. Jordan also monitors students who excel in various subjects for enrollment in special schools that cater to high achievers. All educational stages are free for Jordanian citizens, but only primary education is compulsory.

New Zealand. Education in New Zealand is compulsory for students between the ages of six and 16. At the same time, older students up to the age of 19 also have a right to attend school. Students between the ages of five and 11 attend primary school (grades 1 to 6). New Zealand also offers a "full primary school" model that includes grades 1 to 8 (ages five to 13). School levels in New Zealand are determined by the year (from 1 to 13). Essentially, years 1 through

6 constitute primary school, 7 and 8 intermediate school, and 9 through 13 secondary school.

Peru. In Peru primary education is compulsory and requires students between the ages of six through 11 to attend school. Primary education is divided into two parts: one four-year period and a second two-year period. The Peru Ministry of Education maintains that the goal of primary education is to develop critical and independent thinking in addition to the instruction of content in science, language, civics, mathematics, and physical education. In addition, vocational subjects are provided for students who are leaning toward nonacademic careers, especially in the last two-year segment of study.

Russia. Compulsory education in Russia lasts from age six to 15. The first level of primary school lasts for four years (ages six to 10). Upon completion of primary school, students enter what is known as "basic general secondary school," the duration of which is five years (ages 10 to 15). During the Soviet period, primary (and secondary) education was much more centralized than it is at the present time. It was primarily based on a Marxist-Leninist approach to curriculum that emphasized a communist ideology. During the period of perestroika and into the 1990s, schools underwent a system of restructuring that proved difficult to accomplish. Financial difficulties and demographic changes are the primary reasons why school restructuring has become a difficult task.

Tanzania. Primary education in Tanzania is the only compulsory period. Students must attend primary school for seven years, from about the age of seven to age 14 or 15. In 2000 the percentage of primary school students was slightly over 50 percent of all eligible schoolchildren. By 2005 nearly 90 percent had completed the fifth grade, and the majority of primary school students finished the seven-year compulsory period. One important reason for the increase in completion is that tuition for primary schools was removed in 2002.

United Kingdom. All children in England and Wales must attend school between the ages of five and 16. In Northern Ireland, all children must begin formal schooling at age four. Although the required age range for students in Scotland is the same as for England and Wales, education in Scotland is run by the Scottish regional government. The duration of primary education in the United Kingdom is approximately seven years.

United States. Primary education in the United States most frequently begins at age five or six. In many school districts throughout the country, kindergarten is mandatory, but compulsory schooling technically commences with first grade. Primary school most often ends with the end of the sixth-grade academic year, but also may end in certain instances in the fourth or fifth grade. In general, education in the United States is under the authority of state governance and not a federal matter. However, with the institutionalization of so-called education czars and the official office of the secretary of education, the federal government usurped some of the states' responsibilities.

Comparisons and Conclusions of Primary Education in Sample

In general, most of the countries in the sample, regardless of economic development, have made primary education compulsory. What differs, however, is the age at which students are required to enter and graduate from primary school. Another difference concerns the graduation and attrition rates in each of the countries mentioned above. Countries with a long-standing history of public education generally have much higher graduation rates than those with a shorter history. The contrast between the primary education systems of the United States and Haiti provide a clear example of this phenomenon.

What Is to Be Learned in the Primary Education Years?

It should be self-evident that no standard curriculum exists for primary schools throughout the world. It is also fair to say that no single country has a consistent curriculum that all of its schools follow. Nevertheless, it is highly probable that the most common goal of curricula among all ministries of education worldwide is to prepare students to learn how to read, write, and speak in the official language of a country. It is interesting to note that many school systems do not prepare students to learn the grammar and syntax of their native language. For example, there are more than 3 million native speakers of Makua, a language spoken in northern Mozambique. Nevertheless, children who attend formal primary school in Mozambique are required to learn Portuguese—the official language of the country. In another instance, although some 10 different languages are spoken in Tanzania, the country's educational ministry has made an effort to prepare students for written and spoken language learning only in Swahili and English; unfortunately, the remaining eight languages are not emphasized in most Tanzanian formal primary schools. In Finland, although the overwhelming majority of the population learns Finnish, the native tongue, Swedish is also taught in the schools, notwithstanding the fact that only a bit less than 500,000 of the country's 5.2 million people (about 10 percent) speak Swedish.

Aside from language, mathematics is a common subject that is introduced in formal primary schools throughout the world. Again, this is not to say that all education ministries emphasize the learning of mathematics. In fact, most students of primary school in developing countries—particularly in certain countries of Africa and Asia—tend to achieve a modicum of skill in language development with little to no emphasis at all in mathematical or quantitative skills.

Children of wealthy families who live in notoriously poor countries have opportunities, unlike their less fortunate peers, to travel to other parts of the world to study various subjects that are not offered in the mother country. In addition to socioeconomic status, gender, too, plays an important role in terms of privilege. In poor nations, girls have fewer opportunities to attend formal schooling than do boys. However, girls are becoming increasingly educated in developing countries compared to past decades.

Daniel Ness and Chia-ling Lin

REFERENCES

British Council. "UK Education Systems." www.britishcouncil. org.

Bureau of Democracy, Human Rights, and Labor. *2009 Human Rights Report: Tanzabia*. Washington, DC: US Department of Labor, 2009.

Fleish, Brahm. *Primary Education in Crisis: Why South African Schoolchildren Underachieve in Reading and Mathematics*. Claremont, South Africa: Juta, 2008.

Gasperini, Lavinia. *The Cuban Education System: Lessons and Dilemmas*. Country Studies: Education Reform and Management Publication Series 1:5 (2000). ERIC Clearinghouse Document No. 454117.

Independent Evaluation Group. "Case Study: Peru." http://ieg. worldbankgroup.org.

Library of Congress. *Country Profile: Haiti*. Washington, DC: Library of Congress, 2006.

Medwell, Jane. *Organizing the Primary Curriculum and the Primary Classroom*. New York: Routledge Falmer, 2010.

UNESCO Institute for Statistics. *Education Counts: Benchmarking Progress in 19 WEI Countries: World Education Indicators–2007*. Montreal: UNESCO, 2007.

SECONDARY EDUCATION

Secondary education is the second compulsory education period for most students throughout the world. It is a generally considered to be the period of education between the last year of primary education—usually a preadolescent grade—and the end of the last compulsory year of education, usually but not always the twelfth grade.

Entrance to Formal Secondary Education

As for age or grade of attendance, secondary education is similar to primary education in that one point of entrance or exit is clear. The two are different in that the point of entry is clear for primary school students while the point of entry for secondary school students is not. The point of exit or graduation for secondary school students is clear, but this is not so consistent for primary school students. Most, but not all, secondary education institutions graduate their students generally after 12 years of schooling. For those countries where secondary education is not compulsory, graduation from primary education usually occurs after fifth or sixth grade—so long as students are able to read and possibly write in the official language and possibly do some math. Although the point of graduation is fairly consistent for secondary school students, namely, the twelfth grade, there is some lack of consistency. One of the causes concerns a rate of attrition. In many countries, especially developing nations, attrition rates, particularly in secondary school, range from low levels to extremely high levels.

Sample Representation of Countries

Below is a description of compulsory secondary education in 15 sample countries and is based on multiple factors—one factor does not outweigh any other factor. Countries selected differ in terms of economic development (i.e., developing or developed), population, and geographic region, among other factors.

Australia. Secondary education in Australia represents a somewhat unique position among the countries of the world because it is comparable with the United States, and not many others, in that the institution of education is the responsibility of the Australian states. Australian secondary education differs, however, from the US model in that each state has its own laws determining the age at which a student can enter secondary school and, more interestingly, graduate and matriculate into tertiary levels of education. Three Australian states—New South Wales, Queensland, and Tasmania—serve as examples. Secondary education in New South Wales is "typical" in the sense that it is most comparable with most states in the United States; secondary grade levels range from grade 7 to grade 12. Northern Territory's system is comparable to that of New South Wales, but contains a so-called middle school component. Queensland differs slightly in that secondary education does not begin until the eighth grade. Secondary education in Tasmania is most interesting in that although students begin their secondary programs in seventh grade, they can matriculate to college after the tenth, as opposed to the twelfth, grade. Approximately two-thirds of all secondary schools in Australia are public in the sense that they are government-run. The remaining schools are private or independent. A large proportion of private high schools are parochial, mostly Catholic.

Brazil. Secondary education in Brazil is unique in that it lasts for three years, and it is one of the few secondary school systems in which students do not take national exit examinations. College entrance is based on student grades and transcripts, among other curricular and noncurricular factors. In recent decades, the Brazilian government seems to have made an attempt to make secondary education universal, so that children of lower socioeconomic levels can receive a college education. In the 1990s, secondary education enrollment nearly doubled from 3.5 million students to nearly 7 million students. In 2001 the Brazilian government established a law called *Diretrizes e Bases* (Directives and Bases), which made the curriculum more flexible so that students with a variety of backgrounds and contexts can be directed into certain disciplines and professions in which they excel.

Cameroon. Despite the rather poor adult literacy rate (68 percent), the primary and secondary education system in Cameroon is somewhat more advanced than in neighboring countries. Nevertheless, most Cameroonian secondary education requires tuition payments and is not fully compulsory. There are both Francophone and Anglophone divisions of secondary education in Cameroon. In the Anglophone group, secondary education is approximately eight years, from ages 12 through 17, with an upper secondary school period for students aged 18 and 19. In the Francophone group, students attend the first part of secondary school for four years (ages 12 through 15), upon which they receive the *Brevet d'Etudes du premier Cycle*, an award for completing the first four years. The second part lasts for three years (ages 16 through 18 or 19), at which time they receive the *Baccalauréat*. Both the Francophone and Anglophone systems prepare students for both academic and technical careers. One major obstacle that still exists, however, is that the gross enrollment ratios are rather low (32 percent), even for an educationally progressive country such as Cameroon.

Ecuador. Education in Ecuador is compulsory for nine years, usually between the ages of six and 15. Although primary education is entirely compulsory, secondary level grades are compulsory depending on the region or district. Generally, the lower three grades of secondary school are mandatory while the upper three are not, thus making grades 1 through 6 (primary) and grades 7, 8, and 9 compulsory. As a developing country, Ecuador is in the process of revitalizing its educational infrastructure. In previous decades, enrollment ratios dropped significantly when comparing grades 1 through 5 with grades 6 through 10. This indicates that few Ecuadorians completed secondary education and even fewer attended college or the university. Private secondary education accounts for over 20 percent of all the secondary schools in Ecuador, thus demonstrating its impact in countries where secondary education is not entirely compulsory.

Germany. In Germany all students must attend school through age 18. *Grundschule*, or primary schooling, lasts for six years, hence six grade levels. Germany is most well known for its multitrack secondary education system. In general, the German secondary school system consists of three tracks:

Gymnasium, Hauptschule, and *Realschule.* The *Gymnasium* prepares students for a rigorously academic college or university education or for a polytechnic institute for students interested in engineering and architecture. Students are often trained in the so-called classics; they learn Greek and Latin, as well as other foreign languages, in addition to mathematics, physical sciences, and social sciences. *Gymnasium* students generally finish their *Arbitur,* or final exams, at the end of their twelfth-grade year.

The *Hauptschule,* in contrast to the *Gymnasium,* prepares students who plan to work in a trade profession or vocation. *Hauptschule* students usually complete their studies by the end of tenth grade. Curriculum in the *Hauptschule* is similar to the *Gymnasium,* but often not as demanding and much more focused on vocational skills. Scholars and educational advocates in the international community have criticized the German educational system on grounds of segregating students of recent immigrants and ill preparing them in language, thus barring them from entrance into the prestigious *Gymnasium.* Nevertheless, students whose grades improve may have the opportunity to switch to the *Gymnasium* in the earlier secondary grades.

The third track in the German secondary school system is the *Realschule.* This type of school was an offshoot of the empiricist philosophical movement that emphasized the importance of empirical knowledge over rationalism. Accordingly, the *Realschule* focuses on preparing students for professions that require a modicum of mathematics and sciences, particularly the banking and health professions. Students must also take a foreign language, usually French or English, and one or more of the social sciences, most often economics. The final examination for the *Realschule* is given at the end of the tenth grade.

Lithuania. Schooling in Lithuania is compulsory from age six to 16. This compulsory period includes four years of primary education (grades 1 through 4) and six years of lower secondary education (grades 5 through 10). However, students who are college-bound will continue for an additional two years in their secondary studies (to the age of 18). After 1989, Lithuania began educational reforms. Since 2003 it has maintained its form of education described above. Nevertheless, other educational structures exist as well, such as the option of entering the four-year *gymnasium* as a transition from the first levels of secondary school.

Iceland. Secondary school in Iceland consists of two parts: lower secondary school and upper secondary school. Lower secondary school is compulsory and consists of grades 8 through 10 (approximately ages 13 to 15 years). Often, but not in all situations, the lower secondary school is attached to, or a part of, the primary school. Upper secondary school consists of four types: grammar schools, industrial-vocational schools, comprehensive schools, and specialized vocational schools. Grammar schools prepare college-bound candidates. Industrial-vocational schools prepare students interested in high-skill professions, such as engineering or medicine. The comprehensive school is for the most part a hybrid between the grammar school and the industrial-vocational school. The specialized vocational school accommodates students interested in everyday skills that do not require higher education. The age range for the upper secondary system is 16 to 20 years.

Libya. Like many national school systems, Libya's educational program consists of nine years of compulsory education—six years of primary school and three years of junior or middle school. It is important to note that the enrollment ratio for both primary and secondary education is roughly the same—over 700,000 students in each—which signifies that attrition levels are relatively low. The second level of secondary education, namely, for students between the ages of 15 and 18, consists of two tracks. The first track is a general education track that prepares students for the university. The second track prepares students for technical schools, vocational schools, teacher training schools, agricultural and industrial institutions, and the like.

Mexico. Compulsory education in Mexico is only six years. The educational system in Mexico is somewhat puzzling, possibly due to inconsistencies in governance. In general, the order of schooling structures is the following: preschool, which is federally funded for four- and five-year-old children; *primaria,* which consists of grades 1 through 6, and is compulsory; middle grades (grades 7 to 9), which is divided into three school types, namely, *secundarias, tecnicas,* and *telesecundarias;* and high school (grades 10 to 12), which consists of two general school types, namely, *preparatorias* and *bachilleratos,* and *tecnologicas* and *comercios.*

Regarding the middle grades, *secundarias* are schools that enroll mostly urban students who intend to continue to the high school that prepares them for a university education. *Tecnicas* are schools that provide vocational education for students who do not intend to go to college. Like the *tecnicas*, the *telesecundarias* are schools for non-college-bound students who mostly live in rural areas of Mexico. Curriculum instruction is often televised due to the difficulty in hiring teachers. Regarding the high school grades, *preparatorias* and *bachilleratos* are schools that prepare students who intend to go to college or the university. Curricula in these schools focus on mathematics and physics, chemical and biological sciences, economics and other social sciences, and disciplines within the humanities. *Tecnologicas* and *comercios* prepare students for vocational occupations.

Monaco. Monaco is slightly less than 1 square mile in area (slightly over 2 square kilometers). So the number of secondary schools (in addition to primary schools) in the principality is few. These institutions include the Collège Charles III Secondary School, which prepares students for a traditional university education, as well as lycées that prepare students for predominantly professional careers. In Monaco, there is an essential need for students who wish to enter the tourist and hotel industry. The lycées help students prepare for these occupations.

Palestine. The education system in the Palestinian Territories is highly systematized and intense. In order to put Palestinian secondary education in context, it is necessary to identify its place within the framework of the entire system. Children must attend school from grades 1 through 10. None of these grades, however, is defined as "secondary" education. Rather, secondary education is composed of grades 11 and 12, which are not compulsory. For the most part, these two grades are intended to prepare prospective students for college and the university. There is, however, a small number of so-called vocational secondary schools that train students in nonacademic professions.

Somalia. Secondary school in Somalia, which enrolls students between the ages of 15 and 18, consists of four grade levels (after eight grade levels of primary education). Instruction is most often conducted in English. Prior to 1980, fewer than 20 percent of all the students who completed primary grades were able to finish their secondary school education. This percentage has increased since then, but a poor economy, war, and other forms of social upheaval seem to have stifled educational progress in Somalia. Students who continue their secondary studies enroll in several subjects, including mathematics, the physical sciences, Arabic, English, and a variety of social sciences, which include geography, economics, and history. Students engage in physical education; however, this subject is not required in most Somali high schools.

South Korea. Compulsory education in the Republic of Korea (i.e., South Korea) consists of six years of primary education and at least three years of secondary education. There is a second level of secondary education that lasts for two to three years for students who wish to attend the university. The first three years of secondary school consists of middle school, whose content is very rigorous. The age range for middle school is from 12 or 13 years old to 15 or 16. Academic performance at the middle school grade levels will determine which route and career path that students will take. The high school in South Korea is based on a track system whereby students select a school based on their abilities and interests. For example, a student who performs well in the sciences will more than likely attend a science high school. A student who exceeds in the humanities and the arts will most likely attend a high school whose curriculum focuses on these subjects. For the most part, Korean tertiary education from a curricular standpoint extends the content of the specialized high schools. In other words, students often continue to a college or university that specializes in a particular area—for example, a polytechnic university, the national university (usually the most prominent in the country), a normal university (i.e., teachers college), or a trade and vocational school. This model is common in other countries in East Asia and the Pacific Rim, including Japan, Singapore, and Taiwan.

Swaziland. The secondary education system in Swaziland is currently in a developing stage due to the fact that only about one in five students who complete their primary education are eligible to continue on to secondary school. In general, primary school is compulsory whereas secondary school is not. Students in primary school must at the very least pass the Swaziland Primary Certificate Exam to be considered for secondary school. Moreover, secondary school requires tuition and fees for books and expenses. Many students, in fact, must live in dormitory facilities at or near the school. Most Swazi secondary schools focus on a liberal arts curriculum, while some include a modicum of vocational and trade curriculum.

Tajikistan. Compulsory schooling in Tajikistan is nine years. The Tajik Ministry of Education, for the most part, kept a large part of the foundation of the former Soviet school system, which emphasized mathematics and the natural sciences. However, in order to accommodate to Tajik culture, the ministry made some educational reforms to both primary and secondary schools. Primary education last four years and is followed by what is referred to as general basic education. Basic education is the first level of secondary education, which consists of five years. Hence, with the four-year primary requirement, Tajik students must complete nine years of education. After this point, Tajik students who pass the general basic tests have the opportunity to ender general secondary school for two years prior to tertiary-level education. General secondary education in Tajikistan is often conducted in English and is mostly one of two types of institutions: gymnasia (schools that integrate most forms of academic and polytechnic studies) or lyceums (schools that focus primarily on academic studies). Students who do not follow this educational route are encouraged to enter one of three levels of professional education, which trains them for various vocations and professions.

Comparisons and Conclusions of Secondary Education Sample

For the most part, in terms of compulsory education, it is difficult to generalize about the secondary education systems of the countries in the sample. It is possible to generalize that the ages at which students are required to enter and graduate from secondary school differ considerably from one nation to another. One consistent theme throughout, however, is that countries with relatively stable public education histories generally have much higher graduation rates than those with shorter histories.

What Is to Be Learned in the Secondary Education Years?

No standard curriculum exists for secondary schools throughout the world. Likewise, no single country has a consistent curriculum that all of its schools follow. Unlike primary school, which most often prepares students to read, write, and speak in the official language of a country, the role of secondary education is somewhat different. The goals of most countries' secondary education programs are two-fold: preparation for tertiary education (i.e., college or the university level), or preparation for a trade or profession.

Further, just as in primary education practices throughout the world, secondary school students, particularly in developing countries, are often not educated in the grammar and syntax of their native language. For example, there are more than 3 million native speakers of Makua in Mozambique, many of whom are either not taught language formally or taught Portuguese, the country's official language. In fact, most teachers in secondary schools in the developing nations of Africa and in regions of Asia instruct their students in the so-called official language of the specific country's previous colonizer (e.g., Portuguese in Mozambique, Brazil, and Macau; French in Benin; Dutch in Angola; Spanish in Mexico).

Secondary education throughout the world also differs from lower-level education in that the content is more diverse and generally more rigorous. The subject of natural science, for example, is divided into different types of natural sciences—botany, chemistry, biology, physics, earth and marine science, and astronomy. Some high schools, particularly private institutions, divide the so-called social studies into many categories: history, social science (sociology), psychology, anthropology, geography, and economics. In addition, some elite secondary schools provide either mandatory or elective courses in the so-called classical languages and the fine and performing arts.

Finally, children of affluent families, regardless of citizenship, have greater opportunities to excel in their education than students whose families' incomes are near or below the poverty line. In addition to socioeconomic status, students' gender, race, ethnicity, and sexual orientation can affect their educational outcomes. A society that condones prejudices based on one or more of these factors will adversely affect the educational outcomes of its citizens. In recent years, there has been a slight increase in tolerance regarding these factors. Nevertheless, all societies have much more to do to increase the potentials of all members of society.

Daniel Ness and Chia-ling Lin

REFERENCES

Ajab Amin, Aloysius, and Wilfred J. Awung. "Economic Analysis of Private Returns to Investment in Education in Cameroon." In *Developing a Sustainable Economy in Cameroon*, ed. A. Ajab Amin, 219–234. Dakar, Senegal: Council for the Development of Social Science Research in Africa.

Australian Government Department of Immigration and Citizenship. *What Is the Australian Education System?* www.immi.gov.au.

Di Gropello, Emanuela. *Meeting the Challenges of Secondary Education in Latin America and East Asia: Improving Efficiency and Resource Mobilization*. Washington, DC: World Bank, 2006.

Iceland Ministry of Education, Science, and Culture. http://eng.menntamalaraduneyti.is.

Korean Ministry of Education, Science, and Technology. http://english.mest.go.kr.

Kouega, J.P. "Promoting French-English Individual Bilingualism Through Education in Cameroon." *Journal of Third World Studies* 22 (2005): 185–196.

McCowan, Tristan. "Expansion Without Equity: An Analysis of Current Policy on Access to Higher Education in Brazil." *Higher Education* 53:5 (2007): 579–598.

McLaughlin, H. James. *Schooling in Mexico: A Brief Guide for U.S. Educators*. Washington, DC: ERIC, 2002.

Ministry of Education of the Republic of Tajikistan. *National Strategy for Education Development of the Republic of Tajikistan*. Dushanbe, Tajikistan: Ministry of Education of the Republic of Tajikistan, 2005.

Nicolai, Susan. *Fragmented Foundations: Education and Chronic Crisis in the Occupied Palestinian Territory*. Paris: UNESCO International Institute for Educational Planning and Save the Children UK, 2007.

Zorrilla, Juan F. "Anomie and Education: The Politics of Innovation in a Mexican High School." In *Educational Qualitative Research in Latin America: The Struggle for Paradigm*, ed. Gary L. Anderson and Martha Montero-Sieburth, 117–135. New York: Garland, 1998.

TERTIARY EDUCATION

Tertiary education is the third formal education period, after primary education and secondary education. It is generally the period of education that a student pursues after graduating from a secondary school system—usually at age 16, 17, or 18, or at the end of the twelfth grade. Unlike nearly all primary education systems and most secondary education systems, tertiary education is not compulsory.

However, in most postindustrial countries—such as Australia, Canada, New Zealand, the United States, most countries in Europe, and most countries in the Pacific Rim—students are strongly urged to enter college or university and are frequently compelled, either by family or by economy, to enter some type of formal education after the twelfth grade of high school. The acquisition of a tertiary education degree, such as an associate's degree, baccalaureate, master's degree, or doctorate, increases human capital—that is, the knowledge, ability, and personal attributes that people need in order to increase the economic value of a given nation's system.

Entrance to Tertiary Education Institutions

The beginning of tertiary education is clear—namely, upon graduation from secondary school. However, high-achieving students frequently take college-level courses as a means of earning college credit before high school graduation.

It is also important to consider that the last grade level in secondary education differs considerably depending on the tertiary institution. For students entering traditional higher education institutions, the standard terminal secondary school level is the twelfth grade. For those seeking higher education institutions that specialize in vocations and trades, many countries require these students to complete tenth grade before they enter the vocational school. The United States offers an interesting contrast to countries with track systems in that nearly every state requires completion of 12 grade levels before college level, regardless of the student's academic level or potential.

Types of Tertiary Education Institutions

There are many types of tertiary education institutions. Traditionally, tertiary education meant college- or university-level education. However, during the twentieth century, the definition of tertiary education broadened considerably. Many European systems, notably the education system of Germany, instituted track systems, whereby students entered a field of study based on both interest and ability. In the early years of tracking, students capable of rigorous academic performance would enter a traditional academic secondary school (called a "gymnasium" in Germany and other European nations) in preparation for a university education, whereas those who did not pass exit examinations at the primary education levels or did not persist in strong academic achievement would exit the primary level and engage in a vocation that either required schooling that terminated at the secondary level or did not require additional schooling at all. During the twentieth century, however, particularly after World War II, much changed with regard to postprimary schooling. Tertiary institutions were at this point major players at the higher education levels.

Colleges

The origin of the word "college" comes from the Latin *collegium*, which means "gathering together." The term "colleague" too has its origins in the notion of a specified gathering. "College" eventually came to refer to the meeting place for the education of clergy and future leaders. Over the centuries, the term was associated with a campus where elite students, usually males, had the opportunity to learn the classics, law, and possibly religion in preparation for privileged positions in society. At present, the term "college" has multiple meanings. Some colleges are part of a university. Other colleges stand alone as separate autonomous entities. In either case, a college generally offers baccalaureate and sometimes master's degrees, but seldom, if ever, doctorates. Many, but not all, present-day universities in the United Kingdom and the United States began as colleges but, perhaps with later influence from the traditionally research-oriented German university model, developed into universities.

Universities

The university is considered the largest institution of higher education. Like colleges, universities grant both undergraduate and graduate degrees. The first universities were established in the late eleventh to early thirteenth centuries, in Bologna as early as 1080, and then in Paris, Oxford, Cambridge, and Salamanca. The primary reasons for the establishment of universities were, first, to reassimilate content knowledge that had been lost upon the fall of Rome and, second, to use this knowledge as part of a scholastic curriculum that combined Christian theology with classic philosophy in line with the subjects of the trivium (grammar, rhetoric, and logic) and quadrivium (arithmetic, geometry, astronomy, and music). Early university personnel intended to revive the works and study of the ancient Greek philosophers Pythagoras, Plato, and Aristotle; ancient Greek poets, playwrights, and historians, including Homer, Aeschylus, Sophocles, and Euripides; and famous Roman writers such as Cicero, Virgil, Ovid, and Livy. The early universities also investigated the sciences, particularly as it applied to medicine. The university became the vehicle through which new knowledge became reintegrated into Western society. In addition, the precedent of academic freedom began with the early universities; scholars were generally not brought up on charges of heresy, especially if they belonged to a university.

Most (but not all) competitive and elite universities today generally share the model of the early university. Although accommodating themselves to greater scientific discovery, universities have maintained the liberal arts education, which essentially evolved from the trivium and quadrivium. Most universities are complex conglomerates of several colleges that emphasize different disciplines and award different degrees.

Polytechnic Institutes

Polytechnic institutes emerged in the nineteenth century as an alternative to the traditional university. Engineering programs, traditionally housed in military institutions, such as West Point or the Virginia Military Institute, were created along with programs in physics and mathematics in newly established private institutions, such as the Massachusetts Institute of Technology (MIT) and, later, the California Institute of Technology (Cal Tech). In the twentieth century, these institutions were funded by the federal government to assist in several war efforts, from World War I to the war in Vietnam. Today polytechnic institutes enroll young men and women in countries throughout the world, including Argentina, Canada, China, France, Germany, Iran, Israel, Italy, Japan, Pakistan, Russia, Singapore, Taiwan, Turkey, and the United Kingdom. At present, these institutions still represent the so-called cutting edge of scientific research.

Normal Schools and Teachers Colleges

The term "normal school" is essentially synonymous with "teachers college"; both are educational institutions whose mission is to prepare teachers to work in both public and private schools throughout the world. Normal schools were traditionally institutions in the United States and Europe that emerged in the middle of the nineteenth century for the purpose of training future teachers to educate the rapidly growing masses of children who, before this point, did not receive formal education. At present, normal schools are common in most countries throughout the world. In Taiwan, for example, normal schools prepare students to become teachers, usually in secondary schools, in the discipline of interest (e.g., mathematics, biology, chemistry, language). The primary school equivalent is the primary normal school. Taiwanese normal schools eventually developed into teachers colleges with a liberal arts component. In Canada and the United States, teachers colleges are most often affiliated with or attached to universities. In most European countries, the teachers college is a form of tertiary education that serves as one of several tracks of study.

Community Colleges

The community college is an American invention, and the majority of community colleges are public institutions that award associates degrees. These degrees are designed to be completed within a two-year period; however, given the diversity of experiences and needs of community college students, degree completion can take much longer than two years. Although the first community college, Joliet Junior College, in Joliet, Illinois, was established in 1901, the overwhelming majority of community colleges were established between the 1950s and 1970s, mostly to accommodate World War II and Korean War veterans, as well as a growing number of students who are the first in their families to attend college. In the United States, there are currently over 1,000 community colleges. Between 1974 and 2007, there was a 17 percent increase in the number of community colleges established. Countries that followed the United States in establishing community colleges include Australia, Canada, Malaysia, the Philippines, and the United Kingdom.

In general, community colleges have four essential missions. (1) Many students enroll in a community college for two years intending to transfer to a four-year traditional college or university. Community colleges, then, serve the purpose of educating these students in traditional subjects taught at the four-year baccalaureate level. (2) Developmental education offers remedial courses for both college students (for many of whom English or the official language is not the language spoken in the home) and high school students who are preparing for college. (3) Career education and training enables students who do not necessarily have academic inclinations to gain skills in vocational careers. In this case, the community college serves as an alternative to the vocational school. (4) Finally, continuing education serves the community or region at large by offering mostly noncredit courses that emphasize personal interests (such as courses in yoga, health and first aid, painting, or swimming).

Vocational and Trade Schools

Vocational and trade schools, which appear in nearly all countries throughout the world, are two related forms of tertiary educational institutions that prepare students for professional trades that do not require a traditional liberal arts education. Students do not necessarily need baccalaureate or graduate degrees in order to become skilled in a particular trade. Vocational schools prepare students for both blue-collar and white-collar trades and vocations, such as artisan work; business and administration; paralegal jobs; machinist, plumbing, and electrician jobs; forestry; nursing; catering; and information technology.

Rather than granting degrees, vocational schools generally provide licenses or a similar type of accrediting certificate to indicate that a graduate is skilled in a particular vocation. Besides the numerous vocational institutions in the United States, public and private community colleges and for-profit institutions have shared the role of preparing students for vocations.

For-Profit Colleges and Universities

For-profit colleges and universities pride themselves on the idea that anyone who enrolls can obtain a baccalaureate, master's degree, or doctorate. Their stakeholders contribute millions of dollars for advertisements highlighting the institution's technologies and practitioner-oriented instructors. For-profit colleges and universities include the Apollo Group Inc., which runs the University of Phoenix; Capella Education Company, which controls Capella University; Education Management Corporation, which runs Argosy University; DeVry University; and Sylvan Learning Systems Inc., which controls Walden University. Although for-profit institutions have been popularized in the United States for the past two decades, they are growing entities in other countries as well, most notably the Philippines.

Despite the seemingly promising future of for-profit institutions, their current role as players in the realm of higher education appears to be diminishing, especially in highly volatile economies. Their possibly tenuous future in higher education has to do with a number of factors that seem to have worked against each other—tuition costs, poor global economies at various point in time, and the degree that these schools offer. Tuition costs at for-profit institutions are often comparable to those of traditional colleges, universities, technological institutions, teachers colleges, and the like. During periods of economic recession, the hiring committees of businesses and industries, especially those that are not affiliated with for-profit institutions, tend to reject job candidates who hold for-profit college or university degrees in favor of applicants with traditional higher education degrees. As a result, because for-profit institution graduates have difficulty in finding employment, a majority of them will find it burdensome, if not difficult, to pay their student loans. Some researchers even predict that this situation is contributing to a subprime education crisis (a term taken from the subprime mortgage crisis that began in 2008), thus leading to a for-profit education bubble. The global economic downturn in 2009 and 2010 demonstrates this emerging trend.

Present and Future of Tertiary Education

There is no question that the number of students with postsecondary degrees from tertiary institutions is on the rise worldwide. The seminal issue that a number of educators and researchers are contemplating, however, is the extent to which traditional tertiary education—the traditional liberal arts education at the college or university level—increases potential and human capital and thereby fosters the success of world economies. In the United States, for example, nearly 55 percent of the population receives a so-called traditional college education. It is difficult to determine, however, whether all those who do receive this education have equal potential. Educators, researchers, and political educational advocates in all nations may need to question the viability of tertiary education for all citizens. Rather than equalizing educational attainment for everyone, educators, researchers, and policy makers may need to consider equality in salary for all forms of labor as an alternative and more favorable outcome.

Tertiary education in developing countries often has low enrollment and high attrition rates, largely due to students' family circumstances, lack of funds for tuition, and need to find employment. Low enrollment figures seem to indicate that many of these countries need to consider the role of women in higher education. Although the situation has improved somewhat within the last 20 years, men still outnumber women, particularly in countries in the Middle East and North Africa, in tertiary education attendance and graduation. Another problem with both secondary education and tertiary education is lack of resources and technology. When these institutions have comparable resources in quality and in quantity to institutions in developed countries, they will be able to compete in the global market.

Another important issue to consider is the ever-changing forms of knowledge and, hence, occupations that will be needed in the future. Evolving technologies and new research will necessitate new forms of employment that today might seem unthinkable. Predictions of new areas of expertise and forms of employment include those in the biological sciences and health professions as well as those in the physical sciences and mathematics. Stem cell research, for example, may be one of the new frontiers not only for research but also for medical practice. Tertiary institution administrators and stakeholders will need to address these and related issues if they consider themselves actors within the global economy.

Daniel Ness and Chia-ling Lin

REFERENCES

Cowen, Tyler, and Sam Papenfuss. "The Economics of For-Profit Education." In *Doing More with Less: Making Colleges Work Better*, ed. J.C. Hall, 177–193. New York: Springer, 2010.

Salmi, Jamil. "Constructing Knowledge Societies: New Challenges for Tertiary Education." *Higher Education in Europe* 28:1 (2003): 65–69.

Vaughn, George. B. *The Community College Story*. 3rd ed. Washington, DC: Community College Press, 2006.

Wechsler, Harold S., Lester F. Goodchild, and Linda Eisenmann. *The History of Higher Education*. 3rd ed. Upper Saddle River, NJ: Pearson, 2008.

INTERNATIONAL COMPARISONS IN ACADEMIC SUBJECTS

An international comparison in one or more academic subjects is a device that measures the academic proficiency primarily of a nation's primary and secondary school student population in relationship to other nations. Well-known comparisons include the Trends in International Mathematics and Science Study (TIMSS) and the Programme in International Student Assessment (PISA). International comparisons of adult academic proficiency, such as the Adult Literacy and Lifeskills (ALL) Survey, are also becoming increasingly popular. Although an international comparison is generally used to identify levels of academic proficiency among postindustrial countries throughout the world, the device, nevertheless, has much deeper political implications. For one thing, an international comparison may be illustrative and representative of a nation's awareness of economic progress. Low scores on international rankings in one or more academic subjects can possibly lead to both justifiable and unreasonable internal crisis. Citizens of a given country showing low achievement levels will often identify their ranking in comparison to higher-scoring nations as a cause for alarm.

Historical Background of International Comparisons

The activity of comparing students of different nations in terms of their proficiency in academic sub-jects is a relatively recent phenomenon, popular for perhaps a bit more than two decades; in comparison, the history of formal education for the masses spans about two centuries. During the early part of the Great Depression, the newly inaugurated president of Harvard, James B. Conant, wrote that standardized testing might be the solution for admitting students to universities such as Harvard not solely by their wealth or last name. Given the growing acceptance of intelligence testing at this time, Conant's idea was to devise examinations that would separate people with academic merit from those who simply had privilege. This spawned the standardized achievement test movement.

The overarching purpose of the standardized admissions test was to base students' acceptance to prestigious institutions such as Harvard, Princeton, and Stanford on merit, not on family connections and ties. Since Conant's installation of the college admissions test, the role of high-stakes assessment became increasingly important, eventually making its way to lower grade levels. As a result, certain grade levels became so-called benchmark grade levels because it was at these points in students' schooling that educational administrators believed key academic topics were to be mastered. In most states, the fourth and eighth grades became common benchmark grades.

In addition to the origin of benchmark grade levels, education attainment and curriculum gradually became a crucial agenda for political leaders after the end of World War II. The major impetus for this phenomenon was the Cold War. In competing for dominance, both militarily and psychologically, the United States and the Soviet Union adopted several initiatives that attempted to outdo the other side—either NATO or the Warsaw Pact. The crucial initiative in this postwar period was space exploration. After the Soviet launching of *Sputnik* in 1957, the United States instituted a national mathematics and science curriculum that all states had the option of adopting. Most states eventually did. However, due to the cognitively advanced nature of the content, this curriculum eventually led to generally poor academic performance by the 1970s, causing great alarm among political figures and national educators. By the 1980s, it was determined that students in other countries, particularly in mathematics and the sciences, outperformed students in the United States. This conclusion was determined and confirmed by research studies, particularly those headed by Harold Stevenson, a University of Michigan psychologist that compared academic performance of samples of students from Japan, Germany, and the United States. These events contributed in part to the national publication *A Nation at Risk* in 1983. Since the 1980s, then, international educational comparisons have become increasingly fashionable in the field of international education studies.

A Sample of International Comparisons

Perhaps the most important organization that has contributed to the collection of international data on educational levels and ability is the National Center for Educational Statistics (NCES). The NCES website provides a listing of most, but not all, of the international comparisons that are used for analysis. The following list describes four international comparisons—TIMMS, PIRLS, CivEd, and PISA—in general terms.

TIMSS

TIMSS is the oldest international comparison study. It is intended to measure mathematics and science ability among fourth- and eighth-grade students in countries throughout the world. TIMSS stands for Trends in International Mathematics and Science Study. However, the original name varied depending on the date that the assessments associated with the Study were administered. The first study, in the 1960s, was actually called FIMSS (the First International Mathematics and Science Study), followed by SIMMS (the Second International Mathematics and Science Study) in the 1980s and finally TIMSS, originally intended as the Third International Mathematics and Science Study in 1995, but then changed to "Trends" for each subsequent study. From that point, TIMSS has been scheduled for four-year periods (1999, 2003, 2007, and 2011).

TIMSS was developed by the International Association for the Evaluation of Educational Achievement, housed at Boston College in Chestnut Hill, Massachusetts, an organization that later developed PIRLS (discussed below). In 2011 the most recent administration of TIMSS, 47 countries participated. TIMSS results are almost always the same: a select number of countries in East Asia at the top of the list (most often Singapore and Hong Kong), followed by a mixture of other countries from this region and Europe (most often Taiwan, Japan, Belgium, South Korea, and the Netherlands), and eventually Canada and then the United States. The major problem with TIMSS is that it generally fails to take multiple factors of achievement into account—most notably, poverty, gender, and ethnic background (which are sometimes correlated with socioeconomic status).

PIRLS

The Progress in International Reading Literacy Study (PIRLS) is administered internationally approximately every five years, beginning in 2001. PIRLS is designed to measure the reading skills of fourth graders from 36 countries throughout the world. Questions in PIRLS measure a variety of skills, including literary experience; acquiring and using information; focusing on and retrieving explicit information and ideas; making inferences; interpreting and integrating ideas and information; and examining and evaluating content, language, and text. Tests are administered in students' native languages. The countries participating in PIRLS are Argentina and Colombia in South America; Belize, Canada, and the United States in North America; Bulgaria, Cyprus, Czech Republic, England, France, Germany, Greece, Hungary, Iceland, Italy, Latvia, Lithuania, Macedonia, Moldova, Netherlands, Norway, Romania, Russia, Scotland, Slovakia, Slovenia, Sweden, and Turkey in Europe; Iran, Israel, and Kuwait in the Middle East; Hong Kong and Singapore in East Asia; Morocco and South Africa in Africa; and New Zealand.

CivEd

CivEd, which stands for Civic Education Survey, is a comparative study that provides information about ninth graders' knowledge of democratic government and civics. Most recently conducted in 1999, CivEd compares results from the United States and 27 other participating countries. In addition to students from the United States, most participants were from Europe—namely, Belgium, Bulgaria, Cyprus, Czech Republic, Denmark, Estonia, Finland, Germany,

Table: **Comparisons of TIMSS Mathematics Scale Scores of Eighth-Grade Students and PISA Mathematics Scale Scores of Students Age 13 by Country, 2003**

TIMSS Rankings			PISA Rankings		
Ranking	Country	Average	Ranking	Country	Average
1	Singapore	605	1	Finland	544
2	South Korea	589	2	South Korea	542
3	Hong Kong	586	3	Netherlands	538
4	Taiwan	585	4	Japan	534
5	Japan	570	5	Canada	532
6	Belgium	537	6	Belgium	529
7	Netherlands	536	7	Switzerland	527
8	Estonia	531	8	Australia	524
9	Hungary	529	9	New Zealand	523
10	Malaysia	508	10	Czech Republic	516
11	Latvia	508	11	Iceland	515
12	Russia	508	12	Denmark	514
13	Slovakia	508	13	Sweden	511
14	Australia	505	14	Austria	506
15	United States	504	15	France	503
16	Lithuania	502	16	Germany	503
17	Sweden	499	17	Ireland	503
18	Scotland	498		**International Average**	500
19	Israel	496	18	Slovakia	498
20	New Zealand	494	19	Norway	495
21	Slovenia	493	20	Luxembourg	493
22	Italy	484	21	Poland	490
23	Armenia	478	22	Hungary	490
24	Serbia	477	23	Spain	485
25	Bulgaria	476	24	United States	483
26	Romania	475	25	Italy	466
	International Average	466	26	Portugal	466
27	Norway	461	27	Greece	445
28	Moldova	460	28	Turkey	423
29	Cyprus	459	29	Mexico	385
30	Lebanon	433			
31	Jordan	424			
32	Iran	411			
33	Indonesia	411			
34	Tunisia	410			
35	Egypt	406			
36	Bahrain	401			
37	Palestinian N.A.	390			
38	Chile	387			
39	Morocco	387			
40	Philippines	378			
41	Botswana	366			
42	Saudi Arabia	332			
43	Ghana	276			
44	South Africa	264			

Note: Countries in italics participated in both studies.

Greece, Hungary, Italy, Latvia, Lithuania, Norway, Poland, Portugal, Romania, Russia, Slovakia, Slovenia, Sweden, Switzerland, and the United Kingdom. Also participating were Australia, Hong Kong, Chile, and Colombia. For the entire pool of students, scores ranged from 53 percent to 83 percent of items answered correctly.

PISA

PISA stands for Programme for International Student Assessment. PISA is an interesting alternative to TIMSS and PIRLS because one of its primary goals is to use data for improving educational systems that have been either nonexistent or disadvantaged in the past. It can be argued, then, that PISA attempts to gauge where international students should be (analogous to criterion referencing) rather than simply comparing how they perform (analogous to norm referencing). PISA, which was developed by the Organization for Economic Cooperation and Development, measures students' performance in reading, mathematics, and science.

In order to appreciate the possibilities of relationships between two different international comparison studies, it is important to find two separate studies that measure similar content in the same subject, for similar grade or age levels, and in the same year of administration. The Table (see page 112) identifies the mathematics scores of all the countries that participated in both the TIMSS 2003 study and the PISA 2003 study. One particular feature that stands out is that students of nearly any given country performed differently on one test when compared with the other. There were 12 different countries that participated in both studies in 2003 (e.g., see the two scores for the United States, New Zealand, or Hungary).

The Figure shows correlations among the 12 countries whose students participated in both studies. The correlation is mixed. In other words, it is not very strong, but not too weak either ($r = .67$). This means that countries whose students participated in both studies had TIMSS scores that did not always match the corresponding PISA scores. Again, Hungary, New Zealand, and the United States are good examples. Moreover, when comparing the international averages in both studies, there is quite a disparity (466 for the TIMSS when compared to 500 for the PISA).

International comparisons of students' content knowledge began as a result of a manufactured crisis—in other words, the notion that students of a given country were not performing at a baseline level, which could affect the country's economy, military strength, political dominance, and so forth. The problem is determining whether such a crisis is justified. At present, however, genuine crises in education are those in developing industrial nations where poverty has always been a norm. Nevertheless, international comparisons almost always involve countries with more or less established educational systems, where compulsory education lasts for at least nine or 10 years and a large segment of the population attends tertiary-level institutions. Moreover, international

Figure: **Correlation of Mathematics Scores of Countries That Appear on Both TIMSS 2003 and PISA 2003**

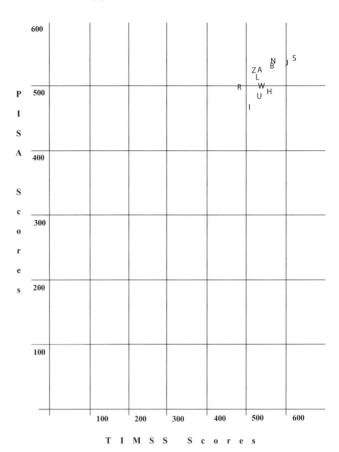

Key:

A	=	Australia	N	=	Netherlands
B	=	Belgium	R	=	Norway
H	=	Hungary	S	=	South Korea
I	=	Italy	U	=	United States
J	=	Japan	W	=	Sweden
L	=	Slovakia	Z	=	New Zealand

Correlation: $r = .67$

South Korea	589	542
Netherlands	536	538
Japan	570	534
Belgium	537	529
Australia	505	524
Hungary	529	490
Slovakia	508	498
United States	504	483
Sweden	499	511
Norway	461	495
New Zealand	494	523
Italy	484	466

comparisons seem to have evolved into a trend, and therefore, no urgency in comparison is needed.

Daniel Ness and Chia-ling Lin

REFERENCES

National Center for Education Statistics. International Activities Program. http://nces.ed.gov/surveys/international/.

———. "The Reading Literacy of U.S. Fourth-Grade Students in an International Context: Results From the 2001 and 2006 Progress in International Reading Literacy Study (PIRLS)." 2007. http://nces.ed.gov/pubsearch.

National Commission on Excellence in Education. *A Nation at Risk: The Imperative for Educational Reform.* Washington, DC: U.S. Department of Education, 1983.

PIRLS. *International Association for the Evaluation of Educational Achievement.* Chestnut Hill, MA: TIMSS & PIRLS International Study Center, 2005.

TIMSS. *International Association for the Evaluation of Educational Achievement.* Chestnut Hill, MA: TIMSS & PIRLS International Study Center, 2005.

ACCREDITATION AND LICENSURE

The notion of formal education implies at least three entities: a school system, which includes a building (or more than one building) with classrooms or perhaps just a single classroom; students, most of whom are between the ages of five and 18, but including some individuals older than 18 as well; and teachers. Accreditation and licensure has to do with teachers, the last of these entities, and the methods that educational ministries or administrations use to determine how they should be prepared in order to be engaged in the business of teaching students.

In order to enter the teaching profession, it should be self-evident that teachers, first and perhaps foremost, should possess knowledge. This knowledge comes in a variety of forms: content knowledge, pedagogical knowledge, pedagogical content knowledge, and knowledge of students from a developmental perspective. First, content knowledge provides students with the tools and strategies that they need to succeed in various disciplines—such as mathematics, history, grammar and writing, and the like. It is important because if the primary goal of schooling is a functional

one—namely, to prepare students for future economic endeavors—then it is essential that students gain the content knowledge and skills that are necessary for workplace success. Second, pedagogical knowledge refers to a teacher's ability to deliver content to students (i.e., to instruct) in ways that increase their success and mastery in comprehension, analysis, and synthesis of knowledge. Third, pedagogical content knowledge demonstrates teachers' overt awareness of actual content and the methods that they need to use to reflect the diversity of knowledge levels of each of their students. This suggests the fourth type of knowledge—that is, knowledge of students from a development perspective. Teachers need to be acutely aware of their students' knowledge, dispositions, strengths, weaknesses, and emotions.

Who should become a teacher? And what method should society use to determine who can become one? Both of these questions are difficult to answer because, unlike an examination in mathematics or history, the task of finding excellence in teaching skills is not quantitative. Rather, it is a highly subjective undertaking. Nevertheless, as formal schooling began to take in the late nineteenth century, especially as urban centers began to grow at exponential rates, political leaders and administrative managers, many of whom never had any experience in educating students, attempted to find methods of assessing teachers' abilities and skills. In the early nineteenth century, nearly all schoolteachers were men. The women's movement at this time emphasized differences—not similarities (as it did in the late twentieth century)—between men and women. The notion that men were "intellectual" and "political" while women were "moral" and "spiritual" contributed to the belief that men were best able to run a business and join the workforce, while women were "best able" to raise children and run the home. But this attitude changed rapidly toward the end of the century, primarily with the development of increasing numbers of normal schools, institutions of higher learning devoted solely to the training and preparation of teachers. Normal schools were eventually called "teachers colleges" by the middle of the twentieth century. When economic conditions ebbed in the late nineteenth century, many women had to work in order for families to make ends meet. As a result, an increasing number of women became teachers, primarily teachers of young students. By the early twentieth century, both men and women became teachers in large numbers, and it became more profitable, in terms of earnings and stability, to graduate from normal schools. These normal schools eventually attached themselves to colleges and universities throughout the United States, later becoming higher educational institutions. By midcentury, normal schools became increasingly popular throughout the world, particularly in Europe and East Asia.

Due to greater profitability, then, increasing numbers of students began to enroll in normal schools and teachers colleges. In the United States, this increase contributed to the decision by policy makers to accredit institutions that graduated the best teacher candidates—that is, the institutions that the policy makers—who may have had little or no teacher training or knowledge of students—believed to be the best. So accreditation became a process by which policy makers give authorization to an institution for the purpose of establishing its official status. It is important to note, however, that accreditation has nothing to do with how well an institution performs or how well teachers perform in their occupation.

Historical Overview of Teacher Accreditation

Accreditation in education is not a new phenomenon. In fact, accreditation of higher education institutions in the United States began shortly after the American Revolution. As early as 1787, even before it achieved statehood, the colony of New York legally had accredited colleges. This procedure served as a precedent for other institutions of higher education, which began to set standards of their own. Generally, college faculty controlled curriculum, instruction, and assessment—until recent decades, when school, college, and university administrators felt the necessity to outsource the process of accreditation. Since the 1980s, accreditation policies have changed. At present, national boards and organizations have assumed the authority of institutions to set their own standards. External agencies dictate policy to most educational institutions—particularly those that are in the business of preparing primary and secondary school teachers—regardless of the institutions' prominence. One common criticism of the officials and functionaries of these outside agencies is that most

of them have little, if any experience in the areas of education research or practice.

As fields of inquiry and professional disciplines emerged and developed, the thrust of the argument in favor of teacher institution accreditation seems to have originated from the putative need for protection from incompetent practitioners. As David Tyack suggests in *The One Best System*, this notion of distinguishing a competent group from an incompetent one seems to have close parallels with the fields of medicine, law, and law enforcement. Given that liberal arts and science institutions were not traditionally involved in teacher preparation, teacher education accreditation was granted only to teachers colleges and normal schools as early as 1927. Shortly after, the American Association of Teachers Colleges issued a set of criteria that teachers colleges throughout the country were asked to follow in order to be considered for membership. Liberal arts institutions began to collaborate with teachers colleges in the training of teachers and teacher educators because they saw this venture as an economic boon. The formation of the American Association of Colleges for Teacher Education (AACTE) in 1948 opened the teacher-training doors to liberal arts colleges and universities. As a result, there was a growing interest in the creation of teacher education standards. On July 1, 1954, the National Council for the Accreditation of Teacher Education (NCATE) was formed by AACTE along with four other administrative organizations. During that time, nearly 300 teachers colleges and liberal arts colleges and universities with schools and programs in education were members of AACTE.

With the launching of *Sputnik* by the Soviet Union in 1957, the US government began to question the rank of American education in comparison to those of other countries. Many policy makers believed that American primary and secondary students were not of the same academic caliber as their Soviet counterparts, especially in the disciplines of mathematics and the earth, physical, and life sciences. This perception caused a great alarm in both political and educational circles. As a result, the federal government began to issue grants to colleges and universities to push mathematics and science content on prospective teachers. Cold War officials clearly wanted to increase the number of mathematicians and physicists so as to compete with the Soviet Union. This funding contributed to what was referred to as the "new-math and science" movement—the period in United States education history from the late 1950s to the early 1980s.

By the late 1970s, it was becoming increasingly clear that fewer teachers than expected were becoming proficient, let alone skillful, in the physical sciences and mathematics. Indeed, students were failing in mathematics and the sciences for at least two reasons: first, the mathematics content in the primary and early secondary years that students needed in order to become adept in physics and chemistry, as well as advanced mathematics, was difficult because the curriculum overlooked the necessity of basic mathematics and science concepts; second, a number of the mathematics and science concepts taught became outdated (e.g., mathematics in bases other than base 10, modular arithmetic, and theories of sets in the early grades).

Teacher accreditation bodies like NCATE were aware of the political and educational debates in the American school system during the 1960s and 1970s. By 1960 AACTE and certain federal policy makers gave NCATE the authority to define teacher education institutions. As Lindley Stiles and James Bils maintain in their article "National Accrediting" (1973), "NCATE had autonomous authority to prescribe what teacher education should be, and there was no due-process procedure by which policies and decisions could be challenged. One by one, colleges and universities preparing teachers were being forced to comply with mandates of the council." During the 1960s, the decade that NCATE was granted this authority, the University of Wisconsin–Madison School of Education challenged external agencies that were given carte blanche to usurp authority from college and university faculty—the very individuals who control curriculum and other internal matters. Accordingly, the School of Education at Madison withdrew from NCATE and has since remained apart from external accreditation agencies. Afterward, many originally NCATE-accredited institutions (e.g., Arizona State University, UCLA, University of Chicago, Boston University, Wayne State University, University of New Hampshire, and University of Northern Iowa) have followed in the footsteps of Madison.

The year 1983 saw the publication of *A Nation at Risk*, a federally published book written by members of education team of William Bennett, the Secretary of Education in the Reagan administration. This publication condemned the American education sys-

tem for avoiding the so-called basics in mathematics and science and therefore attacked the "new math" movement. It also spawned the standards movement, which began in the 1980s and picked up momentum during the administration of George W. Bush. Given its close adherence to education policy cycles (given the Republican administration during the 1980s), NCATE developed nineteen standards for teacher performance, which were eventually trimmed down to six standards in 2000:

Standard 1—   Candidate knowledge, skills, and dispositions
Standard 2—   Assessment system and unit evaluation
Standard 3—   Field experiences and clinical practice
Standard 4—   Diversity
Standard 5—   Faculty qualifications, performance, and development
Standard 6—   Unit governance and resources

Future Prospects

At present, there are two federally recognized teacher education accreditation agencies: NCATE and Teacher Education Accreditation Council (TEAC). Given their general neglect of the constituents—students—whom they should be advocating, accreditation bodies are almost entirely political entities that have historically attempted to usurp as much power as they can from local, regional, and federal legislatures. They have gained more influence in recent years as a result of the No Child Left Behind legislation under George W. Bush and its continuation under the Obama administration. Consequently, educational accrediting bodies have found their niche not only in the United States, but also in many countries throughout the world. NCATE administrators, in fact, have courted political leaders in the United Arab Emirates and other nearby nations of the Middle East. But current evidence regarding the efficacy of teacher education accreditors demonstrates that teachers who graduate from NCATE- or TEAC-accredited institutions are no better or worse than those who have graduated from institutions that are not accredited by external accrediting bodies.

Daniel Ness and Chia-ling Lin

References

Johnson, Dale, Bonnie Johnson, Stephen J. Farenga, and Daniel Ness. *Trivializing Teacher Education: The Accreditation Squeeze.* Lanham, MD: Rowman & Littlefield, 2005.

Lindsey, Margaret. *New Horizons for the Teaching Profession: A Report of the Task Force on New Horizons in Teacher Education and Professional Standards.* Washington, DC: National Education Association of the United States, 1961.

National Commission on Excellence in Education. *A Nation at Risk: The Imperative for Educational Reform.* Washington, DC: U.S. Government Printing Office, 1983.

Stiles, Lindley, and James A. Bils. "National Accrediting." In *New Perspectives on Teacher Education*, ed. Donald J. McCarty. San Francisco: Jossey-Bass, 1973.

Taubman, Peter. *Teaching by Numbers: Deconstructing the Discourse of Standards and Accountability in Education.* New York: Routledge, 2009.

Tyack, David. *The One Best System: A History of American Urban Education.* Cambridge, MA: Harvard University Press, 1974.

Teacher Preparation Around the World

Teacher preparation refers to a method by which an individual is educated and subsequently officially confirmed or certified to teach students. If formal education is the undertaking of a society in schooling its population in organized settings, then there must be two sets of players visible in a schooling system: teachers and students. The teacher's role is to transmit information in the form of knowledge and provide a model of environmentally or culturally appropriate behavior for students. Teacher preparation and training is a subjective area of investigation. Unlike other aspects of formal schooling where it is possible for laypersons and educational researchers to rate or possibly rank different countries' systems of education (such as overall levels of educational achievement), teacher preparation does not allow for such ratings. The question that must be answered, then, is the following: How are teachers prepared in different learning environments? This question assumes that different environments mean different countries or geographic regions with different economic levels of development, among other variations.

The need for preparing individuals to enter the teaching profession stems from the need to educate the masses of students and not simply a privileged few. Before the beginning of the nineteenth century, the so-called teaching profession was not such a complex phenomenon—essentially, if a family had the financial resources, then the children, mostly male children, would have the privilege of becoming formally educated. Teachers were generally private tutors who were college or university graduates. Most of these tutors prepared for professional disciplines, such as the priesthood, law, public service, or teaching. In short, the business of training teachers did not commence until the middle of the nineteenth century, after the establishment of formal schooling for children in the United States and in several European nations.

Examples of teacher preparation from the perspective of four countries—namely, Germany, Namibia, Taiwan (Republic of China), and the United States—can help provide readers with a broad overview of general approaches to teacher education, training, and preparedness as well as an overall generalization of how pre-service and in-service teachers are trained throughout the world. Nevertheless, it is important to note that this examination is not intended to provide an exhaustive explanation of every country's methods of teacher preparation.

Germany

In Germany students take essentially one route to train to become teachers—a university education. Teacher education regulations in Germany require teacher candidates, regardless of teaching grade level, to major in a specific content area in addition to training in pedagogical methods. New teachers in Germany differ from those in other postindustrial nations in that they have an unparalleled support system that provides numerous benefits and services for recent teacher graduates. As a result, the attrition rate of teachers within the first five years of the profession is relatively low. New in-service teachers also have a reduced class schedule, initially serving as assistants in the classroom. They also receive regular professional development.

In recent decades, teaching has become a growing profession in Germany. According to the German Standing Conference of the Ministers of Education and Cultural Affairs (KMK), more than 20 percent of all freshmen at German universities began what is known as *Lehramtstudium*—the teacher-training program—

in the 1980s. In the next decade, teacher education programs attracted approximately 16 percent of the university student population. The slight drop had to do with declining enrollments in K–12 schools.

Students in Germany who decide to enter the teaching profession must do so during twelfth grade, essentially the last year of secondary school. They need to pass a comprehensive exit examination and be eligible to qualify for the *Abitur*, or qualification for admission to the university. Students are given the opportunity to apply to a university of their choice. As long as they pass the *Abitur*, they can enroll in a teacher preparation program; that is, they need not take an entrance examination to enter teacher training once they are enrolled in the university.

However, in some German states, teacher-training enrollment is quite competitive. This is due to either too many students enrolling in teacher preparation programs or increasing shortages of K–12 students in certain areas. For example, in Nordrhein-Westfalen, students who decide to enter the teaching profession are required to apply to the Zentralstelle fur die Vergabe von Studenplatzen (ZVS), a centralized organization that mediates the number of student teacher candidates and determines the university which each student will attend. In a few other states, *numerus clausus* (Latin for "closed number") is used as a means of admission of students who wish to enter teacher preparation programs. The criterion used when implementing *numerus clausus* is academic achievement: only students with above-average grade point averages are eligible for admission.

As in the United States, the responsibility of teacher training in Germany is given to each of the 16 German states. In contrast, however, universities in each German state must follow curriculum guidelines set forth by the KMK. Teacher preparation is divided into two parts: the completion of a university degree and student teaching—the first preceding the second. During the first part, progress toward completion of a university degree, or *Lehramtstudium*, students must identify a major for a discipline, which will include subjects that they will eventually teach. Second, students must enroll in social science courses, including psychology, sociology, anthropology, economics, and history (among others), as part of their educational training. Third, students are required to take courses in pedagogy and didactical training that are specific and applicable to their primary area of study. The chief

difference between students aiming at primary school careers and those preparing for secondary education is the duration of their university study; students training to become teachers at the primary level tend to spend less time than those who plan to teach at the *Gymasium* or most other secondary school levels. Before completion of a university degree, students must pass a comprehensive exit examination—also called the First State Examination—that is essentially tantamount with receiving a university degree. This examination is also required for students if they are to continue to the next level of teacher training—student teaching. Guided student teaching, known as *Vorbereitungsdienst* or *Referendarzeit*, is a continuous program of teacher training and development that lasts for about two years. It is a form of practicum whereby the student teacher works with a supervising mentor. The student teachers must also attend student teaching seminars where they discuss their experiences of classroom teaching. The final trial in the education training process is the Second State Examination. Upon passing this examination, students become certified to teach in German schools as a profession.

Namibia

According to the United States Agency for International Development Pilot Study on Teacher Professional Development, teacher preparation in Namibia does not necessarily take a direct route, such as a professional college degree or teacher certification. Karima Barrow and Elizabeth Leu in *Cross-National Synthesis on Educational Quality* (2006) demonstrate that policies regarding the education of teachers in Namibia strongly focus on a foundation of constructivism, learning as an active process, and learner-centered education. Given the strong need for well-trained teachers in Namibia and other African nations, both in-service and preservice teachers are prepared in the constructivist, learner-centered paradigm.

After more than a century of colonial domination and apartheid subjugation by Germany and subsequently South Africa, Namibia became an independent state on March 21, 1990. As Nahas Angula, the Namibian minister of higher education, training and employment creation (MHETEC), asserts, Namibian independence did not come solely on diplomatic terms, but as the result of continuous struggles by the Namibian people. The previous apartheid policies had granted privilege to the white minority that had assumed political and economic authority. The ruling elite set out to exclude and oppress the Namibian majority by severely limiting the amount of education services provided to the various ethnic groups while widening the social and economic gap between the black majority and white minority by rendering high-quality educational services for the small white population. Thus, in 1990 Namibia inherited a racially and ethnically segregated society.

After Namibian independence, the fledgling government began an initiative to equalize society. To do this, it was necessary to reconstruct the educational system. The entire educational system needed drastic transformation and reformation that was aligned with the major post-independence goals of access, equity, quality (pedagogical effectiveness and internal efficiency), and democratic participation. As a result, a great paradigm shift ensued from a predominantly content-based, teacher-centered model to a learner-centered and knowledge-based model that purportedly would accommodate a larger school population. Given the new model, teacher education and preparation had to be drastically modified in order to suit the new educational model. Critical-practitioner inquiry and reflective practice were adopted from praxis-based schools of thought that were fashionable in many universities in Europe and the United States. In essence, the new cognitive, learner-centered approach became the primary model for directing teacher education.

Of the nearly 13,500 teachers throughout Namibia, nearly 5,000 (more than one-third) have little, if any, teacher training. Accordingly, it is difficult to generalize about how primary and secondary school teachers are prepared. Namibian universities offer pre-baccalaureate certificates of teaching. A number of teachers follow this route and many of them continue for bachelor's degrees and beyond, some in Namibian universities, and others in foreign higher education institutions. The roughly 5,000 teachers with limited training are strongly encouraged by the government to enter in-service training. Regardless of training, teachers are required to be trained, or retrained, using the student-centered knowledge model and dispense with the teacher-centered approach.

The paradox, however, is that these policies are often understood in a very narrow sense, and the conceptual learning aspects of learner-centered education are only minimally practiced. Barrow and Leu's findings support school-based teacher professional development programs, associated with whole-school improvement programs, as very promising ways of increasing understanding and effective implementation of active-learning policies.

Taiwan

Teacher education students in Taiwan must attend the university in order to teach in K–12 schools. Universities are generally categorized by levels of education. For example, students who wish to teach in the primary school (K–6) attend different institutions than those wishing to teach in secondary school. Most institutions of higher education offer teacher education programs for certification. Most of these programs are four years long. Prospective teachers then engage in at least a six-month internship. Only then is it possible for teachers to apply for teacher certification.

Normal universities still exist in Taiwan and other nations of the Pacific Rim. Prospective teachers generally attend education colleges, depending on the grade levels they intend to teach. Unlike teacher preparation in Germany, where all teacher candidates, regardless of preferred grade level of teaching, must have a content-specific major, teacher preparation policies in Taiwan expect only those who plan to teach at the secondary school level to attend a normal university. The curricula at normal universities in Taiwan typically expect students to be highly specialized, depending on the area that the candidate wishes to teach. For example, mathematics teacher candidates are expected to engage in rigorous mathematical training, similar to that of a so-called pure mathematics major. However, this expectation is currently being challenged as a result of a push to adapt a more cognitively based model, such as numerous teacher education programs in the United States, for teacher candidates in Taiwan.

United States

Depending mostly on state residence, there are two general ways that individuals can obtain teacher certification in the United States. One is the traditional college education, which will often include specialization in the graduate level. The second method is through a nontraditional educational setting, such as a museum or child enrichment center, that has been approved as an accredited body by the state where the setting is located.

Since the inception of formal schooling for the masses in the United States, teacher training was initially carried out by college graduates, who would otherwise have become tutors (much more prominent and academically prepared in early times than at present) in colleges, attorneys at law, or members of the clergy. In the second half of the nineteenth century, there was a growing need to hire large numbers of teachers to accommodate the masses of children, many of whom were offspring of recent immigrants. To do so, normal schools, those specifically designed to prepare teachers, were established. Normal schools were generally autonomous educational institutions that trained K–12 teachers. By the early twentieth century, normal schools were common in most industrial societies throughout the world. Between the 1890s and 1920s, there was a growing interest, especially in highly competitive universities, to initially prepare future teachers, like students of other disciplines and professional areas, with a strong liberal education. As a result, an increasing number of normal schools essentially became attached to universities as separate schools or colleges, as they exist to the present day. After World War II, autonomous normal schools began to fade. Given the present tenuous condition of schools of education in the twenty-first century (as a result of the increase in nontraditional settings, as described below), it is unclear what the future holds in terms of institutional changes in teacher preparation and training in the United States.

Commencing in July 2010, certain states began to permit both nonprofit and for-profit, non-college-related organizations to certify teachers. These organizations vary in type and in sources of income. These organizations include tutoring centers; learning and education centers; private organizations that obtain funding from Title I (i.e., education) funds; museums; zoological parks; aquariums; botanical gardens; private schools; and schools with so-called laboratories of teacher training.

It is important to note that this nontraditional method of certifying teachers seems to be the beginning of a new trend in teacher education. In fact, many education and policy scholars are predicting that by 2020, with the exception of a few so-called premiere graduate education schools, most schools of education will close their doors as a result of their inability to compete financially with nonprofit organizations with large endowments, such as large art and science museums, children's museums, science centers, zoological parks, and aquariums. Moreover, these organizations have the necessary physical resources to combine theory and praxis in teacher education. Prospective teachers, it is argued, need to learn to combine education theory with practical, every day, real-life activities as a form of preparation. Museums and learning centers often have the necessary facilities that traditional schools of education do not.

The four contrasted examples above provide a general overview of teacher preparation practices across the globe. It should be clear from these cases that there is no single direct route to becoming a teacher. Teaching preparation philosophies and paradigms vary from one country to another. Uniform paradigms of teacher preparation have become increasingly popular within individual countries, especially those with centralized educational systems, but not at an international level.

Daniel Ness and Chia-ling Lin

REFERENCES

Barrow, Karima, and Elizabeth Leu. *Cross-National Synthesis on Educational Quality: Report No. 1.* Washington, DC: United States Agency for International Development, 2006.

Hwang, Chien-hou, and Suh-ching Deng. "The Selection of Teacher Training Candidates in Taiwan." Paper presented at the World Assembly of the International Council on Education for Teaching, Washington, DC, 1983.

Lin, Chia-ling, and Daniel Ness. "Mathematics Teacher Education in Taiwan: An Investigation of the Origins and Influences of the Mathematics Program at National Taiwan Normal University." Paper presented at the Annual Conference of the American Educational Research Association, San Diego, CA, 2009.

Pomuti, Herta, et al. *Practicing Critical Reflection in Teacher Education in Namibia.* Tunis, Tunisia: Association for the Development of Education in Africa, 2003.

Swarts, Patti S. "The Transformation of Teacher Education in Namibia: The Development of Reflective Practice." Unpublished thesis, Oxford Brookes University, Oxford, UK, 1998.

Tyack, David. *The One Best System: A History of American Urban Education.* Cambridge, MA: Harvard University Press, 1974.

University of Southern California. "The Future of Schools of Education." *The Navigator* 3:1 (2003): 6–7.

INFORMAL EDUCATION

EXPERIENTIAL EDUCATION

Experiential education is an educational philosophy that was developed in the late nineteenth century and has been incorporated into numerous fields, including outdoor education, environmental education, service learning, internships, cooperative education, field studies, leadership development, and organizational development and training. Since the introduction of the concept of "discovery learning" described by John Dewey in *The School and Society* in 1902, numerous theories have evolved that support the idea that students learn more when they are actively engaged in problem-solving activities. These theories include Jean Lave's apprenticeship model, the cognitive apprenticeship project, and problem-based learning and guided discovery.

Experiential education is based on the premise that all learning is experiential—meaning that the learner must interact with and form a personal relationship with the subject. Learning must begin with the individual's relationship to the topic. The learner applies theories and concepts in a real-world situation and acquires knowledge directly through the experience. Experiential education has made a positive impact on students, creating a context for learning and making learning more meaningful.

The experiential learning model is based on a *do*, *apply*, and *reflect* process. Learning occurs through experience. In this model, experience is the primary activity and it is critical that the youth gains the experience with minimal direction. The leader's role is to facilitate the process and develop self-directed young people. Next, students share and describe the outcomes of their exploration, their observations, and their reactions to the experience. The students then process their reflections through comparisons and an analysis of the experience. While the experience is a critical element in the process, it is the reflection that turns it into experiential education. The process is known as the "action-reflection" cycle that is ongoing and everbuilding.

Experiential education is based on a five-stage model. The first stage in the cycle is *focus*. The focus stage defines the task and prepares the participants for the subsequent challenging action. Focus activities may include discussions of expectations, reading information related to the task, and the teacher's explanation of the next activity.

The *action* stage places learners in a stressful situation designed to force them to face the problem presented and utilize new skills or knowledge. The action—which may be physical, mental, emotional, or spiritual—utilizes the participants' attention and energy. The participants and their brains are responsible for the learning process.

The *support* phase encourages the learners to challenge themselves and to experiment in new situations. Support can be obvious or subtle and can be manifested in multiple ways: physical, verbal, or written. It demonstrates that the learners are not alone and that assistance is available if needed.

Feedback is provided throughout the learning process to ensure that the participants have sufficient information regarding the action being undertaken in order to complete it. It may include comments about the nature of the task or the participants' performance. Feedback is most beneficial when it is specific and when examples are given to clarify the meaning.

In the *debrief* stage of the model, the learning is articulated and evaluated. The participants have the opportunity to learn from the experience by sorting and analyzing the information and examining personal perceptions and beliefs. In experiential education, debrief must be made publicly verifiable. Participants can generalize new understandings and connect them to real-world examples through group discussions, presentations, writing summary papers, sharing personal journals, role-playing, posters, music, or art. The public nature of debrief ensures that the participants' conclusions about the experience are verified across a broader body of perception.

Service learning is a particular type of experiential education program. The characterization of service learning has been debated by education researchers and practitioners for more than a quarter of a century. One view of service learning is that it is an experiential education approach that is based on "reciprocal learning," whereby both the providers and recipients of the service benefit from the experience. The National Society for Experiential Education defines it more broadly as any service experience that is based upon intentional learning goals and in which the student actively reflects on the learning experience. The Corporation for National Service sees it as carefully organized service experiences that meet a community need and are part of the students' school curriculum, but extend student learning beyond the classroom.

In his research, Andrew Furco provides distinctions among various types of service-oriented experiential education programs, including volunteer, community service, internship programs, and field education. He places them on a continuum that is determined by the intended beneficiary and balance between service and learning.

Volunteerism is the engagement of students in service activities of their own choice and without pay. The primary beneficiary is the service recipient. For example, a student might volunteer in a hospital or nursing home.

Community service programs engage students in activities that focus on a particular type of service or a cause that meets a community need, such as providing food for the homeless. The students benefit by learning about the impact of their service on the lives of the recipients.

Internship programs provide students with hands-on experiences that enhance their academic learning or vocational development, as well as broaden their understanding of specific issues related to an area of study. For instance, students interested in the legal profession may undertake an internship in a law firm.

Field education programs primarily enhance students' understanding of a field of study. For example, university students in teacher education programs typically spend a year as student teachers to develop their teaching skills and better understand the teaching profession. These student teachers reflect upon how their service impacts those who receive it.

Outdoor education was influenced in the past by advocates of camping education and nature study. Over time, outdoor education has broadened its scope to include objectives and experiences in many areas and is used as a context for learning. Experiential education is used by outdoor and adventure educators as a way of using real-life experiences to achieve certain learning goals. The focus on "learning by doing" is enhanced by reflection and critical analysis.

Environmental education emerged into prominence in the late 1960s with the first Earth Day and the initial publication of the *Journal of Environmental Education*. The goal of environmental education is to promote the development of an environmentally literate citizenry who have the concepts and skills necessary to take responsible action to protect and preserve the natural environment. For example, the Youth Enrichment Adventure Program provides out-of-school-time, environmental education opportunities for learning to low-income, traditionally underrepresented students in Santa Barbara, California. It enhances students' environmental knowledge, behaviors, and attitudes by implementing a month-long summer enrichment program that integrates mathematics, science, language arts, and technology. Its Leadership Program also incorporates issue investigation, action training, and peer-to-peer sharing of results.

Vishna A. Herrity

REFERENCES

Collins, Allan, John S. Brown, and Susan E. Newman. "Cognitive Apprenticeship: Teaching the Craft of Reading, Writing, and Mathematics." In *Knowing, Learning, and Instruction: Essays in Honor of Robert Glaser*, ed. Lauren B. Resnick. Hillsdale, NJ: Lawrence Erlbaum, 1989.

Collins, Allan, and Albert L. Stevens. "A Cognitive Theory of Interactive Teaching." In *Instructional Design Theories and Models: An Overview of Their Current Status*, ed. Charles M. Reigeluth. Hillsdale, NJ: Lawrence Erlbaum, 1983.

Cullen, Gerald R., and Trudi L. Volk. "Effects of an Extended Case Study on Environmental Behavior and Associated Variables in Seventh- and Eighth-Grade Students." *Journal of Environmental Education* 31 (2000): 9–15.

Dewey, John. *The School and Society*. Carbondale: Southern Illinois University Press, 1902/1980.

Furco, Andrew. "Service-Learning: A Balanced Approach to Experiential Education." In *Expanding Boundaries: Service and Learning*. Washington, DC: Corporation for National Service, 1996.

Herrity, Vishna A., Julie Haight, Mary E. Brenner, and Yukari Okamoto. *Youth Enrichment Adventure Evaluation Report, 2002–2003 to the Whittier Family Foundations*. Santa Barbara: Gevirtz Research Center, University of California, 2004.

Hungerford, Harold R., and Trudi L. Volk. "Changing Learner Behavior through Environmental Education." *Journal of Environmental Education* 21 (1990): 8–21.

Krajcik, Joseph S., Charlene L. Czerniak, and Carl Berger. *Teaching Children Science: A Project-Based Approach*. Boston: McGraw-Hill, 1999.

Lave, Jean. *Cognition in Practice: Mind, Mathematics and Culture in Everyday Life*. Cambridge, UK: Cambridge University Press, 1988.

Ramsey, John M., and Harold R. Hungerford. "The Effects of Issue Investigation and Action Training on Environmental Behavior in Seventh Grade Students." *Journal of Environmental Education* 20 (1989): 29–34.

EXPERT/NOVICE SITUATIONS

Much of the scientific research on successful learning in expert/novice situations stems from the study of individuals who have developed expertise in areas such as chess, physics, mathematics, electronics, and history. The study of expertise provides important insights into the nature of thinking and problem solving and demonstrates the outcome of successful learning. While expert learners have well-organized knowledge that goes beyond problem-solving strategies, they are not general problem solvers who apply a set of strategies across all areas. Their expertise is field-dependent and does not transfer directly to other fields.

Expertise exists on a continuum that goes from novice to expert. Research findings on differences between experts and novices suggest that experts have extensive knowledge that affects how they identify problems, organize information, represent data, and formulate solutions. This knowledge impacts their memory and the way in which they reason and solve problems. In the book *How People Learn: Brain, Mind, Experience, and School* (1999), John Bransford and colleagues identify key principles of experts' knowledge and their potential implications for learning and instruction:

1. Experts notice features and meaningful patterns of information that are not noticed by novices.
2. Experts have acquired a great deal of content knowledge that is organized in ways that reflect a deep understanding of their subject matter.
3. Experts' knowledge cannot be reduced to sets of isolated facts or propositions, but instead reflects contexts of applicability: that is, the knowledge is "conditionalized" on a set of circumstances.
4. Experts are able to flexibly retrieve important aspects of their knowledge with little attentional effort.
5. Though experts know their disciplines thoroughly, this does not guarantee that they are able to teach others.
6. Experts have varying levels of flexibility in their approach to new situations.

Pioneering research studies with chess masters and novice chess players demonstrated that experts perceive and understand a stimulus differently depending on previous knowledge that is brought to the task. While both experts and novices explored various possibilities for moves, the chess masters considered possibilities that were of higher quality than novice players. The knowledge acquired over thousands of hours of chess playing gave the chess masters an advantage in seeing patterns and configurations. Expertise in certain domains enables experts to develop sensitivity to patterns of meaningful information that may not be evident to novices. Research in mathematics found that expert knowledge that enables individuals to recognize problem types involves the development of organized conceptual structures, called schemas, which indicate how problems are represented.

Experts' knowledge is organized around key concepts, principles, and laws. Experts are able to respond to contextual clues and self-regulate their focus on specific tasks. In contrast, novices solve problems by searching for correct formulas. In *Enhanc-*

ing Thinking Skills in the Sciences and Mathematics (1992), R. Glaser posits that students can be guided into thinking more like experts in mathematics and science. This suggests that curricula, whether in formal or informal programs, should be organized in a manner that promotes conceptual understanding rather than just factual information. Having students participate in learning activities that make visible the thinking processes is more beneficial than simply focusing on the conclusions of their thinking. Modeling expert thinking and emphasizing the techniques that are particular to expert thinking is also valuable in developing expertise.

The Third International Mathematics and Science Survey (TIMSS) was critical of the "mile wide and an inch deep" curricula prevalent in some countries. Curricula focusing on the breadth of knowledge limit students' in-depth learning and ability to organize knowledge effectively. Research on expertise suggests that deeper understanding of critical concepts may enhance student competencies and better prepare them for future learning and problem solving. Novice learners could benefit greatly from the models and strategies used by experts in problem solving. Researchers claim that it is important to provide students with educational experiences that enhance their abilities to recognize meaningful patterns of information. Pattern recognition triggers the ability to access knowledge related to a particular task or situation, thus enhancing student competence.

In research studies on human learning, Donovan, Bransford, and Pellegrino provide important findings on how people learn. The authors make significant implications for teaching and learning: (1) Children begin to make sense of the world at a young age and come to school with numerous preconceptions about how the world works. Thus, teaching must integrate preexisting knowledge with new knowledge in order to maximize learning. (2) Research comparing the performance of experts and novices on learning and transfer suggests that students must have a deep understanding of the factual knowledge, develop a conceptual framework, and organize knowledge in particular ways that promote rapid retrieval and application to new domains. (3) Research on the performance of experts in relation to metacognition suggests that learners can be taught to define their learning aspirations and monitor their progress in achieving their goals.

A model of expert and novice learning that is being promoted internationally with children using educational technology in informal, collaborative learning environments is the programs of the Fifth Dimension. It provides opportunities for children to volunteer to engage in a variety of activities in out-of-school time. Participants play computer and board games, draw pictures, read and write stories, and interact with children at 25 Fifth Dimension sites worldwide through telecommunications and by using multimedia and software. In addition to regional sites headquartered in California and North Carolina, Fifth Dimension also has international sites in Sweden, Denmark, Russia, Israel, Mexico, and Australia.

The children learn perseverance and the ability to organize their problem-solving skills in a collaborative manner. By creating a coherent mixture of play, interaction, and affiliation, the Fifth Dimension provides a way in which students can engage in a socially oriented educational activity.

University students, adult volunteers, high school students, and other experienced Fifth Dimension members assist the younger students in setting goals, making decisions, and developing strategies to achieve goals. They adhere to a teaching philosophy of providing help to children only when it is needed. Instruction is viewed as a joint activity or the co-construction of what Lev Vygotsky, in *Mind in Society* (1978), calls a "zone of proximal development by two or more participants that is mediated through communication and other cultural tools." In the process of sense making, children are encouraged to discuss what is important to know about playing a game, how they know that they are successful in playing the game, how the game is organized, and how the game is similar to other games they have played.

In *Teaching and the 5th Dimension* (2008), researchers from the University of Miami describe the expert/novice teaching instruction. In a collaborative teaching situation, one adult facilitator typically has more expertise than another, serving as an expert in the teaching situation. The other participant may be the novice who is developing instructional skills for working with children. In providing instruction, the expert tends to anticipate when a child needs assistance, uses precise speech and exact names for items in the learning task, and takes risks or experiments to try new problem-solving strategies. The novice waits for the child to ask for assistance, views the task as the responsibility of the child, and may abandon a task upon becoming frustrated with it. The expert models a strategy for solving a problem in a game with confidence, while the novice often lacks confidence and may take over an activity rather than model a specific behavior for the child. In terms of questioning techniques, the expert asks leading questions closely related to the goals of the activity and checks for understanding. In contrast, the novice asks fewer questions related to assisting performance and tends to ask questions for personal clarification. The expert offers purposeful feedback with extensive explanation while the novice provides less verbal feedback, resulting in periods of silence. The novice cannot always explain why a strategy does not work. As participants travel through the "zone of proximal development," the level of expertise changes for both the expert and the novice.

Vishna A. Herrity

REFERENCES

Blanton, W.E., G.B. Moorman, and S.J. Zimmerman. *Ways of Knowing, Ways of Doing, Ways of Transporting: Mastering Social Practices in the Fifth Dimension.* National Child Care Information and Technical Assistance Center, 2000. http://nccic.acf.hhs.gov.

Bransford, J.D., A.L. Brown, and R.R. Cocking, eds. *How People Learn: Brain, Mind, Experience, and School.* Committee on Developments in the Science of Learning, Commission on Behavioral and Social Sciences and Education, National Research Council. Washington, DC: National Academy Press, 1999.

Bransford, J.D., J.J. Franks, N.J. Vye, and R.D. Sherwood. "New Approaches to Instruction: Because Wisdom Can't Be Told." In *Similarity and Analogical Reasoning*, ed. S. Vosniadou and A. Ortony. Cambridge, UK: Cambridge University Press, 1989.

Cole, M. *Cultural Psychology: A Once and Future Discipline.* Cambridge, MA: Harvard University Press, 1996.

DeGroot, A.D. *Thought and Choice in Chess.* The Hague: Mouton, 1965.

Donovan, M.S., J.D. Bransford, and J.W. Pellegrino, eds. *How People Learn: Bridging Research and Practice.* Washington, DC: National Academy Press, 1999.

Glaser, R. "Expert Knowledge and Processes of Thinking." In *Enhancing Thinking Skills in the Sciences and Mathematics*, ed. D.F. Halpern, 63–75. Hillsdale, NJ: Lawrence Erlbaum, 1992.

Glaser, R., and M.T.H. Chi. "Overview." In *The Nature of Expertise*, ed. M.T.H. Chi, R. Glaser, and M.J. Farr, xv–xxvii. Hillsdale, NJ: Lawrence Erlbaum, 1988.

Nicolopoulou, A., and M. Cole. "Generation and Transmission of Shared Knowledge in the Culture of Collaborative Learning: The Fifth Dimension, Its Play-World, and Its Institutional Contexts." In *Contexts for Learning: Sociocultural Dynamics in Children's Development*, ed. E.A. Forman, N. Minick, and C.A. Stone, 283–314. New York: Oxford University Press, 1993.

Schmidt, W.H., C.C. McKnight, and S. Raizen. *A Splintered Vision: An Investigation of U.S. Science and Mathematics Education.* U.S. National Research Center for the Third International Mathematics and Science Study. Dordrecht: Kluwer Academic, 1997.

Schustack, M.W., C. King, M.A. Gallego, and O.A. Vasquez. "A Computer-Oriented After-School Activity: Children's Learning in the Fifth Dimension and La Clase Magica." In *New Directions for Child Development: Environments for Socialization and Learning*, ed. R.M. Lerner and A. Villaurruel, 35–50. San Francisco: Jossey-Bass, 1994.

Simon, H.A. "Problem Solving and Education." In *Problem Solving and Education: Issues in Teaching and Research*, ed. D.T. Tuma and R. Reif, 81–96. Hillsdale, NJ: Lawrence Erlbaum, 1980.

University of Miami, School of Education. *Teaching and the 5th Dimension.* 2008. www.education.miami.edu/blantonw/5dClhse/teachibng/expert.html.

Vygotsky, L.S. *Mind in Society: The Development of Higher Psychological Processes.* Cambridge, MA: Harvard University Press, 1978.

HOME, MUSEUMS, AND LIBRARIES

A critical element for the successful recruitment, participation, and retention of participating youth learners in out-of-school-time programs is the participation of the family as well. Informal learning experiences that include both parents and children provide a supportive family environment for learning. Research conducted on family group interactions and learning in informal education settings demonstrates that sharing experiences, discoveries, and excitement is conducive to children's retention of knowledge. Social interactions with the family in out-of-school settings are critical, as they are the most effective source of positive attitudes toward science. Programs that encourage families to work together using investigative skills and science processes have been well received in alternative educational settings. The Family Math Program, for example, developed at the Lawrence Hall of Science at the University of California, Berkeley, provides opportunities for parents to engage in exciting, hands-on learning experiences with their children that are related to the real world.

Home and Family

A challenge for informal learning practitioners is to provide equitable access to resources for all families, particularly those with low levels of education and self-confidence to serve as facilitators for science learning. Language barriers and cultural misconceptions leave many parents of underserved youth without the realization that their participation is crucial to their child's educational success. Research on family life activities demonstrates that they provide dimensions of learning across the lifespan. Greater opportunities for families to participate in out-of-school-time science, technology, engineering, and mathematics education activities would help parents gain an increased cultural awareness of education and the importance of lifelong learning.

Museums

Informal learning environments, such as museums, provide free-choice, self-paced, and multisensory experiences. Virtual museums are another valuable resource for informal learning. Based on specific curriculum themes, they demonstrate electronic museum collections including photographs, paintings, artifacts, databases, and web links to other resources worldwide.

Learning in a museum uses fewer verbal and written symbols for communication than classrooms, allowing learners to interact with real-world objects without having to learn confusing terminology. According to Linda Ramey-Gassert and colleagues, "Museum learning has many potential advantages: nurturing curiosity, improving motivation and attitudes, engaging the audience through participation and social interaction, and enrichment. By nurturing curiosity, the desire to learn can be enhanced."

An exhibit in a science museum is designed for individuals to interact with objects, to read some information or instructions, and to experience a connection with a scientific principle. It usually stands alone as a learning experience and the interactions are typically one-time and brief. Informal science environments provide direct nonverbal experiences,

objects, and visual displays rather than lectures to convey information. Informal science learning enables students to observe and investigate natural phenomena and live specimens in ways that are not possible using textbooks alone.

Exploration and discovery are essential for promoting the development of a child's natural curiosity, thereby laying the foundation for conceptual science learning. In a study of the effects of social interactions on learning in Scotland's first interactive science center, The Stratosphere, students tended to remember the information from exhibits that required active mental and physical involvement, rather than simply visual displays. The students also engaged in peer teaching, which reinforced the conceptual knowledge that was developed.

Museum schools have emerged as a new phenomenon that blends formal and informal learning. These schools are founded on a partnership between local museums and school districts to establish a curriculum that incorporates the district-mandated learning goals into long-range projects that allow students to create new projects or exhibits. Examples in the United States include the New York City Museum School, the Museum Magnet Schools of St. Paul, Minnesota, and the Robert Brent Elementary School and Stuart-Hobson Middle School at the Smithsonian Institution in the District of Columbia. According to a paper presented to the American Educational Research Association by Kira King in 1998, these partnerships create interdependence among the collaborating institutions resulting in a "continuum of partnership structure" as partnerships move from institutional cooperation through alliances to virtual corporations. In addition to providing informal learning opportunities for students, many science centers and museums provide professional development for teachers based on research-based models of promising practices.

Libraries

Public libraries play a major role in lifelong learning. In 1996 UNESCO created the Public Library Manifesto declaring that "the public library, the local gateway to knowledge, provides a basic condition for lifelong learning, independent decision-making, and cultural development of the individual and social groups." Public libraries have a long-standing tradition of serving the community through numerous educational programs and services. Most major cities, suburbs, and small towns have a library. Admission is free and doors are open to everyone. Libraries are accessible during after-school hours and on weekends.

Libraries are optimal places for informal learning. They provide ongoing access to learning for acquiring and renewing the skills necessary for sustained participation in the knowledge society. Although their mission is to serve learners of all ages, they particularly promote student success in academic achievement through summer reading programs, homework assistance, and access to technology. Researchers have proposed some general principles for effective library programs, including reflecting the culture of the communities they serve, engaging families, incorporating strategic collaborations and partnerships, and providing services that are developmentally appropriate for their target populations. With the proliferation of information and communication technologies, libraries connect local learning institutions with global resources of information and knowledge. Moreover, they provide the training and guidance to empower users in the search for worldwide sources of information.

Public libraries are valuable partners in the educational process. Many libraries form partnerships and work collaboratively with school systems, youth-based organizations, businesses, foundations and other community agencies. The Learning in Libraries Initiative is an example of a successful partnership that was established in 2003 between the Wallace Foundation, the Urban Libraries Council, and three New York City library systems to provide activities and programs that enrich children's lives during out-of-school hours. The Wallace Foundation awarded $2 million in grant funding to each of the three library systems. The Learning in Libraries Initiative has had the following positive outcomes:

1. The Queens Library provided leadership on the creation of a joint summer reading program that increased enrollment by 30 percent.
2. The New York Public Library developed an online homework help website—www. homeworkNYC.org—that is available to all New York City students. The site provides live assistance from teachers and offers valuable resources for parents so they can help their children reach their optimal potential.

3. The Brooklyn Public Library created a citywide staff development curriculum, "Everyone Serves Youth," which has been implemented by all three library systems and has trained more than 3,500 employees.
4. The branch libraries have enhanced other after-school services including teen mentoring and advisory councils, book buddy programs, homework assistance, writing workshops, and arts activities.

There are many other examples of libraries in America supporting the informal learning of children and teens during out-of-school time. In Broward County, Florida, more than 300 children participate in the Afterschool @ Your Library enrichment program each day at 10 branches of the county library system. In Cuyahoga County, Ohio, the public library provides homework help centers for K–6 graders at eight branches. Trained volunteers assist with tutoring in school subjects. The Free Library of Philadelphia provides the Learn, Enjoy and Play (LEAP) program for students in grades K–12 at all 35 branches. The program offers homework instruction, computer-assisted learning, and multicultural enrichment for more than 57,000 students. The Los Angeles Public Library (LAPL) brings children living in downtown hotels and shelters to the central library through the Camp LAPL program. Children engage in storytelling workshops, magic shows, science projects, crafts, performing arts, and the Summer Reading Club.

Vishna A. Herrity

REFERENCES

Beer, Valorie. "Do Museums Have 'Curriculum'?" *Journal of Museum Education* 12:3 (1987): 10–13.

Black, Susan. "Museum Learning." *American School Board Journal* 189:1 (January 2002): 34–36.

Dierking, Lynn D., and John H. Falk. "Family Behavior and Learning in Informal Science Settings: A Review of the Research." *Science Education* 78:1 (1994): 57–72.

Falk, John H., John J. Koran Jr., and Lynn D. Dierking. "The Things of Science: Assessing the Learning Potential of Science Museums." *Science Education* 70:5 (1986): 503–508.

Gerzer-Sass, Annemarie. "Family Skills as a Potential Source of Innovative Human Resources Development." In *Trading Up: Potential and Performance in Non-Formal Learning*, ed. Lynne Chisholm, Bryony Hoskins, and Christian Glahn. Strasbourg, France: Council of Europe Publications, 2005.

Haggstrom, Britt M. *The Role of Libraries in Lifelong Learning.* Final Report of the IFLA Project Under the Section for Public Libraries. 2004. http://archive.ifla.org.

King, Kira S. "Museum Schools: Institutional Partnership and Museum Learning." Paper presented at the annual meeting of the American Educational Research Association, San Diego, CA, April 13–17, 1998.

Miller, Jon D. "The Roots of Scientific Literacy: The Role of Informal Learning." In *Science Learning in the Informal Setting: Proceedings of the Symposium of the Chicago Academy of Sciences,* ed. Paul G. Heltne and Linda A. Marquardt, 172–182. Chicago: University of Chicago Press, 1987.

Osborne, Jonathan, and Justin Dillon. "Research on Learning in Informal Contexts: Advancing the Field?" *International Journal of Science Education* 29:12 (2007): 1441–1445.

Ramey-Gassert, Linda. "Learning Science Beyond the Classroom." *Elementary School Journal* 97:4 (1997): 433–451.

Ramey-Gassert, Linda, Herbert J. Walberg III, and Herbert J. Walberg. "Museums as Science Learning Environments: Re-examining Connections." *Science Education* 78:4 (1994): 345–363.

Semper, Robert J. "Science Museums as Environments for Learning." *Physics Today* 43 (1990): 2–8.

Steineger, Melissa. "Families First: A Willamette Valley Preschool Program Strengthens Parents' Role in Children's Education." *NW Educational* 1:1 (1996): 29–33.

Tuckey, Catherine J. "School Children's Reactions to an Interactive Science Center." *Curator* 35:1 (1992): 28–38.

Walter, Virginia A., Cindy Mediavilla, Linda Braun, and Elaine Meyers. *Learning in Libraries: White Paper on Principles and Practices for Public Library Services to Children and Young Adults during Out-of-School-Time.* Chicago: Urban Libraries Council, April 2005.

ISSUES AND CHALLENGES OF INFORMAL EDUCATION

Educational programs provided by museums, botanic gardens, and other informal institutions are grounded in the belief that they are responsible for promoting the knowledge of the citizens in the community at large. Since informal education institutions serve diverse audiences, they strive to provide innovative educational opportunities to underserved communities in order to extend learning beyond the classroom. One of the challenges faced by informal education institutions is how to implement effective curricula in multiple contexts.

Dissemination of Informal Education Programs

The dissemination of successful programs beyond the domain of a particular institution is based on the sustainability and transportability of curricula. Research on successfully disseminated programs has identified several common features, including accessibility, comprehensive nature, use of validated practices, interactivity, and training and technical assistance related to user needs. While the experiences of students in community-based informal education programs will not be the same as those in a museum, similar goals can be achieved by adjusting the curriculum, instructor training, and recruitment process and by leveraging the resources and expertise of the museum.

Research on Formal, Informal, and Nonformal Education

For over a century, formal education has been the subject of a large body of scholarly research. In comparison, the research on informal and nonformal education is significantly less prevalent.

Formal Education

Formal education is the process of teaching and learning that occurs within a school-based context. The curriculum used in a formal education environment is one by which the learner must practice using organized systems—such as the use of algorithms, formulas, and categorizations—as a means of acquiring knowledge. With formal instruction, learners engage in scientific thinking when solving problems in various fields of inquiry. Scientific thinking does not necessarily refer directly to the meaning of science as "natural sciences" (e.g., life sciences versus physical sciences); rather, it refers to the formalized and systematic thought processes that one needs in order to carry out certain procedures for producing an end product of a question, problem, or larger project.

Non-formal Education

Non-formal education is similar to formal education in that both forms are processes that take place in the context of school. It differs, however, from formal education in that the curriculum of non-formal education practice may not necessarily focus primarily on the study of standard subjects of most school curricula—namely, reading and language arts, mathematics, natural science, and social science (or social studies). Moreover, the methods of instruction in non-formal educational settings differ from those of formal settings. Common formats of study in non-formal education include the conference seminar, workshop, lifelong learning courses (short courses in-class, on tape, or video), weekend courses, or as community-based courses. Non-formal education can take place in schools, museums, community colleges, four-year colleges, or universities. Curriculum can include the four areas of inquiry (mentioned earlier), but also include foreign language study (e.g., Teaching English to Speakers of Other Languages [TESOL]), advanced studies in formal areas of inquiry for lifelong learners (i.e., learners of all ages), vocational and technical training, the teaching of skills in music and other arts and crafts, and basic subject area skills.

Informal Education

Unlike formal education, informal education is the process of learning that occurs predominantly outside the school environment. It occurs at home, at work, during play, or while engaging in daily tasks or routines. The subject matter of the informal education environment can vary from basic ideas that may involve single word utterances based on word recognition or number counting to highly advanced cognitive skills that may entail highly complex concepts and procedures needed for solving problems. Informal learning can take place in almost any setting: a playground, a park, the office, a car, a basketball court or football field, a plane, and even on school grounds when formal instruction does not occur. Participants range in age from infant to senior. Also, informal education entails basic habits and cultural specifics that are associated with language and communication, as well as the use of numbers and other aspects of mathematics that is needed in everyday contexts.

Research in the areas of non-formal and informal learning does have a theoretical basis and both forms of education provide implications for practice. The study of learning in formal contexts is easier because such learning is more structured and occurs in con-tained spaces. In informal and nonformal contexts, the researcher has less control over the environment and more difficulty structuring interactions with the activity under study. Moreover, there is a lack of appropriate research instruments to measure learning in informal and nonformal contexts.

In an effort to expand research, scholarship, and leadership in the field of informal learning, the US National Science Foundation funded the Center for Informal Learning and Schools (CILS). CILS is a collaborative partnership between the University of California Santa Cruz, San Francisco Exploratorium, and King's College in London. CILS explores the relationship between informal science institutions and schools and strives to build programmatic bridges to connect the two contexts for learning.

Reconceptualizing Terms

The contemporary discourse in the literature on formal, informal, and nonformal education is being integrated into the context of lifelong learning or education. This discourse presents a unified sense of education stretching throughout a person's entire life, both lifelong and life-wide.

Some researchers believe that formal, informal, and nonformal educational environments are complementary. They argue that there are successful strategies inherent in each approach, while others claim that lifelong education offers a process for promoting and improving learning and acknowledge the contributions of nonformal and informal educational influences on lifelong education. Another group of researchers have called for the reconceptualization of boundaries between formal, nonformal, and informal lifelong learning. Proposals have also been made to drop these terms in favor of the notion of flexible schooling or participatory education. As we look to the future of research in education, Carlos Torres, in *The Politics of Non-formal Education in Latin America* (2001), claims that the distinctions are irrelevant and will be no longer necessary: "Within the lifelong learning paradigm, conventional classifications will regroup around new categories. . . . All over the world, programs exist that resist traditional classifications. They are challenging the formal/non-formal, school/out-of-school barriers, building bridges and creating hybrids."

This new conceptualization of formal, informal,

and nonformal education will require multiple, creative methodologies for assessing learning in a variety of circumstances. The need for innovative research designs, methodologies, and analyses is paramount. There should be a focus on the refinement and validation of instruments that are appropriate for learning in informal and nonformal contexts. Moreover, scholarly research should promote collaborative research between informal, nonformal, and formal education researchers to explore possible intersections and benefits for learning.

Vishna A. Herrity

REFERENCES

Atchoarena, David, and Steven Hite. "Lifelong Learning Policies in Low Development Contexts: An African Perspective." In *International Handbook of Lifelong Learning*, ed. David Aspin Judith Chapman, Michael Hatton, and Yukiko Sawano, 201–228. London: Kluwer, 2001.

Osborne, Jonathan, and Justin Dillon. "Research on Learning in Informal Contexts: Advancing the Field?" *International Journal of Science Education* 29:12 (2007): 1441–1445.

Owens, Thomas. *Dissemination: A Key Element of the ATE Program*. Kalamazoo: Evaluation Center, Western Michigan University, 2001.

Percy, Keith. "On Formal, Nonformal, and Informal Lifelong Learning: Reconceptualising the Boundaries for Research, Theory, and Practice." *Proceedings of SCUTREA 27th Conference*, Warwick, UK: University of Warwick, 1997.

Rogers, Alan. *Non-formal Education: Flexible Schooling or Participatory Education?* Comparative Education Research Centre, University of Hong Kong: Kluwer Academic, 2004.

Schwarz Ballard, Jennifer. "Primero la ciencia: Transforming an Urban Science Summer Camp." Paper presented at the American Educational Research Association conference, San Francisco, 2006.

Torres, Carlos A. *The Politics of Non-Formal Education in Latin America*. New York: Praeger, 1990.

Wright, Cream. "Learning How to Mainstream: Experiential Knowledge and Grounded Theory." Paper presented at the ADEA meeting, Tanzania, October 2001.

LEARNING AT WORK

The workplace can be seen as an opportunity for continuous learning that is embedded in daily experiences. It can support continued learning through spe-cialized courses, on-the-job training, and professional development workshops. The modern workplace requires workers to adapt to changing technologies, skill requirements, and work conditions. Employees need to continually expand their knowledge base to pursue lifelong learning.

The Workplace Learning Environment

In *Studies in Continuing Education* (2004), Michael Eraut classifies workplace learning as nonformal, rather than informal learning, considering the latter term less precise. The author provides a schema for identifying different types of nonformal learning based on the timing of the stimulus (past, current, future), the extent to which the learning is tacit (tacit, reactive, or deliberative), as either individual or social, and either implicit or explicit. Eraut believes that learning at work must have outcomes that contribute to significant changes in capability or understanding.

Informal learning in the workplace is unique to the individual; the control of learning is maintained by the learner. Research by Phil Hodkinson at Leeds University, UK, suggests that the workplace has a learning culture that influences the degree that learning is possible. According to the author, the most effective learning cultures are synergistic and the greatest learning occurs in an expansive learning culture. Phil Hodkinson and Heather Hodkinson produced a matrix of the types of workplace learning with two intersecting dimensions. The first categorized learning that was intentional and planned in contrast to learning that was unintentional and unplanned. The second dimension considered the source of the knowledge—whether there was an existing source of expertise available or whether the learning was not known by anyone and was new in the workplace.

In their studies on learning, John Bell and Margaret Dale suggest that informal learning should be used to complement formal learning activities and not replace them. Utilizing informal learning in the workplace alone may have some drawbacks, including the legalities of accreditation when formal qualifications are necessary and, as a result of the lack of transferability of skills, the employee learns only a portion of a task.

According to Bell and Dale, informal learning in

the workplace has a number of benefits. By enhancing the knowledge and competencies necessary for specific jobs, it closes the gaps in the skills of workers. Informal learning fosters a sense of self-worth and leads to an increase in motivation and productivity at work. Learning at work promotes the development of learning organizations whereby all individuals use knowledge and skills to create a continuous cycle of innovation.

Strategies for Facilitation

There are several strategies for facilitating informal learning in the work environment. Personal development plans that are created with managers and an external learning facilitator promote natural learning that takes place outside of the formal classroom and can be coordinated with more structured courses. Membership in related professional associations encourages workers to enter mentoring relationships, attain leadership positions, develop new perspectives on management processes, and learn new skills that may be beneficial for future employment responsibilities or promotions. Research also suggests reading and study groups, brown-bag discussions, and book clubs as methods of facilitating informal learning in the workplace. In a journal article titled "Twelve Opportunities for Learning in the Workplace" (1996), Anne Marrelli proposes information exchanges that "can encourage employees to share their intellectual wealth." These exchanges of knowledge can be structured as stand-alone sessions or included as part of staff meetings.

Technologies for Learning at Work

With recent advances in technology, information exchanges can be facilitated through Internet websites, chat rooms, discussion boards, e-mail list-serves, and other distance-learning software. Such e-learning imparts content knowledge through electronic information and communications technologies. Many Canadian employers, for example, are embracing technology in an effort to become more productive. They utilize e-learning to build a skilled workforce and create self-directed lifelong learners among their employees; in these workplaces, moreover, e-learning is integrated with knowledge management, performance management, and communication systems. A positive aspect of e-learning is that workers are able to incorporate learning into the workplace more effectively because the tools and technology used for learning are the same as those used for their jobs. Besides being convenient and flexible, e-learning gives employees more control over their learning.

Effectiveness of Learning at Work

Victoria Marsick and Marie Volpe (1999) make suggestions for increasing the effectiveness of informal learning in the workplace. The internal and external environment should be scanned to determine the needs and goals for informal learning. It is important to make time and space for informal learning on a regular basis and integrate it into daily work routines. Since informal learning is an inductive process of action and reflection, an inductive mind-set must be nurtured and reflective skills developed.

In case studies of action learning projects, some educational researchers have provided strategies for on- and off-the-job training. Communication with learners on a one-to-one basis is important to ensure there is a fit between the assignment and the learner's work requirements. Key skills need to be developed at the earliest time possible and there should be effective assessment, monitoring, and feedback to ensure that the relevant individuals are informed about the learner's progress. Additionally, employers should consider taking on a mentoring role to support the learners.

Content of Learning at Work

As a result of globalization and widespread use of information technology, there is a growing need for workers to be highly skilled, particularly in the areas of science and mathematics, and for countries to be competitive internationally. In testimony before the US Senate on April 14, 2005, Brian Fitzgerald summarized four serious threats to the capability of the US workforce: (1) increasing demands for US workers with higher levels of mathematics and science skills; (2) disappointing performance trends of American students on comparative international mathematics and science assessments; (3) decreasing numbers of science and engineering degrees awarded to American citizens; and (4) a critical shortage of qualified mathematics and science teachers.

Reform efforts in the United States have advocated for incorporating inquiry-based and investigation-based learning into school science curricula and increased use of learner-centered pedagogy and collaborative learning. These methodologies are central features of informal science institutions. Therefore, when informal science institutions collaborate with school systems, they contribute to K–12 science education reform efforts. The most beneficial programs are those that allow informal science institutions to connect their collections and pedagogy directly with students.

Workplace Learning and Partnerships

To address the critical need to develop a highly capable workforce, increasing numbers of partnerships are being created between educational institutions and business. For example, the New Jersey Academic-Business Connections initiative builds and maintains effective partnerships among American businesses, schools, and colleges to promote school-to-career programs in the state. Our Piece of the Pie, another youth employment program in Hartford, Connecticut, develops entrepreneurial experiences to engage at-risk youth in school-based learning.

In *Working Knowledge* (2004), a study of high school and community college interns participating in work-based learning, Thomas Bailey and colleagues analyze the pedagogical processes of workplace learning by providing key strategies and examples of corresponding tactics:

1. Front-loaded instruction (prior to the start of a task): Lecturing; modeling and demonstrating; providing opportunities for observation; putting the learner through a dry run; touring the facility; pointing out work processes, personnel, and technologies; and giving an overview of the organization.
2. On-the-job training (as a work activity progresses): Giving orders and instructions; encouraging the learner to "help out"; allowing for trial and error; encouraging questions (and providing answers); and providing opportunities to practice.
3. Back-loaded instruction (after a work activity is completed): Providing formal feedback following a supervisory session; checking and testing; giving reminders about key points; disciplining (in extreme cases); storytelling (narratives that illustrate significant knowledge about the organization and the work).
4. Mentoring (more holistic than supervising, mentoring may be manifested before, during, and after the work activity): Offering advice, instruction, and feedback; explaining workplace culture; modeling appropriate and effective behavior; and generally supporting the newcomer's learning, development, and well-being.

Johanna Lasonen and Pirkka Vesterinen (2002) report on the role of project-based learning in the development of working life skills by three Finnish higher vocational education institutions. The authors claim that project-based learning helps to integrate theory and practice: "True integration of theoretical and practical knowledge is fostered most effectively when students transform abstract theories and formal knowledge for use in practical situations and, correspondingly, when they employ practical knowledge to construct principles and conceptual models."

Vishna A. Herrity

REFERENCES

Bailey, Thomas, Kathryn Hughes, and David Moore. *Working Knowledge: Work-Based Learning and Education Reform*. New York: Routledge Falmer, 2004.

Bell, Chip R. "Informal Learning in Organizations." *Personnel Journal* 56:6 (June 1977): 280–283, 313.

Bell, John, and Margaret Dale. "Informal Learning in the Workplace." *Department for Education and Employment Research Report No. 134.* London: Department for Education and Employment, August 1999.

Dobbs, Kevin. "Simple Moments of Learning." *Training* 35:1 (January 2000): 52–58.

Education Development Center. "Investigating Informal Learning." 2012. www.ltd.edc.org/investigating-informal-learning.

Eraut, Michael. "Informal Learning in the Workplace." *Studies in Continuing Education* 26:2 (2004): 247–273.

Falk, John H., and Lynn Dierking. "The Museum Experience." Washington, DC: Whalesback, 1992.

Fitzgerald, Brian K. "Testimony to the Health, Education, Labor, and Pensions Committee of the United States Senate." *Business–Higher Education Forum*, April 14, 2005.

Hodkinson, Phil. "Improving Workplace Learning: Learning Cultures the Key." *THINKPIECE eZine.* March 2008.

Hodkinson, Phil, and Heather Hodkinson. "Problems of Measuring Learning and Attainment in the Workplace: Complexity, Reflexivity and the Localized Nature of Understanding." Paper presented at the conference Context, Power, and Perspective: Confronting the Challenges to Improving Attainment in Learning at Work. University College Northampton, Northampton, UK, November 8–10, 2001.

Lasonen, Johanna, and Pirkko Vesterinen. "Work-Based Learning in Higher Vocational Education Programs: A Finnish Case of Project Learning." *International Journal of Vocational Education and Training* 10:1 (2002): 21–42.

Marrelli, Anne F. "Twelve Opportunities for Learning in the Workplace." *Performance Improvement* 35:10 (November–December 1996): 26–28.

Marsick, Victoria J., and Marie Volpe, eds. "Informal Learning on the Job." In *Advances in Developing Human Resources, No. 3.* San Francisco: Berrett-Koehler, 1999.

Marsick, Victoria J., and Karen E. Watkins. "Lessons from Incidental and Informal Learning." In *Management Learning: Integrating Perspectives in Theory and Practice,* ed. John Burgoyne and Michael Reynolds. Thousand Oaks, CA: Sage, 1997.

Natrins, Lesley, and Vikki Smith. *Rethinking the Process: Strategies for Integrating On- and Off-the-Job Training.* London: Learning and Skills Development Agency, 2004.

Phillips, Michelle, Doreen Finkelstein, and Saundra Wever-Frerichs. "School Site to Museum Floor: How Informal Science Institutions Work with Schools." *International Journal of Science Education* 29:12 (2007): 1489–1507.

Rennie, Léonie J., Elsa Feher, Lynn D. Dierking, and John H. Falk. "Toward an Agenda for Advancing Research on Science Learning in Out-of-School Settings." *Journal of Research in Science Teaching* 40:2 (2003): 112–120.

Rusaw, A. Carol. "Learning by Association: Professional Associations as Learning Agents." *Human Resource Development Quarterly* 6:2 (1995): 215–226.

Stamps, David. "Learning Ecologies." *Training* 35:1 (January 1998): 32–38.

Out-of-School-Time Programs

Out-of-school time (OST) is defined as curriculum program offerings for children and adolescents that are available before school, after school, on weekends, and during the summer and other school breaks. Typically they are designed to offer safe environments where students can learn, explore interests, and develop life skills. They are characterized by their discretionary opportunity, choice, and flexibility. Most out-of-school-time programs are structured for a particular academic or recreational purpose. Examples of after-school programs are Boys and Girls Clubs, the YMCA, Big Brothers/Big Sisters, 4-H programs, library programs, faith-based programs, and municipal parks and recreation programs. Research shows that extracurricular learning activities, such as summer school and structured after-school programs, help youth from diverse backgrounds gain extra educational experiences that supplement formal education.

OST for Underserved Populations

Many children are home alone while their parents are at work. A study by the After School Alliance in the United States found that approximately 14 million, or 25 percent, of children in grades K–12 spend some time alone, while only 14 percent participate in after-school programs. Law enforcement studies indicate that after-school hours between 3:00 and 6:00 P.M. on school days are peak hours for children to become victims of crimes or to commit crimes themselves. These are also primary hours for drug and alcohol abuse and automobile accidents involving children. Since children spend only 18 percent of their waking hours in school, high quality out-of-school-time activities may help students reach their full potential in school.

With the passage of the No Child Left Behind Act of 2001 in the United States, after-school programs have emerged nationally and are perceived to supplement academic learning. They promote enrichment and social development for underserved, at-risk students. In 2004 the US Department of Education commissioned the National Partnership for Quality After-School Learning to identify and validate exemplary after-school practices that offer high-quality, research-based academic content and retain students. Research shows that the most successful programs are designed for the appropriate age group; provide highly motivational and challenging activities that relate to the lives of the children; combine and balance cultural, recreational, social, and academic activities; and incorporate a format that is very different form the regular school day. In order for after-school programs to be successful, research findings demonstrate the importance of program management components including leadership skills, support, and staff capital (i.e., personal characteristics, relational skills, and subject matter knowledge) to promote high-quality instruction and ensure student retention.

OST as an Antidote for Behavior Problems and Crime

Research suggests that after-school programs have numerous positive impacts on children and society in general by reducing risk-taking behavior, decreasing crime, making the streets safer, and improving student learning. There is increasing evidence that quality OST programs improve academic performance, promote regular school attendance, and enhance student behavior, particularly among disadvantaged youth. A report of California's statewide evaluation of the After School Learning and Safe Neighborhoods Partnerships Program further substantiates positive results in student achievement, attendance, behavior, and reductions in grade repetition. The most marked improvements were in achievement among the most high-risk students, including those initially demonstrating low achievement on standardized test scores and English language learners.

Communities across the United States are establishing partnerships to support out-of-school-time learning. For example, the $23-million After-School for All Partnership involving Harvard University, the city of Boston, and nine other nonprofit and for-profit institutions aims to improve children's after-school educational opportunities, support established after-school programs, strengthen the after-school infrastructure in Boston, and help students reach high academic and developmental goals.

Research suggests that there may be valuable economic benefits resulting from OST programs. A study conducted by the Rose Institute of State and Local Government in Claremont, California, found that for every dollar invested in out-of-school-time programs, taxpayers will save approximately three dollars spent on other services.

Informal education programs offered after school, on weekends, and during the summer months may also play an important role in promoting scientific and mathematical literacy among youth. Research shows that students' motivation and interest in science has decreased not only in the United States but also globally. It has also been shown that students' motivation for academic tasks declines steadily from mid-elementary through high school. Girls' and minority students' interest in science and mathematics also begins to decline in middle school. Science learning in schools is frequently decontextualized and not relevant to daily life. The decline in motivation and interest among middle school youth appears to coincide with a lack of out-of-school-time science education programs, a link confirmed by a needs assessment conducted by the Gevirtz Research Center.

Types of OST

Traditionally, out-of-school learning for youth has been limited to one-day field trips to institutions such as museums, science centers, and botanic gardens. Research from the California Department of Education has shown that education rooted in the local environment over extensive periods of time makes for the best teaching and learning. Wetlands and watersheds, for example, provide ubiquitous contexts for engaging youth in their local environment outside of the classroom. Out-of-school-time programs provide free-choice, self-paced, multisensory, and socially interactive opportunities for hands-on learning.

One of the benefits of environmental education programs provided by informal education institutions is that they promote "scientific literacy," a term coined by the American Association for the Advancement of Science and the National Research Council. Scientific literacy enables learners to identify important environmental issues, develop a sense of personal and civic responsibility for stewardship of the environment, and take action on environmental issues. Environmental education typically promotes problem solving, decision making, applying scientific knowledge to solve real problems, and understanding environmental and social problems from a scientific perspective. Moreover, it stimulates students' interest in science. Research has shown that attitudes toward science and academic achievement in science are correlated, particularly when students actively participate in environmental education activities.

Literature reviews identify various factors, including tracking, gender biases, parental education, parental involvement, family structure and income, and language, that contribute to the underrepresented youth's lack of presence in science, technology, engineering, and mathematics education. Teachers, reflecting society's expectations, tend to offer students limited opportunities for experiential scientific inquiry. The mainstream education research community has given relatively little attention to equity issues relating to ethnicity and almost no attention to interactions among ethnicity, social class, and gender. A survey of 3,011 mathematics education research articles published between 1982 and 1998 revealed that only three articles examined interrelated factors such as ethnicity, class, and gender.

Research indicates that both informal and formal education programs that target underrepresented groups as they move through the K–12 pipeline are critical in promoting student success. Such programs, according to Marcia Linn and Janet Hyde, "provide scaffolding so that the participants can acquire new skills, encourage sharing of ideas so that the learners can make realistic appraisals of their own contributions, provide extensive feedback and encouragement so that the learners can recognize their own strengths, and may well increase the persistence among those less confident."

For many students, formal schooling is not sufficient for high academic achievement. Inequity in access to nonschool supports limits the effectiveness of schools and promotes a chronic achievement gap, harming particularly disadvantaged and ethnic minority students. All students should have supplementary education opportunities—formal and informal opportunities for enriched learning outside of school and beyond the regular school day or academic year. High academic achievement is linked with exposure to informal supports such as after-school programs that incorporate academic instruction, recreational activities, and interaction with students' families. Informal education programs have the potential to promote enrichment and social development, particularly for underserved youth and at-risk populations.

Vishna A. Herrity

REFERENCES

Aikenhead, Glen. *Science Education for Everyday Life: Evidence-Based Practice.* New York: Teachers College, 2005.

American Youth Policy Forum. *Helping Youth Succeed Through Out-of-School-Time Programs.* January 2006. www.aypf.org.

Athman, Julie A., and Martha C. Monroe. *Elements of Effective Environmental Education Programs.* School of Forest Resources and Conservation, University of Florida, 2002.

California Department of Education. *Education and the Environment: Strategic Initiatives for Enhancing Education in California.* Sacramento: California Department of Education Press, 2002.

Cooper, Harris, Kelly Charlton, Jeff C. Valentine, and Laura Muhlenbruck. "Making the Most of Summer School: A Meta-Analytic and Narrative Review." *Monographs of the Society for Research in Child Development* 260:65 (2000).

Durlak, Joseph A., and Roger Weissberg. *The Impact of After School Programs That Promote Personal and Social Skills.* Chicago: Collaborative for Academic, Social, and Emotional Learning, 2007.

Eccles, Jacqueline S., and Janice Templeton. "Extracurricular and Other After-School Activities for Youth." *Review of Research in Education* 26 (2002): 113–180.

Gordon, Edmund W., Beatrice L. Bridglall, and Aundra S. Meroe. *Supplementary Education: The Hidden Curriculum of High Academic Achievement.* Lanham, MD: Rowman & Littlefield, 2004.

Herrity, Vishna A., Julie Haight, Mary E. Brenner, and Yukari Okamoto. *Youth Enrichment Adventure Evaluation Report, 2002–2003 to the Whittier Family Foundations.* Santa Barbara: Gevirtz Research Center, University of California, Santa Barbara, 2004.

Huang, Denise. "Staff Characteristics and Professional Development in Quality After School Programs." *Evaluation Exchange* 11:4 (2006): 18.

Linn, Marcia C., and Janet S. Hyde. "Gender, Mathematics, and Science." *Educational Researcher* 18:8 (1989): 17–19, 22–27.

Lubienski, Sarah T., and Andrew Bowen. "Who's Counting? A Survey of Mathematics Education Research 1982–1998." *Journal for Research in Mathematics Education* 31:5 (2002): 626–633.

National Institute on Out-of-School Time. *Making an Impact on Out-Of-School Time: A Guide for Corporation for National Service Programs Engaged in After School, Summer, and Weekend Activities for Young People.* Washington, DC: Corporation for National Service and National Institute on Out-of-School Time, 2000.

Osborne, Jonathan F., Shirley Simon, and Susan Collins. "Attitudes towards Science: A Review of the Literature and Its Implications." *International Journal of Science Education* 25:9 (2003): 1049–1079.

Rose Institute of State and Local Government. *The Estimated Costs and Benefits of After School Education and Safety Programs Act of 2002.* Claremont, CA: Claremont McKenna College, 2002.

CONTENT, CURRICULUM, AND RESOURCES

CURRICULUM IN EDUCATION FROM A HISTORICAL PERSPECTIVE

The human condition can be defined as the product of what has been taught, experienced, and discovered. Had humans not been able to transmit knowledge from generation to generation, people would not have evolved in the same way or explored the world with the same eyes. Within the world of education, parents are responsible for educating their offspring and preparing them to enter their society. School is responsible for showing students the world of knowledge to help them better understand their universe. It is intended not only to fill the need for knowledge, but also to prepare children to play a future role in their society and the world in general.

Given that the world is constantly changing, skills and professions appear and disappear. Accordingly, schools must adapt to these rapid changes. Education no longer takes place only at a certain time in life; it is part of a lifelong process. Given its connection with intellectual growth, education is closely linked with a society's development. Education contributes to the process of developing the artists, scientists, politicians, and citizens of tomorrow. In order to appreciate the role that education plays in fostering intellectual development, it is important to examine the phenomenon from a historical perspective.

History of Education from Early Times to Late Antiquity

Throughout history, schooling has always been a controversial subject of heated debate. Knowledge was first transmitted by word of mouth. Before writing was devised, our ancestors must have used an oral tradition to transmit knowledge, as some cultures still do today. In those distant times, people passed on their knowledge through narratives. These narratives included stories, tales, songs, and legends that conveyed all people knew about the world around them. Unquestionably, knowledge was transmitted from one generation to another long before there were schools. This transmission took place through direct firsthand experience and observations when people participated in the cultural rituals of the society. This was the way in which children learned to succeed—that is, to cope and survive—in the world. During this point in the development of human culture, it was indeed hardly, if at all, necessary to be schooled in order for these processes to function.

Onset of Written Communication: Education in Sumer

Formal education may have begun in Sumer. About 3500 BCE, educational methods were revolutionized. The invention of writing was finally the necessary and the sufficient condition for the establishment of schools and schooling. As soon as there was a system whereby abstract thought could be preserved, encoded, decoded, and thus passed down as written record, then clearly there needed to be institutions or mechanisms for transmitting those skills. Written communication is not acquired naturally; it not acquired necessarily by accident or by coincidence. The result of learning how to write resulted in the rise of schools.

The question of which culture discovered writing is difficult to answer. Nevertheless, the discovery of clay tablets covered with symbols and words to be studied confirmed that the Sumerians did have schools in order to transmit the skills of reading and writing. Sumerian students worked from dawn to dusk and had six days free per month. It took these students many years of hard work to learn the 2,000 or more pictograms that constituted their written language. By the time they finished their studies, scribes had a broad range of knowledge. Some became teachers while others became notaries, surveyors, builders, archivists, or advisers to their rulers. There was also a need for scribes to write, keep, and interpret important documents. People would go to a scribe if a letter had to be written and sent to someone else. The scribe, who was always an adult male, would then be paid for his services. Schools became important for a particular social class. Usually the wealthy in a particular society sent their sons to school. It is important to make this distinction because schooling was exclusively for boys. Daughters were not formally educated; rather, they were taught at home.

Education in Ancient Egypt

In Egypt schooling played a major role. The curriculum concentrated on teaching hieroglyphics, mathematics, music, and geometry. Students' homework involved the solution to problems dealing with the profit of a piece of land as well as shipbuilding. Students needed to learn how to calculate the volume of a pyramid or the surface area of a sphere. The aim of instruction of all early schools—and for perfectly understandable reasons—was not to promote innovation, originality, and individuality, but rather to impart what was regarded as a sacred and sacrosanct culture. The purpose was to transmit that culture unchanged, inviolate, and in the form in which it had been handed down throughout the course of many successive generations. This was thought to be essential to the survival of the people of the society and of the culture. Therefore, innovation and change, far from being appreciated, were understandably discouraged in nearly all early societies that developed formal schooling.

Education in Ancient Greece

Education in Greece marked a clear departure in education from previous civilizations. Rather than promoting conservation of a culture's habits and traditions, Greek philosophers worked to encourage the development of the individual. They considered that schools were responsible for preparing citizens to take an interest in politics, the arts, law, and theater. Under Greek law, parents were required to provide an education for their sons. From the ages of seven to 18, students attended private schools supervised by slaves who were referred to as pedagogues. These pedagogues would take sons of families to schools or gymnasiums and look after their education and well-being. If parents were wealthy, their sons would begin higher studies in mathematics and astronomy at the age of 21. They were also taught philosophy and the art of oratory. The Greeks believed in the power of speech as a means for advancing knowledge and civilization. Further, they believed and admired the master of the spoken word, and hence oratory, rhetoric, and the arts of public address were highly regarded and taught in school curricula almost from their inception.

Roman Education

Among the Romans, children were traditionally taught by their fathers. When Rome conquered Greece in the second century BCE, this model of paternal education was superseded by the Greek educational method of using a pedagogue, a family slave who served as a mentor to the children of a given family. Roman education was thus essentially borrowed from the Greek model. The elementary school, or the misnomer "play school," was also a direct imitation of a model that had long before been established in Greece. The oratorical schools of Rome were very much in the tradition of the Greek oratorical schools. Young Romans studied Greek so that they could discover poetry and philosophy. As in all ancient societies, girls were not sent to formal schooling. Many women were very well educated, but they were educated by family slaves or they were taught by their fathers how to read and write.

The Romans spread their culture throughout their empire. By doing so, they also spread Greek culture. They trained local elites who eventually abandoned their native languages to speak Latin. In the late years of the western part of the Empire, the noble Martianus Minneus Felix Capella completed the *De septem disciplinis*, or *Seven Disciplines*, which attempted to compile the entire body of Roman knowledge in an encyclopedia of several volumes. The seven disciplines were grammar, rhetoric, logic (the trivium) and geometry, arithmetic, music, and astronomy (the quadrivium). These important volumes were to become the prime reference in education for the next 1,000 years.

The School as It Relates to Church and State

Schooling gained importance in connection with the church and its relationship with state matters after the fall of the Roman Empire. From about the fifth century CE to the dawn of the Renaissance, at the end of the thirteenth and the beginning of the fourteenth centuries, church and state were inextricably linked. To achieve status, schooling was offered to boys exclusively. In addition, during this millennium the university emerged as a general symbol of educational achievement and preparation for positions in the church, law, and politics.

Education in the Middle Ages

During the Middle Ages in Europe, monasteries became the last refuge of culture on the continent. Some of them were monastic schools that provided education for the clergy, but these schools were rare. The European world lost a great deal of the knowledge bequeathed to its people by the ancients. It is important to note, however, that intellectualism was thriving in the Middle East and Near East, particularly in Muslim lands. In fact, the works of Aristotle and Plato were transcribed by numerous scribes, not from Europe, but from Persia and India. Education in these regions was given to boys who learned from skilled experts.

In Europe the church retained a monopoly on teaching for centuries. In matters of education, one figure dominates in the Middle Ages—the emperor Charles, later to be known as Charlemagne. Although Charlemagne was often thought of as "barbarian" in one sense—he could not read or write as a youth and adolescent—he kept a tablet under his bed, and he would take it out and practice writing at night because he really wanted to be an educated man. He was very important in encouraging education, especially the cathedral schools, during the Middle Ages. In 800 CE, after he conquered most of Europe, Charlemagne

was crowned Christian Emperor of the West by Pope Leo III. From then on, Christendom was subject to the political authority of one single monarch. Charlemagne wanted to unify all of Western Europe over which he ruled. To do this, he needed clerks who would be responsible for keeping records. He needed writs that were copied properly so that there would be no discrepancies or deviations and therefore no confrontations, and so that he could govern from a distance through capitularies (i.e., legislation or administrative documents) or through ordinances. These capitularies, or laws, spread throughout the empire. Charlemagne believed that those involved with the act of learning should not be content solely to live a life of piety but should also undertake the task of teaching. Although he claimed the importance of good actions, Charlemagne believed that one cannot act well if one does not know anything. However, cathedral schools accepted only a minority of the population—almost exclusively boys.

The first universities appeared early in the thirteenth century. Oxford University, which still enjoys great prestige today, was founded in Oxford, England, in 1206. One of the major reasons for the appearance of the universities was the increasingly urgent need to reassimilate information that had been lost upon the Roman invasions in late antiquity. Universities, then, recovered the writings of Aristotle, as well as information about medicine that had been preserved in places like Baghdad, Samarkand, and other centers in the Middle East. As returning crusaders brought knowledge from the Greco-Roman period back to Europe, the university was the vehicle through which this information was reintegrated into the Western Eurocentric worldview.

Education in the Sixteenth and Seventeenth Centuries

In the sixteenth century, German Protestants were the first to translate the Bible into a language other than Latin. Numerous Lutheran and Calvinist leaders argued that the word of God, and not the words of priests, exceeded all else. Accordingly, one of the tenets of the Reformation was that all believers must be able to read the Bible in the vernacular. Protestants held that people needed direct access to books so that they could read the Holy Scriptures for themselves without having to rely on an intermediary—that is, a priest. The literacy movement thus was strong in places where the Reformation was strong. In short, in regions where the Reformation had thrived, so did literacy creation and schooling, even for commoners and girls. The Counter-Reformation movement had to take this into account.

In the spirit of the Counter-Reformation, the Jesuits decided to occupy the entire field of Catholic education. During the seventeenth century, the Jesuits founded more than 500 colleges and universities. Their model of classical education inherited from the Greeks spread throughout the entire world and was to hold sway through the twentieth century. The Jesuits chose their students based on ability and talent. Therefore, it was possible for boys of modest background to move up the social scale.

Education in the Eighteenth and Nineteenth Centuries

The eighteenth century saw the beginning of another revolution in the history of education—the Enlightenment. The Enlightenment emphasized the power of human reason, encouraging people to think for themselves and use their reason in order to make sense of the world around them. This event evokes the changes that took place in education in Greece during the fourth and third centuries BCE, when emphasis was given not to cultural tradition, but to individual growth and development. The Enlightenment questioned what the church was teaching people to think about and follow. If people could think for themselves, then they did not need others to think for them. This period also coincided with the birth of modern science and the birth of political theory.

A growing number of Europeans had begun to believe in education as a right and not a privilege. In 1717 Prussia became the first European state to adopt the notion of compulsory public education. On the eve of the French Revolution, Jean-Jacques Rousseau published *Émile*, a novel that questioned all the educational methods used in schools at the time. The important contribution of Rousseau is not that he laid down a blueprint or a framework within which one could build a school or modern school system, but that he developed the very modern proposition of the possibility of estrangement or alienation of the individual from the social fabric and structure. The question he asked was this: if schools are instru-

ments of the dominant culture and if that culture is profoundly alienating, then how can one create schools that will produce authentic and autonomous individuals to function in their own right?

Rousseau, then, opened the door to the new trend of modern educational thinking. This trend emphasizes individuality rather than conformity—learning to think rather than learning by rote. With the French Revolution, the state began to take over the schools and many other institutions. But education did not become free, compulsory, and secular until the appearance of Jules-François-Camille Ferry, a parliamentarian and anticlerical. In Ferry's words, "I made a vow to myself, among all the crying needs of these days, among all the problems, I will choose one to which I will devote everything I have of intelligence, heart, physical, and moral strength—the education of the people. We have an unequal system of education. That being so, I defy you ever to provide equal rights—not theoretical equality, but real equality."

Conservatives fiercely opposed nonconfessional schools. Gradually prayer and catechism gave way to civic instruction in the schools. Students were educated to become good republicans, free to exercise their critical faculties. The principle of the public school soon spread throughout other Western countries. Education spread rapidly as countries such as France, Great Britain, and Germany became heavily industrialized. Thus, it should be clear that a link exists between industrialization and mass education. During this period (1830s–1840s), formal education for the masses was also developing in the United States as many individuals, most notably Horace Mann in Massachusetts, fought for the institutionalization of formal education practice—that is, making school compulsory for children.

In contrast to Western countries, China had a non-industrialized culture during the nineteenth century. Education was not easily accessible to all; that is, very few people were educated. Similarly, the vast majority of the population in czarist Russia was not taught to read and write. It was not in the czar's interest to have an educated, literate population, especially since most of the people in the Russian empire were serfs.

Schooling in the Modern World

Today, primary school education is compulsory in almost every country in the world. However, in developing countries, there is a deep gulf between the principle and practice of education. In several countries in Africa, Latin America, and Southeast Asia, only 65 percent of children attend school. In rural areas, this proportion drops even further. Some very poor families see little reason to send their children to school. Others do not have the means to pay all the expenses. In other cases, there is simply no school to send the children to. Even if there is a school, the classrooms are filled to capacity. In *Child's Right to Education* (1977), Gaston Mialaret, professor emeritus of the Université de Caen in France, states that he saw "a grade 1 class in Togo with 250 pupils. At that time, I was chair of the inspection board. And the teacher asked me, 'What would you do, sir?' I answered, 'I couldn't do better than you!' She was doing the best she could. What do you do with 250 children with a slate and a piece of chalk? You can't teach them all. It is impossible."

In South Africa, with the abolition of apartheid in the early 1990s, young blacks flooded into an education system where everything was in short supply—teachers, classrooms, and books. Although developing countries devote a large part of their budgets to education, the proportion per student remains far lower than that allotted in developed countries. The great challenge for many developing countries of Africa, Asia, and elsewhere is this: When resources are scarce, how much education and of what sort should they invest in? Should they seek to produce a mass public school system that begins from the ground up with basic literacy skills? Or should they start with a select few universities and train a new generation of leaders with the hope that they, in turn, will preside over a development process that will allow for a fuller and more extensive school systems later on? Demographic growth is another important consideration. In the Middle East, Latin Asia, and Southeast Asia, 40 percent of the population is of school age. In Africa it is almost 50 percent of the population. The countries themselves and major international bodies like UNESCO are trying hard to get more children into school. Although the percentages obtained in African countries do not match the rates in Europe and North America, there is still progress being made. At the same time, it is evident that the literacy movement still has not attained the goals it has set for itself.

In developing countries, people often use learning techniques inherited from colonial times. Even today, memorization and simple repetition of words—practices of colonial schooling—are used on a regular basis. Students are taught abstract rules that are of no use to them in their society. In rural regions the school schedule ignores both harvest time and the requirements of work in the fields. Life in a village can be transformed when someone, a priest or a teacher, sinks a well, allowing every villager to have a garden and grow vegetables. Perhaps learning how and where to dig a well is as important as learning how to read. To illustrate, in Haiti, people working on a reforestation project will attend literacy classes after their day's work. In Burkina Faso, training in mechanics is available to young women (not only men) who want to fight unemployment and their society's taboos. These are isolated experiments, but even if they were part of a concerted policy, it is unclear whether they would ensure prosperity.

Not long ago, people believed that education and economic development necessarily went hand in hand. For example, South Korea's growth rate has been climbing as quickly as its percentage of children attending school. Today, we know that this is not an infallible rule. It is obvious that people need to read and to calculate. Residents who cannot read or write are not equipped to play a part in a village cooperative, for instance. But school must not be seen as the basic element for economic development. There are economic, technical, political, and religious forces that are much stronger than educational forces. Nevertheless, for an individual, a few years spent in a classroom can make a tremendous difference. A child who learns how to read and write will be better prepared to face the future. A woman from a developing country with at least a minimum of education will tend to have fewer children. Limiting the number of children does not seem like a major accomplishment for people in more developed countries, but in overpopulated countries where each mouth to feed is an additional burden, it could mean hope for a better life.

Until the 1960s, education was considered a promise for the future. However, for the last four decades, earning a baccalaureate degree has no longer been enough for success. People need to be even more highly educated and multiskilled to find a place in the labor market. Yet thousands of young people are dropping out of high school. The dropout rate for many urban minority students ranges between 35 percent and 50 percent. The first reason why urban minority students and working-class white students drop out is that they do not see a value in their education or think that education is going to matter to them in the long run. In their neighborhoods and everyday environments, they do not have role models for whom education has made a difference. In contrast, many students in mostly middle- and upper-middle-class suburban areas can identify and appreciate how education has made a difference for their families, friends, and siblings. Therefore, they are willing to sacrifice in the short term for long-term gains. If long-term gains through education do not seem a possibility, a student is much more likely to drop out.

The public school of today faces very different challenges from those faced by the elitist schools of the past; it is trying to cope with so many students that there is some question whether public education can meet the needs of each one. Schools must continually integrate new knowledge if they are to satisfy the requirements of a labor market that is continually changing and modifying in structure. Schools are having trouble adapting to these changes. Countless reorganizations, reviews, revisions, and changes to curricula and teaching methods have occurred throughout the years. In addition, budgets are stagnating, causing fears that the quality of education is threatened.

Higher education in the United States has become a consumer product sold in the marketplace. And as universities battle for their market share to attract students, higher education has become not much different from any other consumer product. Students, primarily university students, treat higher education as a consumer product. Thus, they place demands on professors to be less rigorous and to require less work. Given the tendency of university administrators to reward professors who get favorable teaching evaluations and punish those who do not, the current trend is often to lower standards and to make fewer demands on students so that a professor will be popular.

In most developed societies, schools are generally open to the entire population. At the same time, they are open to all the social dilemmas in their communities. To be sure, it is difficult to teach a child who comes to school hungry and therefore cannot

concentrate. Poverty, violence, and drug abuse—all of which can potentially contribute to the onslaught of learning disabilities—are some of the grim realities facing schools today. Although schools cannot replace families, they must grapple with all these issues. Unfortunately, the reality is that many children do not come to school already prepared to read. Moreover, their parents are seldom involved (let alone active) in the school community and they rarely engage and convince their children of the importance of education. It is thus the decision of each individual school body to identify and enact provisions—both socially and academically—for the sole purpose of educating its children. This includes the notion that schools take over the roles that once were the responsibility of parents and families.

In order to ensure success in developing an educated society, schools are obliged to broaden not only their social role, but also their clientele. Lifelong, or continuing, education has become a fact of life in developed societies. As lower-echelon jobs have been eliminated by robotics and information technology, workers must return to the classroom to acquire new skills. Society is changing dramatically, and schools are deeply involved in all these changes. Torn between the demands of some and needs of others, global educational initiatives will need to overcome many challenges.

Education is not only a lifelong process; it also starts at much earlier ages, particularly in so-called developed societies. To give young children every chance for success, the minority parents who are involved in their children's education are enrolling their one-year-olds in reading and mathematical development classes. One question frequently asked concerns the ideal age to start school. Although kindergarten seems to provide a useful transition that helps children adapt to elementary school, there is little, if any, irrefutable research evidence that this is the case. Nevertheless, in practice, children who go to kindergarten adapt more easily to elementary school than children who do not.

Schools of the Future

Article 26 of the 1948 Universal Declaration of Human Rights (UDHR) states that the goal of education is to help all human beings achieve their full potential and learn to respect basic freedoms. There are three

Figure: **Article 26 of the Universal
Declaration of Human Rights**

1. Everyone has the right to education. Education shall be free, at least in the elementary and fundamental stages. Elementary education shall be compulsory. Technical and professional education shall be made generally available and higher education shall be equally accessible to all on the basis of merit.
2. Education shall be directed to the full development of the human personality and to the strengthening of respect for human rights and fundamental freedoms. It shall promote understanding, tolerance and friendship among all nations, racial or religious groups, and shall further the activities of the United Nations for the maintenance of peace.
3. Parents have a prior right to choose the kind of education that shall be given to their children.

main responsibilities that the school system must accomplish in order to achieve these ends. The first is to provide a setting for the child's transition from the limited circle of the family to the broader circle of the community and society at large. This will assist the process of social integration. The second basic responsibility is to provide a link between each individual and society's past, present, and the future. Without this link, many people will not appreciate the intrinsic importance of education in preparing individuals for a constantly changing workforce with different needs and goals. The third basic responsibility is to start from the circumscribed culture of the community and to introduce the individual to a universal culture—in other words, to humanity.

Around the world, there are still 230 million children and 900 million adults who are illiterate, and two-thirds (more than 750 million) of them are women. In wealthier countries, school no longer has a monopoly on knowledge; the media inundate children with striking images and appeal so strongly to their emotions that it becomes hard for schools to teach students how to analyze information. Making links between items of information, integrating them into a body of knowledge, and giving them meaning

is a much more demanding exercise than merely reacting emotionally to stimuli.

In recent years, government authorities have reduced funding for education. As a result, educational institutions have increasingly attempted to seek the funds they need from the private sector. Thus, there is a fear that, in the long term, school curricula will be tailored to fit the needs of industry instead of training future citizens to be free to use their own judgment. In short, curricula seem to be based more and more on the needs of economies instead of encouraging students to learn concepts for their own sake.

Rather than basing curricula on market outcomes, education systems must continue to make strenuous efforts to adapt to changes in society. There is a tradition in many countries, including the United States, of prizing diversity in both public and private schools. For example, in the public sector, many school districts have poured resources into so-called alternative or magnet schools in an effort to make them sufficiently desirable that they will bring in a diverse mixture of students by race, ethnicity, and social class background. In the private sector, there is strong interest in preserving the role of sectarian or denominational schools, operated under the auspices of churches, sects, and denominations. Moreover, many private alternative and preparatory schools offer features that are not available in the public schools. The private sector also lays claim to secular education that emphasizes the importance of keeping pace with changes taking place in all societies throughout the world.

At present, a large amount of financial capital and personal and organizational effort is expended on the integration of new technologies into education. The positive aspects of computer technology are to be found, for example, on the Internet. Students can investigate topics, places, people, and things that, in the past, they could have seen only by traveling to. Students, for example, can examine and investigate information from numerous organizations that only a decade ago was completely unavailable. If the educational community at large considers technology as a tool that augments learning, then the role of technology in teaching and learning will more than likely yield positive outcomes. However, if technology is used to replace teachers, replace the act of thinking and analysis, or act as a surrogate for the learning process in general, it will have undoubtedly have profoundly adverse effects on students.

Nearly all students have been profoundly influenced by certain teachers who taught them to consider the world in diverse ways. If the school is to transmit essential knowledge and values, then schooling must be viewed as a valuable product of society. The success of the school of the future rests on whether it continues to pursue four basic goals: teaching people how to learn, how to do or make things, how to live humanely with others, and how to become civic-minded individuals. Beyond economic, cultural, and religious differences, the school plays a vital role in building a climate of respect, justice, and equality.

Daniel Ness and Chia-ling Lin

REFERENCES

Lucas, Christopher. *Foundations of Education: Schooling and the Social Order.* Upper Saddle River, NJ: Prentice-Hall, 1984.

Mialaret, Gaston. *Child's Right to Education.* New York: Unipub, 1977.

Rousseau, Jean-Jacques. *Emile.* 1762. Translated by Christopher Kelly and Allan Bloom. Hanover, NH: Dartmouth College Press, 2009.

Semel, Susan. *Foundations of Education: The Essential Texts.* New York: Routledge, 2010.

Semel, Susan, and Alan Sadovnik. *Schools of Tomorrow, Schools of Today: What Happened to Progressive Education.* New York: Peter Lang, 1998.

Universal Declaration of Human Rights (UDHR), G.A. res. 217A (III), U.N. Doc A/810 at 71 (1948).

ETHNOMATHEMATICS

Ethnomathematics is a relatively new discipline that scholars describe as the study of mathematics and mathematical thinking from anthropological, sociological, and historical perspectives. Since the early 1980s, ethnomathematics has carried different meanings for different people, an inconsistency that results from the context in which individuals become acquainted with the term. The distortion of ethnomathematics as a crude version of school mathematics is not uncommon. In a number of educational institutions, the distortionists sanction ethnomathematics courses due to their misconceptions. One misconception is that ethnomathematics deals solely with exotica or the quaint and folkloristic components of mathematics, commonly associated with ethnicity (ethnic-mathematics) rather than culturally defined mathematics (ethno-mathematics). Another view is that ethnomathematics highlights mathematics practiced within the confines of geographic regions, while others believe the sole purpose of ethnomathematics is to serve as a motivating tool for so-called mathematically reluctant students. Others, still, refer to the mathematics of ethnomathematics, suggesting that ethnomathematicians endeavor outside mathematics, thus "muddling" mathematical content with interdisciplinary currents. Although this distortionist position in particular recognizes the interdisciplinarity of ethnomathematics, those in favor of it argue that such practice obfuscates the so-called universality of mathematical truths and the logico-deductive process that they claim to be at the core of written or formal mathematics.

There have been several attempts by culturalists to counter these misconceptions of ethnomathematics. Some culturalists have classified ethnomathematics into schools of thought by codifying its theories and premises. Patrick Scott categorizes ethnomathematics by differentiating between ethnomathematics of so-called third-world countries and the ethnomathematics of first-world countries. He argues that the former model bridges the gap between the mathematics of the native culture and the mathematics of the academy while the latter one focuses on encouraging schools to bring the mathematics of other cultures into the classroom as a means of demonstrating how mathematics may be used in various cultures or in everyday life. Examples of the third-world model include a number of writings of Ubiratan D'Ambrosio and Paulus Gerdes, while those of the "postindustrial" model, Scott maintains, include works by Marcia Ascher and Claudia Zaslavsky. By the same token, Alan Bishop classifies ethnomathematics into three groups, all of which seem to link to one or more areas in the social sciences: mathematical knowledge in traditional cultures, which focuses primarily on the anthropological nature of mathematics; mathematical knowledge in non-Western societies, which emphasizes the history and origins of various mathematics concepts and ideas; and the mathematics of different groups in society, which deals with sociological and psychological issues relating to how various groups or individuals use mathematics. Other perspectives include those by Ron Eglash, who argues for an

Table: **Codification of Ethnomathematical Conceptions**

Theorist	Discipline	Definition	Position	Argument
Ubiratan D'Ambrosio	Mathematics	Crossroads of mathematics and anthropology	All-inclusive; political	Ethnomathematics aids in the emancipation of populations in poverty through social activism.
Paulus Gerdes	Mathematics; anthropology	The mathematics implicit in each practice	All-inclusive; political; historical	Ethnomathematics includes the manners and mores of all the world's cultures—including Mozambican artisans, Angolan sand drawers, university-employed mathematicians, and young children.
Marcia Ascher	Education	Mathematical ideas of nonliterate peoples	Exclusive; anthropological	The field encompasses all mathematical activity found in non-European cultures—particularly those whose members do not read or write.
Ron Eglash	Technology studies	Intentionality versus epistemology	All inclusive; philosophical	The field enables members of all cultural groups to appreciate the importance of mathematical ways of knowing.
Gelsa Knijnik	Mathematics	Traditions and practices of a subordinated social group	Exclusive; political	Ethnomathematics is exclusively a political field in which underrepresented populations can benefit.
Norma Presmeg	Education	Mathematics of cultural practice	Exclusive; cultural (for purposes of mathematics curriculum)	The field is essential in broadening students' awareness of mathematical activities undertaken by cultures other than their own.

all-inclusive definition of Ethnomathematics that includes all cultural groups, and Norma Presmeg, who takes a more Eurocentric approach to the topic.

While these classifications may serve as a basis for a codification of ethnomathematics research, it is important to recognize that a number of ideas from each category of the classifications may overlap. Moreover, in avoiding the political implications and motives of the origin of mathematical concepts and the institutionalization of mathematics education, these attempts to classify ethnomathematics do not seem to challenge putative misconceptions of the origin and development of mathematical ideas, particularly those referring to the formal mathematics in school or at the college or university.

Ethnomathematics, an area that has often been grossly ill defined and misinterpreted, is a relatively new intellectual current that critically examines these issues. Ethnomathematicians seek to demystify distorted histories and commonly held myths related to the origins of mathematical ideas, particularly those held by individuals who argue in favor of mathematics as a universal, culture-free construct. However, without considering this factor, it can be inferred that ethnomathematics is an entirely new area of study. D'Ambrosio dissuades us from concluding

that ethnomathematics is the result of revisionist or postmodern philosophy. Despite D'Ambrosio's contention, however, the notion of mathematics as a culturally specific phenomenon is by no means a novel one; strands of research conducted before World War II indicate that the conceptualization of mathematics as a culturally specific product was not uncommon. A few of the numerous examples include the research of the anthropologist A. Bernard Deacon (1920s), the mathematician Marianne Schmidl (early twentieth century), and the early and mid-nineteenth-century educator Warren Colburn, among others.

Definitions of Ethnomathematics

Initially defining ethnomathematics as "the study of mathematical ideas of non-literate peoples," Marcia Ascher and Robert Ascher redefine the term by replacing "non-literate" with "traditional." Without distinguishing between different cultures' levels of literacy, Ubiratan D'Ambrosio, who coined the term "ethnomathematics" in 1985, defines the term as "the mathematics . . . practiced among identifiable cultural groups, such as national-tribal societies, labor groups, children of a certain age bracket, professional classes . . . [which] depends largely on focuses of interest, on motivation, and on certain codes and jargons which do not belong to the realm of academic mathematics." Included within the scope of this definition, D'Ambrosio refers to the nonrigorous forms of calculus used by engineers and the mathematics used by construction workers, weavers, and tailors among others.

Although most ethnomathematicians seem to have accepted D'Ambrosio's definition, a number of additions have been made to this seemingly all-inclusive conceptualization of ethnomathematics. Gelsa Knijnik defines ethnomathematics in terms of its political associations by referring to "the traditions, practices, and mathematical concepts of a subordinated social group." She argues that ethnomathematics "establish[es] comparisons between [these concepts] and academic knowledge, thus being able to analyze the power relations involved in the use of both these kinds of knowledge." Although not explicitly defining the term, Gloria Gilmer adds the dimension of respect for, or in deference to, the mathematical products of each culture and the people who create them as an essential characteristic of understanding ethnomathematics. Taking most of the definitions into perspective, ethnomathematics does not exclude academic mathematics. In accordance with these definitions, academic mathematics is seen as one of numerous types of mathematical manners and mores which therefore can be included under the umbrella of ethnomathematics, a cultural product that the distortionist position may view as absolute, objective, and taken as universal truth. Ethnomathematicians, then, do not excoriate academic mathematics as a cultural product in and of itself; rather, they see ethnomathematics as a vehicle for questioning the Eurocentrism, or political domination, of academic mathematics while investigating the mathematical ideas of non-European or nonacademic cultures whose mathematical tools and products have developed either independently or in conjunction with school or postsecondary mathematics.

The Confluence of Mathematics and the Social Sciences

D'Ambrosio expanded on his definition by referring to ethnomathematics as the crossroads between the history of mathematics and cultural anthropology. In embracing the anthropological underpinnings of ethnomathematics, some authors have examined how the mathematics of cultures of different ethnic backgrounds appear to be no less sophisticated than the mathematics of academia. Paulus Gerdes, one of the most prolific authors in the field, discovered several forms of geometrical artifacts and ways of knowing in Mozambican society that lay dormant for several decades, primarily those during the country's colonial period, a form of mathematics that he refers to as "frozen" mathematics. Mozambican students, many of whom are the sons and daughters of peasants, often counter the idea that they actually do use geometry (in the same way that Euclid and his colleagues recorded it) in their everyday lives and, for the most part, use it in ways much different from the axioms that are considered fundamental in Euclidean geometry—the geometry created and recorded by Euclid and his clique during the third century BCE that has since been canonized and thus institutionalized in various forms (evident in K–12 mathematics education and nearly all mathematics textbooks). Gerdes offers two different construction techniques, or axioms, clearly distinct from their Euclidean counterparts, for creating the foundation of a house. He also provides several other geometric examples that essentially bridge the gap between "practical" and "abstract" geometry. Moreover, Gerdes's examples are presented as a means of "culturally conscientializing" mathematics educators. Gerdes takes the term "cultural conscientialization" from Paulo Freire's concept of "concientização" in his book *Pedagogy of the Oppressed* (1970), referring to the ways in which people learn to grapple with socioeconomic and political contradictions and challenge oppression.

Pinxten's and Pinxten, Van Dooren, and Harvey's work in ethnomathematics is devoted to the spatial and geometrical concepts of the Navajo Indians of northeastern Arizona and northwestern New Mexico, and how their culture has contributed to their thinking of space in comparison to the so-called Western model. Unlike the Navajo knowledge system, space in Western knowledge terms is finite, bounded, and absolute. Conversely, space in Navajo terms, in addition to the objects within its path, is dynamic; that is, it is considered to be "engaged in continuous processes" qualitative in nature, not necessarily quantifiable or static in the Western context—a conception that is consistent with Freire, who insists that knowledge is not static. Since the Navajo model is incommensurable with the Western model, Pinxten, Van Dooren, and Harvey propose to integrate the Western system "in a Navajo-biased frame, with both politically and educationally justified ends." They argue that mathematical instruction of Navajo children within the Western system would only serve to alienate and subordinate them from the start. First, Pinxten, Van Dooren, and Harvey show that there is much that Western science can learn from the worldviews of non-Western cultures. They use the example of the influence of Chinese developments in mathematics on Leibniz's contributions to mathematics and physics. For Pinxten, Van Dooren, and Harvey, it would be senseless to dismiss the Navajo system on grounds that Western mathematics and science are "superior" to other systems. In addition, imposing a solely Western-based frame demonstrates a lack of respect and sensitivity to the Navajo worldview.

Interdisciplinary in nature, ethnomathematical research has been conducted by those who specialize in cognitive psychology and sociology—two areas that have not been traditionally associated with academic mathematics per se. Herbert Ginsburg and Jill Posner confirm that poor children are as apt to do well in school mathematics as their privileged peers. They found that unschooled Dioula children from Côte d'Ivoire outdo their American schooled counterparts in mental addition, a finding that seems to corroborate Constance Kamii's argument that learning mathematics by way of algorithms in the academic setting, as is often the case in schools in former colonized countries and in so-called developed countries, may actually impede children's development of doing mathematics. Ginsburg defends the clinical interview as a sound method in determining any child or adult's mathematical understanding. This methodology, as opposed to standardized tests and other forms of evaluation, seems to break several dichotomies. One is the split between student and teacher; rather than teaching the child, in the clinical interview protocol, the teacher-interviewer asks questions that are intended to elicit useful responses and that may indicate not necessarily what the child knows mathematically, but how the child arrives at certain conclusions. Ginsburg further contends that psychological theories that focus on the current cognitive structure of individuals should be treated with skepticism, for they emphasize current cognitive processes, not what actually can occur, or the

learning potential of an individual—a conception closely linked with Vygotsky's concept of the zone of proximal development. Although cognitive deficit theories are less credible now than in the past, Ginsburg stresses the need for broadening the research areas so as to include learning potential, motivational issues, and the role of social and political factors that undoubtedly influence the very ways in which poor children learn mathematics.

Valerie Walkerdine argues that an individual who practices within a certain profession in which mathematics is used to produce a certain goal may begin a task by planning a strategy of actually achieving that goal, say, cooking dinner. At some point, the product of the task—the dinner itself—becomes peripheral to the mathematics involved in carrying out the process of completing this task. Cooking the dinner, then, is not the mathematics, but instead becomes marginal until the mathematical process is completed. "This concentration," Walkerdine asserts, "on the mathematical string for its own sake, moving away from the product, is typical of the mathematical tasks . . . observed in early education." Walkerdine provides another example of children playing the game of "shopping," in which each child is required to "buy" an item on a card that costs fewer than 10 pence (about 16 cents). Children are further required to calculate the differences on a piece of paper. In this example, Walkerdine claims that the child's transition from the role of "shopper" (buying an item) to that of a student (performing calculations) is not one from the practical to the abstract, but rather from one discursive practice to another. Moreover, as a discursive practice, school mathematics "has its own mode of regulation and subjectification" where each child becomes a unique subject. This subjectification adversely affects the success of oppressed and working-class children within the school context. The subjection and indoctrination of the oppressed, as Walkerdine suggests, relieves the dominant groups' fear of recalcitrance and potential uprising.

Finding the motive for any mathematical undertaking seems to be intimately linked to the definition of "problem." Marcelo Borba posits that a problem must be distinguished from a superficial question that requires little or no reflection. A problem arises either when something arouses curiosity for someone or when there is a need for something to be accomplished. But the questions that may contribute to accomplishing these needs may be unanswerable for a certain length of time, or perhaps indefinitely. Ethnomathematics, then, is "intrinsically linked to a cultural group and to its interest." This "interest" of a particular cultural group is essentially the "problem." At the same time, Borba convincingly distinguishes between a cultural interest or motive, on the one hand, and what students may construe as being a mathematical problem, namely, that which appears in print in a textbook, on the other. Borba defines these latter "problems" as pseudo-problems because they are not of utmost priority to most students and not imperative in students' lives or everyday activities. Unfortunately, Borba does not fully elaborate on the distinction between pseudo-problems and academic mathematics problems. Unlike pseudo-problems, academic mathematics problems are solved initially by an individual or a group. The results may be published and are sometimes known as theorems, lemmas, or the like. However, many of these problems, which are later introduced into school textbooks and in most cases turn into pseudo-problems. They are analogous to, say, movie reruns; although they may arouse initial interest, their practical use or potential for aesthetic pleasure or intrinsic interest is limited the second time around, perhaps only to serve the purpose of mnemonics or recalling particular moments. Pseudo-problems behave the same way in that they serve as mnemonic devices for students in recalling formulas and performing rote calculations, not necessarily learning or understanding concepts.

In another work that seems to link mathematics with social issues, Mary Harris's study on mathematics and gender presents examples demonstrating how sexism has permeated the academy in both formal and informal mathematical circles. Harris's main argument is that mathematics courses relating mathematics to everyday activities tend to emphasize traditional men's work—such as carpet laying, construction work, and carpentry—as examples of mathematical practice. Mathematics educators, Harris claims, often dismiss the fact that weavers, for example, are also mathematicians, almost certainly because most weavers lack formal schooling, are illiterate, and are, more often than not, female.

As Brian Martin suggests, another interesting sociological and historical issue concerns the role that other mathematical models have played within the context of academic mathematics. Linear programming, for instance, can be used as a mathematical model associated with managerial science that enables the corporate world to allocate acquired resources for the purpose of maximizing profit and minimizing cost and work time. Nearly all applied mathematical models in current textbooks are based on the fundamental notion of optimizing a particular variable for some desired outcome. In some cases, for instance, a maximum outcome is desired, such as a corporation's net income, while in other circumstances, minimum outcomes, such as cost or job layoffs due to computerized or robotic labor, are desired. Most current mathematics textbooks argue that linear programming originated during World War II as a way of optimizing planning and scheduling strategies for the Allies. George Dantzig, the individual credited with the invention of the linear program technique called the simplex method, even asserts this. Undoubtedly, the verification that linear programming techniques were initially documented and published during the late 1940s is irrefutable. That this area of study, however, never surfaced before then seems speculative, especially if the definition of mathematics is broadened so as to include both written and oral forms. In fact, according to George Joseph, the mathematics devised by the ancient Egyptians and Babylonians included methods of obtaining optimal feed mixtures for poultry and livestock. If, perchance, ethnomathematics research verifies this example as historical evidence, we can then maintain that linear programming was used more than, say, 2,500 years before Dantzig's "creation" of it.

One of the greatest misconceptions, according to ethnomathematical theory, is the notion that present-day academic mathematics is solely a product of a European tradition that stems from Hellenic Greece. For centuries, this notion has been not only held as fact, but canonized in most history of mathematics textbooks. Martin Bernal presents several arguments in "Animadversions on the Origins of Western Science" (1992) that clarify "the rich mathematical—particularly geometrical—and astronomical traditions in Egypt by the time Greek scholars came in contact with Egyptian learned priests." In challenging the notion of the Greek origins of mathematics, Beatrice Lumpkin, historian and mathematics educator, argues that the evidence confirming Euclid's ancestors as Greek is severely lacking. Moreover, Lumpkin argues that most evidence seems to support Euclid's largely Egyptian or North African ancestry. By demonstrating that mathematics was thriving after the so-called fall of the Roman Empire, particularly in the Indian sub-continent, East and Southeast Asia, Egypt, and Persia, George Joseph argues that the so-called Dark Ages never existed, even within the political boundaries of present-day Europe. What Joseph unfortunately does not inform the reader, however, is that highly advanced mathematical systems were being developed and practiced in the precolonial Americas and in a number of areas in sub-Saharan Africa during the same time.

In elaborating on the notion of academic mathematics from a European historical perspective, the mathematician Dirk Struik provides one of the first accounts of Karl Marx's displeasure with the foundations of calculus and the individuals (Newton, Leibniz, D'Alembert, Cauchy) to whom the calculus and its clarifications are attributed in mathematics texts and histories. This is a convincing example of how academic mathematics behaves as one of many types of ethnomathematics within a social, historical, and cultural context. Struik shows how dialectic materialism contributed to Marx's understanding of the calculus. To illustrate, Struik elaborates on Marx's criticisms of the processes by which Leibniz, D'Alembert, and Cauchy each grappled with the concept of differentiation in calculus, or the means of obtaining the slope of a line that behaves tangent to a particular curve in question. In short, Marx argued that these individuals' representations lacked systematic development in that the treatment of each mathematician's method of differentiating yielded an answer that preceded the final result during the process of differentiation. Using the function $f(x) = x^3$ as an example, Struik maintains that Marx was quite dissatisfied with the lack of development in each mathematician's procedure. "Marx's objection," he argues, "is that though [the treatment of the methods is] formally correct, the derivative, $f'(x) = 3x^2$, is already present . . . before [the process of] differentiation" actually takes place. That is, the derivative, or final outcome, is present before the act of differentiating actually occurs.

Ethnomathematics: Practice and Research

Perhaps one of the most common concerns of mathematics educators is how ethnomathematics reconciles with the established mathematics curriculum in schools. Richard Kitchen and Jerry Becker argue that this issue is not often addressed satisfactorily. Other scholars who have addressed this topic are Claudia Zaslavsky, whose seminal book *Africa Counts: Number and Pattern in African Culture* has inspired many ethnomathematicians' activities and research; Sam Anderson, activist and mathematics educator, who argues that mathematics in the classroom cannot be taught without a historical framework; Munir Fasheh, whose "Mathematics, Culture and Authority" examines the relationship between the teaching of mathematics and how one's approach in teaching may affect students' outcomes, particularly as it relates to methods of teaching mathematics in the West Bank; and Marcelo Borba, whose work was discussed earlier.

In addition to these, perhaps one of the most fundamental themes linking ethnomathematics and school mathematics concerns the educator's ability to help students' recognize how school mathematics may be related to their everyday mathematical practices. In order to do this, instructors would need to accept the social constructivist stance or the notion that every day or spontaneous mathematics exists. As Ginsburg argues, it is essential to forgo standardized testing and instead use alternative methods of evaluation, such as the clinical interview or naturalistic observation, that will allow teachers "to capture the distinctive nature of the [student's] thought." In embracing this philosophy, the teacher should initially identify each student's everyday mathematics. This can be done during clinical interviews, when instructors can observe students construct their own mathematical ideas. Once the spontaneous or informal mathematical construct or artifact has been identified, the teacher should find ways to foster a conducive environment in which students can identify the connections between their spontaneous construct and formal mathematical concepts. Moreover, since ethnomathematics involves empowering students of formerly colonized countries, making these connections need not take place only in schools of first-world societies. As a case in point, a number of researchers from Mozambique investigated the ways in which Mozambicans use mathematics in trade, in art, or simply in their daily experiences. The next step in their research was to relate such conventions as a means of helping students in Mozambican schools construct or identify patterns between informal and formal mathematics. Of course, the recognition of patterns and the identification of relationships between two or more properties are two means of stimulating the intellect and promoting fascination with numbers and geometric and spatial concepts. In sum, the most effective method that can potentially empower students mathematically calls for reducing the gap between their formal and informal mathematical understanding. This is precisely where ethnomathematics can benefit the mathematics curriculum.

Although educational practitioners can embed an ethnomathematical perspective into school mathematics curricula, at the same time it is necessary to consider ethnomathematics as a field research, especially if the mathematical goings-on of a culture had been taken away, or "frozen," as a result of colonialism. Readers interested in examining past and current research in ethnomathematics, its history, its methodologies, and its direction should consult Gerdes's exhaustive "Survey of Current Work in Ethnomathematics" (1997). Gerdes delineates what he calls the gestation that served as an impetus to the current ethnomathematics program: the study of indigenous mathematics emphasizes the importance of understanding the mathematics of a culture as a starting point. "Sociomathematics," a term coined by Zaslavsky, shows the interactions between a particular cultural group and the mathematics used within its ways of knowing. In the early stages of devising the current ethnomathematics program, D'Ambrosio and many of his students explored the role of spontaneous mathematics or everyday mathematical concepts. Gerdes has researched the mathematics that he calls "hidden," or the mathematics that is said to be manifest in "old production techniques, like that of basketry," and "frozen" mathematics that, as mentioned above, had been repressed or outright extirpated by colonization.

Researchers in ethnomathematics in general have succeeded in gathering evidence that, on the one hand, disproves the blatant, commonly held myths and distortions concerning the origin and development of academic mathematics and, on the other, convincingly argues in support of the notion of mathematics as a culturally bound product. However, there are a number of provocative critiques of ethnomathematics. A number of specialists, in fact, have disputed several ethnomathematical assertions. For example, some critics are skeptical that mathematics occurs in certain environments, particularly those in which the mathematics may not be an explicit part of an individual's or group's activity—that is, without the actor or participant of a group or culture acknowledging that mathematics was actually manifest on a conscious level. Furthermore, these critics argue that this so-called mathematics may not even exist in a latent form, especially if a level of mathematical awareness does not exist. Critics argue that in such environments, the "alleged" mathematics taking place undermines more apparent cultural products or activities. For them, this form of mathematics may play merely a subconscious part in the mind of the actor and therefore should not be considered a mathematical product. Examples of such types of mathematics may include what Paulus Gerdes has referred to as "hidden" or "frozen" mathematics (mentioned earlier) or Ubiratan D'Ambrosio's concept of spontaneous mathematics, such as the mental arithmetic of unschooled merchants or some of the mathematics practiced by preschool children. One such critic is Yves Chevallard, who caustically passes Gerdes's concepts off as "sheer propaganda" and a "private myth [and] a wish-fulfilling daydream." In addition to Chevallard's critique, Renuka Vithal and Ole Skovsmose argue from a linguistic standpoint that D'Ambrosio's conception of "ethno" as referring to the notion of "culture" is flawed in that it serves as a negative connotation in South Africa, for culture, ethnicity, and race are not only thought of as interwoven concepts, but are used divisively in that society. They also posit that sentiment of cultural difference had been a major contributing factor in the formation of apartheid and other racist tactics.

Daniel Ness and Chia-ling Lin

REFERENCES

Anderson, Sam. "Worldmath Curriculum: Fighting Eurocentrism in Mathematics." *Journal of Negro Education* 59:3 (1990): 348–359.

Ascher, Marcia. *Ethnomathematics: A Multicultural View of Mathematical Ideas*. New York: Chapman and Hall, 1991.

Bernal, Martin. "Animadversions on the Origins of Western Science." *Isis* 83 (1992): 596–607.

Bishop, Alan. "Cultural Conflicts in Mathematics Education: Developing a Research Agenda." *For the Learning of Mathematics* 14:2 (1994): 15–18.

Borba, Marcelo. "Ethnomathematics and Education." *For the Learning of Mathematics* 10:1 (1990): 39–43.

Chevallard, Yves. "On Mathematics Education and Culture: Critical Afterthoughts." *Educational Studies in Mathematics* 21 (1990): 3–27.

D'Ambrosio, Ubiratan. *Etnomatemática: arte ou técnica de explicar e conhecer* [Ethnomathematics: Art or technique of explaining and knowing]. São Paulo: Editora Ática, 1990.

———. *Socio-Cultural Bases for Mathematics Education.* Campinas, Brazil: UNICAMP, 1985.

———. "Where Does Ethnomathematics Stand Nowadays?" *For the Learning of Mathematics* 17:2 (1997): 13–17.

Draisma, Jan. "How to Handle the Theorem 8 + 12 = 13 in (Teacher) Education." In *Explorations in Ethnomathematics and Ethnoscience in Mozambique*, ed. Paulus Gerdes. Maputo, Mozambique: Instituto Superior Pedagógico, 1994.

Fasheh, Munir. "Mathematics, Culture, and Authority." *For the Learning of Mathematics* 3:2 (1982): 2–8.

Freire, Paulo. *Pedagogy of the Oppressed.* New York: Continuum, 1970/1996.

Gerdes, Paulus. *Ethnomathematics and Education in Africa.* Stockholm: Stockholms Universitet, 1995.

———. "Survey of Current Work in Ethnomathematics." *Ethnomathematics: Challenging Eurocentrism in Mathematics Education*, ed. Arthur B. Powell and Marilyn Frankenstein, 331–372. Albany: State University of New York Press, 1997.

Gilmer, Gloria F. *Ethnomathematics: An African American Perspective On Developing Women In Mathematics.* Nottingham, UK: Centre for the Study of Mathematics Education, 2004.

Ginsburg, Herbert P. *Entering the Child's Mind: The Clinical Interview in Psychological Research and Practice.* New York: Cambridge University Press, 1997.

Ginsburg, Herbert P., Jill K. Posner, and Robert L. Russell. "The Development of Knowledge Concerning Written Arithmetic: A Cross-Cultural Study." *International Journal of Psychology* 16 (1981): 13–34.

Harris, Mary. "An Example of Traditional Women's Work as a Mathematics Resource." *For the Learning of Mathematics* 7:3 (1987): 26–28.

Joseph, George G. "Foundations of Eurocentrism in Mathematics." *Race and Class* 28:3 (1987): 13–28.

Kamii, Constance, and Ann Dominick. "To Teach or Not to Teach Algorithms." *Journal of Mathematical Behavior* 16:1 (1997): 51–61.

Kitchen, Richard S., and Jerry R. Becker. "Mathematics, Culture, and Power." *Journal of Research in Mathematics Education* 29:3 (1998): 357–363.

Knijnik, Gelsa. "An Ethnomathematical Approach to Mathematics Education: Culture, Mathematics, Education, and the Landless of Southern Brazil." *For the Learning of Mathematics* 13:3 (1992): 21–24.

Lumpkin, Beatrice. "Africa in the Mainstream of Mathematics History." In *Blacks in Science: Ancient and Modern*, ed. Ivan van Sertima, 100–109. Piscataway, NJ: Transaction, 1983.

Mapapá, Abflio. "Symmetries and Metal Grates in Maputo: Didactic Experimentation." In *Explorations in Ethnomathematics and Ethnoscience in Mozambique*, ed. Paulus Gerdes. Maputo, Mozambique: Instituto Superior Pedagógico, 1994.

Martin, Brian. "Mathematics and Social Interests." *Search: Science and Technology in Australia and New Zealand* 19:4 (1988): 209–214.

Mellin-Olsen, Stieg. *The Politics of Mathematics Education.* Dordrecht, Netherlands: D. Reidel, 1987.

Pinxten, Rik. "An Anthropologist in the Mathematics Classroom?" In *Cultural Perspectives on the Mathematics Classroom*, ed. Stephen Lerman, 85–98. Dordrecht, Netherlands: Kluwer Academic, 1994.

Pinxten, Rik, Ingrid Van Dooren, and Frank Harvey. *Anthropology of Space: Explorations into the Natural Philosophy and Semantics of the Navajo.* Philadelphia: University of Pennsylvania Press, 1983.

Powell, Arthur B., and Frankenstein, Marilyn. *Ethnomathematics: Challenging Eurocentrism in Mathemathematics Education.* Albany, NY: State University of New York Press, 1997.

Scott, Patrick. "What Can We Expect from Ethnomathematics?" In *Mathematics, Education and Society*, ed. K. Keitel, A. Bishop, P. Damerow, and P. Gerdes. Paris: UNESCO, Science and Technology Education Document Series, No. 35, 1989.

Struik, Dirk J. "Marx and Mathematics." *Science and Society* 12:1 (1948): 181–196.

Trivett, John. "The Multiplication Table: To Be Memorized or Mastered?" *For the Learning of Mathematics* 1:1 (1980): 21–25.

Vithal, Renuka, and O. Skovsmose. "The End of Innocence: A Critique of 'Ethnomathematics.'" *Educational Studies in Mathematics* 34 (1997): 131–157.

Walkerdine, Valerie. "Difference, Cognition, and Mathematics Education." *For the Learning of Mathematics* 10:3 (1990): 52–55.

Zaslavsky, Claudia. *Africa Counts: Number and Pattern in African Culture.* Brooklyn: Lawrence Hill Books, 1973/1979.

ETHNOSCIENCE

Ethnoscience is the study of the ways in which different cultures systematize and classify knowledge. One example of a culture's method of classifying knowledge is its taxonomy of plants and animals. Oswald Werner, in "The Basic Assumptions of Ethnoscience"

(1969), differentiates between ethnographic ethnoscience and ethnologic ethnoscience. The ethnographic form of ethnoscience emphasizes the study of ways in which different cultures categorize elements within scientific subareas, such as anatomy, botany, and zoology. The ethnologic form of ethnoscience deals with theoretical issues that involve the formulation of universal laws that accommodate the ways in which most cultures construe classification techniques. Ethnologic ethnoscience, then, takes a comparative perspective in the categorization of scientific knowledge. As an example, knowledge of the digestive process in animals diverges when comparing Navajo perspectives with the so-called Western perspective or with the Ainu (native Russo-Japanese) perspective.

Ethnoscience: Life Sciences vs. Physical Sciences

The root "ethno" comes from Greek and means "people," "culture," or "race." This root is combined to form compound words, such as "ethnography," "ethnological," and "ethnic." As stated above, the term "ethnoscience" has a generally clear meaning; the study of classification systems in different cultural contexts is perhaps the most predominant definition. It is interesting to note the clarity in meaning of ethnoscience when compared to that of "ethnomathematics." Unlike ethnoscience, the term "ethnomathematics" is more ill-defined in that different individuals construe its meaning in different ways. As a result of its political, geographical, anthropological, and sociological positions, ethnomathematics researchers tend to disagree with regard to the meaning of ethnomathematics. In contrast, ethnoscience, as it pertains to schools in Western society, is primarily concerned with a methodological approach to the study of classified systems. Science in these schools is investigated through the lens of individuals who themselves are labeled "scientists," whose expertise is based on years of study in institutions of higher education. These schools also consider the sciences in two primary categories: life sciences and physical sciences. The life sciences are studied more intensively in the discipline known as biology. Another life science discipline is botany. The physical sciences are often divided into two areas: geology (earth science) and physics. Chemistry is often considered to borrow from both the life sciences and the physical sciences.

Astronomy

Astronomy refers to the scientific study of celestial bodies and the phenomena (particularly physical forces) that act on them. Ethnoastronomy is generally defined in anthropological terms as the ways in which humans have engaged with the meaning of celestial bodies and the skies in general from various cultural perspectives. The term is often paired with archaeoastronomy, which deals with the ways in which cultures have used astronomy as a means of engaging in various physical pursuits—particularly construction.

Biology

Biology is simply the study of life. We can also refer to the subject as the study of living organisms—both plant and animal organisms. The term "ethnobiology" has been formed to indicate the study of biological classification systems. It has also taken on a similar meaning to that of ethnobotany—namely, that ethnobiologists examine the ways in which members of the world's cultures deal with various organic life forms.

Botany

Botany is the study of plants and plant life. It is generally not taught as frequently in Western secondary schools as biology is. Historically, since the European Renaissance, botany has been a common science subject at the college level. Nevertheless, the term has recently been subsumed by many curriculum programs under biology. Coined in 1895 by John William Harshberger, ethnobotany refers to the study of the ways in which the world's cultures have interacted with plant life. It took a century, however, with the work of the ethnobotanist Gary J. Martin, for the term to include all the world's cultures—both developing and developed—not simply those outside so-called Western society. Those who study ethnobotany are interested in examining and explaining these interactions in a variety of ways. They are mainly interested in how humans classify and use plants in a variety of contexts. These contexts include edibles, medicines, cosmetics, tools for farming and textile manufacturing, clothing, ritualistic exercises, constructions, and dye materials.

Chemistry

Chemistry is the study of elements and compounds. Different forms of energy can act on certain types of elements and compounds in different ways—some harmless, others volatile. Little, however, has been written on ethnochemistry. Scholars who have discussed the topic seem to consider it similar to ethnobotany in that ethnochemistry examines the ways in which humans have worked with various substances and matter in their own cultural context. Instead of a primary focus on plants, ethnochemistry focuses on interactions between people of a particular culture and the ways in which they treat different substances (e.g., using heat or other chemicals) in their environment.

Geology

Geology is the study of the earth. In particular, it investigates how the contents of the earth—rocks, molten lava, and the like—act on each other. People who study ethnogeology identify the history of various interpretations of how the earth has developed over time. Although most ethnogeologists study so-called non-Western peoples, it is important to consider all cultural contexts that have made contributions to the study of earth's development.

Physics

Like ethnochemistry, the term "ethnophysics" has been scantly used in the literature. It is generally difficult to examine how members of one culture can view physics, the scientific study of the inter-relationship between matter and energy, differently from another. Nevertheless, the term is confined to the ways in which people throughout the world have construed how objects act and react from a historical perspective.

Ethnoscience Through the Comparative History of Scientific Ideas

Ethnoscience can also be studied through the lens of past events—in particular, the study of different scientific perspectives at various times and places in history. To study the history of scientific perspectives from different cultural standpoints, it might be necessary to use an epistemological approach—namely, a method that investigates the origins of knowledge of a given science within a distinct cultural group. For example, in "An Anthropologist in the Mathematics Classroom?" (1994), Rik Pinxten outlines the Navajo scientific mind-set by comparing spatial constructions in the Western worldview with parallel constructions from the Navajo perspective. Similarly, Gordon Tucker compares the differences in mindset between the Western world views of botany with that of China. In the context of schools and educational settings, ethnoscience can be valuable in that it provides the opportunity for students to engage in the various uses of organic and inorganic matter from different cultural perspectives.

Environmentalism and Green Science

Overlapping with the general framework of physical, life, and earth sciences is the important concept of environmental conservation—a topic that is often considered along with ethnoscience techniques and practices. Today, this topic often involves the ways in which different societies grapple with the problems of global warming and overuse of fossil fuels and other forms of energy that may pose a potential risk to the environment. One of the topics within an ethnoscience curriculum is the problem of finance and subsidies for environmental conservation and sustainability. In the past five decades, the world's wealthy countries demonstrated the ability to provide essential capital for funding projects to improve the earth's environmental conditions. Research needs to be undertaken to continue efforts in promoting environmental awareness and action in less affluent nations.

Daniel Ness and Chia-ling Lin

REFERENCES

Cotton, Charles M. *Ethnobotany: Principles and Applications.* New York: Wiley, 1996.

Pinxten, Rik. "An Anthropologist in the Mathematics Classroom?" In *Cultural Perspectives on the Mathematics Classroom*, ed. Stephen Lerman, 85–98. Dordrecht, Netherlands: Kluwer Academic, 1994.

Rist, Stephan, and Farid Dahdouh-Guebas. "Ethnosciences: A Step Towards the Integration of Scientific and Indigenous Forms of Knowledge in the Management of Natural Resources for the Future." *Environment, Development, and Sustainability* 8 (2006): 467–493.

Sanghamitra, Nusrat J.M. "Let Us Go Green." *Reviews in Environmental Science and Biotechnology* 9:1 (2010): 3–5.

Tucker. Gordon C. "Teaching Ethnobotany in China." Berkeley, CA: Berkeley Electronic Press. 2011.

Werner, Oswald. "The Basic Assumptions of Ethnoscience." *Semiotica* 1:3 (1969): 329–338.

HUMANITIES, ARTS, AND EDUCATION

The visual and performing arts have historically been important characteristics of cultures throughout the world. Although the humanities, visual arts, and performing arts continue to be prevalent staples of society, their level of value in particular milieus demonstrates the ebb and flow of support among constituents. To study the humanities and the arts from a transcultural point of view, it is important to consider the role of ethnoaesthetics, a concept referring to a philosophy of beauty that is founded on a culture's system of beliefs and values.

Ethnoaesthetics

Ethnoaesthetics is a form of analysis that allows one to analyze art in a comparative way. Philip Dark defines ethnoaesthetics as the "analysis of art as a cross-cultural phenomenon." Accordingly, in order to study ethnoaesthetics, it is necessary to examine comparative philosophies from international and intercultural perspectives. To do so, one can investigate the humanities and the arts as separate, yet interrelated, entities.

Humanities

The humanities can generally be defined as areas of expertise having to do with the intellectual systems of knowledge that are deemed of high value for any given culture. These systems of knowledge generally necessitate the study of languages and the study of philosophy. In a universal context, a philosophical perspective is one that considers beliefs and traditions of behavior and knowledge. To be evenhanded, it is important to distinguish philosophy in the universal context from religion in that philosophical ideas need not consider the sacred or spiritual realm, although in many societies there is a great deal of overlap between philosophy and religion.

The notion of "humanities," strictly speaking, developed in Western civilization in relatively modern times. It developed from the necessity of learning the essentials of writing—particularly the grammar of language and other forms of symbolism and their interpretations, such as mathematics and music—in educational settings. In early times, it was important for a student to master the liberal arts (*artes liberales*) known as the trivium, namely, grammar, rhetoric, and logic, in order to engage in occupations having to do with law, political service, or priesthood. The term "liberal arts" refers to the so-called free man, as opposed to the slave, who had no rights or education, or the lower-class citizen, whose only educational opportunity was technical or vocational in nature. The trivium along with the quadrivium—arithmetic, geometry, music, and astronomy—became the foundation of what is referred to in the modern Western sense as the humanities. In Western societies, the humanities consist of academic disciplines associated with all aspects of language and philosophy; they are set apart from professional and vocational areas of study within the context of postsecondary study.

Of course, it is not only Western societies that consider the significance of language and philosophy. The important knowledge and behavior of a particular culture represent and reflect the philosophy of that culture. It is clear from historical sources, for example, that Chinese philosophy is rooted in the ideas of Confucius and the writings of his disciples—most significantly, the *Analects*. Despite some overlap of philosophical ideas with Western traditions, Chinese philosophy is exclusive in the sense that it originated and developed within its own historical and cultural context.

According to the Kenyan philosopher Henry Odera Oruka in *Sage Philosophy* (1990), the notion of an African philosophy is a relevant phenomenon that considers the individualized philosophies of thinkers in numerous indigenous cultures. African philosophy is rooted in the idea that philosophical positions are numerous and form the foundational underpinnings of all cultures within and outside of the African continent. This position can be described as sage philosophy because it deems all cultural traditions of what we know and how we should behave as important components of livelihood. Oruka also developed the notion of ethnophilosophy, a term that underscores the importance of finding universals in the study of the philosophies of various cultures and subcultures throughout Africa.

Fine and Performing Arts

The question that forms the basis of the fine and performing arts as they relate to education is this: for what reason is a work of art created? In order to answer this difficult question, it is necessary to consider the many factors that go into an artwork's creation. First, the creation may not necessarily have aesthetic—that is, artistic—value to the creator of the work. Second, depending on the culture, a work of art can be everlasting or ephemeral. Next, it can be for an audience of thousands or an audience of one; it can be created by a group of people or created by an individual. Finally, it can be made with many things or made of nothing. In the Western cultural tradition, works of art generally have an everlasting value to their observers or listeners; in other cultures, this is not necessarily so. For example, *sona* sand drawings made by tribe leaders in the Kalahari Desert in southwestern Africa are not considered works of art in the so-called Western sense by the people who create them. From the sona drawer's standpoint, a sona drawing is intended as a wise or important maxim, saying, or portent that is to be taken as advice or direction for other members of the tribe. For the outsider, however, sand drawings may be considered artistic and possibly aesthetically pleasing. The sand drawing is not meant to last forever. It is ephemeral in that its purpose is to instruct the participant in the present—not in the future. Indeed, a sand drawing will erode or wither in a strong wind or if someone inadvertently walks on it. The sona sand drawing is not meant for a large audience. For typical students in school settings, sona sand drawings are fine examples of aesthetic creations that do not conform to the notion of art in the Western tradition.

Another example is ritual music, such as Asante *kete* drumming in southern Ghana. Kete performers may not necessarily be cognizant of the highly complex rhythmic and, to a large extent, mathematical nature of their music. Like sona, kete drumming may not be considered an aesthetic art form (in contrast to painting or sculpture) by the communities that engage in kete performances.

In contrast to sona sand drawing or kete drumming, artistic creativity in the so-called dominant society emphasizes the uniqueness of the singular artist and his or her artistic work. The artwork is meant to be eternal, although it does not often become part of tradition. It is also meant to convey an aesthetic quality or significance that possibly unifies the work or connects it with something of value to an individual or group. In addition, with the exception of certain forms of performance art (such as mime), it is produced with objects (e.g., a musical instrument, paint brush, clay for sculpting) that allow the audience to connect with the artwork through the use of their visual, tactile, or auditory senses.

Humanities and Arts Education in the World

It is difficult to make generalizations about how education in the humanities and arts is administered throughout the world. As for art, aesthetic education in the so-called formal setting seems to be predominant in school systems of developed nations. In the United States, arts education began somewhat modestly with the picture study movement in the middle 1800s. This movement emphasized mostly the beautification of schools and their surroundings. Art education was most greatly influenced by John Dewey, who propounded its importance in the schools as early as the 1890s. Dewey put his views on arts and aesthetics in education in his book *Art as Experience*, first published in 1934. He expounds on the idea that since art is an inextricable part of one's community, it must play a significant role in the educative process in order to maintain the strength of one's culture and background. Art and aesthetics education in the United States reached its peak in the 1960s and 1970s. With the onset of educational reform initiatives that insisted on increased test scores in language and mathematics (since more time had to be devoted to these areas), art and aesthetic education began to decline—especially with the introduction of Goals 2000 under the William J. Clinton administration. Arts and aesthetic education began a precipitous decline about 10 years later with the No Child Left Behind legislation under the George W. Bush administration, and even with Race to the Top under the Obama administration.

In contrast to art and aesthetics education, it is very difficult to identify or, for that matter, objectify the notion of "humanities education" per se. In other words, humanities education, or the study of the meaning, origin, and history of the humanities, has not been considered an area of academic inquiry, despite the fact that traditional humanities subjects in the Western context form the basis of liberal arts education in colleges and universities throughout the world. However, hermeneutics, the study of interpretation of art or written texts, may provide a way for students to consider how arts and humanities subjects establish the foundation of a particular culture or society.

Daniel Ness and Chia-ling Lin

REFERENCES

Dark, Philip. "The Ethno-Aesthetic Method." In *Essays on the Verbal and Visual Arts: Proceedings of the 1966 Annual Spring Meeting of the American Ethnological Society*, ed. June Helm. Seattle: University of Washington Press, 1966.

Dewey, John. *Art as Experience.* New York: Perigee Trade, 1934/2005.

Nealon, Jeffrey, and Susan Searls Giroux. *The Theory Toolbox: Critical Concepts for the Humanities, Arts, and Social Sciences.* Lanham, MD: Rowman & Littlefield, 2012.

Oruka, Henry Odera. *Sage Philosophy: Indigenous Thinkers and Modern Debate on African Philosophy.* Boston: Brill Academic, 1990.

WORKER EDUCATION, EDUCATION FOR EMANCIPATION, AND EDUCATION UNIONS

Worker education is the schooling or instruction of individuals who, as a subset of a country's population, form the overwhelming majority of the labor force. This form of education is mainly for people who, for the most part, do not possess terminal secondary or tertiary degrees in a particular field or profession. The International Labour Organization (ILO), a subsidiary office of the United Nations, defines the education of workers as "a means of providing workers and their representatives with the training they need to play an effective role in the economic and social life of their societies." The term is widely held to refer to the education of low-income, working-class individuals and the working poor—in general, members of the proletariat. Sociologists seem to suggest that one-third to one-half of the world's population can be categorized as such. The role of workers and their education has only recently gained ground in worldwide importance. There are at least two reasons that have contributed to this increased interest in worker education. One is the emergence of developing countries and their transition from developing to industrial economies. The second reason has to do with the worsening national economies throughout the world in both developing and developed nations.

As indicated above, most individuals who qualify for entrance into worker education programs are those who did not complete educational or academic degrees, mostly at the secondary or tertiary educational levels. The formation of educational programs for such workers began to achieve momentum in the 1960s and 1970s. The ILO website enumerates the following objectives of worker education programs: (1) to strengthen unions and their influence on the education of workers; (2) to increase the capacity of unions to develop and administer educational programs; (3) to strengthen staff development in unions; (4) to develop human resources in workers' organizations; and (5) to promote gender equity in all the activities involving trade union development of union networks with the support of information technology and the exchange of union practices and policies. It can be concluded from this list that unions are seminal in the formation of worker education programs and development.

Historically, unions have played an important role in achieving the rights and civil liberties of workers throughout the world. Unions have historically been involved in the development of worker education programs as well. The reasons for union influence in the education of workers are perhaps self-evident. First, unions were created and developed to represent workers—primarily the proletariat. Therefore, they have attempted with overall success to justify their influence in worker education programs. Second, since worker education programs often provide free service for their participants, given their nonprofit status, their revenue overwhelmingly comes from union coffers.

The study of curriculum as a tool for liberating various cultural groups is quite broad in scope. From a twenty-first-century standpoint, worker education curriculum often focuses on issues related to present and future issues, including environmental concerns; medicine and health-care policy and administration; education policy and preparation for teaching both literate and illiterate populations; development of new and current forms of transportation; and techniques in building and construction. A number of these problems are addressed in numerous programs in colleges, universities, and organizations throughout the world. Such programs include those in urban studies, administration and public policy, health care, government and political science, labor studies, paralegal studies, and engineering. The Consortium for Worker Education in New York City is a private, nonprofit agency that accommodates displaced workers, furloughed workers, recent immigrants in search of employment, and others who may not have completed terminal degrees. It offers courses free of charge to its participants. Within the consortium's curriculum, participants are educated in the area of employment preparation for individuals entering the workforce or changing their careers. In addition, the organization offers English as a second language (ESL) courses, seminars in running businesses, and education for union employees. In general, the consortium and other similar organizations have an overall mission to educate and empower their members so they can compete on an equal footing with other workers. Other worker education curricula provide workshop-level education programs for the purpose of awareness and safety issues. For example, the National Institute for Environmental Health Sciences offers programs geared to employees who deal with on-the-job hazardous materials and waste. These programs, which help employees meet Occupational Safety and Health Administration requirements, are crucial in developing strategies for avoiding injury or death in perilous occupations that involve rescue or hazardous cleanup.

Traditional academic subjects are also evident in worker education curricula. In defining mathematics in terms of a distinct cultural group's mathematical traditions and practices, particularly those of subordinated social groups within a dominant society, Gelsa Knijnik (1992) outlines methods that members of these subordinated cultural groups can implement as a means for emancipation and perhaps liberation from governing forces. One of these methods concerns mathematical instruction as a channel for opportunity and cultural growth. In particular, she investigates oral mathematical knowledge as a form of social and political mobility from the vantage point of the landless Brazilians. In identifying this oral mathematics through the process of qualitative research methodology, Knijnik developed a system that enables teachers to reinterpret oral mathematical tradition in formal concepts that allow the landless people to understand and appreciate how mathematics can be used to advance all members of a particular society. Paulus Gerdes, another ethnomathematics researcher who has investigated the study of mathematics as a means of social mobility and as a tool for liberation, examines the oral and written traditions of sub-Saharan cultures.

Daniel Ness and Chia-ling Lin

REFERENCES

Gerdes, Paulus. "Exploration of Technologies, Emerging from African Cultural Practices, in Mathematics (Teacher) Education." *ZDM, The International Journal of Mathematics Education* 42:1 (2010): 11–17.

Henslin, James M. *Essentials of Sociology: A Down-to-Earth Approach.* Needham Heights, MA: Allyn & Bacon, 2001.

International Labour Organization (ILO). Workers' Education. www.ilo.org.

Knijnik, Gelsa. "An Ethnomathematical Approach to Mathematics Education: Culture, Mathematics, Education, and the Landless of Southern Brazil." *For the Learning of Mathematics* 13:3 (1992): 21–24.

INTELLECTUAL AND MOTOR DEVELOPMENT

COGNITION AND LEARNING: AN INTERNATIONAL PERSPECTIVE

Cognition has to do with the ways in which humans gain knowledge about the world. Cognition can also be defined as some internal representation of the external world. Learning in these terms, therefore, demands that the individual strive to find the most accurate representation possible. The individual can use these types of representations to solve problems. This idea differs greatly from learning as defined in behaviorist terms, referring to the ways in which humans behave in the world as a result of external stimuli. The foundations of the former term lies in the work of the early developmental theorists of the twentieth century—namely, Jean Piaget and Lev Vygotsky. The latter term refers primarily to the works of the great behavioral theorists, the most noted being B.F. Skinner.

Piagetian Origins

Cognition in education played an increasingly significant role, specifically in the early and middle twentieth century, primarily as a result of the implications of student academic outcomes and also as an alternative theoretical position to the behaviorist model. Piaget was precocious as a boy, publishing his first research article on the albino sparrow at the age of ten. His interests clearly were devoted to biology, in which discipline he earned his PhD at the age of 22. Upon his residence at the Grange-Aux-Belles in Paris, a school that implemented the Binet intelligence test, Piaget noticed that certain students, depending on their age, would make consistent errors in their answers to the same questions. It was not until several years later that these children would be able to answer the same questions correctly. Piaget's experience at Grange-Aux-Belles motivated him to study the development of human knowledge. In order to do so, Piaget insisted that one must identify the origins of knowledge through the study of epistemology—the study of the nature of knowledge and cognitive processes. More specifically, Piaget argued that in order to appreciate the structure and processes of human cognition, it is necessary to study its origins—more specifically, the field of genetic epistemology. For Piaget and subsequent developmental psychologists, the term "genetic" does not refer to nativism; rather, it refers to origin ("genesis"). In general, Piaget's general theory of intellectual development is based on the premise that humans actively—not passively—engage in their environment. Piaget was greatly influenced by the philosophies of Rousseau and Kant, which are generally based on the rationalist tradition—the idea that humans must actively shape their lives in order to avoid corrupt environments. Subsequent influences included the works of Henri Bergson, Charles Darwin, and, to an extent, Sigmund Freud.

Schema

Piaget observed his three children as infants and took painstaking notes on nearly every utterance or movement they made that was a result of some impulse or drive. For example, when his daughter Jacqueline was eight months old, Piaget would say "pa pa" and his daughter would repeat the same phrase. He would continue with "pa pa pa pa" and Jacqueline then added a few more syllables (for example, "pa pa pa pa pa"), indicating that even as early as infancy, repetition through imitation is a basic evolutionary human cognitive process. Through his investigation of infant cognitive development, he argued that nearly all human cognition emanates from schema (the plural of "scheme"), elemental constructs of knowledge that contribute to new knowledge. The three primary schema, Piaget argues, are sucking, grasping, and gazing (or looking), for these are the biological bases for all future knowledge. For example, an infant is biologically endowed with the ability to suck in order to obtain nourishment. Eventually, within two weeks to one month of birth, the infant accommodates a new and related scheme—the ability to suck its finger or thumb. That is, the infant may haphazardly move its hand next to its sucking mouth and will acclimate to the new scheme of sucking a part of the body—the finger or hand. Schema occur throughout the lifespan. A child develops the scheme for adding "ed" to form the past tense of a verb. Later, a new scheme is accommodated for irregular verbs—those that do not take on "ed" (catch → caught; run → ran). All humans—older children, adolescents, and adults—accommodate new schema when realizing the necessity to view the world differently through new knowledge (e.g., when learning that trees get their mass not from sunlight or water, but as a result of carbon dioxide, whereby carbon turns from a gas into a solid). Piaget argued that schema help humans base their existing knowledge on previously acquired knowledge for solving new problems. Accordingly, Piaget is known as the first constructivist thinker. Constructivism—the idea that any pursuit of knowledge or the solving of problems requires the application of previously acquired knowledge—became a staple in developmental psychology and, perhaps more significantly, in education.

Aside from observing his three children during infancy, Piaget collected a large corpus of data from his application of the clinical method—a means by which he was able to study cognitive development of children from early childhood to adolescence. The clinical method involves the implementation of the interview (or clinical interview), a one-on-one, two-way question-and-answer communication between an interviewer and the child, who is usually between the age of two and 16 or 17. The clinical method allows the interviewer to ask specific, directed questions that are based on a protocol—a list of tasks that the inter-

viewer wishes to examine. The protocol can be based on a variety of intellectual or cognitive domains, such as mathematical thinking, scientific thinking, language development, morality, and cognitive tasks directed toward the identification of a child's stage of development (Piagetian developmental stages are discussed below).

Assimilation and Accommodation

Piaget argues that the two processes of assimilation and accommodation guide and direct cognitive development. According to constructivism, human knowledge is predicated on what can be processed through prior knowledge; humans use their current, preexisting schema as a means to validate what they know from the environment. This is the process of assimilation: bits of information are essentially assimilated into preexisting knowledge. As noted above, an infant is born with the sucking scheme and is able to suck anything that is placed in its mouth. The infant immediately sucks when a nipple-like object is placed on the lips. The infant assimilates the sucking scheme when placing its finger in its mouth. That is, the sucking scheme is applied to the finger—not the nipple. Similarly, an older child will develop a scheme for a car—a place with seats and four wheels that takes you from one place to another in a relatively shorter time than walking or riding a bicycle. If the child then sees a two-door hatchback, the car scheme will be applied and the child will identify the two-door hatchback as a "car."

The difficulty in living a life solely by assimilating information, however, is that the human mind would be unable to make exceptions to general rules. In other words, assimilation allows humans to generalize information to the point that it would be difficult to realize another individual's point of view. To be able to avoid overgeneralization in cognitive development, the human must accommodate new information. Humans will need to make adjustments to the ways they approach new knowledge. In sum, assimilation allows people to generalize and apply their knowledge to many different situations. However, it has the tendency to distort reality to the point at which knowledge becomes meaningless. As described above in the example on verbs in the past tense, the adding of "ed" is a generalizable formula but it cannot be used on every occasion. Accordingly, individuals assimilate the general formula (e.g., "walk" and "walked" or "cook" and "cooked") until an obstacle prevents them to go further (as in "to go" and "goed" instead of "went"). Assimilation defies restructuring and modification of schema. In order to avoid over-generalization, accommodation, the complementary process to assimilation, must be employed.

According to Piaget, accommodation reorganizes and modifies our current schema so that it is possible to process new information. Accommodation, then, is the adjustment of reality, which allows the individual to avoid the distortion of reality. The process enables the individual to change existing schema entirely so that they can suit more diverse and varied conditions and situations. In addition to the adjustment and modification of existing schema, the process of accommodation involves the formation and conception of new schema. For example, infants develop the new scheme for sucking the finger. Later they encounter a new object—a drinking cup. The sucking reflex, however, will not produce the same results when the child sucks the top of a drinking cup as when sucking the nipple of a bottle. The infant, then, may decide to apply another scheme to the drinking cup, perhaps biting or licking. This demonstrates evidence of novel schema. However, these schema will not yield results for the infant. Eventually the infant will accommodate the scheme for drinking liquids from the drinking cup. In a similar manner, older children might refer to a truck as a car because it has four wheels and carries people from one place to another. The child will eventually accommodate the scheme of trucks as being quite different from the car scheme (trucks are bigger, they carry larger loads, etc.). At this point, the child will need to make adjustments and reorganize knowledge of motor vehicles so that a differentiation between cars and trucks becomes apparent. To accommodate the new truck scheme, the child will jettison previously held ideas that do not seem to work—such as the car classification—and introduce new ideas that present the new scheme in a way that avoids distortion and encourages better alignment with reality. While assimilation also allows individuals to generalize between different phenomena and identify conditions through classification, accommodations allow for the modification of reality for the purpose of avoiding distortion and overgeneralization.

The complementary processes of assimilation and accommodation lead to equilibration, since, as living organisms, humans desire a sense of equilibrium and balance. Humans are generally motivated to assimilate preexisting schema and accommodate new schema in the environment. This constant engagement leads to equilibrium. In contrast, individuals are in a state of disequilibrium when unable to assimilate preexisting schema and accommodate new schema.

Four General Stages

Through his two primary methods of inquiry—observation and the clinical interview—Piaget identifies four general stages of development: the sensorimotor stage, the preoperational stage, the concrete-operational stage, and the formal-operational stage. These four stages seem to serve as the quintessential model of human intellectual stage theory among developmental psychologists.

Sensorimotor Stage

By the term "sensorimotor," Piaget refers to two attributes that seem to contribute jointly toward the unfolding of infant cognition: the use of senses and the organization of motor skills. Piaget argues that the human at birth is equipped with the five senses in tandem with the movement of joints through musculoskeletal activity. The infant begins a lifelong journey of knowledge through the initial ability to employ the senses concurrently with motor skills. Examples of sensorimotor skills have been discussed earlier—particularly with regard to the initial biological schema (sucking, grasping, and looking) that unfold and form new schema.

Preoperational Stage

Piaget believes that by the end of infancy, young children begin to use words as a means of applying them to specific referents—objects or ideas that are not necessarily in sight. This ability, which Piaget labels "the semiotic function," is an accomplishment for the soon-to-be two-year-old child. Nevertheless, the young post-sensorimotor child is unable to perform certain tasks that show logical, deductive thinking. To demonstrate this lack of knowledge, Piaget introduces two specific intellectual tasks: conservation and seriation. By conservation, Piaget does not mean the protection of environmental resources; rather, he defines conservation as the ability to identify two identical quantities or amounts as being the same or equal despite any physical changes or arrangements that modify one of those quantities. Piaget argues that the preoperational child, generally between the ages of two and six, is unable to conserve quantities or amounts. For example, the interviewer will show a preoperational child two identical balls of clay (i.e., the same amount of clay in each ball) and then flatten one of the balls of clay into a disk. When asked whether the two pieces have the same amount of clay, the preoperational child will say that the spherical piece of clay contains more clay than the flattened disk. In other words, the child is not conserving mass or amount. Another intellectual task that Piaget devised to determine preoperational thinking is seriation. In this task, the interviewer places three or more rods of different lengths on a table and asks the child to determine the rank order of each rod in terms of length. Preoperational children, according to Piaget, are unable to accomplish this task because the rod that they mistakenly interpret as having the shortest length will be the one that is nearest the edge of the table on the side where the they are sitting, while the rod appearing to be the longest will be the one that they mistakenly interpret to be closest to the edge of the table, furthest from where they are sitting.

Concrete-Operational Stage

Unlike preoperational children, Piaget argues that children at the concrete-operational stage (generally between six or seven years and 10 or 11 years of age) are able to solve the conservation or seriation tasks that are presented to them. For example, the child will realize that the flattened piece of clay has the same amount of clay as the ball of clay. Likewise, the child will identify the lengths of the rods in the seriation task based on the length of the distance of each rod from one end to the other, and not in terms of the placement of the rods. This is quite an accomplishment for the concrete-operational child; however, there are still limitations in concrete-operational thinking. For example, concrete operational children might be able to follow directions in an experiment or a project. However, they might be unable to explain the significance of the experiment or what they are doing. Moreover, when the concrete thinker is given

an abstract problem to solve, such as the ages of three or more individuals, there will be gaps in terms of a logical explanation.

Formal-Operational Stage

Children who reach the formal-operational stage, according to Piaget, are able to think abstractly about problems. They do not need objects or manipulatives to help them. They can think deductively. For example, they might be given the following problem: Jane is older than Linda. Barbara is older than Jane. Rank these individuals from youngest to oldest. In this case, while the concrete-operational child will be unable to solve this problem, the formal-operational child (usually over 11 or 12 years of age) can solve this problem deductively by arguing that Linda is the youngest, Jane is in the middle, and Barbara is the eldest. In general, according to Piaget, abstract argumentation is possible under formal operations.

Piagetian Research from an International Perspective

The idea that researchers in cognitive psychology are referred to as "post-Piagetian" means either that their work is primarily an offshoot of Piagetian theory or that they take Piaget's arguments to a level in which they can be critiqued. The work of Geoffrey Saxe, described in a *Journal of Educational Psychology* article in 1982, is a prime example of Piagetian research that has been conducted in order to validate the stage theory construct as it relates to intellectual development. Saxe employed the Piagetian framework in his investigation of the cognitive capacities of children in so-called underdeveloped societies. He worked primarily with the Oksapmin people in the Sandaun province of Papua New Guinea. His main hypothesis was that differences in intellectual development between Oksapmin children and children of postindustrial societies were negligible. Through the use of specified cultural tools, Saxe posed questions that were consistent with the conventions and traditions of the Oksapmin people. More specifically, Saxe employed the Piagetian clinical interview, with, however, major modifications. One major modification was the environment in which the interview was conducted. With an interpreter, Saxe interviewed Oksapmin children individually outdoors—without a table, chairs, and manufactured props (e.g., seriation rods, beakers and graduated cylinders for conservation tasks). Instead, Saxe borrowed from Oksapmin traditions and customs to generate conservation tasks for the children to solve. One such tradition is the crafting of handbags. For example, preoperational children were asked to put their arm inside a handbag. In nearly all cases, the top of the handbag reached their shoulders. When the adult interviewer put his hand inside the same handbag, the top of the handbag reached his elbow. The preoperational children said that the handbag they used was larger than the one used by the interviewer even though the bag was identical. Concrete operational children understood that both handbags were the same size. In general, Saxe concluded that there is little, if any, difference between Oksapmin children and children of the United States and Europe.

Vygotsky: Sociocultural Influences on Cognition

Saxe's investigation connecting Piaget's framework of intellectual development with a non-European society brings up a number of issues concerning social and cultural influences on cognitive development. One issue has to do with whether cognitive development occurs individually, without interaction with others, or whether one's cognitive propensities are increased or strengthened only in the context of social interaction—that is, with one or more people. Another issue has to do with the extent to which one's cultural background and history influences intellectual development. A third issue concerns the extent to which children's behaviors traditionally labeled trivial—such as play or egocentric speech—are rather productive elements that strongly influence cognition. These questions, among numerous others, were of primary interest to the Russian developmental psychologist Lev Vygotsky.

Cognitive Mediation Theory

In *Mind in Society* (1978), Vygotsky argues that language, specifically artificial language (e.g., English, Mandarin, Russian), is not only culturally bound but also the primary construct that separates the cognitive abilities of humans and nonhuman species. Humans, Vygotsky maintains, possess the ability to communicate through language and therefore are able to plan their behavior. This is not possible with members of the animal kingdom. Cognitive mediation theory, then, emphasizes the belief that human cognition is mediated through psychological tools, the most important being language. Vygotsky challenged the behaviorists on grounds that human beings do not shape their behavior as a result of successive stimuli and responses. Rather, if (or when) a stimulus occurs, humans have the capability to use language to mediate behavior, thereby not necessarily responding to a stimulus in an automatic, instinctual manner. In short, the stimulus does not dictate the individual's response; rather, language and other psychological tools mediate between the stimulus and a desired response.

Psychological Tools

According to Vygotsky, psychological tools are the mechanisms that enable the human and animal kingdom to function through the use of signs and symbols. The most common psychological tool is language. But virtually any symbol system that enables the individual to communicate, such as musical sign systems, paintings, and mathematical symbolism, is a psychological tool. As stated above, Vygotsky distinguishes between humans and nonhumans in that the former use psychological tools not only for communication, but also for planning and setting goals.

Dialectic

In addition to the influence of Karl Marx, Vygotsky was also greatly indebted to the work of the philosopher Georg Hegel, who introduced the concept of dialectic as a way of interpreting interaction in various forms: art, science, music, and aesthetics as a whole. Vygotsky introduces this concept when considering the roles humans play when interacting with each other. In general, dialectic involves three components: thesis, antithesis, and synthesis. It begins when someone proposes a thesis, which can be construed as an argument or even a general statement about something or someone. Another individual, that is, the recipient of the thesis, proposes an antithesis, which can be thought of as a counterargument or counterstatement to the original statement. Depending on how different or contrary the two (or more) arguments posed happen to be, the dialogue between the two (or more) individuals unfolds in such a way that the goal is to find a meeting ground—that is, a point of agreement between the people in communication. This point of agreement, or the awareness of the opposing side's point of view, is referred to as synthesis.

Concept Formation

Vygotsky argues that there are two types of concepts: spontaneous concepts and scientific concepts. Spontaneous concepts are those that individuals develop within their everyday environment. They are both contextually and culturally specific. These concepts are powerful in what concerns the situation at hand, what the individual observes in the everyday context (i.e., the empirical), and what is achieved through practical experience. Contemporary researchers have reinterpreted the term "spontaneous concept" and instead call it an "everyday concept," given that not all contextually driven concepts are formulated spontaneously. In contrast, scientific concepts refer to a hierarchical system of interrelated ideas. Scientific concepts are highly organized and systematic. School instruction, for example, makes the individual self-conscious of these concepts. Experts in mathematics, physics, sociology, music, linguistics, or indeed any academic discipline make regular use of scientific concepts. Contemporary researchers have also reinterpreted the term "scientific concept" and instead call it a "conventionally systematic concept" in order to convey that not all concepts designed by experts in a particular field are literally "scientific"—that is, having to do with constructs in the natural or social sciences. One key example is in music—conventionally systematic concepts in music are those that involve the reading and performing of music based on symbolism that is common to a group of individuals who can interpret that symbolism.

The foundations of systematization enter the individual's mind through scientific concepts. According to Vygotsky, instruction in scientific concepts is necessary because it provides school-age children with broader frameworks in which they can place their spontaneous concepts. For example, an eight-year-old child might develop the spontaneous concept of "car" primarily based on an image of her parents' four-door sedan. If asked to define the term "car," she

might reply, "It's something that you get into to take you to school or on a trip to the store. The engine is in the front and the trunk is in the back. You also need to sit in a special child's seat behind Mom and Dad." Formal instruction, in which an adult diagrams different meanings of cars—such as the different sections of trains, or perhaps hatchbacks or station wagons—can give the learner a broader framework in which to place her spontaneous concept and help her understand what a car really is. Vygotsky argues that spontaneous concepts move upward while scientific concepts have a downward movement: "The upward everyday [spontaneous] concept clears a way for a scientific [conventionally systematic] concept and its downward development. Scientific concepts provide structures in turn for everyday concepts by making them conscious and deliberate."

Zone of Proximal Development

The zone of proximal development (ZPD) is perhaps the most celebrated construct in Vygotsky's theory of cognitive mediation. Vygotsky argues that ZPD extends from the level at which individuals have already completely mastered so-called lower-level skills and knowledge to the level at the upper limit of the individuals' ability, where they can use a skill or develop knowledge in the best of circumstances. Vygotsky defines the lower level of ZPD as the actual level of development. All knowledge below this level has already been mastered—that is, it constitutes a person's prior knowledge. All knowledge above this level is not yet achievable or attainable and beyond the individual's limits. It is possibly attainable, however, in some future time. Vygotsky calls this upper level the potential level. Everything between the actual level and the potential level is in ZPD and is potentially achievable by the individual. This area is called ZPD because this range covers the problems, challenges, and tasks that are proximal to, or possibly adjacent to, the individual's last fully developed level of abilities. ZPD can also be defined as the difference between the potential level and the actual level of development.

Rather than referring to ZPD as a distinct point in time within the course of a learner's cognitive development, Vygotsky proposes a zone because the successful performance of a given task or the solution to a problem depends on numerous environmental factors—for example, whether a problem is written clearly, whether a problem has a simple solution or a complicated one, whether there is another person serving as a facilitator, or whether aids, cues, or hints are provided.

Vygotsky and Educational Practice

The integration of Vygotsky's contributions to the fields of psychology and education was the work of several American and Russian psychologists who identified both the depth and breadth of Vygotsky's ideas and made them known to psychologists and educators throughout the world. These individuals include Jerome Bruner, Michael Cole, Vera Johns-Steiner, Alex Kozulin, and Sylvia Scribner. A number of constructs and areas of inquiry have emerged from Vygotsky's theory of cognitive mediation. These include Jean Lave's concepts of situated learning and cognition, Valerie Walkerdine's cultural and gender theory as it relates to cognitive development, medical and sociocultural psychology as construed by Kozulin, and Bruner's instructional scaffolding. Scaffolding, an instructional and educational process developed by Jerome Bruner, is perhaps the most popularized instructional technique that is attributed in part to the work of Vygotsky. The technique of scaffolding involves the overt participation of an adult in the child's learning process. During scaffolding, the adult does not explicitly teach the child, but rather serves as a form of support through which the child is provided clues and hints during the learning process. Scaffolding is gaining popularity not only in the United States and in European countries, but also in educational systems in East Asia, Australia, New Zealand, Israel, and countries in South America as well.

Post-Piagetian and -Vygotskyan Research

After the 1960s, research in cognitive psychology and its interrelationship with the education of young children and adolescents blossomed, and as a result, many subfields within the intersection of cognitive science, psychology, and education began to emerge. Some of these subfields fall under the categories of mathematical thinking, scientific thinking, and language development. In each of these categories, there are several areas of specialization that researchers have investigated within the last three decades. One of the main criticisms of the Piagetian and possibly the Vygotskyan frameworks is that they seem to overlook innate characteristics of intellectual ability. What follows is a discussion of a select number of research areas investigated by leading post-Piagetian and post-Vygotskyan researchers in cognitive development. A number of the researchers discussed below argue in favor of both a nativist model and a developmental-environmental approach to intellectual development.

One branch of cognitive development concerning infants and young children involves physical reasoning. One major question in this area has to do with the manner in which infants and young children predict and determine the outcomes of various physical events. Renee Baillargeon's research investigates various points during development when infants show signs of predicting outcomes of physical events. For example, through the method of inspection time, also referred to as preferential looking, it is posited that young infants spend a longer period of time looking at a picture showing an object in midair and off a table than when looking at a picture showing the same object positioned on a table, thus suggesting that an object in midair will fall to the ground.

Numerous studies have posited the innate characteristics of mathematical reasoning. One of the initial studies in this area was undertaken by Rochel Gelman, who found that relatively young infants—between five months and eight months—were able to differentiate between slides projected on a screen showing two objects versus those showing three. Gelman also used inspection time as a method of inquiry. Karen Wynn studied the extent to which infants can comprehend number. Her initial findings suggest that infants only a few days old can differentiate between "one" and "more than one" and by four or five months can add and subtract using small numbers. Mix, Huttenlocher, and Levine have shown, however, that young infants' mathematical cognition is not so clear-cut as Wynn has argued.

In addition to the nativist argument, some researchers in mathematical cognition embrace a more developmentalist model. These researchers include Herbert Ginsburg, Arthur Baroody, and Douglas Clements. Ginsburg has advanced the Piagetian clinical interview method as a means of identifying the strengths and weaknesses of young children's mathematical abilities. He and his colleagues have also implemented naturalistic observation methodology as a means of identifying the length of time that young children are engaged in mathematical activity. Baroody also takes a developmentalist approach in studying young children's arithmetic abilities. Similarly, Clements has investigated young children's spatial and geometric development.

There has been a great deal of debate in recent years about the most efficient way to teach language. Proponents of whole-language learning promote a method of instruction that emphasizes meaning and context. Those who embrace phonics, on the other hand, emphasize the learning of language through sounds and elemental grammatical structures, such as the phoneme, as a means of identifying words and their eventual meanings.

Another area of inquiry is language cognition. Ee Clark's research focuses primarily on the acquisition of meaning and semantic relationships. Other researchers include Lois Bloom, who investigates the transitional points when infants use language as a form of expression, and Benedicte de Boysson-Bardies, who has examined the role of babbling and the transition from babbling to artificial language.

Daniel Ness and Chia-ling Lin

REFERENCES

Baillargeon, Renee. "The Acquisition of Physical Knowledge in Infancy: A Summary in Eight Lessons." In *Blackwell Handbook of Childhood Cognitive Development*, ed. U. Goswami, 46–83. Oxford: Blackwell, 2002.

Baroody, Arthur J. "The Development of Adaptive Expertise and Flexibility: The Integration of Conceptual and Procedural Knowledge. In *The Development of Arithmetic Concepts and Skills*, ed. Arthur J. Baroody and Ann Dowker, 1–34. Mahwah, NJ: Lawrence Erlbaum, 2003.

Bloom, Lois. *The Transition from Infancy to Language: Acquiring the Power of Expression*. New York: Cambridge University Press, 1995.

Boysson-Bardies, Benedicte de. *How Language Comes to Children: From Birth to Two Years*. Cambridge: MIT Press, 2001.

Bruner, Jerome. *The Process of Education*. Cambridge, MA: Harvard University Press, 1960.

Clark, Eve V. *The Lexicon in Acquisition*. Cambridge, UK: Cambridge University Press, 1993.

Clements, Douglas H. "Linking research and curriculum development." In *Handbook of International Research in Mathematics Education*, ed. Lynn D. English, 589–625. New York: Taylor & Francis, 2008.

Ginsburg, Herbert P. *Entering the Child's Mind*. New York: Cambridge University Press, 1997.

Ginsburg, Herbert P., and Sylvia Opper. *Piaget's Theory of Intellectual Development*. Englewood Cliffs, NJ: Prentice Hall, 1987.

Ginsburg, Herbert P., Noriyuki Inoue, and Kyoung-Hye Seo. "Young Children Doing Mathematics: Observations of Everyday Activities." In *Mathematics in the Early Years*, ed. Juanita Copley, 88–99. Reston, VA: National Council of Teachers of Mathematics, 1999.

Kirschner, David, and James A. Whitson. *Situated Cognition: Social, Semiotic, and Psychological Perspectives*. Mahwah, NJ: Lawrence Erlbaum, 1997.

Kozulin, Alex. *Psychological Tools: A Sociocultural Approach to Education*. Cambridge, MA: Harvard University Press, 2001.

Lave, Jean. *Cognition in Practice: Mind, Mathematics, and Culture in Everyday Life*. New York: Cambridge University Press, 1988.

Mix, Kelly, Janellen Huttenlocher, and Susan C. Levine. *Quantitative Development in Infancy and Early Childhood*. Oxford: Oxford University Press, 2002.

Piaget, Jean. *The Child's Conception of the World*. Totowa, NJ: Littlefield Addams, 1929.

Saxe, Geoffrey. "Effects of Schooling on Arithmetical Understanding: Studies with Oksapmin Children in Papua New Guinea." *Journal of Educational Psychology* 77:5 (1982): 503–513.

Vygotsky, Lev. *Mind in Society*. Cambridge, MA: Harvard University Press, 1978.

Walkerdine, Valerie. *The Mastery of Reason*. London: Routledge, 1988.

Wynn, Karen. "Addition and Subtraction by Human Infants." *Nature* 358 (1992): 749–750.

BASIC COGNITIVE FUNCTIONS

Scholars in the fields of psychology and education have studied cognition since the early twentieth century. However, the implementation of cognition as a means to support educational practice is a relatively novel venture that did not really take shape until the early 1970s. At the present time, the principles of cognition play a major role in the shaping and development of educational curriculum, instruction, and assessment. What follows are definitions and descriptions of basic cognitive functions that are necessary for future learning.

Perception

The external world provides a bath of stimulation for an organism. Perception is one of the most evident aspects of cognition because it is one of the first ways that humans begin to make sense of the world. One apparent way of defining perception is to construe it as a transaction or mediating process between the percipient and the observable world. There are two ways to deal with how humans perceive the world. First, we see things that are viewable in our environment. Second, we use what we perceive as a means for directing our way within this environment; that is, we see what we are looking for, what we have an affinity for, or what we at one time had meaningful experiences of. Perception, then, is selective. Humans perceive selectively in two fundamentally different ways, both of which are forms of filtering. The first form is fixed filtering, in which what is perceived is determined by the functional and structural features of the sensory systems themselves. For example, in terms of vision, humans can respond to wavelengths within the range of 360 to 760 nanometers. This perception is much different for other organisms, such as the honeybee, which senses objects primarily in the ultraviolet range. The second form is selected filtering, which is achieved through attention and memory—two characteristics of cognition that are discussed below.

Filtering mechanisms, which are required in order to exclude extraneous stimuli, are governed by passive filtration. Since humans do not respond to all wavelengths of light, no matter what the range of radiation might be, we will see only a small portion. The mechanisms of perception contain two kinds of filters. The first is a passive filter, which behaves in the same way trial after trial and event after event. For example, in vision, the retinal receptors—the rods and cones—contain pigments. These pigments must be acted on by quanta of light, which, in turn, strike molecules of pigments. Subsequently, the pigments undergo decomposition. Humans do not see all electromagnetic radiation, only the range called the visible range—again between 360 and 760 nanometers; humans do not see ultraviolet light like the honeybee can. Therefore, passive filtration determines that humans can see within a visible range and that beyond that range (less than 360 nanometers and more than 760 nanometers), no vision is possible. The same

is true for the auditory system. Humans can hear sounds that are between 20 hertz and 20,000 hertz (i.e., cycles per second). Dogs, unlike humans, can hear sounds greater than 20,000 hertz. The human auditory system, then, has fixed—passive—filtering capacities, simply due to the physical nature of the human ear. The eardrum does not accept frequencies higher than the audible range. It is designed in a certain way that limits the frequency range. All human and animal perceptual systems have these fixed filter features.

There are also active filters that shape our perceptions. Humans are able to filter things out quite selectively with a selectivity that depends in part on learning and also seems to depend to some extent on certain innate predispositions. There are many examples of active filtering that we use all the time. One important example is the "cocktail party" effect. The "cocktail party" effect works as follows: Sandy is at a party with dozens of other people. Groups of people are engaged in separate conversations all around her. Music is playing in the background. The room is alive with sound. Sandy is solely preoccupied with the conversation she is having, notwithstanding the fact that her auditory system is able to accept all these other sounds. However, these other sounds are all supra threshold—they have been shut out unintentionally. Next, suppose Sandy hears someone in a distant corner of the room mention her name. The speaker in the corner of the room does not know who Sandy is; he is talking to another person who has the same name—Sandy—as she. Sandy will most likely stop in the middle of her conversation and turn around and look over to the corner of the room. She might even walk over to the speaker and say, "Did I hear you mention my name?"

The cocktail party effect demonstrates two phenomena. First, humans have a highly selective filter—in other words, a filtering mechanism that keeps away everything that is not central to the conversation. Second, the effect is variable in that if something in the acoustic environment is meaningful, like a person's own name, the filter will accept it. The active nature of the auditory system exemplifies the basic characteristics of human attention (discussed below).

The problem with understanding visual perception is the fact that determining exactly what we see is a difficult thing to do. For example, examine the shape in Figure 1 (see page 166). What is it, and why do we see it in the way we do? Nearly all readers will agree that the shape is a circle. Now examine the shape in Figure 2 and answer the same question. Again, we can agree that the shape we see in Figure 2 is an ellipse. It can be argued, however, that what we see in Figure 1 and what we see in Figure 2 are exactly identical. We do not view them as identical individually because we are not basing our conclusions on additional information or contextual clues. However, we can perceive the circle and the ellipse as the same shape by examining the cylinder in Figure 3.

Attention

The value of visual (and auditory) perception is crucial to how we pay attention to certain stimuli and not to others. Assuming that there is some initial cognitive processing occurring, attention can be defined as continuous cognitive processing. Like perception, attention has two properties. First, attention is limited in that all continuous cognitive processing at some point will come to an end and will be directed elsewhere. Second, attention is also selective. An individual will spend time on a particular mental activity through cognitive processing if that very activity is deemed important. The fact that attention is selective presupposes the fact that it is limited—if we do not want to expend mental currency on a particular cognitive task, we will revert to some other task. Hence, each cognitive task cannot last forever.

The cocktail party effect was described in the discussion of human perception above. It showed that humans within an ambient acoustic environment can pick up specific words that will direct their attention elsewhere. Colin Cherry's study, described in "Some Experiments on the Recognition of Speech, with One and with Two Ears" (1953), was one of the first studies (and perhaps the most significant at the time) that outlined and examined the human potential of attention. Cherry questioned which factors had the greatest influence on human attention when an individual was engaged in listening to two separate aurally verbal monologues simultaneously, as opposed to a single monologue.

It is extremely common to listen to single monologues, a form of discourse that attentional cognitive scientists have labeled monaural attention. People engage in this act every day—listening to a teacher give a lecture, a sole comedian cracking jokes on stage,

Figure 1: **Visual Perception: Circle**

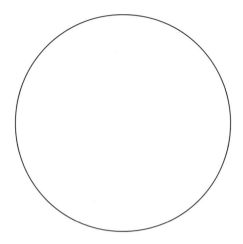

Figure 2: **Visual Perception: Ellipse**

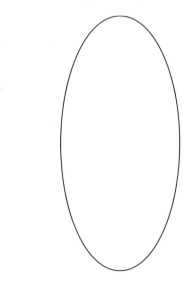

Figure 3: **Visual Perception: Cylinder**

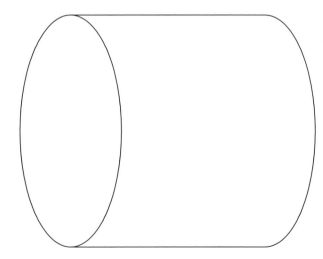

a religious leader giving a sermon, or a newscaster on television. But monaural attention is not informative in explaining the specific features that individuals cognitively select when listening to a single conversation. In other words, it is difficult to determine which parts of a monologue humans focus, or center, on as a way to pay attention. Cherry's attention studies and attention researchers who followed him have provided a conducive experimental environment in investigating attention. The simultaneous double monologue method solved the problems that monaural attention studies could not. Accordingly, monaural attention studies were replaced by dichotic attention (simultaneous double monologue) studies. In one classic dichotic attention study, an individual would put on a headphone and hear two separate conversations—one entering the left ear and the other the right. On the left side, the investigators would play a professor's lecture that the subject would hear in the left ear. On the right side, the investigators would play an entirely different conversation—most often a sequence of numbers, or possibly a well-known passage from a famous poem or text—that the subject would hear in the right ear. Several important findings emanated from this study and many that followed. First, dichotic attention is difficult to do; humans find it quite difficult to pay attention to two separate conversations going on simultaneously. Prior to these studies, this difficulty may have seemed intuitively self-evident, but it had not been shown scientifically. Second, and related to the first finding, subjects were quite attentive, through their ability to describe what they heard in the professor's lecture (i.e., left ear) and not to the number sequence, word repetition, or well-known passage. In other words, each subject could explain the content of the lecture that was entering the left ear but was unable to recite the content entering the right ear. However, most subjects were able to describe the overall contextual features of the right-ear conversation (e.g., "It sounded like a pattern"; "Numbers were involved but I'm not sure which ones"; "The content was connected [or detached], but I couldn't tell you what was said"). Although it might seem self-evident that some people would be more attentive to a poem than the professor's lecture, results show that participants were more attentive to the lecture than the reading of a poem. Factors such as the way in which the poem was recited or the structure of the poem may have been distractors for participants.

Memory

Memory is a necessary component of cognitive processes. Without memory, most people would find it very difficult to construct ideas from previously acquired knowledge. Nevertheless, there have been many examples of individuals who cannot remember anything prior to several seconds in the past, yet they are able to memorize the contours and rhythms of musical compositions after listening to them. It is important to consider, however, that memory alone is not the only factor in cognition. Schooling processes over the last two centuries have, in part, instilled a culture of knowledge based on students' memory practices as a means of knowledge acquisition. This can be seen most vividly during periods when students learn mathematics. For years, teachers would approach concepts in arithmetic and other topics in mathematics by encouraging and fostering speed and accuracy of number facts, thus making memory the sine qua non of knowledge acquisition. Nevertheless, without memory, it is unclear what the trajectory of knowledge acquisition would look like. To investigate what people remember, it is necessary to examine the nature of memory retrieval—that is, sensory memory, primary memory, and secondary memory.

It is more productive to think of memory not in terms of short-term versus long-term memories, but in terms of the interrelationship between sensory stimulation, a staging ground for deciding what is important (secondary memory) and what is not (primary memory), and repetition. Sensory memory is the memory that is produced when the brain is stimulated by objects or events in the external environment. The essential question in discussing sensory memory is this: how much information can people absorb spontaneously? Sensory memory emanates from what we apprehend instantaneously and subsequently deem important enough to pay attention to. Two important types of sensory memory are iconic memory and echoic memory. Iconic memory refers to contact with the sensory environment through visual stimulation, while echoic memory refers to contact with external stimuli through auditory stimulation.

Primary memory, as stated above, is like a staging ground or holding pen for incoming stimuli. One example of primary memory is the short list of groceries we need to buy in a supermarket—for example, broccoli, milk, bread, and fish. We tend to hold this information for a very short period of time—specifically until the groceries are brought to the counter for purchase. The so-called shelf life of primary memory is shortened due to forgetting. There are three types of forgetting that shorten and eventually extinguish primary memories: proactive interference, retroactive interference, and decay. Proactive interference occurs when the learning of a subject is followed immediately by the learning of a second subject. For example, if someone studies biology in the morning and subsequently studies chemistry in the early afternoon for a late afternoon chemistry test, the earlier time spent studying biology will interfere with the performance on the chemistry test. Retroactive interference will occur if the same person studies chemistry in the morning followed by biology in the early afternoon, followed by a chemistry test in the late afternoon (i.e., switching the order of what was studied). Decay is the extinction of what is being represented within primary memory over time.

Secondary memory refers to the concepts that we store over very long periods of time. If asked how many legs a dog has, a five-year-old child will undoubtedly say "four," which is the answer that is stored as secondary memory. The idea that dogs have four legs is one that the child learned initially through sensory memory, perhaps due to early exposure to pets or a related environmental stimulus, and subsequently through primary memory, possibly as the child categorizes "dog" by connecting "dog" with "four legs." The child will then rehearse this idea many times before it is stored into secondary memory. Examples of secondary memory span the range of concepts from simple to complex. It should be clear that historians, geographers, physicists, linguists, and engineers store information that is essential to their academic domains in secondary memory, where it is available for retrieval at some later point. In sum, it is possible to construe memory retrieval in the following way:

1. The external environment sets off the sensory systems—that is, the sensory memory—in which the auditory, visual, tactile, olfactory, or taste senses react. These reactions send signals, via neural activity, to the brain. If these reactions allow for greater attention, then short-term memory is activated. If these reactions contribute to meager stimulation or no stimulation at all, then sensory memory is forgotten.

2. If that short-term memory is activated, then the individual must be attentive in some way to sensory memory. But like sensory memory, short-term memory could be forgotten if the information that was inputted is not necessary for the future. The grocery store scenario above is a prime example of this. However, if it is necessary for a student to learn the process of photosynthesis in order to become a botanist, it will be essential for that individual to identify the interrelated ideas that are involved in plant growth. In short, the individual must practice or rehearse (and even re-rehearse) certain content in order to master concepts and theories within a particular academic domain.

3. Long-term memory for the most part is not forgotten. It is the memory that remains in one's mind even for a lifetime. It accepts the content that was rehearsed and re-rehearsed in short-term memory by retrieving necessary concepts.

Imagery

Imagery is a component of cognition that is connected with perception: we perceive images—both symbolic and spatial—as a means of making sense of the world. Visual imagery generally refers to two conditions: images that are formed through sight and images that are formed based on what we think something looks like. The idea of visual or mental imagery was an emerging topic in the early days of psychology in the late nineteenth century, particularly in reference to cognitive studies. Experimental psychologists used introspection as a means of identifying one's cognitive behaviors. It seemed conclusive to the introspectionists (such as Wilhelm Wundt and his student Edward B. Titchener) that thought was virtually the same as imagery. This assumption changed with the advent of behaviorism in the United States during the early decades of the twentieth century. Behaviorism slowed the discussion of imagery among psychologists for at least 50 years. Imagery reemerged in 1963 when Alan Paivio introduced the topic in relation to concrete versus abstract words in an article in the *Canadian*

Journal of Psychology. Paivio would give two words to a subject to memorize. On a later day, the researcher would ask the subject to recall the second word of a pair when given the first word, which is the stimulus word. So, for example, a subject would be given the pair "potato–lamp" and at a later point asked to produce the word that goes with "potato"—namely, "lamp." Paivio concluded that subjects had a more difficult time when given abstract stimulus words (e.g., "justice–cereal") than when given concrete stimulus words (e.g., "potato-lamp"). In a later study, Paivio and Dennis Foth proposed the dual coding hypothesis, which states that there are two ways to represent concepts. One way is through a verbal representation and the other is through mental imagery. People generally represent abstract concepts more effectively through verbal discourse and represent concrete concepts more effectively using some form of mental imagery.

In more recent decades the subject of visual imagery underwent a great deal of scrutiny because some scholars argued that all human thinking could be represented verbally (see Pylyshyn 1973, 1981, 2003). The debate revolved around propositional representation versus analog representation. Advocates of propositional representation argued that images are not needed to represent behavior; rather, all cognitive activity is reducible to the proposition, which is the basic construct for determining whether something is true or false. In contrast to the propositional representation argument, advocates of analog representation argued that relying solely on verbal representation does not account for situations that describe a specific relation, nonsyntactical representation (since propositional representation is based on syntax), and spatial considerations (see Kosslyn 1980, 1995). Moreover, propositional representations rely on the truth or fallaciousness of something considered, while a mental image does not.

The debate between the two arguments seemed to have been resolved by brain imaging. During the 1990s, neuroscientists and cognitive psychologists used positron emission tomography (PET) and functional magnetic resonance imaging (fMRI) as a means of settling the question. In sum, researchers found that when subjects used mental imagery to explain a concept, the primary visual cortex of the brain was most active; when subjects used verbal representation

as an explanation, then the language centers of the brain were most active.

Mental imagery is also important because its use can be beneficial in educational settings. Given that mental symbolism in mathematics or in a particular language is often difficult for young children to use, manipulatives—hands-on objects that are designed for learning—are often used as a means of showing alternative methods for solving problems. For example, counters or small blocks can be used when children demonstrate that they know the addition or subtraction concept. Manipulatives allow children to create visual images of problems that are otherwise provided with words alone. When children engage in visual imagery, they are asked to represent something based on what it looks like. With spatial imagery, children are asked to identify where an object is in the context of its place or location in space.

Concepts and Procedures

In the traditional view, concepts are associated with the process of categorization because a concept refers to a list that can be categorized under a particular heading. For example, the animals that are named poodle, cocker spaniel, collie, German shepherd, and Labrador retriever all fall under the concept of "dog." More specifically, a concept is a required and sufficient condition that satisfies membership within a particular category. It serves as a mental representation of any class of objects or ideas. In a more contemporary view, concepts are the blocks of ideas that develop as a result of the interrelationship between different aspects of factual knowledge. In terms of educational subjects such as science or mathematics, concepts are generally considered of fundamental importance because they are thought to be essential in long-term, secondary memory storage. That is, the more one builds on conceptual knowledge, the more facile one will be in a particular academic domain. Conceptual knowledge bridges the gap between novice and expert knowledge. In science, one might think of the concept of states of matter, in which "liquid" would be essential in understanding this concept. In mathematics, one might think of the concept of place value, in which Hindu-Arabic numerals are written in a manner that represents positions in the base-ten system.

Educational researchers, practitioners, and psychologists often pit conceptual knowledge in opposition to procedural knowledge. In this case, procedures are the instructions one carries out in order to obtain a result in a particular task. In science, this can be done by following instructions in conducting a laboratory task. In mathematics, procedures can be conducted by following step-by-step instructions or using an algorithm. It is relatively easy to use procedural knowledge when attempting to solve mathematical problems. Unfortunately, when problems become too difficult or when students forget which procedure to use for a given problem—given that procedures without a conceptual basis are generally stored in short-term memory—procedural knowledge alone can impede one's mastery in a given practical or academic domain. Procedural knowledge and application should be preceded by conceptual knowledge in order to obtain optimal results and eventual expertise in an academic subject.

Daniel Ness and Chia-ling Lin

REFERENCES

Cherry, Colin. "Some Experiments on the Recognition of Speech, with One and with Two Ears." *Journal of the Acoustical Society of America* 23 (1953): 915–919.

Kosslyn, Stephen M. *Image and Mind*. Cambridge, MA: Harvard University Press, 1980.

———. "Mental Imagery." In *Visual Cognition: An Invitation to Cognitive Science*, vol. 2, ed. Stephen M. Kosslyn, 267–296. Cambridge: MIT Press, 1995.

Paivio, Alan. "Learning the Adjective-Noun Paired Associates as a Function of Adjective-Noun Word Order and Noun Abstractness." *Canadian Journal of Psychology* 17:4 (1963): 370–379.

Paivio, Alan, and Dennis Foth. "Imaginal and Verbal Mediators and Noun Concreteness in Paired-associate Learning: The Elusive Interaction." *Journal of Verbal Learning and Verbal Behavior* 9:4 (1970): 384–390.

Pylyshyn, Zenon W. "The Imagery Debate: Analogue Media Versus Tacit Knowledge." *Psychological Review* 88:1 (1981): 16–45.

———. "Return of the Mental Image: Are There Really Pictures in the Brain?" *Trends in Cognitive Sciences* 7 (2003): 113–118.

———. "What the Mind's Eye Tells the Mind's Brain: A Critique of Mental Imagery." *Psychological Bulletin* 80:1 (1973): 1–24.

Sacks, Oliver. *Musicophilia*. New York: Vintage Books, 2008.

Willingham, Daniel. *Cognition: The Thinking Animal*. Upper Saddle River, NJ: Prentice-Hall, 2008.

COMPLEX COGNITIVE FUNCTIONS

In addition to basic cognitive functions, humans are also capable of carrying out more advanced cognitive behaviors as well. What follows are definitions and descriptions of complex cognitive functions that individuals use in order to plan their behaviors: deductive and inductive reasoning, algorithms and heuristics, formal and informal logic, problem solving and cognitive development, neuroscience, and artificial intelligence.

Argumentation

Cognition is a central component to the process of argumentation. The term "argumentation" has been used pejoratively in common discourse because it contains the root word "argument," which is often associated with the notion of bickering or fighting. But argumentation is a positive form of engagement between two or more parties because it is a way for one side to convince or sway the other side. Through discourse, argumentation, in the best-case scenario, does not (and most researchers would posit should not) involve the use of propaganda, pandering, or bias when attempting to convince an audience one way or another. Rather, it should promote and employ dialogue that invokes critical inquiry and challenging questions.

In general, it seems to be the case that humans strive in the direction of perfection when performing tasks. But human effort seldom reaches that point. As young children develop intellectually, they identify ways of achieving solutions to tasks that are more efficient than they have attempted any time before. For example, a young child of three years, five months might count seven gummy bears by pushing each one aside when counting. That same child one year later might use a more efficient strategy when counting seven objects, such as counting them by tagging—that is, touching or pointing at each of them when counting. As humans age, there is a gradually greater tendency to optimize our attempts to solve problems by considering the speed at which we problem solve and the accuracy for which we strive when attempting a solution. But sometimes we simply do not have the time, and perhaps the ability, to maximize our strengths or optimize our strategies when making decisions or solving problems in our everyday lives. Satisficing, a term coined by psychologist Herbert Simon in 1956, is what we do when we are not necessarily concerned with obtaining the *best* or *optimal* solution, but simply a *good* or *fair* one.

Algorithms vs. Heuristics: Decision-Making Shortcuts

Algorithms are formalized symbolic structures that are used to solve problems. They should have a reliable accuracy rate of 1.00; that is, if executed correctly, solutions should be 100 percent accurate. Algorithms can be used in any academic domain, but are most frequently associated with mathematics and the sciences. They can be standard—that is, common to the general schooled public—or invented, in which the algorithm is defined by a single individual for a particular (nonstandard) purpose. For example, the standard algorithm for multiplying 23 by 4 is the following:

$$\begin{array}{r} 2\,^{1}3 \\ \times\ 4 \\ \hline 9\ 2 \end{array}$$

In this case, the standard algorithm for multiplication indicates that the 4 must be multiplied by 3. The product, "12," is indicated by placing the "2" in the ones place of the final product. The "1" in the tens place of the number "12" is placed next to the "2" of "23." So, 4 times 20 is 80, and 80 plus 10 (which is symbolized as the small "1") is 90. The "9" for "90" is placed in the tens place of the final product. An example for a contrived, invented algorithm for the same problem would be the repeated addition of the number "23" (i.e., 23 + 23 + 23 + 23) or 4 times 20 plus 4 times 3.

Like algorithms, heuristics are devices that are used to reach a solution to a problem. They differ, however, from algorithms in that their accuracy rate is less than 100 percent. Heuristics can be developed and used consciously or even without necessarily realizing that one has been constructed in the mind. For example, consider the following problem: If a farm consists of cows and chickens and there are 8 heads and 22 legs, how many cows and chickens are there? To solve this problem, a student can develop a heuristic by drawing a diagram of eight circles (representing heads) and then adding two line strokes (representing legs) to each circle. If this student is aware that chickens have two legs and cows have four, then two additional legs will be drawn for each head until 22 legs have been drawn altogether. (Farmer Smith has 3 cows and 5 chickens.)

Formal Logic vs. Informal Logic

One who employs formal logic often uses categorical, conditional, or disjunctive syllogisms as a means of attempting to convince listeners or readers. For example, examine the following categorical syllogism:

A: All skyscrapers are made of cheese.
B: The Empire State Building is a skyscraper.
C: Therefore, the Empire State Building is made of cheese.

Three issues arise when examining this syllogism. First, with the exception of B, the content is untrue; we know that skyscrapers are not made of cheese. Second, unlike the content, the form of the argument is actually valid and convincing. Despite the fact that the content is false, the syllogism's form is valid in that if A is true, and if B is included in A, then C must be true. Third, the conclusion, C, is not new—it appears in some context in parts A or B. That is, C states that the Empire State Building is a skyscraper (B) that is made of cheese (A).

Formal Logic

Deductive reasoning was considered the most effective method of argumentation for more than two millennia. Aristotle was one of the first architects and originators of deductive reasoning for the purpose of argumentation and its place as the foundation of rhetoric. With only slight modification, Aristotelian logic continued to govern how argumentation would be conducted for the next 2,000 years. Deductive reasoning was one of the only methods used during ancient, medieval, and modern litigation practices as a means of winning court cases or gaining political advantage over an opponent. Given a strong association with formal logic, the argumentation process was always seen as absolute; to prevail in an argument meant that one's support was based on certainty—that is, through the use of syllogisms.

By the early twentieth century, however, it became clear that formal logic was a highly flawed method in litigation. In addition, with the expansion of research in the physical and social sciences, formal logic became a defective approach for purposes of inquiry. There was a growing awareness of what the approaches to deductive reasoning omitted. This led to dissatisfaction with the formal-deductive model for reasoning. Although the deductive argument's form is valid, the possibility of injecting false content into its framework is apparent. In order to rectify these shortcomings, people presenting arguments will invoke informal logic instead.

Informal Logic

There are three primary components of informal logic: the claim, its evidence, and the inferences that link the evidence with the claim (Zarefsky 2002).

Claims

A claim is essentially identical to the resolution of some type of controversy in which an audience will be asked to reject or accept one side of the argument. Different types of claims raise different types of issues. There are four types of claims: claims of fact, claims of definition, claims of value, and claims of policy. Claims of fact do not require a great deal of evidence because the claim is based on factual information. For example, we can claim that water freezes at 0° Celsius. Someone can verify the evidence with a thermometer or from print or electronic resources. Factual claims are descriptive for the very reason that they can be verified in a source. Claims of definition are based on interpretation because definitions are not neutral. Someone, for example, might claim that a field is an open region consisting of grassland or a related kind of turf. The listener or reader might ask whether the claim can be interpreted in a different way. Claims of value are based on one's judgment. The claim, for example, "Students whose teachers use cognitively guided instruction perform better than those whose teachers do not" is a value claim. Its conclusion cannot be verified in a book (such as a claim of fact) or examined through a definition (as in a claim of definition). Finally, claims of policy are based

on action, or what should be done in a particular situation. For example, it can be argued that the United States should nationalize education curriculum. The counterclaim would be that the country should not adopt a national curriculum. The problem that arises with claims of policy is that they have no influence without evidence to support them.

Evidence

Evidence serves as the basis of a claim. Questions such as "How do you know?" or "What do you have to go on?" are common ones. Three common types of evidence can be grouped under the headings of objective data, social consensus, and credibility (Newman and Newman 1969; Rieke and Sillars 1997). Objective data may be in the form of cases, statistical studies, historical documents, and testimony. Each of these data types may be used to support different types of research. For example, testimony would not be used to support the existence of a cause-and-effect relationship between two phenomena. It usually is not as credible as the use of inferential statistics. Social consensus refers to the beliefs of a particular population group that function almost like facts. Social consensus evidence includes "common knowledge," shared value judgments, previously established conclusions, and stipulations in a particular discussion. Different types of social consensus are used to support different types of research. The main problem with social consensus is that popular opinion has the potential to distort reality. The credibility of a person is also a form of evidence for claims. It is often meant as a function of trust and competence. Like the two previous forms of evidence, credibility is also problematic because a listener will need to determine if the individual cited is an authority on the subject. Also, the listener will need to determine if the individual is biased toward or against something or someone and if there is a vested interest that serves as the basis of the bias.

Inferences

Inferences support the link between evidence and claim, and warrants serve to define the importance of particular inferences. There are six types of inference: analogy, narrative, example, correlation, cause-and-effect, and form. Analogy is often invoked as an inference to link evidence with claim because it allows individuals to show fallacies through the use of relationships between two ideas or situations. Analogy comes in two forms: literal analogy and figurative analogy. Literal analogies are direct comparisons of objects or events that are related to the same situation. Literal analogies are weak as a form of effective reasoning because they are difficult to generalize. Figurative analogies, however, are useful in effective reasoning because they rely on general relationships between objects, events, or situations and not merely on the specific comparisons between them. Narrative inferences are those based on the structure of stories. The use of narrative is an attempt to personalize a story so that the listeners or readers can imagine themselves within the story as participants. The story serves as a means to compare its plot, conflict, and resolution to the actual controversy itself. From this comparison, listeners or readers may be convinced to accept or reject one side of an argument (Zarefsky 2002). Example inferences are used to derive a general statement from one or more specific examples. Two types of inference from example will allow someone to make a generalization by comparing the part to the whole: the statistical generalization and the anecdotal generalization. The statistical generalization is used when a researcher draws on a sample of an entire population and relates the conclusion to the entire population because of what is true of the sample. The anecdotal generalization is used when someone cites a few specific anecdotal references and then draws a conclusion based on those few cases.

Correlational inferences are often used as a means to demonstrate the strength of evidence that supports a claim through relationships between two or more items or events. Inference of correlation can show the existence of a statistically relevant relationship between two or more variables. When using correlation, the individual is concerned only about the existence of a relationship between two things—not whether one thing is the cause of the other. Causal inferences are used to explain relationships in which one phenomenon has influence on another. Causation is more difficult to realize than other forms of inference because it involves abstractions—not observation (as in correlation). Inferences of form are based on an argument's structure. The conclusion seems as if it follows with certainty but it is really based on probability that something is or is not evident.

Problem Solving and Cognitive Development

Problem solving is a major component in the course of cognitive development. It is a characteristic of cognitive behavior that is apparent in humans and higher-order organisms, such as primates, dogs, and certain birds and sea life. It enables organisms to obtain a desired result, such as figuring out how to obtain food that is too far to reach, how to approach a question in mathematics, how to play a cluster chord on the piano, or how to fix a machine that does not work properly.

Problem Solving Through Comparative Cognitive Studies

Studies of cognitive abilities from a comparative perspective (i.e., between humans and animals) began in the early twentieth century with the work of the Gestalt psychologists, particularly Wolfgang Kohler. In one of his definitive studies, Kohler shows that stimulus response theory fails to provide reasons for various behaviors of animals, particularly primates. For example, an ape in a cage about the size of a midsize room locates bananas on the roof of the cage. But the ape cannot reach the bananas. Kohler presents the ape with a pair of long sticks. The ape attempts to use the sticks to get the bananas, but one stick alone will not reach them. After several hours of observation, Kohler notices that, through trial and error, the ape was able to connect the sticks so that the length of both sticks together is greater than the distance between the ape and the bananas. That is, the ape identified a method to obtain the bananas through solving a problem—namely, attaching the two sticks end to end.

Kohler's studies provide an alternative to the popular operant conditioning argument proposed by behavioral psychologists, whose primary vehicle for acquiring knowledge was stimulus followed by response. Instead, Kohler's investigations lead the reader to conclude that knowledge acquisition is more cognitive and less behaviorist; rather than stimulus followed by response, the ape showed evidence of stimulus—noticing bananas, followed by second stimulus—finding two sticks, followed by third—putting the sticks together to make a longer stick, and so forth.

Another important study that was contemporaneous to the work of Kohler was that of Edward Tolman, a psychologist at the University of California at Berkeley. Tolman's well-known article "Cognitive Maps in Rats and Men" (1948) contradicts a great deal of what behavioral psychology says about knowledge acquisition. Tolman and his colleagues initially placed laboratory rats in a maze. The rats would then run through the maze, ending up in locations that did not lead them to the exit of the maze. Many of the rats would not even try to find how to leave the maze, but would instead sniff around corners for several hours. The rats were then strapped in miniature wheelbarrows. The experimenters then wheeled the rats through a maze correctly (i.e., so that the rats in the wheelbarrows would exit the maze where food was often located). Tolman and his colleagues did this for several trials, and then they set the rats free to run through the maze. This time, the rats found the exit of the maze with little difficulty. In a subsequent experiment, Tolman flooded the maze to see if the rats would eventually be able to swim to the exit of the maze. The rats, in fact, were able to demonstrate an ability to swim to the maze's exit.

Behaviorists would argue that organisms learn new knowledge through operant conditioning—that is, the organisms would be rewarded and thus follow the appropriate steps to learn a novel task. If this were true, then, if one were to condition a rat to correctly solve a maze, the rat would repetitively solve the maze by following all the left and right turns toward the exit where the food is, even if the maze were taken away. But this is simply not the case. A rat that learns the directions to exit a maze will not follow the left and right patterns if the maze is removed; rather, the rat will run directly to where the food is.

Algorithmic and Heuristic Approaches to Solve School-Related Problems

One of the most important developers in the field of problem solving was George Pólya, a Hungarian mathematician who emigrated to the United States before World War II. As a mathematician, Pólya was an anomaly—he was no child prodigy, nor was he particularly successful as a student of mathematics in primary school. His interest in mathematics grew when he was a young college student, as he was

greatly influenced by one of his mathematics professors. Despite this seemingly slow introduction to the subject, Pólya came to be known as one of the major mathematical thinkers of the twentieth century, and perhaps the best-known professor of mathematics at Stanford University. Pólya did not put all his energies solely into mathematical research, however. One of his many other interests was the changing nature of mathematical teaching and learning in American public (and private) schools, an interest that was sparked in the 1930s when he was developing algorithms for the United States military. During this time, Pólya was searching not only for algorithms that would enable the functioning of various applications—he was also searching for the maximization and optimization of the application's efficiency. This interest led Pólya to examine methods of problem solving that could be used not only for academic purposes, but for educational purposes as well.

Pólya developed a four-step method for solving mathematical problems that turned out to be one of the most valuable applications in mathematics education of the twentieth century. Pólya's method for problem solving seems self-evident and intuitive to most people today. But back in the 1930s, it was not so evident. The general approach is the following:

1. Understand the problem. Understanding is not simply a matter of reading a problem. Reading any type of written text does not mean that one is clear about what is being asked. The problem solver must be clear about what the problem entails and what type of solution is appropriate.

2. Devise a plan to solve the problem. In this step, it is assumed that the problem solver will need to identify prior knowledge as a means of formulating a strategy for solving the problem. The strategy could entail the ability to know which algorithm or set of algorithms to use or perhaps to utilize one or more heuristics that will approximate a solution.

3. Carry out the plan. This step simply calls for the problem solver to execute the plan that was devised in step 2. Again, the execution of the plan may involve anywhere from one instruction to multiple algorithms or heuristics in a chronological and orderly manner. It is in this step that the solution appears.

4. Check the result or solution. It is important to ensure that the solution that was found is both accurate and reliable. Students of all ages often fail to check their results, thus running the risk of erroneous solutions.

As mentioned in step 2 above, Pólya offers two possibilities for solving mathematical problems—algorithms and heuristics. For example, in determining the importance of a particular issue, such as economics, in a presidential campaign, a political scientist or sociologist might develop a heuristic that is capable of counting the number of times each presidential candidate uses words that have associations with economics (e.g., financial, recession, banks, Wall Street, pocketbook).

In another example in which algorithms must be employed, a student is given the following problem: "A calculator's screen functions correctly, but the keypad does not. Only the buttons for "7," "+," "−," "×," "÷," and "=" work. How might it be possible to obtain a reading of "34" on the screen when using only these buttons?" To answer this question, the student must use arithmetic algorithms. More important, however, the student must execute these algorithms in the correct sequence. To do so, the student must use prior knowledge, mostly through long-term memory. Without prior knowledge, one's ability to solve problems would be futile. In solving this problem, a student should realize, first, that it is necessary to operate on "7" in such a way as to make the outcome larger—that is, by initially adding or multiplying 7 with 7, and not subtracting or dividing. Next, the student should realize that 7 is not a factor of 34, so it will take a long time to add 7s repetitively to the point that a multiple of 34 is reached. So it might be more fruitful to multiply. The student knows that 7 × 7 is 49. But 49 is not a multiple of 34, so the student might now multiply 49 by 7 and get 343. The student then subtracts 7 from 343 and then divides 336 by 7, getting 48. The next step is to subtract 7 from 48 and another 7 from 41 to obtain "34" on the screen.

Neuroscience

Neuroscience is the study of the physiological makeup of the brain. One studies neuroscience in connection with cognition and learning in an effort to under-

stand how the physiology of the brain changes as a result of various forms of cognitive activity. The study of neuroscience emerged in the nineteenth century when scientists were interested in determining where certain cognitive constructs—such as memory, sound, intensity of sound (loud vs. soft), vision, and language—were located in the brain. Within the last two to three decades, the processes of scanning and neuroimaging have taken scientific inquiry of cognitive activity to new heights. For example, in the study of mental imagery discussed earlier, neuroscientists make use of specific scans, such as MRIs or PET scans, as a means of identifying the location of activity in the brain when a certain stimulus is presented to the subject.

Neuroscience can be very helpful in education as well. The use of MRIs can help doctors identify specific conditions that might be the causes (at least in part) of certain actions and behaviors in the school setting. For example, the use of an MRI can help identify brain changes that contribute to language deficits in autistic children. Despite the rather large intersection between studies in neuroscience and cognition, this area of study represents one of the new frontiers of inquiry for the psychologist and educator.

Artificial Intelligence

One of the most pressing questions in cognitive studies and in education in general is whether nonhuman entities can perform the same tasks that humans can do. Perhaps more important, if nonhuman entities can perform these human tasks, can they perform them better? The answers to these questions fall under the heading of artificial intelligence (AI). In general, AI is a form of problem-solving performance that is achieved by a programmed computational device. A strong AI argument is that machines are able to do the types of things that humans do when engaged in behavior that is regarded as intelligent. If something made up of various components can function in the same way that humans can function, then it would be difficult to argue that humans are not reducible to "component parts."

There are several foundations for the rationale of AI. One point of departure is the field of information sciences, developed by Warren Weaver and Claude Shannon. In their book *The Mathematical Theory of Communication* (1963), Weaver and Shannon developed a theory of information that generated the notion that all problems, no matter how complex, are reducible to a series of yes–no, or 1–0, responses. In the computational sciences, the work of the mathematician Alan Turing contributed to the formulation of a strong argument for AI. While developing heuristics for problem-solving strategies, Turing developed a technique for determining whether a given problem is computable. In order to aid in this project, he created one of the first computers. His initial goal was to determine whether a machine—a computer—can be regarded as an intelligent being or structure, regardless of appearance. According to Turing, the appropriate kind of test should evaluate whether or not the machine's responses are relevantly intelligent. We can make these evaluations on the basis of the degree to which the responses of the machine are similar to a human's responses. Another form of evaluation was to create a program for playing chess. The development of this program was based on a premise that chess playing—a highly computational activity—is the essence of what it means to be intelligent like a human being.

In general, there are two sides to the argument of AI. One side argues that the data on AI show positive signs that AI could reach human intelligence. Advocates suggest that current computers are simply a foretaste of what is to come in the ensuing decades. The other side argues whether such a device can engage in creative language and communication with regard to meaning and expression as humans do. The philosopher John Searle has argued against the notion of AI intelligence by posing the Chinese Room scenario. In sum, the Chinese Room is analogous to what is happening within the AI device as it develops a response. The subject in the Chinese Room is engaged in the sorting and compiling of cards with Chinese ideograms according to a specified program or instruction. It takes someone who is fluent in reading Chinese to actually go well beyond the mere sorting and compiling—that is, making sense and meaning from what was sorted and compiled.

Daniel Ness and Chia-ling Lin

REFERENCES

Newman, Robert P., and Dale R. Newman. *Evidence*. Boston: Houghton Mifflin, 1969.

Pólya, George. *How to Solve It.* Princeton, NJ: Princeton University Press, 1948.

Rieke, Richard D., and Malcolm O. Sillars. *Argumentation and Critical Decision Making.* 4th ed. New York: Longman, 1997.

Saxe, Geoffrey B. "Developing Forms of Arithmetic Operations among the Oksapmin of Papua New Guinea." *Development Psychology* 18:4 (1982): 583–594.

Tolman, Edward C. "Cognitive Maps in Rats and Men." *Psychological Review* 55:4 (1948): 189–208.

Weaver, Warren, and Claude E. Shannon. *The Mathematical Theory of Communication.* Champaign: University of Illinois Press, 1963.

Willingham, Daniel. *Cognition: The Thinking Animal.* Upper Saddle River, NJ: Prentice-Hall, 2008.

Zarefsky, David. *Public Speaking: Strategies for Success.* 3rd ed. Boston: Allyn & Bacon, 2002.

LINGUISTIC DEVELOPMENT

Linguistic development refers to the process by which human cognitive functions of communication unfold over time. The tool that humans use for progressing linguistic development is language. Any compilation of a list of uniquely human attributes will most likely include language. Possibly beginning with the Stoic philosophers in the third century BCE, it became a common belief among philosophers, scholastics, intellectuals, and, in the modern era, scientists that language was the essential factor that distinguished humans from nonhumans. The idea was that humans, unlike any other organism, were able to represent the world abstractly in propositional form and solve problems that are far beyond the range of possibilities for the nonlinguistic entity.

Language understood in behavioristic terms becomes one particular category of behavior and is entirely musculoskeletal. Instead of producing an effect on the environment through movement, an acoustic effect is produced, which becomes the necessary condition to be satisfied for some reinforcer to occur. One key question in defining language has to do with what is meant when we refer to some form of communication as linguistic. Language as traditionally understood contains at least two elements: denotations and connotations. Denotations represent actual objects in the real world. These elements can be defined in an ostensible manner. An object is described ostensibly by pointing at it. So, for example, if an individual wishes to learn the meaning of the word "book," another person could point at something that falls under the category "book." The term "book," then, is a denotative term in that the word denotes an actual object. Language also contains connotations—terms that have meaning but do not represent an object. If A asks B for a book, B can hand A a distinct object. However, if A asks B for ingenuity, B would have no object to give to A. In order to show ingenuity, B would have to display a certain disposition that matches up not with an object in the external world but with a principle or particular behavior. For example, showing ingenuity would involve outcomes demonstrating initiative, cleverness, and creativity in solving problems, completing tasks, and the like. Humans engage in patterns of meaning in which linguistic elements are mostly connotative. Accordingly, language is inundated with cultural and anthropological considerations.

Language Levels

When an infant babbles and the babbling results in nothing, the babbling tends to decrease. When an infant cries and the crying leads to an outcome (e.g., the baby gets a bottle), the crying tends to wane. The infant may be crying so that some condition of need does get satisfied. The infant may have purposes, but not in the sense of an intentional purpose. According to behaviorist psychology, certain linguistic behaviors are extinguished over time when a particular desire or outcome is not achieved (e.g., babbling to get a bottle of milk), while other linguistic behaviors, such as crying, can be useful in obtaining desired outcomes. But this is not a reliable way of examining human linguistic development, since certain manners of conduct (e.g., crying) become extinguished even if they do initially provide desired outcomes. Instead, in order to understand the development of language, it is important to examine language levels. Language levels must be examined separately because each level has rules that govern what is allowable in terms of form and structure.

Phonemes

The lowest level of language is the phoneme. Phonemes are individual speech sounds that crudely correspond to the letters of the alphabet. Some of the letters perform more than one task when representing speech sounds. For example, the letter i is pronounced differently in "tight" and "hill," and gh produces different sounds in the words "rough" and "ghost." So the i sound in "tight" and the i sound in "hill" are two different phonemes. Interestingly, there are 46 phonemes used in English and about 200 phonemes used in the nearly 6,700 languages throughout the world. Some phonemes that are available in languages other than English can be pronounced by many English speakers. For example, the phoneme x in German is almost like a soft-k sound (almost like kh) and is sounded in the German word $buch$ (which is translated in English as "book"). Some phonemes cannot even be pronounced by native English speakers, for example, certain phonemes in a number of East Asian languages and languages from southern Africa. Some phonemes are thought to be identical when in fact they are not. For example, the n in "night" (n) and in "sing" ($ŋ$) are slightly different phonemes. These related yet different phonemes are called allophones.

Words

When combined in various ways, the 46 phonemes in English produce approximately 600,000 words, the second level of language. Note that these 46 phonemes do not exhaust all combinations in the English language. In other words, there are some patterns of phonemic structure in non-English languages, such as Croatian or Bantu, which would be prohibited in English. For example, the spelling of the geographical place name Krk, an island in the northern Adriatic, is acceptable in Croatian but would not be permitted in English. Stop consonants (i.e., p, t, k, b, d, g) in English are sounded as air is stopped during utterance. So words that begin with a stop consonant cannot have a stop consonant as a second letter (i.e., "gket").

Sentences

The third level of language is the sentence. In the same way that rules are violated when phonemes occur incorrectly to form words, rules can also be violated when words occur incorrectly—that is, in an ungrammatical order—to form sentences. Like accurate phonemic structure (as it pertains to English), words must be placed appropriately in sentences in order to make sense. For example, the sentence "store went The to boy the" makes little sense because the function of the words is lost as a result of grammatical inconsistency. Indeed, "The boy went to the store" is clear and understandable. But word order is not necessarily the only factor in sentence construction when forming thoughts for communication. The sentence "Jill odiously expressed green books without salt on them" makes little sense. The grammatical structure is satisfactory, but the words themselves do not convey anything meaningful to the reader.

Texts/Paragraphs

In the fourth level of language, texts are groups of sentences that form paragraphs, which in turn can be extended into groups of paragraphs. A paragraph is constructed in such a manner in which sentences are organized with a sense of agreement in mind. This agreement can be in the form of, among other things, sentences exhibiting chronological order, an expression of logical coherence, or an expression of causal relationship. The following text illustrates an example of a paragraph that lacks agreement:

> Betty was disappointed because she didn't know what transportation she could take to the art gallery in time for her show. After boarding the train to go downtown to visit the art gallery, Betty heard a shrieking sound. Betty was really eager to visit the art gallery since her artwork was on exhibit. The train made a sudden stop, and the conductor instructed all the riders to disembark. Before Betty left for the gallery, she prepared something to eat at home, and subsequently made sure that all the knobs on the stove were turned off.

Clearly, each sentence of this paragraph should make sense to the reader, but the sentences are in the incorrect order (the correct order is sentences 3, 5, 2, 4, 1). The lack of order prevents the reader from determining the meaning and context of what the author is attempting to convey. Textual constructions are also culturally bound. Many stories in the form of texts might make sense to one culture but seem peculiar or odd to another.

Grammar

At this point, the four levels of languages—phonemes, words, sentences, and texts—have been discussed in terms of their meanings, functions, and rules that govern their use within a particular language. The problem, however, is that with these rules alone—those for each language level—it is not possible to determine how the mind produces and recognizes language, particularly as it results in communication or dialogue. This is particularly the case when examining sentence structure. More than phonemic structure and word structure, the structure of sentences has been studied by linguists and psychologists for decades because, unlike the structures of the other three language levels, rules of sentence structure in essence govern a great deal of human cognitive processes when deciphering the meaning of a particular form of verbal communication. Thus, grammar is an essential component, not only in terms of structural governance, but also of meaning and context. It is true that the grammars of English and geographically close languages—such as French or German—are related; however, they are in no way the same. It should be clear that the grammar of one language is different from the grammar of others. Nevertheless, one goal of the linguist and cognitive psychologist is to identify the similarities of these various grammars and how the rules of these seemingly differing grammars can be applied to what Noam Chomsky and other scholars refer to as a universal grammar.

For the most part, grammar refers to a set of rules that, when followed, will produce accepted sentences within a particular language. Chomsky refers to two aspects of one's grammar: competence and performance. Competence is the grammatical knowledge that humans possess. Performance is the ways in which people talk, which may or may not be grammatically accurate. There are many parameters that may affect one's grammar during performance, including starts and stops of a train of thought, socially accepted discourse (e.g., talking with friends versus talking with a teacher or professor), or a partial lack of grammatical rules. Psychologists and linguists have examined phrase structure grammars to demonstrate sentence structure within a hierarchy.

Linguistic Frameworks

The topic of language acquisition has been investigated by philosophers and theorists for many centuries. Only in the twentieth century did it become an increasingly developed research agenda. The well-known German philosopher Ludwig Wittgenstein posited that language is an entirely cultural construct and that the language that one individual uses to refer to a particular object might very well be the same language that another individual uses to refer to an entirely different object. He argued this position in his famous "beetle-in-the-box" scenario, in which several people in a room are each given a closed box. At a certain agreed-upon time, each box can be opened simultaneously. At that point, it is entirely possible for each person to open her or his box and say "beetle." But the content of one box might be entirely different from the content of other boxes. Wittgenstein's "beetle-in-the-box" scenario is a powerful example of how language can be vague, amorphous, and possibly even deceiving. One important aspect that unfolds from this view is that one's culture is responsible for the formalized language systems that each individual uses. In other words, Arabic, Bantu, English, French, German, Hindi, Italian, Japanese, Mandarin, Polish, Russian, Spanish, and the remaining 6,000 or so of the world's languages are what Wittgenstein scholars would refer to as artificial languages: they are products of the societies that have used them over the centuries. The diametric opposite to artificial language is natural language. The content of natural language contains no similarities with artificial language. Young children's language is paradigmatic of artificial language, particularly the language of infants and toddlers. The sounds of a baby crying, cooing, or producing syllables that are not referents to any object, event, person, place, or idea in any artificial language are elements of natural language. Natural language is used when a child scrapes his elbow and begins to cry. An adult who scrapes her elbow will often use an interjection ("Ouch!") that may be construed as natural, but might then continue with "I need to put a bandage on that!" which is entirely artificial.

Here are just some of the numerous questions that linguists have attempted to answer within the last several decades: When do humans acquire the ability to communicate? What is the nature of language acquisition? Does it involve a modicum of stimuli and responses, as the behaviorist psychologists would argue? Is it a matter of development and maturation, as a number of early developmental psychologists would argue? Or does it have something to do with an innate characteristic that all humans possess? Further, what might the trajectories of language acquisition look like

in terms of abilities? Ten scholars—Maria Montessori, Jean Piaget, B.F. Skinner, Edward Sapir and Benjamin Lee Whorf, Noam Chomsky, Charles Hockett, Michael Halliday, Eve Clark, and Steven Pinker—have attempted to answer these questions using the language acquisition frameworks discussed below.

Montessori's Sensitive Periods

Maria Montessori, perhaps most well known for her contributions to early childhood education, was also an established theorist in childhood development, both physical-social development and cognitive development. One of her primary contributions in her theoretical writings was the role of sensitive periods in children's initial five years of life. Two of the six sensitive periods were based on the influence of language. The first sensitive period concerned the ages from birth to 36 months. In this period, the infant begins uttering monosyllabic words, often repeating them over time. These words, which may seem nonsensical to the typical observer, are crucial to development because, by 12 months of age, their utterance leads to words possessing more complex syllables. In general, before the age of three, children develop a sense of speech in which they move from cooing to speaking in complete and somewhat coherent sentences. One interpretation of the first three years is a period of practice for the young child as a means of developing a way to communicate clearly and coherently. It is also possible to argue that the young child, initially using natural language, common to all humans in the early stages, is eventually engaged in the traditions of the culture and develops a system of communicating in the artificial language used by adults. The second language period, from age three to the end of age five, is further development of the artificial language spoken in a particular society. It is also a time when the grammatical structure of the language becomes more concise and formalized. It can be argued that Montessori's notion of sensitive periods is a precursor to the position that a child's acquisition of grammar is innate—foreshadowing the work of Noam Chomsky.

Piaget's Semiotic Function

Jean Piaget believed that the fundamental criterion that defined the last few months of the sensorimotor period was the onset of language—most particularly, the language that identifies abstractions or objects that are not present in the child's environment. In order to understand Piaget's interpretation of the semiotic function, it is important for the reader to be familiarized with Piaget's overall account of development discussed in *The Child's Conception of the World*.

According to Piaget, the main characteristic that can be identified through play, imagination, and concept development is the semiotic function—which is represented through symbolism. He argues that children do not acquire the semiotic function through society; rather, the semiotic function is something that children acquire individually before they interact with others. Two components are essential and must occur in tandem in order for the semiotic function to come about: imitation and play. Through the process of accommodation, imitation provides the signifiers, which occur as mental images. These images can be a concrete or abstract imitation of an absent model. Through the process of assimilation, play provides meanings to the earlier imitation, also referred to as the signified. The earlier schemas that developed during the sensorimotor period lead to individual symbols and subsequently are combined with collective forms of symbolism that are mutually understood during the preoperational stage. The development of symbolism, then, contributes to the development of concepts that emerge during the concrete operational stage.

Chomsky critiqued Piaget's semiotic function on the grounds that it did not consider the notion of humans being equipped with a universal grammar.

Skinner's Verbal Behavior

In the late 1930s, B.F. Skinner argued that learning occurs through a set of stimuli and responses—possibly several thousand of them—that occur over time. In his view, development plays no role in how humans (and animals) acquire knowledge. About 20 years later, Skinner's book *Verbal Behavior* was published. In this controversial book, Skinner advanced his theory of operant conditioning by applying it to language acquisition. That is, over time, a child will undergo thousands of positive and negative reinforcements through the use of speech that will shape that individual's language capability. For example, a child's monosyllabic speech at 10 months of age

unfolds into bisyllabic speech shortly thereafter, possibly at the end of the tenth month or the beginning of the eleventh, as a result of several hundred or thousand positive and negative reinforcements. These reinforcements might take the following form: the child says "da . . ."; the child's mother says "daddy" (on perhaps 20 occasions); the child says "daddy" and receives a reward, which can be either verbal or material. This process will continue for days and months until the child eventually puts two words together (at approximately 14 months), three words (18 months), four words (20 months), five words (21 months), and eventually coherent sentences (before the child's second birthday).

Edward Sapir and Benjamin Lee Whorf

It is true that how and what we think affects how we speak and how we write. In other words, there is an inextricable link between thought and language. The question that Edward Sapir had was whether cognitive processes differ in two people whose native languages are entirely different. Sapir argued that language inclines people of one language to engage in certain habits and mores that would not necessarily be the case for speakers of other languages. Benjamin Lee Whorf, a student of Sapir, elaborated on Sapir's argument and developed a position known as the Sapir-Whorf hypothesis, which states that each language is unique in that it engenders patterns within its vocabulary and grammatical structure that influence the thinking of its speakers; in other words, some languages favor certain patterns of thinking over other languages. There is a strong and weak interpretation of the Sapir-Whorf hypothesis. A proponent who favors the strong interpretation will argue that thought and language are so intimately bound that a thought generated in one language cannot be generated in another. A proponent of the weak interpretation will argue that, at the very least, some languages favor certain thought modalities when compared to other languages. Take the classical Greek word *eudaimonia*. For one thing, this word's meaning is difficult to translate into English. A rough translation of *eudaimonia* in English is "happiness," a term that connotes pleasure and possibly hedonism. But that is not how the Greeks intended to define the term. They defined it as "human flourishing allowing one to thrive in a particular discipline." So the Sapir-Whorf proponent would argue, in favor of the weak interpretation, that even with some type of translation, the way one thinks of *eudaimonia* in Greek would be different from the way used by an English speaker.

Chomsky's Theory of Universal Grammar

Noam Chomsky, perhaps the most noted linguist in the last 60 years, essentially gained his reputation in the late 1950s as a result of his insightful critique of Skinner's book. Chomsky was a strong opponent of learning theory and Skinner's view of language as a succession of positive and negative reinforcements based on stimulus-response. In Chomsky's view, language does not emerge from the baby's repetitive babble; in other words, continuous, repetitive babble does not contribute to the utterance of a word as a means of reinforcement. In addition, children do not acquire the meaning of new vocabulary merely by stumbling upon newly encountered words. Chomsky's overarching argument is that native language acquisition is not a result of thousands of sets of stimuli and responses. Rather, early language ability, specifically the ability to put words together (i.e., grammar) for the purpose of communicating (i.e., semantics), is an innate characteristic of humans. Chomsky completed his book *Syntactic Structures* (1957) in the same year that he published a critique of Skinner's *Verbal Behavior*. *Syntactic Structures* lays the groundwork for Chomsky's view of the innateness of grammatical structure.

Another theory that was predominant prior to Chomsky's theory of universal grammar was the so-called storage bin theory, which focused on the premise that children base their acquisition of grammatical structure on imitation of adults and peers. As storage bin theorists would argue, imitation allows children to acquire strings of sentences that are then essentially stored in the mind. Accordingly, they usurp words and sentences from memory when needed— depending on the context of conversation.

Chomsky has demonstrated the flaws in the storage bin model of grammar acquisition, arguing that the number of words, phrases, sentences, and the like that a person calls up from memory would be very limited. In addition, the person would struggle when communicating to others who use grammatical structures that the person had not heard prior to the communication. That is, the continuous retrieval of previously stored sentence structures would not allow individuals to understand sentences that they had never heard on previous occasions. Individuals do usurp a particular grammatical structure when writing stories, essays, articles, and the like. However, although people reuse previously learned words, they still create novel sentences each time they speak. Chomsky identifies this characteristic as an internal rule that helps speakers recreate their verbal communication as they progress in daily life. Chomsky argues that a child's linguistic abilities during short periods of time are so advanced that it becomes difficult to explain the development of grammar through inputs from the external environment. It is important to note that although children are acquainted with only a limited grammatical structure, they are generally able to master complex grammatical structures well beyond what they experience in the everyday world. Chomsky argues that there exists a genetic blueprint that enables young children to engage in more complex forms of grammar than the forms that they are generally exposed to. Chomsky calls this the "innateness hypothesis."

In comparison with Piaget, Chomsky's theoretical work presents an alternative approach to the study of language acquisition. The two scholars are similar in that they do not believe that children develop passively through external environmental agents (as illustrated above in the comparison with Skinner). Instead, they develop physically and cognitively through active and spontaneous engagement with the external environment. Piaget believes that cognitive development has almost everything to do with the child's own active constructions of previously learned ideas in making sense of the world. Chomsky, on the other hand, argues that language is prewired for the child. Based on the universality of grammar and spoken syntax, the child then will create grammatical structures automatically. The theory of universal grammar initially posed by Chomsky has gained momentum in the scientific community with the recent correlation made between the FOXP2 (Forkhead box protein P2) protein and the argument that language is a prewired neurological characteristic—one that now serves as evidence demonstrating the evolutionary periods of linguistic development in humans.

Charles Hockett's Thirteen Linguistic Universals

Although Charles Hockett's career began before that of Noam Chomsky, we discuss Hockett after as one of the leading critics of Chomsky's theory of universal grammar. Hockett was an eminent linguistic theorist whose career began in the middle of the twentieth century. He claimed that all the world's languages, in some ways, were related to each other. During the late 1950s and early 1960s, Hockett (1960, 1966) proposed 13 linguistic universals that characterized the similarities that exist among all languages. Furthermore, he posited that these 13 universals clarify the distinctions between human languages and communication among animals. Hockett was critical of Chomsky's approach to language acquisition, arguing that natural language and cultural patterns play a greater role in the process.

Hockett's 13 linguistic universals are arbitrariness, broadcast transmission and directional reception, cultural transmission, discreteness, displacement, duality of patterning, interchangeability, productivity, rapid fading, semanticity, specialization, total feedback, and the vocal-auditory channel. Each of these universals will be discussed briefly.

Arbitrariness refers to the idea that few, if any, examples exist in the world's languages of situations in which word meanings have direct associations to the words themselves. For example, we know what "boat" means; it is a vessel used for water transportation. But the word "boat," in and of itself, has no connection to its meaning. The primary exceptions to this rule are uses of onomatopoeia ("ding," "pop," and the like).

The transmission of language is public, given that what we say is transmitted in all directions and therefore heard by all those in range. This universal characteristic is what Hockett refers to as broadcast transmission and directional reception; in all languages, there is a source (i.e., the speaker) and a listener or group of listeners within the range of transmission.

Unlike genetic factors, such as mating tendencies among animal species, language is entirely a cultural phenomenon among all humans. This is evident by the way in which members of one cultural heritage interpret a concept when compared with the way in which members of another culture interpret the same concept.

Sounds within a particular language system are perceived categorically. They are not perceived continuously, despite the fact that sound, in general, is continuous if one considers the slight shades of change that occur in frequency of pitch. In other words, we generally alter our pitch in a gradual way when pronouncing a word. Thus discreteness is a universal characteristic of language whereby the sounds of words fall within a very small range of frequency—small enough so that it can be categorized as having a particular sound pattern.

Displacement refers to the ability of humans to communicate events that occur not only in the present, but in the past and future as well. In other words, in every language system, there is a way to conjugate verbs to indicate past and future in addition to present. This implies that memory plays an extremely important role in communication as it relates to time.

All languages are based on a small set of phonemes, which generally do not have meaning in and of themselves. However, when selections of these phonemes are organized and permutated, we form words and sentences, which do, in fact, have meaning. This is what Hockett refers to as duality of patterning.

Hockett argues that within certain animal groups, there may be a form of communication by one animal that another animal will not be able to repeat back. This is evident, for example, when a member of a particular species is able to communicate through sound or movement to another member of the same species when a food source has been discovered. In contrast, humans do possess the ability to repeat back a sentence that was communicated to them by another human because it is assumed that the listener understands what the original speaker stated. This is called interchangeability.

Hockett defines productivity as a characteristic that emphasizes the novelty of language and the utterances of words. When someone produces a statement, it is more than likely that the statement was never before produced the same way by the same individual or by another individual.

Hockett argues that the transmission of language is transitory: the speaker must say what is necessary at the right moment; otherwise, the listener will lose the context of what was said. In other words, language fades due to the ways in which we communicate. For example, if one person starts a conversation by talking about the weather, the context of communication will be lost if the speaker responds to the listener several minutes later, with or without other content discussed in the interim.

It might be self-evident that semanticity refers to the fact that words possess meaning. Hockett stresses this point as a means of distinguishing words that we use to communicate from other sounds that humans produce, such as sneezes, coughs, deep breaths, sighs, and the like. This, of course, assumes that the cough or sigh was not intentionally used as a form of expression to imply sarcasm or boredom.

Specialization refers to the notion that a listener can detect sounds that convey meaning through language in contrast to nonlinguistic sounds. This is closely associated with the differences between so-called natural language versus artificial language mentioned earlier.

In total feedback, the speaker has the ability to hear what is being transmitted to the listener. The speaker can thus adjust the sounds of speech, depending on the circumstances of the communication. For example, the speaker can adjust the communication depending on the change of distance of the listener.

Hockett refers to the vocal-auditory channel as the conduit in which all forms of verbal communication takes place. In other words, when talking as a form of communication, we use our vocal cords. Writing as a form of communication is excluded here because it is an invented form of communication.

Halliday's Seven Functions of Language in the Early Years

Michael Alexander Kirkwood Halliday is a contemporary Australian linguist (born in England) who has identified seven functions of language for young children, particularly in the early years—from birth to about three years of age. Halliday developed a model in linguistics known as systemic functional grammar, which focuses not solely on meaning and syntax, but also on the ways in which humans use grammar for their own purpose. The seven functions of language in the early years are divided into two categories. The first four functions serve young children's physical and social needs, while the remaining three functions

serve their environmental and cognitive needs. The first four functions are (1) the instrumental function, in which children use words to express something needed or wanted; (2) the regulatory function, which is used when a child commands someone to do something; (3) the interactional function, for the purpose of communicating with others; and (4) the personal function, for the purpose of expressing feelings. The remaining three are (5) the heuristic function, which allows children to use language for gaining knowledge; (6) the imaginative function, for telling jokes or understanding stories; and (7) the representational function, in which young children use language to state facts and ideas.

Eve Clark and the Interactionist Model

Eve Clark, a faculty member at Stanford University, is noted for her work on first language acquisition in children. Unlike the nativist perspective of Noam Chomsky, Clark explains first language acquisition using an interactionist approach, attempting to bridge the gap between environmental influences and nativist explanations of cognitive abilities. In general, interactionists attempt to make a connection between basic cognitive processes on language development, on the one hand, and environmental factors that influence language, on the other. Clark posits that there are certain ages that serve as benchmarks for specific language changes. For example, at two and one-half years, children generally establish two separate words for the same object. Clark also argues that vocabulary development is not merely an increase in the number of words that a child acquires during a particular period of time; it also involves fundamental changes—particularly in meaning—in the ways in which the same words are used, as well as contextual factors that direct the ways in which words and sentences are constructed. Clark, among other researchers of linguistic development, argues that the underpinnings of language development begin practically from the time the baby is born. Children will accomplish a great deal of language structure before they enter formal schooling. According to Clark's book *The Lexicon in Acquisition* (1993), the child acquires knowledge of approximately 14,000 words before entrance to formal schooling.

Steven Pinker

Steven Pinker is a professor of cognitive psychology at Harvard University whose work on language acquisition became popularized with the publication of his book *The Language Instinct* (1994). As the title of the book suggests, Pinker argues that language is instinctual. He bases this premise on his assertions that human language ability is founded on an evolutionary component. This component controls the language capacity of humans. Pinker, unlike Chomsky, believes that although language is innate, there is a strong biological component in the acquisition of grammar and that much of language, one of several characteristics of cognitive abilities, is adaptable. As a strong proponent of evolutionary psychology, Pinker attempts to link the human language capacity to natural selection, arguing that language, like various parts of the human body, evolved in a manner that demonstrated the elimination of some cognitively related features of language that were unfavorable heritable traits, and the progression of other features that were favorable.

Daniel Ness and Chia-ling Lin

REFERENCES

Chomsky, Noam. *Syntactic Structures.* The Hague: Mouton, 1957.

Clark, Eve V. "Later Lexical Development and Word Formation." In *The Handbook of Child Language*, ed. Paul Fletcher and Brian MacWhinney. Malden, MA: Blackwell, 1995.

———. *The Lexicon in Acquisition.* Cambridge, UK: Cambridge University Press, 1993.

Hockett, Charles F. "The Origins of Speech." *Scientific American* 203 (1960): 89–96.

———. "The Problem of Universals in Language." In *Universals of Language*, ed. Joseph H. Greenberg, 1–29. Cambridge: MIT Press, 1966.

Piaget, Jean. *The Child's Conception of the World.* Totowa, NJ: Littlefield Addams, 1929.

Pinker, Steven. *The Language Instinct.* New York: William Morrow, 1994.

Sapir, Edward. *Culture, Language, and Personality.* Berkeley: University of California Press, 1956.

Skinner, Burrhus F. *Verbal Behavior.* New York: Appleton, 1957.

Whorf, Benjamin Lee. *Language, Thought, and Reality: Selected Writings.* Cambridge: MIT Press, 1956.

LEVELS OF INTELLECTUAL DEVELOPMENT

One of the most pressing problems for teachers in formal education settings is to know how to align curriculum with students at particular grade levels. Educational systems and bureaucracies throughout the world have generally applied the term "developmentally appropriate practice" to serve as a mantra for what content is to be taught at any one grade level. It has been posited that both researchers and educational practitioners marveled at the notion that specific subject matter content can be taught not according to grade levels, but according to whether a child has reached a particular stage or substage of development based on Piaget's theory of intellectual development. In other words, educators with highly Utopian notions of aligning curriculum with cognitive levels in teaching and learning held the view that teachers would determine when to teach a particular topic based on specific traits that children would exhibit in their behavior. For example, a child who the teacher believes is exhibiting knowledge of single- and double-digit multiplication problems but cannot generalize the pattern to the sequence of perfect square numbers (1, 4, 9, 16, 25, etc.) or the Fibonacci sequence (0, 1, 1, 2, 3, 5, 8, etc.) might be categorized using the Piagetian framework as concrete-operational. In a similar manner, another child might be labeled preoperational if he exhibits the ability to add single digits but makes errors with larger numbers, or adds "ed" to all verbs in past tense.

However, this view is highly unrealistic and unlikely to come to fruition for one main reason: humans are immensely diverse in their cognitive abilities at any one given time. To make matters more complex for those who embrace this point of view, from a comparative standpoint, students possess individual differences when considering one academic domain. Therefore, given the numerous fields of inquiry, the identification of a generalizable developmentally appropriate curriculum for any age or grade level group is all the more difficult to determine.

Thus, although grade levels might serve as adequate indicators in grouping students by age, they are rather poor benchmarks for determining individual student abilities in any specific cognitive domain. Educators have an even more difficult time adhering to curriculum because within any one grade level, the diversity of cognitive abilities is often so extreme that some students need to be placed in separate learning environments either because they are unable to grasp the content understood by their mainstream peers (i.e., students with learning disabilities) or they are exceeding the levels of their mainstream peers (i.e., so-called gifted and talented students). What follows is a discussion of these three levels of cognitive ability.

Students Identified Under "Special Education"

Special education is a form of classroom instruction and assessment in which the teacher attempts to accommodate students who may have either innate or developmental disabilities that negatively affect their cognitive ability. These accommodations include provisions for students with hearing impairment, speech impairment, visual impairment, cognitive dysfunction involving verbal or mathematical abnormalities (e.g., dyslexia, aphasia, dyscalculia), mental retardation, motor-physical impairment, and general learning disabilities that are not categorized under the previous headings.

One of the main problems with the "special education" label is that many students do not belong in special education classes because they simply do not have any type of physical disability or learning deficit or because it is difficult to identify any learning deficit since there are no tests that can conclusively diagnose any condition.

Students with severe disabilities, on the other hand, need substantial assistance in their education. These individuals need extensive instruction, support, assistance, and adaptation to the educational setting in order to eventually contribute and participate in a meaningful and significant way in their everyday lives. These students may experience one or possibly several significantly acute intellectual, emotional, or physical disabilities, such as mental retardation, developmental disabilities, autism, pervasive developmental disorders, traumatic brain injury, deafness, and blindness. A diagnosis of any of the above conditions, however, does not necessarily mean that a student is severely handicapped; on the contrary, students with severe

disabilities constitute a subset of those diagnosed. It should be noted that the majority of students with mental retardation need only limited support and are therefore generally able to function independently in society. It is estimated that approximately 1 percent of the general population has severe disabilities that will affect their abilities in school. Students who do possess severe physical and intellectual disabilities constitute a heterogeneous population, with a diverse range of physical, emotional, and intellectual features. The notion of "severe disabilities" emanated from The Association for Persons with Severe Disabilities (TASH) during the 1970s. As a result of litigation and changes in legislation, TASH was organized as a means of establishing legal rights to education and related services for students with severe disabilities who traditionally had been excluded from school and therefore denied the right to education and participation in mainstream society.

In general, special education researchers and practitioners have categorized special education settings in three ways: inclusion, mainstreaming, and exclusion.

Inclusion

Inclusion is a model of special education practice whose proponents embrace a classroom in which all students, regardless of special needs, are grouped together. There are different types of inclusion settings. In the regular inclusion setting, students with disabilities learn with their mainstream peers approximately half the time. During the other half of the class day, special education providers come to the classroom to assist students, depending on their disability, with special needs. Partial inclusion involves a classroom in which special education students learn with their mainstream peers for the entire day, but may attend special education instruction outside of school. Full inclusion also entails the grouping of special needs, mainstream, and high-ability students in the same classroom. Unlike the other inclusion types, however, full inclusion involves the presence of a special needs instructor to work with special needs children during the entire day.

Mainstreaming

Similar to inclusion, mainstreaming is a model of special education in which regular education classes are combined with special education classes. Unlike inclusion practices, special education students who are mainstreamed engage in learning with their non–special education peers, but are taken out of their regular classes to attend smaller classes that focus on their specific disabilities. Advocates of both inclusion and mainstreaming argue that students with special needs (particularly those with disabilities) benefit the most when they engage in learning with their non–special needs peers because it better prepares them to be functioning members of society. Research, however, shows mixed findings as to the academic and social advantages of inclusion and mainstream models. One major disadvantage is cost. According to the National Education Association, the average per student spending in the United States in the 2007–2008 school year was $10,297, while the average per special needs student was almost $19,000, a difference of nearly $9,000. The average expenditure for students with learning needs is nearly 2.5 times greater than so-called mainstream students.

Exclusion

Special needs students in an exclusion setting do not share learning experiences with other students in the regular schooling environment. These students are either taught at home in a one-on-one setting or are sent to special education schools. In one type of exclusion setting, often referred to as segregation, a student engages in full-time special education classrooms with no contact in regular classrooms.

Students Identified as High-Ability or "Gifted and Talented"

The education of the gifted is a category of education by student grouping that is rich in history and, at the same time, abundant with cultural variation. Earliest evidence of intellectual giftedness suggests that rulers during the Tang Dynasty in China (ca. 618 BCE) encouraged the scouting of youth who performed at high levels on some of the earliest standardized tests available in recorded history. In the *Analects*, Confucius called for the creation of educational establishments to accommodate students with exceptional intellectual aptitude. Talented students would then be eligible, through standardized testing, for positions as civil servants and other highly prestigious positions. The Confucian tradition of examination has influenced educational practice in China even to the present day.

In the West, the first record that identifies the need to promote and foster intellectual potential and excellence is explicated in the work of Plato. In Book 7 of the *Republic*, Plato associates the notion of ruler or statesman with the quality of giftedness and intellectual precocity. In the dialogue between Socrates and Glaucon, Plato writes:

> Socrates: You remember, I said, how the rulers were chosen before. . . .
> Glaucon: Certainly, [he said].
> Socrates: The same natures must still be chosen, and the preference again given to the surest and the bravest, and, if possible, to the fairest; and, having noble and generous tempers, they should also have the natural gifts which will facilitate their education.
> Glaucon: And what are these?
> Socrates: Such gifts as keenness and ready powers of acquisition. . . . Further, he of whom we are in search should have a good memory . . . he must have natural gifts.

In general, Plato's argument that the leaders of Athens—whom he called philosopher kings—were to have intellectual capacities far beyond the so-called common citizen depended upon an education that fostered and developed strong intellectual powers. This argument influenced the role and trajectory of gifted education to the present day. The formal education of any individual prior to the eighteenth century can be considered "special" or "gifted," given that formal education in general was limited to a privileged class whose members were chosen by birth, piety, or even intelligence.

In the sixteenth century, Suleiman the Magnificent, the Sultan of the Ottoman Empire from 1520 to 1566, established a number of schools for talented youth. As a means of recruitment, he conducted a search for gifted youth throughout the Ottoman Empire. These individuals would then prepare to become leaders and administrators. Areas of instruction included art and drawing, literature, martial arts, natural sciences, philosophy, and religion. These subjects were believed to be the best means of preparing selected individuals to serve and uphold the strictures of the Empire.

Conceptions of giftedness were fairly similar in China and in the Western world. However, in other areas of the world, giftedness has been judged by different sets of criteria. For example, leadership ability (which might be construed as oratory ability), linguistic skill, and facility and dexterity in a particular skill were regarded as important criteria for selecting young individuals for specific high-ranking roles in many African societies. Some of these individuals would train to become interpreters, drummers, or scribes—positions deemed of highest value and, at the same time, not based on heredity, but on talent or manual skill. In short, the criteria that might be important for defining giftedness in one time period or culture are not necessarily the same for other times or other cultures.

Prior to the twentieth century, the construct of "the gifted child" did not exist. The notion of giftedness arose with the invention of the IQ test. In fin de siècle France, the famous psychologist Alfred Binet was hired by the French government to identify a way in which children whose families were emigrating from the rural parts of France and nearby countries to Paris and other urban areas could be categorized in terms of their academic and intellectual achievement. This categorization process, which developed into the first IQ test, served as the primary criterion for directing children to their appropriate schools based on their current academic and intellectual achievement levels. In the following decade (about 1920), American psychologists transformed the IQ test to identify gifted and genius levels of intelligence. Unfortunately, this transformation led to the categorization of children and adolescents by associating intelligence with race, religion, or country of origin. It is at this time that, many researchers would argue, the term "gifted" was applied to youth who were said to possess high intellectual prowess, particularly with the publication of *Classroom Problems in the Education of Gifted Children* by Theodore Henry in 1920. At the same time, the public viewed giftedness in a somewhat negative light, linking it with eccentricity and idiosyncrasy. Reports of the lives of geniuses by biographers were transformed by the media to give the impression that individuals with high intelligence were peculiar. Even today, the mathematics or science whiz is often characterized as peculiar or different from mainstream peers.

In 1921, however, Lewis Terman countered this popular perception of the relationship between high intellectual ability and personality peculiarities through his longitudinal study of 1,500 children in California who were categorized as gifted. Terman's findings corroborated the earlier conjectures of Binet that the gifted child was as well adjusted to society as the average individual.

With the encouragement of many notable mathematicians and physicists, particularly the Hungarian physicist Baron Loránd von Eötvös, schools for the mathematically and scientifically gifted began to flourish in the early twentieth century. By the middle of the twentieth century, both public and private schools had begun to develop gifted education curricula as a means of accommodating those students who had been labeled "gifted." At the present day, researchers on the topic of giftedness are leaning toward the argument that the notion of giftedness is merely a historical construct that served the interests of people in control of the educational system. In "Gifted Education without Gifted Children" (2005), James Borland argues that although there might be the need for a gifted curriculum, there is no such thing as a gifted child. Another term often used in the same context as "giftedness" is the construct of "creativity." Unlike giftedness, the idea of creativity is not solely dependent on historical context, given that something that is synthesized is essentially created by an individual. Moreover, while giftedness is mostly applied to a student's ability in the areas of verbal construction, scientific inquiry, and mathematical problem solving, creativity is applied more to a student's ability in artistic endeavors, particularly in the fine and performing arts.

At the kindergarten or possibly the first-grade level, in most educational settings, students are often given either individual or group IQ examinations. The dominant individual IQ examinations are the Stanford-Binet Intelligence Test and the Wechsler tests (i.e., Wechsler Intelligence Scale for Children and Wechsler Adult Intelligence Scale). The prominent group tests are the Multidimensional Aptitude Battery, the Cognitive Abilities test, and the Scholastic Assessment Tests. Students who are then identified as gifted are often sent to other classroom environments—often in the same school—where they follow an accelerated curriculum. Many parochial schools that are unable to accommodate students who fall at both ends of the intellectual spectrum—the learning disabled and the intellectually gifted—send them on particular school days to other schools, mostly public schools, that can support programs in these areas.

There are several countries throughout the world that support high-ability, or gifted, programs within their school systems. In addition to the United States, these countries include Argentina, Canada, China, Costa Rica, Cuba, France, Germany, Hungary, Israel, Japan, Jordan, North Korea, Russia, Singapore, South Korea, Taiwan, and the United Kingdom.

Students Identified as Mainstream Learners

Perhaps the most underrepresented students in terms of local, state, and federal government programs and grants are those students who have no label—the so-called mainstream students. The students are unquestionably, and perhaps overwhelmingly, the majority in any classroom setting in any part of the world. The terms "mainstream" and "average" are often used as euphemisms for mediocre academic performance. Although parents often associate "average" ability with their own or other children with little difficulty, the term is often perceived in a negative light.

Since the early twentieth century, students' academic ability has been measured according to intelligence—that is, IQ—tests that provide educators with the so-called crystal ball to predict potential achievement. These tests measure some type of ability either by scaling and ranking in terms of mental age or by analyzing correlations among mental tests using factor analysis. Although the IQ test is not used as frequently as it was in the past, other high-stakes tests have replaced it. Academic achievement and cognitive ability as measured by high-stakes tests often exclude the contributions related to higher-order thinking, creativity, and persistence for success.

There has been a recent trend among some researchers to reexamine the role of intelligence beyond school achievement. The academic community is only beginning to realize and take seriously that the goal of education is to produce an individual who can make important contributions to society. With this in mind, researchers suggest that functional intelligence may be composed of numerous attributes not fully explained by one theoretical position on intelligence. Accordingly, David Perkins has categorized the numerous theoretical models explaining

intelligence into three broad categories: neurological endowment, experience in a domain, and reflective abilities. Each of these categories appears to account for some aspect of human intelligence. However, researchers are not entirely certain as to how much each theoretical perspective accounts for a person's overall intelligence or success quotient. In addition, the relationship between intelligence and how the brain functions is not fully understood. Despite these uncertainties, there is some general agreement in the field that the neurological model, which is primarily indexed to a biological endowment (genetic component), remains relatively stable even after interventions. Even though researchers have suggested that certain aspects of IQ are highly heritable, IQ can also be affected by environmental conditions. In fact, in 1994 52 professors, all experts in human intelligence and allied fields, signed a position statement on the nature of intelligence in the *Wall Street Journal*, stating, "Individuals are not born with fixed, unchangeable levels of intelligence (no one claims they are). IQs do gradually stabilize during childhood, however, and generally change little thereafter." They go on to argue that although the environment is influential in intellectual development, there is a great deal of controversy as to how much the environment plays a role in raising long-term scores in intelligence.

An important point to consider with regard to levels of intelligence is the apparent critical relationship between time and resources. An individual's or organization's provision of even unlimited resources may be futile after a certain critical time period. A cursory investigation of the biological world provides a great deal of support for this argument. A sapling, for example, needs water to thrive. During a long period of drought, the sapling will undergo desiccation, making it likely to die within a short time. At a certain point during the desiccative process, no amount of water will return the plant to its original, healthy state; even an abundance of rainwater and other forms of nourishment after the drought ends would fail to rejuvenate the sapling. The same idea often applies to the child who is not labeled exceptional—either learning disabled or intellectually gifted.

It is possible that the environment can be manipulated so that students who are labeled with "average" abilities are capable of exceptional achievement in school. In support, a research field known as epigenetics has demonstrated that environmental factors can differentiate gene behavior or expression. However, the answer to how the environment causes the variation in gene behavior is still under investigation. Given the significance of recent scientific findings in the field of epigenetics, early intervention (i.e., neonatal development) and conducive learning environments may be more important than once believed in affecting genetic expression. In response, it can be suggested that three conditions must be met in order for the interventions to be successful: early intervention carried out over a long period of time integrating the environments of both home and school; quality of the educators carrying out the intervention; and consistency among the providers of the intervention—in short, consistency, quality, and time.

Based on the research involving the three broad theories of intelligence (neurological endowment, experience in a domain, and reflective abilities), many researchers believe that it is important to have at least average intelligence—average "g"—in order to ensure that the individual utilizes the experiential and reflective components as a means of increasing intelligence. According to Heidi Goodrich Andrade and David Perkins, both experiential and reflective intelligence can be nurtured and developed. Therefore, average intelligence can become the precursor to above-average achievement and performance. However, there is a paradox: on the one hand, students may require average ability to take advantage of experiential and reflective training; on the other hand, students who lack a classification or who are not labeled—that is, who are average—are not entitled to specialized services. Unfortunately, this situation puts the average or mainstream student at a disadvantage. Essentially, the lack of classification means that the child receives no extra services. It can be concluded, then, that a student's level of intelligence serves as perhaps the most important threshold for receiving special services. Either limited intelligence on the one hand or abundant intelligence on the other may qualify one for support.

Since the end of World War II, increases in the funding of educational endeavors and enterprises in the United States followed the crisis model: if no crisis exists, then no additional funds and services will be provided. In stark contrast, when a particular presidential administration attempts to paint a picture of crisis and emergency as a result of a seeming lack of academic preparedness (e.g., after the Soviet launching of *Sputnik*) or in general cross-national educational and political comparisons (e.g., the unwarranted conclusions in the infamous publication *A Nation at Risk*), then all organizations that wish to embrace a call to "end" the alleged educational pandemonium receive both federal and private funding and services. As David Berliner and Bruce Biddle note in *The Manufactured Crisis* (1995), in most cases, the "crisis" does not end because the organizations that receive funding for ending the crisis wish to perpetuate the problem in order to get more funding. The irony is that in many schools across the country students need to perform below or above their present grade levels in order to benefit from additional monies and special services. The tendency to fund educational services based on students' performance below or above grade level leaves a number of questions unanswered. The first has to do with who is ignored by this method of funding. Second, it is important to learn the factors that are the best predictors of success in the real world. Third, one needs to ask why academic achievement as measured by high-stakes tests often excludes the contributions of higher-order thinking, creativity, and persistence. A fourth question deals with how intelligence as measured by IQ tests establishes predetermined categories that serve as holding patterns for students throughout the school years. Fifth, it is important to consider how parents can challenge school policies in order to promote their children's achievement. Finally, it is necessary to determine where this leaves the average student who may require additional encouragement in order to maximize potential. Federal and state governments appear only to act in the presence of a national crisis.

Those advocating support for students who do not fall into a particular categorization (i.e., the great majority of students) call for redirection of educational services, arguing that it is direly needed in order to maintain a competitive workforce globally. It is argued that average students are an untapped natural resource that, if given the attention that their peers receive, could provide the momentum for changing the economic environment. As much of the world shifts from an industrial to a technological and service-related workforce, a greater number of highly qualified individuals will be needed to fill positions in the technology and service-related ventures. These positions demand that researchers broaden their conception of intelligence and realize the importance of the potential contributions of the average individual. Theoretical frameworks that discuss social and emotional intelligences, along with the habits of highly successful people, have only touched upon the task of recognizing the need to maximize human potential. These frameworks emphasize specific life skills and goals that often rely on a variety of traits that are neglected or not fostered in traditional educational settings, nor are they measured by high-stakes tests. Even as intellect, persistence, creativity, and practical abilities are valued by the arts, the professions, and the business community, some still question their relevance in academic venues. In an environment that is mesmerized by numbers, concepts and abilities that evade measurement are circumspect. Therefore, the average student who possesses an unquantifiable number of various attributes might be neglected and the possibility of extraordinary accomplishments will be lost.

Daniel Ness and Chia-ling Lin

REFERENCES

Andrade, Heidi Goodrich, and David N. Perkins. "Learnable Intelligence and Intelligent Learning." In *Intelligence, Instruction, and Assessment: Theory into Practice*, ed. Robert J. Sternberg and Wendy M. Williams. Mahwah, NJ: Lawrence Erlbaum, 1998.

Berliner, David C., and Bruce J. Biddle. *The Manufactured Crisis: Myths, Fraud, and the Attack on America's Public Schools.* Cambridge, MA: Perseus, 1995.

Borland, James H. "Gifted Education Without Gifted Children." In *Conceptions of Giftedness*, 2nd ed., ed. Robert J. Sternberg and Janet E. Davidson, 1–19. New York: Cambridge University Press, 2005.

Brody, Nathan. *Intelligence*. New York: Academic Press, 1992.

Campbell, Frances A., and Craig T. Ramey. "Effects of Early Intervention on Intellectual and Academic Achievement: A Follow-Up Study of Children from Low-Income Families." *Child Development* 65 (1994): 684–698.

Ceci, Stephen J. *On Intelligence . . . More or Less: A Bioecological Treatise on Intellectual Development*. Englewood Cliffs, NJ: Prentice-Hall, 1990.

Colangelo, Nicholas, and Gary A. Davis, eds. *Handbook of Gifted Education*. 2nd ed. Needham Heights, MA: Allyn & Bacon, 1997.

Darlington, Richard B., et al. "Preschool Programs and Later School Competence of Children from Low-Income Families." *Science* 208 (1980): 202–204.

Gardner, Howard. *Frames of Mind*. New York: Basic Books, 1983.

Gould, Stephen Jay. *The Mismeasure of Man*. New York: Norton, 1996.

Guilford, J.P. *The Nature of Human Intelligence*. New York: McGraw-Hill, 1967.

Henry, Theodore S. *Classroom Problems in the Education of Gifted Children: The Nineteenth Yearbook of the National Society for the Study of Education* (Part II). Chicago: University of Chicago Press, 1920.

Jensen, Arthur R. *The g-Factor: The Science of Mental Ability*. Westport, CT: Greenwood, 1998.

———. "How Much Can We Boost IQ and Scholastic Achievement?" *Harvard Educational Review* 39 (1969): 1–123.

———. "The Nonmanipulable and Effectively Manipulable Variables of Education." *Education and Society* 1:1 (1983): 51–52.

Johnson, Dale D., and Bonnie Johnson. *High Stakes: Children, Testing, and Failure in American Schools*. Lanham, MD: Rowman & Littlefield, 2002.

Kinross, Patrick. *The Ottoman Centuries: The Rise and Fall of the Turkish Empire*. New York: Morrow, 1979.

Perkins, David N. *Outsmarting IQ: The Emerging Science of Learnable Intelligence*. New York: Free Press, 1995.

Plato. *The Dialogues*. Edited by Benjamin Jowett. New York: Random House, 1937.

Sternberg, Robert J. *Beyond IQ: A Triarchic Theory of Human Intelligence*. New York: Cambridge University Press, 1985.

Terman, Lewis M. *The Measurement of Intelligence*. Boston: Houghton Mifflin, 1916.

Wall Street Journal Position Paper. "Mainstream Science on Intelligence." *Wall Street Journal*, December 13, 1994.

Weiss, Rick. "How DNA Is Influenced." *Washington Post*, July 6, 2005.

PSYCHOMOTOR DEVELOPMENT

Psychomotor development has to do with the acquisition of skills through the use of both mental and physical activity. Psychomotor development is similar to cognitive-intellectual development in that both forms of development necessitate the use of the human brain and nervous system.

Motor Control

Motor control is an area of study in psychomotor development that investigates how one accomplishes a goal, rather than selecting a goal—which would be the more intellectual endeavor. It concerns the physical processes that one needs to engage in so that a particular movement can be carried out. It has little to do with why one needs to engage in a particular movement. Overall, there are three general classes of theories that account for the basic question that researchers have addressed in movement science: how does one select a particular movement? These three classes of theories are efficiency theories, synergy theories, and the mass spring theory. In order to explain these ideas, it is necessary to clarify two terms that refer to the ways in which one engages in movement: "trajectory" and "effector." In general, a trajectory is the path taken by a person's arm, foot, or other extremity to accomplish a movement goal. An effector is the part of the body that one uses to engage in a particular movement.

Efficiency theories emphasize that some movements are more efficient than others when a person attempts to solve a particular task, such as reaching for or grasping something. For example, when reaching for a light switch, one does not twist the arm and flex the elbow. Rather, it is much easier to keep the arm straight when engaging in this task. There are a great number of ways in which we can measure the efficiency of a movement. One can move the shortest distance possible by moving an effector to accomplish something. The problem that is encountered, however, is whether the efficient movement involves the movement of an effector rectilinearly (in a Cartesian format) or in terms of joint space—the way one plans the movement of an effector using joints in an angular format.

Synergy theories differ from efficiency theories in that they describe a particular movement as determined by a group of joints or muscles that work together in performing a task. In other words, although it might be more efficient for one particular joint or muscle to engage in a movement (e.g., reaching for a book on a desk), certain bodily reactions might favor a group of muscles to work concurrently as a means of carrying out the movement. Synergy, then, refers to the interrelationships between certain muscles that are used to carry out a movement, even though the use of single muscle to do the same movement might be more efficient. For example, it has been shown that certain muscles and joint movements do go together when performing different types of

tasks. For example, it is easier to flex or extend the wrist and elbow together than to flex or extend one without the other.

In the mass spring theory, movement scientists argue that the way our joints move is similar to the way a saloon door operates: when the saloon door is opened, it swings back and forth and eventually stops moving when it is even with the door jamb. Our joints behave in the same way: if a limb can be moved in one direction, it can be moved the same distance in the other in order to perform a movement task.

Motor Development

Motor development is the sequence of periods in which one demonstrates changes in controlling physical movement. This movement is carried out through the collaboration between the brain, bones, and muscles. Motor development specialists have identified two types of skills that allow humans to function from the perspective of movement: gross motor skills and fine motor skills. Gross motor skills are the skills needed to function for walking, sitting, reclining, and general moving from one location to another. Fine motor skills are those skills that allow for more specified movement activity and that are dependent on movement of smaller muscles. Fine motor ability allows people to write, draw pictures, develop hand-eye coordination, and work with small objects. For example, watchmakers must have well-developed fine motor skills. Dynamic systems theory (DST) is a contemporary framework in motor development that has been used for the purpose of supporting research in the field. According to David Gallahue and J.C. Ozmun in *Motor Development* (2002), DST is a theory based on an ecological approach—in other words, one that focuses on environmental factors that either promote or impede development.

Motor Learning

Motor learning, or motor skill learning, refers to the improved exactness and precision of motor skills that occur through repetitive practice. This form of learning involves both spatial and temporal accuracy. Learning how to use a crayon or pencil, riding a bicycle, and typing on a keyboard of a typewriter or computer are just three examples of motor skill learning in an educational context during the course of one's life.

There are three properties of motor skill learning: generalization, retention, and automaticity.

When a person learns how to do something for the first time, it might take hours, days, if not weeks, to accomplish without error. Generalization accounts for the fact that after someone learns how to do something, the task can be accomplished at other times and using different objects. For example, a person learning how to play the piano may take years before achieving errorless performance. At that point, however, the individual will be able to perform anywhere, and on any piano, not just the piano that was used initially. Similarly, after a child masters the ability to ride a bicycle, it will be possible to ride any bicycle, large or small, and regardless of location. Furthermore, once someone learns how to do something, the person retains the knowledge of how to do it one year, ten years, or thirty years later. The bassoon player who quits playing but picks up the instrument 30 years later will still be able to play the instrument, although probably not all that well. Similarly, most adults who learn how to ride a bicycle during childhood can still do so as an adult, even though they may not have ridden a bicycle for years.

When performing a task for the first time, learners have to pay constant attention to the task. But as they perfect their abilities to do the task, the amount of attention they give to the task steadily decreases. This is the case with most general tasks. After long-term retention, tasks become automatic—people do them without consciously thinking about the processes that these tasks entail. The properties of generalization and retention hold up fairly well in laboratory environments, although some tasks serve as exceptions. Automaticity, on the other hand, holds up quite well when investigated under laboratory constraints.

Motor Program Theories

Researchers who have proposed the idea of motor programs argue that these programs are equated to complex motor skills. The motor program is analogous to a computer program in that each has a list of commands that need to be executed in a certain manner. Motor program theories have three general characteristics. First, each program has a set of commands for each type of movement. Second, commands can be carried out without the need of perceptual feedback. Third, the commands of the program can be executed for various sets of muscle groups and effectors. Studies in this area seem to have shown the hierarchical nature of motor programs. In a hierarchical diagram, there are movement nodes and control nodes. The movement nodes identify which muscles are to be used for a particular task. The control notes identify what exactly the muscles are supposed to do to execute the task. In addition, there seems to be strong evidence of hierarchical organization of muscle movement in the brain.

Perception and Movement

The study of perception has traditionally been a topic in the psychological subfield of cognition and intellectual development. However, perception is also related to movement and motor skills. In other words, we base much of what we do in terms of movement by what we perceive in the everyday world. When we reach for a book, we do so based on our perception of what the book looks like and how far away the book is. There are basically two ways in which humans use their perceptions as a means of engaging in their movements. One way is through the use of vision, and the other is through proprioception.

Vision

Vision plays an important role in connection with psychomotor development. First, vision helps us determine what we are looking for when searching or getting an object. Also, it informs us how we are going to get it. For example, will we reach for it? Or will we grasp it? Of course, it all depends on the object's location and placement. One important question that movement study researchers have investigated is the extent to which vision is necessary in the procurement of an object. They investigated whether vision was applied only during the planning of reaching or grasping, or whether it was applied during the reaching or grasping process. Visual information is often not needed, particularly when a subject is asked to intercept an object, like a moving projectile, or ball.

Proprioception

At times, vision cannot be used when attempting to accomplish a movement. When this happens, proprioception takes over. Proprioception is the sensation of the location of different parts of a person's body. Proprioception refers to the ability to engage in a movement activity without the sense of vision; in this case, special subcutaneous receptors in the joints and muscles take over and detect the location of the parts of one's body during movement.

Physical Education

The topic of physical education serves as an extension to the preceding discussion on movement and motor skill development. Universities throughout the world include physical education departments that might be named the department of kinesiology (given that this term essentially means the science of human movement), exercise science, movement science, or human performance. The subdiscipline of physical education that now focuses on curriculum, teaching, and teacher education is called sport pedagogy. Prior to the 1970s, the broad field of physical education was not yet considered a field of research. It was not until the work of Lawrence Locke that the field gained research status. Of the many current subfields in physical education, the following ones have been emphasized in recent decades: standards-based curriculum development, current curricular approaches in physical education, and student development.

Daniel Ness and Chia-ling Lin

REFERENCES

Gallahue, David, and J.C. Ozmun. *Motor Development: Infants, Children, Adolescents, Adults.* 5th ed. Boston: McGraw-Hill, 2002.

Keele, Steven. "Behavioral Analysis of Movement." In *Handbook of Physiology*, vol. 2, *Motor Control*, ed. John M. Brookhart, Vernon B. Mountcastle, and Vernon B. Brooks, 1391–1414. Bethesda, MD: American Physiological Society, 1981.

Locke, Lawrence, F. "Qualitative Research as a Form of Scientific Inquiry in Sport and Physical Education." *Research Quarterly for Exercise and Sport* 60:1 (1989): 1–20.

Santello, Marcello, Martha Flanders, and John F. Soechting. "Postural Hand Synergies for Tool Use." *Journal of Neuroscience* 18 (1998): 10105–10115.

Silverman, Steven. "Research on Teaching in Physical Education." *Research Quarterly for Exercise and Sport* 62 (1991): 352–364.

Todorov, Emanuel. "Optimality Principles in Sensorimotor Control." *Nature Neuroscience* 7 (2004): 907–915.

QUANTITATIVE DEVELOPMENT

Quantitative development refers to the processes by which humans have the capacity to work with numbers or numerical quantities. This topic is discussed through the examination of number recognition in infancy, early childhood mathematical development as it relates specifically to spontaneous concepts, mathematical symbolism, and formal operations that students encounter for the first time in school.

Mathematical Development in Infancy

For a long time, cognitive research was mixed as to when humans acquire the ability to think mathematically. Since the early 1990s, research has suggested that mathematical thinking begins shortly after birth; the infant reacts to quantity as either discrete numbers or amount. There is a large body of research on mathematical thinking during infancy, quantitative reasoning in particular.

Renee Baillargeon conducted a number of studies to tap whether infants may have much more cognitive appreciation of the physical world and reality than Jean Piaget would have contended, based on his writing on the sensorimotor stage. Baillargeon's approach in studying infant numerical cognition is sweeping in that it involves a broad list of cognitive tasks, which she investigates by presenting infants with pictures of various objects shown in various situations. For example, one picture shows a table top with a box firmly set in the middle of it. The second picture shows the box placed very close to the edge of the table—half on and half off. In the third picture, the box has been moved off the table and is hanging in midair (see Figure 1 on page 194).

Baillargeon uses a method known as inspection time (also known as "looking time")—in other words, the number of seconds (or minutes) that a child is looking or gazing at something as evidence of recognition or interest. A three-month-old infant will spend very little time (perhaps only one second) looking at the depiction of the box on the table. The same infant will spend a little more time (a few seconds) looking at the box at the edge of that table. The movement of the box from the center of the table to the edge of the table is called the habituation event. If the box is suspended in midair

Figure 1:　**Baillargeon's Pictures of Objects On/Off the Table**

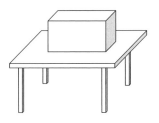

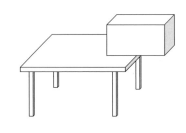

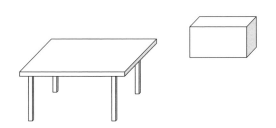

and away from the table without any supports, the same three-month-old infant will stare at the picture for a long period of time (several seconds, perhaps as long as one minute). The evidence of the infant's uncertainty is clear in videotapes of infants who are shown these and similar pictures. Baillargeon's findings suggest that infants already have a conception of how objects in the external world are supposed to behave. When a baby notices that an object in the external world, even in the form of an artistic depiction, is violating what seems to be the laws of physics, it may be necessary to reconsider when cognition in general and spatial sense in particular really begin.

This type of investigation is part of a large body of research that challenges Piaget's stage theory. Children are able to do things at much earlier points than Piaget's theory would suggest. It is not even quite clear whether the stage concept is the most valid concept. Different infants differ in abilities related to perception of spatial structures; some researchers have argued that cognitive development is a rising

and falling of certain waves of ability and prowess. But what can be said is that the more one learns about infants, the more one learns what they know.

Karen Wynn's research also involves the use of a display of a small number of objects. She uses a method involving infants' inspection time as a means of tapping into infant numerical development. The sequence of events in Wynn's experiments adheres to the following procedure:

1. An object is placed in the infant's view by hand in a large open box.
2. A screen is then used to cover the box so that the object is hidden from the infant's view.
3. The hand leaves the scene empty.
4. A second object is then added, also in the infant's view. So either two objects are present, or one object is present and the second object that was considered is placed out of sight behind the screen.
5. The hand leaves the scene empty.

In Wynn's study, two situations may occur: (1) two objects behind the screen are revealed, or (2) only one object behind the screen is revealed. Wynn found that infants showed more evidence of suspense and longer intervals of inspection time when the number of objects remaining (e.g., the one object in the above scenario) did not match the number of items in the change that had occurred, namely, the addition of another object. This strongly indicates that the infant expected more than one object to be present. Wynn's research is one of the first examples in which we find that infants show evidence of the ability to distinguish between one object and more than one object.

Wynn and others have contributed much to our understanding of the origins of mathematical development in humans. The results of a number of these infant cognition studies led many in the field of cognitive science to conclude that quantitative ability is an innate part of human cognition. Other cognitive researchers do not necessarily embrace the nativist argument, however. Mix, Huttenlocher, and Levine argue that the origins of mathematical thinking in infants are based on the role of overall amount. In other words, infants are not necessarily universally equipped to distinguish between discrete numerical values (i.e., natural numbers, such as 1, 2, 3); they rather view the world in terms of amount (i.e., more versus less).

Mathematical Development in Early Childhood

Early in the child's life, everyday mathematical activity—given that it is not taught to the child—is for the most part a spontaneous activity. Spontaneous mathematics is associated with the everyday mathematical concepts learned before entrance to formal schooling. Constructivist philosophy supports the notion that the development of knowledge is strongly situated with the idea that learning unfolds due to the interaction of initial schema (i.e., sucking, grasping, and gazing) that develop shortly after birth. This unfolding process contributes to children's abilities as they invent new, untaught strategies for solving problems based on prior situations. A large number of these problems involve quantitative and spatial thinking processes.

In addition to the term "spontaneous mathematics," mathematical development specialists also use the terms "informal mathematics," "everyday mathematics," and sometimes "practical arithmetic." Informal mathematics is associated with any mathematical activity that is not written—more specifically, the mathematics that does not make explicit use of the scientific and conventionally systematic notation that is learned in school. Everyday mathematics is often used to describe children who are engaged in both written and nonwritten mathematical activity outside of school. These meanings are not entirely definitive for they are used casually in research and in reference to classroom activity.

In order to identify the significance of spontaneous procedures in solving mathematical problems, researchers have developed assessment techniques that are suitable for identifying such behavior. Standardized assessments like multiple choice examinations are unsuitable for measuring such activity because they fail to tap children's cognitive abilities. Instead, developmental psychologists and mathematics educators rely on observational techniques for the most part to identify children's spontaneous cognitive behavior. Preschool free play hours are perhaps most conducive to naturalistic observation, since children in this setting are more interested in their playing than in wondering why a grownup is observing them. Preschoolers in general are engaged in spontaneous mathematical activity nearly 50 percent of the time during free play. There seems to be an increase in spontaneous mathematical activity during free play and other informal contexts as children increase in age. In addition, there are no gender differences or social class differences when considering frequency of children's spontaneous mathematical activity. In other words, girls and boys engage in mathematically related tasks and activities for roughly the same amounts of time. The same is true for children of different socioeconomic status (SES) groups: children in lower SES groups perform as well and engage in mathematically related activities for approximately the same amount of time as their middle and upper SES counterparts.

Counting and Numbers

Very early in life, young children develop informal strategies for counting various objects. Given its universality in nearly every world culture, the ability to count in many ways represents the foundation of formal mathematical instruction. Therefore, educators and psychologists have developed assessment techniques, such as the clinical interview and observation, as methods for identifying young children's spontaneous strategies in determining cardinality of sets and one-to-one correspondence—two indispensable criteria for counting objects properly. Through the process of counting objects and ideas in a one-by-one manner, children begin to master the counting procedure, and their accuracy improves greatly with time. However, counting itself is only one part of spontaneous mathematical activity. The strategies for counting provide even more evidence that spontaneous mathematics occurs. The following are some of these spontaneous strategies:

1. *Pushing aside.* One important strategy that children use to develop more efficient counting using spontaneous techniques is the process of pushing aside. Children spontaneously discover a simple and elegant procedure for counting one by one: after they count an object, they simply move it to the side, away from those that remain to be counted. This strategy is extremely powerful because it minimizes strain on the child's memory. At this point, it is not necessary to remember which individual objects in a random collection have and have not been

counted. Having pushed to the side each object counted, the child need only remember to count all remaining items. Invention of this simple strategy results in a tremendous increase in accuracy.

2. *Tagging.* Pushing aside demonstrates a spontaneous action on the part of the child to facilitate counting in an efficient manner. However, one step above this action is the process of tagging, which does not account for the time spent pushing objects aside from the ones that are not yet counted. Instead, tagging involves making a one-to-one correspondence between a child's finger, which points to, or touches, an object of a set, and the objects themselves. This procedure allows the child to arrive at answers and conclusions about sets slightly more quickly than pushing aside alone.

3. *Subitizing.* There is an obstacle to pushing aside, however; as time progresses, children develop ways to become more efficient in their problem solving. This problem solving is associated with mathematical thinking. After using more primitive strategies, like pushing aside or tagging, children learn to "see" small numbers directly so that they do not need to count small collections—that is, those consisting of two, three, four, or five—to know their number. They can perceive ♦ ♦ ♦ ♦ ♦ as "five," just as they can directly convert the letter *w* into the sound "double you." This kind of spontaneous recognition of number is called subitizing, which comes from the Italian *subito*, often found in musical notation, and means "immediate." Children practice subitizing when they repeatedly count sets and remember the results. If children count to a number enough times, they learn to "see" that number without actually counting each object of the set.

4. *Grouping.* After mastery of immediate recognition of number with regard to objects, children develop grouping strategies that allow them to determine numbers in increasingly efficient ways. Often they begin by grouping objects by twos. Instead of counting one by one, a child may count "two, four, six . . ." to yield a result. As seen in Figure 2, a child in the third grade might determine the number of dots in the set

Figure 2: **Grouping by Threes to the Number 17**

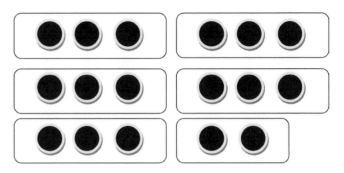

by identifying five groups of three dots and adding two—17 dots altogether.

5. *Arithmetic procedures.* Older children use relatively advanced forms of arithmetic in basically the same strategy. In solving the "dot" problem in Figure 2, another third grader might say, "I know that 5 times 3 is 15, plus 2 is 17." Indeed, this strategy is easier than counting and, if developed properly, just as accurate. As seen from the above spontaneous strategies, children proceed from counting one by one to applying operations to groups of objects of a set.

Although scholars do not necessarily agree on exactly when mathematical thinking begins in connection with human cognitive development, there is general agreement in the research communities in both education and psychology that mathematical thinking occurs well before the beginning of formal schooling. The literature in mathematical cognition is also very clear with respect to young children's quantitative and spatial abilities. Educational and psychological research has demonstrated that children build ideas about quantity and ideas about space through active performance, not merely through passive viewing. They engage in a considerable amount of mathematical activity during free play. Mathematical activity of several types in everyday free play is evident in children of all socioeconomic backgrounds and is indifferent to gender.

Piaget's conservation of equivalent relations task underscores how young children compare with older children when confronted with numerical problems. In the problem depicted in Figure 3, the child is asked to determine whether the two sets of objects are equal or whether one set is greater than the other. In this figure, the child is presented with five toy dogs and five toy bones. The interviewer asks: Each dog is supposed to get one bone. Is this possible? The interviewer then spreads out the five bones and keeps the five toy dogs where they were. Now the interviewer asks: Does each dog get one bone? In other words, is there the same number of dogs as bones, or is the number of dogs different from the number of bones? The young, preoperational child will say that the number of bones is greater than the number of dogs because they are spread apart. That is, according to Piaget, the preoperational child is unable to conserve equivalence relations—the two sets are not equal (according to the child) because the set of bones is spread out and the set of dogs is not. The general idea here is that the young, preoperational child is unable to differentiate between the number of objects and the physical location of objects.

Numerical Symbolism

Adults generally take for granted the ease with which an individual comprehends the numerals 1, 2, 3, 4, 5, and so on. As members of postindustrial society, it is even effortless for adults to see 5 + 8 = 13 and know exactly what it means. However, in societies that do not have formalized numerical systems—in the present day, such societies are very few—these numerals are not used in the everyday goings-on of life. At the same time, these societies demonstrate a heritage that is rich in mathematical ideas. For example, Paulus Gerdes writes eloquently of the highly complex mathematical systems known as *sona* used by the Cokwe people of Angola when conveying and interpreting messages. In other works, Gerdes examines the sophisticated mathematical underpinnings involved in the work of Mozambican artisans and craftspeople. In general, the Hindu-Arabic numerical system is not universal; rather it consists of a large set of symbols that originated more than 2,000 years ago and evolved into what postindustrial and developing societies use today.

The Number Concept

Given appropriate instructional techniques, formal schooling can be quite beneficial in advancing children's knowledge of number concepts. There is a great deal of research supporting the existence of

Figure 3: **The Task of Conservation of Equivalent Relations**

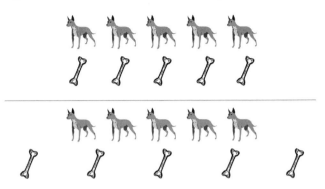

young children's everyday mathematics. The term "enumeration" has to do with one's understanding of the concept of number. As a necessary component of mathematical development, it is very important for adults to be aware of students' strengths and weaknesses in enumeration. Accordingly, it is essential that adults—parents, teachers, school psychologists, among others—know what underlies a student's ability to enumerate. In other words, adults need to know when a student understands the meaning of number—that is, number sense. The following is an outline of the essential benchmarks for concluding that a child comprehends the concept of number:

First, a child needs to know the counting words. But knowing the counting words alone does not necessarily mean that a child understands the concept of number.

Second, the child needs to say the number words in their accurate sequence—"one, two, three, four . . ." (the stable-order principle). Again, this does not demonstrate a child's mastery of number sense.

Third, the child must count each member of a collection of items once and only once (one-to-one principle). Young children often count objects of a set more than once or may "combine" two objects that are close in proximity as one item.

Fourth, the child must recognize that the counting words do not have to be assigned to particular objects (order relevance principle). For example, if we see a row of nine checkers, whether we start counting from the left, the right, or the middle, we still should end up with nine checkers. This may pose a major obstacle for many young children.

Fifth, the child has to learn that the physical arrangement of these objects is irrelevant to the total number of objects. Piaget's conservation of number task, mentioned above, is an illustrative example.

Still, the recognition of the equivalence of two sets does not indicate a child's understanding of the concept of number.

Sixth, counting objects indicates the total number of objects in a relevant collection (cardinality principle). For example, the number "5" is not the name of the fifth object or sixth one. Rather, it says something about the total number of objects in the set—the cardinal number. Mastery of cardinality is strong evidence that a child's conceptual knowledge of number is forming and taking shape.

Finally, the child needs to know that the last number in a sequence relates to other numbers in unique ways. That is, 5 is one more than 4, 5 is one less than 6, 10 is double 5, and so forth. This knowledge of a number in relation to other numbers in a complex system provides the definitive role of number concepts. In addition, at this point, the child understands that anything can be counted, even if the objects counted are not of the same kind (the abstraction principle).

Research in mathematics instruction suggests that teachers and other practitioners will obtain the best results when they use different concrete models with their students in the early grades. This will allow students in the later grades to be able to appreciate the different ways to represent equal quantities. Often, however, teachers implement materials or models using rote procedures, thus running the risk of failing to bridge the gap between students' informal, everyday mathematical knowledge and formal mathematical concepts.

Most teachers, especially those who teach young children, have often associated the concepts of number and operations with the teaching and learning of mathematics in general. Nevertheless, despite this association, children's mastery of number concepts provides a strong foundation for learning more complex and challenging mathematical concepts in the later grades.

Children's mastery has an additional benefit: if developed appropriately, children's understanding of the concept of the numbers 0 through 12 will enable them to improve their number fact knowledge—operations on numbers between 0 and 12—in subsequent grade levels. Subsequent stages of symbolic development occur when young children are introduced to operator symbols (+, −, ×, ÷). For many years, research in mathematics education was unclear as to children's understanding of operator meanings. These studies questioned whether cognitive acquisition of these symbols was gradual through the learning of arithmetic operations or whether it is a question of transition from one developmental stage to another. Today, cognitive psychologists seem to conclude that the learning of mathematical symbolism, or any symbolism for that matter, has little if anything to do with stage theory or levels of development. Rather, as Daniel Willingham notes in *Cognition* (2008), it is the continuous overlapping of, and acquaintance with, various ideas and concepts that unfold during the course of human life. Research seems to be consistent with respect to the level of difficulty in understanding each of the operation symbols.

Daniel Ness and Chia-ling Lin

REFERENCES

Ben-Zeev, Talia, and Robert Sternberg. *The Nature of Mathematical Thinking.* Mahwah, NJ: Lawrence Erlbaum, 1996.

Dretske, Fred. I. "Perception from an Epistemological Point of View." *Journal of Philosophy* 66 (1971): 584–591.

Ginsburg, Herbert P., Chia-ling Lin, Daniel Ness, and Seo Kyoung-Hye. "Young American and Chinese Children's Everyday Mathematical Activity." *Mathematical Thinking and Learning* 5:4 (2003): 235–258.

Lesser, Gerald S., Gordon Fifer, and Donald H. Clark. "Mental Abilities of Children from Different Social-class and Cultural Groups." *Monographs of the Society for Research in Child Development*, Serial No. 102, 20:4 (1965).

Mix, Kelly S., Janellen Huttenlocher, and Susan C. Levine. *Quantitative Development in Infancy and Early Childhood.* New York: Oxford University Press, 2002.

Ness, Daniel, and Stephen J. Farenga. *Knowledge under Construction: The Importance of Play in Developing Children's Spatial and Geometric Thinking.* Lanham, MD: Rowman & Littlefield, 2007.

Piaget, Jean. *The Construction of Reality in the Child.* New York: Basic Books, 1954.

Willingham, Daniel. *Cognition: The Thinking Animal.* Upper Saddle River, NJ: Prentice-Hall, 2008.

Wynn, Karen. "Infants Possess a System of Numerical Knowledge." *Current Direction in Psychological Science* 4:6 (1995): 172–177.

SPATIAL DEVELOPMENT

Spatial development is a generic term often defined as the process of unfolding an individual's intellectual capabilities as regards to space. In the fields of psychology and education, one might causally talk about the development of spatial thinking, which refers to the unfolding of biological and mental processes connected with spatial thinking over time. In addition, when the construct of "development" is included, one might infer the existence of periods, or stages, of increasing (rarely decreasing) levels of ability over the course of a certain time period or duration.

Theories Concerning the Development of Spatial and Geometric Thinking

Four dominant theories of spatial and geometric thinking have been developed within the last century—the Piagetian perspective, the Vygotskyan perspective, the nativist perspective, and the interactionist perspective. A fifth perspective, the everyday spatial thinking model, is a more recent view.

Piagetian Perspective

Jean Piaget and Bärbel Inhelder advanced a general theory of spatial and geometrical development—particularly the theoretical underpinnings of the topological primacy thesis—by intensively observing and interviewing approximately 140 children between the ages of two and a half years and seven years in a task Piaget refers to as haptic perception, or a child's representation (drawing) of an object after touching it.

Topological space refers to children's conception of space from birth to six or seven years of age. Children at this level view objects in space in a somewhat plastic or re-forming way. In other words, the disposition of objects is not considered in terms of their association to polygons (e.g., a bowl is like a circle) but rather in terms of their physical appearance in relation to other objects (e.g., a bowl is like a dish, whereas a coffee mug is like a doughnut because they both have holes). In addition, spatial development at this early level is closely connected with how close objects are (proximity); how two or more objects are distinguishable (separation); how and when two or more objects appear (order); the location of a middle object (enclosure); and sequences of objects (continuity).

Projective space, from the Piagetian perspective, refers to the child's conception of objects that are associated with their polygon equivalents. Children

exhibiting concepts of space from a projective standpoint are usually between four and 10 years old (or possibly 12). In order for children to represent an object through drawing, they will need a frame of reference to complete the figure. For example, if a child is asked to draw a triangle, one of the edges of the triangle will be parallel with the edge of the table. Children's drawings, especially during the early part of the projective period, will often fail to treat an object as three-dimensional and will instead represent it as a two-dimensional figure.

Finally, Euclidean space, which is based on precepts of Euclidean geometry, refers to a child's ability to represent objects in a way that closely conforms to their appearance. These children will exhibit knowledge of parallel or perpendicular lines with respect to rectilinear objects (e.g., drawing a window or a house) and will not depend on frames of reference (e.g., table edges). Children who exhibit Euclidean tendencies are generally older than seven years of age.

Vygotskyan Approach

The Vygotskyan perspective, named after the well-known Russian theorist Lev Vygotsky, is intrinsically associated with the cultural implications of cognitive development and the ways in which spatial sense contributes to that development. For the proponents of this perspective of spatial thinking, culture is the most important attribute on which any area of cognitive study depends, including that of spatial and geometric thinking. Vygotskyan researchers argue that mapping becomes more cognitively accessible when it is contextualized for the individual reading the map. Lack of contextualization limits the individual's cognitive ability to identify and decipher the meanings and symbolic representations associated with maps. Vygotskyans often implement the scaffolding metaphor to illustrate this point even further. The scaffold serves to mediate between the child's misunderstandings of a given subject and the actual attainment of that knowledge. Unlike the Piagetian perspective, which views mapping—in relation to spatial thinking—as an individualistic phenomenon, only reached once the child surpasses projective space and understands the precepts of Euclidean space, the Vygotskyan method focuses on the expert-apprentice model, whereby researchers concern themselves with individual situational factors in spatial thinking that involve experiential learning within a sociological context.

There are several researchers whose work falls into this category. In *Anthropology of Space* (1983), Rik Pinxten outlines a framework of spatial ability that views spatial sense from a universalist standpoint, rather than solely a Western one. Unlike Piaget's adherents and other present-day developmental psychologists focusing on spatial thinking from a Piagetian perspective, Pinxten challenges the idea that space and spatial thinking are entirely self-evident, truthful (i.e., a priori) constructions. Instead, he argues in favor of cultural boundedness of epistemological systems. In other words, the nature of knowledge with regard to universal concepts—like space—is dependent upon the norms or patterns of a particular culture. Yet, at the same time, his research concerning the development of a posteriori universals enables researchers to analyze the similarities between two or more cultural groups.

Pinxten discusses cultural universals of spatial thinking and presents an argument for a culturally bound geometry curriculum in the early grades. He addresses this curriculum specifically toward Navajo children, but contends its usefulness in the learning of space and geometry for most populations. Pinxten challenges the notion of the strict universality of so-called Western geometry and instead demonstrates how the Western conception of geometric and spatial thinking is incommensurable with the Navajo perspective.

Prior to the publication of *Anthropology of Space*, Pinxten developed a system for understanding universal aspects of space so that researchers are able to identify spatial behaviors characteristic of all cultures studied. He calls this system the universal frame of reference (UFOR). UFOR was developed as a means of identifying universal spatial relations through semantic categorizations of specific spatial concepts. Pinxten's UFOR framework is important because the categorization of universal spatial concepts was developed through the study of culturally specific values that are not based on absolute truths, but can be generalized through analyzing methods of different cultures (i.e., a posteriori). UFOR is a product of detailed analyses from fieldwork. Each code or category is based on an empirical approach used while studying the spatial characteristics of several distinct cultures. For Pinxten, the universality

of spatial thinking is situated not solely in the tenets of the Western philosophical tradition regarding the meaning of space and geometry. Instead, it is based on empirical data collected from both Western and non-Western cultural systems of knowledge.

Nativism

The nativist perspective in spatial thinking embraces the notion of a genetic component to spatial development. Nativists argue that spatial thinking is a universal attribute. From the middle of the nineteenth to the middle of the twentieth century, researchers believed that the left hemisphere of the brain controlled one's verbal ability and that losing access to the right hemisphere was not as crucial. It was not until the late 1960s and early 1970s that research shed light on the importance of the right hemisphere, especially in spatial and geometric competencies.

Nativist theorists and researchers generally will argue the existence of innate factors that contribute to a particular intellectual ability. For example, Prentice Starkey, Elizabeth Spelke, and Rochel Gelman observed that six-month-old infants can discriminate between two everyday objects and three everyday objects when looking at pictures of these objects on slides. In her well-known empirical research, Karen Wynn concluded that infants as young as two or three days old can discern between different numerosities (e.g., one object versus a set of objects—more than one). In general, the nativist perspective emphasizes the heritable, or brain-based origins of concepts and intellect, at the expense of environmental or developmental (stage-related) factors.

Interactionism

The interactionist approach in the development of spatial thinking was introduced by Nora Newcombe and Janellen Huttenlocher. This approach suggests that spatial thinking, among other cognitive domains, is a construct that is influenced by a nativist, a developmentalist, and an environmental influence. In this approach, human biological factors interact with environmental and contextual factors. Eventually, this interaction will influence the development of spatial thinking during early and middle childhood.

The supporters of an interactionist approach initially examine the ways in which adults think about space and spatial structures. Doing so provides a general overview of how one might approach the origins of spatial cognition. Newcombe and Huttenlocher refer to the process of spatial coding as a way to determine the spatial abilities of individuals at various age levels. Their application of spatial coding emanates from the works of Piaget and Inhelder, who argued that adult competence at any mental task was an end whereby one would be able to identify the means—that is, developmental factors contributing to a particular cognitive ability.

Newcombe and Huttenlocher caution the reader not to overextend the eclectic nature of the interactionist approach. To do so would be possibly to lose oneself in the multifaceted characteristics of various outlooks. For example, an overemphasis on contextual factors that impinge on spatial thinking muddles the equally important factors having to do with biological mechanisms that influence human spatial thinking processes.

Related Topics

In addition to perspectives in spatial and geometric development from a global standpoint, research in this domain identifies several related categories. These include spatial perception, spatial representation, spatial cognition, spatial orientation, spatial sense, and spatial relations.

Spatial Perception

Spatial perception generally refers to one's extraction of the local environment and one's self. The sources of spatial perception, as the empirical philosophers would have it, are the external senses. For example, sight delivers light, hearing delivers sound, and touch delivers the physical makeup of objects. One of the difficulties with spatial perception is one's ability to distinguish between reality and fiction. Philosophers seem to dichotomize spatial perception into two fairly broad categories: fact perception and object perception. Fact perception, unlike object perception, considers the cognitive systems of the mind, such as conceptual understanding, procedural understanding, and memory, whereas object or event perception does not require us to "remember" the way we see a large object in the road or the chalkboard in the classroom.

Spatial Representation

Spatial representation refers to the way in which one mentally organizes, describes, or constructs an image, depiction, or account of an object (or objects) in its given place. In "The Development of Spatial Cognition" (1973), Roger Hart and Gary Moore refer to two types of spatial representation: internalized and external. Internalized cognitive representations of space refer to the ways individuals construct space through mental reproduction, in other words, by reflecting on spatial attributes through thought and without the aid of external objects or symbols. External cognitive representations of space refer to the ways in which individuals construct models of space. Examples of external spatial (or geometric) representation include children's drawings, a tenth-grader's written representation of a traversal intersecting two parallel lines, an architect's blueprint, and an experimental psychologist's map of psychophysical phenomena.

Spatial Cognition

Spatial cognition refers to any behavior or activity of an organism that involves space or location with the premise that this behavior is mediated by cerebral functioning. In other words, spatial cognition deals with any characteristic of space—both visual and navigational—so long as the premise of any cognitive attribute of spatial features refers back to the neurological bases of behavior. Each branch of research in these areas has its own position on the definition or description of an exhaustive or comprehensive concept of spatial knowledge. Hart and Moore review the literature on space by focusing on spatial cognition as the all-encompassing domain. They define spatial cognition as "the knowledge and internal or cognitive representation of the structure, entities, and relations of space" or "the internalized reflection and reconstruction of space in thought."

Further, Hart and Moore argue that spatial cognition encompasses all the modes of an individual's knowledge of the subject of space—namely, perception, thinking, reasoning, and judgment. At the same time, however, they argue that all these subareas interact with each other and may influence spatial cognition. In addition, Hart and Moore suggest that spatial cognition encompasses other modes of spatial knowledge as well. This assertion is based on a connection they have made between Piaget's figurative and operative distinction—two aspects of how individuals know the world. The figurative form deals with percepts based on fleeting, perceptual configurations of pictures and images that individuals create upon direct contact, whereas the operative concerns the ways in which individuals operate on or transform two or more successive states into reconstructed patterns or arrangements. Hart and Moore associate the figurative knowledge with spatial or visual perception, while operative knowledge is associated with spatial cognition, or intelligence. In other words, they argue that spatial cognition includes all the various attributes of spatial (or geometric) knowledge—namely, perceiving, thinking, imaging, reasoning, judging, remembering, representing, orienting, relating, and associating.

Spatial Orientation

Distinctions have also been made between the concept of spatial (and geometric) orientation and other forms of spatial knowledge. Spatial orientation refers to the manner in which location is determined within one's immediate environment. In "Geometric and Spatial Thinking in Young Children" (1999), Douglas Clements defines spatial orientation as "understanding and operating on relationships between different positions in space, especially with respect to your own position." Spatial orientation also involves navigational abilities as well. That is, when we orient ourselves from one place to another, we need to consider factors of location of place (topos) and direction from one location to another. This ability in orienteering, then, is very much related to the construct of spatial orientation. To be spatially oriented assumes the use of frames of reference and their relationship to the environment. Spatial (or geographic) orientation specifically calls for the individual's construction of either mental images or physical representations that are specifically related to the environment and that utilize frames of reference.

Spatial Sense

Researchers in mathematics education often use the term "spatial sense." Such terminology seems to be associated with the idea of what children need to know in order to succeed in their spatial and geometric knowledge abilities. Clements argues that having spatial abilities presupposes spatial sense and that spatial orientation and spatial visualization are two important types of spatial abilities.

The term "spatial sense" can unfortunately be construed as a subjective quality that cannot be identified or measured in any empirical or quantifiable manner. "Spatial sense" is often used with regard to what the common individual needs to know about space in order to function in everyday life. This meaning of the term gives rise to a number of problems. First, the term implies a sense of cultural neutrality—that is, all individuals, regardless of their cultural and social upbringing, should have a way of thinking about space that is not culturally bound. Second, by its semantic associations, "spatial sense" also can imply a way of experiencing the world empirically, through the sense organs. If this were the case, then humans would have developed a sense for space in the same manner in which they possess senses for tactile, visual, olfactory, auditory, and taste behaviors. "Spatial sense" defined in this manner would be redundant if people use the same phenomena for "spatial sense" as we would for the visual sense.

It is very important to distinguish between spatial sense, as it relates to noncognitive associations with brain behavior, and spatial thinking, which is entirely dependent on the study of human cognitive abilities. The former seems to be very much connected with human memory, while the latter has more to do with cognitive ability and does not by any means rely on memory alone.

Spatial Relations (or Relationships)

The notion of "spatial relations" (or relationships) is another term used in the literature. Spatial relations cannot exist with one object alone; there must be a second object to which one can compare the first. In "The Development of Spatial Thinking in School Children" (1991), Yakimanskaya defines spatial relations as the closeness between or among various objects in space, or between or among the spatial attributes of these objects. This is related to topics such as direction, distance, magnitude and comparison, physical location, and physical dimensions of distinct objects.

Cross-National Differences in Spatial and Geometric Thinking

Cross-national studies on the cognitive processes of space and geometry are very limited in number. One study attempted to compare intellectual competencies of immigrant children of four ethnic groups living in New York City. One area in which the children were tested involved spatial thinking, in which the Chinese children scored roughly the same as the Jewish children and significantly better than African American and Latino children. This study, however, employed only standardized methods of assessment and did not provide sufficiently rich or accurate information concerning what children of varying ethnic backgrounds really know about spatial relationships or other areas of knowledge. A more recent study compared the differences in spatial structures and drawings of 210 four-, six-, eight-, and ten-year-old children from Canada and China. The results, mostly descriptive, show that the drawings of the Chinese children tended to be more complete, with more attention given to line precision, than the drawings of their Canadian peers.

Using the method of naturalistic observation, a third study compared Chinese and American children from four to six years old in terms of the amount of time each group engaged in mathematical activity as well as the types of mathematical activity that were involved. The results indicate that the Chinese children engaged in more mathematical activity that involved spatial and geometric relations than did their American counterparts. Surprisingly, although much cross-national research emphasizes East Asian children's adeptness in the use of number, there was no significant difference in each group's engagement in enumeration activity. However, with the exception of this investigation, cross-national research is bereft of studies investigating comparisons of spatial and geometric thinking in the everyday context.

Intersection of Quantitative and Spatial Thinking

Despite the plethora of research studies suggesting that quantitative thinking begins only moments after birth and continues to develop throughout the lifespan, some experts believe that numerical knowledge during infancy is not as unequivocal and

as manifest as it might seem. Mix, Huttenlocher, and Levine argue that the findings of most post-Piagetian researchers in the area of quantitative thinking trumped up claims about infants' and young children's extensive abilities in mathematics.

Daniel Ness and Chia-ling Lin

REFERENCES

Clements, Douglas H. "Geometric and Spatial Thinking in Young Children." In *Mathematics in the Early Years*, ed. Juanita V. Copley, 66–79. Reston, VA: National Council of Teachers of Mathematics, 1999.

Gerdes, Paulus. *Geometry from Africa: Mathematical and Educational Explorations.* Washington, DC: MAA, 1999.

———. *Sona Geometry from Angola: Mathematics of an African Tradition.* Milan, Italy: Polimetrica International Scientific, 2006.

Hart, Roger A., and Gary T. Moore. "The Development of Spatial Cognition: A Review." In *Image and Environment: Cognitive Mapping and Spatial Behavior*, ed. Roger M. Downs and David Stea, 248–295. Chicago: Aldine, 1973.

Newcombe, Nora S., and Janellen Huttenlocher. *Making Space: The Development of Spatial Representation and Reasoning.* Cambridge, MA: MIT Press, 2003.

Okamoto, Y., R. Case, C. Bleiker, and B. Henderson. "Cross-Cultural Investigations: The Role of Central Conceptual Structures in the Development of Children's Thought." *Monographs of the Society for Research in Child Development*, Serial No. 246, 61:1–2 (1996).

Piaget, Jean, and Bärbel Inhelder. *The Child's Conception of Space.* Translated by F.J. Langdon and J.L. Lunzer. London: Routledge & Kegan Paul, 1956/1967.

Piaget, Jean, Bärbel Inhelder, and Anna Szeminska. *The Child's Conception of Geometry.* Translated by E.A. Lunzer. New York: Basic Books, 1960.

Pinxten, Rik. *Anthropology of Space: Explorations into the Natural Philosophy and Semantics of the Navajo.* Philadelphia: University of Pennsylvania Press, 1983.

———. *Universalism Versus Relativism in Language and Thought.* The Hague: Mouton, 1976.

Starkey, Prentice, Elizabeth Spelke, and Rochel Gelman. "Number Confidence in Infants: Sensitivity to Numeric Invariance and Numeric Change." Paper presented at the meeting of the International Conference of Infant Studies, New Haven, CT, April 1980.

Yakimanskaya, I.S. "The Development of Spatial Thinking in School Children." *Soviet Studies in Mathematics Education*, vol. 3. Reston, VA: National Council of Teachers of Mathematics, 1991.

TECHNOLOGIES AND GLOBAL EDUCATION

HISTORY AND DEVELOPMENT OF TECHNOLOGY EDUCATION

Technology in education, or education technology, emerged about 80 years ago and has evolved symbiotically with the second generation of the Web 2.0, and new improved technologies. However, the integration of technology into the educational curriculum from a global perspective categorically lags behind the development of the Internet and tools of technology. This disparity and the dearth of technology tools in many educational systems worldwide, which negatively affect hundreds of thousands of individuals, are metaphorically referred to as the "Digital Divide."

The definitions of technology education have also changed over time and at present reflect the demands of a global economy where students are exposed to and trained in the use of the tools that will enable them to become productive citizens in the Information Age. Research concurs that effectual definitions of educational technology include not only the tools of technology but the strategies for integrating them into the curriculum. Thus operative educational technology today incorporates both instructional strategies and activities whereby students become proficient in online learning and the use of asynchronous and synchronous learning tools, and upon graduation are work ready and equipped with the technological skills necessitated by the global economy.

The history and development of technology in education is generally based on three developmental stages: mainframes and minicomputers, microcomputers, and the Internet. The following sections succinctly highlight predominating views, usage, and new and emerging technologies.

Mainframes and Minicomputers

From the mid-1930s to the early 1950s, technology in education normally referred to media and audiovisual communications, specifically the use of slide projectors, films, and tape recorders to enhance learning. It was not until the late 1940s that business, industry, military, and educational leaders foresaw the potential use of technology as an instructional tool and its ability to transform the educational system. During this period, applications were primarily designed by programmers and system analysts for use in business, industry, and military settings. Starting in 1948, the first-generation digital computer, Project Whirlwind, grew out of the US military defense need in the Cold War to train bomber crews on flight simulators. With the continuation of the Cold War and the advent of *Sputnik* in 1957, US governmental leaders focused their attention on the need to develop technology to enhance space exploration.

The first documented case of instructional technology is IBM's 1959 pilot initiative to aid precocious youth in the hard sciences. In 1964 Patrick Suppes of the Institute for Mathematical Studies in the Social Sciences at Stanford University initiated the first tutorial "drill and practice" program on mathematical logic. This instructional software, termed computer-assisted instruction (CAI), was piloted to 41 fourth-graders using a teletype machine, telephone lines, and the institute's mainframe. These applications were written using a high-level programming language, titled Courseswriter, and were utilized in conjunction with the IBM 1500 Instructional Systems.

Private businesses foresaw the marketplace in designing educational programs and were the first stakeholders to initiate contracts. The first commercial instructional system dedicated solely for educational use and marketing was designed by IBM in the early 1960s. By the later part of the decade, IBM refined its 1500 Instructional Systems Model to support 32 student stations that were equipped with integrated student terminal configurations, graphics, audio, and static film projections. In retrospect, the IBM 1500 was akin to the personal computers of the early 1990s but never achieved its full potential due to short shelf life. IBM discontinued support in 1975 due to lack of funding from educational systems.

During the 1970s, educators on all levels increasingly became interested in computer-based technology and envisioned it as a possible panacea in educating youth. Mainframe-based computer systems and minicomputers, in conjunction with the development of sophisticated computer programming languages, such as Fortran in 1967 and Pascal in 1971, took hold and gained momentum in colleges and universities.

The most successful and sophisticated cost-effective CAI system created was PLATO—Programmed Logic for Automatic Teaching Operation. PLATO was spearheaded by Donald Bitzer of the University of Illinois and developed out of the partnership between the university, Control Data Corporation, and the National Science Foundation. PLATO used a specialized programming language called Tutor to write educational software. With the introduction of PLATO IV in the early 1970s, the PLATO system progressed into a large time-sharing system in which multiple courseware users, professors and students alike, could simultaneously access interactive software and resources on a network of terminals that were connected to a mainframe terminal. PLATO enabled professors to write tutorial lessons and course syllabi while students were accessing the software and instructional materials. It was also the first CAI system to combine graphics and touch-sensitive screens (plasma display) for interactive training. Within a decade in the United States and in conjunction with newer technologies, the PLATO system grew from 20 terminals in the early 1970s to approximately 1,000 terminals in the early 1980s. By the mid-1980s, more than 100 PLATO systems were operating worldwide, with about 60 percent of them running full-time.

In 1972 the Mitre Corporation in conjunction with Brigham Young University developed Time-Shared, Interactive, Computer-Controlled, Information Television (TICCIT), an instructional system that combined minicomputers with color television receivers to deliver CAI lessons and educational programs to college students. Both PLATO and TICCIT are credited with introducing effective computer-assisted instruction in educational systems.

However, interest in CAI instructional methodology eventually declined due to lack of pedagogical knowledge of programming, lack of pedagogical input in designing instructional software, and virtually nonexistent ongoing professional development for teachers on applications. In addition, most of the software developed from the early 1960s through the late 1970s was targeted toward vocational, scientific, industrial, and military training. Contributing to the diaspora of PLATO and other mainframe-based architectures was the introduction of the cost-effective personal computer by IBM in 1977.

Microcomputers

In 1977 IBM developed the first microcomputer that permitted local control of software and peripherals. Educators were no longer dependent upon their local school district or external commercial companies who chose the instructional applications and resources to be uploaded to the mainframe. Educators had a renewed interest in acquiring computer literacy for both themselves and their students. Due to cost-effectiveness reasons, specifically the acquisition of site licenses, integrated learning systems (ILS), or microcomputers networked to a central server, soon became the norm.

During this same time period, the work of Massachusetts Institute of Technology (MIT) mathematician Seymour Papert, who co-founded the MIT Artificial Intelligence Laboratory and first advocated giving every child a laptop, had a profound influence on computer instruction. Papert's student-centered, constructivist philosophy was a direct result of years of collaboration with his mentor, the developmental psychologist Jean Piaget. Strongly influenced by Piaget's prose, Papert believed that young children, like sponges, could absorb knowledge in bountiful quantities and, if provided with the tools to explore and experiment with the language of programming, could learn simple algorithms as easily as they learn their native language.

In 1967 Papert developed LOGO—a computer language targeted for children. LOGO was student-centered and aimed at the student's use of "explora-toration and skills" to solve problems. Throughout the 1970s the language of LOGO continued to evolve, gained momentum internationally, especially in Scotland and Australia, and became widespread with the advent of the personal computer. The first pilot projects utilizing TI 99/4 and later Apple II computers were implemented in the 1980s in the Lamplighter Schools in Dallas, Texas, and the New York Academy of Sciences and Community School Districts 2, 3, and 9 in New York City. The tenets of Papert's philosophy and LOGO were published in his popular book *Mindstorms* (1980), which ignited both educators and commercial companies, such as Atari Logo and Commodore Logo, throughout the world. In the 1980s, the developers of LOGO expanded the host of programs to include word processing, multimedia capabilities, and gaming capabilities using video-style graphics that became extremely popular in Europe, Japan, and South America. Although LOGO is still in use today on an international level, interest in Papert's program nearly vanished in the educational system in the mid-1980s due to unmet instructional objectives.

Revolutionary to instructional technology was the innovation of Mosaic in 1994, which now presented information over the Internet using a combination of graphics and text.

The Internet

Although professors from the University of California, Los Angeles (UCLA) and Stanford Research Institute played integral roles in the creation of the innovative packet-switching ARPANET in 1969, the predecessor of today's global Internet, the power of the Internet as an educational tool and resource did not come to fruition till the development and subsequent commercialization of the graphics browser Mosaic in 1994. Mosaic was free, reliable, easy to install, and quick to gain popularity as it was the first browser to embed images with text in the same window.

Most educators, like most individuals during this period, became familiar with the Internet through e-mail usage. However, educators' use of e-mail and the emerging technologies was directly related to their training and exposure to Internet connectivity. Primary and secondary schools provided little or no

training as most of these institutions had no Internet access. Institutions of higher education were the first educational environments to implement technological infrastructures and provide professional development. Thus, educators who worked for institutions that supplied operable access to the Internet envisioned multiple ways for integrating the Internet into the classroom.

With the development of Really Simple Syndication (RSS) technologies and the second generation of the Internet, Web 2.0, Internet usage exploded as users became participatory and could now interact on the Internet. Web usage continues to grow exponentially The medium of the Internet is collectively valued for its universal social, educational, and commercial attributes as it literally can create "web storefronts" for all organizations. The Miniwatts Marketing Group on Internet World Statistics reported that as of March 31, 2011, there were more than 2 billion Internet users worldwide, with the largest population of Internet usage in Asia (44 percent), followed by Europe (22.7 percent), North America (13 percent), and Latin America and the Caribbean (10.3 percent). The populations' Internet usage in Africa, the Middle East, and Oceania and Australia ranges from 5.7 to 1 percent. There are more than 922 million Internet users in Asia, the greatest number of users of any world region. The top 10 languages utilized on the Internet are English (26.8 percent), Chinese (24.2 percent), Spanish (7.8 percent), Japanese (4.7 percent), Portuguese (3.9 percent), German (3.6 percent), Arabic (3.3 percent), French (3.0 percent), Russian, (3.0 percent), and Korean (2.0 percent). These 10 languages represent 82.2 percent of all Internet users.

The fastest growing use of the Internet in all educational systems is distance learning—with growth rates exceeding the growth in overall higher education enrollment. The Sloan Consortium's eighth annual *Sloan Survey of Online Learning* in the United States found that approximately 5.6 million students were enrolled in at least one online course during the Fall 2009 term—a 21 percent increase of nearly 1 million students from the previous year. Nearly three-fourths of the 2,500 colleges and universities surveyed reported that the economic downturn had increased demand nationwide for distance learning courses and programs (Allen and Seaman 2010).

Similarly, the establishment of the Open University in the United Kingdom, which provides support for both faculty and students through an integrated distance teaching system, spurred the proliferation of other open universities in varied areas such as Sudan, South Africa, Australia, China, Germany, India, Indonesia, Malaysia, Netherlands, Pakistan, Philippines, Sri Lanka, Thailand, and the United States. Distance learning institutions and course offerings continue to mushroom throughout the world, making higher education more accessible.

Educational Technology Policies

Critical to the successful integration of technology in education are the educational technology policies, plans, visions, assessment strategies, and procedures to address the ever-shrinking shelf life of technology that nations employ. Likewise, the lack of a systematic educational technology plan or policy in educational settings inhibits intellectual productivity as critical Global Age competencies—specifically asynchronous and synchronous skills—are either omitted from the curriculum or inadequately taught.

Educational technology policies play a critical role in the development of technology in education, because these policies not only point out the direction of development, but also, more importantly, affect research and practices through the allocation of funding. The main goals of educational technology policies include improving a nation's economic competitiveness, achieving democratic and human development goals, addressing challenges in teaching and learning, and catalyzing various other changes in education.

Propelled to achieve these economic, educational, social, and cultural goals, many countries have publicized their national educational technology plans. Funded by government and corporate sponsors, developed countries have launched four waves of strategic information and communication technologies (ICT) planning for education. The first wave focused on equipping classrooms with hardware and software to increase students' access to technology; the second wave focused on integrating technology into teaching and learning practices; and the third wave focused on the contextual understanding of ICT integration at the micro level (i.e., local or regional) and how it affects society. With the rapid development of ICT, the fourth wave of educational technology planning

has emerged internationally, with a focus on the use of new technologies and Internet interactive learning tools for teaching and learning.

Sharon Anne O'Connor-Petruso and Jing Lei

REFERENCES

Allen, I. Elaine, and Jeff Seaman. "Class Differences and Online Education in the United States." Babson Survey Research Group. 2010. http://sloanconsortium.org/publications/survey/class_differences.

Bardini, Thierry, and Michael Friedewald. "Chronicle of the Death of a Laboratory: Douglas Engelbart and the Failure of the Knowledge Workshop." *History of Technology* 23 (2002): 1–22. www.friedewald-family.de/Publikationen/hot2002.pdf.

Bruce, Bertram C. "Innovation and Social Change." In *Network-Based Classrooms: Promises and Realities*, ed. Bertam C. Bruce, Joy K. Peyton, and Trent Batson. New York: Cambridge University Press, 1993.

Buck, George, and Stephen Hunka. "Development of the IBM 1500 Computer-Assisted Instructional System." *IEEE Annals of the History of Computing* 17:1 (1995): 19–3. doi.ieeecomputersociety.org/10.1109/85.366508.

Center for Digital Education. The Next National Turning Point in Education. Folsom, CA: e.Republic, 2007.

Conway, Paul F., and Yong Zhao. "The Global Reach of Educational Technology Planning: Images of Students and Teachers." Paper presented at the International Study Association on Teachers and Teaching (ISATT), Leiden, Netherlands, July 2003.

Cuban, Larry. *Oversold and Underused: Computers in the Classroom.* Amherst, MA: Harvard University Press, 2001.

Dewey, John. *Democracy and Education.* New York: Macmillan, 1916.

Internet World Stats—Usage and Population Statistics (2001–2011). "Internet Users in the World: Distribution by World Regions—2011." Miniwatts Marketing Group. www.internetworldstats.com/stats.htm.

Internet World Stats—Usage and Population Statistics (2001–2011). "Internet World Users by Language." Miniwatts Marketing Group. www.internetworldstats.com/stats7.htm.

Kleinrock, Leonard. "The History of the Internet." www.lk.cs.ucla.edu/internet_first_words.html.

Papert, Seymour. *Mindstorms: Children, Computers, and Powerful Ideas.* New York: Basic Books, 1980.

———. "Tomorrow's Classrooms?" *Times Educational Supplement*, March 5, 1982, 31–32, 41. www.papert.org/articles/Tomorrows Classrooms.html.

Roblyer, M.D., and Aaron H. Doering. *Integrating Educational Technology into Teaching*, 5th ed. Englewood Cliffs, NJ: Merrill, 2009.

Suppes, Patrick, and Elizabeth Macken. "The Historical Path from Research and Development to Operation Use of CAI." *Educational Technology* 18:4 (1978): 9–11.

Woolley, D.R. "PLATO: The Emergence of On-line Community." *Computer-Mediated Communication Magazine* 1:3 (July 1, 1994). www.ibiblio.org/cmc/mag/1994/jul/plato.html.

Zhao, Yong, and Kenneth Frank. "Factors Affecting Technology Uses in Schools: An Ecological Perspective." *American Educational Research Journal* 40:4 (Winter 2003): 807–840.

Zhao, Yong, Jing Lei, and Paul F. Conway. "A Global Perspective on Political Definitions of e-Learning: Commonalities and Differences in National Educational Technology Plans." In *The International Handbook of Virtual Learning Environments*, ed. J. Weiss et al., 673–697. Dordrecht, Netherlands: Springer, 2006.

Information and Communication Technologies and Challenges

The implementation of information and communication technology (ICT) throughout the world continues to increase thanks to organizations dedicated to bridging the "Digital Divide," such as the World Bank, UNESCO, and the Global Development Learning Network, and each government's determination to enact sound ICT policies that will equip its citizens with global age skills. Consequently, all citizens become accountable as government and business leaders must provide funding and funding initiatives to implement broadband connection throughout their region, maintain pragmatic Information Age infrastructures, consistently update hardware and software, and provide ongoing professional development on new and emerging technologies in adolescent, primary, and secondary educational environments and institutions of higher education.

ICT Implementation and Development

The following is a snapshot of ICT implementation and development in educational environments in both the Western and Eastern hemispheres. Although school structures, technological infrastructures, language, and cultures vary, one tenet is abundantly clear—all nations are revising their educational systems to become competitive within the global economy.

United States

Educational technology policies in the United States have increasingly gained momentum since the 1980s, when the nation was rebounding from a dismal national report, *A Nation at Risk* (1983). In addition to the three national educational technology plans since 1996, more than 30 well-publicized key policy documents have focused on topics of educational technology.

As the US Department of Education notes in *Adult Literacy and New Technologies* (1993), at the onset of globalization in the early 1990s, the federal government began to provide funding to states that agreed to establish technology literacy; however, no accountability measures were implemented and individual states defined their understanding of technology literacy. Hence numerous definitions arose and no common standard exists today. In addition, accountability measures such as testing are not mandated, although many states receive annual funding from the Enhancing Education Through Technology (EETT) initiative under the No Child Left Behind (NCLB) Act, which stipulates that all students must be technologically literate by the end of eighth grade. In order to be in compliance with NCLB, states need only to certify that they are working toward NCLB's tech-literacy goals. Some states, such as Arizona and Hawaii, administer technology assessments on their own.

In 2003—in response to Congress's request on the status of educational technology in the K–12 school system—the staff of the US Department of Education reported that over the past 10 years, 99 percent of the schools had been connected to the Internet with a 5:1 student-to-computer ratio. However, integrating technology into the curriculum was not the norm as computers were often segregated in computer rooms, poorly maintained, and rarely used by teachers who were given no training on applications. The Department of Education staff concluded that students mainly learned about the realm of the Internet at home.

Consequently, the US government implemented

the 2004 National Technology Plan titled *Toward a New Golden Age in American Education: How the Internet, the Law and Today's Students Are Revolutionizing Expectations*, which focused on the fourth wave of ICT planning—the use of e-learning and mobile learning to facilitate individualized learning. The report acknowledged the rapidly increasing global competition and the combined responsibility of government leaders, policy makers, and the educational enterprise to prepare students with global age skills. The report recommended the following seven steps to achieve these goals: (1) strengthen leadership, (2) consider innovative budgeting, (3) improve teacher training, (4) support e-learning and virtual schools, (5) encourage broadband access, (6) move toward digital content, and (7) integrate data systems.

The government also acknowledged in its well-publicized report that educators and students are displaying a growing fervor for e-learning and virtual schools; that the American educational community is playing catch-up in technology as compared to industry; that a large "digital disconnect" currently exists between high school teachers and their techno-savvy students, causing major frustration; and that public schools that do not implement asynchronous and synchronous e-learning risk becoming extraneous.

The key objectives of the 2012 National Education Technology Plan (NETP) are to engage and empower the student's learning experiences in a globally networked society, use technology-based assessments to continuously monitor learning outcomes, connect teachers to student data and technological resources, provide educators and students with a comprehensive cyber infrastructure, and redesign processes and structures to efficiently take full advantage of technology to support lifelong learning. The NETP recommendations also call for research and development initiatives to solve crucial long-term problems. The bold vision of NETP is for the United States to lead the world in the proportion of college graduates by 2020, thereby ensuring America's competitiveness in the global economy.

In line with ICT planning of infrastructure, content, and pedagogical training, every state plus the US Virgin Islands now has a statewide, long-range strategic technology plan for improving students' academic performance through new and emerging technologies. In addition, other widely accepted nationwide technology standards for students, teachers, and administrators were drafted by the International Society for Technology in Education between 2007 and 2009.

In the quest to make the US workforce globally competitive, businesses have long been partnering with schools throughout the nation in the disciplines of science, technology, engineering, and mathematics (STEM). At the 1996 National Education Summit, business and government leaders pledged to work together to raise academic standards throughout the public school system, improve accountability and assessment measures, and promote college and work readiness with competencies in the STEM subjects. Prominent examples include Bayer Corporation's company-wide initiative "Making Science Make Sense," implemented throughout the country, and Boeing Corporation's long-standing partnership with a 72,000-student district in Mesa, Arizona, where students attend an aviation camp that combines lessons in mathematics with flight simulators, aeronautics, and space shuttle missions. Large corporate foundations such as Carnegie, Rockefeller, and Gates continue to provide funding for America's school system; the Bill and Melinda Gates Foundation has pledged more than $2 billion to schools and agencies that advocate academic and ICT improvement.

In addition, Archive, a nonprofit organization created at the 1996 National Education Summit, hosts an online toolkit, "Business Tools for Better Schools," in order to produce college graduates who are work ready, produce more STEM workers and data-driven decision makers, and ultimately increase the role of business in the public school system.

European Union

In light of globalization and the digital culture, the development of ICT in education throughout the European Union (EU) has been supported by numerous national plans and policies in all European countries. At the Lisbon European Council in March 2000, the heads of state and government of EU declared the need to increase and update ICTs throughout the region. The European Commission adopted the eLearning: Designing Tomorrow's Education initiative as part of the so-called 2000 eEurope Action Plan, which also included guidelines for employment and social cohesion.

The eLearning Action Plan, a part of the eEurope

Action Plan that was adopted in 2001, pledged to connect all schools to the Internet by the end of 2002, increase student use of multimedia technologies, and provide support services and training, together with online platforms for students, parents, and teachers. Additional objectives to be completed by the end of 2003 under the eEurope Action Plan included digital literacy for all school leavers, the implementation of technology-based lesson plans by teachers, and digital literacy for all workers, who would be given the opportunity to become technologically savvy through the lifelong learning system.

According to Olivier Debande, writing in the *European Journal of Education* (2004), 80 percent of the European countries (with the exception of Austria, Portugal, and Greece) were connected to the Internet by the end of 2001; however, the percentage of schools where students had Internet access was substantially lower in Germany, Spain, and Luxembourg than that of schools in other European nations. In addition, a majority of the teachers cited lack of Internet connectivity in their school as the main reason for not implementing technology-based plans, although, except for Greek teachers, they used the Internet at home. Debande also found that the Internet was more developed, in terms of integrated services digital network (ISDN) and broadband connections, in Sweden, Finland, and Denmark than it had been in other countries of Europe; Sweden and Denmark also received government and school sponsorship.

The *eEurope 2002 Benchmarking Report* concluded that although a majority of the schools reached their objective for Internet connectivity, there was not equal access to the Internet, and their focus will turn toward pragmatic educational use and widespread availability and connectivity. Thus the Barcelona European Council in 2002 requested the European Commission to draft the successor plan, the eEurope 2005 Action Plan, which targeted broadband connection for all schools and universities that implemented e-learning initiatives (partnerships with museums, libraries, and archives), virtual campuses, a dynamic environment for e-business and e-health, and pilot projects that use advanced computing systems and broadband networks for optimum learning environments. The eEurope 2005 Action Plan was endorsed by the Council of Ministries in the eEurope Resolution of 2003.

The European Commission report *Benchmarking Access and Use of ICT in European Schools 2006* found that computers were used in approximately 100 percent of European schools. However, large variations existed in the number of computers per 100 students, the level of ICT equipment, the type of connectivity, and the level of schooling. Higher-level schools, such as vocational schools, were almost twice as likely to have computer access and connectivity as compared to primary schools. Only three member states of the EU, Germany, Luxembourg, and Malta, evinced high ICT in primary schools.

The report found the most advanced countries in ICT use in the classroom were the United Kingdom, Sweden, Finland, the Netherlands, Denmark, Norway, and Austria. In terms of teachers integrating the Internet in most of their subjects, the variations were large, with the UK reporting 94 percent of its schools as compared to 42 percent in Greece and 44 percent in Latvia. The report noted that although new member states of the EU (Estonia, Hungary, Italy, Latvia, Lithuania, Poland, Portugal, Slovenia, and Spain) are still playing catch-up with new technologies, high ICT in lesson planning (more than 50 percent) was reported by teachers in Hungary, Poland, and Portugal. Greek teachers also reported high ICT use in lesson planning. The report, however, noted skepticism by 16 percent of the teachers in the EU, who believed that the benefits of ICT in student achievement were unproven; in particular, 48 percent of the German teachers were not using ICT in lesson planning. Nonetheless, the report found a 10 percent increase in teacher use of the computer from 2001 to 2006. The report concluded that overall broadband access in the EU schools had increased and that better ICT maintenance and equipment were key to helping two-thirds of the European schools, as evidenced in the level of student, parent, and teacher satisfaction in the advanced Norwegian schools.

The European Commission's strategic policy framework, i2010–Information Space Innovation & Innovation in R & D Inclusion, launched at the end of 2005, provided multiple proactive policies and strategies for harnessing the digital economy, including online public services, and was steadfast in trying to prepare society for the skills necessary in the global age. The i2010 framework is referred to as "EU's renewed Lisbon strategy for growth and jobs." The EU's most recent growth policy for the ensuing decade, Europe 2020, continues to focus on education and research and development innovation, with each member state setting its own national target.

Asia

Most developing and emerging economies in Asia view ICT as a key factor and a potential turning point in improving their global economic competitiveness. In the last decade many Asian countries have witnessed a rapid development in educational technology, supported by generous investment in and strong advocacy of integrating technology into educational settings.

Most Asian countries have developed national educational plans so schools can reap the benefits of available information and communication technologies. Among them, Singapore and South Korea stand out in integrating ICT into the education system. In 1997 Singapore launched its first master plan for IT in education, intended to provide teachers and students with access to information technology. This effort has proved very effective. According to *Global Competitiveness Report 2001–2002*, Singapore was ranked second in the world for the availability of Internet access in schools. Singapore's second master plan, publicized in 2002, emphasized the crucial importance of teachers as the key to the effective use of IT in enhancing teaching and learning. Singapore's ICT for Education project (2006–2008) established technology standards and policies and encouraged local ownership by schools. South Korea has published three five-year master plans for ICT in education since 1996, focusing on installation of basic infrastructure, enhancing teachers' capabilities for ICT application and development of ICT-based educational content, and adapting education to the Information Age, respectively. As of April 2001, all schools in South Korea have free access to the Internet, and the student-to-computer ratio was 10:1 in primary schools, 7:1 in middle schools, and 5:1 in high schools. In 2008 Korea developed national standards for e-learning.

The Japanese government enacted five e-Japan Priority Policies from 2001 to 2006 that aimed at achieving broadband access, preparing ICT personnel, and promoting ICT learning. The 2006 U-Japan Policy (ubiquitous network Japan) is presently focused upon creating a ubiquitous network environment where everyone can receive services from wired and wireless networks without fear of security or privacy breaches; the policy is based on the premise that enhanced ICT usage has the potential to help resolve social issues. India's ICT plan, initially developed in 2000, specified detailed technology literacy standards for students and provided curriculum guidelines and syllabi for information technology. The current five-year ICT plan (2012–2017) includes telecom, software and hardware services and resources, IT enabled services, and broadcasting.

In 1982 the Chinese government started putting computers in classrooms. By 2004 China had spent about $13.2 billion on educational technology, including hardware, software, Internet, and teachers' professional development. The annual expense has been increasing rapidly. After three decades of investment, the number of computers in Chinese schools has increased dramatically. However, given the large student and teacher population, convenient access to technology is still a problem for most schools.

Still, a number of Asian countries are making their best efforts to integrate technology into education despite serious challenges and a lack of resources. For example, the ASEAN (Association of Southeast Asian Nations: Brunei, Cambodia, Indonesia, Laos, Malaysia, Myanmar, Philippines, Singapore, Thailand, and Vietnam) 2015 ICT master plan focuses upon bridging the Digital Divide by providing affordable and equitable ICT access and broadband infrastructure to all populations, including rural residents. The master plan also nurtures innovation and creativity at school by ensuring that every child has ongoing access to broadband Internet. ASEAN's six key strategic objectives clearly acknowledge ICT as a key driver in economic and social transformation. Several countries, such as Laos, Vietnam, and Bangladesh, have equipped schools with secondhand computers. These countries have also started training teachers, connecting schools and classrooms to the Internet, and integrating technology into teaching and learning practices. However, it is clear that there is a long way to go in terms of both technology facilities and the use of technology in education.

In addition to increasing technology access in schools, preparing teachers to better use technology in classrooms is another area strongly emphasized. To motivate teachers to learn and use ICT in their classrooms, South Korea developed several programs to evaluate and certify teachers, such as the Information Ability Evaluation program, which encourages teachers to develop interest in ICT utilization and increase their use of ICT in carrying out their duties. In China, the Ministry of Education published *The Educational Technology Standards for Elementary and Secondary School Teachers* in 2004, which covers four components in using technology in education: awareness and attitude, knowledge and skills, application and innovation, and social responsibilities. From 2005 to 2007, the Chinese education ministry implemented the National Educational Technology Development Plan for Elementary and Secondary School Teachers, which required all grade 1–12 teachers to receive a minimum of 50 hours of professional development in educational technology. This plan focused upon building a national system to train and certify teachers in the area of educational technology.

Most Asian countries, like other developing nations and continents, are facing a serious challenge—the Digital Divide. The disparity is reflected in the differences in access to technology hardware and software between the "haves" and the "have-nots" due to social-economic status, ethnicity, locality, or gender. In China, for example, the disparity between urban schools and rural schools in access to technology is huge. The severity of educational inequity caused by the Digital Divide has been well recognized, and great effort has been made to narrow the gap. From 2003 to 2007, China promoted its Modern Distance Learning Project for Rural Elementary and Secondary Schools, which was designed to build computers labs and satellite receiving stations in rural schools; however, it did not achieve its ultimate goal of increasing technology access for students from poor and rural areas due to funding issues and improper planning. Working with the government, the Li Ka Shing Distance Education in Western China Project also invested millions of dollars to support a number of technology initiatives in underdeveloped western China, including providing an intercollege network to improve teaching and research in higher education and setting up a satellite transmission advance network for distance learning in K–12 schools. In Cambodia, solar energy has been used to introduce computers in rural schools without electricity. The ICT plan of India also addresses the Digital Divide between genders, with specific instructional strategies

that can be adopted by teachers to make IT-based activities in the school free from gender bias.

Another challenge that many Asian countries face is a shortage of educational software and resources; in China, for example, teachers report a "lack of teaching and learning resources and technology facilities" as the major barrier in using technology in teaching. The ICT plan of South Korea identified a special council to coordinate the development of new educational software to meet the demands of specific school levels, grades, and curricula.

Many international organizations and companies have developed programs to help Asian countries integrate technology into education. For example, IntelTeach to the Future program has trained subject teachers from many provinces in China to help them integrate technology into their classroom teaching. Intel, IBM, Microsoft, and Coca Cola have funded massive teacher training programs in countries such as India, Malaysia, the Philippines, and Thailand.

Challenges in Technology and Education

Worldwide, technology in education is facing a number of serious challenges. The first challenge is the slow adoption of technology in teaching and learning. With continuous investment in technology in education and strong emphasis on the importance of technology in improving education, the student-to-computer ratio continues to drop, and both the number and the variety of technologies available in schools continue to grow. However, sufficient information technology access does not naturally translate into sufficient technology use. Researchers have found that technologies in classrooms are unused or underused. The slow adoption of technology innovation has been a serious concern of educators and researchers. Great efforts have been made to investigate why technologies are not used in schools, what conditions influence teachers' technology use, how technology innovations are integrated or rejected, and how technology innovations transform and are transformed by existing practices. Technology in schools still remains largely a high-access but low-use "technology puzzle." To the disappointment of many educational technology advocates, technology to date has not fundamentally transformed education.

Some researchers suggest an evolutionary perspective to study technology in education. According to this perspective, technology and education shape each other and evolve together. On the one hand, how educational organizations function affects what technology survives in schools, what technology is selected out, and how technology evolves. On the other hand, technology is playing a very active role in changing schools and education. Technology has not only changed how schools are laid out, how schools function, and how teaching and learning are conducted, but also has created new educational organizations such as virtual schools and virtual universities.

The second challenge is dealing with the social, cultural, and legal issues created by the use of information and communication technologies, especially in the online virtual community. Technology in education has experienced an unprecedentedly rapid development and expansion worldwide in the last two decades. However, the social norms and regulations regarding the use of technology are not yet fully established. Technology, especially the Internet, has brought great risks and promises to education. Serious concerns have arisen around children's online safety. For example, research shows that young people are exposed to the potential harm of online harassment, cyberbullying, and unwanted sexual materials and solicitations. They are easy targets of phishing experts and are at risk of becoming potential victims of cybercrime as well as getting involved in committing cybercrimes. To protect children from online victimization, a number of national and state laws—such as the Child Online Protection Act and the Children's Online Privacy Protection Act—have been passed.

Other social and ethical problems such as plagiarism, copyright violation, security threats, cybercrime, spam, invasion of individual privacy, and computer fraud also must be addressed as we move toward improved education through technology use.

Another serious challenge is the Digital Divide. The gap between students who have access to technology and those who do not is a serious challenge to education equity. Affluent parents and children have regular access to Internet resources, digital reference resources, and the tools of digital commerce and interaction. Students at risk are not only denied these routine benefits, but they often fail to appreciate them because of unfamiliarity or lack of exposure.

The inequality of ICT access further creates inequality in learning experiences, abilities, and opportunities in the global economy. National statistics show that many disadvantaged students use the Internet only at school. When their technology access in school is limited or denied, they are deprived of the only opportunity to learn about and with technology.

Researchers point out that access issues include not only who can afford a computer and get an online connection, but also who can use the Internet and operate the software. Users who cannot participate effectively across the full range of opportunities that information technologies provide cannot be said to have "access." In addition, the disparity in the quality of access further widens the Digital Divide because advanced technology hardware and software always cost more and therefore are out of reach of children from less economically advanced families and communities.

The digital global age cannot go fast or go far without funding and full participation of government, business, community, and educational leaders.

Sharon Anne O'Connor-Petruso and Jing Lei

REFERENCES

Achieve.org. "Business Tools for Better Schools: Promoting More Effective Business Involvement in America's Public Schools." 2012. www.biztools4schools.org.

A Nation at Risk. "Archived Information—Recommendations." 1983. www.ed.gov/pubs/NatAtRisk/recomm.html.

ASEAN. "We're Stronger When We're Connected. ASEAN ICT Masterplan 2015." 2011. www.asean.org.

Berman, Paul, and Edward W. Pauley. *Federal Programs Supporting Educational Change*, vol. 2, *Factors Affecting Change Agent Projects.* Santa Monica, CA: RAND Corporation, 1975.

Burbules, Nicholas, and Thomas. Callister Jr. *Watch IT: The Promises and Risks of New Information Technologies for Education.* Boulder, CO: Westview, 2000.

Business Wire. "Bayer Launches New STEM Education Guide Aimed at Forging Business-Education Partnerships." September 28, 2006.

Commission of the European Communities. eEurope 2005: *eEurope 2005: An Information Society for All.* Brussels: Commission of the European Communities, 2002.

Cornelius, Peter K., and John W. McArthur. *Global Competitiveness Report, 2001–2002.* New York: Oxford University Press, 2002.

Cuban, Larry. *Teachers and Machines: The Classroom Use of Technology since 1920*. New York: Teachers College, Columbia University Press, 1986.

Debande, Olivier. "ICT's and the Development of eLearning in Europe: The Role of the Public and Private Sectors." *European Journal of Education* 39:2 (2004): 191–208.

Education Week. "School-Business Partnerships Target STEM Subjects." June 19, 2007.

European Commission. "Europe 2020 Targets." http://ec.europa.eu/europe2020/.

European Commission, Information Society and Media Directorate General. *Benchmarking Access and Use of ICT in European Schools 2006*. Brussels: Empirica, August 2006. http://ec.europa.eu.

Europe's Information Society. "ICT and Lisbon Strategy." European Commission. http://ec.europa.eu/information_society.

Harris, Judith B., and Neal Grandgenett. "Correlates with Use of Telecomputing Tools: K–12 Teachers' Beliefs and Demographics." *Journal of Research on Computing in Education* 31:4 (1999): 327–340.

Honey, Margaret, and Babette Moeller. *Teacher's Beliefs and Technology Integration: Different Values, Different Understandings* (Technical Report 6). New York: Center for Children and Technology, 1990.

Japanese Ministry of Internal Affairs and Communications. "Contributing to Future Deployment of e-Japan Strategies." 2007. www.soumu.go.jp/menu_seisaku/ict/u-japan_en.

Lei, Jing, Paul F. Conway, and Yong Zhao. *The Digital Pencil: One-to-One Computing for Children*. Mahwah, NJ: Lawrence Erlbaum, 2007.

No Child Left Behind Act of 2001. 20 USC 6301 (2002).

Park, Jonghwi. "ICT in Education in Asia-Pacific. Asia-Pacific Regional Forum on ICT Applications." May 19, 2011. www.itu.int.

Schofield, Janet W., and Ann L. Davidson. *Bringing the Internet to School: Lessons from an Urban District*. San Francisco: Jossey-Bass, 2001.

Shanmugaratnam, Tharman. "IT in Learning: Preparing for a Different Future." Speech delivered by Tharman Shanmugaratnam, Senior Minister of State for Trade and Industry and Education, at iTopia 2002 conference, Suntec City, Singapore, July 24, 2002. www.moe.gov.sg/media/speeches/2011.

Teach to the Future. www.teachfuture.com.

US Department of Education, National Center for Education Statistics. *Adult Literacy and New Technologies, Tools for a Lifetime*. Washington, DC: NCES, 2003.

———. *Internet Access in U.S. Public Schools and Classrooms*. Washington, DC: NCES, 2003.

———. *Young Children's Access to Computers and School*. Washington, DC: NCES, 2003.

US Department of Education, Office of Educational Technology. *Transforming American Education: Learning Powered by Technology*. Washington, DC: 2012. www.ed.gov.

Wolak, Janis, Kimberly Mitchell, and David Finkelhor. *Online Victimization of Youth: Five Years Later*. 2006. www.missingkids.com.

Yu, S.Q., and Minjuan J. Wang. "Modern Distance Education Project for the Rural Schools in China: Recent Development and Problems." *Journal of Computer Assisted Learning* 22 (2006): 273–283.

Yumlembam, Dayananda. "IIM–A Prof to Help Frame 5-Year Plan for India's ICT Sector." *The Times of India*, May 22, 2011.

Zhang, Jianwei. "A Cultural Look at Information and Communication Technologies in Eastern Education." *Education Technology, Research and Development*, 55 (2007): 301–314.

Zhao, Yong, Kevin Pugh, Steve Sheldon, and Joe L. Byers. "Conditions for Classroom Technology Innovations." *Teachers College Record* 104:3 (2002): 482–515.

Zhu, Z. "Breaking the Application Bottle Neck to Lead the Development of Information Technology in Schools." Paper presented at the National Forum of Principals in Educational Technology, China, 2005.

SYNCHRONOUS AND ASYNCHRONOUS E-LEARNING

Electronic/synchronous and asynchronous learning refer to all the electronic communication tools that continue to emerge, known as emergent technologies, into both the onsite and offsite educational learning systems from early childhood to institutes of higher education (IHE). The nomenclatures or categories, "synchronous and asynchronous," refer to the type and speed of information or communication delivery and provide a classification system for electronic communication tools. Educators throughout the world utilize and value this type of e-learning (electronic learning) through the benefits of the communication tools each type of system provides.

Synchronous Delivery and Communication Tools

Synchronous delivery refers to the instant transfer of communication in real time. Onsite class instruction that provides instant feedback is an example of synchronous delivery. Common synchronous communication tools include chat rooms and video-based communication tools

Chat tools allow users to communicate directly with each other in real time by instant text messaging or sound using various media such as the computer or telephone, via the Internet. Examples of popular instant text messaging include iGoogle Chat Online, Yahoo Messenger, MSN Messenger, and AOL Instant Messenger.

Internet phone calls provide global voice communication via the Internet at a relatively low cost. This is a direct result of increased bandwidth, lower costs in audio hardware, and the long-distance infrastructure provided by the Public Switched Telephone Network (PSTN). PSTN is the world's collection of public and private (government and commercially owned), interconnected and aggregated circuit-switching telephone network. The Luxembourg-based program Skype, available in multiple languages, is very popular and touted with success by several universities, especially when paired with point-to-point video conferencing technologies. In addition to video and conference calling, Skype offers free conference calling with up to twenty-five people worldwide.

Live chats on the web usually target large, sometimes unlimited group discussion on a particular subject or interest. Live chats are scheduled well in advance by a plethora of educational and commercials sites and are usually free. Chat tool components have also become commonplace in educational course management systems such as Blackboard, Sakai, Moodle, and WebCT.

Video-based communication tools include online streaming, webcams, and videoconferencing. Due to improved technologies, online streaming capabilities have continued to evolve. Students are able to interact with other students around the world as well as with experts such as museum curators, scientists, and astronauts. One very notable project that amply incorporates video streaming into its global community of teachers and students is the Jason Project (2007–2012). The Jason Project, founded in 1989 by Dr. Robert D. Ballard, connects middle school students with scientists and researchers in synchronous and near-synchronous virtual and physical science learning experiences.

Webcams, or Web cameras, are able to supply instant images or videos over the Internet. Webcams usually use a real-time digital video camera, are transmitted via satellite, and can be viewed instantaneously over the web. However, webcams also can be posted to a website for later viewing and are thus not considered "real time." Real-time webcams are

commonly used for traffic reports, weather reports, and sports games—utilized mainly on the college level. Dan Carnevale reports in the *Chronicle of Higher Education* (2007) that smaller universities are joining large universities in airing SportsCams, to the delight of students, alumni, and parents who are miles away, since sports activities at small, lesser known colleges and universities are usually not aired by large television networks, such as ESPN.

Videoconferencing, also known as video conference, or video and voice over IP networks, is increasing in use in both the corporate and educational sectors due to improved quality and performance and increased cost effectiveness since its emergence in the early 1980s. Video conferencing between two parties is referred to as point-to-point and among more parties is referred to as multipoint. The benefits of live video communication over the Internet are manifold, if not limitless, as students, teachers, professors, and educational administrators located in distant cities, countries, and continents can instantaneously interact with each other as long as all parties have access to videoconferencing equipment and the necessary technological infrastructure. To date, students from early adolescence to college level have been able to build and share their knowledge on particular subjects and issues through their visual collaboration with peers, scientists, engineers, astronauts, artists, historians, curators, and mavens worldwide.

A growing number of videoconferencing networks, listservs, and directories include asynchronous collaborative and learning tools available via the Internet; however, most of these newer sites require membership or a fee. A very popular videoconferencing directory with a history of longevity is AT&T's Knowledge Network Explorer, a free online videoconferencing listserv and directory which links a host of educational institutions, content providers, and community organizations around the world. In addition, this open source website provides a global hotlist of uniform resource locators, or URLs, of other videoconferencing directories and resources.

The fastest growing use of videoconferencing is seen on the college level, most notably in virtual schooling. A virtual school is an online school whose students use both synchronous and asynchronous tools to complete their coursework. Virtual schooling is discussed below under the heading Distance Learning.

Asynchronous Delivery and Communication Tools

Asynchronous delivery refers to the transfer of archived and stored communication that is delayed, or not instantaneous, and can be later accessed. Reading e-mail and accessing a CD-ROM are examples of asynchronous delivery. Common asynchronous communication tools include e-mail, electronic media, bulletin boards or discussion boards, blogs, wikis, podcasts, interactive and noninteractive websites, and distance learning/virtual schooling.

E-mail

One of the most widely utilized asynchronous tools worldwide is electronic mail, or e-mail. In 1971 Ray Tomlinson developed the first ARPANET e-mail application that allowed copying of files over the network. He chose the "@" symbol to combine user and host—that is, user@host—which remains the standard today. Although the early programs had simple functionality, they set the conceptual standard for the electronic mail model utilized today as every e-mail user has a mailbox. The Radicati Group, a technology market research firm, reported that worldwide e-mail accounts mushroomed to about 2.9 billion users in 2010 and are forecasted to increase to over 3.8 billion by 2014, with approximately 75 percent of e-mail accounts belonging to consumers.

Most e-mail systems worldwide use a simple text editor, allow users to send messages to multiple recipients at once (known as broadcasting), and permit file attachments with varying file size limits. Data can be entered from the keyboard or a variety of electronic storage devices and media, deleted, edited, or saved in a mailbox. Although different e-mail services and Internet service providers utilize different formats, they all have an Internet gateway that permits communication with other computer systems, thus allowing the users to access e-mail from other systems worldwide. Electronic mail and messaging systems continue to grow in use worldwide due to effectiveness, user-friendliness, speed, low cost, and incredible exceptional power. In 1985 the RAND Corporation acknowledged and reported to the National Science Foundation the incredible commanding power of electronic mail, which the organization termed a fundamentally new medium, and correctly prophesied its explosive worldwide expansion over the next decade in homes, educational settings, and work environments as it evolved into a key if not the dominant mode of communication.

Bulletin Boards and Discussion Boards

Bulletin boards and discussion boards are asynchronous communication tools that allow members of the respective website to post comments or upload files in chronological order. From the late 1970s to the mid-1990s, both the business and private sector enjoyed using the Bulletin Board System (BBS) to post messages through both private e-mail and public message boards; however, the BBS eventually lost popularity due to new and emerging technologies and the growing use of the Internet. The BBS is considered by many today to be the precursor of social networking sites (SNS).

Discussion Boards, also known as discussion groups, discussion forums, message boards, and online forums, originated from the BBS. Discussion boards use a variety of web applications and programming languages and offer diversified features from text-only posts (which are called threads) to advanced multimedia features. Discussion board forums are managed by an administrator, can be public or private, engage users on topics of interest or profession, and are used on many web hosting systems, such as wikispaces.com, and free and proprietary course management systems, such as Moodle, Blackboard, and Sakai. Many educators utilize discussion boards to augment their lectures and assignments.

Electronic Portable Storage Devices

Electronic media have collectively evolved into smaller and more durable pieces of technology compared to the original 5.25-inch floppy disk. Today's electronic portable storage devices hold more memory, are usually hot swappable (they can be inserted or removed from the computer without rebooting the computer), work on both the Mac and PC, and can have the capacity to be rewritable.

Popular media include the flash drive or jump drive (also referred to as a "stick" in Europe) and the CD-ROM (compact disk read-only memory). Although 3.5-inch floppy disks are still being used in the educational system, they are losing popularity due to their limited memory size (1.44 megabytes) and incompatibility with newer computers. Newer computers focus primarily upon supplying universal serial bus (USB) ports for USB flash drives and CD-ROMs that have the ability to store much larger amounts of memory. At present, flash drives have the capacity to hold an astounding 256 gigabytes of memory.

Web 2.0

With the advent of the second generation of the Internet, known as Web 2.0 or the "participatory net," communication tools and technologies have robustly improved. One of the main goals of Web 2.0 was the harnessing of collective intelligence, the sharing of knowledge, and the promotion of user contributions. New tools such as blogs, wikis, and podcasts and improved technologies, most notably RSS (Really Simple Syndication or Rich Site Summary), which allow users to subscribe to web pages and be informed every time they it changes, have taken a strong foothold and continue to burgeon worldwide.

Blogs

Spearheading the way in interactive websites are web logs, known as blogs. A blogger is a person who creates a blog. Blogging, or interacting with a web log, whether as creator or as a reader accessing and responding to it, is one of the most touted features of Web 2.0. Blogs focus on particular subjects or topics of interest, including autobiographies and biographies. Popular blogs which have various multimedia characteristics such as text, music, and video and are interactive. Commentaries are posted chronologically and permit multiple threads (posts) by different users.

The commercial website Technorati, self-proclaimed as one of the world's leading blog search companies, has tracked more than 92 million blogs and reports over 175,000 new blogs being added to its their site every day. In its State of the Blogosphere 2010 report, Technorati lists the top geographic locations of bloggers, with the largest groups in the United States (49 percent) and Europe (29 percent), followed by Asia and the Pacific (12 percent), Canada and Mexico (7 percent), and South America (3 percent). Technorati also found in 2010 that blogging was in transition, with significant growth attributed

to the advent of mobile blogging on smart phones and tablets and an increase in the number of women and mothers blogging.

Blogging has gained increasing popularity in the educational community since its inception in 1997. American cable specialty TV channels, such as the Learning Channel, Discovery Channel, and Animal Planet, which are viewed worldwide, have jumped on the bandwagon and post blogs. In addition to the growing number of student bloggers, there is an increase in the number of teachers, librarians, professors, and school leaders who are creating blogs for their peers and classroom. Some school officials believe that blogging will make education more relevant to student bloggers by giving them a larger voice, fostering pride in their work, and promoting reflection, intellectual interaction, and writing.

Wiki

A wiki is a collaborative, participatory, group website that permits instant editing by anyone who has access to it. The first wiki was developed by an American computer programmer, Ward Cunningham. Cunningham developed the software in 1994 and posted the first wiki in 1995. The term "wiki" comes from the Hawaiian language, meaning "fast" or "quick." Users tout wikis for their simplicity, freedom, and power that allow users to directly add or delete new content in an instant. Although the number of wiki websites continue to grow internationally, controversy exists as to the validity of content posted on many wikis, as anyone can create a wiki and add or delete information.

One of the most popular international wiki sites is The Wikimedia Foundation, a nonprofit organization registered in Florida and maintained by a growing, global volunteer community and a professional staff committed to international projects that provide free access to information sharing. Their projects include free multilingual encyclopedias, famous quotations, dictionaries, books, content texts, a species database on taxonomy, news, educational materials and resources, and a central repository for photographs, diagrams, maps, videos, animations, music, sounds, spoken texts, and other free media.

One of Wikimedia's most prolific sites, utilized widely in the education field is the Wikipedia Project, launched in 2001. Its primary goal is to build free encyclopedias in all languages of the world. To date, there are more than 20 million articles available in over 283 languages. The largest Wikipedia is in English, comprising approximately 4 million articles, followed by German, French, Italian, Polish, Spanish, Russian, Japanese, Portuguese and Chinese editions, each comprising more than half a million articles.

Other popular educational wikis that offer free web hosting and a variety of Web 2.0 tools allowing individuals to create, edit, and share information collaboratively are wikispaces.com, wetpaint.com, and wikidot.com. The wiki tool is also available on free course management systems, such as Moodle, Sakai, and Wordpress.

Podcasts

Podcasts are a new method of distribution for rich media files, such as audio or video, over the Internet. They emerged in 2004 as a direct result of Web 2.0 and RSS technologies. Podcasts are essentially radio programming that can be produced with a standard computer, microphone, or free software; they play standard MP3 audio files and can be listened to on the Internet. Podcasts continue to grow in popularity worldwide. Research analysts from eMarketer Digital Intelligence predict that the podcast audience will continue to grow with approximately 38 million people downloading podcasts in 2013—a significant increase from 17 million podcast users in 2008. In addition, numerous podcast or podcasting directories are available on a plethora of websites, categorized by subject, interest, educational level, professions, schools, colleges, and universities.

Elementary and secondary schools and institutions of higher education (IHEs) report using podcasts as successful educational tools with the help of corporate and government sponsors and innovative educational leaders with the help of corporate and government sponsors and innovative educational leaders. Early podcasts were created with the help of Apple's iTunes free service. Apple Computers also reports on its website the successful use of audio and video podcasts in K–12 and IHE environments worldwide. School websites hosting podcasts by their students, such as the elementary, middle, and high schools in the Bavaria District in Germany, are also on the rise.

Today, universities around the world, including Duke, Purdue, George Washington, Vanderbilt, and the University of Florida in the United States; Bradford University in the United Kingdom; and Melbourne University and the University of Sydney in Australia, have incorporated podcasting into their curriculum by posting lectures, assignments, and study notes. In addition, IHEs are increasingly launching podcast initiatives for the purpose of bringing together a global audience of educational leaders and innovators to discuss key issues and events. Such key initiatives are seen in Boston College's Center for International Higher Education Podcast Initiative, the University of Warwick (UK) Podcast Browser, and at the University of Sydney.

Interactive and Noninteractive Websites

There is a proliferating number of international educational, organizational, and commercial websites, both interactive and noninteractive, that provide information and digital media on diversified subjects and interests, hyperlinks to similar sites, and discussion boards for students, teachers, professors, and subject area mavens. The Discovery Channel, the National Aeronautics and Space Administration (NASA), Merlot, and BrainPop are a small sampling of such popular websites.

Popular educational websites for both students and teachers also include many free resources. The vast listing of advertised resources and tools available includes downloadable lesson plans on diversified subjects, theme units, classroom projects, math manipulatives, newsletters, graphic organizers, state and federal reports, news, maps, videos, podcasts, and DVDs. Popular websites include Teachers Planet, School Express, ABC Teach, Education World, and By Teachers.Org. In addition, numerous commercial, government, and organizational websites offer free resources to teachers, students, and parents.

There are also social networking sites (interactive web-based sites whose members share a common interest or activity) created solely for educational purposes, such as Educational Networking, which provides a global list of social networks encompassing common educational interests, resources, and instructional activities for students, parents, and educators. Members of these sites are required to supply a profile that usually includes an e-mail address, a photo, and a short dossier. These sites are found on both proprietary web platforms such as Ning and free web social networking sites such as Facebook and Linked-in.

Distance Learning

Distance learning, also known as virtual schooling, refers to online instruction allowing students to complete coursework and communicate with classmates and the instructor through asynchronous and synchronous tools via the Internet. Virtual schooling refers to all coursework offered by the institution only online. This type of instruction is the fastest-growing form of instruction worldwide.

The Guide to Online Schools reports that the majority of distance learning offerings are undergraduate computer and business courses, with Canada as the leader per capita for the number of online courses offered, and the United States offering more than 25,000 courses to over 3 million American students. The expanding programs at the Open University offer four advanced research degrees and approximately 600 courses toward more than 250 qualifications to over 250,000 students in the United Kingdom, Ireland, Europe, and their partnerships. The International Association for Distance Learning (IADL) provides a comprehensive list of accredited bodies for distance learning worldwide and a legion of global distance learning associations.

The number of new distance learning courses continues to accelerate. Their easy accessibility from any computer with Internet capabilities is touted by students for whom on-site classes are unaffordable or unavailable.

Advantages and Disadvantages of E-Learning

Educational leaders across the globe praise the opportunities synchronous tools provide as astronauts, scientists, curators, professors, educators, mavens, and peers become accessible to students either through text, audio, or videoconferencing. However, educators also acknowledge the potential disadvantages associated with e-learning.

Educators concur that their students' knowledge base is increased since students are highly motivated to interact and participate in synchronous learning activities. Text chat tools also benefit students who are deaf or hard of hearing. Positive aspects of asynchronous learning tools such as blogs, wikis, and so on also promote high student motivation and participation, thus increasing the students' knowledge base. In addition, distance learning is touted as the premier educational vehicle for students in rural areas who do not have access to on-site locations due to difficult traveling conditions or personal constraints.

Nevertheless, educators have to deal with some negative aspects of using synchronous tools. Some problems are traceable to the manufacturer and relate directly to the quality and performance of audio and video tools, screen size, keypad function, accessibility, and size. Other problems are directly attributable to the instructor, webmaster, blogger, or podcaster. Discussion boards and websites may not be available or updated; new information and material may not be posted on a timely basis. Teachers have also questioned the educational validity and usefulness of various sites. Bloggers and podcasters are confronted with possible liability and defamation issues. Educators have also expressed concern over the lack of face-to-face human interaction in distance learning courses and questioned instructor competencies in designing online courses that elicit student understanding of curricular objectives.

Critical Components for Successful E-Learning

Prior to the Information Age, the efficacy of all learning systems was were contingent upon the instructor's expertise and delivery, the availability of updated curricular materials and resources, and the students' understanding of curricular objectives. Although these tenets remain steadfast, educational strategies, conditions, and levels of instructor expertise have become vastly more demanding. Asynchronous and synchronous tools and online learning are on the rise in educational institutions worldwide. Critical components for success in electronic synchronous and asynchronous learning environments include the support of government, business, educational leaders, and other key stakeholders, who must lobby to supply funding for the implementation of sound technological infrastructures, on-site instructional technologists, updated software, and ongoing professional development to train instructors at all levels on both the new tools of technology and effective strategies for incorporating e-tools into the learning environment. Globalization demands a literate and highly skilled, technologically competent workforce, and educational systems are the vehicle to this new way of Information Age learning. Electronic synchronous and asynchronous learning or lack of e-learning will have a profound effect on an individual's intellectual, educational, social, and economic development.

Sharon Anne O'Connor-Petruso

REFERENCES

Apple in Education. "Education Profile." Apple Inc. www.apple.com/education.

AT&T Education. "Welcome to the Knowledge Network Explorer." Videoconferencing for Learning. www.kn.pacbell.com/vidconf/index.html.

Bavaria District Superintendent's Office. "Podcasting in the Bavaria District." Bavaria School District, DoDDS/European Area. www.bav-dso.eu.dodea.edu/Podcast.htm.

Borja, Rhea. R. "'Blogs' Catching On as Tool for Instruction." *Education Week* 25:15 (2005): 1–17.

Boston College, Center for International Higher Education. "CIHE Podcasts." www.bc.edu/research/cihe.html.

Carnevale, Dan. "Colleges Too Small for Prime Time Take Sports Online." *Chronicle of Higher Education, Information Technology* 53:40 (2007): A26.

Education Podcast Network. "What Is a Podcast?" http://epnweb.org.

Educational Networking. "List of Networks." www.educational-networking.com.

"Growth in Virtual Learning, Data Management, Blogging and Podcasting Expected in 2006." *Electronic Education Report. Business Intelligence on Opportunities in the Educational Software Industry* 13:2 (2006): 1–4.

Guide to Online Schools. "Distance Learning 101: The Ins and Outs of Online Education." www.guidetoonlineschools.com.

Gunawardena, Charlotte N., and Marina S. McIsaac. "Distance Education." In *Handbook of Research for Educational Communications and Technology*, 2nd ed., ed. D.H. Johannassen, 355–431. Mahwah, NJ: Lawrence Erlbaum, 2004.

Jason Project. "Jason Science. Education through Exploration." 2007–2012. www.jason.org.

Open University. "Study at the OU." www3.open.ac.uk/study/.

O'Reilly, Tim. "What Is Web 2.0? Design Patterns and Business Models for the Next Generation of Software." 2005. www.oreilly.com.

Radicati, Sara. "Email Statistics Report, 2010." Microsoft Exchange Server and Outlook Market Analysis, 2010–2014, Executive Summary. www.radicati.com/wp/wp-content/uploads/2010/04/Email-Statistics-Report-2010-2014-Executive-Summary2.pdf.

Read, Brock. "How to Podcast Campus Lectures." *Chronicle of Higher Education, Information Technology* 54:21 (2007): 32.

Salah, Khaled. "Analytic Approach for Deploying Desktop Videoconferencing." *Communications, IEE Proceedings* 153:3 (2006): 434–444.

Shapiro, Norman Z., and Robert H. Anderson. *Toward an Ethics and Etiquette for Electronic Mail*. Santa Monica, CA: Rand Corporation R-3283-NSF/RC, 1985.

Sobel, Jon. "State of the Blogosphere 2010: Introduction." November 30, 2010. http://technorati.com/blogging/article/state-of-the-blogosphere-2010-introduction/.

Thompson, Ann. "Multi-Tasking with Technology: Expanding Our Conversations." *Journal of Computing in Teacher Education* 22:4 (2006): 122.

Tomlinson, Ray. "The First Network Email." http://openmap.bbn.com/percent7Etomlinso/ray/firstemailframe.html. http://openmap.bbn.com/~tomlinso/ray/firstemailframe.html

University of Melbourne, Learning Environments Learning Management System. "Podcasts and Lecture Capture." www.lms.unimelb.edu.au.

Vonderwell, Selma, Xin Liang, and Kay Alderman. "Asynchronous Discussions and Assessment in Online Learning." *Journal of Research on Technology in Education* 39:3 (2007): 309–328.

Wikimedia. http://wikimediafoundation.org/wiki/Home.

THE INTERNET

The first use of the Internet in the early 1960s was to share information on research and development in scientific and military fields and to provide a communication network. Researchers at MIT and UCLA developed a system for Internet connection. The Internet had many acronyms in its developing stages: DARPA, ARPANET, ARPA. In 1969 initially four major computers at UCLA, Stanford, University of California, Santa Barbara, and the University of Utah were connected online. Later MIT, Harvard, Carnegie-Mellon, and various research labs were added.

Computer experts, engineers, scientists, and librarians used the early Internet. Knowledge of its use was very intricate. In the late 1960s libraries began cataloging its holdings on this automated system. In 1972 network e-mail was developed and the @ symbol was instituted to link the username with the address. Throughout this decade the Internet system advanced in its technology. By 1978 discussion groups evolved, linking information throughout the world, and in 1981 BITNET (Because It's Time Network) connected IBM mainframes to the educational community and the world, thus providing mail services. Listservs evolved with this new hookup. Those with access were not able to share files and resources. As the Internet grew, more tools were required to index all the resources that were available; in 1989 a group at McGill University in Montreal created a searchable index called Archie. Now, with databases on the rise and an increase in use, a set of Internet standards were established.

By the 1990s, the World Wide Web evolved as a system of links in text to other text. The National Science Foundation (NSF) Net provided the funding for Internet use; however, it was only for research, education, and government dealings. As commercial networks grew, they sidestepped the government-funded sites, causing both an end to the NSF sponsorship and the birth of AOL, Prodigy, and CompuServe. Microsoft and Windows 98 completed the commercially based Internet.

High-speed connections with 56K modems soon became outdated. The industry sought cable and digital capabilities and more recently universal wireless access.

Education and the Internet

In the early 1990s computers collected dust in the classroom, but by the early twenty-first century more schools were using the computers for word-processing and accessing information. The National Center for Education Statistics reported in 2003 that 91 percent of American children from nursery school (age three) through grade 12 use computers, and about 59 percent use the Internet. With the advent of Web 2.0 and the twenty-first century, effective curricula included interactive websites, streaming video, and exposure or use of blogs, wikis, and podcasts. Successful instructional practices engaged students in the electronic learning (e-learning) process. The role of the pedagogue evolved into facilitator in the discovery process of new technologies. Consequently, instructors needed to be technologically competent in order to guide or turnkey Information Age tools to their students.

However, many school systems throughout the world, especially in countries with low gross national product (GNP), do not have the technological infrastructure to provide the Internet, have outdated hardware and software that cannot access these new tools, or lack professional development for the teachers who are struggling with these new tools. Without support, change is slow.

Transcending the Boundaries of the Classroom

The world has been shrinking. This is a statement commonly heard since the advent of the Internet. It has provided people with the means by which to communicate with each other worldwide. No longer do we rely solely on paper letters for correspondence. E-mail has become the new Pony Express. Schools from kindergarten to the university have taken advantage of this service by connecting students around the world. Initially, pen-pal programs developed not only for students to learn about another child's life in a distant land but also to gain knowledge of the other country. Some programs are international and some involve students in neighboring cities. Students have traveled to visit their pen-pals when possible. Now, as a direct result of the Internet, more and more students throughout the world have electronic pen pals.

The new age of technology has categorically transcended national boundaries. The Information Age provides an opportunity for students to study other countries' cultures and thereby create comparisons and strengthen one's own cultural identity. Programs have been developed for the purpose of establishing cross-cultural connections, improving computer skills, and collaborating with other students worldwide. One such program is the Global Virtual Classroom (GVC) from Fairleigh Dickinson University. The GVC provides an opportunity for students from different countries to work with and learn from each other by creating a website on a topic of their choice. The program spans the primary through the secondary school levels.

With more than two decades of experience in online project-based learning, the nonprofit educational organization Global School Net (GSN) offers interactive and collaborative e-learning projects in diversified subject areas and multicultural content to thousands of students worldwide. One such flourishing global learning portal from GSN (launched in

1999) is Friend and Flags, which offers a cultural exchange on collaborative learning projects in English. Hundreds of K–12 classrooms worldwide interact through e-mail, blogs, discussion boards, and a project website. Thus both English and non-English speakers interact globally, learn new content, increase their knowledge of English vocabulary, and improve their reading, comprehension, and writing skills.

The mushrooming Global Learning and Observations to Benefit the Environment (GLOBE) program unites elementary and secondary students and teachers with scientists who collaborate on inquiry-based investigations on the study of Earth and its environment. From its fledgling project Earth Day in 2004, participation has grown to over 1.5 million students representing 111 countries which conduct scientific experiments and share their results on the GLOBE database, which currently contains more than 22 million measurements for use in their inquiry-based science projects.

Another successful nonprofit organization, launched in 2000 and dedicated to connecting schools in the United Kingdom and around the world through the medium of videoconferencing, is Global Leap. Such programs are an enriching experience allowing students to participate in celebrating ideas, events, cultures, and festivals with their connecting schools.

Collaborative learning online, as addressed by the aforementioned global projects, develops critical thinking skills and fosters creativity and brainstorming; students also improve their writing skills. Each individual learner assumes responsibility for his or her contribution to the group's success. A key component of collaborative learning is shared decision making. When students become part of the process, motivation and interest are maintained and active analysis of each project results in suggestions for improvements for future endeavors.

Today's technology has also enhanced college students' note taking. Recording the lesson has become commonplace as many students miss important information during lecture. Recordings allow students to playback the instructor's lesson and select content to be included in their notes. Students come to class with their laptops, smart phones, or tablets ready to access information or contact friends and family through Skype or text messaging who might help with their questions.

College libraries offer electronic resources with many databases, abstracts, journals, and e-journal articles. On the web students can also access musical selections, graphics, and art images necessary for their classes. Schools across the globe are investing in laptops, smart boards, digital cameras, and an assortment of software and services.

In addition, the number of distance learning programs and classes continues to grow each year. Students are able to enroll in courses from around the globe. This means that the regional boundaries of the university no longer limit access to its programs. Individual instructors can reach students from distant states and countries. Summer courses can be accessed from anywhere there are Internet connections. Some universities and colleges allow students to complete a degree using only distance learning classes, forfeiting the requirement of on-campus courses. Distance learning affords the student the opportunity to "attend" class without interfering with family or work commitments. The professors provide course materials, pose questions, and give assignments. Students now take responsibility for their own learning. The instructor is no longer the sole dispenser of knowledge. The professor becomes the "guide by the side," acting as a facilitator.

The Internet is also home to several commendable student organizations. Founded by a group of students from Western Washington University, the Global Technology Academy (GTA) is an organization dedicated to providing digital literacy to underserved areas such as Arusha, Tanzania, where GTA provided 60 laptops and installed three computer labs in a primary school, a teacher training college, and a medical clinic. A program called iEARN (International Education and Resource Network) engages over 2 million students each day in over 150 collaborative online research projects that examine alternatives for solving the world's problems. Numerous global student organizations dedicated to humanitarian projects are found on university websites, social networking sites, and open-source (free) web hosting sites. These budding professionals are making a real difference in the world.

Globalization is also driving the demand for an internationally "literate" workforce that demonstrates competencies in the universal languages of English and mathematics, but also proficiency in multiple languages and technology. New security challenges require greater proficiency in world languages, a greater understanding of world regions, and respect and concern for other cultures. US-based multinational corporations are seeking employees with knowledge of foreign languages and cultures in order to be successful in the global marketplace. Flex hours have expanded to flex places. Communication worldwide has made it possible for workers to work anywhere and anytime. Global production teams are becoming commonplace.

In the United States, the College Board has increased the number of advanced placement courses in multiple languages. The Virtual High School Consortium offers hard-to-find advanced placement courses, especially those with a focus on international studies. Online discussions with students from a variety of countries, cultures, and economic backgrounds are an integral component of these courses.

Teacher education programs are also revising their course requirements to include intense study of history, social studies, language arts, and technology. Teachers are developing units of instruction and sharing them via the web with colleagues in teacher education departments across the globe. There are numerous educational, organizational, commercial, and teacher-created websites where educators share lesson plans, assessment tools, and diversified resources.

The influence of the Internet on learning is still being explored. However, it is clear that educators must embrace the concepts put forth in both e-learning and collaborative learning. As we approach the next generation of the Internet, Web 3.0, it is critical that all educators become competent in using new and emerging technologies so they can prepare students to be "literate" and work-ready for the global economy.

Marilyn Verna, Sharon Anne O'Connor-Petruso,
and James R. Campbell

References

DeBell, Matthew, and Chris Chapman. 2006. Computer and Internet Use by Students in 2003 (NCES 2006-065). U.S. Department of Education. Washington, DC: National Center for Education Statistics.

Globe Program. http://globe.gov/about.

Global SchoolNet.org. www.globalschoolnet.org.

Global Technology Academy, Western Washington University. http://gta-wwu.org.

Gokhale, Anuradha A. "Collaborative Learning Enhances Critical Thinking." *Journal of Technology Education* 7:1 (1995).

iEARN (International Education and Resource Network). www.iearn.org/about.

Kalgan, Sharon Lynn, and Vivien Stewart. "Putting the World into World-Class Education: Introduction." *Phi Delta Kappan* 86:3 (2004): 195–196.

Kelly, James A. "Teaching the World: A New Requirement for Teacher Preparation." *Phi Delta Kappan* 86:3 (2004): 219–221.

Roberts, Linda G. "Harnessing Information Technology for International Education." *Phi Delta Kappan* 86:3 (2004): 225–228.

US Department of Education, Office of Innovation and Improvement. "Connecting Students to Advanced Courses Online." 2007. www2.ed.gov.

Technology in Rich and Poor Countries

Since the 1980s, technology has revolutionized the capitalist economy in countries across the world, integrating them economically, politically, and culturally to varying degrees. The application of technology to economic activities has not only catapulted the economic development of countries, but may have created a great divide between rich and poor nations and peoples. The themes for consideration in this chapter are technological inventions as the engine of economic development from the earliest times to this new century; the contributions of technology to the emergent state of globalization; an assessment of who benefits and who loses from globalization; and the reduction of poverty through the use of technology.

Technology: The Engine of Development of Civilizations

History has shown that technological inventions have been the single most important catalyst in the development of civilizations. In Europe, North America, and parts of Asia, where geographical and environmental resources have been amenable to technological developments, great inventions have been made, industries have emerged, and economies grew, whereas in regions like sub-Saharan Africa and southeastern Asia, where these resources were largely absent, inventions and economies have remained mostly agrarian, and economic growth has remained vastly underdeveloped.

Scholars have described technology as an engine of development that had its genesis in the fourth millennium BCE, when tools made from stone and later bronze and iron were developed and applied in areas such as the Fertile Crescent of Mesopotamia, Egypt, the Indus Valley, and the Yellow River Valley in China. The use of technology enabled these civilizations to forsake old agricultural economies and pursue manufacturing and distribution of economic goods and the building of cities. In Egypt empirical mathematics emerged as a means of solving practical problems; for example, engineering projects led to architectural achievements such as the pyramid tomb of Giza in 2,500 BCE. In China technology was used in the construction of roads, bridges, and the Great Wall of China, the latter an architectural monument built for the defense of the country against invaders. In their extensive trading activities, the Chinese used metallic currency as the medium of exchange, and the axial rudder used in shipbuilding facilitated sailing overseas. Historians have theorized that by using empirical science as a technological tool, the Chinese invented the magnetic needle, gunpowder, bombs, porcelain, and printing; in 105 CE, China began the use of paper, which was introduced to the West by Islam in the eighth century.

Technology was diffused to Europe and became the basis of the civilizations of the Greco-Roman empires of the last century BCE and first century CE. Concrete and glass were applied to projects in construction of aqueducts, elevators, roads, and bridges, and also in the development of towns and military fortifications, like the defensive Hadrian's Wall in Britain. The beginnings of a mechanical age marked the transition to modern Europe, with inventions like gunpowder; the mariner's compass, which made it possible for ships to traverse the oceans and facilitated the growth of commerce and empires; and movable type, invented by Johann Gutenberg in the 1440s, which made printing possible and revolutionized communication until the advent of the computer. The next era, called the Enlightenment, saw the emergence of scientific principles. For example, mathematics was used in the military; according to historian Dirk Struik in *A Concise History of Mathematics* (1987), "the excellence

of the French navy was due to the fact that in construction of frigates and ships of the time, the faster shipbuilder was partly led by mathematics." Sir Isaac Newton was a pioneer in integrating mathematics and science with the invention of calculus, which made possible the infinitesimal calculations needed in the building of rockets for travel into space. The fusion of science and mathematics led to the invention of instruments such as the clock, barometer, telescope, and microscope. Antoine Lavoisier, the founder of modern chemistry, designed the first thermometer. Physics became important when William Gilbert, while experimenting with the force developed by rubbing amber on soft cloth, discovered and coined the name for electricity; also, the invention of X-rays advanced the practice of medicine. The Industrial Revolution of the eighteenth and nineteenth centuries represented a milestone in the use of industrial technology, which modernized the world. Beginning in Great Britain, it involved the invention of machinery and its application to manufacturing using coal, iron, steel, and textiles, and to transportation by trains, railways, and shipping. Indeed, because of the application of technology, Western civilization emerged in Europe, with countries like Britain and France in possession of extensive empires that subordinated many of the countries that are now classified as poor.

The Age of Technology and the Digital Age are the names used to describe the twentieth and twenty-first centuries. With the leadership of the United States, technological advances introduced materials like aluminum, concrete, plastics, porcelain, rubber, steel, and titanium; equipment like electronics; procedures like genetic engineering, photography, magnetic resonance imaging, and organ transplants; and power from hydroelectrical, petroleum, nuclear, and solar sources. Alexander Graham Bell invented the telephone in 1875, Thomas Edison the first electric bulb in 1879; Henry Ford's assembly line for the manufacture of automobiles in 1913 revolutionized mass production methods, and in 1927 Charles Lindbergh completed his nonstop trans-Atlantic flight in an aeroplane. Household appliances made lifestyles easier, pharmaceuticals made people healthier, and film, radio and television added to life's enjoyment. After World War II, the commercial computer was invented, based on matrix and Boolean algebra critical to the design of both computers and the programming that ran them. The computer could be used to solve problems in academics, business, finance, industry, medicine, and space exploration. Inventions like the Internet, satellite communication, wireless telephone, and electronic transfers facilitate international movement of information across countries, space, and time zones. Indeed, technological inventions have made America the dominant and richest country worldwide.

Globalization: A Worldwide Order Created by Technology

In the second half of the twentieth century and into the twenty-first century, there emerged a spectacular modern civilization, a new world order, which embraces and integrates all willing and prepared economies and cultures of the world and is based on the application of science to practical tasks. The development of this integrated civilization is called globalization, or the age of globalization; its main engine is technology. Globalization is best defined by journalist Thomas Friedman in *The Lexus and the Olive Tree* (1999) as "the inexorable integration of markets, nation-states, and technologies to a degree never witnessed before." The central instrument of this dramatic economic growth and transformation and of the great advances in communications and digital technology, which facilitate the movement of capital and information, was the invention of the semiconductor in the 1960s. In *The Reluctant Welfare State* (2001), social welfare theorist Bruce Jansson describes elements of globalization in this way: "Corporations move portions of their operations to other nations, and skilled persons take employment abroad. International trade increases as a percentage of the total economic activity of specific nations. Ideas float across national boundaries via the Internet." He argues further that such globalization has intensified at the same time that technology has developed at an increasing rate, whether through computers, use of robots, advances in biotechnology, or communication innovations like wireless phones and the use of the Internet. Other scholars have proposed that just as economies have been integrated by technology, cultures have also converged; the nature of employment has become cross-national, and workers are bound together by similar technological skills and common behaviors and values; they have become citizens of the globalized world. It is technology such as cheap air travel, the satellite, the Internet, telephones, global radio, television, teleconferencing, and the like that has facilitated and integrated communication and distribution of goods across the world's economies.

Globalization: Who Benefits and Who Loses?

Globalization, a product of multinational corporations' search for profit maximization, benefits rich countries and corporations as a result of cheap labor costs. In 1980 the World Bank grouped countries of the world based on gross domestic product (GDP) per capita into three categories: 25 percent were developed countries with high incomes, such as the countries in the Organization for Economic Cooperation and Development; 45 percent were semideveloped, middle-income countries like those in the former Soviet bloc, the Middle East, and Latin America; and 30 percent were low-income countries—both countries with emerging economies like the Asian tigers, China, India, and Indonesia, and poor countries like those in sub-Saharan Africa. The low-income group comprises approximately half the world's population.

As political scientist Geoffrey Garret noted in a *Foreign Affairs* article in (2004), "after two decades of globalization (1980–2000), technological change and international integration of markets have spurred growth in countries categorized as high income in 1980, by roughly 50 percent in real terms, due to innovation fueled by advances in biotech and information and communication technology." Average GDP per capita in these economies was $20,000. Several low-income countries, some ironically named, had phenomenal growth in their economies, up to 160 percent, due to large-scale export of manufactured goods ranging from steel to shoes to computers. However, due to their large populations, their GDP per capita was an average of $300 (e.g., $750 in China, $640 in Indonesia, and $440 in India). These countries exploited their comparative advantage in cheap labor to gain large shares of the global marketplace. Many corporations are notorious for their "sweatshop" operations in countries where products are shipped and sold at huge profit levels, while the corporations take advantage of the lack of organized labor by paying below-subsistence-level wages and little or no health and other benefits to workers. In describing wage levels, the World Watch Institute reported that the percentage of people working below

$2 per day was 53.1 percent in China, 66.1 percent in Indonesia, and 86.2 percent in India (comparatively, the national minimum wage in the United States was $5.85 per hour on July 24, 2007). Thus, while the GDP of countries with emerging economies was growing exponentially, the distribution of that income per capita was inequitable. The workers who possess low-level skills and perform routine tasks derived the least benefit. Poor people in low-income countries such as those in southeastern Asia have not profited greatly from globalization, despite the enormous benefits to corporations and their governments. As one scholar has pointed out, for Bangladesh, the forces of globalization have contributed positively to poverty reduction by increasing the scope of remunerative employment opportunities of the poor. At the same time, say scholars, unless education levels improve, the poor will not be able to take advantage of the economic opportunities globalization generates. Further, globalization has had little impact on countries in sub-Saharan Africa. Indeed, some scholars have placed Africa into what they called the fourth world, in which the vastly expanding informal economy has become a key source of income for both urban and rural people. However, in "Globalization in the New Millennium" (2003), South African scholar Devan Pillay attributes Africa's underdevelopment not only to "factors such as state patronage, elite corruption, ethnic rivalry, and an underdeveloped civil society" but also to its failure to participate in the use of technology. As the World Bank notes, "Africa needs to be integrated into the world economy in order to develop." Technology may well be the instrument for development of that region.

In essence, countries have had relative benefits from globalization based on their uses of technology. The data above show that the low-income countries with emerging economies that use high technology, like China, India, and Indonesia, derive the greatest benefits, improving their economies by an average growth rate of 160 percent. The traditionally developed countries of Europe, as well as Japan and the United States, which have high incomes and growth rates averaging 50 percent, rank second in derived benefits. Countries in Latin America and the Middle East, which are categorized as middle income and still largely rely on old technologies, rank third, and the countries of sub-Saharan Africa and southeastern Asia, which use little technology, are the poorest.

Reducing Poverty Through Technology: A Human Capital Approach

Human capital theory posits that the poor are poor because of low economic productivity levels. From this perspective, it would be argued that the poor are lacking in such areas of human capital as education, marketable skills, and training. A significant proportion of the world's poor fit into this category, with many living in parts of the world that experience persistent poverty and underdevelopment, thereby lacking the necessary resources for building the productivity-enhancement capabilities of their people. Respected economists seem to agree that success at adopting new techniques used by more advanced societies will lead to better standards of living in poor countries. Indeed, the United Nations Millennium Development Goals, adopted by the world community around the common agenda of eradicating extreme poverty and improving the quality of life for the peoples of the world by 2015, are predicated on the strength of the belief in the role of technology in realizing such an ambitious goal.

With growing intensity, the information and knowledge technologies are leaving their mark. The "new economy" emerging in industrialized countries suggests that a substantial share of GDP growth is attributable to the information technologies sector, while in the developing world, information and communications technologies (ICTs) are proving formidable and cost-effective development tools. Properly used, they can reduce poverty; empower people; build capacities, skills, and networks; inspire new governance mechanisms; and reinforce popular participation on all levels. The range of applications is limitless, from electronic commerce to empowerment of communities, women, and youth; from the promotion of good governance and decentralization to advocacy programs, including the observance of human rights; from long-distance education to tele-health and environmental monitoring. Creatively implemented, modern technology can help educate the poor, thereby allowing underdeveloped countries to compete and thus narrowing the gap between the rich and the poor countries and peoples. Unequal access to technology based on income and educational levels, race, gender, and geography threaten a digital divide.

Revolutionary changes in technology have had enormous impact on the world's social, economic, and political equilibrium. Technology conveys access to new markets, with major consequences for the world's populations. Not only has technology brought about the openness of the world communities, but it has provided the necessary tools for corporations to maximize profits and for workers to grow intellectually, economically, and socially. Poor countries, however, have only been remotely touched by globalization. As in developed countries, education may be the strong catalyst for providing the skills and knowledge that will enable the poor to become self-reliant creators of wealth. Technology such as distance learning may provide access to world-class education and training opportunities for developing countries to diversify and expand their economies, especially in areas of telecommunications, agriculture, and financial services. Indeed, technology may provide the poor with the genius necessary to make inventions and become creative and dynamic participants in low-income and emerging economies and indeed in civilizations.

Velta Clarke and Annettee Mahoney

REFERENCES

Amin, Samir. *Empire of Chaos*. New York: Monthly Review Press, 1992.

———. "Globalization Resource Documents for the WCAR NGO Forum, Durban August/September 2001." Pretoria: Africa Institute of South Africa, 2001.

Brumgart, John K. "History of Algebra." In *Historical Topics for Mathematics Classrooms*. Virginia: National Council of Teachers of Mathematics, 1993.

Castells, Manuel. *The End of Millennium*, vol. 3, *The Information Age: Economy, Society and Culture*. Oxford: Blackwell, 1998.

Clarke, Velta. *Effective Strategies in the Teaching of Mathematics: A Light from Mathematics to Technology*. Lanham, MD: University Press of America, 2003.

———. "Students' Global Awareness and Attitudes to Internationalism in a World of Cultural Convergence." *Journal of Research in International Education* 3:1 (2004): 51–70.

Friedman, Thomas L. *The Lexus and the Olive Tree*. New York: Farrar, Straus and Giroux, 1999.

Garret, Geoffrey. "Globalization's Missing Middle." *Foreign Affairs* 83:6 (November/December 2004): 84–96.

Jansson, Bruce. *The Reluctant Welfare State*. Pacific Grove, CA: Brooks Cole, 2001.

Pender, John. "Agricultural Technology Choices for Poor Farmers in Less-Favored Areas of the South and East Asia." Washington, DC: International Food Policy Research Institute, 2007.

Pillay, Devan. "Globalisation in the New Millennium: Implications for Development and Democracy in Africa." *Society in Transition* 34:2 (2003): 252–271.

Polack, Robert. "Social Justice and the Global Economy: New Challenges for Social Work in the 21st Century." *Social Work* 49:2 (April 2004): 281–290.

Saadi, Mir Lutful Kabir. "View from Bangladesh: The New Literacy." *Ubiquity* (July 2002).

Struik, Dirk J. *A Concise History of Mathematics*. New York: Dover, 1987.

World Watch Institute. *State of the World*. New York: W.W. Norton, 2001.

TECHNOLOGY AND THE CURRICULUM

The use of computer technology in the classroom is a trend that began in the late twentieth century, after computers had become compact in size and relatively affordable, when educators determined that computers could play a role in the learning process. Early uses of computers in the classroom included computer-based instruction (software programs) and the teaching of programming to students. Many school systems included computer programming (often in Basic language) as part of the curriculum because educators thought that it would be important for all students to have this skill. The requirement to learn programming skills was largely abandoned when educators realized that it was unnecessary for all students. Just as one does not need to be a mechanical engineer to drive a car, one does not need programming skills to use a computer.

Although some people associate classroom use of technology with computers, technology really encompasses much more. Technology may be considered both a product (hardware and software) and a process (developing consistent and replicable outcomes to tasks) or some combination of both (especially when the process and product cannot be separated). In this section, technology generally refers to hardware and software, but is not limited to computers only.

Classroom technology encompasses many different products besides computers and related items (e.g., scanners, digital visual presenters, assistive technology). Counted among technologies in present schools are televisions (satellite, cable, and interactive), videocassette recorders (VCRs) and players, digital videodisc (DVD) burners and players, camcorders, still cameras, overhead projectors, graphing calculators, telephones (both landlines and cell phones), laminating machines, copy machines, interactive white boards, laptop keyboards (e.g., AlphaSmarts), personal response systems (PRSs or clickers), personal digital assistants (PDAs), iPods, iPads, and noncomputer assistive technologies (including electronic book devices like the Kindle and Nook). Among the older technologies are film projectors, slide projectors, filmstrip projectors, opaque projectors, tape recorders, record players, and radios. Many of the old technologies have been replaced by newer ones, but the old machines are still occasionally found in a classroom or tucked away in a school storage closet. Despite the availability of both old and new tools, technological innovations are not always used to enhance classroom teaching and learning.

Restructuring Education with Technology

A common image of a classroom from 100 years ago depicts a teacher standing at the front of the room and students sitting in rows of individual desks. The teacher, the fountain of knowledge, imparts information to the students. The school year, based on an agrarian society, is closed during the summer so that children are available to help on the farm. In many instances, the classroom of the twenty-first century is not so different from the classroom of the last century. In contrast, if we compare a hospital from 100 years ago versus one in the twenty-first century, a lot has changed. Hospital personnel take advantage of new technologies to update their knowledge and improve patient care. Our educational system can also use technology to change the way teachers teach and students learn.

Some educators are using technology to restructure education and change what and how students learn. With an abundance of information (and misinformation) available, students need skills to access information, absorb it, synthesize, and analyze it. It is no longer sufficient to merely memorize information provided by teachers and textbooks to recall at a later time. Proponents of change propose that students learn through exploration, collaboration in groups, and critical examination. Technology plays an important role in the teaching and learning pro-

cess by providing a ready source of information. The classroom becomes less teacher-directed and more student-centered. The teacher no longer has to be the proverbial "sage on the stage" dispensing knowledge but can take on the role of facilitator or "guide on the side" who leads students to find needed information. The importance of teaching students to be self-reliant knowledge seekers cannot be minimized, especially given the enormous amount of information that is available and growing exponentially every day on the web as well as in more traditional media resources.

A technology-infused classroom provides opportunities for teachers to change the way they teach. When questions arise in class, the teacher does not need to be responsible for giving all the answers and solving all the problems. Instead, the teacher can ask students to go to various information resources, including the web, and to collaborate and cooperate with others to find the necessary information to answer the question or solve the problem. Eliciting the correct answer is not as important as identifying the process that solves the problem. A discussion of how the information was found, how to judge the reliability of the source, and how the problem was solved is an important part of the learning process that enables students to be good communicators and collaborators, lifelong learners, and knowledgeable members of society.

Computers in Teaching and Learning

In the classroom, the computer can be used as an object of instruction and as a tool to help teaching and learning. As an object of instruction, students may learn how computers can be useful in society, how to operate a computer, or how to program various computer languages.

The computer can also be used as a tool for learning. A very popular use of the computer is as a source of information, especially from the Internet. It is also a tool for presenting and composing information (e.g., PowerPoint, multimedia), for writing (e.g., word processing, desktop publishing), for calculating, for retrieving information (e.g., from a database), for recording data (e.g., from handheld probes), and for communicating (e.g., e-mail, texting). The use of technology helps learners by fostering creativity, allowing students to explore and create their own knowledge, inside and outside the classroom, and providing students with tutorials and practice as needed. The computer tool enables students to find answers to questions and problems so students can develop their own knowledge. They can then use computer software to make a presentation to share this information with others.

Technology tools can also be used to help the instructor plan lessons, present instructional materials (e.g., share ideas or animate learning concepts in geometry), prepare handouts, and keep grades. The computer tool supports varying instructional formats. For example, from a teacher-directed perspective, computer-assisted instruction (software) enables teachers to provide instruction and/or practice to aid student learning.

Integrating Technology Across the Curriculum

Teachers often teach in the way they were taught unless there is an intervention—for example, a course or a teacher who models an alternate way. Many teachers, especially those coming from traditional teacher-directed environments, are unsure how and when they might include technology in the curriculum, so it is important to provide training and practice. Many schools of education provide educational technology courses that allow teachers (both preservice and in-service) to explore various technologies and their classroom uses. However, it is important for schools to also provide on-going training and support as new teachers join the faculty and new technologies become available.

Technology use should be thoughtfully designed. In *Integrating Educational Technology into Teaching* (2003), M.D. Roblyer suggests the following plan for integrating technology into any area of the curriculum:

1. *Determine the goals and objectives of the unit or lesson.* It is important to keep in mind that technology use in the classroom should be aligned with the goals and objectives that the teacher has delineated for the unit or lesson. The goals and objectives should in turn be aligned with the standards (e.g., national, state, discipline). If the technology does not help to meet the standards, goals, and objec-

tives, it should not be used. Technology is not a panacea for all problems nor should it be a substitute for the teacher. On the other hand, it can be a very powerful tool for teachers and students in all areas of the curriculum.

2. *Consider the relative advantage of using technology.* Whenever teachers wish to use technology tools for teaching and learning, they should consider the relative advantage of doing so. Will the goals and objectives of the lesson be reached more quickly, more efficiently, or more effectively with the use of the technology? Will the lesson be more relevant or engaging for the students? The use of technology often enables students to have actual hands-on experiences or work with real data, which tends to make learning more meaningful. On the other hand, if the technology serves merely as an automated page turner, it may not significantly improve the learning experiences of the students. When technologies are integrated into target subject matter (for both elementary and secondary levels), students learn significantly more than when technologies are not integrated into the subject matter.

3. *Choose appropriate assessment strategies.* How will learning be assessed? There may be several separate assessments or there may be several parts of a single assessment, perhaps one part for the learning objective, one part for the use of the technology, and another part for group work and collaboration. Assessments should always be aligned with the stated objectives. A rubric is often provided to help students determine what the teacher expects and what effort students need to expend for a particular grade. A rubric can also make grading more objective for the teacher.

4. *Select appropriate integration strategies.* The procedure or sequence of activities that will accomplish the goals and objectives of the unit or lesson should be described. What role will the teacher play? What background information will the students need to carry out their tasks? What will the students do and how will they do it?

5. *Resolve the logistics of preparing the environment and instructional materials.* The environment and needed materials should be

prepared prior to the lesson. Where will the lesson take place? Options may include the classroom, a library media center, a computer lab, or an outdoor classroom. What arrangements will be made to accommodate student learning? What technologies are needed? Are computers available? Will a laptop cart be used? Sometimes equipment needs to be checked out or reserved. If students will use software, it should be loaded on the computers before the lesson begins. If students will access websites, teachers should check ahead of time that the site addresses are still active and bookmark the sites on the computers the students will use. If cameras are used, equipment should be checked ahead of time to ensure everything is in working condition (e.g., batteries are charged). Any written materials should be ready for distribution. It is useful to have a backup lesson prepared in case the technology does not work as planned.

6. *Evaluate and revise the strategies used.* After the lesson is taught, the teacher should review student work and reflect on what occurred. Were goals and objectives met? Were students engaged in the activities? Is there anything that might be changed to improve the lesson?

Sometimes teachers, preservice teachers, and administrators who have not had much experience using technology tools in the classroom have trouble envisioning technology-integrated lessons. An excellent website called InTime (www.intime.uni.edu/) provides online video vignettes of actual teachers in pre-K–12 classrooms teaching in various curricular areas using diverse strategies. *VisionQuest* (www.edci. purdue.edu/vquest/) is another website that provides digital models of three technology-rich classrooms, again with the purpose of helping teachers integrate technology into their own teaching.

Some researchers discuss the elements necessary for successful technology integration. Access to technology, support, and training are important components for integrating technology into preservice teachers' field experiences. The technology plan for the state of Nevada delineates four main goals for successfully integrating technology into the curriculum: (1) funding for repairs and maintenance, (2) high-quality instructional materials, (3) teacher

access to technology and professional development, and (4) reliable, timely technical support. In spite of their best intentions, sometimes teachers are unable to use technology tools in the classroom. The lack of necessary components will obviously be a barrier to technology integration.

Although many states require that preservice teachers take educational technology courses prior to certification, the content of the courses and how they are taught varies. Many K–12 students are adept technology users. As these students age and join the teaching ranks, they may be familiar with many technologies. However, they may not be so familiar teaching with them to help student learning. Therefore, training should be available for all teachers so they are not only competent and comfortable using the technology, but also confident using it in classroom situations. Appropriate technology use should be discussed and modeled, and teachers should have time to practice with it. Training should be ongoing throughout the year, not merely in one-day workshops, and geared to the teachers' current level of use. Teachers need time to develop and practice skills with various technologies.

Technology tools used in the classroom occasionally break down and need to be repaired. If the equipment is not fixed in a timely way, teachers may get discouraged and stop using it even after it is again available. School administrators need to believe that classroom technology use is important for student learning in order to ensure that care of equipment, along with training and support, are school priorities.

Sometimes budgetary difficulties prevent schools from purchasing new technologies or updating old ones. Far-sighted administrators who realize the important role that technology can play in the teaching and learning process will do their best to place technologies as needed and provide funding for maintenance and replacement.

All students should have access to computer technology at school, where student use should be scheduled as needed. Computer labs are sometimes unavailable to certain populations or classes, making computer use inequitable in the school.

New Technologies

For years technology has been used by educators to enable communication with others. For example, educators and students commonly use e-mail to stay in touch. Students can correspond with other students, teachers, or other adults in various places within a school, city, or country when teachers set up key pal (e-pal or electronic pen pal) projects. Discussion lists enable participants to explore topics outside of class. However, technology is constantly being updated, and teachers are constantly updating and inventing ways to use new technology tools in the classroom to help their students learn. One such communication tool is the blog (web log), an online journal that others can access and comment on. For example, instructors can use a blog to dialogue with a student or group of students, or a college professor can ask students to set up personal blogs to monitor their progress as they write their master's theses.

Podcasting is also relatively new. A podcast is a prerecorded digital media file (audio and video) distributed over the Internet using syndication feeds for playback on a portable media player or a personal computer. Educators can tap into this new technology by recording lectures or other material that students could download at a later date. Distance learners or absent students might find this especially useful. Students could post projects that they created so that not only their classmates, but virtually anyone with the appropriate equipment would be able to view their work.

Another new technology phenomenon is the wiki, and in particular, Wikipedia, an online, multilingual, collaboratively written encyclopedia. Anyone can edit or contribute to a wiki. With more than 20 million articles in over 283 languages, Wikipedia is the biggest, broadest encyclopedia ever compiled, and it continues to expand. Because it is written by volunteers rather than scholars, Wikipedia has been criticized in terms of its accuracy and reliability and the possibility of false information, possibly even deliberate contributions of malicious false information. The consensus seems to be that falsehoods are corrected quickly and that the information posted is generally accurate. When everyone has free and open access, peer review is worldwide. However, researchers have found instances when falsehoods were not removed for several months. When anyone can contribute and change the content, errors are likely to occur. However, the usefulness of wiki documents is that the information comes from the community of its contributors.

Text messaging by students in school is often viewed by teachers as problematic because they feel it interferes with teaching and learning. Teachers worry that students might exchange answers on tests or discuss issues that are not relevant to classroom learning. However, in the future this could change. Creative educators will find ways to make text messaging a useful technology tool perhaps through commentary of ongoing discussions or by facilitating students' collaboration with each other on projects. While technology tools can divert students from learning, they also have the potential to be vehicles for greatly enhancing the learning process.

Because technology tools are constantly being invented and updated, educators cannot predict what will be useful and what will not. In an article titled "Technology Immersion" (2005), Dennis Peterson reports that about 10 percent of his school district's technology funds are allotted for the discovery of new tools to help student learning. Educators are finding imaginative ways to use new technology—for example, using a YouTube video as a motivating lesson starter. It is likely that in the future creative teachers will continue to find ways to use new technology tools to enhance the teaching and learning process.

Barbara Rosenfeld

REFERENCES

ChanLin, Lih-Juan, et al. "Factors Influencing Technology Integration in Teaching: A Taiwanese Perspective." *Innovations in Education & Teaching International* 43:1 (2006): 57–68.

Devereaux, Michelle. "The Web 2.0 Visual Glossary." *Technology and Learning* 27:11 (2007): 40–44.

Friedman, Thomas L. *The World Is Flat: A Brief History of the Twenty-First Century.* Updated and expanded ed. New York: Farrar, Straus & Giroux. 2006.

Judge, Sharon, and Blanche O'Bannon. "Integrating Technology into Field-Based Experiences: A Model That Fosters Change." *Computers in Human Behavior* 23:1 (2007): 286–302.

Knapp, Linda Roehrig, and Allen D. Glenn. *Restructuring Schools with Technology.* Boston: Allyn & Bacon, 1996.

LoParrino, Camille. *How Are Teachers at a Technologically-Advanced NYC School Site Integrating Educational Technology into the Curriculum?* (2006). (ERIC Document Reproduction Service No. ED491685)

Nevada Commission on Educational Technology. *Nevada State Educational Technology Plan.* August 12, 2005. www.eric.ed.gov (ERIC Document Reproduction Service No. ED492899).

Newby, Timothy J., Donald A. Stepich, James D. Lehman, and James D. Russell. *Educational Technology for Teaching and Learning.* 3rd ed. Upper Saddle River, NJ: Pearson, 2006.

November, Alan. "Banning Student 'Containers.'" *Technology and Learning* 27:11 (2007): 24–26.

Peterson, Dennis L. "Technology Immersion: New Tools in the Hands of Well-Trained Staff Transform Teaching and Learning." *School Administrator* 62:7 (2005): 16–19.

Roblyer, M.D. *Integrating Educational Technology into Teaching.* 3rd ed. Upper Saddle River, NJ: Pearson, 2003.

Smaldino, Sharon E., Deborah L. Lowther, and James D. Russell. *Instructional Technology and Media for Learning.* 10th ed. Upper Saddle River, NJ: Pearson, 2012.

Taylor, Lydotta M., Donna J. Casto, and Richard T. Walls. "Learning With versus Without Technology in Elementary and Secondary School." *Computers in Human Behavior* 23 (2007): 798–811.

Warlick, David. "The Executive Wiki." *Technology and Learning* 27:11 (2007): 36–38.

FUTURE OF TECHNOLOGY

Across the globe, the unprecedented growth of technology has transformed every aspect of life from education to economics. Not too long ago, people debated the role of technology in education. Should it be just an additional tool teachers can use or can it transform teaching and learning? Rod Paige, former US Secretary of Education, believes that education is still based on an agricultural timeline in an industrial setting, that it has not caught up to the Digital Age, and that educators are still debating the value and usefulness of technology. Technology, however, is embedded in student life today, and an increasing number of educators recognize they no longer have any choice in whether or not to use technology. The pace of the technological revolution has increased the students' need for a richer learning environment. Educators now have the responsibility to integrate technology into teaching and learning in order to prepare students for the twenty-first-century workforce. According to Project Tomorrow's annual report, "Speak Up 2010," approximately "30% of the teachers in the United States are using podcasts and videos in their classroom—an increase of over 50% from 2008"; over three-quarters support the potential (albeit there are concerns) for using mobile devices, handheld computer devices such as smart phones, and personal digital assistants (PDAs) for instruction; and they overwhelmingly report that the use of technology for both schoolwork and homework has enhanced student performance and achievement; however, the use of digital content is still nascent in the classroom and dependent upon grade level assignment.

The definition of technology is not confined to computing technologies or the Internet. Technology includes any digital application or equipment that provides access to communication and information. David Engler, in an essay titled "Instructional Technology and the Curriculum" (1972), views technology as inextricably related to education: "If we view the ecology of education as the Web of relationships between and among learners, teachers, and the environment in which they operate, then it becomes apparent that these relationships are largely defined by the prevailing technology of instruction." Forty years after Engler's definition, educators, scientists, industry leaders, humane organizations, and pundits worldwide, who are well aware of the critical synergy between education and technology, are collaborating globally to bring new and emerging technologies to all students.

Implementations and Challenges

An overall goal for most educational institutions is to determine how technology can improve the quality of academic life. As we consider the future of technology, we must address the issues that arise from the implementations, challenges, and trends in different countries. We can also forecast future developments in technology based on key trends in a global context.

Implementations

Many countries have adopted a technology plan for their education systems, and national governments are taking an interventionist position to assist every student in crossing the Digital Divide. In the United States, the portion of the No Child Left Behind Act known as the Enhancing Education Through Technology Act of 2001 has the goal of ensuring that every student is technologically literate by the end of eighth grade, regardless of the student's race, ethnicity, gender, family income, geographic location, or disability. These requirements are defined and supported through a required Technology Application curriculum. All learners and educators are required to use technology to acquire knowledge, solve problems, and communicate in order to thrive in the twenty-first century. Dozens of states and school districts in the United States have programs to bring computers to classrooms and connect schools with the infrastructure necessary to enrich learning activities and allow increased interactions among students, teachers, and parents. The government of the United Kingdom has created a fund to support schools in developing information technology confidence and competence in education and for using information technology as a core activity to enhance student achievement in the future.

Southeast Asian countries have undertaken a number of initiatives to integrate technology in education. For example, Singapore allocates a very large budget for information technology education and assisting infrastructure development in the schools. China has also made great efforts to increase the number of computers and the level of connectivity in its schools. The UNESCO SchoolNet project, "Strengthening ICT in Schools and SchoolNet Project in ASEAN (Association of South East Asian Nations) Settings," launched in 2003, has assisted Asian-Pacific teachers in integrating information and communication technologies (ICTs) into their curricula by supporting Internet, broadband, and satellite connectivity and creating a network of collaborative schools. To date, SchoolNet activities include open source software and gaming in several primary and secondary educational environments in the ASEAN region.

The UNESCO European SchoolNet network, launched in 2004, consists of more than 30 ministries of education in Europe and beyond. Their goal is to encourage innovation in teaching and learning in the areas of mathematics, science, and technology by building a Learning Resource Exchange (LRE) that permits both teachers and students to share educational resources. To date, the LRE lists over 40,000 resources and over 100,000 learning assets.

Many countries are investing in professional development training for educators. In the UK, teachers will have the opportunity to access training to help them use technology in the classroom. The training programs are designed around teachers' needs and are offered in a variety of modes. The UNESCO Asia-Pacific Regional Bureau has done extensive work on providing professional training for teachers. The teacher training activities are implemented either by the government or in partnership with nongovernmental organizations and/or the international community.

Challenges

When implementing any technology plan, it is important to identify what works well, recognize what is not successful, and learn from any weaknesses identified. During this process, the challenges of implementation may be considered in terms of three categories: people, cost, and infrastructure.

In the people category, one common challenge identified by many countries is professional development. Technology cannot be effectively used in the classroom unless teachers understand and are knowledgeable about diverse strategies to create a rich learning environment and enhance learning outcomes. The trend in the UK is to provide both initial training for all teachers and ongoing professional development so teachers can maintain progress, design curriculum applications, and finally discuss and share best-practice and management methods.

The US National Education Technology Plan 2010 (NEPT) candidly acknowledges that many educators do not have the same understanding and skill level in using new and emerging technologies that other professionals in other sectors use on a daily basis. Hence, NEPT calls for colleges of education and other institutions that prepare teachers for the global economy to train educators in technology-based learning and technology-based assessment systems and to continuously generate digital data that will drive decisions to improve student learning.

Another significant challenge related to people is the impact of governmental policies. The Global Information Society Watch (GISW) is an international project that monitors information and communication technology implementation in 53 countries in Africa, the Caribbean, Europe, the Middle East, North America, and South America. The GISW 2010 Report found that common challenges in the aforementioned countries are related to ICT policies on environmental sustainability and in the fields of ICT with climate change and electronic waste (e-waste).

In the second category, the lack of funding is also

a major problem in many countries. The biggest concerns in relation to ICT implementation in schools in China are the lack of funding and how to make effective investments. Likewise, due to the limited funding in Indonesia, only 3 percent of the population has Internet access, and Internet access costs are still prohibitive. Most of the more than 7 billion people who inhabit Earth, especially those in developing nations, have not encountered the Digital Age.

In the third category, it is implicit that effective ICT implementation can be possible only if the infrastructure, equipment, and software are available. Improving technology infrastructure in schools is an emphasis in education policies, but it is still a major barrier for many countries. Lack of access to technology for teachers and students also has been identified as a major challenge in many countries, especially developing countries. The Digital Divide, the gap between those who benefit from digital and information technology and those who do not, is also a product of insufficient infrastructure and other digital equipment. The Digital Divide not only reflects the inconsistent availability of digital and information technology, but also how the benefits derived from it are not equally available. Given the "great disparities in opportunity to access the Internet and the information and educational/business opportunities tied to this access . . . between developed and developing countries" (Lu 2001), the Digital Divide is "a constraint to the improvement of educational quality, equity, and access" (Gasperini and Mclean 2000).

There is no simple solution to the challenges of integrating technology into education in many countries. Nevertheless, technology is being asked to play an increasingly important role in creating learning environments in homes, schools, and communities.

The Knowledge-Making Kitchen

When preparing food in a kitchen, a cook will see what foods and seasonings are available and search for the appropriate cookware and appliances. The selection of foods, seasonings, and tools might differ each day, yet some processes, such as mixing and heating, remain essential. Finally, the cook will choose the appropriate dinnerware to display the food. The food-preparation procedure is analogous to learning in the classroom. Students always have some materials

and tools to use when learning and some available ways to express or present their learning. A classroom can be described as a "knowledge-making kitchen." However, compared to a traditional classroom with limited knowledge-making resources and tools, a technology-infused classroom provides access to unlimited resources, a variety of new and emerging tools to use, and different ways to describe or present concepts.

The key concepts in the technology-infused learning environment are understanding the power of technology, and the changes in the role and needs of both teacher and student. Moreover, this kitchen metaphor implies two directions for the future: technology use in education and technological innovations. The changing role of both the teacher and student in future technology-infused learning environments will affect the use of technology and future innovations.

The Roles of Teacher and Student in the Technology-Infused Learning Environment

The move toward the increased use of technology in education encourages teachers to consider how future instruction may be improved. In a "knowledge-making kitchen," teachers may worry that they must know every new or old tool and resource to teach their students, but they do not. Michael Davino, superintendent of Springfield, New Jersey, Public Schools and former chief administrator of New York City Schools, says that teachers simply need to understand the power of the technology and that students will show them the details. He thinks this approach "breaks down the Digital Divide between teachers and students, and builds a new kind of interaction that is highly beneficial" (The Greaves Group, The Hayes Connection 2006). The teacher need not be the source of all knowledge, but rather a facilitator, mentor, and ongoing learner of new technologies and strategies in order to integrate these tools into the curriculum.

The rate of students' acceptance of using technology in learning and daily life is almost as fast as technological development. In *Educating the Net Generation* (2005), Diana G. Oblinger writes, "Student's skills that new technology has actually enhanced—which have profound implications for their learning—are almost totally ignored by educators." The traditional model of schooling in which the teacher is the source of knowledge and the student is the receiver of knowledge is not adequate for the twenty-first century. Students must be active participants in the creation of knowledge instead of merely absorbing it. Rather than being told information, students would rather construct their own learning and assemble information, tools, and framework from a variety of resources. Getting the right resources into students' hands during learning processes will boost motivation and interest in learning. In addition to extant paper-based assessments, students have more options for exhibiting their understanding of learning objectives or projects using technology. Teachers also have more ways to assess different types of student work, thus maximizing each student's potential.

Teacher and Student Needs in a Technology-Infused Learning Environment

When the roles of teachers and students change, teachers and students have different needs. Teachers need new strategies for curriculum, instruction, and assessment. It is crucial for teachers to understand in today's (and tomorrow's) technology-rich world how students differ from students in the past, what learning activities are most engaging, and how to use technology to make learning more successful. Consequently, teachers need professional training to help them visualize, internalize, and create effective technology-enhanced learning environments and technology-based assessment systems.

Having grown up with widespread access to technology, students are accustomed to technology without an instruction manual, but Oblinger and Oblinger note that students' "understanding of technology and source quality may be shallow." Students tend to use the Internet to search for information they need rather than reviewing resources from the library. However, according to the Online Computer Library Center (2002), two-thirds of students know how to find valid information on the web, but the web does not meet all their information needs. Regarding technology integration in the classroom, students are more concerned about the activities enabled by technology and less concerned about whether their teachers use the latest technologies or not. In other words, students care

more about the ways in which teachers use technology to meet their learning needs of communication and social networking, first-person learning, interaction, immediacy, and multiple media literacy.

Technology, Globalization, and Education

Information and communication technologies make the process of globalization real and fast. In *The World Is Flat* (2006), Thomas Friedman describes the stages of the process of globalization: "Globalization 3.0 is shrinking the world from a size small to a size tiny and flattening the playing field at the same time. And while the dynamic force in Globalization 1.0 was countries globalizing, and the dynamics of Globalization 2.0 was companies globalizing, the dynamic force in Globalization 3.0—the force that gives it its unique character—is the newfound power for individuals to collaborate and compete globally." This global sharing of expertise and work is made possible through a "flat-world play field." As a result of new and emerging technologies and effective education, each individual has the power to contribute and collaborate in the ongoing and never-ending process of globalization. In many countries, education is identified as an essential part of their strategy for the country's economic future and plays a vital role in equipping students with the skills needed to create a strong economic environment. Often, the belief in the importance of education is accompanied by a desire to see how technology might improve education and a belief that technology will bring greater success in the global market. Thus more developed countries, emerging economies, and developing countries are under great pressure to improve their economic competitiveness by integrating ICT into education in order to either maintain their current advantage in the global economy or to catch up with more developed countries. As globalization brings disparate communities together, the context for education and work is radically changing. As a consequence, governments and educators are concerned whether students are aware of this changed global context and, more importantly, if students are adequately prepared to learn and live in the global economy.

The United States plays a leading role in the global economy, and much research has been done to examine the country's potential to remain dominant in the future. The 2006 NetDay Speak Up National Research Project nationwide survey collected the views of 232,781 K–12 students, 21,272 K–12 teachers, and 15,316 parents. The three main findings related to preparation for jobs and careers in the twenty-first century are as follows:

- Although 86 percent of students in grades K–2 are interested in specific careers in science and/or math, their interest starts to decrease in grade 3. In grades 3–12, over one-third of the students state they are not interested in careers in science, math, technology, or engineering.
- Only 47 percent of teachers believe their school is doing a good job of preparing students to compete for jobs and careers in the twenty-first century, and they have a variety of ideas on how to fix the situation.
- A majority of parents (52 percent) do not believe their child's school is doing a good job of preparing their child to compete for jobs and careers in the twenty-first century; however, they have a long list of their own ideas on how to fix this situation.

There is no doubt that better education and training are expected to produce more professionals and experts in science, technology, and engineering. Nevertheless, national initiatives are needed to create opportunities for citizens to participate in economic, political, and cultural life through the use of information and communication technologies.

Current Trends

The desired goal of technology integration in education is for technology to be used effectively by students and teachers to meet most learning and teaching needs and to prepare students with necessary learning and living skills and abilities for the global economy.

Low-Cost Technology

There has been a gradual shift toward applying technology to promote teaching and learning in the world. Therefore, the creation of low-cost technologies becomes an important goal for the future. Open source software and web-based software are common examples. Open source is defined as "a

development method for software that harnesses the power of distributed peer review and transparency of process. The promise of open source is better quality, higher reliability, more flexibility, lower or no cost" (www.opensource.org). Open source (free) software continues to grow in popularity in both industry and education and is especially needed in developing countries that cannot afford propriety software licenses. The free and open source software (FOSS) movement is a development that offers resources and opportunities for governmental, private, and educational institutions. For example, there is a growing critical mass in Colombia, especially in the educational institutions, in favor of the adoption of FOSS. In addition, Bulgaria uses FOSS to implement e-government projects.

Another trend in technology development is web-based software. The move of software development toward a web-based environment has grown significantly. The primary advantage of web-based software or applications is that they are easier to use and cheaper to develop, deploy, and update than desktop solutions. We may see widespread improvements in open source and web-based software in the future.

Universal Design

Making resources available online for all people, developing new global partnerships, and increasing students' knowledge of global issues are ICT trends in many countries. In the GISW 2007 Report, international efforts have been focused on the following:

- Supporting educational, scientific, and cultural institutions, including libraries, archives, and museums, in their role of (1) developing diverse and varied content, (2) providing equitable, open, and affordable access, (3) preserving in digital form, (4) supporting informal and formal education, research and innovation, and (5) improving ICT literacy and community connectivity, particularly in underserved communities.
- Strengthening the creation of quality e-content on national, regional, and international levels.
- Promoting the use of traditional and new media to foster universal access to information, culture, and knowledge for all people, especially vulnerable populations and populations in developing countries.

Likewise, curriculum directors in the United States rank adherence to a universal digital format as the top factor in successful digital learning (The Greaves Group, The Hayes Connection 2006). As a result, it is hoped that future technologies will provide more tools and resources to make these processes easier and more successful. Moreover, to facilitate communication between people in different countries, web-based language translation tools will become increasingly important.

Infrastructure

The use of technology in education should maximize outcomes of the teaching and learning processes. This can occur only if technological infrastructures are in place and updated, and if both pedagogy and technology are integrated. According to the US Department of Education, National Center of Education Statistics (2011), 100 percent of public schools had at least one computer with Internet access and 97 percent of the schools had at least one computer with Internet access in each classroom. In addition, 91 percent of the computers were used for instructional purposes.

The benchmarks for the European Union's (EU) Education and Training 2020 work program (ET 2020) within all levels of education include adoption of ICT and promotion of multilingualism, innovation, and creativity. The EU's "Digital Agenda and Union Initiative" focuses on equipping all students with basic skills, including those that enable the use of modern technologies to produce a skilled workforce (Official Journal of the European Union 2011).

The synergy between quality education, technology, and a thriving economy is well known as is the lack of these three key ingredients in underdeveloped countries. To date, more than one-half of the world's population needs the technological infrastructure to become active participants in the Digital Age.

Safety and Health

According to many scholars, online predators, inappropriate websites, and privacy issues are the top Internet safety concerns for most teachers and students. As the Internet is used more and more in daily life and in schools, educators need to make sure it is also a safe learning environment. In addition, future tech-nology should avoid health-related problems, such as eyestrain and the effect of electromagnetic radiation, which is a common characteristic of computer use.

Tomorrow's Children

The growing power of technology encourages teachers to rethink how to integrate existing technology into the classroom in order to provide more individualized and differentiated instruction, to stimulate students and help them visualize structure and process, to support formative and summative assessments, and to create a rich learning environment that will promote student learning. It is hoped that future technology will provide more applications for teaching and learning. When technology is no longer considered optional in education, the expectations and responsibilities of technology development will also increase.

At the most basic level, technology is a means to create better education for students in every country. The work, tools, communication, and information in the future will be different from those of today. However, we must keep in sight what technology can mean to future generations. By so doing we will be better prepared to connect new technology to the wide range of educational purposes and possibilities that the children of tomorrow's world will face.

In *Lead the Field* (1973), Earl Nightingale mused, "We become what we think about." Technology, if applied properly, can provide tools to bring the thoughts of students to reality. In light of worldwide strategic technology plans and humane organizations to provide educators with both effective infrastructures and professional development in new and emerging technologies, students will reach their full potential and become globally competitive.

*Chia-Jung Chung and
Sharon Anne O'Connor-Petruso*

REFERENCES

Ali, Mohammed. "E-learning in the Indonesian Education System." *Asia-Pacific Cybereducation Journal* 1:2 (2005): 15–24.

APC and Hivos. "Global Information Society Watch 2010: Focus on ICTs and Environmental Sustainability." www.giswatch.org.

APC and ITeM. "Global Information Society Watch 2007–Participants." www.giswatch.org.

Asian Foundation. "The ASEAN Foundation Discussing the Future of ICT Programs for ASEAN Community." ENews, August 1, 2011. www.aseanfoundation.org.

Cabanatan, Priscilla G. "Using ICT in the Classroom: Status and Prospects in Southeast Asia." *Asia-Pacific Cybereducation Journal* 1:2 (2005): 65–72.

Engler, David. "Instructional Technology and the Curriculum." In *Technology in Education: Challenge and Change*, ed. F.J. Pula and R.J. Goff, 58–64. Worthington, OH: Charles A. Jones, 1972.

European Commission Education & Training. "Strategic Framework for Education and Training." February 17, 2011. http://ec.europa.eu.

European Schoolnet. "About." EUN Partnership AISBL. www.europeanschoolnet.org.

Friedman, T. *The World Is Flat: The Globalized World in the Twenty-First Century.* London: Penguin Books, 2006.

Gasperini, Lavinia, and Scott Mclean. "Education for Agriculture and Rural Development in Low-Income Countries: Implications of the Digital Divide." Paper presented at the Global Junior Challenge, Rome, Italy, 2000.

The Greaves Group. *America's Digital Schools: A Five-year Forecast.* 2006. www.ads2006.org/ads2006/pdf/ADS2006KF.pdf.

The Greaves Group, The Hayes Connection. "America's Digital Schools 2006: A Five-Year Forecast." 2006. http://ads2006.net.

Lu, Ming-te. "Digital Divide in Developing Countries." *Journal of Global Information Technology Management* 4:3 (2001): 1–4.

Nightingale, Earl. *Lead the Field.* Niles, IL: Nightingale-Conant, 1973.

No Child Left Behind Act of 2001, 20 USC 6319, Section D, Enhancing Education Through Technology Act of 2001.

Oblinger, Diana. "Is It Age or IT: First Steps toward Understanding the Net Generation." In *Educating the Net Generation*, ed. D.G. Oblinger and J.L. Oblinger, 2.1–2.20. Boulder, CO: EDUCAUSE, 2005.

Official Journal of the European Union. "IV Notices from European Union Institutions, Bodies, Offices and Agencies (C70)." April 3, 2011.

Online Computer Library Center Inc. "OCLC White Paper on the Information Habits of College Students: How Academic Librarians Can Influence Students' Web-Based Information Choices." 2002. www5.oclc.org/downloads/community/informationhabits.pdf.

Open Source Initiative. www.opensource.org.

Project Tomorrow. "Speak Up 2010 National Findings. The New 3 E's of Education: Enabled, Engaged, Empowered." May 2011. www.tomorrow.org/speakup.

SIS Newslog. "UNESCO SchoolNet Project in South-East Asian Countries." January 31, 2010. www.itu.int.

US Department of Education. "Visions 2020.2: Student Views on Transforming Education and Training through Advanced Technologies." www.ed.gov.

US Department of Education, National Center for Education Statistics. "Educational Technology in U.S. Public Schools." NCES 2010–034.

US Department of Education, Office of Educational Technology. "Transforming American Education: Learning Powered by Technology: Executive Summary." National Education Technology Plan 2011. www.ed.gov.

Yuan, Li, and John Gardner. "Examining Trends in the Use of Computers in Education in China from a Wood's National Policy Models Perspective." *Asia-Pacific Cybereducation Journal* 2:2 (2006): 1–21.

INSTITUTIONS OF EDUCATION THROUGHOUT THE WORLD

GLOBAL MONETARY AGENCIES FOR EDUCATION

Global monetary agencies (GMAs), such as the Asian Development Bank and the World Bank, not only offer monetary support for education in developing countries but also provide policy advisement to their governments. Because GMAs often consider education as an investment in poverty alleviation and sustainable economic development of developing countries, the support they provide includes the rehabilitation of postconflict countries and the assistance they offer is through projects and programs in a cost-effective and efficient manner. GMAs tend to be very influential in assisting the education sector in developing countries. They consist primarily of two types of institutions: multilateral agencies and bilateral agencies. Multilateral agencies are further divided into two categories: global institutions and regional institutions. Although GMAs are independent of each other in terms of funding, nowadays it is not uncommon to find them collaborating with one another by cofinancing education projects and programs.

Multilateral Agencies

Multilateral agencies are characterized by their multiple memberships, and both developing countries and developed countries are usually included in the membership. Other than regional perspectives, multilateral agencies are categorized further by the character of memberships. A category of multilateral agencies that operates with wide membership structures is known as international development organizations; examples include the World Bank, International Monetary Fund, African Development Bank, and Inter-American Development Bank. Another category has narrower membership structures and focuses on specific activities pertaining to the education sector. Such GMAs include the International Fund for Agricultural Development, Islamic Development Bank, and OPEC Fund for International Development. The roles of seven of these GMAs are presented below.

World Bank

The World Bank (WB) was established in 1945 with its headquarters in Washington, DC, and more than 100 country offices spread across the globe, the majority in developing countries. WB consists of five institutions: International Bank for Reconstruction and Development (IBRD), International Development Association (IDA), International Finance Cooperation (IFC), Multilateral Investment Guarantee Agency, and International Center for the Settlement of Investment Disputes. Among these institutions, IBRD, IDA, and IFC provide support for the education sector. IBRD provides support to governments of middle-income countries, while IDA supports the government of poor countries. IFC supports the private sector on education.

Historically, WB started its operation in the education sector in 1960 and invested in it for the first time in 1963. WB's first education lending was for vocational education in Tunisia. Since then, the total amount of loans and credits for education (both IBRD and IDA) has reached more than US$39 billion. Both the amount of loans and credits as well as the share of WB's total amount of lending have increased substantially, as seen by the increase in the former from US$5 million in 1963 to about US$2 billion in 2010, and the increase in the latter's education share total lending from 0.7 percent in 1963 to 8.6 percent in 2010. Indeed, WB is currently the single largest external financier in the education sector. It has recently focused on primary education, which is considered the most profitable investment in developing countries.

Within the WB, three lending trends are observed in the education sector. First, WB initially focused more on tertiary education than primary education; however, the lending share for tertiary education has gradually decreased, while that for primary education has increased since the early 1980s. Currently, the lending share for primary education is the largest compared to that for tertiary and secondary education. Moreover, a comparison of the lending trends for general and vocational education at the secondary level shows that lending for general education has increased considerably since the 1980s, while lending for vocational education has decreased. Furthermore, WB's project activities have changed since the 1960s. Within a span of two decades from the 1960s to the 1980s, activities focusing on "hardware," such as infrastructure and rehabilitation of schools, proved to be the major educational inputs. On the other hand, from the 1980s to the 1990s, the number of education specialists at the WB has increased, with the focus shifting to "software" type of activities, including curriculum reform and teaching materials.

Geographically, WB has provided assistance to all regions across the globe. WB has invested in Latin America and the Caribbean region the most; 35.8 percent of its total investment has been in this area. Currently, WB has two main themes for education; one is to assist countries to achieve Education for All (EFA), which is an international commitment to providing quality basic education for all children, youth, and adults.

WB identifies itself as a knowledge bank by providing policy advisement to the governments and private sectors in developing countries. In addition, WB also considers education to be a knowledge economy and assists client countries to equip themselves with highly skilled and flexible human capital needed to compete effectively in today's dynamic global markets. Since 2002, after the G8 summit in Kananaskis, Canada, the Education for All: Fast Track Initiative Secretariat was established within the WB, dedicated to achieving the Millennium Development Goals (MDGs), specifically to achieve universal primary school completion

by 2015 with adequate quality of education as well as equitable gender enrollment. The Fast Track Initiative has increased the achievement of the goal in numerous targeted countries; currently, many multilateral and bilateral agencies have committed themselves to this initiative.

International Monetary Fund

The International Monetary Fund (IMF) was established in 1945 and began operation in 1947. Headquartered in Washington, DC, next to the World Bank, IMF's primary operation revolves around the stabilizing of international monetary and financial systems by means of surveillance and financial as well as technical assistance. IMF plays an important role in supporting developing countries mainly through financial assistance, as lending is one of the most effective tools that IMF uses. In the 1980s, IMF established the Structural Adjustment Program with WB as a conditionality of the latter's lending. Specifically, both the IMF and WB requested developing countries that desired to borrow money to reform their internal structures. Open market, adjustment of foreign exchange rate, and privatization are some examples of these reforms. As a result of the adjustment program, many developing countries had to tighten their national budgets; consequently, the budgets for social sectors such as health and education were reduced. Problems and issues in the education sector then began to emerge, and progress in education was largely obstructed.

There are currently two lending programs conducted by the IMF: the Poverty Reduction and Growth Facility and the Exogenous Shocks Facility, both of which are based on the Poverty Reduction Strategy Paper (PRSP). The PRSP covers economic and social development issues, including education, which implies that the IMF indirectly provides lending to the education sector rather than by direct means. IMF established a Joint Development Committee with WB in 1974. This committee provides advice on development issues and financial resources to the board of governors of the WB and IMF.

Asian Development Bank

The Asian Development Bank (ADB) is a regional development bank overlooking the Asia and Pacific region. ADB was established in 1966 with its head-quarters in Manila, the Philippines, and it started its funding in the education sector in 1970. ADB supports education by means of two instruments, lending and technical assistance. In 2006 a total of US$251 million in loans and US$47 million in grants were approved for the education sector. These amounts increased slightly in 2010. In its founding years, the primary focus of the ADB was on technical and vocational training, but it shifted to basic education and education sector development in recent years. Southeast Asia is the region wherein ADB has financed the most heavily in the period between 1991 and 2006. For example, 49 percent of the ADB's total lending and 50 percent of total technical assistance in that period were distributed within Southeast Asia. Clearly, the ADB has set its priorities on educational development assistance; its principle priorities consist of six components: (1) to increase access, equity, and retention (especially for the poor, women, and other marginalized groups); (2) to improve the quality of education; (3) to strengthen management, governance, and efficiency, and emphasize further stakeholder participation; (4) to mobilize resources for sustainable education delivery, particularly facilitating the role of the private sector, while protecting access by poor students to affordable basic education; (5) to strengthen collaboration with partners and beneficiaries; and (6) to emphasize more experimentation with and dissemination of innovative strategies and technologies.

Currently, one of ADB's major goals is to assist governments in developing countries to achieve Education for All and Millennium Development Goals by 2020. In order to tackle many challenges in achieving these goals, ADB pays considerable attention to concerns such as community-based approaches, quality teaching, curriculum, materials development, and provision of facilities.

Inter-American Development Bank

The Inter-American Development Bank (IDB) was established in 1959 and covers the Latin American and Caribbean regions. Also headquartered in Washington, DC, IDB assists the education sector through loans and technical cooperation with three major objectives: (1) training of human resources for development, (2) equality of educational opportunities, and (3) efficiency of investments in education. From 1962 to 2010, close to US$5.54 billion of loans were approved for distribution in the education sector. IDB covers a wide range in education—adult and nonformal education, education management and reform, higher education, preschool and early childhood education, primary and secondary education, rural and distance education, science and technology, and teacher training.

As for the trend of loans since 1998, IDB provided loans at relatively the same level in 1998, 1999, and 2000 (US$263.3 million in 1998, US$250.2 million in 1999, and US$233.0 million in 2000), with the largest amount being US$687.5 million in 2001. After 2001 the amount decreased substantively. In 2006 the distribution of loans and guarantees for the education sector totaled US$60.5 million, which represented 0.9 percent of IDB's total lending. As for grants, the amounts totaled US$18.61 million in 1998 and US$23.9 million in 1999, decreasing considerably after 1999.

African Development Bank

The African Development Bank (AfDB) was established in 1964 and covers all the African countries. Its headquarters was initially established in Abidjan, Côte d'Ivoire; however, since February 2003, AfDB has operated in Tunis, Tunisia, because of political instability in Côte d'Ivoire. Four grants were approved for the education sector, with a total sum of US$97.8 million, of which 13.2 percent was total grants and 2.8 percent was a combination of total loans and grants. Further, 26.6 percent of the total financing amount was approved for the education sector. AfDB focuses on basic and vocational education as well as adult education and training. AfDB is progressively supporting the EFA Fast Track Initiative in many African countries, particularly in Burkina Faso, Cameroon, Chad, Democratic Republic of Congo, Mali, and Niger.

In the future, the AfDB plans to expand access to primary education by ensuring affordability, with particular focus on enrolling and retaining female students, enhancing the probability of youth and adult employment through literacy, providing vocational and basic skills training, providing teaching materials, and encouraging public expenditure management reforms. In higher education, the AfDB focuses on the areas of critical skill shortages and research concerning poverty and poverty alleviation, particularly thorough public-private partnership programs.

Islamic Development Bank

The Islamic Development Bank (IsDB) was formally opened in 1975, headquartered in Jeddah, Saudi Arabia. The IsDB Group consists of five institutions: Islamic Development Bank, Islamic Research and Training Institute, Islamic Corporation for the Development of the Private Sector, Islamic Corporation for the Insurance of Investment and Export Credit, and International Islamic Trade Finance Corporation. Among these institutions, IsDB provides support in development issues; its goal is to foster economic and social development of its member countries and Muslim communities in nonmember countries individually as well as jointly in accordance with the principles of Sharia. Although a regional bank, IsDB differs from other regional banks such as the ADB in that member countries are not limited to specific geographic regions but are spread across the world; obviously IsDB is a big supporter of Islamic countries and communities. Of the 56 member countries, the sub-Saharan African region has the biggest share (38 percent) in terms of the number of countries, followed by the Middle East and North Africa region (32 percent).

IsDB supports the education sector by means of many instruments, one of which is funds through the World Waqf Foundation. Another type of assistance is provided to the education sector through scholarship programs—for example, the IsDB Scholarship Programme for Muslim Communities. Since this scholarship program began in 1983, a total of US$62 million has been used to provide scholarships to 7,450 poor and merit students from 48 countries. Another example is the IsDB Merit Scholarship Programme for High Technology. Since this scholarship started in 1990, a total of US$13 million has been used by 339 scholars, including 197 PhD holders. Last but not least, the Master of Science Scholarship Programme for the Least Developed Member Countries, which was established in 1997, has spent US$0.95 million on scholarships for 183 students.

OPEC Fund for International Development

The OPEC Fund for International Development (OFID) was established in Vienna, Austria, in 1976 with twelve members, namely, Algeria, Gabon, Indonesia, Iran, Iraq, Kuwait, Libya, Nigeria, Qatar, Saudi Arabia, United Arab Emirates, and Venezuela. With an initial endowment of US$800 million, OFID's resources doubled within a period of less than one year. By the end of 1977, it had extended 71 loans to 58 developing countries and it was channeling donations from its member countries to other development institutions through the IMF Trust Fund and the International Fund for Agricultural Development. The OFID became a fully functional and permanent international development agency in May 1980. Its chief aim is to foster social and economic progress in developing countries by means of financial assistance. OFID covers a wide range of geographic regions; 119 countries in Africa, Asia, the Caribbean, Europe, Latin America, and the Middle East have benefited from OFID's assistance. In addition, OFID covers a wide variety of field and activities, including public sector lending, private sector facility, trade finance facility, grant program, HIV/AIDS special account, and Palestine special account. There is no specific lending category for the education sector within OFID; however, there are some projects in the education sector. For example, in 2002, OFID set up the Special Grant Account for Palestine to provide new-curriculum textbooks in order to improve the quality of education in Palestine. The total amount of this grant is US$2.5 million. About 9 million books for grades 1–12 will be printed and distributed among Palestinian schools, benefiting at least 1 million students. The Islamic Development Bank is regarded as one of the OFID sister institutions.

Bilateral Agencies

Bilateral agencies are organizations that are based in developed countries and work to improve educational infrastructure an opportunity in developing countries. Multilateral agencies differ from bilateral agencies in that the former include international institutions that function along with government membership in conducting development projects in developing countries. Bilateral agencies are different from multilateral agencies in terms of membership. Bilateral agencies do not have country-wide membership as multilateral agencies do; in fact, because bilateral agencies are established by national governments themselves, they tend to be significantly affected by government policies and political expediency.

Japan Bank for International Cooperation

The Japan Bank for International Cooperation (JBIC) is one of the providers of Japanese Official Development Assistance (ODA) by means of loans. JBIC was established in 1999 with two main operations: International Financial Operation and Overseas Economic Cooperation Operation (OECO). Through OECO, JBIC has provided numerous loans to developing countries, among them loans to the education sector. In 2010 the total amount of JBIC's loan commitment was slightly more than US$9 billion, with over 80 percent allocated to the Asian region (with about 10 percent to Africa and slightly less to Latin America).

Approximately 5 percent of this loan commitment was allocated to the education sector, amounting to roughly US$0.477 billion in 2010 (4.1 percent was toward total ODA and four projects were committed). JBIC started its loan program for the education sector in 1977; its first loan was to Indonesia in the amount of US$10.4 million. Within the education sector, JBIC currently provides support primarily to technical vocational education and higher education. In October 2008, the OECO division of JBIC merged with the Japan International Cooperation Agency to offer technical support and collaboration in developing countries.

Kreditanstalt fur Wiederaufbau (KfW)

The KfW Banking Group consists of five different types of banks: KfW Mittelstandsbank, KfW Foderbank, KfW Ipex-bank, KfW Entwicklungsbank, and Deutsche Investitions- und Entwicklungsgesellschaft (DEG). Among them, KfW Entwicklungsbank (KfW) assists developing countries by means of its loans and grants. For example, each year since 2000, the total commitment of grants and loans by KfW amounted to approximately €2.5 billion (about $3.2665 billion), with about 40 percent allocated to

Asia and Oceania (with 15 percent for sub-Saharan Africa, 17 percent for Europe and Caucasus, 18 percent for North Africa and the Middle East, and 10 percent for Latin America).

About 30 percent of the total amount has been allocated to social infrastructure and €96 million allocated to the education sector. Within the education sector, KfW assists many targets such as school construction, school equipment, and teacher training. KfW conducts its activities in primary and secondary education, higher education, and vocational training, funding 75 projects in Africa, Asia, Latin America, and Europe by the end of 2000 with €0.77 billion or the equivalent of $1 billion (59 projects for primary and secondary education, 10 projects for higher education, and six projects for vocational training).

Partnership Among GMAs

Indeed, there is a great deal of diversity of lending, including total funding amounts, funding amounts in the education sector, and assistance instruments (for instance, loans, grants, and technical cooperation) among GMAs. However, stressing the effectiveness of assistance is relatively common among GMAs. Nowadays, GMAs form partnerships with each other to find the most effective and efficient way to enhance their financial lending. An example of such a partnership among GMAs is cofinancing. According to WB, cofinancing refers to any arrangement under which bank funds or guarantees are associated with funds provided by third parties for a particular project or program. Official cofinancing, either through donor government agencies or multilateral financial institutions, constitutes the largest source of cofinancing for bank-assisted operations. In the case of the World Bank, there are several objectives in encouraging cofinance: mobilizing resources in order to fill a financing gap in a specific project or program, establishing closer coordination with donor agencies on country programs, policies, and investment priorities, and providing donor agencies with a cost-effective way of extending assistance based on WB's country experience and capacity of project and program management.

There are several types or concepts related to cofinancing: poverty reduction strategic credit (PRSC), general budget support (GBS), common basket/SWAp (education program), and cofinancing at the project level. PRSC is one type of cofinancing, largely based on the Poverty Reduction Strategy Paper (PRSP). In order to realize the purpose of PRSP, donors provide assistance through the PRSC. On the other hand, GBS is a scheme that allows donors to place their financial resources directly into government budgets. The Department for International Development (DfID) and other donors in Europe are primary promoters of this scheme. Although the GBS itself does not focus on the education sector, this scheme directly affects the national budget in a country, thus tending to influence the education sector.

The common basket is the concept that donors pool and manage their financial resources in one account and use that account effectively. This scheme directly applies in the education sector. The sector-wide approach (SWAp) is one of the schemes that conduct donor coordination in one sector. Therefore, donors are able to cofinance through the common basket in a sector based on SWAp (especially, given this topic, education SWAp).

GMAs play an important role in the education sector of developing countries not only because of their financial influence but also because of their policy perspectives. They assist the governments of developing countries through financial means and technical support. However, GMAs differ from institution to institution in many aspects such as membership, geographical regions, scale of budgets, and strategies. GMAs form partnerships not only with governments and other types of institutions but also with other GMAs by means of cofinancing.

Keiichi Ogawa

REFERENCES

African Development Bank. *Annual Report.* 2007, 2008, 2009, 2010. www.afdb.org.

———. *Assessing Progress in Africa toward the Millennium Development Goals.* Tunis, Tunisia: AfDB, 2010. www.beta.undp.org.

Asian Development Bank. www.adb.org.

———. *ADB Development Effectiveness Review 2010.* Metro Manila, Philippines: ADB, 2011.

———. *Policies and Strategies.* Metro Manila, Philippines: ADB, 2011.

Bhargava, Vinay. "The Role of the International Financial Institutions in Addressing Global Issues." In *Global Issues for Global Citizens: An Introduction to Key Development Challenges,* ed. Vinay Bhargava. Washington, DC: World Bank, 2006.

Education for All Fast Track Initiative. Global Partnership for Education. www.educationfasttrack.org.

Inter-American Development Bank. *IDB Annual Report 2010.* 2011. www.iadb.org.

International Monetary Fund. www.imf.org.

Islamic Development Bank. *Annual Report 1426H.* 2010. www.isdb.org.

———. 2011. *Islamic Development Bank Group in Brief.* 2011. www.isdb.org.

Japan Bank for International Development. *Annual Report 2010.* www.jbic.go.jp/en/.

———. *Loan Activity Report 2010.* www.jbic.go.jp/en/.

Japan International Cooperation Agency. www.jica.go.jp/english.

Kreditanstalt fur Wiederaufbau (KfW). *Semi-Annual Report 2011.* www.kfw.de/kfw_/kfw/en.

Ogawa, Keiichi, Masahiko Ezure, and Harumi Take. *Challenge for Education for All (EFA): Recommendation Toward Japanese ODA.* Tokyo, JICA: 2005.

OPEC Fund for International Development. www.opecfund.org.

Organization for Economic Cooperation and Development (OECD). www.oecd.org.

Psacharopoulos, George. "World Bank Policy on Education: A Personal Account." *International Journal of Education Development* 1.26 (2006): 329–338.

UNESCO. www.unesco.org.

World Bank. *EFA-FTI Progress Report 2006.* www.worldbank.org.

GLOBAL CURRICULUM ORGANIZATIONS

In the ideal situation, global curriculum organizations aim to promote a worldwide approach to curriculum, unifying criteria, identification and respect of regional uniqueness, and responses to a nation's distinctiveness. The purpose of the existence of such organizations is to understand local and global circumstances, maintaining a curriculum that incorporates into the intellectual agenda the concepts and questions related to national and international levels. Dialogue is the key to transforming curriculum, its contents, methodology, application, and evaluation at all levels of formal and nonformal education.

The concept of global curriculum organizations is not well defined in academia. As many scholars state, the internationalization of curriculum is needed in a world where development in education is the target. The internationalization of curriculum creates links to theories and perspectives that have cultural and traditional manifestations, thus linking global curriculum organizations with concepts such as global education, global curriculum networks, and multiculturalism.

Curriculum development manifests itself differently according to context. The many local curriculum products occurring in schools, colleges, and universities are of a different scale than those related to government or to global institutions, which are few and far between.

International associations interested in curriculum often lack mechanisms to give teachers in developing countries opportunities to give their curriculum a global perspective. Also, the use of English as the official language often denies the majority of the population equal access.

However, the dimensions of international curriculum are becoming an important focus for international organizations, nongovernmental organizations (NGOs), governments, intergovernmental organizations, educational planners, teacher trainers, teachers, academic scholars, educational communities, and communities of practice. Guidance and advisory support for curriculum development, especially in HIV/AIDS, human rights, environmental issues, civic education, and vocational education may include global training manuals and those designed for specific countries. Training methodology should be included in the training manuals, while the review, revision, and finalization of previous manuals may be developed to include methodology and the preparation of training toolkits and textbooks. Depending on the country, the recipients would be the army, political agencies, custodial institutions for nonformal education, as well as children, youth, or adults involved in formal education.

The internationalization of global curriculum is important in order to standardize a set of minimum curriculum contents. However, in doing this, care should be taken not to impede the development of curriculum targeted to local, regional, or national perspectives and any associated links to tradition.

Global Curriculum Organizations

Global curriculum organizations may be categorized according to their institutional genesis. Thus there are (1) global community curriculum organizations, where academia and international institutions are involved arguing the relevance of the curriculum studies; (2) government-sponsored curriculum institutions and programs, related to national reforms in curriculum and decentralized experiences; and (3) disciplinary research institutions in curriculum, where the subjects are the main focus, and the curriculum developed by experienced teachers is shown. Differing according to their institutional reach, these organizations attain credibility according to the quality of the educative curriculum they sustain, the activities they promote, their engagement in dialogue and debate, and the degree to which curriculum is improved in the regions they serve.

At the global level there are in academia two organizations for specialists interested in curriculum. One is the World Council on Curriculum and Instruction (WCCI), and the second is the International Association for the Advancement of Curriculum Studies (IAACS). There are also two essential United Nations organizations: the United Nations Educational, Scientific and Cultural Organization International Bureau of Education (UNESCO IBE) and the UNESCO International Institute for Capacity Building in Africa (UNESCO IICBA).

The World Council on Curriculum and Instruction is an affiliate of UNESCO, a nongovernmental and nonprofit organization resulting from the meetings of the United States Association for Supervision and Curriculum Development Committee (ASCD) on international understanding held from 1950 to 1964. Awareness of educational curriculum and practices in a world context was the main reason for promoting an annual conference of ASCD in 1966. The goal of the ASCD Executive Committee was to promote international understanding and cooperation in education. The Commission on International Cooperation in Education (in existence from 1966 to 1969) inaugurated the first world conference on education in 1970 in Asilomar, California. Since then, triennial and biennial world conferences have been held, with regional conferences in intervening years. The constitution was adopted in August 1, 1971, and after four amendments (in 1975, 1983, 1987, and 1998) was ratified in 1999. The sixth triennial world conference, Creative Curriculum Development and Practice, held in Noorwikerhout, The Netherlands, in September 1989, and the eleventh triennial conference, Education for a Worldview: Focus on Globalizing Curriculum and Instruction, held in Wollongong, Australia in July 2004 defined educational curriculum as holistic, in opposition to the existing colonial model. WCCI produces the journal *International Journal of Curriculum and Instruction*, a semester newsletter (spring and fall), and the triennial conference proceedings. Interest groups deal with issues such as community development, early childhood, peace education, media and technology, environmental concerns, global education, ethics and values, women and education, and lifelong education. One of the organization's resolutions vigorously promotes the integration of environmental concerns into curriculum.

The purpose of the International Association for the Advancement of Curriculum Studies is to support the scholarly debates and the work of academia, policy makers, professionals, and students in the field of curriculum, creating a national and regional cross-border exchange. Triennial conferences are held representing the global community of regions (i.e., Asia 2003, Europe 2006, Africa 2009, South America 2012, North America 2015, and Asia 2018). For instance, the Second World Curriculum Studies Conference, Meeting the International and Global Challenges in Curriculum Studies, held in Tampere, Finland, in May 2006, made the assumption that a transnational curriculum studies field would make possible a global public space for enriching theoretical studies through debate. The publications of the IAACS include the *Transnational Curriculum Inquiry* journal and electronic conference papers available online from the organization's website.

UNESCO IBE is the core of curriculum development for developers and curriculum specialists. Based in Switzerland and founded in 1925, it became an integral part of UNESCO in 1969, with the main objective of promotion and construction of curriculum capacity building at international and local levels. The goal is to create a community of practice with experts from all over the world and to promote a positive dialogue for improving practical skills in modern approaches to curriculum design and implementation. The organization updates resources with regard to content, methods, and structure of curriculum that can be shared among practitioners from both private and public sectors. Key actions of the organization include events in five regional communities, global

curriculum data as resource packages, e-forums exchanging ideas and documents, comparative research curricula, development of competences, and university partnerships.

The International Institute for Capacity Building in Africa is the UNESCO decentralized partner in Africa for the construction of the capacity building of individuals and institutions, offering training in curriculum skills development and application. Founded in 1999, it serves 20 African countries at school, local, regional, and national levels through two regional offices based in South Africa and Ethiopia. Narrowing the gap between grassroots and researchers, developers and teachers, the IICBA works to strengthen knowledge and skills and implement curriculum programs, mostly at school and local levels. Key activities include research and development in Africa, construction of institutional networks, and learning from previous actions.

Standardizing Minimum Curriculum

For the purpose of standardizing minimum curriculum at a global level, the Inter-Agency Network for Education in Emergencies (INEE) provides an interesting example. Working as an international network in humanitarian aid since 2000, it consists of individuals (5,700 as of June 2011), intergovernmental and nongovernmental organizations (e.g., CARE, Norwegian Refugee Council, Christian Children's Fund, Save the Children, and the International Rescue Committee, World Bank), and United Nations agencies (e.g., UNESCO, UNICEF, and the Office of the United Nations High Commissioner for Refugees). The Working Group on Minimum Standards for Education in Emergencies, Chronic Crises and Early Reconstruction is the global executor. It is made up of governments (e.g., Ministry of Education, France) and organizations (e.g., AED, CARE, AVSI, Catholic Relief Services, Fundación dos Mundos, GTZ, Norwegian Church Aid, Save the Children, USAID, UNESCO, UNHRC, UNICEF, World Education, and Windle Trust International) with expertise in education during natural and complex emergencies (i.e., crisis and peace building reconstruction) with a commitment to collaboration around the right to education. The handbook for education in emergencies is based on the mutual commitment of the Sphere Project Humanitarian Crisis, a group of humanitarian NGOs, and the Red Cross and the Red Crescent organizations, expressed as "the Convention of the Rights of the Child, the Dakar Education for All framework, and the UN Millennium Development Goals." The handbook is multilingual. Category three of the minimum standards identifies a "Teaching and Learning" focus on curriculum, training, instruction, and assessment. Cross-cutting issues (e.g., community participation, gender parities, human and children's rights, vulnerability, disability, and HIV/AIDS) are included, as well as diversity issues related to learners with special needs, multi-age instruction, nationality, ethnicity, culture, gender, religion, learning capacity, and multilevel instruction. The curriculum is defined as "a plan of action to help learners broaden their knowledge and skill bases," an umbrella of learning aims, contents, methodology, techniques, and instructional materials for nonformal and formal educators. The curricula are designed to be developmentally age-appropriate, adapted to the host country or the country of origin (in the case of formal education for refugees) or facing both ways (in the case of long-term refugee situations), and gender-sensitive, with quality learning content in the teachers' and students' languages. The methodology applied to nonformal education is the learner-centered approach, while for formal education the participatory method would be introduced carefully.

Curriculum in the Regional Programs

The Academy for Educational Development (AED) is based in the United States and has worked in more than thirty countries in Latin America, Asia, and Africa since 1961. Its main objective is to improve the quality of education by promoting gender parity, increasing teacher performance though better preparation, increasing student skills and capacities, assessing community participation, supporting education in complex emergencies, and enhancing the relation between education and technology through educational strategies. The focuses are K–12 education for children with disabilities, students with and from different cultures, and the transformation of learning environments by aligning curriculum and resources with instruction. One of the goals of AED is to promote the availability of teaching materials

in English, French, Spanish, Portuguese, and, soon, Arabic.

The Association for the Development of Education in Africa (ADEA) is a forum for educational policy dialogue among ten sub-Saharan African ministries of education and donor agencies (multilateral, bilateral, and private development organizations) divided by region (Indian Ocean, southern Africa, central Africa, eastern Africa, and western Africa). The antecedent organization was Donors to Africa Education, which was basically derived from World Bank recommendations, with a goal of creating a regional network to promote the dissemination of successful practices and strategies. In 1992 the creation of the UNESCO International Institute of Educational Planning (IIEP) in Paris increased ownership in this idea and serves as the liaison between donors and ministries. Their objectives are to promote exchanges about and understanding of education issues such as educational finance, cooperation in education, and educational quality. Policy coordination comes through the harmonization and cooperation of the donors and the ministers. Through working groups, ADEA promotes the production of books and learning materials, mathematics and science education, the teaching profession, and higher education. Ad hoc groups deal with issues such as HIV/AIDS, education quality, and postprimary education.

Curriculum in the National Programs and Organizations

At the national level, there are several models to consider in curriculum standards and institutions related to curriculum.

A Nation at Risk (1983), a report written by the US National Commission on Excellence in Education, focused on curriculum based on the revision of the 1964–1969 and 1976–1981 high school courses of studies. The findings were critical. The report discovered a predominance of a general rather than subject-matter-oriented curriculum (called a "cafeteria-style curriculum"), low standards, textbooks increasingly written by editors rather than by teachers or scholars, and a decline in the consumption of textbooks and teaching materials. *A Nation at Risk* recommends educational reform to align the individual interests of learners with curriculum contents. The "five new basics" recommended included English (four years), mathematics (three years), science (three years), social studies (three years), computer science (one-half year), and foreign language (two years). The No Child Left Behind Act was introduced in 2002 to improve mathematics, language, and science standards through annual evaluation in grades 3 to 8. As James A. Banks states in *An Introduction to Multicultural Education* (2008), the program has had a negative impact on curriculum development because too much focus on numeracy, literacy, and assessment impedes the development of other subjects and the students' critical thinking.

In Japan, the Japan Curriculum Research and Development Association (JCRDA), based at Hiroshima University, Faculty of Education, was created in 1975. The association publishes four bulletins annually, a journal written in Japanese titled *Japanese Pedagogy Subject Association Journal*, and a journal written in English titled *International Journal of Curriculum Development and Practice*. Both journals promote the exchange of curriculum innovations worldwide and report new ideas in curriculum and instruction, especially in the study of the Japanese language, foreign languages, and social sciences. The members of JCRDA are primarily undergraduate, graduate, and postgraduate students as well as professors and other members of academia.

At Nanyang Technological University in Singapore, the National Institute of Education (NIE) Department of Curriculum is a prestigious international institution for teacher preparation. As the largest research center in the Asian Pacific region, NIE houses the Centre for Research in Pedagogy and Practice, founded in 2002. This center is the core institution for establishing innovative teaching and learning methods. The two main publications of NIE are the *Asia Pacific Journal of Education*, centered on curriculum and pedagogy, educational policy and teaching practice, and *Pedagogies*, focused on the classroom itself. Since 2005, biannual conferences titled Redesigning Pedagogy: Research Policy and Practice provide new paradigms in curriculum and theory.

The official website of the Argentine state was established in 2000. It is an invitation for teachers to join the curriculum studies debate in science, culture and communication, economics, physics, philosophy, web creativity, music, arts, technology, teachers today, and chess. Its educational tools promote the usage of information and communication technology for teachers, e-learning courses for teachers, educational

news, debates, a forum, resources through television, and awards for schools. Its purpose is to reduce the digital divide by creating networks among government, private, and third-party sectors.

Decentralized Curriculum

The nations of Argentina and Brazil, considered provincial and private models, exemplify the decentralization of the curriculum.

In the Argentina of 1980 to 1990, the distribution of knowledge was not egalitarian. The out-of-date information taught in schools did not reflect the changes in society because education law had not been reformulated for 100 years. The resulting curriculum was obsolete for teaching both knowledge and methods. Teachers were expected to conform to curricular documents, follow content and sequence of content, and sometimes carry out certain classroom activities. During this era, the expansion of the educational system was always associated with centralized policies.

The 1993 Federal Law of Education (FLE) changed the educational system and the curriculum. A new model of curricular management emerged, proposing a shift from the traditionally centralized model (welfare state policies) to a decentralized management model (neoliberalism policies). The curriculum transformed to include nongeneral frameworks of basic contents and goals geared to each school's final examination categories. Therefore, through its curricular projects, each school specifics objectives, contents, and educational activities embedded in its own communities, putting into practice education that fits the needs and expectations of the community.

In the case of Buenos Aires province, the discussion of a new reform in the educational system started in April 2004 as a process of consultation and evaluation with the collaboration of all members of the society together with international organizations. The problems detected were the poor quality of students' basic knowledge and difficulties in social behavior that followed society's rules. Pilot projects implemented in Buenos Aires since 2005 at the administrative level were adopted as official policy in March 2006. The Educational Plan 2004/2007, *Document 2: Aims of the Education: A Redefinition for the Secondary Basic Education*, emphasizes the reinforcement of multilinguistic and transterritorial identities included in the curriculum. Teachers, parents, and students of all the jurisdictions were surveyed during 2004–2005. The results obtained for the General Basic Education level were to prioritize the culture and the education state policy and to reinstate identity and values in the curriculum. For parents, the solutions were to educate them in values and to review or to reformulate the curriculum. For students, the emphasis was placed on the lack of content and depth in the subject areas and the lack of correlation among the subjects.

In the case of Córdoba province, the institutionalization of the provincial educational system incorporates private and official services embedded in the political and institutional framework of the province. The basis of the educational system focuses on promoting continued education, instituting democratic principles, providing equal opportunities, accessibility, and permanency of educational goals, and integrating provincial institutions with local and regional counterparts. The system is divided into cycles, including the initial level (consisting of kindergarten and maternal care) and primary, secondary, and superior levels of education.

Hence, curriculum modifications by region, cooperation among diverse local, provincial, and regional groups, the use of mass media as a tool for the reinforcement of national and regional identity, and the use of education as an egalitarian way of consolidating national identity among jurisdictions were the targets for Argentina's education law. On December 13, 2007, a new National Law of Education was passed. As a result, the unification of the Priority Cores of Learning (Núcleos de Aprendizajes Prioritarios) in the entire territory of the country was implemented.

One of the main objectives in the Brazilian education system is "to make possible greater reflection on and understanding of current reality." To achieve this objective, schools are given the "choice of didactic material, ability to elaborate the curriculum, and the professional development of the professors," according to the Brazil Secretariat of Basic Education in 1998. Brazilian national curriculum guidelines stipulate multicultural understanding and identity as main priorities, while special pedagogical projects can be developed at different levels in Brazilian schools with the contexts of different cultures and societies. Guidelines for Brazilian National Curricular Parameters "had been elaborated, on the one hand, to respect regional, cultural diversities, existing politics in the country and, on the other hand, to consider constructing common national references to the educative process in all the Brazilian regions." The government promotes the creation of school conditions that allow the younger generation to have access to socially elaborated knowledge, recognized as necessary in the exercise of citizenship.

International schools are the product of a globalized world. For example, international schools based on the Brazilian education system can be found in Angola, Japan, and the United States.

The Pitagoras System of education is at work in all the states of Brazil and in foreign countries that have ties to Brazil. Created in 1960, it is a nonprofit organization, having as its mission the improvement of the management of organizations contributing to the development of the quality of education, particularly with regard to educational curricula.

The second example is the Positive System of education. It initiated its activities in 1972 in Curitiba, Brazil, with a mission to offer preparatory courses for entrance to university. At the present time its focus is primarily the development of educational curriculum, didactic material, and methodology for teaching practices. Schools in the United States and Japan use its teaching materials and curricula, which are adapted to different societies, taking into account their cultures and traditions.

Disciplinary Curriculum Organizations

Curriculum organizations based in the disciplines are abundant. For example, the Biological Sciences Curriculum Studies, Center for Curriculum Development, in Colorado Springs, Colorado, is based on the natural sciences; the Center for Civic Education in Woodland Hills, California, is based in the discipline of civics.

The number of teachers' global websites has increased, especially those based on associations devoted to curriculum improvement in higher education—for example, the Staff and Educational Development Association in the United Kingdom and the International Consortium on Educational Development in Australia.

Further investigations should focus on the ways global curriculum organizations spread their products and knowledge. This can be done, for example, by analyzing their usage and the effects of new technologies on curriculum development; examining the implementation of multilingual headlines in educational periodicals; and developing lesson plans based on the kinds of powerful, higher-level concepts that exist in a truly multicultural curriculum.

Mariana Coolican

REFERENCES

Adamson, Bob, and Paul Morris. "Comparing Curricula." In *Comparative Education Research: Approaches and Methods*, ed. Mark Bray, Bob Adamson, and Mark Mason, 263–282. New York: Springer, 2007.

Anderson, Allison, et al. *Standards Put to the Test: Implementing the INEE Minimum Standards for Education in Emergencies, Chronic Crises and Early Reconstruction*. Humanitarian Practice Network, United Kingdom: Overseas Development Institute, No. 57, 2006.

Banks, James A. *An Introduction to Multicultural Education*. 4th ed. Upper Saddle River, NJ: Pearson Education, 2008.

Braslavsky, Cecilia, ed. *Textbooks and Quality Learning for All: Some Lessons Learned from International Experiences*. Studies in Comparative Education series. Geneva: UNESCO–IBE, 2006.

Gvirtz, Silvina. "Curricular Reforms in Latin America with Special Emphasis on the Argentine Case." *Comparative Education* 38:4 (2000): 453–459.

Inter-Agency Network for Education in Emergencies (INEE). *Minimum Standards for Education in Emergencies, Chronic Crises and Early Reconstruction*. London: DS Print/Redesign, 2006.

International Institute for Capacity Building in Africa. *Gender and Curriculum Issues in African Education, Bi-Annual Newsletter in English and French* 7:1 (June 2005): 5–6.

Pinar, William F., ed. *International Handbook of Curriculum Research*. Mahwah, NJ: Lawrence Erlbaum, 2003.

———. "Curriculum." In *Encyclopedia on Education and Human Development*, ed. Stephen J. Farenga and Daniel Ness, 3–39. Armonk, NY: M.E. Sharpe, 2005.

Sigsworth, Alan, and Karl J. Solstad. "Strategies for Planning the Curriculum." In *Making Small Schools Work: A Handbook for Teachers in Small Rural Schools*, 55–65. Addis Ababa, Ethiopia: UNESCO International Institute for Capacity Building in Africa, 2001.

Trueit, Donna, et al., eds. *The Internationalization of Curriculum Studies*. New York: Peter Lang, 2003.

US Department of Education, National Commission on Excellence in Education. *A Nation at Risk: The Imperative for Educational Reform*. April 1983. www.ed.gov/pubs/NatAtRisk.

GLOBAL HEALTH AND WELL-BEING ORGANIZATIONS

Globalization in recent years has had mixed effects on people's health. High economic growth and technological advancement have enhanced health and life expectancy in many populations. In contrast, global processes of change—including climate change, human migration, and economic and political instability—have affected the epidemiology of many diseases. Particularly, uneven economic growth worsens new patterns in the spread of infectious diseases to poor and disadvantaged populations. Although wealthier populations generally have a lesser burden of these diseases, the spread of both unhealthy dietary culture and sedentary lifestyles contributes to the spread of noncommunicable diseases (NCDs).

In fact, the world faces a global health crisis, characterized by an increasing disparity in health status among people, groups, and countries. The gaps in health status are widest between the poorest nations and middle- and high-income countries.

The rate of premature mortality has been accelerating in sub-Saharan Africa, some parts of eastern Europe and the former Soviet Union, and in war-torn countries such as Afghanistan, Iraq, and Sudan. This increase presents a sharp contrast to health advances achieved elsewhere, such as in newly industrialized countries. In spite of some health gains in poor countries, such as the near eradication of polio and the continuing decline in deaths from diarrhea diseases, these gains are almost offset by the high prevalence of HIV/AIDS.

Infectious diseases, which used to be the major hazard in industrialized countries, have been substantially reduced since the twentieth century by mass immunization, the use of antimicrobials, and the steady development of living standards. Today, however, infectious diseases remain a major public health problem in low-income developing countries. Continued progress in the public health sector is challenged in the face of emerging pathogens, such as HIV/AIDS, new influenza strains, and forms of diseases like tuberculosis that are resistant to existing treatments or antibiotics.

Noncommunicable diseases are predominant in

high-income countries, where population age and population risk factors change. However, NCDs are also increasing in low-income countries, which are, accordingly, faced with double burdens of diseases; before alleviating communicable diseases significantly, they are already challenged by NCDs.

Health Inequalities

Since World War II, average life expectancy has increased worldwide by about 20 years to 65 years; in particular, low- and middle-income countries have seen the highest increase rates. This advance reflects improved sanitation, access to clean water, and the diffusion of immunization and primary education.

Nevertheless, average life expectancy at birth ranges from 81.4 years for women in Western Europe, North America, Japan, Australia, and New Zealand down to 48.1 years for men in sub-Saharan Africa. sub-Saharan countries are affected most severely by HIV/AIDS; life expectancy fell by 20 years since the epidemic broke out there in the early 1990s. Furthermore, the resurgence of tuberculosis, which used to be well contained, is mainly induced by HIV-related susceptibility to opportunistic infection.

The World Health Organization (WHO) estimates that approximately 56.844 million people died in 2009. Of those who died, 8.1 million (14 percent) were children less than five years of age. Although these data represent a 6 percent drop in child mortality since 2000 (children constituted 20 percent of all who died in 2000), the Millennium Development Goals have not reached considerable success in lowering the incidence of child mortality as close as possible to zero percent. Of these child deaths, nearly 99 per cent occurred in developing countries and can be attributed to some preventable conditions—pneumonia, diarrhea diseases, malaria, measles, and malnutrition—that overlap and are worsened by poverty.

The global difference in average life expectancy is largely determined by mortality rates for children, especially in the first five years of life. Despite remarkable decreases in children's deaths under five years of age in low- and middle-income countries, gaps in child health between and within countries are growing. The average probability of dying before the age of five in sub-Saharan countries is about nine times that in Europe, according to UNICEF.

Maternal death rates are equally distressing; they are estimated to be more than 100 times higher in sub-Saharan Africa than in high-income countries.

The impact of gender on health inequalities is one of the most serious issues. Striking inequalities related to gender are observed in a number of low- and middle-income countries. The World Health Organization reports that, globally, girls five years or younger are more likely to have problems of obesity than boys of the same age—a problem that can significantly contribute to higher risk of diabetes, cardiovascular disease, some forms of cancer, and musculoskeletal conditions. It is clear that discrimination against female children persists, together with inequalities in access to health care services across low-income countries. On the other hand, there is complex evidence of growing gender inequalities against males. For example, in some parts of the former Soviet Union, life expectancy for males has fallen sharply and is ten years shorter than for females.

New Infectious Diseases

In the 1960s, the public health community envisaged that deaths from infection would be virtually eliminated by the end of the millennium. However, about 26 percent of the 57 million deaths in 2002 were attributed to communicable diseases caused by transmitted bacteria, viruses, protozoa, or multicellular parasites. The world of infectious diseases cannot be conquered once and for all because it is a constantly changing world that raises new challenges. Roughly 170 emerging infectious diseases (EIDs) have been identified. EIDs are either newly identified illnesses caused by a previously unknown pathogen, such as HIV, or old diseases reemerging as a significant threat. New disease-causing agents include HIV, hepatitis C, Nipah virus, Ebola virus, and *Borrelia burgdorferi*. At the same time, reemerging diseases that were believed to be under control, at least in high-income countries, have been rising in number and spreading regionally, often in more malicious forms (e.g., tuberculosis, plague, diphtheria, malaria, yellow fever, dengue fever, and cholera). The spread of drug-resistant strains of diseases such as tuberculosis and malaria is causing grave concern.

In 2003 a novel coronavirus was identified as the agent responsible for the epidemic of sudden acute respiratory syndrome (SARS), which spread to about

30 countries. The SARS epidemic illustrates the speed with which infection can now travel around the world due to increased air transport. In addition, Japanese encephalitis virus spread to Australia, possibly via mosquitoes that traveled in an aircraft. Cases of West Nile fever appeared even in eastern and western Europe and the United States. Oceangoing shipping is another route by which infection can spread globally.

Another contributor to the growing threat from infectious diseases is global climate change, which is widening the habitats for insect vectors such as mosquitoes, ticks, and rodents.

The list of health risks has to include infection from unsafe health-care practices, such as contaminated injections, blood transfusions, and organ transplants. About half a million deaths a year are associated with this cause, mainly because of transmission of blood-borne pathogens such as HIV and hepatitis B and C viruses.

Global Risk Factors for Noncommunicable Diseases

Reflecting their contagious nature, communicable diseases are frequently addressed in relation to globalization, but noncommunicable diseases are now the leading cause of death in the world. NCDs are estimated to account for 60 percent of the total number of deaths globally. In the future, NCDs will dominate the global pattern of death and disability. Even in low-income countries, NCDs are increasing not only among the highest income groups, but spreading into the poorest as well. Evidence worldwide shows that the global spread of risk factors (e.g., tobacco use and diet, physical inactivity and obesity) is higher in low-income populations than in the past.

Tobacco consumption now kills about 5 million people per year, and the death rates are rising. In China alone, annual deaths attributed to smoking are expected to rise three times by 2050. Tobacco related illness and diseases are shifting from high-income to low-income countries. Thus, these countries are expected to see a noticeable increase in tobacco-related diseases.

Dietary transitions are in progress in all but the low-income countries. A higher proportion of fatty and sugary foods and lower consumption of whole grains and vegetables increasingly characterize diet.

Energy intake from nutrients (e.g., sugar, fats) associated with NCDs is increasing, while consumption of protective factors (dietary fiber, micronutrients) is decreasing. This trend is emerging in various developing countries, too. In fact, the rapid increase of poor nutrition that contributes to NCDs among urban children below seven years is well confirmed.

Tobacco and dietary and nutrition transitions are all integrated under the global networks of tobacco industry and food production businesses. This highly developed system organizes efficient production, distribution, and consumption. Marketing campaigns by these companies promote a global brand in worldwide markets and are often tailored to diversified local preferences. The globally organized production system creates an environment where seemingly rich choices are substantially turned into narrow selections. This powerful marketing campaign easily targets children and teenagers. This is true not only for food and beverages, but also for tobacco.

Traffic Injuries

Traffic accidents cause the death of about 1.2 million people worldwide annually. About two-thirds of traffic-related deaths and the burden of disability from injuries are estimated to occur in low- and middle-income countries. The fatality rates per 10,000 vehicles are already 30 to 40 times greater in some developing countries than the average of high-income countries. Moreover, pedestrians, cyclists, and passengers on public transport are most affected; that is, traffic accidents within a population tend to be unevenly distributed on low-income people. Males are almost three times more likely to suffer injury or death on the road than are females. WHO projects that as the traffic volume continues to rise worldwide, over 80 percent of total road-traffic deaths will happen in developing countries in the coming decade or so.

Policy Directions

Concerning the highly complex agenda of public health, many international and national health policies have been developed over the last two decades. In particularly, the Millennium Development Goals (MDGs) and the Ottawa Charter for Health Promotion have been frequently referred to in the public health community and still receive considerable attention.

MDGs were established by the Organization for Economic Cooperation and Development (OECD) as a normative framework to guide policies and programs for global health efforts. The goals and targets are closely interrelated, promoting the vital link between health, development, and alleviation of poverty. The targets range from halving extreme poverty to halting the spread of HIV/AIDS and providing universal primary education, all by the target date of 2015. Therefore, achieving the MDGs demands determination by the international community to reduce health inequalities. Despite difficulties in achieving the goals, it is essential to continue to monitor progress against the indicators concerned. MDGs practically constitute a blueprint agreed to by all the world's countries and leading development institutions. They have galvanized unprecedented efforts to meet the needs of the world's poorest people.

An international conference in Ottawa in 1986 laid a foundation for improving people's health worldwide in the Ottawa Charter for Health Promotion, which is generally regarded as having promulgated a new public health policy worldwide, thereby endorsing the process of enabling people to increase control over and improve their health. The charter clarified five action areas: providing safe and supportive environments, developing healthy public policy, developing personal skills, promoting community action, and reorienting the health service. Thus, it concluded that the attainment of global health is not merely the business of health professionals, but that significant measures must be enhanced beyond the narrowly defined professional areas. These action areas demand collaborative partnerships across sectors and refocusing on the individual as a whole person who participates in health actions.

The Ottawa Charter is widely accepted as guiding principles for designing comprehensive health strategies and methodologies based on the five approaches. The critical importance of participatory and interdisciplinary approaches in public health is now much better understood.

Role of Governments

Governments all over the world have played a vital role in improving people's health. They have come to have a massive role in the financing, delivery, and regulation of health care. Government obligations in providing health care are essential to maintaining a sound regulatory environment in which public and private actors in health care work in an orderly, effective manner to improve people's welfare levels. The following general principles describe a government's roles in health care, at least based on experiences in high-income and middle-income countries.

First, governments are obliged to establish a set of policies on major components of the health sector and the direction of any reforms that may be required. Second, under the policies established, governments must properly regulate the health care sector to ensure adequate quality of care and effective mobilization of health resources. Third, governments gather and disseminate health information (which is certainly a public good). Along with this, the surveillance of disease and the identification of epidemics are also government responsibilities. Fourth, governments need to be involved in health finance as a central player, because governments have a crucial role to increase both public and private expenditures to a reasonable level. Equity is one of the main issues in health care provision.

However, many low-income countries with weak institutional capacity are unable to implement these principal roles of government. Thus, there is an immense need for innovative partnerships between the government domain and nongovernmental involvements. The Ottawa Charter suggests the importance of the five approaches; healthy public policies require the formulation of a good framework for coordinated action to foster equity. Creating a supportive environment emphasizes a socioecological approach to health in the form of reciprocal maintenance. This is connected with strengthening community action, which entails the empowerment of communities and their ownership of health efforts. Therefore, developing personal skills is crucial for increasing the options available to people to exercise more control over their own health. Accordingly, reorienting health services indicates that health sectors are obliged to pursue public health beyond conventional service provisions.

Global Partnerships for Health

There must be a general, strong commitment to cooperation between the government and nongovernment sectors. Our increasingly interrelated global society needs to establish an effective system for the prevention, control, and treatment of infectious diseases. It is necessary to break through traditional boundaries, between nation-states, within government and nongovernmental organizations (NGOs), and between the public and private sector. Diseases do not respect national borders, and a single state alone is unable to prevent their spread effectively. Well-functioning global health cooperation is essential to promoting international health.

The inequality problems with health status are closely linked to a widening gap in socioeconomic conditions among populations and limited institutional capacity of concerned governments. Limited access to health care is persistent as a significant factor at the very root of large-scale poverty. On the policy front, a wide range of factors contributes to this deterioration in global health, including distortion of health priorities at national and global levels; a narrow, top-down, service-oriented approach to health; coercive privatization of health services; and reduced government subsidies.

A multiplicity of actors in the global health arena, which could be a major strength, has at the same time become a complex problem because of the shortage in coordination among agencies and duplication of efforts on the international and national levels. These actors include international and national institutions, governmental agencies, and NGOs. Unfortunately, these actors often compete rather than cooperate with each other to formulate and establish values and rules for global governance.

For example, when governments of low-income countries need to allocate more funds for health expenditure, the International Monetary Fund (IMF), which is responsible for macroeconomic stability on a global scale, often advises them to reduce overall public expenditure and to balance their budgets. The influence of the World Bank and regional development banks has increased in the health sector, and their economic prescriptions have led to budgetary cutbacks of more than half in already lean health budgets of various developing countries. On the other hand, the World Health Organization (WHO), which is expected to be the directing and coordinating authority for health within the United Nations system, faces institutional capacity problems like other UN technical agencies. WHO officially states that it is responsible for providing leadership on global health matters, shaping the health research agenda, setting norms and standards, articulating evidence-based policy options, providing technical support to countries, and monitoring and assessing health trends. WHO has pointed out several crucial issues in relation to the World Bank–driven health policy; for example, continued warnings of indiscriminate privatization of the health sector; the concept of efficiency, which was emphasized excessively at the cost of equity; and so forth. Although WHO faces financial difficulties in keeping itself as the lead agency for world health, it is making some efforts to modify its organizational character to become a more energetic organization. The biomedical paradigm used to characterize the organization and its narrow mode of thinking; however, it is now promoting broad, intersectoral approaches to health and health-related problems, as expressed well in the Ottawa Charter and other declarations, such as the Jakarta Declaration on Health Promotion. WHO set up priorities for the twenty-first century around increased investment, expansion of partnership, social responsibility, sustainability, community capacity and empowerment, and the securing of an infrastructure for the promotion of health.

NGOs and Philanthropic Organizations for Global Health

Apart from the conventional setups and limited operational capacity of UN organizations, very well-funded NGOs or philanthropic organizations and innovative networks have emerged since the turn of the century. Interestingly, these new institutions have already come to play a powerful and influential role in international cooperation and coordination for global health. Some of them have an unprecedented financial position and operational capacity; the most notable examples are the Global Fund to Fight AIDS, Tuberculosis and Malaria and the Bill and Melinda Gates Foundation. On the research front, an innovative research network of health fields was created in Switzerland, the Council on Health Research for Development (COHRED).

The Global Fund to Fight AIDS, Tuberculosis and Malaria was created to finance a dramatic turnaround in the fight against these diseases. These diseases kill more than 6 million people each year, and the numbers are growing. To date, the Global Fund has committed US$10 billion in 136 countries to support aggressive interventions against all three diseases. The Global Fund is committed to relying on existing financial management, monitoring, and reporting systems, where possible. As a financing mechanism, the Global Fund works closely with other multilateral and bilateral organizations involved in health and development issues to ensure that newly funded programs are coordinated with existing ones. In many cases, these partners participate in local country coordinating mechanisms, providing important technical assistance during the development of proposals and implementation of programs.

The Bill and Melinda Gates Foundation was created in 2000 to reduce inequities in the United States and around the world. The foundation supports health, education, and other social development activities. The mission of its Global Health Program is to encourage the development of lifesaving medical advances and to ensure that they reach the people who are disproportionately affected. The Gates Foundation focuses its funding in two main areas: (1) access to existing vaccines, drugs, and other tools to fight diseases common in developing countries, and (2) research to develop new health solutions that are effective, affordable, and practical.

A global health research coordination initiative produced the Council on Health Research for Development in 1993 as an international organization with a strong network. COHRED builds the foundations of a new set of services for strengthening national health research for countries and the international community of development organizations and professionals that support health research. At the core of this approach is the creation of a set of services, approaches, and tools that countries can use to map, assess performance, and strengthen their systems for health research. COHRED also enables countries to put in place and use health research to foster health, health equity, and development. It works globally, prioritizing the poorest countries.

Unlike traditional international approaches, these forefront philanthropic organizations and their partners aim to bring together shared interests across nation-states, civil society, and the business community for a comprehensive effort to deal with persistent inequalities in health within and across countries. For example, both the Global Fund and the Gates Foundation work closely with other inter-national and national organizations involved in health and development issues to ensure that newly funded programs should be well coordinated with existing ones. On the other hand, COHRED operates in a way that strengthens institutions interested in working for health research for development (e.g., academic, research, governmental, or nongovernmental organizations). If there is a serious commitment to health research for development, COHRED collaborates and develops joint activities or even joint units or centers that can assist in implementing COHRED's mission and activities in several countries and regions. These institutions and networks are very likely to activate rules and mechanisms of the global partnership for health.

Yasuo Uchida

REFERENCES

Central Intelligence Agency. *World Factbook*. New York: Skyhorse, 2011.

UNICEF. *Levels and Trends in Child Mortality: Report 2010—Estimates Developed by the UN Inter-Agency Group for Child Mortality Estimation*. Paris: UNICEF, 2010.

World Health Organization. *Women's Health: Factsheet No. 334*. 2009. www.who.int/en/.

———. *The World Health Report: Health Systems Financing—The Path to Universal Coverage*. Geneva: WHO, 2010.

EDUCATIONAL ACTIVIST ASSOCIATIONS

The aim of educational activist associations is to advocate and foster political dialogue on various educational issues that are controlled by decision makers in the public sector. They may also deliver actual educational services both in formal and nonformal settings, but it is not always necessary for them to deal with these activities. Educational activist associations include teachers' unions, foundations, academic associations and societies, student organizations, and nongovernmental organizations (NGOs) working in diverse fields related to education. Although such NGOs may also be labeled as nonprofit organizations or private voluntary organizations, the term "NGO" refers to organizations that are both nongovernmental and nonprofit.

It should be noted that those organizations categorized as educational activist associations have been widely considered as important members of civil society. Thus, this section discusses the characteristics and roles of civil society organizations in the education sector in general and educational activist associations in particular.

It is also important to note that educational activist associations operate in both industrialized and developing countries. While some of them only conduct their activities domestically, many others expand their activities across domestic borders as well. Therefore, this section focuses on those educational activist associations operating internationally, particularly in the context of international cooperation in education in developing countries.

Civil Society Organizations and International Cooperation in Education

Civil society is becoming much more open globally, forming a community that goes beyond the borders of nation-states and is regarded as a medium for private bodies to fulfill public responsibilities. Civil society organizations conduct their activities in both public and private domains and are characterized both internationally and domestically by multiple organizations with different agendas, interests, and functions. It is important to note that the public regulations governing civil society organizations in carrying out their activities include not only regulations imposed by the state, but also those based on mutual agreement of the bodies comprising civil society. Under such voluntary self-regulation, the pursuit of private gain is kept in check and order is maintained among civil society organizations, including educational activist associations.

International cooperation in education is conducted on the basis of partnerships among different actors of diverse positions, namely governments of developing countries, bilateral and multilateral aid agencies, and civil society organizations. Among these actors, civil society organizations, including educational activist associations, have been playing considerably important roles in recent years.

The Dakar Framework for Action, which was adopted at the World Education Forum held in Dakar, Senegal, in April 2000, reaffirms the goals of Education for All (EFA) originally set at the World Conference on Education for All in Jomtien, Thailand, in 1990 to promote basic education, mainly in developing countries. This framework stresses that the promotion of basic education is a national and international responsibility since the provision of educational opportunities to fulfill basic learning needs is a guaranteed right of all children, young people, and adults. The framework also emphasizes that the engagement and participation of civil society should be ensured in the process of formulating, implementing, and monitoring the strategies for promoting education in developing countries. These expectations are discerned in the support that donors and the governments of developing countries have shown in developing various national education plans and strategies through a more transparent and democratic process involving the various stakeholders, which include representatives of the public, community leaders, parents, learners, NGOs, and other civil society organizations.

In line with such trends, the following three areas of activity have been recognized as conventional roles for civil society organizations: (1) as implementing agencies and service providers, particularly at the grassroots level, (2) as innovators who can make efforts that the public sector cannot as easily make, and (3) as informed critics of the public sector and advocates for public opinion. Today, in addition to these roles, civil society organizations have been increasingly recognized as policy partners for governments and international agencies. Many educational activist associations are also playing this role of being active policy partners, particularly through the international networks to be described later in this section.

Civil society should be regarded not only as a political domain but also as an arena for economic and social relationships. This approach leads to multiplicity within the definition of civil society. For instance, at the 46th Session of the International Conference on Education held in Geneva in September 2001, delegates from Africa drew attention to rich precolonial traditions with regard to civil society, strongly stating that "the wise people, the third generation, or traditional professional associations . . . are not as visible as modern NGOs in the eyes of international partners." Nevertheless, in African civil society, these are also important constituents of educational activist associations.

Networks of Educational Activist Associations

In recent international cooperation efforts in education promoted by civil society organizations, the most significant example of becoming policy partners for governments and international agencies is the formation of the Global Campaign for Education (GCE), a coalition of civil society organizations working in the field of education and related areas in both industrialized and developing countries. Prior to the World Education Forum, international educational activist associations, including Education International, Oxfam International, Global March Against Child Labor, ActionAid, and national NGO networks from Bangladesh, Brazil, and South Africa, strongly called for solidarity of the civil society. In response, the GCE was formed in 1999 to bring together major NGOs and teachers' unions in more than 150 countries around the world. Since then, many other major international, regional, and national groups active in the fields of education, human rights, social justice, and the eradication of poverty have joined the coalition.

The GCE, which engages in advocacy and lobbying in an attempt to ensuring that everyone in the world has the right to receive education, is a representative organization driven by its members. This campaign has been an important mechanism for expressing the views and opinions of civil society organizations, particularly for small, domestic organizations that normally do not have the means to send their messages to a wider audience, including governments and donor agencies.

Participation in the GCE is determined by the free will of its members. They come together once every three years at the World Assembly, where they discuss future directions of the campaign and elect members of the board. Although the board "makes policy decisions, oversees the development of campaign strategy, manages the budget and guides the work of a small secretariat," all members of the GCE are equal in theory and there is no institutional leader. Instead, the chair of the board represents the body at international conferences and similar events.

The GCE encourages and supports the formation of national platforms, bringing together community groups, unions, education NGOs, churches, young people, women, and other stakeholders to create broad-based citizen pressure for action on the EFA goals. The GCE has been very active in lobbying governments and donor agencies to encourage them to provide more financial support to promote basic education in developing countries. Moreover, in collaboration with the United Nations Educational, Scientific and Cultural Organization (UNESCO), the GCE supports the annual EFA Action Week, held every April to celebrate the anniversary of the World Education Forum, one of whose aims is to mobilize political leadership and communities in promoting EFA in many countries.

Another network of educational activist associations, the Collective Consultation of NGOs on Education for All (CCNGO/EFA), was set up by UNESCO after the World Education Forum in 2000 and functions alongside the other educational organizations. This network has been considered a vehicle for facilitating the participation of civil society organizations in international cooperation in education and a mechanism for reflecting the voice of civil society organizations in the policies of national governments and international agencies. Thus, similar to the functions of the GCE, this network aims at providing more people with the opportunity to communicate and exchange their views. The key difference between the CCNGO/EFA and GCE, even though members of these two networks overlap considerably, is that the former was created as an official channel with UNESCO mainly for consultations on UNESCO's roles to coordinate the global, regional, and national EFA movements, while the latter was developed through the initiatives of civil society organizations and covers a much wider area of interests and activities.

As of spring 2007, over 600 international, regional, and national NGOs have registered with CCNGO/EFA. These groups form a network for promoting EFA and regularly conduct opinion and information exchanges with international agencies centered on UNESCO. Members of the CCNGO/EFA have been invited to regional and global EFA meetings as well as other UNESCO consultation meetings and conferences. This is an indication that this network of civil society organizations is clearly regarded as an equal partner of state governments and international agencies.

Civil society organizations today are expected to play a wide range of roles, as mentioned above.

Thus, the importance of networks such as the GCE and CCNGO/EFA is likely to continue to increase among educational activist associations. Above all, greater diversity in the networks will be required. To this end, these networks are establishing voluntary regulations and structures based on mutual agreement among member organizations, while at the same time respecting flexible affiliation. They urge participation not only from large international NGOs, typified by Oxfam and ActionAid Alliance, but also from local NGOs in developing countries. With the growth of these networks, local NGOs are confronted with the need to maintain specific language abilities, in languages such as French, Spanish, and Arabic, but usually in English, the lingua franca of international discussions. Other practical impediments also exist that make it difficult for members to participate in such international networks.

While each network is eager to gather opinions at the grassroots level, the reality is that a certain kind of hierarchy is emerging among NGOs. Differences are also developing within this hierarchy between international and local NGOs. For example, staff members educated at graduate schools in Western countries or who have experience working for international agencies are increasing in many international NGOs, which raises the quality and competitiveness of the work carried out by these organizations. This is why reasonable discussions and assertions made by international NGOs are often readily understood by international agencies, but act as a detriment to local NGOs. Given this situation, further examination must be attempted of the public dimension of partnerships between civil society organizations and governments or international agencies.

For these networks of educational activist associations, the World Social Forum provides an important venue for people to share knowledge and experiences and exchange views and opinions not only with those in the education field but also those in many other fields of interest. As a counter arena to the World Economic Forum, an annual event in Davos, Switzerland, bringing together political and business leaders from around the globe since 1971, the World Social Forum mobilizes activists, social movements, networks, coalitions, and other progressive forces from all over the world who are concerned about the influences of neoliberalism ideology on the political and economic situations facing vulnerable people in many societies.

The first meeting of the World Social Forum, held in Pôrto Alegre, Brazil, in January 2001, was attended by about 20,000 people from over 100 countries. At the annual global forum as well as regional and thematic forums, participants discuss a variety of issues, including economic justice, human rights, youth and women, the environment, and labor. Among various economic, political, and social issues discussed at the World Social Forum, education, including issues of child labor, is often considered one of the most important topics for many societies. A significant number of educational activist associations taking part in the GCE and CCNGO/EFA are joining these forums as a way to share with a wider audience their views and experiences concerning the promotion of education around the world.

Student Political Activism

Because there is no prevailing theoretical explanation for student political activism, the issue is fraught with complexity. It is important, however, for political leaders, academic communities, and activists themselves to be aware of the history, politics, and potential of student political activities because of the impact these activities have in many countries, particularly in developing countries.

Many years ago, American sociologist C.W. Mills saw in intellectuals and students a major potential mass base for emerging political movements. Today, intellectuals and students remain a source of new radical leadership and mass support. In a chapter of *The Student Revolution* (1970), Seymour Lipset points out that students' politics are affected to a considerable degree by the social position and political values of the intellectual community in their countries, because "intellectuals who are resentful of their society often stimulate rebellious 'apprentice intellectuals'—students."

Student movements have occupied an important position among various agents of social change. Student political activities have sometimes led in forcing changes in national policies or overthrowing governments and have been instrumental in various kinds of cultural revivals. Particularly, this has happened in many developing countries. As Philip Altbach points out, "the achievement of independence after World War II for many of the developing countries brought substantial change for the student movement." Political leaders in these countries are normally more interested in training manpower to develop their country's social and economic conditions than in supporting student political activism. Furthermore, student political activism is usually restricted or even suppressed because a strong, independent student movement is seen to oppose the governing regimes.

It is thus important to distinguish between student political activism in industrialized countries and similar movements in developing countries. In general, students in developing countries have always been, and remain, a major political force. Student activists in developing countries have sustained their political influence in society, which places them in a significantly different position compared to their counterparts in industrialized countries. Student political activism focuses on key political issues, particularly in developing countries, and sometimes even leads to the downfall of a regime. In many developing countries where students have an established place in the society's political sphere, their political activities are often seen as a normal part of the political system. On the other hand, students in industrialized countries are generally not seen as legitimate political actors, and society and established authorities both have much less tolerance for student political activism.

It should also be noted that student activism is generally antiestablishment, but not necessarily leftist. In many developing countries, nationalism has been leftist in orientation, often influenced by Marxism. However, as Altbach emphasizes, students are "cultural nationalists" and not necessarily leftist in orientation. Thus, student organizations, an important form of educational activism in many developing countries, often try to represent the mass public and assert the importance of respecting traditional values and strengthening national identity rather than westernizing their society and promoting economic growth in their country.

Intellectual Contributions of Educational Activist Associations

It is essential for intellectuals conducting research and fieldwork in education to recognize the importance of mentality and morality. We find intellectuals not only in academic associations and societies as expected, but in other forms of educational activist associations as well. Intellectuals are not only education specialists who limit themselves within their specific interests and/or disciplines, but also responsible persons who constructively criticize the way education is promoted by society.

An intellectual can be defined as a person who has the ability to maintain a critical attitude toward the existing social system of education promotion, to examine it intellectually and comprehensively, to show how it should be changed if necessary, and to express opinions persuasively. Through these activities, intellectuals always need to be critical not only of the existing social system of promoting education but also of their philosophical stances as intellectuals. Recognizing the importance of such an attitude of intellectuals who work in the field of education, Henry Giroux claims in *Border Crossings* (2005) that intellectual educationalists need to play their roles as "cultural workers" who stand for and connect to people. Intellectual educationalists working in educational activist associations are no exception; they are always seeking ways they can contribute to their society.

As important members of civil society, educational activist associations are expected to provide intellectual as well as practical contributions to society in order to promote and improve educational conditions around the world, particularly in developing countries, through international cooperation in the education sector. For this purpose, educational activist associations need to continue playing their roles in advocacy and promoting political dialogue with decision makers on emerging and challenging issues in the education sector in all corners of the globe.

Yuto Kitamura

REFERENCES

Altbach, Philip G. "Perspectives on Student Political Activism." In *Student Political Activism: An International Reference Handbook*, ed. P.G. Altbach, 1–17. New York: Greenwood Press, 1989.

———, ed. *The Student Revolution: A Global Analysis*. Bombay: Lalvani, 1970.

Collective Consultation of Non-Governmental Organizations on Education for All (CCNGO/EFA). www.unesco.org/education.

Giroux, Henry A. *Border Crossings: Cultural Workers and the Politics of Education*. New York: Routledge, 2005.

Global Campaign for Education (GCE). www.campaignforeducation.org.

Lipset, Seymour M. "Students and Politics in Comparative Perspective." In *The Student Revolution: A Global Analysis*, ed. P.G. Altbach, 29–49. Bombay: Lalvani, 1970.

UNESCO. *The Dakar Framework for Action. Education for All: Meeting Our Collective Commitments*. Paris: UNESCO, 2000.

———. *Synthesis Report: Special Session on the Involvement of Civil Society in Education for All*. Paris: UNESCO, 2001.

Walzer, Michael. *Toward a Global Civil Society*. Oxford: Berghahn Books, 1995.

World Social Forum India. www.wsfindia.org.

TEACHERS COLLEGES

Teachers colleges are educational institutions intended for training teachers, with the purpose of establishing teaching standards. The role of teachers colleges is to foster the development of personnel with wide visions and broad expertise, who can act as leaders and contribute to establishing school education systems. As Susan Fuhrman, the president of Teachers College, Columbia University, indicates, the founding vision of the oldest teachers college in the United States was to provide educational opportunities to all members of society. It is a simple but fundamental statement of the role of teacher education.

With the advent of the new century, teacher education has become increasingly complex in modern society. This trend makes the discipline of education more than a system of vocational knowledge and expertise to be acquired by students who wish to become teachers. Teacher education is now expected to display its unique characteristics and contribute to human civilization. Besides, teacher education also aims to prepare students for careers in fields other than education.

The teachers college, department of education, or faculty of education in a university usually draws on a wide range of research strategies and traditions and has a commitment to conducting research of high quality and practical value for cultivating teachers. Listed below are descriptions of the educational studies at 18 universities spread across five continents. These institutions represent the oldest and largest colleges and universities of education in the world, as well as those highly regarded in terms of educational research and scholarship.

Europe

The Faculty of Education at the University of Cambridge and the Institute of Education (IOE) at the University of London are good cases to analyze. As one of the oldest universities and most important centers for teaching and research in the world, Cambridge is famous for its heritage of scholarship; the Faculty of Education reflects a strategy of future teacher education. IOE at the University of London has long been recognized as a leading center of education studies, hosts over 100 research projects, and is an intellectually rich and diverse learning community.

University of Cambridge

In 1891 the University of Cambridge set up the Day Training College for Teachers in Cambridge; Oscar Browning served as the first principal from 1891 to 1909. In 1911 Day Training College for Teachers changed its name to the Cambridge University Training College for School Masters.

From then on, teacher education has existed on the campus of Cambridge. The Training College for School Masters became the Department of Education in 1939. In 1968 it was reconstituted as the Faculty of Education and in 1997 as the School of Education. The Education Tripos was inaugurated in 1979. The degree of master of philosophy in education was established in 1981. The MEd, formerly offered by the Institute of Education, was taken on by the university on amalgamation with the Institute in 1992. The Faculty of Education was reinstated in August 2001. In 2004 a new home opened for the Faculty of Education on a site next to Homerton College in Cambridge.

The wide range of expertise in the faculty covers all stages of formal education. The faculty's teaching programs are basically divided into two broad categories. The first category integrates courses that concentrate on the academic study of the process of education itself. The second category involves courses of teacher education, either at the initial level or through the continuing professional development of those already in the teaching profession.

For the undergraduate degree program, the faculty provides a joint-honors degree combining the study of education with another subject. The aims of the program are (1) to draw on a wide range of intellectual resources, theoretical perspectives, and academic disciplines to provide an understanding of education and the contexts in which it takes place; (2) to enable students to study the foundation disciplines of education and to appreciate their contribution to educational policy and the process and practice of education; and (3) to equip students with the skills to conduct research and enquiry within the field of education, thus enabling them to pursue postgraduate study in education.

The master of philosophy program is aimed at students who aspire to positions of professional leadership and responsibility or careers in educational research. The master of education program offers educational development for experienced teachers, lecturers, and others with substantial ability. The PhD program aims to develop research skills and in-depth knowledge within a particular field; it involves the completion of a substantial piece of original research.

Institute of Education, University of London

The Institute of Education was founded in 1902 to deliver high-quality training for teachers by the London County Council. As the London Day Training College (LDTC), it opened on October 6, 1902, with fifty-eight students. The college was open to "duly qualified students of either sex who were engaged in, or intended to enter, any branch of the teaching profession; or who were making a special study of the theory, history and practice of education."

Professor Sir John Adams was the first principal of the London Day Training College from 1902 to 1922. Professor Sir Percy Nunn succeeded Adams as second principal in 1922, by which time the LDTC had become the "intellectual and professional centre for London's teachers." In 1932, after 30 years, LDTC converted into a member of the federation of the University of London, when it received its present name. Nunn retired in 1936 and was succeeded by Fred Clarke as director. From 1948 to 1975, the institute developed into a multipurpose organization, undertaking research, advanced studies, and overseas work, as well as initial training. The IOE was granted a royal charter in 1988.

As a graduate college of the federal University of London, it is a distinguished center of excellence for research, teacher training, higher degrees, and consultancy in education and education-related areas of social science. The IOE offers an unrivalled range of part-time, full-time, and distance-learning postgraduate courses, including initial teacher education, further professional development, and research degree programs.

The IOE has the largest education research body and portfolio of postgraduate programs in education in the United Kingdom. As it looks ahead, the IOE is increasingly taking advantage of new technologies for teaching and learning, offering students additional opportunities for interaction and engagement, and greater flexibility in access to courses. The IOE's mission is to pursue excellence in education and related areas of social science and professional practice. To this end, it plans to engage in the promotion of new ideas in policy and professional practice grounded in its research and teaching expertise, and consultancy and other services to support and develop the quality of educational systems and related fields of policy and practice.

North America

As the oldest and largest graduate school of education in the world, Teachers College at Columbia University is an institution with a rich and distinguished record in the field of education. The college plays a leading role in the United States in devising, designing, and implementing education reforms. The School of Education at Stanford University advocates the integration of practice and research by maintaining close collaborations with administrators, teachers, and policy makers. Additionally, pioneer courses are always emphasized by the school. The Faculty of Education of the University of British Columbia in Canada is a cross-disciplinary body that provides instruction, research, and public service; in instruction and research sectors, the faculty prepares professionals for practice in a wide range of education-related fields from preschool through adulthood.

Teachers College, Columbia University

Teachers College of Columbia University was founded in 1887 by Grace Hoadley Dodge, a philanthropist, and Nicholas Murray Butler, a philosopher, as the

New York School for the Training of Teachers. Butler was appointed as its first president. The founders recognized that professional teachers need reliable knowledge about the conditions under which children learn most effectively. They insisted that education must be combined with clear ideas about ethics and the nature of a good society. In 1892 a permanent charter was granted and the name changed to Teachers College. Teachers College became affiliated with Columbia University as a professional school for the training of teachers in 1898, with James Earl Russell named as dean of the college. Since then, Teachers College has served as a comprehensive school of education as an affiliate of Columbia University.

It is worth mentioning that Dean Russell developed four goals of teacher education that would guide Teachers College in its work: general culture, special scholarship, professional knowledge, and technical skills. In 1899 the first PhD degree was conferred on a Teachers College student; in 1935 the first EdD degree was conferred. The Institute of International Studies was established in 1964, and the Institute for Urban and Minority Education in 1973. The Institute for Education and the Economy and the Institute for Learning Technologies were established in 1986. The National Center for Restructuring Education, Schools, and Teaching was established in 1990, and Hechinger Institute on Education and the Media in 1997.

Now Teachers College is the largest and most comprehensive graduate and professional school of education in the United States, primarily embracing the disciplines of psychology, health, and education. The college offers master of arts (MA), master of education (EdM), master of science (MS), doctor of education (EdD), and doctor of philosophy (PhD) degrees to students selected.

It is worth mentioning that Teachers College offers the Programs in International Educational Development (IED) and Comparative and International Education (CIE). IED is based on a concentration in a professional field of education, while the CIE program is based on a concentration in an academic discipline within the social sciences. There are primarily three types of professions that graduates of the programs pursue: educational research, international development work, or the general field of education.

In the field of research, many graduates of CIE continue doing comparative educational studies, working for such national and international organizations as the American Educational Research Association (AERA), Educational Resources Information Center (ERIC), and the Organization for Economic Cooperation and Development (OECD). In the field of international development, graduates choose to work in such nongovernmental organizations as the Academy for Educational Development, Africare, CARE International, Catholic Relief Services, I-EARN, International Rescue Committee, Lutheran World Relief, Save the Children, World Teach, or World Vision. Many also work in government or government-affiliated organizations such as the World Bank and the United Nations.

Stanford University

The Stanford University School of Education, also known as SUSE, was founded in 1891. The Department of History and Art of Education, one of 21 original departments at Stanford University, was renamed the School of Education in 1917. In 1916 the first PhD degree was conferred on an education student, and the first EdD was granted in 1929. In addition, the Stanford Teacher Education Program was established with funding from the Ford Foundation.

The Stanford International Development Education Center (SIDEC) was established with funding from the Department of Education of the United States and the Ford Foundation in 1965; the teaching objective of SIDEC is to encourage foreign nationals to return to their countries and establish effective educational systems. The Stanford Institute of Behavioral Counseling was founded in 1969 to provide educated students with an opportunity to obtain counseling experience under the supervision of faculty; the Center for Educational Research at Stanford was constructed as part of a national network of educational research centers in 1972.

The Center for Research on the Context of Teaching was founded in 1987. The Stanford Center on Adolescence and the National Center for Postsecondary Improvement were established in 1996 to research topics related to national and global changes in the environment for postsecondary education. The School Redesign Network was founded in 2001.

The Stanford University School of Education highlights education as concerned with the development of physical and interpersonal skills, emotional and attitudinal predispositions, character formation and work habits, as well as cognitive abilities and subject-matter expertise. The school offers numerous bachelors, masters and doctoral degree programs, which prepare students for leadership roles in groundbreaking, cross-disciplinary inquiry that shape educational practices around the globe.

The school is committed to developing new knowledge, ensuring the usefulness of the knowledge produced, and enhancing training opportunities for students. For this purpose, doctoral students work with faculty as part of a research team. Furthermore, the school provides help for students in gaining field experience and locating internships that will enhance opportunities for employment upon graduation. Master's students are encouraged to pursue individual research projects.

University of British Columbia

The University of British Columbia (UBC) was built in 1908, with a Vancouver campus located at the western tip of the Point Grey Peninsula, close to the city of Vancouver in British Columbia, Canada. UBC provides instruction, research, and public service that contribute to the economic, social, and cultural progress of the people of British Columbia and Canada.

The Faculty of Education at UBC prepares professionals for practice in a wide range of education-related fields from preschool through adulthood. The faculty consists of four departments: Department of Curriculum Studies; Department of Educational and Counseling Psychology, and Special Education; Department of Educational Studies; and Department of Language and Literacy Education.

The Department of Educational Studies was formed in July 1994, through the amalgamation of the former Department of Administrative, Adult and Higher Education with the Department of Social and Educational Studies. It offers PhD, EdD, MA, and MEd degrees. The PhD and MA degrees are intended for students wanting to pursue educational research either professionally or out of personal interest. The EdD and MEd degrees are designed primarily for students wishing to pursue professional study in education or to prepare for positions of leadership in varied settings.

Oceania

Most colleges of education in New Zealand have gradually amalgamated in recent years. For instance, the Massey University College of Education was established after the merger of the Faculty of Education and Palmerston North College of Education in 1996. The Faculty of Education at the University of Auckland was created through the combination of the former Auckland College of Education and the University's School of Education on September 1, 2004.

Wellington College of Education and Victoria University of Wellington formally merged on January 1, 2005. The University of Otago and the Dunedin College of Education officially merged and the new University of Otago College of Education came into being on January 1, 2007. In that same year, the Christchurch College of Education amalgamated with the University of Canterbury. These mergers in New Zealand created a very strong faculty with teaching and research expertise in teacher education and support and the study of education.

The University of Sydney was the first university established in Australia, and it has an international reputation for teacher education. The Faculty of Education at the University of Melbourne is one of the largest institutes in the university; its international links with research institutions ensure faculty major contributions to knowledge and practice in education.

University of Sydney

The University of Sydney was the first university to be established in Australia, in October 1850, with the inauguration ceremony on October 11, 1852. The first teacher training college in Australia was established in the city of Sydney in the late nineteenth century. In 1906 several teachers colleges were combined to form Sydney Teachers College. The first chair in education at the university was inaugurated in 1911, when the principal of Sydney Teachers College, Alexander Mackie, became a professor of education in the Faculty of Arts.

In 1940 the Education Department was established in the Faculty of Arts. In 1986 the Faculty of Education was born comprising three schools: the School of Teaching and Curriculum Studies; the School of

Educational Measurement, Psychology and Technology; and the School of Social and Policy Studies in Education. The founding dean of the Faculty of Education was Professor Cliff Turney.

In 1990 the Sydney Institute of Education was amalgamated with the Faculty of Education. In 1998 the Faculty of Education was restructured to form three new schools: the School of Educational Psychology, Literacy and Learning; the School of Professional Studies; and the School of Social, Policy and Curriculum Studies. In 2001 the faculty was again restructured to form two schools: the School of Development and Learning and the School of Policy and Practice. In 2003 the Department of Social Work was compounded with the Faculty of Education to form the School of Social Work and Policy Studies in the new Faculty of Education and Social Work in 2003. In January 2006 it was restructured to form a one-school faculty.

The daily work of the Faculty of Education and Social Work is administered through seven divisions: the Division of Graduate Studies, the Division of International Relations, the Division of Professional Learning, the Division of Research, the Division of Teaching and Learning, the Division of Undergraduate Studies, and the Division of Professional Experiences.

University of Melbourne

Very early in the history of the colony of Queen Victoria, the legislation establishing the University of Melbourne was introduced late in 1852 and passed early in 1853. The foundation was laid in July 1854, and the first four professors arrived early in 1855.

After World War II, with a growing demand for higher education, the University of Melbourne transformed from a small to a large institution offering diverse courses. During the 1980s and 1990s, the university merged with a number of colleges, including Melbourne College of Advanced Education and Victorian College of the Arts, enhancing the university's role as a broadly based teaching and research institution.

The Faculty of Education is one of the University of Melbourne's largest faculties, and it covers every aspect of education and training. With its responsibility through teaching and research to advance and disseminate knowledge in the field of education and

training, the faculty provides both undergraduate and postgraduate courses to those aiming to teach in preschools, primary and secondary schools, post-secondary schools, and other educational institutions and to contribute to the design, development, administration, or policy formulation of education and training programs and institutions.

The objective of the faculty is to improve education theory and practice by promoting research and development programs. The faculty has access to a comprehensive network within the wider education community, including school principals, teachers, school course advisers, educational organizations, government bodies, and other educational institutions.

The aim of the bachelor of education program in the faculty is to qualify students for registration and employment as generalist teachers in primary schools. Master's qualifications can be taken as either coursework or research degrees, depending on whether students wish to complete a thesis. Doctoral degrees seek to develop graduates who demonstrate academic leadership, increasing independence, creativity, and innovation in their research work.

Africa

In Africa, teachers are faced with an educational transition; from precolonial times to the postcolonial period, the teacher has always been respected in African societies. Teacher education in Africa plays the role of social and economic development. As one of the top teacher-training institutes, Kenyatta University's teacher education program in Kenya is one of the largest education schools in sub-Saharan Africa. Makerere University in Uganda was a university affiliated with the University College of London from 1949 to 1963. The School of Education on its campus offers diversified programs and has connections with several international universities. The University of Pretoria is one of the leading research universities in South Africa, offering diversified academic programs in two of the official languages, Afrikaans and English; it comprises the most diverse Faculty of Education in South Africa. The University of the Western Cape (UWC) is another South African university, whose Faculty of Education supports the general positioning of UWC as a partner in the broad democratic movement for political change in South

Africa. The mission statement of UWC portrays the university as "committed to excellence in teaching and research, to responding in critical and creative ways to the needs of a society in transition. Drawing on its proud experience in the liberation struggle, the university is aware of a distinctive academic role in helping build an equitable and dynamic society."

Kenyatta University

Kenyatta University is located about 14 miles from the city of Nairobi. Kenyatta College, the university's forerunner, was founded in 1965. In its early days, it was divided into two sections, the Secondary Education Division (SED) and the Teacher Education Division (TED). The Teacher Education Division offered the three-year Post-Ordinary Secondary Teacher's Certificate and a one-year Post-Advanced Secondary Teacher's Certificate.

In 1970, following an Act of Parliament announcement, Kenyatta College became a constituent college of the University of Nairobi. In 1972 the name changed from Kenyatta College to Kenyatta University College—the year when the first class of 200 matriculated students had begun the bachelor of education degree program. In July 1978, the Faculty of Education of the University of Nairobi moved to Kenyatta University College Campus. The Kenyatta University status was achieved on August 23, 1985; the new university was inaugurated on December 17, 1985.

The School of Education in Kenyatta University is the oldest institution in Kenya. It includes 30 academic programs and seven departments: Department of Educational Administration Planning and Curriculum Development, Department of Early Childhood Studies, Department of Educational Communication and Technology, Department of Education Foundation, Department of Library Studies, Department of Educational Psychology, and Department of Special Education.

The School of Education also runs the Kenya School Improvement Project, which was developed out of the need to uplift the educational standards of primary school teachers. The School of Education has established cooperation with the education departments of other institutions of higher education in the region, such as Makerere University, Kyambogo University in Uganda, and Dar es Salaam University in Tanzania.

Kenyatta University's main role is to help students achieve their potential and become what they want to be and what society needs them to be. The objectives are to promote the development and expansion of higher education opportunities through initiation of new programs and alternative modes of delivery, using, among other things, modern technologies. The aim is also to provide facilities in collaboration with other institutions for enhancing access to higher education. The university vision is to be "a dynamic, an inclusive and a competitive centre of excellence in teaching, learning, research and service to humanity."

Makerere University

Makerere University was established in 1922 as a technical school and later renamed Uganda Technical College; located on Makerere Hill, in the capital city of Uganda, it is one of the largest institutions of higher learning in eastern and central Africa. After opening its doors to 14 day students who studied carpentry, it expanded over the years to become a university college affiliated with University College of London in 1949 and then became the University of East Africa on June 29, 1963, the same day it ended the intimate relationship with the University of London. On July 1, 1970, Makerere became an independent national university of Uganda, offering undergraduate and postgraduate courses.

The School of Education in Makerere University is committed to excellence in teaching, learning, and research, to nurturing the cultural diversity of Uganda, and to responding in critical and creative ways to the needs of a society in transition. The aims of the school are to design curricula and research programs appropriate for the Ugandan context; to assist educationally disadvantaged students to gain access to higher education; to seek racial and gender equality and help the historically marginalized participate fully in the life of the nation; to conserve and explore the environmental and cultural resources of the Ugandan region, and to encourage a wide awareness of them in the community; and to produce competent teachers, lecturers, education managers, and administrators to carry out various activities that support education and country development.

The School of Education, which offers day and evening programs to students, is currently comprised of six departments: Department of Curriculum, Teaching and Media; Department of Educational Foundations and Management; Department of Higher Education; Department of Language Education; Department of Social Sciences and Arts Education; and Department of Science and Technical Education.

Makerere University has a vision "to be a center of academic excellence" and a mission "to provide quality teaching, carry out research and offer professional services to meet the changing needs of society in Uganda."

University of Pretoria

The University of Pretoria has its origins in the establishment of the Pretoria Centre of Transvaal University College in 1908. The college opened its doors as an Afrikaans language institution housed in Kya Rosa and started off with four professors, three lecturers, and 32 enrolled students. On October 10, 1930, an act of Parliament changed the name to the University of Pretoria. The university currently offers courses in both English and Afrikaans and has transformed from a mainly white, Afrikaner institution to a multicultural and multiracial university.

The Faculty of Education is the largest facility in South Africa for the initial and advanced training of education professionals. The bachelor of education program in the Faculty of Education offers training at all levels of schooling and in all the major subject areas. Additionally, students for the MEd degree must have a minimum of one academic year for the research program or two years for the course-work packages. After one year as PhD doctoral candidates, students must have a minimum duration of study at the university of at least two years after complying with all the requirements for a master's degree

The mission of the Faculty of Education in the future is to create flexible, lifelong learning opportunities; enable students to become well-rounded, creative people, responsible, productive citizens, and future leaders; undertake active and constructive involvement in community development and service; and contribute to the prosperity, competitiveness, and quality of life in South Africa.

University of the Western Cape

The University of the Western Cape, located in the northern suburbs of greater Cape Town in the city of Tygerberg, was established in 1959 as a constituent college of the University of South Africa for people classified as "Colored." The first group of 166 students enrolled in 1960. The university has a long history of its creative struggle against oppression, discrimination, and disadvantage. Through the University of the Western Cape Act of 1983, the university gained its autonomy.

The Faculty of Education was one of the first faculties in the university with its main task being the training of "colored" teachers only for "colored" secondary schools. The Teacher In-Service Project was established in the early 1990s as a nongovernmental organization working from UWC.

The university introduced four-year, school-based BSc (education) and BEd qualifications in 2004. Facing the new era, the university's primary aim is to create and maintain a sense of hope for the nation while helping to build an equitable and dynamic society.

The Faculty of Education at the University of the Western Cape offers a wide range of professional and academic programs at undergraduate and postgraduate levels. The bachelor of education program consists of modules in a variety of areas. The master's degree offers students the opportunity to pursue more advanced studies in education and to conduct independent research. Students have two approaches to obtain their master's degree; they may conduct independent research work, writing a full thesis, or they may follow a structured program, which includes courses and a mini-thesis or research paper. The doctoral degree in education is for students who are well established in their fields to undertake advanced and original research.

Asia

In addition to the Department of Education, international cooperation studies in education are very special courses in Japan. These programs aim to cultivate quality human expertise in international cooperation and to contribute to educational development in developing countries. The Graduate School of International Cooperation Studies (GSICS) at Kobe University, the Graduate School for International Development and Cooperation (IDEC) at Hiroshima University, and the Graduate School of International Development (GSID) at Nagoya University play a large and significant role in international cooperation education.

The term "normal school" is translated from the French *école normale*. In China, Taiwan, and the Philippines, the term "normal university" or "normal college" refers to a teachers university or teachers college: for example, National Taiwan Normal University, Beijing Normal University, South China Normal University, and Philippine Normal University. The purpose of the normal university is to train teachers, chiefly for the elementary grades. Other universities in the region also offer teacher-training courses in their education departments. For example, National Chengchi University in Taiwan has earned a reputation as an institution of higher education celebrated for its studies in its College of Education.

Hiroshima University

Hiroshima University was established in May 1949 by combining eight prewar educational institutions in Hiroshima Prefecture. This venture included Hiroshima School of Secondary Education, Hiroshima School of Education, Hiroshima Women's School of Secondary Education, and Hiroshima School of Education for Youth, and others.

As one of the two centers for training middle-school teachers in Japan, Hiroshima School of Secondary Education, founded in 1902, had a distinguished name before World War II. The present Hiroshima University, which was basically created by the training institutions for teachers, today continues to hold an important position in these fields in Japan.

The Faculty of Education covers all aspects of education from preschool teaching to higher education, as well as lifelong learning. Besides being based on the key concept of learning, the Graduate School of Education has an objective of establishing a new system for a broad range of educational sciences. The Faculty of Education's goal is to foster personnel with wide vision and broad expertise, who can act as leaders and contribute to establishing school education systems and learning societies suitable for the new century.

In international cooperation studies, Hiroshima University maintains the purpose to contribute to the creation of new educational science and to develop international cooperation on education. The campus possesses the Center for the Study of International

Cooperation in Education (CICE) and the Graduate School for International Development and Cooperation (IDEC). CICE was established in April 1997 with the aim of providing action-oriented research and training related to educational development in developing countries in order to contribute to the effective and efficient implementation of Japanese educational aid. The mission of IDEC is the construction of a theoretical framework and a practical methodology of international cooperation.

Research activities in CICE focus on a variety of issues and topics, including the following: educational cooperation in sub-Saharan African countries; educational cooperation policies of major developed countries and international organizations; and the promotion of education for women and the underprivileged in developing countries. In addition, IDEC courses cover two divisions: (1) the Division of Development Science and (2) the Division of Educational Development and Cultural and Regional Studies Student Complement. The Division of Development Science has three sub-institutes, which are the Department of Development Policy, the Department of Development Technology, and the Department of Peace and Coexistence. The Division of Educational Development and Cultural and Regional Studies Student Complement has two sub-institutes, which are the Department of Educational Development and the Department of Cultural and Regional Studies.

Kobe University

The Graduate School of International Cooperation Studies (GSICS) at Kobe University was established in 1992. It has been directly engaged in practical contributions to the international community, with the aim of contributing to the development of the international community by cultivating the capabilities of students who are interested in pursuing careers in international cooperation. GSICS offers four education and research programs: International Studies, Development and Economics, International Law and Institution Building, and Political Science.

The education studies in GSICS emphasize development of both expertise and multidisciplinary knowledge. The school offers unique overseas internships and training opportunities for students as a formal class with credit in international and other development organizations in many different countries, including Cambodia, Indonesia, Laos, Switzerland, Tanzania, Yemen, and Zambia. In addition, some students have also taken part in internships in the World Bank, Inter-American Development Bank, UNICEF, Japan International Cooperation Agency (JICA), and Japan Bank for International Cooperation (JBIC).

GSICS offers masters and doctoral programs in both Japanese and English. Moreover, Yemen Project, Laos Project, and Young Leaders' Program are significant ongoing educational and research activities in GSICS. The Yemen Project, initiated in 2005 as a joint venture with a development consultancy firm, has been working toward the development of girls' education in the Tail Governorate in Yemen. This project has provided both teaching staff and students the opportunity to participate. Through different activities, GSICS provides students with opportunities to gain practical work experience in international cooperation. Graduates of GSICS have participated in a diverse spectrum of professional jobs, including NGOs, the World Bank, United Nations organizations, and national and local governments in the education and welfare sectors.

The University of Tokyo

Established in 1877, the highly reputable University of Tokyo is the oldest university in Japan. As a representative of Japan, it has greatly contributed to the development of the modern state. After World War II, recognizing the necessity of developing educational sciences, the Faculty of Education, which had existed within the Faculty of Literature since 1919, was founded in 1949 as its own faculty. The Graduate School of Education adjunct to the faculty was founded in 1953.

The Faculty of Education offers six courses to undergraduate students which are the same as graduate school courses: History and Philosophy of Education; Social Sciences in Education; Educational Psychology; Teaching, Curriculum, and Learning Environments; Lifelong Educational Planning; and Physical and Health Education. The Graduate School offers a master's program, a PhD program, and the Foreign Research Student Program. Candidates for the Foreign Research Student Program are sometimes already enrolled in a PhD program outside of Japan.

National Taiwan Normal University

The forerunner of the National Taiwan Normal University (NTNU) was founded in 1946 as the Taiwan Provincial Teachers College and changed its name to NTNU in 1967. The goal of the university is to train qualified secondary education teachers. NTNU is composed of 28 academic departments and 24 separate graduate institutes, divided into seven distinct colleges.

The College of Education includes seven departments. The Department of Education was established in June 1946, with the mission to cultivate students for schoolteachers, academic researchers, school administrators, and educational administrators. The other departments are the Department of Educational Psychology and Counseling; Department of Adult and Continuing Education; Department of Health Education; Department of Human Development and Family Studies; Department of Civil Education and Leadership; and Department of Special Education. Furthermore, the Mandarin Training Center at NTNU, established in 1956, offers language courses at all levels; it is the largest and most well-known language center in Taiwan for non-Chinese-speaking people who wish to study Mandarin.

The vision of NTNU is to become a teacher-training-based and well-concentrated multiple-disciplinary university. In conjunction with this vision, NTNU not only continues preparing schoolteachers, but also prepares to provide more social services and to train more professionals who take leading roles in special education.

Beijing Normal University

Beijing Normal University (BNU) has grown out of the Faculty of Education of Capital Metropolitan University, established in 1902. BNU was renamed Beijing Normal University in 1923. Over the last 100 years, BNU has gradually developed into a vital education and research base; it is a comprehensive university that prepares students in basic disciplines in science, humanities, teacher education, and educational science.

BNU is the first university in China that has been authorized to grant doctoral degrees in educational technology. BNU appeals to outstanding scholars from all over the world through projects such as

Outstanding Scholars Attraction Project, Promising Young Scholars Attraction Programs, and Human Resources Sharing Program.

As one of the key national universities, BNU was one of the first six normal universities sanctioned by the Ministry of Education in 2002 to set up its own degree programs. BNU has 19 colleges or schools, six separate departments, and 13 research centers covering almost all the subjects in humanity, social science, and natural science.

BNU's mission is to produce outstanding leaders in education science as well as in other fields. In the past few years, several effective measures have been implemented, such as multiple-mode of education, innovative education, new mode of teacher education, and new learning system. Zhuhai campus in Guangdong Province, near Macau and Hong Kong, is a new branch of BNU directly affiliated with its main campus in Beijing. It was founded in 2002, the centennial of BNU, with the primary goal to accommodate more teachers in an increasingly competitive region.

National Chengchi University

National Chengchi University (NCCU) was founded in 1927 and reestablished from China to Taipei, Taiwan, in 1954 with four graduate schools, one of which was the Graduate School of Citizenship Education, renamed the Graduate School of Education in 1955. This pioneer institute became the first graduate school offering master's degree programs in Taiwan. NCCU has four cooperative affiliations: experimental kindergarten, elementary school, junior high school, and senior high school.

The College of Education is one of nine colleges in the university. The Department of Education provides systematic education for undergraduate students through doctoral students. The undergraduate program is divided into two tracks, devoted to elementary and secondary school teaching. Basically, students are allowed to take courses in both tracks. Master's degree programs and doctoral programs focus on educational philosophy and guidance.

The undergraduate program aims are to prepare teachers for elementary and secondary schools, to develop outstanding education administrators, and to provide elementary and secondary school teachers with in-service education and coordinate with national policies. The graduate program objectives are to cultivate research professionals in the fields of educational philosophy, educational administration, and educational psychology and guidance; to advance executives working in the field of educational administration; and to develop professional individuals involved in guidance and counseling.

The Graduate Institute of Early Childhood Education, established in 2000, has a mission to develop early childhood education teachers, professionals, and leaders with a mastery of both early childhood education and management competence. The Graduate Institute of Teacher Education provides an opportunity for students who seek to become a junior high school or high school teacher.

The long-term goals of the College of Education include (1) compiling an interdisciplinary database gleaned from researchers working in the fields of education, literature, law, business, languages, social sciences, and applied sciences, and (2) establishing an education research center and working with already existing programs to provide a support base for professional researchers and a source of information for policy makers at the highest levels of government and education.

South China Normal University

The Teachers College of Guangdong Provincial Xiangqin University, the predecessor of South China Normal University (SCNU), was established in 1933 by Lin Liru, a Chinese contemporary educationist. It was later developed as the independent Guangdong Provincial College of Liberal Arts and Science, together with National Zhongshan (Sun Yat Sen) University. In 1951 South China Normal College was founded with the merging of the Teachers College of Zhongshan University and the Education Department of the South China United University. In 1952, under the national policy of education reform, the Education Department of Lingnan University, the Russian Department of Nanfang University, and several departments of universities in southern China were also merged into the college.

In 1978 the college was approved as a key provincial college in Guangdong. South China Normal College formally changed its name to South China Normal University in October 1982. In October 1996, SCNU was approved as a member of Project

211, a national policy that offers more government financial support for the construction of 100 key national universities in the twenty-first century, which means that SCNU is seen as a paradigm for other institutions with regard to both teaching and research.

The Faculty of Education Sciences (FES) in SCNU serves as three centers in Guangdong province: the Centre for Educational Scientific Research, the Centre for Research in Basic Education, and the Centre for Teacher Education. FES consists of five departments and six institutes and runs three magazines: *Primary School Moral Education*, *Modern Education Forum*, and *Textbooks and Teaching Arts in Primary and Middle Schools*.

FES offers four undergraduate programs in education science: Program of Education Science, Program of Early Childhood Education, Program of Psychology, and Program of Applied Psychology. Master's programs in FES cover all disciplines in education and psychology. At the doctoral level, the faculty offers two disciplines in education science and psychology.

Education is often considered the door to success, and education is also a fundamental issue that affects society as a whole. Education today must make full use of philosophical, historical, psychological, sociological, and administrative approaches and insights in the humanities, social sciences, and natural sciences. The mission of education colleges is to place emphasis on fundamental and quality education, while placing equal emphasis on the cultivation of talent, application skills, and research abilities.

Chang Jia-chung

REFERENCES

Aldrich, Richard. *Education for the Nation*. London: Continuum International, 1996.

Cooper, Hilary. *The Teaching of History in Primary Schools: Implementing the Revised National Curriculum*. London: David Fulton, 2004.

Halstead, Mark, and Monica J. Taylor, eds. *Values in Education and Education in Values*. Abingdon, UK: Routledge Falmer, 1995.

Leedham-Green, Elisabeth S. *A Concise History of the University of Cambridge*. Cambridge: Cambridge University Press, 1996.

Musisi, Nakanyike, and Nansozi K. Muwanga. *Makerere University in Transition, 1993–2000: Opportunities and Challenges*. Oxford, UK: James Currey, 2003.

Ritchie, William. *The History of the SA College: 1829–1918*. Cape Town: Maskew Miller, 1918.

Robson, Joycelyn. *Teacher Professionalism in Further and Higher Education: Overcoming Obstacles and Creating Opportunities*. Abingdon, UK: Routledge Falmer, 2005.

Searby, Peter. *The Training of Teachers in Cambridge University: The First Sixty Years, 1879–1939*. Cambridge: Cambridge University Department of Education, 1982.

Sicherman, Carol. *Becoming an African University: Makerere, 1922–2000*. Trenton, NJ: Africa World Press, 2005.

Walker, Eric A. *The SA College and the University of Cape Town: 1829–1929*. Cape Town, South Africa: Council of the University of Cape Town, 1929.

II

SYSTEMS OF EDUCATION THROUGHOUT THE WORLD

Systems of Education Throughout the World: Introduction

Part II of *International Education: An Encyclopedia of Contemporary Issues and Systems* considers the educational systems in 171 of the 193 sovereign member states of the United Nations as well as four nonmember states (Bahamas, Kosovo, Palestine, and Taiwan), 175 in total. The important consideration in this treatment of educational systems was to determine criteria for inclusion. Embarking on this endeavor proved to be a painstaking enterprise in that decisions had to be made in order to determine the lengths of entries and which systems would be excluded from discussion.

Rationale

At least two criteria were used to determine the countries that were selected for an examination of their educational systems. The first criterion was a country's population. A country with a large population will most likely have mandates or regulations regarding the schooling of youth. Albeit not in every case, these mandates and regulations serve as evidence that a country possesses an educational infrastructure. The general rule was to identify all countries with populations over 1 million persons. The "1 million person" benchmark generally suggests that the child and adolescent population of a country is significant in size—usually 10 to 20 percent of the country's total population. The population factor accounts for the vast majority of countries with educational infrastructures. It should be noted, however, that some states with populations fewer than 1 million persons (e.g., Fiji and Guyana) were selected based on another criterion. The second criterion for selection concerned the uniqueness of the educational system (e.g., Liechtenstein and Palestine). The uniqueness of an educational system can be defined in a number of

ways. First, it might be a time-honored system that perhaps influenced other systems. Second, it might be an innovative system that may challenge the norms of neighboring systems of education. In addition, uniqueness might refer to a system that has achieved success for its students, where success is defined as the number of students who gain successful employment as well as the impact of the system on the nation's economy.

It is important to note that the educational systems not included in Part II are by no means inconsequential; in fact, these systems, despite the relatively small populations (all under 1 million persons) and small geographic areas of their respective countries, are extremely significant in that they are either remnant systems of former colonial powers or systems that have accepted aid and support from countries whose educational systems serve as prototypes (such as the United States [US], the United Kingdom [UK], France, Germany, Portugal, and Japan). Sovereign United Nations member nations that fall under this category are Antigua and Barbuda (UK), Brunei-Darussalam (UK), Cape Verde (Portugal), Comoros (France), Grenada (UK), Kiribati (UK), Maldives (UK), Malta (UK), the Marshall Islands (US), the Federated States of Micronesia (Germany and Japan), Nauru (UK), Palau (US), Saint Kitts and Nevis (UK), Saint Lucia (UK), Saint Vincent and the Grenadines (UK), Samoa (US), São Tomé and Principe (Portugal), Seychelles (UK), Solomon Islands (UK), Tonga (UK), Tuvalu (UK), and Vanuatu (France and UK).

Categorizing Educational Systems

There is no one way to categorize educational systems. In fact, there are numerous possibilities. One way of categorizing education by country is by listing each chapter alphabetically. From an investigative or inquiry-based standpoint, this makes a great deal of sense; clearly, through alphabetization, each chapter will be easy to find. This method of categorization, however, undermines the unique characteristics of individual regions that often maintain similar systems of education. To be sure, placing the entry for Denmark before that of Djibouti (as would be the case in alphabetical order)—two markedly different educational systems—says little, if anything about the educational systems of neighboring countries.

It is also possible to categorize the countries in terms of religious or so-called ethnic boundaries. Examples of such categories include "The Middle East and North Africa," "Sub-Saharan Africa," "The Western World," and "The Pacific Rim." Doing so, however, runs the risk of oversimplifying the education systems and indeed the cultures and subcultures of a region by associating them, possibly erroneously, to both pre- and postcolonial societal norms inherent in that particular part of the world.

Organization

In Part II, chapters are organized primarily by geographic location. This organization was planned for two major reasons. First, this method of organization emphasizes the important role of the world economy in general and its relationship to each country's funding for education in particular. To be sure, socioeconomic status and financial revenue are fairly reliable indicators of a successful educational system. Second, it deemphasizes the role of culture or belief systems, which generally have little, if any, correlation with the educational success of a country. The data in the Table demonstrate this point by showing that countries with high numbers of children between the ages of five and 14 in labor by force or necessity and high numbers of children who are not attending school are mostly the same countries that have high levels of adult illiteracy. High adult illiteracy is an indicator of poor school infrastructure and a lack of financial resources to spend on education.

Systems of Education Throughout the World (Part II) is therefore organized into eight sections: Africa; East Asia; Australia, New Zealand, and Melanesia; Europe; Middle East and South Central Asia; North America and Caribbean; South America; and Post-Soviet Nations. Each of the 175 entries is included

within one of these sections. In most of the entries, institutions that engage in the practice of schooling are identified through their categorization of education level. This categorization is based on the International Standard Classification of Education (ISCED) that was developed in the 1970s by UNESCO. The most recent version of ISCED, updated in 1997, consists of seven levels (Levels 0 through 6). They are as follows:

0. Preprimary education: Education for children usually under six years of age. With the exception of Cuba, preprimary education is not compulsory. Curriculum generally emphasizes social skills and very basic symbolic recognition of letters of an alphabet or characters of a language system. Little, if any, other type of formal subject matter is included at this level. Given the noncompulsory nature of preprimary education, reasons for sending children to schools at this level range from day care to primary school preparation.

1. Primary education: In nearly every country, primary education is the first level of compulsory education. Basic subject matter is introduced at this level. Subjects generally include language (particularly the ability to read, write, and communicate verbally in one's native language), mathematics, natural science, and social studies. Students also engage in physical education and sometimes the fine and performing arts. Primary education spans a period from as few as four to as many as seven years.

2. Lower secondary education: Lower secondary education generally consists of two to four years of schooling beyond the primary school level. It generally covers and elaborates the subject matter and curriculum of primary school. In some countries, lower secondary school is defined as middle school or junior high school. In other contexts, it is simply a continuation of primary school. In addition, many countries view lower secondary education as the last period of compulsory schooling. But this is certainly not the case from a global perspective.

3. Upper secondary education: Upper secondary education prepares students for a variety of purposes. Most notably, it prepares academically inclined students for college- or

Table: **A Comparison of Children (ages 5–14) in Forced Labor, Number of Children Out of School, and Adult Literacy Rate of 172 Countries**

Country	Children in labor by force or necessity (ages 5–14, in percent)	Number of children not attending school (in thousands)	Adult literacy rate (individuals 15 years and older, in percent)
Afghanistan	30	1,816	28
Albania	12	13	99
Algeria	5	177	75
Andorra	no data	0	100
Angola	26	824	67
Argentina	7	61	98
Armenia	4	2	100
Australia	no data	66	100
Austria	no data	9	100
Azerbaijan	7	133	99
Bahamas	no data	4	100
Bahrain	5	2	89
Bangladesh	13	3,347	54
Belarus	5	38	100
Belgium	no data	19	100
Belize	40	2	77
Benin	46	492	41
Bhutan	19	29	56
Bolivia	22	309	90
Bosnia and Herzegovina	5	18	97
Botswana	no data	49	83
Brazil	6	773	91
Brunei	no data	2	95
Bulgaria	no data	20	98
Burkina Faso	47	1,303	29
Burundi	19	337	59
Cambodia	45	205	76
Cameroon	31	475	68
Canada	no data	11	100
Central African Republic	47	291	49
Chad	53	1,186	26
Chile	3	no data	99
China	no data	655	93
Colombia	5	524	94
Congo, Republic of	25	84	87
Costa Rica	5	41	96
Côte d'Ivoire	35	1,164	49
Croatia	no data	18	99
Cuba	no data	29	100
Cyprus	no data	0	98
Czech Republic	no data	34	99
Democratic People's Republic of Korea	no data	no data	99
Democratic Republic of the Congo	32	5,203	67
Denmark	no data	19	100
Djibouti	8	26	68
Dominican Republic	10	288	89
Ecuador	8	56	93
Egypt	7	400	72
El Salvador	6	54	86
Equatorial Guinea	28	26	87
Eritrea	no data	334	59
Estonia	no data	4	100
Ethiopia	53	7,511	36
Fiji	no data	10	94
Finland	no data	11	100
France	no data	53	100
Gabon	no data	10	86
Gambia	25	99	40
Georgia	18	16	100
Germany	no data	55	100

Country	Children in labor by force or necessity (ages 5–14, in percent)	Number of children not attending school (in thousands)	Adult literacy rate (individuals 15 years and older, in percent)
Ghana	34	992	65
Greece	no data	3	98
Guatemala	29	120	73
Guinea	25	719	30
Guinea Bissau	39	132	65
Guyana	16	4	99
Haiti	21	706	62
Honduras	16	233	83
Hungary	no data	47	99
Iceland	no data	0	100
India	12	20,670	66
Indonesia	4	1,138	91
Iran	no data	275	85
Iraq	11	533	74
Ireland	no data	24	100
Israel	no data	23	100
Italy	no data	36	99
Jamaica	6	9	86
Japan	no data	15	99
Jordan	no data	89	93
Kazakhstan	2	18	100
Kenya	26	1,458	83
Kuwait	no data	36	94
Kyrgyzstan	4	33	99
Laos	11	122	73
Latvia	no data	7	100
Lebanon	7	84	88
Lesotho	23	56	82
Liberia	21	391	56
Libya	no data	no data	87
Liechtenstein	no data	0	100
Lithuania	no data	15	100
Luxembourg	no data	1	100
Macedonia	6	8	97
Madagascar	32	675	71
Malawi	26	224	72
Malaysia	no data	5	92
Mali	34	837	23
Mauritania	16	204	56
Mauritius	no data	5	87
Mexico	16	293	92
Monaco	no data	no data	100
Mongolia	18	6	97
Montenegro	4	0	100
Morocco	8	430	56
Mozambique	22	1,655	44
Myanmar*	13	697	90
Namibia	13	34	88
Nepal	31	569	57
Netherlands	no data	23	100
New Zealand	no data	2	100
Nicaragua	15	85	81
Niger	43	1,501	30
Nigeria	13	9,000	72
Norway	no data	9	100
Occupied Palestinian Territory	no data	118	93
Oman	no data	89	84
Pakistan*	8	8,497	55
Panama	3	5	93
Papua New Guinea***	16	no data	58
Paraguay	15	48	94
Peru	19	125	91
Philippines	12	1,028	93

Country	Children in labor by force or necessity (ages 5–14, in percent)	Number of children not attending school (in thousands)	Adult literacy rate (individuals 15 years and older, in percent)
Poland	no data	95	99
Portugal	3	14	95
Qatar	no data	4	90
Republic of Korea	no data	120	100
Republic of Moldova	32	23	99
Romania	1	62	98
Russian Federation	no data	470	100
Rwanda	35	212	65
San Marino	no data	no data	100
São Tomé and Principe	8	0	88
Saudi Arabia	no data	no data	85
Senegal	22	801	45
Serbia	10	23	96
Sierra Leone	48	285	38
Singapore	no data	no data	94
Slovakia	no data	17	100
Slovenia	no data	4	100
Somalia	49	1,280	38
South Africa	3	834	88
Spain	no data	8	98
Sri Lanka	8	38	92
Sudan	13	2,798	61
Suriname	6	2	90
Swaziland	9	33	80
Sweden	no data	31	100
Switzerland	no data	56	100
Syria	4	102	83
Taiwan	no data	no data	100
Tajikistan	10	77	100
Tanzania	36	1,998	72
Thailand	8	310	94
Timor Leste	4	48	59
Togo	29	215	53
Trinidad and Tobago	1	3	99
Tunisia	no data	39	78
Turkey	5	721	89
Turkmenistan	no data	3	100
Uganda	36	1,168	74
Ukraine	7	50	100
United Arab Emirates	no data	33	90
United Kingdom	no data	66	100
United States	no data	2,070	100
Uruguay	8	0	98
Uzbekistan	no data	5	97
Venezuela	8	297	93
Vietnam	16	no data	90
Yemen	23	957	59
Zambia	12	1,020	68
Zimbabwe	13	293	91

Note: Unless otherwise noted, all data are from UNICEF 2012. *ILO 2009; **ILO 2010; ***ILO 2011.

university-level education. It also serves to prepare most students for the workforce by instituting courses that provide students with both low- and high-level skills to gain employment upon graduation. For most countries in the world, stable and secure employment with a comfortable annual wage does not require students to obtain college or university education (as is often the case in the United States). Upper secondary education is the last compulsory education period in countries where lower secondary education is not the last compulsory education period.

4. Postsecondary nontertiary education: This level of education is conceived in many ways. First and foremost, it is often described as

an intermediate education level that enables students to increase skills for more stable employment opportunities. It is an educational level that is provided for students who have completed secondary education but either do not wish to attend college or need education credits for the purpose of transferring to a college or university.

5. Tertiary education, stage 1: The first stage of tertiary education usually entails the attainment of a four-year degree—most often a baccalaureate.

6. Tertiary education, stage 2: The second and last stage of tertiary education is for students who wish to go beyond the baccalaureate degree. These students enroll in graduate programs for the purpose of gaining expertise in a profession, such as high school teaching, college or university teaching or research, medicine, law, business or management, or highly skilled work in services or industry.

Entry Tables

Each entry of Part II includes at least one table, which indicates important general information and educational statistics of a country. These tables are divided into two parts: General Information and Formal Educational Information. The General Information section includes the following general items and figures: capital; population; languages; literacy rate; per capita gross domestic product (GDP); percentage of persons below poverty line; number of phones and Internet users per 100 persons; number of Internet hosts; and life expectancy.

The inclusion of a country's capital allows for the overall identification of a country's center of government and possible identification of embassy information in the event readers wish to conduct further research. Population provides readers with an overall perspective on the number of school-age students compared to the overall number of people in the country. Knowledge of language and literacy rate gives the reader a fairly broad idea about how government policies in the given country provide education for its citizens. It also can indicate if there are disparities among different population groups. For example, in most developing nations, males tend to possess higher literacy rates than do females. This also might be indicative of traditional, ritualistic, or religious practices that have historically alienated females from the education process. Next is per capita GDP, followed by percentage of persons below the international poverty line. These indicators provide readers with an understanding of the interrelationship between socioeconomic status and education systems. Based on much of the data provided in subsequent chapters, there is a positive relationship between low socioeconomic status among the overwhelming majority of a country's population and that country's educational system and training. Most often, these countries, most of which are labeled as "developing," have overcrowded classrooms, especially in the primary grade levels, and an overwhelming number of students who do not complete primary education. The identification of the number of landline phones per 100 people, the number of Internet users per 100 people, and the total number of Internet hosts in a given country is crucial because it is a strong indicator of the stability and staying power of the country's educational system. In addition, it is a powerful indicator of the country's technological changes related to education and schooling. Finally, the life expectancy of a country is included herein because it is highly correlated with the level of educational progress and the success of a country's economy.

The Formal Educational Information section includes the following general items and figures: primary school age population; secondary school age population; primary school age population (percentage); number of years of education (primary); number of years of education (secondary); pupil/teacher ratio (primary); pupil/teacher ratio (secondary); primary school gross enrollment ratio (GER); primary school entrants (percentage) reaching grade 5; secondary school GER; and child labor (percentage ages five to 14).

The primary school and secondary school populations provide a general sense of the number of children compared to the number of adults in a given country. The number of years of primary and secondary education is included in the tables because these data differ considerably by country. Pupil/teacher ratios help in understanding how much attention students obtain in school-based settings. They also serve as a somewhat crude indicator of a country's class size. It is important to note, however, that multiple teachers might be present in classrooms with extremely large numbers of students.

The gross enrollment ratio and net enrollment ratio are common terms to most educators and educational researchers. These indicators describe the nature of school attendance as determined by the number of children in a given country when compared with the number of children and adolescents attending school. Both the GER and NER are determined by dividing the number of individuals attending school either by the child and adolescent population attending a particular educational level, which determines GER, or by the child and adolescent population as a whole, which determines NER. Thus, GER is the total number of children of all ages divided by the total number of children in the official school age group, while NER refers to the total number of children enrolled in school and in the official school age group divided by the total number of children in the official school age group. Both GER and NER outcomes can be interpreted as a decimal, and then converted into a percentage, which, in statistical terminology, is represented as $\hat{p}$ ("p hat"). GER and NER often appear in the research literature as whole numbers because they are interpreted as percentages of a population. Accordingly, $\hat{p}$ is given exclusively as a whole number and never as a decimal. When GER exceeds 100 percent, the data include both students who are both older and younger than the prescribed age of the educational level in question (e.g., primary, lower secondary, upper secondary) as determined by the country's education ministry or administrative authority. For instance, in a number of sub-Saharan African education systems, large numbers of 12- or 13-year-old students might be enrolled in primary school—a level that is typically (but by no means exclusively) for children between the ages of five and 11 years. Therefore, the GER can be greater than 100 percent. The NER will never be greater than 100 percent because many children or adolescents within the prescribed age range for a given educational level or official school age group do not attend school.

Entry Text Format

The entries themselves are outlined as follows: general introduction (not labeled); "educational system"; "teacher education"; "informal education"; "system economics"; and "future prospects." Based on the geographic size, date of independence, and population of a given country, some of these categories are combined. This procedure was undertaken when examining the schooling systems of countries having limited educational data or small student populations. For example, due to Swaziland's relatively small geographic area and population just slightly over 1 million people, the entry on Swaziland combines the sections on system of education, teacher education, and informal education into one general section on education in the country. In contrast, the entry on China is an expansive treatment of schooling practices in the world's most populous nation. This entry includes additional sections concerning special education, minority education, and curriculum, instruction, and assessment.

Educational System

The heading "educational system" includes general background information on a country's regulations and laws regarding compulsory education, specific ages that students are required to attend particular educational levels, and informative description of particular characteristics inherent in each of the levels of schooling. Depending on the country's population, this section is often divided into subsections that include discussion of preprimary (i.e., nursery school, preschool, and kindergarten), primary, lower secondary, upper secondary, and postcompulsory (i.e., tertiary or higher education) levels. This section often includes a historical delineation of the country's educational system—from nascent stages to the present.

Teacher Education

Next comes the heading "teacher education," which expounds on the institutionalization of teacher education and training practices in a country. Each sovereign nation has its own methods of training teachers. Some have multifarious procedures while others have single routes. Some provide education only in teacher training education programs affiliated with a central university; others have multiple centers and alternative route training facilities that provide certification and licensure and even degrees in teacher education. Some align their teacher training practices with those of other countries; others attempt to identify their own methods of teacher education. In many cases, however, educational ministries whose systems are most successful tend to borrow practices from other nations and modify them to fit the needs of their own populations. This is evident in schooling practices in several countries of East Asia.

Informal Education

The next heading is "informal education." The issue of informal education is included for a number of reasons. First, it enables readers to determine how a given country either maintains or implements multimodal media (e.g., verbal discourse, computer technology, visual learning through both digital and nondigital recording devices) in expanding students' knowledge base and inquiry in various academic domains for both its compulsory education population and adult population. Second, informal education practices often indicate how children and adolescent populations transfer content knowledge from one academic domain to another or apply that knowledge to everyday situations. Third, informal education practices indicate how education can potentially boost a nation's economy through the application of knowledge transfer techniques in adult education practice. Such practice has been shown to increase employee marketability by diversifying the abilities of second- or third-career adults. In addition, informal education practices have been instrumental in contributing to the eradication of illiteracy in countries throughout the world. Moreover, such practices have helped equal female and male literacy rates and graduation rates.

System Economics

The section on "system economics" provides an overview of a country's fiscal contributions to education and schooling. This, too, demonstrates differences among the world's sovereign nations. One factor that helps determine fiscal contribution is the source of financial support for education practice. For the most part, federal governments generally allocate a certain percentage of their GDPs (between 0 and 17 percent among 163 countries listed in the *CIA World Factbook*) for education purposes. In some countries, particularly those with high poverty rates or those engaging in ongoing war, education support is seldom provided by the central government or through a percentage of GDP. In these situations, educational support often comes from the coffers and assets of wealthy individuals or from the financial reserves of nongovernmental organizations (NGOs). It is difficult to obtain current data for fiscal contributions to education because such data are often obtained after population censuses are taken as a means of determining changes in student populations—usually once every five to 10 years.

Future Prospects

Finally, "future prospects" considers up-to-date information on educational trends in a given country. Predictions based on current data are provided in determining the path of a country's educational system. In determining trends and predictions, patterns of educational practice and techniques of curriculum, instruction, and assessment are considered, as is a country's economic circumstances. For example, a country's execution of austerity measures can influence the amount of financial contributions to education (as has been the case in several members of the European Union since 2008).

Daniel Ness and Chia-ling Lin

REFERENCES

Central Intelligence Agency. *The CIA World Factbook*. New York: Skyhorse, 2012. https://www.cia.gov/library/publications/the-world-factbook/index.html.

International Labor Organization. *Accelerating Action Against Child Labour: Global Report Under the Follow-up to the ILO Declaration on Fundamental Principles and Rights at Work, 2010*. Geneva: Author, 2010.

———. *Child Labour in Papua New Guinea: Report on the Rapid Assessment in Port Moresby on Commercial Sexual Exploitation of Children and Children Working on the Streets, 2011*. Geneva: Author, 2011.

———. *World of Work Report 2009: The Global Jobs Crisis and Beyond*. Geneva. Author, 2009.

UNESCO. *Global Education Digest 2012. Comparing Education Statistics across the World*. Montreal: UNESCO Institute for Statistics, 2012.

UNICEF. "Percentage of Children Aged 5–14 Engaged in Child Labor." *Childinfo: Monitoring the Situation of Children and Women*. New York: Statistics and Monitoring Division of Policy and Practice, 2012.

World Bank Education Statistics. 2011. www.worldbank.org.

AFRICA

INTRODUCTION

Without question, the educational systems in African countries rank among the lowest in the world. This is due to extreme levels of poverty and war-ravaged states—many of which have seldom witnessed periods of peace and stability.

Although education is compulsory in many African nations, the highest rates of student attrition and truancy where person or institution is held accountable (despite the presence of compulsory education) can be found in countries on the African continent. There are numerous direct and tangential explanations for the poor quality of education in countries of Africa. The most direct explanations are substandard economies, unethical treatment of children, and the chronically poor conditions concerning health care and diseases. Most of the indicators related to education point to Africa as having the lowest rankings.

Undoubtedly, poor education in Africa is the result of the lack of financial, infrastructural, and material resources for schooling children and adolescents throughout the continent. On average, the gross domestic product (GDP) of African countries is US$1.185 trillion. This seemingly large amount ranks the lowest when compared with other world regions. For example, with a GDP of approximately US$4.06 trillion, South America ranks lower than Europe and North America, but significantly higher than Africa. Poor infrastructure and lack of educational resources adversely affect children of families in rural communities because they lack the means of travel to school. Physical infrastructures whose purpose is to provide educational services and that have clean running water and electricity are often located many miles (often over 50 miles) away from where rural families are living. These families often have to pay school fees, regardless of whether governments and legislatures—assuming that they function on peaceful and stable terms—mandate compulsory and free schooling.

Poor educational conditions in Africa are also the result of high levels of child labor for children between the ages of five and 14 years. According to UNICEF, of the 42 countries throughout the world where more than 20 percent of children aged 5 to 14 are engaged in child labor, 32 (78.5 percent) of them are in Africa. This overwhelming number of countries in Africa whose governments condone the labor of children, either forcibly or willingly, warrants specific concern on the part of educators and policy makers. The African countries with more than 20 percent of children engaged in labor are Angola, Benin, Burkina Faso, Cameroon, Central African Republic, Chad, Republic of The Congo, Comoros, Democratic Republic of The Congo, Côte D'Ivoire, Equatorial Guinea, Ethiopia, Gambia, Ghana, Guinea, Guinea-Bissau, Kenya, Lesotho, Liberia, Madagascar, Malawi, Mali, Mozambique, Niger, Rwanda, Senegal, Sierra Leone, Somalia, Togo, Uganda, Tanzania, and Zambia. Moreover, the African governments of Algeria, Botswana, Burundi, Djibouti, Egypt, Mauritania, Morocco, Namibia, Nigeria, São Tomé and Principe, Sudan, Swaziland, and Zimbabwe also allow child labor to persist within their borders, although the percentage is less than 20 percent of children. It is also important to note a degree of child labor in Libya and Tunisia as well. Global March International Secretariat (2011) has indicated that both countries engage in a degree of child slavery, child trafficking (mostly children from Sudan), hiring children to engage in criminal acts, and recruiting child soldiers. Also, many of the countries with more than 20 percent of their children at work engage on a regular basis in forced labor practices. These unconscionable practices have contributed to educational and economic stagnation. Most importantly, child labor, particularly government- or regime-sanctioned forced labor, has contributed to deplorable living conditions for children engaged in these actions and their families.

To make matters worse, in 2009, people of sub-Saharan Africa accounted for more than two-thirds of the world's HIV/AIDS cases (Joint UN Programme 2010). Of the nearly 33.3 million people with HIV/AIDS, approximately 22.5 million adults and children in these countries of Africa live with this potentially life-threatening condition. In addition, nearly all the countries of Africa, particularly sub-Saharan Africa, are at risk of malaria-related illnesses. According to Douglas Gollin and Christian Zimmermann in their report Malaria (2007), more than 90 percent of the world's malaria cases are found in Africa. Their data also suggest that malaria is most prevalent in countries with tropical climates, such as those in Africa, where levels of poverty are the highest and living conditions are the poorest. Communities with squalid living conditions and environmental conditions that allow water to frequently pool, creating nesting sites for mosquitoes, are prime locations for malaria and related illnesses. These grave statistics regarding disease and outbreak in African nations are strongly connected to low GDP, shoddy medical practices, and inadequate health-care establishments.

There are enormous disparities when comparing gross primary and secondary school enrollment ratios and net enrollment ratios in the countries of Africa. These disparities indicate the low numbers of students who are actually attending school. In other words, even when schooling—most often primary schooling—is compulsory (which is the case in most countries of Africa), the total number of school-age children almost never attend school. Further, with the exception of South Africa and possibly Tunisia, the percentage of children finishing primary school is below 80 percent. In fact, the percentage is below 30 percent in a number of countries. These dismal statistics are the result of conditions mentioned above, as well as a lack of initiative on the part of both governments and the people themselves to move away from economic systems that perpetuate agrarian and industrial sources of revenue. These systems also

tend to contribute to the status quo of child labor practice. In addition, there is an overwhelming lack of movement toward information and communication technologies and service-related economies in general. Finally, it is more than likely the case that students who are attending school in Africa can do so because their families can afford private education. These families most often live in urban settings. It should also be noted that because there is little, if any, formal education practice in countries of Africa, transition between school and work in these nations is extremely poor or simply nonexistent.

Daniel Ness and Chia-ling Lin

REFERENCES

Global March International Secretariat. "Global March Against Child Labor." www.globalmarch.org.

Gollin, Douglas, and Christian Zimmermann. *Malaria: Disease Impacts and Long-Run Income Differences*. Discussion Paper No. 2997. Bonn: Institute for the Study of Labor, 2007.

Joint United Nations Programme on HIV/AIDS. *Global Report: UNAIDS Report on the Global AIDS Epidemic*. Geneva: UNAIDS, 2010.

UNICEF. *Childinfo: Monitoring the Situation of Children and Women*. New York: UNICEF, 2011. www.childinfo.org/labour_countrydata.php.

ALGERIA

Algeria is a large country in North Africa. The official language is Arabic although French is also used for commerce and in some colleges and universities. Berber is also spoken in some areas. Roughly 99 percent of the population is Arab-Berber. In other words, although most Algerians are Berber, few Algerians identify themselves as such. The remaining 1 percent of the population is European. Approximately 99 percent of the population is Sunni Muslim. The remaining 1 percent is Christian and Jewish.

Like its North African neighbors, Algeria has a rich history that dates back to ancient Roman times. The Numidians were an ancient civilization that occupied present-day Algeria. The northern region of the country eventually became a province of the Roman Empire. For the most part, present-day Berbers are descendants of the Numidians. Algeria was colonized by France in the mid-nineteenth century. The country became independent in 1962. By the 1990s, the country was in turmoil due to the instability of two of its parties—the National Liberation Front, which was the single ruling party after independence, and the Islamic Salvation Front, which grew out of the National Liberation Front and was believed by moderates to be too extreme in its politics. After nearly nine years of civil war and over 100,000 deaths, the fighting ended in 1998. Algeria faces numerous problems today. The country must deal with growing Berber resentment and pressure for autonomy from a smaller non-Berber government. Second, it must grapple with a decrepit infrastructure, lack of water and electricity for its citizens, and growing unemployment. Clearly, based on these adverse trends, the education system is not faring well; the illiteracy rate is 30 percent.

Educational System

Algeria's education system improved after the countries gained independence. After the countries' independence, their educational systems slowly emerged in the 1960s and 1970s with an emphasis on Arabic. Education is one of the major national concerns in both countries. However, despite these seemingly similar educational concerns and the generally similar contexts in which both educational systems exist, the two are different in terms of infrastructure and student educational success rates, whereby success is determined by growth of a nation's economy in connection with options and employment of recent graduates.

Compulsory Education

The duration of compulsory education in Algeria is 12 years—from ages six to 17 years. However, Algerian education suffers from numerous problems, most of which are a direct result of an erratic political system that has adversely affected social and economic growth. Although primary education maintains a fairly high enrollment rate, only half of the secondary school population actually attends secondary school. In addition, literacy is slightly below the 70 percent mark. Despite more gender equity in comparison with other Arab nations, females in Algeria lag behind males in terms of literacy nearly 20 percentage

points. In addition, Algeria faces a shortage of teachers due to the large growth in population of children between five and 14 years. These difficulties persist despite the fact that 4.3 percent of the nation's GDP is allocated toward education. Arabic is the language that is used in primary school instruction. In recent years, Berber has also been used in schools with large Berber populations.

Tertiary Education

There are 34 universities in Algeria. The oldest and most well-known is the University of Algiers, which was established in 1879 during French colonization. Despite Islamic fundamentalist influence on higher education during the 1960s and 1970s, this influence waned dramatically by 2000 and is now only a fringe element Algerian colleges and universities. The country also has numerous technical institutions, religious education facilities, and schools for teacher training.

Teacher Education

Primary school teacher preparation in Algeria requires that students enroll in institutes of educational technology. Preparation lasts for two years—coursework for the first year and student teaching in the second. Successful completion of this program enables preservice teachers to receive the certificate of general culture. The education ministry also provides students with an education to become middle school teachers. Middle school teacher preparation requires students to enroll in a middle school teacher training institute for middle school teacher certification. Secondary school teacher preparation provides students who wish to teach at the secondary school level the opportunity to enroll in either one of several teachers colleges or national institutes for higher education.

Informal Education

Informal education plays an important role in Algeria. After World War II, these countries had a literacy rate well below the 10 percent mark. One of the achievements of the Algerian education system in the early years of the republic was the creation of the Conquest of Literacy program, which enabled individuals to learn Arabic and French. Given that salary for

Algeria Education at a Glance

General Information

Capital	Algiers
Population	33.3 million
Languages	Arabic, French, Berber
Literacy rate	70%
GDP per capita	US$7,600
People below poverty line	25%
Number of phones per 100 people	8
Number of Internet users per 100 people	6
Number of Internet hosts	1,202
Life expectancy at birth (years)	74

Formal Educational Information

Primary school age population	3.8 million
Primary school age population	11.5%
Number of years of primary education	6 (ages 6–11)
Student/teacher ratio (primary)	25
Student/teacher ratio (secondary)	21
Primary school gross enrollment ratio	111.7%
Primary school entrants reaching grade 5	95%
Secondary school gross enrollment ratio	68%
Child labor (ages 5–14)	5%

Note: Unless otherwise indicated, all data are based on sources from 2011.

teachers is abysmally low, if nonexistent, in Algeria, many volunteers have provided for language learning at students' homes or outdoors. It is interesting to note that the lack of printed material often obliged teachers to use either the Quran or various political pamphlets that were made available as a means of learning language. By the mid-1970s, programs that promoted literacy utilized various forms of media outlets, including radio and newspapers. The World Bank was seminal in supporting these programs. As a result of many initiatives over the last 50 years, literacy in Algeria increased nearly sevenfold. At present, literacy is at the 69 percent mark. Despite this improvement, much more needs to be done to eradicate illiteracy in Algeria. In addition, given the very poor salaries of teachers, informal adult education in areas of technological skill and career advancement is only in its early stages. The Algerian education system has had difficulty in recent years eradicating illiteracy of both children and adults.

System Economics

According to the United Nations Development Programme (2011), total public expenditures on education in Algeria represented 4.3 percent of the gross domestic product in 2008. This amounts to nearly $10.4 billion, or $1,256 per student (total amount equivalent to US dollars divided by 2,517,000, the approximate number of students in the country). The only other country spending 4.3 percent of its GDP on education is Italy.

Future Prospects

The main educational concern in Algeria is to refurbish an old school infrastructure that is founded on French colonial models. Education access remains unequally distributed in Algeria on many levels. First, despite indications of increased gender equality, males still outnumber females in educational attainment. Second, minority populations remain disadvantaged in educational achievement. In addition, large gaps in educational achievement are based on socioeconomic status; clearly, wealthy Algerians are more likely to reach higher educational levels. Despite these disparities, there are indications that show an effort to improve the overall education systems in both countries. Further, the increased number of information and communications technologies in both countries has improved the quality of classroom practices. Nevertheless, more investment in teacher quality, more incentives for teachers to enter the field of education, and an overhauled infrastructure will be the challenge for both countries in the years and decades to come.

Daniel Ness and Chia-ling Lin

REFERENCES

Central Intelligence Agency. *The CIA World Factbook.* New York: Skyhorse, 2011. https://www.cia.gov/library/publications/the-world-factbook/index.html.

Nation Master. 2011. www.nationmaster.com.

UNESCO. *Global Education Digest 2012: Comparing Education Statistics Across the World.* Montreal: UNESCO Institute for Statistics, 2012.

———. "Strong Foundations: Early Childhood Care and Education." *Education for All Global Monitoring Report.* Paris: UNESCO, 2006.

UNESCO–IBE. www.ibe.unesco.org/countries/Algeria.htm.

UNESCO–UIS. www.uis.unesco.org.

United Nations Development Programme. *Human Development Report 2011.* http://hdr.undp.org/en.

World Bank Education Statistics. 2011. www.worldbank.org.

ANGOLA

Angola is a country located in southwestern Africa. The official language of Portuguese is spoken by more than 60 percent of the population. In addition, there are at least six national languages (Umbundu, Kimbundu, Kikongo, Tuchokwe, Ukwanyama, and Ganguela), as well as numerous regional languages (which include Kung, Kwadi, Kunda, Ndonga, and Yauma Ju). One problem, then, is to reconcile formal education practice in a so-called common language and the preservation and survival of indigenous, regional languages. Angola gained independence from Portugal in 1975. The current system of government is a republic.

Educational System

Education in Angola reflects the history of overall instability in the formal education systems throughout the continent of Africa. Nearly all present-day republics in sub-Saharan Africa were subjugated during various times in history by European colonial powers—the United Kingdom, Portugal, France, Spain, the Netherlands, Germany, and Italy, to name a few. Colonialism had formally begun during the Middle Ages, when European empires and kingdoms searched for trade routes to the Far East as well as additional land to support growing agricultural economies. Many inhabitants of the west coast of the African continent were eventually affected by the slave trade between Africa and the Americas and Europe. Between 1580—when the region was first colonized by Portuguese settlers—and the 1820s, nearly 1 million Angolans and Namibians to the south were exported to the Americas—particularly Brazil—in the Atlantic slave trade. After this time, Portugal maintained an overall agrarian society in the region. So formal education in Angola, as well as Namibia and Botswana, during the nineteenth and most of the twentieth century was not even the slightest bit considered an option.

After winning independence from Portugal in 1975, Angola suffered a civil war between the People's Movement for a Liberated Angola and the National Union for the Total Independence of Angola (an anticommunist movement)—a conflict that compounded the problem of establishing a strong educational system even more. Thousands of children between the ages of five and 14 were either enlisted as soldiers or forced into child labor. Further, as many as 8,000 underage girls either were forced into marriage with National Union for the Total Independence of Angola (UNITA) soldiers or suffered sexual abuse from soldiers or army personnel. Affecting nearly 4.5 million citizens—over one-third of the country's population—the Angolan Civil War deprived displaced men, women, and children of food, shelter, and basic medical care. The most devastating statistic was the mortality rate of nearly 30 percent of children before age five. Thanks to postwar intervention by several organizations (e.g., World Bank and the United Nations Office for the Coordination of Human Affairs), there has been slight improvement in the welfare and schooling of Angolan children. Nevertheless, the Angolan population remains in dire need of assistance and support.

Precompulsory and Compulsory Education

Precompulsory educational programs in Angola are controlled by the Ministry of Health, not the Ministry of Education. Day care and early childhood programs tend to be underfunded and lack appropriate resources. Nevertheless, parents generally need early childhood and nursery school services in order to make ends meet.

Although secondary education is compulsory, the Education Ministry of Angola has found it extremely difficult, if not impossible, to ensure high attendance rates among students. In general, schools in Angola have extremely high attrition rates. Only 75 percent of all primary school students reach grade 5. In addition, the economy of Angola is still dependent on strong agrarian and industrial systems. As a result, students generally attempt to find employment either during or after their primary school enrollment.

Tertiary Education

Tertiary education is not compulsory at any level. Colleges and universities in the region are few, but maintaining growth in recognition and quality of programs. One important tertiary institution in Angola is the Agostinho Neto University in Luanda. The Agostinho Neto University, established in 1962 while

Angola was still a colony of Portugal, depends heavily on government resources and therefore has not been as successful as fledgling universities in neighboring countries. However, most of the tertiary student population of Angola attends vocational colleges that specialize in agriculture.

Teacher Education

The teacher training standards of Angola are extemporized and lacking in resources. Teacher training does not generally take place in colleges, universities, or specialized teacher training institutions. Instead, teacher training often takes place in informal, makeshift environments that the Education Ministry develops for preservice teachers. Given that there was little, if any, teacher training practice in the country during the Angolan Civil War, most teacher training in Angola has taken place after 2002, generally on an ad hoc basis. New teachers in Angola are often poorly trained, underpaid, and overworked. Although compulsory education is free for the first eight years, some teachers demand bribes from students and their parents for extra services.

Angola Education at a Glance

General Information

Capital	Luanda
Population	13 million
Languages	Portuguese (official), Bantu
Literacy rate	67%
GDP per capita	US$4,400
People below poverty line (2004)	70%
Number of phones per 100 people	.77
Number of Internet users per 100 people	1.5
Number of Internet hosts	2,525
Life expectancy at birth (years)	38

Formal Educational Information

Primary school age population	1.9 million
Primary school age population	16%
Number of years of primary education	4 (age 6–9)
Student/teacher ratio (primary)*	32
Student/teacher ratio (secondary)*	18
Primary school gross enrollment ratio	150%
Primary school entrants reaching grade 5	75%
Secondary school gross enrollment ratio	28%
Child labor (ages 5–14)	24%

Notes: *Despite lack of data, Angola's pupil/teacher ratio is higher than those of other countries in the region.

Unless otherwise indicated, all data are based on sources from 2011.

Informal Education

One major problem with formal education in Angola is the lack of attention given to the strengths and abilities of citizens, particularly those who lack formal educational experience. For example, *sona* sand drawings of highly skilled artisans of the Chokwe tribe of eastern Angola and parts of neighboring countries represent not only an art form but an advanced intellectual skill in the area of mathematics. Recognition of these intellectual proclivities and strengths can lead to more indelible connections between informal and formal educational practice.

The priority of informal education in present-day industrial economies—such as that of Angola—is to (1) identify common intellectual strengths of farmers, artisans, laborers, and other informally educated citizens; (2) find ways of connecting these strengths with a formal education curriculum; (3) and institute programs that enable education for all. In doing so, educational ministries in these countries need to allocate both public and private funding for courses and to find solutions to eradicate student attrition.

System Economics

According to the United Nations Development Programme (see the *CIA World Factbook* 2011), the total public expenditure on education in Angola represented 2.6 percent of the gross domestic product from 2000 to 2002 (comparable to that in Laos, Tajikistan, Gambia, and Rwanda). These countries thus rank 160 of 186 in terms of government expenditures on education. Most of the expenditure is allocated for the primary level.

Future Prospects

A major problem in education in Angola is the attrition rate of students. According to UNESCO, there are an estimated 2 million children of primary school age. Of these, slightly over 1 million (51.5 percent) attend primary school. This problem poses potentially adverse outcomes in future literacy and, perhaps more important, workforce competition within a global economy. There is hope for improvement of the Angolan education system, especially since the end of the country's civil war in 2002. Another factor that has aided in the improvement of education in Angola was the Angolan government's ability to collect revenues from taxes on oil exports and the extraction of diamonds in the region. Both of these natural resources, in tandem, helped increase the educational budget. In recent years, the Angolan Ministry of Education has instituted a mandate to revive the educational system by adopting the so-called Cuban teaching method (Cuba is known to have an advanced system of education and literacy). This implementation began in early 2009, particularly in the more populous regions of the country. Given an illiteracy rate of nearly 40 percent, the ministry's agenda is to eradicate illiteracy in the country by 2015 or shortly thereafter.

Daniel Ness and Chia-ling Lin

REFERENCES

Central Intelligence Agency. *The CIA World Factbook*. New York: Skyhorse, 2011. https://www.cia.gov/library/publications/the-world-factbook/index.html.

Gerdes, Paulus. *Sona Geometry from Angola. Mathematics of an African Tradition*. Monza, Italy: Polimetrica, 2007.

Nation Master. 2011. www.nationmaster.com.

UNESCO. *Global Education Digest 2012: Comparing Education Statistics Across the World*. Montreal: UNESCO Institute for Statistics, 2012.

————. "Strong Foundations: Early Childhood Care and Education." *Education for All Global Monitoring Report*. France: UNESCO, 2006.

UNESCO–IBE. www.ibe.unesco.org/countries/Angola.htm.

United Nations Development Programme. *Human Development Report 2011*. http://hdr.undp.org/en.

World Bank Education Statistics. 2011. www.worldbank.org.

BENIN

Benin is a small country on the Atlantic coast of Africa. Benin's history dates back to the fifteenth century when the region was the West African kingdom of Dahomey. The region eventually became a territory of France in 1872. Like most French lands in Africa, Benin became independent in 1960. Benin was ruled by a sequence of military dictatorships from 1960 to 1972, at which point the Marxist Mathieu Kerekou led the country. Benin's people were able to vote in free elections in 1989. Benin's population is predominantly Christian (43 percent); other religions include Islam (25 percent) and Vodoun (17 percent). Ethnic groups in Benin are numerous and include Fon, Adja, Yoruba, Bariba, Peulh, Ottamari, Yoa-Lokpa, and Dendi.

Educational System

Due to political instability and government coups throughout West Africa, education in the region was in severe disarray in the late 1980s. Only recently has the educational system in Benin demonstrated signs of advancement. According to the Educational Research Network for West and Central Africa, the extremely wide gap in educational attainment between males and females in Benin was one of the most severe among all sub-Saharan nations (Salami 2000). Prior to 2000, the gross enrollment rate of boys exceeded that of girls by approximately 33 percent. This figure is indicative of the gender gap in the literacy rate in the country; with a total adult literacy rate of about 35 percent, approximately 48 percent of Beninese males above the age of 15 can read and write while only 23 percent of females above the age of 15 are able to do so. Although families were required to pay tuition and fees in order to send their children to school, the country abolished school tuition after 2007. The exponential increase in students since the 1990s made it difficult for the Beninese government to accommodate the large influx of students with properly educated and trained teachers. As a result, Benin has one of the highest student/teacher ratios (47:1) in sub-Saharan Africa. Although a great deal remains to be accomplished, the Beninese education system has steadily improved and has instituted efforts to eradicate gender disparities in education—especially education attainment.

Preprimary education in Benin is extremely limited for a number of reasons. First, preschools are not free, so many families, particularly those in the rural north, are unable to pay tuition and fees. Second, poor families as well as those who are not within reach of urban or metropolitan areas are dependent on the agrarian economy for sustenance. As a result, many children who are eligible for preprimary education either stay at home with their families or begin to work in the fields. Many of these children do not enroll in primary school, even though it is compulsory. Third, many families do not yet realize the significance of preprimary education, especially as it prepares children for primary school education. In addition, preschools are predominant in Porto Novo, the country's capital, as well as a few locations in the small, yet densely populated, southern region.

Primary school, the only compulsory education period in Benin, lasts for six years. This education period is for students between the ages of six and 11 years. The curriculum generally consists of the speaking, reading, and writing of French, the official language, arithmetic, arts and crafts, and physical education. After earning a primary education certificate, students are eligible to continue to junior high school. Unfortunately, due to a 52 percent rate of students not completing the fifth grade, few primary school–age students have the opportunity to be promoted to secondary school. Further, child labor is a major factor in Benin; nearly half of all children between five and 14 are engaged in various forms of labor. This factor only compounds the problem of educational promotion in the country.

Secondary education in Benin consists of a junior high school period, which lasts for four years, and senior high school, which lasts for three years. For the most part, a junior high school education is a continuation of the basic education that is provided at the primary school level. Additional subjects may include topics in the natural sciences and mathematics. The junior level also prepares students for vocational and technical training. Students can enter the workforce after graduating from primary school with some experience. However, graduation from junior high school provides students with higher-level skills. The senior high school level prepares students who wish to continue to the university. Senior high school students must pass the so-called A level baccalaureate exam in order to be eligible for university enrollment.

University education in Benin consists of one centralized national university, namely, the National University of Benin (not to be confused with the University of Benin in Benin City, Nigeria), with six campuses and 19 schools. The main campus is located in Cotonou, the largest city in Benin. The National University of Benin houses at least two normal schools (teacher training institutions). Other

Benin Education at a Glance	
General Information	
Capital	Porto-Novo
Population	8 million
Languages	French, Fon, Yoruba
Literacy rate	35%
GDP per capita	US$1,100
People below poverty line (2004)	33%
Number of phones per 100 people	>1
Number of Internet users per 100 people	5
Number of Internet hosts	867
Life expectancy at birth (years)	54
Formal Educational Information	
Primary school age population	1.4 million
Secondary school age population	1.3 million
Primary school age population	18%
Number of years of primary education	6 (age 6–11)
Student/teacher ratio (primary)	47
Student/teacher ratio (secondary)	24
Primary school gross enrollment ratio	96%
Primary school entrants reaching grade 5	52%
Secondary school gross enrollment ratio	35%
Child labor (ages 5–14)	46%

Note: Unless otherwise indicated, all data are based on sources from 2011.

higher education schools include a polytechnic institute, school of arts and sciences, schools of business and economics, a school of mathematics and physical science, a school for agriculture and agronomy, and institutes of languages and cultures. Although vocational training is available in Beninese secondary schools, there are at least five technical and vocational colleges in the country.

System Economics and Future Prospects

According to the United Nations Development Programme (2011), total public expenditures on education in Benin represented 3.6 percent of the gross domestic product in 2008. Given that the GDP of Benin is $14.2 billion, educational expenditure in the country amounts to over $511 million, or $183 per student (total amount equivalent to US dollars divided by 2,792,000, the approximate number of primary and secondary students in the country). Benin ranks 130 of 186 countries in terms of percentage of educational expenditure.

Despite improvements in education for its citizens,

the Beninese government is struggling to equalize educational attainment for both males and females. Although literacy is improving for Beninese women, a literacy gap of more than 20 percent remains between males (47.9 percent) and females (23.3 percent). Given the less than 100 percent gross enrollment rate for Beninese primary school students, the realization of education as a means for economic improvement is still in its early stages. Families, particularly those in rural and northern regions of Benin, still base their livelihood on subsistence farming. As a result, despite six years of compulsory schooling, many children from farming communities do not attend school. School attendance is also low due to limited teacher training programs, inadequate facilities in schools, and difficulty in reaching large rural populations. In addition, the best schools in Benin are not free. Therefore, many families are unable to afford the tuition and fees that are associated with a child's education. Families must also pay for books and supplies as well as travel to and from school. This is difficult, if not impossible, for families in rural regions of the country. The future of education in Benin depends on its citizens' recognition of the importance of educational attainment as well as collaborative efforts between public and private organizations and the Benin government to improve the country's educational infrastructure.

Daniel Ness and Chia-ling Lin

REFERENCES

Central Intelligence Agency. *The CIA World Factbook.* New York: Skyhorse, 2011. https://www.cia.gov/library/publications/the-world-factbook/index.html.

Nation Master. 2011. www.nationmaster.com.

Salami, Naim D. *Study on Decentralization of Education System in Benin.* Bamako, Mali: Educational Research Network for West and Central Africa, 2000.

UNESCO. *Global Education Digest 2012: Comparing Education Statistics Across the World.* Montreal: UNESCO Institute for Statistics, 2012.

———. "Strong Foundations: Early Childhood Care and Education." *Education for All Global Monitoring Report.* Paris: UNESCO, 2006.UNESCO–IBE. www.ibe.unesco.org/countries/Benin.htm.

United Nations Development Programme. *Human Development Report 2011.* http://hdr.undp.org/en.

World Bank Education Statistics. 2011. www.worldbank.org.

BOTSWANA

Botswana is a landlocked country located in the Kalahari Desert region of southern Africa. The country gained independence from the United Kingdom in 1966; its government is a republic. Despite a rather small population (slightly more than 2 million people) for a relatively large country, Botswana is home to numerous languages and dialects. The official language of the country is English; the national language, or second official language, is Setswana, which is spoken by more than half the population. In addition to English and Tswana, there are 27 regional and local languages (including Afrikaans) spoken in the country. These languages range widely in the number of people who speak them, from the Khoisan dialects known as Hua and Nama (each spoken by an estimated population of 200) to the Bantu language Kalanga (spoken by an estimated 150,000 people). The term Batswana describes the people of Batswana while the term Motswana refers to the country of Botswana (e.g., the Motswana government). Given the diversity of language and dialect in Botswana, formal education practice in the country has been a great challenge for the Health and Education Ministries in terms of accommodating all Batswana children, adolescents, and adults.

Educational System

Since its independence, Botswana has achieved one of the highest economic growth rates in the world. Diamond mining and tourism have fueled much of the Motswana economy. This, in turn, has strengthened the country's system of education. The Motswana government has allocated over 8.9 percent of its GDP for educational purposes. With a literacy rate of 81 percent, Botswana has devoted much of its resources to education. The country has made attempts in improving education access for all students of primary and secondary ages, lifelong learning, and innovations in teacher training.

Precompulsory and Compulsory Education

Precompulsory educational programs in Botswana, like those in neighboring Namibia and Angola, are run by the Ministry of Health. Nevertheless, day care and early childhood programs are severely underfunded and lack essential physical and financial resources for functioning adequately. Compulsory education at the primary level in Botswana consists of seven years of schooling (grades 1 through 7). On completion of seven years of primary education in Botswana, students are expected to have acquired language skills in both English and Setswana; developed dispositions that foster the well-being of themselves and others; developed an understanding of the interconnections between science, mathematics, and technology and their effects on society; acquired an understanding of various vocations and skills (e.g., food and industrial arts); developed mathematical skills and critical thinking skills; and honed skills related to physical, artistic, or intellectual abilities.

Secondary education in Botswana is compulsory. However, the Motswana system of education suffers greatly from attrition. This is primarily due to the need for subsistence farming, and most families' ambivalence about reforming their agricultural methods and transitioning to an industrial or service economy. Accordingly, children are needed to engage in farm labor, which thereby limits their time in school. The completion rates and net enrollment ratio in Botswana are slightly higher than those of its neighbors. More than 90 percent of all primary school children reach grade 5. However, the number of children remaining in school then drops precipitously; slightly more than half of secondary age children and adolescents complete secondary school. The net enrollment ratio for primary school in Botswana is 86.2 percent, and that of secondary school is 61.1 percent.

Tertiary Education

Tertiary education is not compulsory in Botswana. Colleges and universities in the region are small in number. The largest institution in Botswana is the University of Botswana, which was established in 1982. The university maintained its independence from a larger flagship university system that included campuses in Lesotho and Swaziland. The University of Botswana in Gaborone has become reputable in the region as a leader in the areas of business, education, engineering, the humanities, and the physical and social sciences. In 2009 it established a partner-

ship with the University of Melbourne in Australia in opening a school of medicine—a timely addition, given the dire need of medical treatment in curbing a relatively low rate of life expectancy. However, most Batswana attend vocational and technical colleges, as well as agricultural institutes.

Teacher Education

Unlike the teacher training in neighboring countries, teacher training in Botswana has shown signs of improving teachers' content knowledge and pedagogical skills that are necessary for accommodating children whose native languages vary in the same classroom. However, the system is still in great need of improvement, given the status of the Motswana economy. The University of Botswana is one of the few tertiary institutions in the region that maintains a program in education and teacher training. The program is one of the first in the region whose aim is to prepare baccalaureate students for the teaching profession as teachers, tutors, lecturers, and related educational personnel. The program is also noted for its emphasis on gender awareness and gender equality in education.

Botswana Education at a Glance

General Information

Capital	Gaborone
Population	1.8 million
Languages	Setswana (78%), Kalanga (8%)
Literacy rate	81%
GDP per capita	US$11,000
People below poverty line (2004)	30%
Number of phones per 100 people	7
Number of Internet users per 100 people	3
Number of Internet hosts	5,500
Life expectancy at birth (years)	51

Formal Educational Information

Primary school age population	304,000
Primary school age population	17%
Number of years of primary education	7 (ages 6–12)
Student/teacher ratio (primary)	25
Student/teacher ratio (secondary)	14
Primary school gross enrollment ratio	108%
Primary school entrants reaching grade 5	95%
Secondary school gross enrollment ratio	79%
Child labor (ages 5–14)	no data

Note: Unless otherwise indicated, all data are based on sources from 2011.

Informal Education

Like the informal education opportunities in neighboring countries, those in Botswana must focus on workaday behaviors of farmers, artisans, and laborers as a means of identifying common themes related to knowledge transfer—namely, the ability to use concepts in one context or domain and apply it to others. This system would allow Batswana who are engaged in agriculture or manual forms of labor to apply their knowledge to other domains as a means of diversifying their skills. Successful implementation of this type of informal education would ease the transition from an agricultural economy to an industrial or service economy.

System Economics

According to the United Nations Development Programme (2011), Botswana spends approximately 8.9 percent of its gross domestic product on education. The country ranks 8 of 186 of the world's countries. Of all countries in Africa, only Lesotho ranks higher. Over $2.5 billion is allocated for education. Given an estimated primary and secondary student population of 524,000, per capita spending amounts to $4,839.

Future Prospects

Given its relatively strong and stable growing economy, Botswana has maintained one of the strongest education systems in the southern African region. Nevertheless, numerous problems remain, thus making the system still far from exemplary. First, although attrition is not as severe in Botswana as it is in neighboring countries, close to half of all children and adolescents who are eligible to attend secondary school do not do so, primarily for economic and societal reasons. Second, school attendance is difficult for many students due to long distances between home and school, the inability of the education system to accommodate students of differing native languages, and food- and weather-related problems that prevent attendance, perhaps as a result of poor scheduling of the school year relative to various harvest seasons. Another major problem concerns the rate of HIV/AIDS infection. Botswana ranks second of 169 countries in the percentage of adults between the ages of 15 and 49 living with HIV/AIDS. Nearly one in four adults lives with the infection—a strong indication that school-age children, too, live with HIV/AIDS. One way leading to solutions to these problems is to mobilize and strengthen information and communication technologies in the country. The Education Ministry instituted technology for schools throughout the country that not only connects remote communities to formal schooling, but also introduces students to the subject of AIDS prevention. This initiative is funded and developed by UNICEF in collaboration with Stanford University personnel.

Daniel Ness and Chia-ling Lin

REFERENCES

Central Intelligence Agency. *The CIA World Factbook*. New York: Skyhorse, 2011. https://www.cia.gov/library/publications/the-world-factbook/index.html.

Nation Master. 2011. www.nationmaster.com.

TeachAIDS. www.teachaids.org.

UNESCO. *Global Education Digest 2012: Comparing Education Statistics Across the World*. Montreal: UNESCO Institute for Statistics, 2012.

———. "Strong Foundations: Early Childhood Care and Education." *Education for All Global Monitoring Report*. Paris: UNESCO, 2006.

UNESCO–IBE. www.ibe.unesco.org/countries/Botswana.htm.

United Nations Development Programme. *Human Development Report 2011*. http://hdr.undp.org/en.

World Bank Education Statistics. 2011. www.worldbank.org.

BURKINA FASO

Burkina Faso is a landlocked country in northwestern Africa. Approximately 50 percent of the country's population is Muslim, about 40 percent have indigenous beliefs, and 10 percent is Christian. Ethnic groups include Mossi, Gurunsi, Senufo, Lobi, Bobo, Mande, and Fulani.

Like most French African colonies, it gained independence in 1960. The 1970s and 1980s were tumultuous years in Burkina Faso, with year after year of civil wars and military coups. However, in the 1990s, the country's citizens witnessed the first free elections. Perhaps the greatest obstacle for the Burkinabe (i.e., citizens of Burkina Faso) is the alarmingly high population growth rate in the already densely populated country. Given that natural resources are minimal, the Burkinabe are finding it more and more difficult to find employment in the country. Many resort to emigrating to nearby countries, many of which make foreign labor a difficult process.

Educational System

Data about the rate of literacy in Burkina Faso are conflicting. The *CIA World Factbook* lists the literacy rate of Burkina Faso at 21.8, making the country the lowest in the world in terms of literacy. The United Nations *Human Development Report* of 2010 lists the country's literacy rate at 28.7, making it the third lowest in the world. Regardless, illiteracy is a major obstacle in Burkinabe education.

Primary school education in Burkina Faso lasts for 11 years, from ages six to 16. Burkina Faso is not atypical when compared to other developing countries of Africa in its promise of free compulsory education. However, the government has a great deal of difficulty in keeping this promise to Burkinabe families. There are few resources for teachers and for schools. Moreover, education institutions are in desperate need of repair—yet another financial obstacle for the country. The Burkinabe government modified its position by maintaining that students in good standing will receive free public school education from primary school to high school. At 56 percent, the primary gross enrollment rates are clearly very low. Three-quarters of all students who enter primary school reach grade 5. The secondary school gross enrollment rate is an abysmal 13 percent, thus indicating that secondary school is out of reach for most children of Burkinabe families. Free and compulsory education in Burkina Faso also does not mean that all students have the opportunity to attend school. Latecomers to classrooms with the maximum of 65 students are often turned away. This occurs most frequently in rural regions. Few secondary schools exist in the country, and most of them are in urban areas. One of the most popular secondary schools in Burkina Faso is the International School of Ouagadougou, which serves to fill the gap for Burkinabe students wishing to continue on for tertiary education. The two main universities in Burkina Faso are the University of Ouagadougou and the Polytechnic University of Bobo-Dioulasso. Students who are fortunate enough to be accepted to these institutions will enjoy much smaller class sizes than those found in primary or secondary school.

Obstacles in Burkina Faso's education system are numerous. First, schools lack resources for the proper social and intellectual development of their students. Second, many schools are decrepit and in dire need of rebuilding. Third, Burkinabe teachers find it difficult to find highly qualified certification centers. Fourth, although education is free, families are compelled to pay supply fees, and in some cases bribes, to teachers and schools. Next, families, particularly agricultural families, are often reluctant to send children to school out of concern that agricultural yields will dwindle without the children's help in the fields. In addition, there are language barriers between teachers and students. Most classes are instructed in French, which is spoken by less than one-fifth of the population.

System Economics and Future Prospects

According to the United Nations Development Programme (2011), along with Zimbabwe, Czech Republic, and Côte d'Ivoire, total public expenditures

---

Burkina Faso Education at a Glance

General Information

Capital	Ouagadougou
Population	14.3 million
Languages	French (official), Sudanic languages (90%)
Literacy rate	22%
GDP per capita	US$1,300
People below poverty line (2004)	45%
Number of phones per 100 people	.68 (>1)
Number of Internet users per 100 people	.45 (>1)
Number of Internet hosts	400
Life expectancy at birth (years)	50

Formal Educational Information

Primary school age population	2.3 million
Secondary school age population	2.2 million
Primary school age population	16%
Number of years of primary education	6 (ages 7–12)
Student/teacher ratio (primary)	47
Student/teacher (secondary)	31
Primary school gross enrollment ratio	56%
Primary school entrants reaching grade 5	75%
Secondary school gross enrollment ratio	13%
Child labor (ages 5–14)	47%

Note: Unless otherwise indicated, all data are based on sources from 2011.

on education in Burkina Faso represented 4.6 percent of the gross domestic product in 2007. Given the GDP of Burkina Faso at $20.06 billion, educational expenditure in the country amounts to nearly $923 million, or $204 per student (total amount equivalent to US dollars divided by 4,530,000, the approximate number of primary and secondary students in the country). Burkina Faso ranks 86 of 124 countries in percentage of educational expenditure.

In order to improve its standing in the world, the Burkinabe government must invest its resources in improving the extremely low literacy rate. This can be done through both formal and informal education programs. Moreover, families must be committed to move beyond a solely agricultural and industrial society to an information-based society that can compete internationally. School attendance is extremely low, and teachers are often poorly educated. Schools in Burkina Faso are in dire need of financial resources for books and supplies and curriculum development. Also, Burkina Faso's rural populations, like those of its neighbors, Mali and Niger, are large, widespread, and often disinclined to change. Like rural families in neighboring countries, those in Burkina Faso are unable to afford travel expenses. Students and families in rural communities are often unwilling to spend numerous hours per day traveling to and from school. Moreover, families must pay for books and supplies as well as travel expenses. Burkina Faso is lagging behind many developing countries of Africa in this regard.

Daniel Ness and Chia-ling Lin

REFERENCES

Central Intelligence Agency. *The CIA World Factbook.* New York: Skyhorse, 2011. https://www.cia.gov/library/publications/the-world-factbook/index.html.

Nation Master. 2011. www.nationmaster.com.

UNESCO. *Global Education Digest 2012: Comparing Education Statistics Across the World.* Montreal: UNESCO Institute for Statistics, 2012.

———. "Strong Foundations: Early Childhood Care and Education." *Education for All Global Monitoring Report.* Paris: UNESCO, 2006.

UNESCO–IBE. www.ibe.unesco.org/countries/Burkinafaso.htm.

United Nations Development Programme. *Human Development Report 2011.* http://hdr.undp.org/en.

World Bank Education Statistics. 2011. www.worldbank.org.

BURUNDI

Burundi is a relatively small country in south-central Africa. The country gained independence from Belgium in 1962. However, its constitution was not written until 2005, almost 43 years later. Unquestionably, the worst chapter in the history of the country was after the assassination of Burundi's first elected president in 1993, when nearly one-quarter of 1 million people died as a result of ethnic violence and nearly 1 million citizens were displaced. As in Rwanda, there was extreme unrest between the Hutu and Tutsi tribes. The decade-long conflict eventually led to peace through a power-sharing treaty between the two factions.

Approximately 70 percent of the country's population is Christian. The remaining 30 percent of the population has indigenous beliefs or is Muslim. Ethnic groups include Hutu (85 percent), Tutsi (14 percent), and Twa, European, or south Asian (1 percent).

Educational System

Burundi's education system consists of primary school and secondary school. With duration of six years, primary school is the only compulsory education period for Burundian students. In recent years, the gross enrollment ratio for primary education increased from about 60 to 82 percent. This is the result of several initiatives provided by both the Burundian government under Hutu leadership and several nongovernmental organizations. Although all-out war between the Hutu and Tutsi people has ended, relationship between the two groups remains tenuous. Nevertheless, the 1990 wars devastated the school infrastructure in Burundi. As a result, some school personnel who were forced to enter the conflict were killed. Only in recent years has the infrastructure begun to show signs of improvement. Despite the somewhat promising signs of primary school attendance, the secondary school gross enrollment rate in Burundi is at a low 13 percent. This statistic is fairly self-evident given that only 67 percent of Burundian students complete the fifth grade.

The country's two primary higher education institutions are the University of Burundi and Hope

Burundi Education at a Glance

General Information

Capital	Bujumbura
Population	8.3 million
Languages	Kirundi, French, Swahili
Literacy rate	59%
GDP per capita	US$700
People below poverty line (2004)	68%
Number of phones per 100 people	>1
Number of Internet users per 100 people	>1
Number of Internet hosts	162
Life expectancy at birth (years)	52

Formal Educational Information

Primary school age population	1.2 million
Secondary school age population	1.3 million
Primary school age population	15%
Number of years of primary education	6 (ages 7–12)
Student/teacher ratio (primary)	49
Student/teacher ratio (secondary)	19
Primary school gross enrollment ratio	82%
Primary school entrants reaching grade 5	67%
Secondary school gross enrollment ratio	13%
Child labor (ages 5–14)	19%

Note: Unless otherwise indicated, all data are based on sources from 2011.

Africa University. The University of Burundi was established after the merging of several academic and technical-professional institutions during the 1970s. Originally, the university was funded by the Roman Catholic Church, but is now an institution subsidized by the Burundian government. The university consists of both colleges that house academic departments and institutes that house professional and vocational departments, including those for the training of teachers.

System Economics and Future Prospects

According to the United Nations Development Programme (2011), along with Tunisia, total public expenditures on education in Burundi represented 7.2 percent of the gross domestic product in 2008. Given the GDP of Burundi at $3.418 billion, educational expenditure in the country amounts to slightly over $246 million, or $94 per student (total amount equivalent to US dollars divided by 2,630,000, the approximate number of primary and secondary students in the country). Despite the fact that Burundi ranks 17 of 186 countries in terms of percentage of educational expenditure, the per capita education expenditure is extremely meager.

In order to improve its standing in the world, the Burundian government must invest its resources in improving the extremely low literacy rate. This can be done through both formal and informal education programs. Families must be committed to move beyond a solely agricultural and industrial society to an information-based society that can compete internationally. School attendance is extremely low, and teachers are often poorly educated. Many of them travel abroad for teacher training and often return with skills that are sometimes incongruent with the needs of the students. Schools in Burundi are no different from those of their neighbors—they often lack adequate facilities and resources. Bujumbura, the nation's capital, is by far the largest city in Burundi; it has seven times more people than Gitega, the second-largest city, with a population of only 45,000. Accordingly, the country's rural populations are large, widespread, and often disinclined to change. Like families in neighboring countries, many Burundian families are unable to afford the fees that are associated with a child's education. Families must pay for books and supplies as well as travel to and from school. Although Burundi is still lagging behind many developing countries of Africa, the country is showing some signs of improvement in its social and financial standing, as well as growing infrastructure.

Daniel Ness and Chia-ling Lin

References

Central Intelligence Agency. *The CIA World Factbook.* New York: Skyhorse, 2011. https://www.cia.gov/library/publications/the-world-factbook/index.html.

Nation Master. 2011. www.nationmaster.com.

UNESCO. *Global Education Digest 2012: Comparing Education Statistics Across the World.* Montreal: UNESCO Institute for Statistics, 2012.

———. "Strong Foundations: Early Childhood Care and Education." *Education for All Global Monitoring Report.* Paris: UNESCO, 2006.

UNESCO–IBE. www.ibe.unesco.org/countries/Burundi.htm.

United Nations Development Programme. *Human Development Report 2011.* http://hdr.undp.org/en.

World Bank Education Statistics. 2011. www.worldbank.org.

CAMEROON

Cameroon is located in west-central Africa. The country became independent in 1960 as a result of the merger between French-colonized Cameroon and a neighboring territory that was subjected to British control. Since its independence, the country has enjoyed a general political stability as a result of agricultural improvements, oil exports, and major infrastructural initiatives involving the building of transportation systems such as railroads and highways. One problem seeming to loom in the background is ethnic rivalry, which has contributed to frequent rigged elections in the country. Approximately 40 percent of Cameroon's people have indigenous beliefs; another 40 percent are Christian, and the remaining population is Muslim. The Cameroonian people are members of several ethnic groups, including Cameroon Highlanders, Equatorial Bantu, Kirdi, Fulani, Northwestern Bantu, and eastern groups.

Educational System

Compared to the educational systems in sub-Saharan African countries, that of Cameroon is ranked one of the highest in terms of students graduating from each of the levels. Education in the country is compulsory for primary education, for children between the ages of seven and 14 years. Although primary education in Cameroon has been compulsory for several decades, it became free for families in 2000. Free education has had a tremendously positive impact on families throughout the country, particularly in rural areas. Despite a relatively low secondary school gross enrollment rate, students in Cameroon tend to remain in school longer than students in other countries in sub-Saharan Africa. The primary school gross enrollment rate is 109 percent, and the percentage of students reaching grade 5 is 64 percent. Unfortunately, fewer students complete secondary school. The secondary school gross enrollment rate is 41 percent—higher than the rate of its neighbors but low according to international standards. Another problem with education in Cameroon is chronic absenteeism in a large part of the student population. According to UNICEF, child labor accounts for over 30 percent of the population of children from to 14 years old. Although many of these children attend school, a large number of them leave school because they find work more economically advantageous, at least in the short run. In addition, most students between the ages of seven and 14 years in the southern part of Cameroon tend to enroll in primary school. Despite compulsory primary schooling, however, students of the same ages in the northern rural panhandle of the country find it extremely difficult to attend school because school centers are often far from home. As a result, it is difficult for families to pay for travel and school supplies.

The principal languages of instruction in both primary and secondary school are English and French. These two languages are evidence of two types of schools that developed during the time when Cameroon was a fledgling democracy in the 1960s. The eastern region of the country was primarily French-speaking, so French was the principal language of instruction in schools in the eastern half of Cameroon. These institutions are commonly referred to as Francophone schools. English, on the other hand, has been the principal language in the western and coastal regions of the country, so schools in the western half of Cameroon adopted English as the principal language of instruction. These institutions are often called Anglophone schools. Students who enroll in noncompulsory high school and pass the General Certificate of Education Advanced Level are eligible to attend colleges or universities either in Cameroon or abroad.

Given the steady dropout rate of students from about the fourth grade to the secondary grade levels, many students in Cameroon resort to employment that does not require advanced skills. Those who do complete secondary school often continue to the university level if they can afford it. Other students travel abroad to obtain a college or university education.

There are 14 universities in Cameroon. The principal university in the country is the University of Yaoundé, a comprehensive institution that offers degrees in numerous disciplines and professions. Like its primary and secondary education system, Cameroon's system of higher education is divided primarily between Francophone- and Anglophone-dominant institutions. The University of Buea is one of the few comprehensive institutions in the country that is primarily an English-speaking university. There are numerous vocational and professional institutions throughout the country, particularly in the southern regions, which tend to be more populated. Schools for teacher training and technological education exist as either separate institutions or colleges that are attached to some of the universities.

System Economics and Future Prospects

According to the United Nations Development Programme (2011), along with Albania, Bahrain, Georgia, Madagascar, Pakistan, Uruguay, and Turkey, total public expenditures on education in Cameroon represented 2.9 percent of the gross domestic product in 2008. Given the GDP of Cameroon at $44.65 billion, educational expenditure in the country amounts to nearly $1.3 billion, or $226 per student (total amount equivalent to US dollars divided by 5,737,000, the approximate number of primary and secondary students in the country). Cameroon ranks 150 of 186 countries in percentage of educational expenditure.

Like its neighbors, the Cameroonian government seems to discriminate against women in education and employment. Fewer girls than boys finish school. Discriminatory practices, however, are not based solely on gender. These practices are evident when comparing schools in urban and suburban environments. Urban schools tend to have many more services available to them than do rural schools. In addition, given the hierarchical, weeding-out approach that the Cameroonian government seems to employ, students who eventually leave school are those who fall behind in academic achievement. As a result, the school dropout rate is high. Children who do not finish school are also subject to sexual victimization. Discrimination against female students is exacerbated with the problem of teen pregnancy.

Despite the high gross enrollment rate for primary school, fewer and fewer students attend school as the school years progress. School attendance is hampered by poor education for teachers, a lack of adequate facilities at schools, and difficulty in reaching large rural populations. Another major problem is that families are unable to afford the fees that are associated with a child's education. Although education is free, poor families in both urban and rural areas are required to pay for books and supplies as well as travel to and from school. Important initiatives for Cameroonian schools include improvement of school infrastructures, the development of school-to-work programs, implementation of information and communication technologies, especially for the benefit of rural populations, and revised curricula that foster motivation and success in economic development.

Daniel Ness and Chia-ling Lin

Cameroon Education at a Glance

General Information

Capital	Yaoundé
Population	18 million
Languages	English and French; 24 major African language groups
Literacy rate	68%
GDP per capita	US$2,400
People below poverty line (2004)	48%
Number of phones per 100 people	>1
Number of Internet users per 100 people	>1
Number of Internet hosts	40
Life expectancy at birth (years)	53

Formal Educational Information

Primary school age population	2.7 million
Secondary school age population	2.9 million
Primary school age population	16%
Number of years of primary education	6 (ages 7–12)
Student/teacher ratio (primary)	48
Student/teacher ratio (secondary)	25
Primary school gross enrollment ratio	109%
Primary school entrants reaching grade 5	64%
Secondary school gross enrollment ratio	41%
Child labor (ages 5–14)	31%

Note: Unless otherwise indicated, all data are based on sources from 2011.

REFERENCES

Central Intelligence Agency. *The CIA World Factbook.* New York: Skyhorse, 2011. https://www.cia.gov/library/publications/the-world-factbook/index.html.

Nation Master. 2011. www.nationmaster.com.

UNESCO. *Global Education Digest 2012: Comparing Education Statistics Across the World.* Montreal: UNESCO Institute for Statistics, 2012.

———. "Strong Foundations: Early Childhood Care and Education." *Education for All Global Monitoring Report.* Paris: UNESCO, 2006.

UNESCO–IBE. www.ibe.unesco.org/countries/Cameroon.htm.

United Nations Development Programme. *Human Development Report 2011.* http://hdr.undp.org/en.

World Bank Education Statistics. 2011. www.worldbank.org.

CENTRAL AFRICAN REPUBLIC

The Central African Republic is a landlocked country in the center of Africa. The country was originally called Ubangi-Shari under French colonization. Three decades of martial rule finally was changed to civilian rule in 1993. After a decade of free society, the government was once again overthrown by a military coup led by one of the military's generals. At present, rural areas are fraught with crime and civil unrest. Approximately 35 percent of the population has indigenous beliefs, 25 percent Catholic, 25 percent Protestant, and 15 percent Muslim. Ethnic groups include Baya, Banda, Mandjia, Sara, Mboum, M'Baka, and Yakoma. At approximately 14 percent, the country has a rather high rate of HIV/AIDS.

Although public education in the Central African Republic is free and compulsory for students between the ages of six and 14, the country lags behind most developing nations in maintaining student attendance. The primary school gross enrollment rate is 77 percent. In addition, only 23 percent of all primary school children complete the fifth grade. As a result, secondary school enrollment is low. The secondary school gross enrollment rate is 11 percent. Few secondary schools are located in rural parts of the country. And students who do successfully complete secondary school often travel abroad for tertiary education. HIV/AIDS poses another threat to public education. Both students and teachers are affected by diseases that result from HIV infection. Teacher deaths as a result of AIDS contributed to postponements of the school year and, in some cases, forced the government to intervene and close school doors.

When formal education institutions were made compulsory in the Central African Republic both before and after independence from France in 1960, native populations were generally reluctant to engage in formal schooling. Despite slight growth in school attendance since 1960, illiteracy in the Central African Republic is extremely high; nearly half of the population cannot read or write. The literacy rate of people 15 years and older is 51 percent. Although Central African families are slightly more inclined than before to send their children to formal schooling, the educational outcomes of students do not adequately translate to the workings of a productive

Central African Republic Education at a Glance	
General Information	
Capital	Bangui
Population	4.3 million
Languages	French, Sangho
Literacy rate	51%
GDP per capita	US$1,200
People below poverty line (2004)	no data
Number of phones per 100 people	>1
Number of Internet users 100 people	>1
Number of Internet hosts	10
Life expectancy at birth (years)	44
Formal Educational Information	
Primary school age population	691,000
Secondary school age population	690,000
Primary school age population	16%
Number of years of primary education	6 (ages 6–11)
Student/teacher ratio (primary)	77
Primary school gross enrollment ratio	54%
Primary school entrants reaching grade 5	23%
Secondary school gross enrollment ratio	11%
Child labor (ages 5–14)	47%

Note: Unless otherwise indicated, all data are based on sources from 2011.

workforce. To be sure, the country suffers from a lack of skilled labor.

According to the United Nations Development Programme (2011), total public expenditures on education in the Central African Republic represented 1.3 percent of the Gross Domestic Product in 2011. Given the GDP of the Central African Republic at $3.672 billion, educational expenditure in the country amounts to nearly $48 million, or a mere $34.57 per student (total amount equivalent to US dollars divided by 1,381,000, the approximate number of primary and secondary students in the country). The Central African Republic ranks 179 of 186 countries in percentage of educational expenditure.

In the Central African Republic, school attendance is hampered by poor education for teachers, high HIV/AIDS rates among both families and teachers, lack of adequate facilities at schools, and difficulty in reaching large rural populations. Another major problem is that families are unable to afford the fees that are associated with a child's education. Although education is free, families must pay for books and supplies as well as travel to and from school. For families in rural communities, this is especially burdensome. Similar to teachers in Chad, teachers in the Central African Republic frequently bribe parents for more money. The Central African Republic government must find ways to ease the burdens for children and families to keep students in school through the secondary level. Until the government is able to rectify these problems, education in the Central African Republic will continue to lag behind that in other developing countries.

Daniel Ness and Chia-ling Lin

REFERENCES

Central Intelligence Agency. *The CIA World Factbook*. New York: Skyhorse, 2011. https://www.cia.gov/library/publications/the-world-factbook/index.html.

Nation Master. 2011. www.nationmaster.com.

UNESCO. *Global Education Digest 2012: Comparing Education Statistics Across the World*. Montreal: UNESCO Institute for Statistics, 2012.

———. "Strong Foundations: Early Childhood Care and Education." *Education for All Global Monitoring Report*. Paris: UNESCO, 2006.

UNESCO–IBE. www.ibe.unesco.org/en/worldwide/unesco-regions/africa/central-african-republic.html.

United Nations Development Programme. *Human Development Report 2011*. http://hdr.undp.org/en.

World Bank Education Statistics. 2011. www.worldbank.org.

CHAD

Chad is a large landlocked country in north-central Africa. As a developing nation, Chad has undergone nearly 30 years of civil war. The Chadian government drafted a constitution in the early 1990s and held elections in 1996 and 2001. Since then, there have been several rebellions in the northern and eastern parts of the country, especially near the border with Sudan. Chad is considered by numerous organizations and periodicals (including *The Atlantic* and *Forbes*) as one of the 10 countries in the world with the highest levels of corruption. With oil as the country's major export, various organizations claim that bribery plays an important role in the goings-on of the oil industry.

Approximately 53 percent of the country is Muslim, 20 percent Catholic, and 14 percent Protestant. The remaining population is atheist, members of animist religions, or of unknown religion. There are numerous ethnic groups, including Sara, Arab, Mayo-Kebbi, Kanem-Bornou, Ouaddai, Hadjarai, Tandjile, Gorane, Fitri-Batha, as well as other indigenous communities.

Like most countries in Africa, Chad's government has focused on primary education. Unfortunately, the literacy rate in the country is below 50 percent, and most families find it difficult to send their children to school, not surprisingly more so in rural regions. The earliest forms of education in Chad were the work of Christian missionaries who traveled and settled in the region. For most of the twentieth century and even today, for the most part, school instruction is conducted in French. Prior to independence, France instituted a national curriculum that was observed by all schools at the time. Given the emphasis on primary education, students who were capable of continuing to secondary school were obliged to travel to other countries, most often Congo Brazzaville. Postindependence education in Chad was more difficult for both students and teachers due to ongoing wars and famines. Teachers found their lives at risk as they traveled from one region to the next to serve children in remote parts of the country. In addition, school attendance is notoriously low in the country. The Chadian government made primary education compulsory. However, this initiative was problematic for several reasons: too few schools, lack of a standard curriculum, and competition between schools—most notably between secular schools and Quranic Muslim schools.

Today, primary education in Chad has not improved much since the 1970s and 1980s. Although the Chadian constitution ensures all citizens between the ages of six and nine years a free education, the government has found it extremely difficult to fund schooling. In reality, teachers are paid by parents who can afford their children's education. Further, families in sparse regions either find it utterly impossible to send their children to school or do not want to have their children educated for personal or social reasons. Only 33 percent of the primary school population reaches grade 5 successfully. School attendance drops even more for Chadian students who continue for secondary school education. The secondary school gross enrollment rate is only 15 percent. To make matters worse, there are gender disparities favoring the education of boys.

By 1960 Chad had no institutions of higher education within its borders. The few students who were able to receive secondary education diplomas were required to study abroad if they wished to attend higher education institutions. The most notable university in the country is the University of Chad, which was established in 1971. In addition to the university, the Chadian government opened the École Normale Supérieure, a teacher training institution that provides an education for future secondary school teachers, as well as several vocational institutions in cities throughout the country. There are two chronological levels for students who wish to enter vocational schools. Subsequent to primary school, students enroll for the initial cycle for three years, which provides low-level skills. Those who wish to continue for an additional three years have the opportunity to receive a diploma in advanced technological training—an education that may qualify them for more highly skilled occupations.

According to the United Nations Development Programme (2011), along with Azerbaijan, China, and the Republic of the Congo, total public expenditures on education in Chad represented 1.9 percent of the gross domestic product in 2011. Given the GDP of Chad at $19.69 billion, educational expenditure in the country amounts to nearly $374.1 million, or $112 per student (total amount equivalent to US dollars divided by 3,347,000, the approximate number of primary and secondary students in the country). Chad ranks 173 of 186 countries in percentage of educational expenditure.

As a developing country, Chad is in dire need of education reform. This is due partly to ongoing armed conflict and cultural dissonance among various groups and partly to the reluctance of rural families to send their children to school. Gross enrollment rates for both primary and secondary education are abysmally low. School attendance is also impeded due to poor education for teachers and a lack of adequate facilities at schools. Another major problem is that families are unable to afford the fees that are associated with a child's education. Although primary education is constitutionally free, families must pay for books and supplies as well as travel to and from school. Moreover, families often pay bribes to teachers who feel that they do not receive enough payment for their services. Therefore, the major initiative of the Chadian government is to relieve the burdens for children and families in order to keep students in school through the secondary level and to convince families that both formal and informal education is necessary in order for the country to pursue economic stability.

Daniel Ness and Chia-ling Lin

REFERENCES

Central Intelligence Agency. *The CIA World Factbook*. New York: Skyhorse, 2011. https://www.cia.gov/library/publications/the-world-factbook/index.html.

Nation Master. 2011. www.nationmaster.com.

UNESCO. *Global Education Digest 2012: Comparing Education Statistics Across the World*. Montreal: UNESCO Institute for Statistics, 2012.

———. "Strong Foundations: Early Childhood Care and Education." *Education for All Global Monitoring Report*. Paris: UNESCO, 2006.

UNESCO–IBE. www.ibe.unesco.org/countries/Chad.htm.

United Nations Development Programme. *Human Development Report 2011*. http://hdr.undp.org/en.

World Bank Education Statistics. 2011. www.worldbank.org.

Chad Education at a Glance

General Information

Capital	N'Djamena (formerly Fort Lamy)
Population	9.8 million
Languages	French, Arabic, Sara; more than 120 other languages
Literacy rate	48%
GDP per capita	US$1,500
People below poverty line (2004)	80%
Number of phones per 100 people	>1
Number of Internet users per 100 people	>1
Number of Internet hosts	10
Life expectancy at birth (years)	47

Formal Educational Information

Primary school age population	1.7 million
Secondary school age population	1.6 million
Primary school age population	18%
Number of years of primary education	6 (ages 6–11)
Student/teacher ratio (primary)	63
Student/teacher ratio (secondary)	34
Primary school gross enrollment ratio	76%
Primary school entrants reaching grade 5	33%
Secondary school gross enrollment ratio	15%
Child labor (ages 5–14)	53%

Note: Unless otherwise indicated, all data are based on sources from 2011.

Congo, Democratic Republic of the

The Democratic Republic of the Congo is a country in central Africa. The official language is French; other languages spoken include Lingala, Kingwana, Kikongo, and Tshiluba. The Democratic Republic of the Congo consists of over 200 ethnic groups, most of which are Bantu-speaking peoples. There are four large tribes—the Mongo, Luba, Kongo, and Mangbetu-Azande—whose members make up nearly one-half of the country's population. Approximately 50 percent of the population is Roman Catholic, 20 percent Protestant Christian, 10 percent Kimbanguist, 10 percent Muslim, and the remaining 10 percent includes members of indigenous syncretic beliefs.

The Democratic Republic of Congo was established as a colony of Belgium in 1908. By 1960 the Republic of Congo gained independence. After a political coup, Col. Joseph Mobutu made himself president and changed the name of the country to Zaire. The country remained in turmoil for over 30 years. By 1994 Zaire witnessed a huge influx of refugees. Civil war broke out between the leading parties and various minority factions, and by 1997, Mobutu was toppled. The country's name was then changed to the Democratic Republic of the Congo.

Educational System

The education system of the Democratic Republic of the Congo is a fledgling infrastructure that is in dire need of great improvement. Compulsory education is for the most part nonexistent. Although remnants of the colonial Belgian school infrastructure remain and are partially in use, the buildings and materials need a large amount of reconstructuring; teachers and schoolchildren often struggle to complete a day of teaching and learning. The nation's position among developing countries ranks low in terms of academic performance. Given civil war and strife within the last several decades, the Democratic Republic of the Congo government's first concern is to grapple with health and basic needs issues.

Precompulsory and Compulsory Education, Curriculum, Assessment, and Instruction

Primary education in the Democratic Republic of the Congo is not compulsory. Moreover, families must pay tuition and fees for their children's education. Data suggest that the gross enrollment rate for primary school students is 61 percent. This figure is not surprising given that 55 percent of all primary school students reach the fifth-grade level. To make educational matters worse, the gross enrollment rate for secondary school students is only 22 percent. As a result, the country has a severe problem in school attendance and levels of attrition. Most tuition is allocated to teacher salaries, and most fees are used to pay for books and materials. The country's civil war in the 1990s made matters worse: more than 5 million children between six and 11 years of age were unable to attend school. Many of these children either had to help their families when older siblings and parents were recruited as soldiers or were recruited themselves as child soldiers. The Democratic Republic of the Congo's education system is administered by the country's several educational ministries. These include the Ministry of Primary Education, the Ministry of Secondary and Professional Education, the Ministry of Higher Education, and the Ministry of Social Affairs.

Tertiary Education

There are five institutions of higher education in the Democratic Republic of the Congo: the University of Goma, the University of Kinshasa, the University of Kisangani, the University of Lubumbashi, and the National Pedagogical University. Unfortunately, education is a privilege for those who can afford it. Accordingly, students who graduate from secondary school may be eligible to continue to one of the country's universities or may be eligible to study abroad.

Teacher Education

Teacher training takes place in higher technical and pedagogical institutes. Unfortunately, due to the dire circumstances of educational attainment in the Democratic Republic of the Congo, new teachers

---

**Democratic Republic of the Congo
Education at a Glance**

General Information

Capital	Kinshasa
Population	70.9 million
Languages	French (official), Lingala, Kingwana
Literacy rate	66%
GDP per capita	US$700
People below poverty line (2004)	no data
Number of phones per 100 people	>1
Number of Internet users per 100 people	>1
Number of Internet hosts	1,200
Life expectancy at birth (years)	57

Formal Educational Information

Primary school age population	10 million
Secondary school age population	8.2 million
Primary school age population	14%
Number of years of primary education	6 (ages 6–11)
Student/teacher ratio (primary)	34
Student/teacher ratio (secondary)	15
Primary school gross enrollment ratio	61%
Primary school entrants reaching grade 5	55%
Secondary school gross enrollment ratio	22%
Child labor (ages 5–14)	25%

Note: Unless otherwise indicated, all data are based on sources from 2011.

---

have difficulty in finding teaching positions. Primary school teachers are usually trained in the secondary school level.

Informal Education

Countries with poor educational systems generally lack programs that emphasize informal education. Given its developing educational system, the Democratic Republic of the Congo would greatly benefit from programs in informal education. Unfortunately, these programs are presently nonexistent. Even if most citizens devote themselves to agriculturally related vocations, informal education programs have the potential of enhancing skills in most fields and can possibly contribute to economic growth. Informal education can also contribute to the elimination of illiteracy, a problem with which the Democratic Republic of the Congo must contend, given a literacy rate of 65 percent of the population.

System Economics

The United Nations Development Programme (2011) does not provide data on total public expenditures on education in the Democratic Republic of the Congo in terms of percentage of the country's gross domestic product. However, according to the Southern African Regional Universities Association Pillay Report (2008), total public educational expenditures of the Democratic Republic of the Congo represented 4.6 percent of the country's GDP. If this datum is accurate, total expenditure amounts to slightly over $1 billion, or slightly less than $58 per student per year (total amount equivalent to US dollars divided by 18,248,000, the approximate number of students in the country). Clearly, this represents a negligible amount per eligible student.

Future Prospects

The largest concern in the Democratic Republic of the Congo is the extremely poor educational infrastructure. The country was ravaged by civil war between 1990 and 2010 and is recovering from its aftermath in the present decade. School attendance rates are extremely low and education access remains unequally distributed among ethnic groups and between genders. To make matters worse, the literacy rate of 65 percent reveals a more than 20 percent gap between males and females (76.2 percent males compared to 55.1 percent females). In addition, with a population growth rate of 3.22 percent, the Democratic Republic of the Congo ranks ninth among the world's countries and thus adds to the problem of what should be done in to improve the education system. Given the somewhat positive correlation between a country's economic standing and gender equality, one important initiative would be to improve the educational standing of the country's female students.

Daniel Ness and Chia-ling Lin

REFERENCES

Central Intelligence Agency. *The CIA World Factbook*. New York: Skyhorse, 2011. https://www.cia.gov/library/publications/the-world-factbook/index.html.

Nation Master. 2011. www.nationmaster.com.

Southern African Regional Universities Association. SARUA Annual Report 2008. Johannesburg: Southern African Regional Universities Association, 2008.

UNESCO. *Global Education Digest 2012: Comparing Education Statistics Across the World*. Montreal: UNESCO Institute for Statistics, 2012.

———. "Strong Foundations: Early Childhood Care and Education." *Education for All Global Monitoring Report*. Paris: UNESCO, 2006.

UNESCO–IBE. www.ibe.unesco.org/en/worldwide/unesco-regions/africa/democratic-republic-of-the-congo.html.

UNESCO–UIS. www.uis.unesco.org.

United Nations Development Programme. *Human Development Report 2011*. http://hdr.undp.org/en.

World Bank Education Statistics. 2011. www.worldbank.org.

CONGO, REPUBLIC OF THE

Republic of the Congo is a country in west-central Africa. Languages spoken include French (the official language), Lingala and Monokutuba (two lingua franca languages used for trade), and numerous indigenous languages. Roughly 48 percent of the population are Kongo, 20 percent Sangha, 12 percent M'Bochi, and 17 percent Teke. Europeans make up 3 percent of the total population. Half the people are Christian, almost the entire other half follow animist religions, and about 2 percent are Muslim.

The Republic of the Congo became independent from France in 1960. An experiment in a Marxist government eventually led to a republic in 1990 with a democratically elected government two years later. The 1997 civil war revived the Marxist government. Stability in the country is currently tenuous as a result of incoming refugees and a gradual depletion of oil reserves that greatly helped the country's economy.

Educational System

Nearly half of the Republic of the Congo's population is under the age of 15. The country's education system invests close to half of its funding on primary school education, approximately 30 percent on secondary school education, and most of the remaining percentage on tertiary education. Given the somewhat tumultuous years after independence, the issue of education has not been a priority in the Republic of the Congo. At present, success in education and achievement is determined by the growth of country's economy in connection with options and employment of recent graduates.

Precompulsory and Compulsory Education, Curriculum, Assessment, and Instruction

In the Republic of the Congo, few, if any, financial resources are allocated to preschool education; as in many other agrarian and industrial societies in Africa, there is little need to send young children to preschool. Primary education in the Republic of the Congo is six years in duration. Students are generally between the ages of six and 12 years. At the end of the sixth year of schooling, Congolese children are expected to take a high-stakes entrance examination if they plan to continue to secondary level education. Secondary school in the Republic of the Congo lasts for seven years, divided into two periods. The first period is a precollege education. The second is referred to as a lycée, which is devoted to higher-level learning. The lycée is divided into three types: general lycée, technical lycée, and agricultural lycée. The general lycée provides general, liberal arts studies for students who pursue university-level education. The technical lycée accommodates students who are interested in engineering, mechanics, architecture, and other technological fields that involve mathematics and science knowledge. Finally, the agricultural lycée prepares students for occupations in agriculture that are intended to exceed general farming knowledge. Elements of technical training are necessary for the agricultural lycée. Students who enter the general lycée have a number of options, including life science and natural science, economics and business, languages, social science, and mathematics and earth science. Students graduate from grade 13 if they pass what is known as the Senior School Higher Certificate Examination.

Tertiary Education

Marien Ngouabi University is the only publicly funded institution of higher education in the Republic of the Congo. Founded in 1971 as the University of Brazzaville, the name of the institution was changed to its present title shortly after the assassination of Marien Ngouabi, the third president of the Republic of The Congo, in 1977. Other tertiary institutions in the Republic of the Congo include the Christian Polytechnic and Professional Institute of Arts, the Institute of Business and Economic Development, and the Mondongo Higher Institute of Agricultural Sciences. One of the benefits of Marien Ngouabi University is its Faculty of Medicine—one of the few in the surrounding region. After passing the Senior School Higher Certificate Examination, students must pass an additional examination to enter the Faculty of Medicine. After seven years of coursework in biology and chemistry, as well as internship, students continue their residencies in hospitals in the region.

Teacher Education

The Ministry of Technical and Professional Education is responsible for teacher training in the Republic of the Congo. There are four colleges for primary school teacher preparation and one college for secondary school teacher preparation. These institutions suffer from a lack of resources, particularly with regard to instructional materials, chairs, desks, and writing instruments. Moreover, given the high risks of HIV/AIDS in the country, the curriculum does not prepare future teachers to grapple with all aspects of prevention of the disease.

Informal Education

Informal education plays a minimal role in the Republic of the Congo. Nevertheless, informal education programs help in maintaining a literacy rate of Congolese adults that is above the average compared to the rate in other African nations. In addition, several programs and initiatives from the United States and Europe have assisted Congolese citizens in gaining life skills for the purpose of curbing problems related to disease as well as skills associated with life enhancement.

System Economics

According to the United Nations Development Programme (2011), total public expenditures on education in the Republic of the Congo represented 1.9 percent of the gross domestic product in 2011. The country ranks 174 out of 186 countries in percentage of educational expenditure. This amounts to nearly $331.5 million, or about $289 per student (total amount equivalent to US dollars divided by 1,145,000, the approximate number of students in the country). Other nations that spend 1.9 percent of their GDP on educational expenditures are Azerbaijan, China, and Chad.

Future Prospects

Like that of the Democratic Republic of the Congo, the Republic of the Congo's main educational concern is to refurbish an old school infrastructure that is founded on French colonial models. Education access remains unequally distributed in the Republic of the Congo on many levels. First, in terms of gender, a disproportionate number of males achieve educational attainment when compared to females. It is also clear that, although the literacy rate in the Republic of the Congo is higher than that of its neighbor—the Democratic Republic of the Congo—there are still disparities in terms of gender and social class. There is a 10 percent gap between males (89.6 percent) and females (78.4 percent) in terms of the literacy rate. Second, minority populations remain disadvantaged in educational achievement. In addition, large gaps in educational achievement exist based on socioeconomic status; wealthy Congolese are more likely to reach higher educational levels. To be sure, more in-

---

Republic of the Congo Education at a Glance

General Information

Capital	Brazzaville
Population	3.8 million
Languages	French (official), Lingala, Monokutuba
Literacy rate	83%
GDP per capita	US$1,400
People below poverty line (2004)	no data
Number of phones per 100 people	>1
Number of Internet users per 100 people	>1
Number of Internet hosts	46
Life expectancy at birth (years)	53

Formal Educational Information

Primary school age population	573,000
Secondary school age population	572,000
Primary school age population	15%
Number of years of primary education	6 (ages 6–11)
Student/teacher ratio (primary)	83
Student/teacher ratio (secondary)	34
Primary school gross enrollment ratio	107%
Primary school entrants reaching grade 5	66%
Secondary school gross enrollment ratio	43%
Child labor (ages 5–14)	25%

Note: Unless otherwise indicated, all data are based on sources from 2011.

vestment in teacher quality, more incentives for teachers to enter the field of education, and an overhauled infrastructure will be the challenge for the Republic of the Congo in the years and decades to come. Promisingly, the National Institute of Pedagogical Research, an organization based in France, is responsible for the development of a curriculum for primary education. The institute has recently provided up-to-date teaching materials that are relevant to the issues facing the country, including HIV/AIDS and the need for various life skills. Also, the US Department of Agricultural Service has assisted in developing school garden projects in both the Republic of the Congo and Rwanda. These gardens help feed students during lunch hours, provide practical fieldwork in addition to school curriculum, and contribute to the social welfare in community organizing.

Daniel Ness and Chia-ling Lin

REFERENCES

Central Intelligence Agency. *The CIA World Factbook*. New York: Skyhorse, 2011. https://www.cia.gov/library/publications/the-world-factbook/index.html.

Nation Master. 2011. www.nationmaster.com.

Southern African Regional Universities Association. *SARUA Annual Report 2008*. Johannesburg: Southern African Regional Universities Association, 2008.

UNESCO. *Global Education Digest 2012: Comparing Education Statistics Across the World*. Montreal: UNESCO Institute for Statistics, 2012.

———. "Strong Foundations: Early Childhood Care and Education." *Education for All Global Monitoring Report*. Paris: UNESCO, 2006.

UNESCO–IBE. www.ibe.unesco.org/en/worldwide/unesco-regions/africa/congo.html.

UNESCO–UIS. www.uis.unesco.org.

United Nations Development Programme. *Human Development Report 2011*. http://hdr.undp.org/en.

World Bank Education Statistics. 2011. www.worldbank.org.

CÔTE D'IVOIRE

Côte D'Ivoire is in western Africa. The country became independent from France in 1960. Côte D'Ivoire is one of the most economically flourishing countries in western Africa due to vast amounts of cocoa production and foreign investment. However,

Côte D'Ivoire has suffered from high degrees of political unrest. The results of a political coup in 1999 put the military junta leader Robert Guei in power. After considerable protest, Laurent Gbagbo became president after it was decided that Guei had engineered the initial election. Several failed coup attempts followed, eventually leading to a rift between factions in the country's northern regions and the southern coastal regions. At present, armed forces from France and other African nations attempt to keep peace in the country. The religious beliefs of most Ivoirians are generally divided equally among Islam, Christianity, and indigenous religions. Muslims make up most of the northern population while Christians make up most of the population in the south and along the coast.

Educational System

Primary school in Côte d'Ivoire lasts for six years—between the ages of six and 11 years. Successful completion of primary school allows students to continue to secondary school, which lasts for seven years. Students who successfully complete secondary education receive a baccalaureate degree and are eligible to study at the university. The only university is located in Abidjan, the country's largest city in population. Other higher education institutions include technical colleges and teacher training institutions.

Private schools of education in the southern part of Côte d'Ivoire are run by the Roman Catholic diocese, while in the northern part of the country, most private schools are Quranic schools. Religion plays no role in public schools throughout the country. Informal adult education is intended to boost the country's literacy rate, which is currently at 51 percent for people 15 years and older. Adults seeking additional education in the northern regions of Côte d'Ivoire must depend on radio and other forms of media that are often provided in community centers.

Educational access is unequal between males and females. Nearly one-third more boys have attended primary school than girls. French is the most frequent language of instruction in Ivoirian primary schools. Children generally receive a basic education in arithmetic, language skills, social studies, science, and the visual and musical arts. Rural primary schools emphasize more agrarian skills than do schools in the cities and along the coast. The sixth-grade examination, which leads to the *certificat d'étude primaires élémentaires*, is a high-stakes assessment that generally determines which students are able to continue to the secondary school level.

Like secondary school systems in other African nations, the secondary school system in Côte d'Ivoire suffers from low enrollment. This is in part due to the inability for many students to pass the sixth-grade primary school examination. It is also worth noting that the inability to pass the primary school examination may be a result of poor schooling and school infrastructure as well as the need for children to work in a largely agrarian society, especially in northern parts of the country. Low secondary school enrollment may also be due to the need of keeping children working in the fields. With a secondary school gross enrollment ratio at 25 percent, students preparing for a college education attend specialized high schools, including the federally funded lycée and the regionally funded *collège*. The duration of secondary study is seven years. During the first four years of study, students prepare to take examinations for an initial secondary education certificate. This certificate allows students who are university-bound to continue their studies for an additional three years. It also allows those who are not university-bound to enter technical colleges or teacher training institutions. Most nongovernmental secondary education schools are run by the Catholic Church. Students who opt for vocational training enter a variety of programs that specialize in agriculture, engineering, transportation, commercial trade, and construction. The only university in the country is the National University of Côte d'Ivoire in Abidjan. The university was initially established in 1959 as the Center for Higher Education and eventually became the University of Abidjan in 1964 and subsequently the National University. Roughly half of the student body is Ivoirian, and a smaller number of students are female. A selection of programs at the university includes law; liberal arts; the physical, natural, and earth sciences; mathematics; engineering; and medicine.

System Economics and Future Prospects

According to the United Nations Development Programme (2011), along with Burkina Faso, Zimbabwe, and Czech Republic, total public expenditures on

Côte D'Ivoire Education at a Glance

General Information

Capital	Yamoussoukro
Population	18 million
Languages	French (official), Dioula, other dialects
Literacy rate	51%
GDP per capita	US$1,600
People below poverty line (2004)	37%
Number of phones per 100 people	1.5
Number of Internet users per 100 people	>1
Number of Internet hosts	2,540
Life expectancy at birth (years)	49

Formal Educational Information

Primary school age population	3 million
Secondary school age population	3.1 million
Primary school age population	17%
Number of years of primary education	6 (ages 6–11)
Student/teacher ratio (primary)	42
Student/teacher ratio (secondary)	29
Primary school gross enrollment ratio	70%
Primary school entrants reaching grade 5	88%
Secondary school gross enrollment ratio	25%
Child labor (ages 5–14)	35%

Note: Unless otherwise indicated, all data are based on sources from 2011.

education in Côte d'Ivoire represented 4.6 percent of the gross domestic product in 2011. Given the GDP of Côte d'Ivoire at $35.6 billion, educational expenditure in the country amounts to nearly $1.738 billion, or $266 per student (total amount equivalent to US dollars divided by 6,170,000, the approximate number of primary and secondary students in the country). Côte d'Ivoire ranks 89 of 186 countries in percentage of educational expenditure. Interestingly, prior to the 1990s, Côte d'Ivoire ranked as one of the highest countries in terms of percentage of GDP allocated for education.

In Côte d'Ivoire, education is compulsory at the primary and secondary school levels. But a large percentage of students do not complete school beyond the fifth-grade level, and even fewer continue to secondary school. As in neighboring countries, school attendance is hampered by poor education for teachers, a lack of adequate facilities at schools, and difficulty in reaching large rural populations. Another major problem is that families are unable to afford the fees that are associated with a child's education. Although education in Côte d'Ivoire is free, families must pay for books and supplies as well as travel to and from school. Rural families find it extremely difficult to send their children to schools mainly because fees are expensive and children are needed by their families for agricultural labor, particularly in the rural north. Therefore, the major initiative of the Ivoirian government is to lessen the burdens for children and families in order to keep students in school through the secondary level.

Daniel Ness and Chia-ling Lin

REFERENCES

Central Intelligence Agency. *The CIA World Factbook*. New York: Skyhorse, 2011. https://www.cia.gov/library/publications/the-world-factbook/index.html.

Nation Master. 2011. www.nationmaster.com.

UNESCO. *Global Education Digest 2012: Comparing Education Statistics Across the World*. Montreal: UNESCO Institute for Statistics, 2012.

———. "Strong Foundations: Early Childhood Care and Education." *Education for All Global Monitoring Report*. Paris: UNESCO, 2006.

UNESCO–IBE. www.ibe.unesco.org/en/worldwide/unesco-regions/africa/cote-divoire.html.

United Nations Development Programme. *Human Development Report 2011*. http://hdr.undp.org/en.

World Bank Education Statistics. 2011. www.worldbank.org.

DJIBOUTI

Djibouti is the smallest country in the so-called horn of Africa region. The country became independent from France in 1977 when the Afar and Issa groups merged. Although a republic, Djibouti was under Issa authoritarian rule, with Hassan Gouled Aptidon as president, for nearly 22 years, until, in 1999, civil war broke out between the Afars and Issas. The war ended in the Afars' favor in that multiparty elections became possible. Since 2001 Djibouti has built strong political ties with the United States, which has its only sub-Saharan military base in the country.

Djibouti is 94 percent Muslim and 6 percent Christian. Ethnic groups include the Somali (60 percent) and the Afar (35 percent).

Educational System

Prior to 2000 education in Djibouti was for families who were able to afford it and was not compulsory for the public. Nevertheless, the country's educational system is unique in that it has one of the longest compulsory periods among all countries of Africa. The primary education period lasts for five years and the lower secondary period for four years—nine years in total. These changes took place as a result of the government-sponsored National Education Forum that took place in 1999. Despite these promising figures, the primary education gross enrollment rate remains at 42 percent, extremely low when compared to countries in western, central, or southern Africa.

Preprimary education in Djibouti, which is not part of the compulsory period, is primarily for families who can afford to enroll their three- to six-year-old children into preschools. The gross enrollment rate at this level is approximately the same for both boys and girls. Curriculum at this level is minimal and focuses primarily on the alphabet and working with numbers.

Primary education in Djibouti is the first compulsory period. Prior to 2005 it was clear from research data that the country was faring poorly with regard to educational access, even at the primary level. The languages of instruction are French and Arabic. Mathematics, the arts, and physical education also play an important role in the Djiboutian primary school curriculum. Although it is somewhat difficult to determine the direction of primary education in Djibouti, it is clear from current educational initiatives that access to primary schools is increasing throughout the country. Unlike in preprimary education, there is a small gender gap in primary schools, since boys have a 10 percent greater gross enrollment rate than girls.

Secondary school is divided into two parts: middle school education and secondary school (i.e., high school) education. Lasting for four years, the middle-level education period is the second and final compulsory period. As in other educational systems, the curriculum of middle-level education in Djibouti is a continuation of the basic education curriculum provided in primary schools. The gender gap at the middle level is approximately a 12 percent difference, with boys having more access to schooling than girls. Students are expected to pass an exit examination in order to continue to the so-called secondary level.

Secondary-level education is a period for students between the ages of 16 and 18 years who intend to continue to the college or university. Curriculum at this level includes more intense and rigorous subjects in the sciences (e.g., physics, chemistry, and biology), mathematics (algebra, geometry, and trigonometry), history, geography, and government. Information and communication technologies are only beginning to play a role in the secondary and tertiary curriculum. Disparities in gender continue at this level with male students gaining greater access than female students. The gross enrollment rate for the entire secondary education period—including both middle-level and secondary-level periods—is 23 percent. However, the gross enrollment rate solely for the secondary education period drops to about 19 percent.

Tertiary education in Djibouti comprises some colleges and one major university, the University of Djibouti, which houses several schools in the natural sciences, social sciences, humanities, and computer technologies. Less than 3,000 Djiboutian students per year enroll in tertiary education programs. Preprimary, primary, and secondary teacher training is available; however, there are severely limited opportunities available for students wishing to pursue teacher training and education. The only institution to date that accommodates future teachers is the Personnel Training Center for National Education, located in the country's capital. Unfortunately, due to its extremely selective enrollment, it is difficult to find qualified teachers in Djibouti.

Djibouti Education at a Glance

General Information

Capital	Djibouti
Population	740,528
Languages	French, Arabic, Somali, Afar
Literacy rate	68%
GDP per capita	US$1,000
People below poverty line (2004)	50%
Number of phones per 100 people	2
Number of Internet users per 100 people	1
Number of Internet hosts	1,540
Life expectancy at birth (years)	43

Formal Educational Information

Primary school age population	122,000
Secondary school age population	135,000
Primary school age population	17%
Number of years of primary education	5 (ages 6–11)
Student/teacher ratio (primary)	35
Student/teacher ratio (secondary)	28
Primary school gross enrollment rate	42%
Primary school entrants reaching grade 5	77%
Secondary school gross enrollment ratio	23%
Child labor (ages 5–14)	8%

Note: Unless otherwise indicated, all data are based on sources from 2011.

System Economics and Future Prospects

According to the United Nations Development Programme (2011), total public expenditures on education in Djibouti represented 8.7 percent of the gross domestic product in 2011. Given the GDP of Djibouti at $2.244 billion, educational expenditure in the country amounts to nearly $183 million, or $760 per student. This amount is based on the US dollar equivalent divided by 257,000, the approximate number of primary- and secondary-school-age students in the country, but not the number of primary and secondary school students actually enrolled. Based on the net enrollment rate, per capita expenditure would be about $2,224. Djibouti ranks 8 of 186 countries in percentage of educational expenditure.

Among the four Horn-of-Africa countries (Djibouti, Eritrea, Ethiopia, and Somalia), Djibouti's education system ranks the best. This rank is based on recent government initiatives to provide greater access to schooling, eliminate illiteracy and innumeracy, institute advancements in information and communication technologies, and reduce gender disparities. Further, the Djiboutian government is making efforts to accommodate broadcast education services for children and students in remote parts of the country; still Djiboutian education system is far from adequate. The gross enrollment rate for primary school is at a low 42 percent, and the gross enrollment ratio for secondary school is only 23 percent. Teacher attrition stands at high levels. School attendance is hampered as a result of a lack of training centers for teachers, a lack of adequate facilities at schools, and difficulty in promoting an egalitarian educational system for both Somali and Afar communities. Another major problem is that families are unable to afford the fees that are associated with a child's education. Despite these obstacles, Djibouti's close ties with the United States have helped the country increase its educational reach. In 2009 the United States gave $8 million as part of the Catalytic Fund (an organization that funds countries that are in some form of transition to postindustrial status) to the Djiboutian government for educational improvements. The government has also instituted a system whereby nomadic families, many of whom have been convinced of the low economic returns in subsistence farming and animal husbandry, are able to send their children to school. The major goal of the Djiboutian government is to lessen the burdens for children and families in order to keep students in school through the secondary level and continue on to college or the university.

Daniel Ness and Chia-ling Lin

REFERENCES

Central Intelligence Agency. *The CIA World Factbook*. New York: Skyhorse, 2011. https://www.cia.gov/library/publications/the-world-factbook/index.html.

Nation Master. 2011. www.nationmaster.com.

UNESCO. *Global Education Digest 2012: Comparing Education Statistics Across the World*. Montreal: UNESCO Institute for Statistics, 2012.

———. "Strong Foundations: Early Childhood Care and Education." *Education for All Global Monitoring Report*. Paris: UNESCO, 2006.

UNESCO–IBE. www.ibe.unesco.org/countries/Djibouti.htm.

United Nations Development Programme. *Human Development Report 2011*. http://hdr.undp.org/en.

World Bank Education Statistics. 2011. www.worldbank.org.

EGYPT

Egypt is located in northeastern Africa. The official language is Arabic; other spoken languages include English and French, especially among the upper income levels. Roughly 98 percent of the population is Egyptian. The remaining 2 percent includes Berber, Nubian, Bedouin, Beja, Greek, Armenian, Italian, and French populations. Approximately 90 percent of the population is Sunni Muslim. Most of the remaining population consists of Coptic Christians, and about 1 percent is Roman Catholic.

Egypt is home to one of the oldest civilizations in the West—one whose origins date to approximately 3,500 BCE. The first of about 30 dynasties, which lasted for nearly 3,000 years, began about 3,200 BCE. Upon the fall of the last dynasty in 341 BCE, Egypt was ruled first by the Persians, then for a short time by the Greeks, and for nearly 600 years by the Romans. Not until the seventh century CE did the region become influenced by Arabic and the new religion of Islam. Egypt is the home of several architectural and infrastructural achievements. These include the pyramids of Giza and neighboring areas, the tombs in the Valley of the Kings, the Suez Canal, and the Aswan Dam, many of which must have required substantial training and education for construction. Currently, Egypt's government is grappling with resolving political instability, rebuilding a decrepit infrastructure, and preparing the third most populous country in Africa for the twenty-first century.

Educational System

Egypt has a rich history in educational practice. Schooling and education were important in ancient Egypt. Most of the curriculum at the time prepared individuals to build infrastructure and work the fields. Therefore, content focused primarily on hieroglyphics, mathematics, music, and geometry. Students would solve problems having to do with how much profit can be made by using a particular parcel of land or the mathematics needed to build sailing vessels. Students were required to learn how to calculate volumes and surface areas of three-dimensional figures that might appear in real life. What is striking, however, is the purpose of an education in ancient Egypt. It was not aimed at promoting innovation, originality, or individuality of any kind. Instead, the goal was to instill what was regarded as a sacred and sacrosanct culture. In other words, the goal was to promote and foster the status quo. It was to transmit the cultural values unchanged and in the form in which they had been handed down generation after generation. Innovation and change were minimized by pharaohs and administrative leaders in early Egyptian civilization.

Education in Egypt saw some improvements under Greek and subsequently Roman rule. The cities of Heliopolis and Alexandria assumed the role of educational hubs during the period of late antiquity. Both cities were centers of Greek thought and philosophical inquiry. On the whole, however, education in Egypt was limited in scope, primarily focusing on religion. Moreover, females had little to no access to education. The fifth century saw the emergence of the use of the Greek alphabet in interpreting hieroglyphics—in other words, Coptic. Schools were created for teaching Coptic until Arabic replaced Coptic in the seventh and eighth centuries. By the tenth century, most schools were madrassas—educational institutions that focused primarily on the study of Arabic.

There are two overarching categories of schools in Egypt: public schools and private schools. The public, government-funded schools consist of two types: Arabic language schools, which conduct most of the curriculum in Arabic, and experimental language schools, which teach most subjects in English. Arabic language schools require students to begin at age six, and experimental language schools require students to begin at age seven. Private schools consist of four types: ordinary schools, language schools, religious schools, and international schools. Ordinary private schools offer the same curriculum as public schools. However, they perform better than their public school counterparts because they devote more time to student development and learning. This is because families of students who attend these schools almost always have a financial edge over those who cannot afford private school. Language schools are private schools that instruct in languages other than Arabic, mostly English. Religious private schools are almost always associated with madrassas or the Catholic Church. International private schools adhere to the curriculum guidelines of other systems. These include the educational systems of the United States, United Kingdom, and France.

Precompulsory and Compulsory Education, Curriculum, Assessment, and Instruction

Compulsory education in Egypt includes primary and secondary education. Although not compulsory, many Egyptian families send their children to preschool. Nearly one-quarter of all children below age six attend preschool. Given a high student/teacher ratio at the early childhood levels and substandard conditions of many preschools in Egypt, the World Bank and other international organizations have agreed to support efforts to promote early childhood education throughout the country. Students at the primary level learn basic subjects—namely, mathematics, natural science, social studies, and Arabic. Depending on the type of school, students are often taught in languages other than Arabic. The lower secondary education period is three years in duration, and it is highly desirable for students to finish this three-year period. Students who drop out early often cannot find work, and many in fact live in poverty. Secondary school consists of three tracks:

the general track, which emphasizes an arts and science curriculum; the vocational technical track; and the dual track. In order to enter secondary school, students must pass a nationwide test, an examination that, if failed, may result in the inability of a student to continue to secondary school or any institution at the tertiary level.

Tertiary Education

At present, there are 17 public universities, 51 public higher education technical institutions, 16 private universities, and 89 private vocational institutions. Of the 51 public higher education institutions, 47 are two-year vocational or technical training institutes. The remaining four are polytechnic institutes that graduate highly skilled students after five years. Nearly 70 percent of all Egyptians do not attend higher education institutions. Of those who do, less than half graduate from the university. As a result, the country lacks a large population of skilled and semiskilled employees.

The oldest tertiary institution in Egypt is Al-Azhar University, which was established as a madrassa, or institute of learning, in 970. For more than a millennium, Al-Azhar University was the center of Arabic study and Sunni Muslim history. In 1961 it became the second higher education institution, after the University of Cairo, to grant degrees in the liberal arts and science disciplines. In contrast to Al-Azhar University, the University of Cairo was primarily a European-influenced institution that promoted the advancement of arts, sciences, and professional fields such as medicine and engineering.

Teacher Education

Teacher education programs in Egypt are not fulfilling their obligation to the more than 19 million children between the ages of six and 17. One reason is the mismanagement of funding in education. Many preservice teachers who have not found employment or who have not benefited financially from teaching in a public or private school resort to private tutoring and other forms of educational entrepreneurship. Another reason is that teacher education programs, for the most part, are affiliated with short-term higher education institutions in large metropolitan areas. Rural communities have few, if any, tertiary programs in teacher education. In some cases, residents in rural parts of Egypt find it more difficult to be schooled than members of rural communities in other African nations. One major future consideration for educational improvement in Egypt is to bolster teacher education programs that not only emphasize modern technologies and innovation but also grapple with the problem of gender inequality in education.

Informal Education

Informal education in Egypt is severely lacking. Hartmann (2008) contends that the only informal aspect of education in Egypt is what she calls the "informal market of education," which describes the sweeping increase of tutoring centers and informal tutoring agencies throughout the country. According to Hartmann, students and families are the consumers and teachers and education entrepreneurs are the providers, whereby education is no longer a societal good but a commodity that can only benefit clients who have the financial capability to afford it. In sum, public education institutions in Egypt do not have the financial resources to provide both children and adults with the opportunities of informal education—opportunities that, one day, might help eliminate illiteracy in a country where only 71 percent of its population (83 percent male and 59 percent female) can read or write.

System Economics

According to the United Nations Development Programme (2011), total public expenditures on education in Egypt represented 3.8 percent of the gross domestic product in 2011. This amounts to approximately $17.8 billion, or $922 per student (total amount equivalent to US dollars divided by 19,300,000, the approximate number of students in the country). Other countries spending 3.8 percent of their GDP on education include Sierra Leone, Panama, Nepal, Mali, Kuwait, Honduras, and Gabon. However, country comparisons are difficult to discern given differences in population and size of GDP. For instance, Egypt is by far the most populous of all of these countries and has the highest GDP. At the same time, although Egypt's population is nearly 30 times greater than that of Kuwait, its GDP is merely 4.5 times larger than Kuwait's GDP. In addition, Kuwait's government spends approximately

Egypt Education at a Glance

General Information

Capital	Cairo
Population	80.4 million
Languages	Arabic, English, French
Literacy rate	72%
GDP per capita	US$4,200
People below poverty line (2004)	20%
Number of phones per 100 people	13
Number of Internet users per 100 people	14
Number of Internet hosts	5,200
Life expectancy at birth (years)	72

Formal Educational Information

Primary school age population	9.4 million
Secondary school age population	9.4 million
Primary school age population	12%
Number of years of education (primary/secondary)	6/6
Student/teacher ratio (primary)	26
Student/teacher ratio (secondary)	17
Primary school gross enrollment ratio	102%
Primary school entrants reaching grade 5	95%
Secondary school gross enrollment ratio	86%
Child labor (ages 5–14)	7%

Note: Unless otherwise indicated, all data are based on sources from 2011.

$10,946 per student, nearly 12 times more funding per student than that of Egypt. This indicates that Kuwait has a much greater per capita GDP and, therefore, that Kuwaiti families have more income, and possibly equity, that can allow for more school choice opportunities.

Future Prospects

The largest educational concern in Egypt is to determine how to manage an extremely large population given the extremely old infrastructure and overwhelmingly large industrial and agricultural economies, which do not tend to increase family incomes, and therefore, adversely affect global competition and progress toward postindustrial status. There has been some improvement since the 1980s. However, education access is unequally distributed in Egypt. It is interesting to note, however, that given the meager education funding in the country, many Egyptian families resort to private tutoring. Moreover, the poor quality of public schooling in Egypt obligates families to send their children to private institutions if they can afford it. The difficulty for upward educational mobility was due in part to long periods of autocratic rule. This form of power eventually ended with the Arab Revolutions (i.e., Arab Spring), which began in 2010 and remain ongoing. It is unclear whether the new government of Egypt will have a positive impact on education.

Given the poor education facilities, youth unemployment is rampant, and the country lacks a population of skilled and semiskilled workers compared to other North African countries. Egypt's priority in coming years and decades is to restructure and foster a skilled and semiskilled labor force in addition to building an infrastructure that accommodates a service economy. There is also the need for the Ministry of Education in Egypt to decrease the economic gap between the wealthy families who benefit from education and the majority of the population who do not have the financial wherewithal to pay for private education. In addition, the ministry should consider alternatives to the nationwide high-stakes test that essentially determines the fate of students after their primary school education.

Daniel Ness and Chia-ling Lin

References

Central Intelligence Agency. *The CIA World Factbook*. New York: Skyhorse, 2011. https://www.cia.gov/library/publications/the-world-factbook/index.html.

Hartmann, Sarah. *The Informal Market of Education in Egypt: Private Tutoring and Its Implications*. Mainz, Germany: Institute for Anthropology and African Studies, 2008.

Nation Master. 2011. www.nationmaster.com.

UNESCO. *Global Education Digest 2012: Comparing Education Statistics Across the World*. Montreal: UNESCO Institute for Statistics, 2012.

———. "Strong Foundations: Early Childhood Care and Education." *Education for All Global Monitoring Report*. Paris: UNESCO, 2006.

UNESCO–IBE. www.ibe.unesco.org/countries/Egypt.htm.

UNESCO–UIS. www.uis.unesco.org.

UNICEF. www.unicef.org/infobycountry/egypt.html.

United Nations Development Programme. *Human Development Report 2011*. http://hdr.undp.org/en.

World Bank Education Statistics. 2011. www.worldbank.org.

Equatorial Guinea

Equatorial Guinea is a small country on the west coast of Africa, along the Atlantic Ocean. It became independent from Spain in 1968. Like many countries of Africa, Equatorial Guinea is a constitutional democracy, but it is perceived by the international community as one whose constitution is blemished as a result of rigged presidential elections. In recent years, the country's economy has benefited from oil exports. At present, after Nigeria and Angola, Equatorial Guinea is the third-largest exporter of oil from sub-Saharan Africa. Despite the promising levels of income for the government, the people see little if any improvement in their own economic situation. The country is generally Christian. Ethnic groups include largely Fang populations, as well as people from the Bubi, Mdowe, Annobon, and Bujeba groups.

Education in Equatorial Guinea

Preprimary education is available for Equatoguinean children between three and six years old. At present, nearly 40 percent of all children within this age range attend preschools. The school-age population of Equatorial Guinea is approximately 140,000. Of these, almost 65,000 children are eligible for primary school, and the remaining 75,000 are eligible for secondary school. Education is free and compulsory for approximately nine years for children between the ages of six and 14 years. Primary education is a five-year period. Although gender has been represented more equally in recent years, girls are still more likely to enter school later or drop out earlier than boys. Schooling is predominantly taught in Spanish and French. Although the primary school gross enrollment rate in Equatorial Guinea is 122 percent, nearly 68 percent of all students fail to continue beyond the fifth-grade level. Despite this indicator, nearly 85 percent of the population above the age of 15 years is literate. Unfortunately, literacy is nearly 20 percentage points higher for men than for women.

Secondary school begins with a four-year period that is essentially an extension of the basic education that is introduced in the primary levels. Students who complete these initial four years may be eligible to continue for three more years of upper secondary school for university preparation. There are few universities in Equatorial Guinea. The principal higher education institution in the country is the National University of Equatorial Guinea, which is located in Malabo. Students pursuing degrees for teacher preparation must enroll in one of the country's universities that house education training programs.

System Economics and Future Prospects

According to the United Nations Development Programme (2011), Equatorial Guinea's total public expenditures on education were 0.6 percent of the gross domestic product in 2003—the second lowest of 186 countries. Given the GDP of Equatorial Guinea at $26.11 billion, educational expenditure in the country amounts to nearly $156 million, or $1,135 per student (total amount equivalent to US dollars divided by 138,000, the approximate number of primary and secondary students in the country).

The Equatorial Guinean government is economically prosperous thanks to the discovery of numerous offshore oil reserves during the 1980s. Unfortunately, because of apparent political corruption in the government, this prosperity is not shared with the Equatoguinean people. As a result of gender inequality, lack of educational mobility, an overwhelming emphasis on fossil fuels for export, and government corruption, most of the population in the country

lives in dire economic circumstances. Moreover, most of the Equatoguinean population on the African mainland lives in rural communities that do not have nearly the same national benefits as those living on Bioko Island. Although the gross enrollment rate for primary school is 122 percent, only one-third of Equatoguinean children living on the mainland reach grade 5. The gross enrollment rate for secondary school is only 32 percent. School attendance is vulnerable as a result of poor education for teachers, a lack of adequate school facilities, and difficulty in reaching large rural populations. In addition, rural families are unable to afford the fees that are associated with a child's education. Although education is free, families must pay for books and supplies as well as travel to and from school. The Equatoguinean government must attempt to make an effort to improve the economic status of the country's people through education and share of wealth in order to experience overall economic prosperity.

Daniel Ness and Chia-ling Lin

REFERENCES

Central Intelligence Agency. *The CIA World Factbook.* New York: Skyhorse, 2011. https://www.cia.gov/library/publications/the-world-factbook/index.html.

Nation Master. 2011. www.nationmaster.com.

UNESCO. *Global Education Digest 2012: Comparing Education Statistics Across the World.* Montreal: UNESCO Institute for Statistics, 2012.

———. "Strong Foundations: Early Childhood Care and Education." *Education for All Global Monitoring Report.* Paris: UNESCO, 2006.

UNESCO–IBE. www.ibe.unesco.org/en/worldwide/unesco-regions/africa/equatorial-guinea.html.

United Nations Development Programme. *Human Development Report 2011.* http://hdr.undp.org/en.

World Bank Education Statistics. 2011. www.worldbank.org.

ERITREA

Eritrea is a relatively new country in Africa that established independence from Ethiopia in 1993. In 1952 Ethiopia annexed the region of Eritrea and claimed it as one of its states. In 1962 Eritrean rebel forces began what was to be a 30-year-long war with Ethiopia. Eritrea finally became independent in 1993,

Equatorial Guinea Education at a Glance

General Information

Capital	Malabo (formerly Santa Isabel)
Population	650,702
Languages	Spanish (65%), French, Fang, Bubi
Literacy rate	86%
GDP per capita	US$50,200
People below poverty line (2004)	no data
Number of phones per 100 people	2
Number of Internet users per 100 people	2
Number of Internet hosts	9
Life expectancy at birth (years)	50

Formal Educational Information

Primary school age population	64,000
Secondary school age population	74,000
Primary school age population	10%
Number of years of education (primary/secondary)	5/7
Student/teacher ratio (primary)	32
Student/teacher ratio (secondary)	23
Primary school gross enrollment ratio	122%
Primary school entrants reaching grade 5	32%
Secondary school gross enrollment ratio	32%
Child labor (ages 5–14)	28%

Note: Unless otherwise indicated, all data are based on sources from 2011.

after the rebel forces defeated the Ethiopian army. A second war between the two nations broke out in 1998 due to disagreement about the border. Casualties have amounted to as many as 200,000 people. At present, despite findings by a UN-led international commission regarding the Eritrean borders with Ethiopia and Djibouti, the country has asked the UN to end its peacekeeping mission in the region.

The prominent religions of Eritrea are Islam, Coptic Christianity, Roman Catholicism, and Protestantism. The major ethnic groups are Tigrinya, Tigre and Kunama, Afar, and Saho. The most spoken languages in the country are Arabic, Afar, Tigre and Kunama, and Tigrinya. English is also spoken, especially in the cities.

Educational System

Education in Eritrea consists of a compulsory period that lasts for eight years. Children enter at age seven and if they finish their primary education, they graduate from primary school at age 14. Prior to 1993, the year of independence, education in Eritrea was similar to that in any of the other ethnically Ethiopian states. Instruction was primarily conducted in English and in Afar, the most commonly spoken native language in the region. However, present schooling trends in the Eritrean education system show an emphasis on language skills in the three main native languages of Afar, Tigre and Kunama, and Tigrinya. Despite the Eritrean government's ambition toward autonomy as a means of improving the country's economy, student enrollment is at abysmal levels. The primary school gross enrollment rate is only 66 percent. It is important to note that this figure compares poorly with the rates of other developing countries in sub-Saharan Africa. Of the students who do enroll in primary school, slightly more than three-fourths reach the fifth grade. The secondary school gross enrollment rate is 30 percent, less than half of the primary school rate. Class sizes are huge; the pupil/teacher ratio for primary school is 48 to 1, while that of secondary school is even larger—51 to 1. In total, there are approximately 850 public primary and secondary schools in the country. There are also private schools in Eritrea that attempt to accommodate gender disparities and other ethnic disparities by providing educational opportunity for underrepresented populations. The major difficulty

Eritrea Education at a Glance

General Information

Capital	Asmara
Population	5.7 million
Languages	Afar, Arabic, Tigre/Kunama, Tigrinya (other Cushitic languages)
Literacy rate	59%
GDP per capita	US$1,000
People below poverty line (2004)	50%
Number of phones per 100 people	>1
Number of Internet users per 100 people	4
Number of Internet hosts	1,241
Life expectancy at birth (years)	60

Formal Educational Information

Primary school age population	585,000
Secondary school age population	733,000
Primary school age population	12%
Number of years of primary education	5 (ages 7–11)
Student/teacher ratio (primary)	48
Student/teacher ratio (secondary)	51
Primary school gross enrollment ratio	66%
Primary school entrants reaching grade 5	79%
Secondary school gross enrollment ratio	30%
Child labor (ages 5–14)	no data

Note: Unless otherwise indicated, all data are based on sources from 2011.

with private school is that many families find it difficult to afford.

The country has two public universities. The largest and oldest is the University of Asmara in the nation's capital. The second is the Eritrea Institute of Technology. Other tertiary-level institutions include colleges, teacher training institutes, and technical schools that accommodate students who complete secondary school, but who wish to enter a profession without having to complete academic requirements or rigorous programs at the university level. Given its large coastline, the country is home to several small colleges specializing in marine and coastal biology as well as agriculture, business, and health professions.

System Economics and Future Prospects

According to the United Nations Development Programme (2011), total public expenditures on education in Eritrea represented 2.0 percent of the gross domestic product in 2006. Given the GDP of Eritrea at $4.178 billion, educational expenditure in the country amounts to nearly $83.5 million, or

$63 per student (total amount equivalent to US dollars divided by 1,318,000, the approximate number of primary and secondary students in the country). Eritrea ranks 168 of 186 countries in percentage of educational expenditure.

The system of education in Eritrea is direr in comparison to the education systems in neighboring countries. The primary gross enrollment rate is 66 percent and the rate for secondary school enrollment is 30 percent or less. Moreover, 79 percent of all Eritrean children reach grade 5. Although no data regarding child labor exist, it seems as if children are encouraged to work or fight border wars rather than to attend school. School attendance is also discouraged due to the lack of quality teacher education, a lack of adequate school facilities, and difficulty in reaching large rural populations. Eritrean families are unable to afford the fees that are associated with a child's education. Although primary education is free, families must pay for books and supplies as well as travel to and from school. Given the current unstable state of the Eritrean government, it is difficult to determine the direction of Eritrean education and the well-being of Eritrean children.

Daniel Ness and Chia-ling Lin

REFERENCES

Central Intelligence Agency. *The CIA World Factbook*. New York: Skyhorse, 2011. https://www.cia.gov/library/publications/the-world-factbook/index.html.

Nation Master. 2011. www.nationmaster.com.

UNESCO. *Global Education Digest 2012: Comparing Education Statistics Across the World*. Montreal: UNESCO Institute for Statistics, 2012.

———. "Strong Foundations: Early Childhood Care and Education." *Education for All Global Monitoring Report*. Paris: UNESCO, 2006.

UNESCO–IBE. www.ibe.unesco.org/countries/Eritrea.htm.

United Nations Development Programme. *Human Development Report 2011*. http://hdr.undp.org/en.

World Bank Education Statistics. 2011. www.worldbank.org.

ETHIOPIA

Ethiopia is a large, landlocked country in Eastern Africa. The major languages of Ethiopia include Amarigna, Oromigna, Tigrigna, Somaligna, Guaragigna, Sidamigna, and Hadiyigna. English is the primary language used for school and university level instruction. The country consists of numerous ethnic groups, some of which include Oromo, Amara, Tigraway, Somalie, Guragie, Sidama, and Welaita. Approximately 61 percent of the population is Christian and 33 percent is Muslim. The remaining 6 percent consists of those who have indigenous beliefs or no beliefs.

Ethiopia is unique among all African nations in that it has been independent from colonial domination for more than 2,000 years—thus making the country the oldest independent nation in Africa and one of the oldest in the world. Within its more than 2,000 year history, it was occupied briefly from 1936 to 1941 by Italy as one of the Axis colonies during World War II. Despite the five-year Italian occupation, Ethiopia was ruled by Emperor Haile Selassie from 1930 to 1974, when he was finally deposed by a military regime that established socialist leaning state. During a period of nearly 20 years, the Ethiopian people endured famine and disease as a result of years of drought. Despite the socialist leaning government, frequent coups and political unrest did not help the dire living situation of the Ethiopian people. The regime that overthrew the Selassie government was finally overthrown itself in 1991 by the Ethiopian People's Revolutionary Democratic Front. By 1995 free elections were held for candidates of different political parties.

Educational System

The system of education in Ethiopia has a long history of both tradition and reform. The institutionalization of education in the country was the result of Ethiopian Orthodox Christian influence, commencing around the twelfth century and continuing to through the nineteenth century. In medieval times, male children would participate in church services at age four. Their church service attendance was also the beginning of their formal education in that after services, children would begin to learn the alphabet using drill. They would also learn to read through recitations of the Psalms of David and other parts of the Hebrew and Christian bible. By the sixteenth century, education in Ethiopia was influenced by both the Coptic Orthodox Church and the Jesuit branch of the Catholic Church. Schools were therefore run by Christian missionaries from Egypt and Southern Europe. The secularization of schools did not occur in Ethiopia until the early years of the twentieth century. However, for most of the twentieth century the education of the Ethiopian people was not always a priority of the Ethiopian government, given volatile shifts of rule and several decades of political unrest. Prior to the revolution that deposed Emperor Selassie in 1974, the country's literacy rate was below 10 percent. The current rate is approximately 43 percent, with males a 50 percent and females at 35 percent. At present, the educational system in Ethiopia is going through transition in order to accommodate the needs of a rapidly growing population—a country with a population growth rate of more than 2 percent per annum.

Precompulsory and Compulsory Education, Curriculum, Assessment, and Instruction

Preschool education in Ethiopia can be seen in both in terms of the traditional education as influenced by the Ethiopian Orthodox Church, when male students learned how to read and write after church services, as well as through western secular influence after the beginning of the twentieth century. With political instability and the devastating drought of the 1980s, preprimary education was not one of the periods of schooling that political leaders thought to be important to support. Education in Ethiopia in general was a privilege for those who were able to afford it. So preprimary education was all the scarcer as a period of education. The first signs of the necessity of preprimary education in Ethiopia occur during the 1990s, when the political status of the country became more stable. Still, preschool in Ethiopia is available primarily to families who can afford and want a preschool education for their children (Hoot, Szente, and Mebratu 2004). Preschool education for poor Ethiopian children less than six years of age might only be possible through initiatives on the part of external organizations and the Ethiopian government that would provide families with both information demonstrating the importance of preschool education (as supported in early education research) and the means of sending their children to early childhood schools.

Primary school in Ethiopia, which lasts for four years, is intended to provide basic compulsory education for children between the ages of seven

and 10 years. English is the official language of instruction in both primary and secondary schools throughout Ethiopia. Ethiopian primary education within the modern educational system had begun to grow during the late 1960s and early 1970s. Unfortunately, severe drought conditions and political instability prevented rapid growth in the country's educational sector. At present, two-thirds of all Ethiopian children who enter primary school actually complete their primary education. To make matters worse, Ethiopia has the some of the worst forms of child labor in the world. UNICEF data show that 53 percent of all children between the ages of five and 14 (i.e., more than half of all Ethiopian children) are engaged in some form of labor. Moreover, although many Ethiopian children engage in subsistence farming and other familial forms of labor, many children are forced into labor that is falls under child abuse and neglect and condemned by the international community. Child prostitution is rampant in Ethiopia. And although data are unavailable, Ethiopia may have one of the highest numbers of incidents of child prostitution in Africa. These figures corroborate the country's less than 100 percent primary gross enrollment rate. At present, there are approximately 9 million children in Ethiopia who fall between seven and 10 years—the period of primary school. More than 8 million of them start primary school and less than 6 million actually finish it. Even more dropouts occur for those entering secondary school.

With a period of eight years, for children between the ages of 10 and 18, secondary education is the longest educational period in Ethiopia. Like primary education, secondary education in Ethiopia is free. But only the first three years of secondary education is compulsory. Prior to 2001, secondary education in Ethiopia lasted from grades 9 through 12. The government altered the curriculum so that secondary school presently commences at the beginning of grade 5. One major educational initiative during the 1970s was the goal to ease the burden for rural families to send their children to school. Despite political upheaval and drought, the number of primary schools in Ethiopia doubled in some areas and the number of secondary schools quadrupled, specifically in urban centers. Another major educational initiative during the 1970s and 1980s was the partial decentralization of schooling, which granted the nine ethnically based states local control of schools. This allowed for schools to instruct lessons in both English and in the specific regional language. However, this initiative dissolved in the 1990s, and as a result, rural communities remain to the present day at an educational disadvantage when compared to children of urban families. In addition, secondary education curriculum began to emphasize both academic and vocational training opportunities. Similar to other sub-Saharan systems of education, most of the secondary education period consists of a curriculum that continues the basic education curriculum of the primary schooling period. Students who successfully complete six years of secondary school and pass a national examination are then eligible to enroll in the eleventh and twelfth grades, which are intended to prepare students for a university education. During these grade levels, students identify their strengths in one of two areas: natural sciences (earth science, biology, chemistry, or physics) or social sciences (geography, civics, economics, or history). Students who are unable to complete the twelfth grade learn to acquire a vocation so that they can enter the workforce. Students who fail national exams for college entrance have the opportunity to enroll in a private college or university if their families have the financial resources.

Tertiary Education

When considering higher education in Ethiopia, it is important to examine the period between 1995 and 2003—one of the highest periods of growth, both in terms of literacy and educational opportunity in all educational sectors. During this period the annual intake of students increased from 3,000 students, to nearly 32,000 students. The total population of higher education students increased dramatically from slightly over 35,000 students to more than 172,000 students by the end of the period. Seen in another light, the student population per 100,000 inhabitants in 1995 was 65; by the end of 2003, that number nearly quadrupled to 220. Approximately 77 percent of the nearly 200,000 students in higher education institutions in Ethiopia in 2004 enrolled in public institutions and 23 percent enrolled in private institutions. At present there are nine higher education institutions under the Ethiopian Ministry of Education and three other institutions that are under different government agencies. In addition, there are

64 accredited private higher education institutions. The oldest and largest university in Ethiopia is Addis Ababa University, which was initially established as a two-year college at the request of the then emperor Haile Selassie. While becoming affiliated with the University of London, the college grew to university status in 1962, at which time it became Addis Ababa University. By 1987 the university offered its first PhD programs.

Between 15 to 20 percent of the total education budget is allocated for higher education. Between 1995 and 2003, the recurrent budget allocation to universities in Ethiopia increased nearly five-fold, from approximately 100 million ETB to more than 500 million ETB. Despite government instability, the universities in Ethiopia have spearheaded natural resources education as a means of grappling with a deteriorating rate of natural resources in the country as a result of deforestation and erosion. At present, natural resource education is primarily housed in departments of agriculture and natural sciences. The main difficulty with natural resources education is its poor link to research in solving everyday problems associated with the country's land use. At present, the public universities are attempting to improve natural resources education as a means of increasing employment in the sciences sector of the workforce. These universities are collaborating with nongovernmental organizations to help ameliorate the perceived difficulty in linking natural resource education with everyday practice.

Teacher Education

Teacher education in Ethiopia is run by schools and programs in either one of the public higher education institutions, the Ethiopian Teachers' Training Institute, Nazareth Technical Teachers College, or in one of the 64 private colleges and universities. Educational reform in Ethiopia has been a contentious issue for several decades. This is primarily due the fact that the country is home to more than 80 different languages and ethnic groups and its recent emergence from civil war. The Amharic speaking groups in the northern part of Ethiopia have ruled the country for centuries. As a result, other ethnic groups faced inequality and discrimination. Thus, education and language remain important issues of upward mobility for the Ethiopian people. In dealing with the major ethnic and language differences in the country, teacher training in Ethiopia, which generally lasts for two years of formal study and student teaching, emphasizes the use of regional language instruction during the primary school period and English instruction during the secondary school period.

Informal Education

Informal education in Ethiopia is primarily in the form of literacy programs and reducing the rate of illiteracy, particularly among women. These programs have become more successful in recent years, especially after the beginning of free elections. According to Molla (2010), another important initiative in Ethiopian informal education is the emergence of lifelong learning programs. The problem, however, with lifelong learning is that given the lack of basic education, many citizens do not necessarily embrace the concept. Another emerging informal education sector is the growth of adult education in the form of vocational skills. Although informal education in the form of the improvement of general and vocational skills is slowly on the rise, the majority of instruction in these areas is provided through the media and the Internet. Actual informal educational settings also take place in schools, churches, and other similar meeting places.

System Economics

According to the United Nations Development Programme (2010), total public expenditures on education of Ethiopia represented 5.5 percent of the Gross Domestic Product in 2011. This amounts to over $5.212 billion, or $217 per student (total amount equivalent to US dollars divided by 24,053,000, the approximate number of students in the country). Ethiopia ranks 44 of 186 countries in terms of percentage of educational expenditure. This relatively high ranking, however, must be examined in light of the country's overall GDP, and the finding that per capita educational expenses amount to less than $200.

Future Prospects

School life expectancy in Ethiopia is slightly under seven years—the number of years of compulsory education. This figure is indicative of the numerous

---

Ethiopia Education at a Glance

General Information

Capital	Addis Ababa
Population	88 million
Languages	Amarigna (33%), Oromigna (32%), other (34%)
Literacy rate	43%
GDP per capita	US$1,000
People below poverty line (2004)	39%
Number of phones per 100 people	1
Number of Internet users per 100 people	>1
Number of Internet hosts	151
Life expectancy at birth (years)	49

Formal Educational Information

Primary school age population	8.9 million
Secondary school age population	15 million
Primary school age population	10%
Secondary school age population	17%
Number of years of primary education	4 (ages 7–10)
Student/teacher ratio (primary)	72
Student/teacher ratio (secondary)	54
Primary school gross enrollment ratio	98%
Primary school entrants reaching last primary grade	67%
Secondary school gross enrollment ratio	35%
Child labor (ages 5–14)	53%

Note: Unless otherwise indicated, all data are based on sources from 2011.

---

problems that the country faces in attempting to improve its educational system. Like other countries throughout Africa, the largest educational concern in Ethiopia is the poor and dilapidated school infrastructure that has remained since colonial times. Another major step that the Ministry must take is to promote gender equality and political neutrality. Education access remains unequally distributed in Ethiopia, with males having more access to education than females. With a literacy rate of almost 43 percent, Ethiopia is grappling with the problem of illiteracy, particularly in rural regions of the country. There is also an approximate gap of 15 percent between males (50 percent) and females (35 percent) in terms of the ability to read and write. Despite indices showing more students graduating from secondary schools, the leaders of the Ethiopian education system must continue to work on reducing the dropout rates throughout the country. At the same time, several educational initiatives are attempting to improve conditions for students through the use of information and communication technologies.

Daniel Ness and Chia-ling Lin

REFERENCES

Central Intelligence Agency. *The CIA World Factbook*. New York. Skyhorse, 2011. https://www.cia.gov/library/publications/the-world-factbook/index.html.

Hoot, J.L., J. Szente, and B. Mebratu. "Early Education in Ethiopia: Progress and Prospects." *Early Childhood Education Journal* 32:1 (2004): 3–8.

Molla, T. "Widening Access to Lifelong learning for Adults in Ethiopia: Opportunities with Recognition of Prior Learning." *Widening Participation and Lifelong Learning* 12:2 (2010): 7–22.

Nation Master. 2011. www.nationmaster.com.

UNESCO. *Global Education Digest 2012: Comparing Education Statistics Across the World*. Montreal: UNESCO Institute for Statistics, 2012.

———. "Strong Foundations: Early Childhood Care and Education." *Education for All Global Monitoring Report*. Paris: UNESCO, 2006.

UNESCO–IBE. www.ibe.unesco.org/countries/Ethiopia.htm.

United Nations Development Programme. *Human Development Report 2011*. http://hdr.undp.org/en.

World Bank Education Statistics. 2011. www.worldbank.org.

GABON

Gabon is an equatorial country in western Africa. Despite autocratic rule, Gabon is one of the most prosperous countries in western Africa, given its abundance of natural resources and foreign aid. In addition, Lambaréné, in the west-central part of the country, is the city where Albert Schweitzer, the world-renowned medical missionary, established the Albert Schweitzer Hospital, a medical institution and education center devoted to the eradication of tropical disease as well as HIV/AIDS.

Two-thirds to three-fourths of the country's citizens are Christian. The overwhelming remainder of the population is animist. Less than 1 percent of the population is Muslim. Ethnic groups include Fang, Bapounou, Nzebi, and Obamba tribes, all of which are part of the larger Bantu population. Roughly 10 percent of the population consists of other African groups. About 20,000 people who live in Gabon are originally from Europe.

Educational System

As the capital and largest city of Gabon, Libreville has the most educational institutions in the country.

French is the chief language of instruction in both Gabonese primary and secondary schools. Although 40 percent of the Gabonese population is below the age of 15, approximately 25 percent of the population consists of students eligible to attend primary and secondary education schools. Primary education is compulsory for 11 years. For the first six years, Gabonese children attend primary school. Secondary school in Gabon starts with one compulsory period that commences after primary school education and lasts for five years. Students who perform well on the initial secondary-level exit examination have the option, if they can afford it, to continue for an additional two years for a baccalaureate degree. Students who wish to earn a baccalaureate may do so in the following disciplines: French, mathematics, physics, biology, earth and marine science, philosophy, and economics. Students with a baccalaureate may be eligible to attend one of Gabon's 11 universities or professional education institutions. Established in 1970, Omar Bongo University, named after the longest-serving president of the country, is the principal comprehensive university in Gabon. Other institutions include the Masuku Science and Technical University, Health Sciences Medical School, Franceville Medical Research International Centre, and Gabon National School of Law. Students preparing for the teaching profession often graduate from the École Normale Supérieure (School of Education).

System Economics and Future Prospects

According to the United Nations Development Programme (2011), along with Egypt, Sierra Leone, Panama, Nepal, Mali, Kuwait, and Honduras, total public expenditures on education in Gabon represented 3.8 percent of the gross domestic product in 2011. Given the GDP of Gabon at $24.28 billion, educational expenditure in the country amounts to nearly $923 million, or $2,347 per student (total amount equivalent to US dollars divided by 393,000, the approximate number of primary and secondary students in the country). Gabon ranks 120 of 186 countries in percentage of educational expenditure.

Despite Gabon's position as a somewhat prosperous developing country in western Africa, the country is in need of educational improvement in order to improve its economic status among world nations as well

Gabon Education at a Glance

General Information

Capital	Libreville
Population	1.5 million
Languages	French, Fang, Myene, Nzebi, Bapounou/Eschira, Bandjabi
Literacy rate	63%
GDP per capita	US$7,100
People below poverty line (2004)	no data
Number of phones per 100 people	2
Number of Internet users per 100 people	6
Number of Internet hosts	90
Life expectancy at birth (years)	54

Formal Educational Information

Primary school age population	184,000
Secondary school age population	209,000
Primary school age population	12%
Number of years of education (primary/secondary)	6/7
Student/teacher ratio (primary)	36
Student/teacher ratio (secondary)	28
Primary school gross enrollment ratio	152%
Primary school entrants reaching grade 5	69%
Secondary school gross enrollment ratio	55%
Child labor (ages 5–14)	no data

Note: Unless otherwise indicated, all data are based on sources from 2011.

as the health and welfare of its people. Education is compulsory for students between the ages of six and 14. There are problems with enrollment, however. Although the gross enrollment rate for primary school is 152 percent, only about 70 percent of these children reach grade 5. The gross enrollment rate for secondary school is 55 percent. Although higher than in neighboring countries, a secondary-level GER of 55 percent needs improvement if the country is to experience both human and economic gains. School attendance is hampered as a result of poor education for teachers, a lack of adequate facilities at schools, and difficulty in reaching large rural populations. Therefore, the major initiative of the Gabonese government is to lessen the burdens for children and families in rural regions in order to keep students in school through the secondary level. One specific initiative can be the institutionalization of information and communication technologies.

Daniel Ness and Chia-ling Lin

REFERENCES

Central Intelligence Agency. *The CIA World Factbook.* New York: Skyhorse, 2011. https://www.cia.gov/library/publications/the-world-factbook/index.html.

Nation Master. 2011. www.nationmaster.com.

UNESCO. *Global Education Digest 2012: Comparing Education Statistics Across the World.* Montreal: UNESCO Institute for Statistics, 2012.

———. "Strong Foundations: Early Childhood Care and Education." *Education for All Global Monitoring Report.* Paris: UNESCO, 2006.

UNESCO–IBE. www.ibe.unesco.org/countries/Gabon.htm.

United Nations Development Programme. *Human Development Report 2011.* http://hdr.undp.org/en.

World Bank Education Statistics. 2011. www.worldbank.org.

THE GAMBIA

The Gambia is a small West African nation. The United Kingdom occupied and colonized the region in the 1800s and half of the 1900s. The Gambia gained independence in 1965. Between 1982 and 1989 it entered into a confederation with Senegal known as Senegambia. The country drafted and passed a constitution in 1996 and has had presidential elections (although most likely rigged) since that time. The population of The Gambia is 90 percent Islam, and 9 percent to 10 percent Christian. English is the official language, but Wolof, Mandinka, and Fula are also used.

Educational System

Like Senegal, The Gambia provides free, compulsory education for students at the primary school level. However, like most African nations, the primary school system suffers from a poor infrastructure, difficulty in hiring qualified teachers, and a lack of materials for teaching. The gross enrollment rates for students are low: 76 percent at the primary level and 45 percent at the secondary level. The educational system of The Gambia is similar to that of Senegal in several ways. For one, education is poorer in rural communities than in urban centers. Second, a disproportionate number of boys receive educational access compared to girls. Education access for girls is even more difficult in rural communities and in areas where Quranic schools are more desirable than public schools. Third, Quranic schools, run by Muslims, serve more than 20 percent of the primary school population and often have more physical and financial resources than do public schools. Yet curriculum in Quranic schools tends to be more limited than in public schools. In addition, the two systems are similar in structure; primary school is a six-year period, followed by a lower secondary period for three years and an upper secondary period for an additional three years. Most Gambian students do not reach upper secondary school. Unlike Senegal, which adheres somewhat to the school model from France, the Gambian school system follows the school model found in the United Kingdom. There are high-stakes exit examinations for each of the three school periods. At the end of the upper secondary school period, students take the West African Senior Secondary Certificate Exam, which prepares them for different tertiary-level tracks. Students with high scores often enter the University of The Gambia. Other students attend the Gambia Technical Training Institute for vocational skills for the industrial or informational workforce. A third option is The Gambia College, which, like the University of The Gambia, has a school of education, as well as a school of agriculture and a school of nursing.

In recent years, the Gambian government attempted to overhaul the educational system by lowering the age of compulsory attendance from eight to seven, and in some cases six, years of age. In addition, the government created an initiative whereby qualified teachers would receive an education that would prepare them to maximize their students' potential. Teacher training centers in The Gambia are in facilities that accommodate teacher education and at the university, which has its own department of education. Further, in collaboration with public and private philanthropic agencies, schools in The Gambia today have many more books and resources for learning than they did prior to 2000. The government's plan was to reach a 100 percent enrollment rate by decade's end; although this did not happen, the initiative is still in place for the ensuing years.

The University of The Gambia, the only public university in the country, was founded in 1999. The university has developed departments and programs in a variety of fields, including law, business and administration, engineering, architecture, information technologies, agricultural science, environmental sciences, education, and the humanities. In an effort to strengthen its medical, nursing, and public health programs, the University of The Gambia partnered with the University of York in the United Kingdom in 2010.

System Economics and Future Prospects

According to the United Nations Development Programme (2011), along with Eritrea and Lebanon, total public expenditures on education in The Gambia represented 2 percent of the gross domestic product in 2011. Given the GDP of The Gambia at $3.774 billion, educational expenditure in the country amounts to nearly $75.4 million, or $169 per student (total amount equivalent to US dollars divided by 448,000, the approximate number of primary and secondary students in the country). The Gambia ranks 170 of 186 countries in percentage of educational expenditure.

The system of education in The Gambia has been more successful than the systems of neighboring countries. However, it is far from satisfactory. Although data do not exist on the percentage of students who do not complete school beyond the fifth-grade level, it is likely that many do not finish

---

The Gambia Education at a Glance

General Information

Capital	Banjul
Population	1.8 million
Languages	English, Mandinka, Wolof, Fula
Literacy rate	40%
GDP per capita	US$2,000
People below poverty line (2004)	no data
Number of phones per 100 people	3
Number of Internet users per 100 people	6
Number of Internet hosts	1,453
Life expectancy at birth (years)	54

Formal Educational Information

Primary school age population	246,000
Secondary school age population	202,000
Primary school age population	13%
Number of years of education (primary/secondary)	6/6
Student/teacher ratio (primary)	35
Student/teacher ratio (secondary)	42
Primary school gross enrollment ratio	76%
Primary school entrants reaching grade 5	no data
Secondary school gross enrollment ratio	45%
Child labor (ages 5–14)	25%

Note: Unless otherwise indicated, all data are based on sources from 2011.

primary school—given the precipitous drop in enrollment from primary school to secondary school. School attendance suffers from a lack of adequate facilities at schools and difficulty in reaching large rural populations. Rural families are often unable to afford fees associated with a child's education, such as books and supplies. The Gambian government and education leaders must find alternative ways to alleviate problems related to poverty so that children in poor families will be able to gain an education.

Daniel Ness and Chia-ling Lin

REFERENCES

Central Intelligence Agency. *The CIA World Factbook.* New York: Skyhorse, 2011. https://www.cia.gov/library/publications/the-world-factbook/index.html.

Nation Master. 2011. www.nationmaster.com.

UNESCO. *Global Education Digest 2012: Comparing Education Statistics Across the World.* Montreal: UNESCO Institute for Statistics, 2012.

———. "Strong Foundations: Early Childhood Care and Education." *Education for All Global Monitoring Report.* Paris: UNESCO, 2006.

UNESCO–IBE. www.ibe.unesco.org/countries/Gambia.htm.

United Nations Development Programme. *Human Development Report 2011.* http://hdr.undp.org/en.

World Bank Education Statistics. 2011. www.worldbank.org.

GHANA

Ghana is a country in western Africa. In 1957 Ghana became the first sub-Saharan colony to become an independent nation after the union of the Gold Coast of Great Britain and the Togoland Trust Territory. The country had a rocky beginning as a result of several coups that prevented free elections. After a decade-long ban on a multiparty system, a new constitution was formed in 1992, which allowed for free elections with candidates of different parties. The country is nearly 70 percent Christian and about 16 percent Muslim. The remaining 14 percent of the population consists of those who have indigenous beliefs or those who have no religion. The principal ethnic group is Akan (45 percent). Other ethnic groups include Mole-Dagbon, Ewe, Ga-Dangme, Guan, Gurma, Grusi, and Mande-Busanga.

Educational System

Primary education in Ghana comprises six grade levels. Compulsory education begins when children turn six years of age. Prior to this point, parents who can afford preprimary education for their children will enroll them in preschools. The most frequently used language of instruction is English; however, in rural regions and in poor urban schools, indigenous languages will often be used. The primary goal for Ghanaian primary school students is to learn how to read and write in English. In some primary schools, French is the language of instruction. Ghana's primary gross enrollment rate is below 100 percent. UNICEF data suggest that 34 percent of children between the ages five and 14 are engaged in child labor practice, thus explaining, in part, the low primary gross enrollment rate. Data also suggest that only 63 percent of primary school entrants reach grade 5. This explains a 46 percent gross enrollment rate for secondary school students.

Children who are able to finish primary education continue to the junior high school level—essentially a three-year extension of the basic curriculum introduced in the primary school. The general curriculum at this level consists of English or French, mathematics, natural science, one of the Ghanaian languages, information and communication technologies, and social science. Vocational training is also introduced in grade 7, especially in order to accommodate students who will not continue beyond compulsory education—unfortunately, children of poor families who attend school turn to vocational tracks more frequently than do their more affluent peers. The most successful junior high school students are those who graduate from private schools. Public junior high schools in Ghana often lack essential resources for teaching.

Junior high school students who pass a national high-stakes examination are eligible to enroll in senior high school. Successful performance at the senior high school level is one of the main credentials for college or university entrance. Senior high school is currently three years in duration—the equivalent of grades 10 to 12. Curricula in Ghanaian secondary schools are similar to those of American high schools in terms of academic content. Students are expected to complete three years of mathematics, social sciences (history, government, geography, economics), and natural sciences (biology, chemistry, and physics). The grading system in Ghanaian schools is inconsistent with those of other countries throughout the world. First, the Ghanaian education system uses numbers, not letters, for grading (i.e., A = 1, B = 2, C = 3, etc.). More striking is the unusual grading system at the university level in Ghana—namely, the numerical equivalent of A is 80 to 100, B is 70 to 79, and C is considered failing.

Tertiary education in Ghana generally comprises four years of higher education. Master's degrees and doctorate degrees are available at most universities in the country. Teacher education in Ghana can be obtained at teacher training institutions of higher education or in programs that are part of universities. There are seven public universities in Ghana. Established in 1948, the University of Ghana is the oldest and largest university in the country. It is also one of the most rigorous higher education institutions in western Africa and offers most tertiary-level degrees leading up to the PhD, MD, EdD (Doctor of Education), DA (Doctor of Arts), and Doctor of Theology. Other tertiary institutions include Kwame Nkrumah University of Science and Technology, University of Cape Coast, Ashesi University, and Regent University.

System Economics and Future Prospects

According to the United Nations Development Programme (2011), along with Austria, Hungary, South Africa, Samoa, and Finland, total public expenditures on education of Ghana represented 5.4 percent of the gross domestic product in 2005. Given the GDP of Ghana at $74.77 billion, educational expenditure in the country amounts to over $4 billion, or $614 per student (total amount equivalent to US dollars divided by 6,580,000, the approximate number of primary and secondary students in the country). Ghana ranks 52 of 186 countries in percentage of educational expenditure.

The strength of education in Ghana lies in the country's tertiary education system. Ghana is a leader in West Africa in college and university education. Along with South Africa, Ghana leads other countries in sub-Saharan Africa in the number of graduates and the academic rigor of its universities. However, the country's educational strengths end here for the most

Ghana Education at a Glance

General Information

Capital	Accra
Population	24.3 million
Languages	Asante, Ewe, Fante, Boron, Dagomba, Dangme, Dagarte, Akyem, Ga, Akuapem, English, other (36%)
Literacy rate	58%
GDP per capita	US$2,700
People below poverty line (2004)	31%
Number of phones per 100 people	1
Number of Internet users per 100 people	4
Number of Internet hosts	41,802
Life expectancy at birth (years)	61

Formal Educational Information

Primary school age population	3.4 million
Secondary school age population	3.1 million
Primary school age population	14%
Number of years of education (primary/secondary)	6/6
Student/teacher ratio (primary)	35
Student/teacher ratio (secondary)	20
Primary school gross enrollment ratio	92%
Primary school entrants reaching grade 5	63%
Secondary school gross enrollment rate	46%
Child labor (ages 5–14)	34%

Note: Unless otherwise indicated, all data are based on sources from 2011.

part. In contrast to the high quality of the Ghanaian tertiary education system, the primary and secondary education system in the country suffers from a lack of resources, poor infrastructure, and high dropout rates, particularly among poor and rural populations. Less than 100 percent of all primary-school-age students actually enroll in primary schools. Less than two-thirds of the primary-school-age population actually completes primary school. And less than one-half of all students complete secondary school. About one-third of all Ghanaian children are engaged in labor, many of whom do not attend school. School attendance dwindles as a result of poor teacher education and experience, a lack of adequate facilities at schools, and difficulty in reaching large rural populations. Families are unable to afford the fees that are associated with a child's education. Although education is free, families must pay for books and supplies as well as travel to and from school. Therefore, the major initiative of the Ghanaian government is to lessen the burdens for children and families in order to keep students in school through the secondary level. One solution to this problem would be the institutionalization of information and communication technologies that are accessible by both urban and rural populations.

Daniel Ness and Chia-ling Lin

REFERENCES

Central Intelligence Agency. *The CIA World Factbook*. New York: Skyhorse, 2010. https://www.cia.gov/library/publications/the-world-factbook/index.html.

Nation Master. 2011. www.nationmaster.com.

UNESCO. *Global Education Digest 2006: Comparing Education Statistics Across the World*. Montreal: UNESCO Institute for Statistics, 2006.

————. "Strong Foundations: Early Childhood Care and Education." *Education for All Global Monitoring Report 2007*. Paris: UNESCO, 2006.

UNESCO–IBE. www.ibe.unesco.org/countries/Ghana.htm.

United Nations Development Programme. *Human Development Report 2010*. New York: Palgrave Macmillan, 2011.

World Bank Education Statistics. 2011. www.worldbank.org.

GUINEA

Guinea is a West African nation. The country became independent from France in 1958. Guinea successfully maintained a stable government despite severe conflict and war in Sierra Leone and Liberia, two of its neighbors to the south. However, in recent years, there has been some political unrest as a result of labor strikes aimed against what strike leaders maintained was a corrupt leadership.

Nearly 85 percent of all Guineans are Muslim. Approximately 8 percent are Christian, and others have indigenous beliefs. The Peuhl make up 40 percent of the population, Malinke 30 percent, and Soussou 20 percent. At 29.5 percent the literacy rate is extremely low, with a nearly 25 percent discrepancy between males (whose literacy rate is 42.6 percent) and females (whose literacy rate is 18.1 percent.

Educational Systems

Education in Guinea is free and compulsory for an eight-year period. Students must attend primary school for a period of six years. Of the seven years of secondary school, the first two years are compulsory and are generally considered a continuation of the basic education that students learn in the primary grades. As in many African nations, there is a great deal of gender disparity between educational access for boys and girls, with twice as many boys attaining education than girls. The primary gross enrollment rate in Guinea is 86 percent, somewhat higher than that of its neighbors. The secondary school gross enrollment rate is 31 percent, which, although a dismal figure, is again slightly higher than the secondary gross enrollment rates of neighboring countries. The Guinean school infrastructure suffers from all the vices that afflict most other sub-Saharan educational infrastructures—lack of resources, poor facilities, limited electricity and running water, and few books. The government is nevertheless committed to improving the education for girls, rebuilding the education infrastructure, which is essentially a remnant of French colonial schools, improving teacher quality, and increasing the level of services. The predominant university in the country is Kofi Annan University in Conakry, which was established in 1996.

System Economics and Future Prospects

According to the United Nations Development Programme (2011), total public expenditures on education in Guinea represented 1.7 percent of the gross domestic product in 2008. Given the GDP of Guinea at $11.53 billion, educational expenditure in the country amounts to nearly $196 million, or $70 per student (total amount equivalent to US dollars divided by 2,809,000, the approximate number of primary and secondary students in the country). Guinea ranks 175 of 186 countries in percentage of educational expenditure.

Despite attempts in improving the quality of education, the relatively stable government of Guinea has been grappling with war that has spilled over into its borders from neighboring Sierra Leone and Liberia. In addition, the coup against President Lansana Conte that resulted in his assassination in December of 2008 did not help the country's dire economic situation. As a result, various international organizations like the International Monetary Fund, the World Bank, and G-8 have divested much of their resources from Guinea. There is widespread corruption throughout the government that has led to the everyday tribulations of its citizens. Schools not only lack books and other

```
┌─────────────────────────────────────────────────┐
│            Guinea Education at a Glance           │
│                                                   │
│  General Information                              │
│  Capital                              Conakry     │
│  Population                        10.3 million   │
│  Languages                     French (official); │
│                     other distinct ethnic languages│
│  Literacy rate                            30%     │
│  GDP per capita                      US$2,100     │
│  People below poverty line                47%     │
│  Number of phones per 100 people           <1     │
│  Number of Internet users per 100 people   <1     │
│  Number of Internet hosts                  14     │
│  Life expectancy at birth (years)          50     │
│                                                   │
│  Formal Educational Information                   │
│  Primary school age population       1.4 million  │
│  Secondary school age population     1.3 million  │
│  Primary school age population            14%     │
│  Secondary school age population        13.5%     │
│  Number of years of education                     │
│     (primary/secondary)                   6/7     │
│  Student/teacher ratio (primary)          45      │
│  Student/teacher ratio (secondary)        36      │
│  Primary school gross enrollment ratio    86%     │
│  Primary school entrants reaching grade 5  76%    │
│  Secondary school gross enrollment ratio  31%     │
│  Child labor (ages 5–14)                  25%     │
│                                                   │
│  Note: Unless otherwise indicated, all data are   │
│  based on sources from 2011.                      │
└─────────────────────────────────────────────────┘
```

educational resources; more importantly, many lack essential facilities, such as clean water and electricity. To make matters worse, a large percentage of students do not complete school beyond the fifth-grade level, and even fewer continue to secondary school. Similar to that of its neighbors, school attendance in Guinea is hampered by poor education for teachers and the difficulty of communications when attempting to reach large rural populations. Families in Guinea, as in neighboring countries, are unable to afford the fees that are associated with a child's education; families must pay for books and supplies as well as travel to and from school. Families in rural communities in the north and east cannot send their children to schools mainly due to the high costs of transportation as well as the presumed necessity of maintaining agricultural labor. It is also worth noting that the country puts nearly 25 percent of its children between the ages of five to 14 to work, mostly in agriculture and also in mining—given that Guinea has nearly half of the world's bauxite reserves. The country struggles with political opposition, which often results in rebellion and pillage. The major initiative of the Guinean government is to determine how to avoid rebellion and theft of philanthropic support from international donors, whose service it is to promote stability and long-term economic progress.

Daniel Ness and Chia-ling Lin

References

Central Intelligence Agency. *The CIA World Factbook*. New York: Skyhorse, 2011. https://www.cia.gov/library/publications/the-world-factbook/index.html.

Nation Master. 2011. www.nationmaster.com.

UNESCO. *Global Education Digest 2012: Comparing Education Statistics Across the World*. Montreal: UNESCO Institute for Statistics, 2012.

———. "Strong Foundations: Early Childhood Care and Education." *Education for All Global Monitoring Report*. Paris: UNESCO, 2006.

UNESCO–IBE. www.ibe.unesco.org/countries/Guinea.htm.

United Nations Development Programme. *Human Development Report 2011*. http://hdr.undp.org/en.

World Bank Education Statistics. 2011. www.worldbank.org.

Guinea Bissau

Guinea Bissau is a West African nation. It was formerly a colony of Portugal. Guinea Bissau, like its southern and eastern neighbors, has witnessed high levels of political and social turmoil as a result of several coup attempts following independence from Portugal in 1974. Military coups in the country began in the 1980s with the establishment of authoritarian Joao Bernardo Vieira as president. Several coups followed in the ensuing decades. The country was also in civil war between 1998 and 1999. Eventually, Vieira came back to power in 2005.

The majority of people in Guinea Bissau have indigenous beliefs. Forty-five percent of the population is Muslim and 5 percent is Christian.

Educational System

Despite compulsory education for six years of primary school (between the ages of seven and 13, the primary school gross enrollment rate is 70 percent, and slightly over half of all school-age children actually go to school. By grades 5 and 6, only a little over one-quarter of school-age children (27 percent) attend primary school and are successful in completing it. Moreover, Guinea Bissau is no different from many of its neighbors in its practice of gender discrimination. Nearly half as many girls attend school as do boys. To make matters worse, with a national literacy rate at 42.4 percent, 58.1 percent of Guinean males are literate, while only 27.4 percent of Guinean females are literate.

Education for Guinean children was put on hold for many families as a result of the 1998–1999 civil war. The country desperately needed assistance from outside agencies to rebuild war-ravaged schools and villages. UNICEF spearheaded efforts to rebuild schools in 2000 and 2001. The organization donated slightly over $5 million to rebuild schools, obtain books and supplies, and support teacher training efforts. This assistance has been essential given that many public school teachers in the country have difficulty in receiving payment for their services. Language has also contributed to the desperate conditions in the educational system in recent years. Portuguese, the official language used by teachers and officials, is being replaced by Creole by many families and their children. This situation is contributing to a major communication problem throughout the nation.

Guinea Bissau Education at a Glance

General Information

Capital	Bissau
Population	1.5 million
Languages	Portuguese (official), Crioulo
Literacy rate	43%
GDP per capita	US$900
People below poverty line	no data
Number of phones per 100 people	<1
Number of Internet users per 100 people	2
Number of Internet hosts	82
Life expectancy at birth (years)	47

Formal Educational Information

Primary school age population	265,000
Secondary school age population	178,000
Primary school age population	17%
Number of years of education (primary/secondary)	6/5
Student/teacher ratio (primary)	44
Student/teacher ratio (secondary)	14
Primary school gross enrollment ratio	70%
Primary school entrants completing primary school	27%
Secondary school gross enrollment ratio	18%
Child labor (ages 5–14)	39%

Note: Unless otherwise indicated, all data are based on sources from 2011.

Despite a great deal of suffering as a result of war and poverty, schoolchildren are learning informally about the adverse effects of climate change through the efforts of the International Union for Conservation of Nature, a mobile laboratory that teaches about the hazards of biomass fuel—charcoal and wood. The organization attempts to teach students about alternative, more sustainable forms of energy that will be safer for the environment in the long run and may potentially provide economic security for the country and surrounding regions.

System Economics and Future Prospects

According to the United Nations Development Programme (2011), along with Belarus, Slovenia, Grenada, Yemen, and Brazil, total public expenditures on education in Guinea Bissau represented 5.2 percent of the gross domestic product in 1999. Given the GDP of Guinea Bissau at $1 billion, educational expenditure in the country amounts to nearly $92 million, or $117 per student (total amount equivalent to US dollars divided by 443,000, the approximate number of primary and secondary students in the country). Guinea Bissau ranks 59 of 186 countries in percentage of educational expenditure.

Like that of neighboring Guinea, the government of Guinea Bissau has been ravaged by instability, civil war, and corruption by which financial resources donated by international organizations have been used to support rebel groups and military rulers. The decrepit state of Bissau, the capital, and its legislative buildings symbolizes the decaying state of affairs in the country. Schools in Guinea Bissau lack books and other resources for education and curriculum purposes, as well as essential facilities, such as clean water and electricity. Only one-quarter of the school-age population actually finish primary school, and even fewer (18 percent) finish secondary school. College or university education is extremely uncommon; the few students who are eligible for tertiary education must go abroad. Further, the country is in dire need of teacher training institutions as well as vocational institutions to promote levels of skills among its citizens. Similar to that of its neighbors, school attendance in Guinea Bissau is low due to poor teacher education facilities, poor communication lines, and a lack of mobility for children in rural communities. Families in Guinea Bissau cannot afford school fees such as books and supplies as well as travel to and from school. Unfortunately, child labor in Guinea Bissau is high. About two-fifths of all children between five and 14 years are put to work in the fields or in the country's mines. Some boys have even been enlisted as soldiers of various rebel groups. The government of Guinea Bissau needs stability before it can consider education infrastructure as well as economic growth in terms of education output and human capital. Only when the country's government can put aside factional differences and instead demonstrate its commitment and obligation to its citizens will it be able to receive support from international donors for promoting long-term educational and economic stability, advancement, and development.

Daniel Ness and Chia-ling Lin

REFERENCES

Central Intelligence Agency. *The CIA World Factbook*. New York: Skyhorse, 2011. https://www.cia.gov/library/publications/the-world-factbook/index.html.

Nation Master. 2011. www.nationmaster.com.

UNESCO. *Global Education Digest 2012: Comparing Education Statistics Across the World*. Montreal: UNESCO Institute for Statistics, 2012.

———. "Strong Foundations: Early Childhood Care and Education." *Education for All Global Monitoring Report*. Paris: UNESCO, 2006.

UNESCO–IBE. www.ibe.unesco.org/en/worldwide/unesco-regions/africa/guinea-bissau.html.

United Nations Development Programme. *Human Development Report 2011*. http://hdr.undp.org/en.

World Bank Education Statistics. 2011. www.worldbank.org.

KENYA

Kenya is located on the eastern coast of Africa, along the Indian Ocean. The official languages are English and Kiswahili (related to Swahili); numerous indigenous and tribal languages are spoken there as well. Ethnic groups in Kenya are 99 percent African, with only 1 percent from Europe, Asia, or the Arabian Peninsula. Approximately 45 percent of the population is Protestant, 33 percent Catholic, 10 percent Muslim, and the remaining 12 percent indigenous religions.

As a former British colony, Kenya emerged as an independent republic, with the help of the revolutionary Jomo Kenyatta, toward the end of 1963. The country was ruled under a one-party system from 1969 to 1991, when President Daniel Toroitich arap Moi agreed to open the country to a multiparty system. The Republic of Kenya consists of seven provinces and one so-called area, which refers to Nairobi and its environs.

Educational System

Kenya's educational system, though needing much improvement, ranks very well when compared to other countries of Africa. Kenya ranks the highest among all African nations in literacy, with an 85 percent literacy rate. However, illiteracy still exists in rural areas. Surprisingly, females do well in language skills. Males perform at high levels in both language skills and in mathematics. Research has also shown that rote skills in mathematics are not performed as well as mathematical problems in real-world, everyday settings.

Kenya still suffers from a continentwide problem in education—namely, private schools outperform public schools in academic performance. This puts urban, coastal families at an advantage in education. Rural students in the Rift Valley and in northern parts of the country do not fare as well academically, because urban residents more often have the opportunity to pay for private school or possibly private tutoring. In addition, private school teachers teach and prepare their students for tests much better than their public school counterparts. Although not as egregious as in schools in neighboring countries, truancy exists throughout Kenya, particularly in rural areas. In addition, public schools run the risk of receiving government funds sporadically during the year; thus it is difficult to plan annual schedules. Given the promising quality of Kenyan schools, mothers in Kenya will have greater opportunity than in the past to obtain primary and possibly secondary education diplomas. As an indicator of human capital, mothers with strong educational backgrounds tend to have children who perform well academically. The country is slightly more egalitarian than its neighbors in that both males and females have an average school life expectancy of 10 years.

Precompulsory and Compulsory Education, Curriculum, Assessment, and Instruction

Unlike in other African countries, about half of all children under six attend preschool in Kenya. Primary schools generally enroll students when they turn six or seven years old or after they complete kindergarten. Students in primary school learn basic subjects—most importantly, Kiswahili, English, mathematics, and some physical science. As in other African school systems, grade promotion is based on a national examination. Similar to the educational system in Tanzania, public primary education in Kenya became tuition-free in 2003. It is not, however, compulsory.

There are three types of secondary schools in Kenya: public or government-funded, harambee, and private. Public schools are grouped into three types: national, provincial, and district-level. Unfortunately, provincial and district-level schools do not fare as well financially or academically when compared to national, government-funded schools. Harambee, which translates from Swahili as "all pulling together," describes a type of school in which students not only learn academic subjects but contribute to the overall upkeep of the school and its environment. These schools receive only partial funding from the government. Private schools, of course, receive no public funding. Acceptance to government-funded secondary schools is based on national test scores from the last year of primary school. The highest-performing students enter the national schools, while those not performing as well have the option of attending the district or provincial schools. Other students who do not perform as well as their national school peers have the opportunity to enter the harambee schools. Many students fail the national primary school exit exam. These students either retake the exam after an additional final primary school year or they enter vocational skills training.

Tertiary Education

Kenya has a total of 30 universities. Seven universities are publicly funded; the remaining 23 are private. The most well-known university in the country is the oldest and largest in enrollment—the University of Nairobi, which was originally part of the University of East Africa in the 1950s and 1960s. In 1970 the University of Nairobi, along with the University of Dar es Salaam in Tanzania and Makerere University in Kampala, Uganda, became independent. As stated above, students who fail the primary school exit examination can apply to two- to three-year postsecondary schools for vocational skills in the areas of business, nursing, teacher education, computer processing, culinary studies, tourism, and other forms of technical training. Students receive certificates or diplomas upon graduation. Curriculums in polytechnic institutions are the most rigorous and usually take longer than those of other higher education institutions to complete.

Teacher Education

Teacher training for primary school teachers takes place in teacher training institutions upon completion of secondary school education. The Kenyan government has also instituted a policy that enables in-service teachers who did not complete their teacher training to do so in the form of distance learning. This enables them to teach while taking classes. Secondary education teacher training takes place at the university level. For example, the University of Nairobi has its own separate college that specializes in education and teacher training at the secondary level.

Informal Education

With nearly 2 million people living with the disease, Kenya ranks 4 in the world in the number of individuals who are HIV-positive or who have AIDS. This number accounts for an astonishing 5 percent of the entire population of the country. Although it is clear that HIV/AIDS in Kenya represents a health crisis, informal education about health and reproduction has the potential of greatly reducing the number of AIDS cases in the country. As in Tanzania, efforts have been made on the part of both religious and secular organizations to promote informal schooling on the topic of healthcare and the control of HIV/AIDS and other potentially deadly diseases. Informal education in Kenya has contributed to the increase in literacy and the country's commitment to lower illiteracy, especially among adults who have little to no education experience. Some organizations, most significantly

```
┌─────────────────────────────────────────────────────┐
│              Kenya Education at a Glance              │
│                                                       │
│  General Information                                  │
│  Capital                                 Nairobi     │
│  Population                            40 million     │
│  Languages            English, Kiswahili, other      │
│                         indigenous languages         │
│  Literacy rate                              85%       │
│  GDP per capita                        US$1,200       │
│  People below poverty line                  50%       │
│  Number of phones per 100 people             <1       │
│  Number of Internet users per 100 people     39       │
│  Number of Internet hosts                47,676       │
│  Life expectancy at birth (years)            55       │
│                                                       │
│  Formal Educational Information                       │
│  Primary school age population        5.7 million    │
│  Secondary school age population      5.1 million    │
│  Primary school age population              14%       │
│  Secondary school age population            13%       │
│  Number of years of education                         │
│     (primary/secondary)                      6/6      │
│  Student/teacher ratio (primary)             40       │
│  Student/teacher ratio (secondary)           32       │
│  Primary school gross enrollment ratio      108%      │
│  Primary school entrants reaching grade 5    83%      │
│  Secondary school gross enrollment ratio     48%      │
│  Child labor (ages 5–14)                     26%      │
│                                                       │
│    Note: Unless otherwise indicated, all data are    │
│  based on sources from 2011.                          │
└─────────────────────────────────────────────────────┘
```

UNESCO, have contributed resources toward the improvement of infrastructure in Kenya, as well as the improvement of skills so that the workforce can remain competitive, not only among its neighbors, but internationally as well. Interestingly, given that primary school is free and universal, Kenya's school system is unique in that adults can go to primary school to learn how to read and write.

System Economics

According to the United Nations Development Programme (2011), expenditures on education in Kenya represented 7 percent of the gross domestic product in 2006. This amounts to over $4.37 billion. There are approximately 10.9 million primary and secondary education students in the country, so per capita expenditure is the equivalent of US$401. This is a meager figure, but surprisingly amounts to more than the per capita education expenditures in neighboring countries. Kenya ranks 16 of 186 countries in terms of government expenditures on education.

Future Prospects

Kenya is not any different from other sub-Saharan African nations in that the ministry of education's main goal is to build upon an older colonial infrastructure that has little use in today's society. International organizations and private donors assist children and adults in Kenya to become skilled in current technologies and high-level professions. This is necessary in order for Kenya to compete in the global marketplace. As in neighboring countries, particularly to the west and south, more needs to be done to reduce the high rates of illiteracy throughout Kenya, educate orphaned children whose parents died of AIDS, and provide education for rural citizens, most of who rely on agriculture for income.

Daniel Ness and Chia-ling Lin

References

Central Intelligence Agency. *The CIA World Factbook.* New York: Skyhorse, 2011. https://www.cia.gov/library/publications/the-world-factbook/index.html.

Nation Master. 2011. www.nationmaster.com.

UNESCO. *Global Education Digest 2012: Comparing Education Statistics Across the World.* Montreal: UNESCO Institute for Statistics, 2012.

———. "Strong Foundations: Early Childhood Care and Education." *Education for All Global Monitoring Report.* Paris: UNESCO, 2006.

UNESCO–IBE. www.ibe.unesco.org/countries/Kenya.htm.

UNESCO–UIS. www.uis.unesco.org.

United Nations Development Programme. *Human Development Report 2011.* http://hdr.undp.org/en.

World Bank Education Statistics. 2011. www.worldbank.org.

Lesotho

Lesotho is a kingdom that is landlocked by South Africa. The country is essentially an enclave within the eastern half of South Africa. It became independent from the United Kingdom in 1966. The Basuto National Party was in power from 1966 to 1992. At that time, King Moshoeshoe returned to the country from exile and was reinstated in 1995. After seven years of military rule, the country went through a short civil war that led to South African and Botswanan military intervention in the late

1990s. Since 2002 the country has held peaceful parliamentary elections.

Educational System

Control of education and schooling in Lesotho is bipartite. In terms of educational management, schools are run by missions and other private institutions. In terms of curriculum, the Ministry of Education controls content, instruction, and assessment practices. Syllabi that reflect the curriculum in schools are developed through the Basotho National Curriculum Development Center, which is overseen by teachers and school administrators. In attempting to keep the gross enrollment rates at high levels, the government has established some initiatives for educational progress: the development of educational competencies that reflect cultural and social values; the development of institutions that enable occupational and technical skills; informal and continuing education programs to increase literacy and numeracy levels; and educational access for all citizens.

As in most countries, Lesotho's education system is divided into primary and secondary school periods. Schools are available throughout the country. If eli-

gible, students who wish to pursue a university education or study at universities abroad often enroll in international schools in Maseru, the country's capital. Despite the government's role in encouraging education for all citizens, it does not mandate compulsory or free education. Classes are taught in Sesotho in the primary schools. Toward the end of primary school and in many secondary schools, English is also used for instruction. It is important to note that unlike in other African countries, female school attendance is much higher than that of males. One reason for this is that nearly 90 percent of the country's population is engaged in subsistence farming. Accordingly, boys are often encouraged to pursue farming as a means of supporting their families while girls are more often sent to school.

System Economics and Future Prospects

Lesotho spends more on education than any other country in Africa. The country ranks 3 of 186 countries in education expenditure. According to the United Nations Development Programme (2011), total public expenditures on education in Lesotho represented 12.4 percent of the gross domestic product in 2008. Given the GDP of Lesotho at $3.67 billion, educational expenditure in the country amounts to nearly $455 million, or $728 per student (total amount equivalent to US dollars divided by 625,000, the approximate number of primary and secondary students in the country). It is worth noting, however, that given the relatively small GDP ($3.31 billion), the per capita educational expenditure per student is rather small despite the large percentage of GDP allocated for education.

Although the gross enrollment rate for primary school is 107 percent, slightly less than three-quarters of these children reach grade 5. The gross enrollment rate for secondary school is only 37 percent. School attendance is hampered as a result of poor education for teachers, a lack of adequate facilities at schools, and difficulty in reaching rural populations. In addition, families are unable to afford the fees that are associated with their children's schooling. Education is neither compulsory nor free, and families must pay for books and supplies as well as travel to and from school. Therefore, the major initiative of the Basotho government is to lessen the burdens for children and

---

Lesotho Education at a Glance

General Information

Capital	Maseru
Population	2.1 million
Languages	Sesotho, English, Zulu, Xhosa
Literacy rate	85%
GDP per capita	US$2,600
People below poverty line	49%
Number of phones per 100 people	3
Number of Internet users per 100 people	4
Number of Internet hosts	632
Life expectancy at birth (years)	40

Formal Educational Information

Primary school age population	371,000
Secondary school age population	254,000
Primary school age population	17%
Number of years of education (primary/secondary)	7/5
Student/teacher ratio (primary)	42
Student/teacher ratio (secondary)	27
Primary school gross enrollment ratio	114%
Primary school entrants reaching grade 5	73%
Secondary school gross enrollment ratio	37%
Child labor (ages 5–14)	23%

Note: Unless otherwise indicated, all data are based on sources from 2011.

families in order to keep students in school through the secondary level.

Daniel Ness and Chia-ling Lin

REFERENCES

Central Intelligence Agency. *The CIA World Factbook.* New York: Skyhorse, 2011. https://www.cia.gov/library/publications/the-world-factbook/index.html.

Nation Master. 2011. www.nationmaster.com.

UNESCO. *Global Education Digest 2012: Comparing Education Statistics Across the World.* Montreal: UNESCO Institute for Statistics, 2012.

———. "Strong Foundations: Early Childhood Care and Education." *Education for All Global Monitoring Report.* Paris: UNESCO, 2006.

UNESCO–IBE. www.ibe.unesco.org/countries/Lesotho.htm.

United Nations Development Programme. *Human Development Report 2011.* http://hdr.undp.org/en.

World Bank Education Statistics. 2011. www.worldbank.org.

LIBERIA

Liberia is a nation in western Africa. In 1822 many freed slaves from the United States and Caribbean Sea settled along the Liberian coast. Descendants of these settlers make up 5 percent of the current population of the country; the other 95 percent are indigenous Africans. The country is 86 percent Christian and 12 percent Muslim.

Liberia became independent in 1847, making it the oldest republic in Africa. Perhaps the most significant leader of Liberia in recent times was William Tubman, who was president of the country from 1944 to 1971. Tubman attempted to improve the economic and political status of Liberia through trade and foreign investment. He also attempted to quell differences between the descendants of the freed American slaves who had immigrated to the region a century earlier and the indigenous populations of the interior regions of the country. From 1980 through 2005, Liberia went through several civil wars and periods of unrest, beginning with a military coup by Samuel Doe, who led by authoritarian rule. Charles Taylor assumed power in 1989 after Doe was killed in a second civil war period. In 2003 Taylor was exiled to Nigeria, and two years later, general democratic elections resumed.

Despite relative calm since 2005, the region remains vulnerable to more civil and military unrest.

Educational System

Education in Liberia is run by the Ministry of Education, which regulates the curriculum and management of schools. Unfortunately, due to constant civil war and rebellion between the late 1970s and 2005, educational institutions were unable to fulfill their obligations for Liberian children and their families. Preschool education exists in Liberia but nearly all preschools are in Monrovia, the country's capital. Primary schools are also mostly centered in urban regions of the country. Therefore, rural populations have a difficult time sending children to school. Primary school in Liberia lasts for a six-year period. Students are expected to learn basic education skills. Following primary education is "junior high school." Again, most junior high schools, or lower-level secondary schools, are located in Monrovia. The curriculum of junior high schools consists mostly of algebra, history, and some physical science and chemistry. Most senior high schools in Liberia are located in and around the environs of Monrovia. Senior high schools are intended for students who plan to go to college or the university. Institutions of higher education in Liberia include the University of Liberia (formerly Liberia College), Cuttington University College, Tubman University (formerly the William V.S. Tubman College of Technology), the African Methodist Episcopal University, Don Bosco Technical College, United Methodist University, Monrovia College, and the African Methodist Episcopal Zion University. Unlike primary and secondary education, tertiary education in Liberia is decentralized. It is important to note that although primary and secondary education struggles to maintain enrollments and acquire resources for teaching, tertiary institutions have been more successful in educating students for the workforce. The university curriculum is diverse in that it prepares students in a variety of fields, ranging from the natural sciences and social sciences to polytechnic professions, such as engineering and architecture. In addition, there are public teacher training institutes, two of which are located in the interior rural regions.

Liberia Education at a Glance

General Information

Capital	Monrovia
Population	3.6 million
Languages*	English (official, 20%)
Literacy rate	58%
GDP per capita	US$900
People below poverty line	80%
Number of phones per 100 people	<.01
Number of Internet users per 100 people	<1
Number of Internet hosts	8
Life expectancy at birth (years)	40

Formal Educational Information

Primary school age population	588,000
Secondary school age population	482,000
Primary school age population	16%
Secondary school age population	13%
Number of years of education (primary/secondary)	6/6
Student/teacher ratio (primary)	38
Student/teacher ratio (secondary)	26
Primary school gross enrollment ratio	100%
Primary school entrants reaching grade 5	no data
Secondary school gross enrollment ratio	32%
Child labor (ages 5–14)	21%

Notes: *In addition to English, the remaining 80 percent of the population speak one of twenty different ethnic languages, most of which cannot be used for correspondence or written communication.

Unless otherwise indicated, all data are based on sources from 2011.

System Economics and Future Prospects

According to the United Nations Development Programme (2011), along with Peru and Libya, total public expenditures on education in Liberia represented 2.7 percent of the gross domestic product in 2008. Given the GDP of Liberia at $1.836 billion, educational expenditure in the country amounts to nearly $49.5 million, or $46 per student (total amount equivalent to US dollars divided by 1,070,000, the approximate number of primary and secondary students in the country). Liberia ranks 157 of 186 countries in percentage of educational expenditure.

Liberian schools have problems with enrollment, especially at the secondary school level. Although the gross enrollment rate for primary school is 100 percent, the proportion of these children reaching grade 5 is unknown. The gross enrollment rate for secondary school is only 32 percent. School attendance is hampered as a result of poor education for

teachers, a lack of adequate facilities at schools, and difficulty in reaching large rural populations. As in other African nations, families are unable to afford the fees that are associated with their children's education. Although education is free, families must pay for books and supplies as well as travel to and from school, a particularly burdensome request for families in rural communities. One major initiative of the Liberian government is to lessen the burdens for children and families in order to keep students in school through the secondary level. In addition, if the political status of the country becomes more stable, there might be a greater possibility for international investment and more resources as well as information technology and communications, enabling students to succeed in school.

Daniel Ness and Chia-ling Lin

REFERENCES

Central Intelligence Agency. *The CIA World Factbook*. New York: Skyhorse, 2011. https://www.cia.gov/library/publications/the-world-factbook/index.html.

Nation Master. 2011. www.nationmaster.com.

UNESCO. *Global Education Digest 2012: Comparing Education Statistics Across the World*. Montreal: UNESCO Institute for Statistics, 2012.

———. "Strong Foundations: Early Childhood Care and Education." *Education for All Global Monitoring Report*. Paris: UNESCO, 2006.

UNESCO–IBE. www.ibe.unesco.org/countries/Liberia.htm.

United Nations Development Programme. *Human Development Report 2011*. http://hdr.undp.org/en.

World Bank Education Statistics. 2011. www.worldbank.org.

LIBYA

Libya is a country in northern Africa on the coast of the Mediterranean Sea. Although the official language of Libya is Arabic, Italian is widely known in the major cities (mostly due to former Italian occupation). Other languages spoken, especially in universities, are English and some French. Roughly 97 percent of the population is Arab-Berber. The remaining 3 percent is from Greece, Italy, Egypt, Tunisia, Turkey, Pakistan, and India. Approximately 97 percent of the population is Sunni Muslim.

Libya's government system is officially a Jamahiriya, which translates as a "state of the people." According to the *CIA World Factbook*, it is an authoritarian regime in practice. Libya was colonized by Italy from 1934 through 1943 and gained its independence after UN intervention in 1951. The kingdom lasted for about 18 years, after which the Jamahiriya government under Col. Muammar Qadhafi was put in place. From the 1970s to the late 1990s, Libya was seen by the many nations of the West as a "state sponsor of terrorism." By 2004 the United States and several of its allies resumed full diplomatic and economic ties with Libya and removed the country from the "state sponsor of terrorism" designation. However, as a consequence of the so-called Arab Spring, the Libyan people ousted Qadhafi, who eventually died after capture by rebel forces.

Educational System

The condition of Libya's educational infrastructure is more promising than that of Algeria in that the political state in Algeria has been notoriously volatile. Prior to 2011 Libya's educational system was founded on ideological tenets of the Qadhafi regime. Given the transitional nature of the Libyan government, the current state of affairs of the educational curriculum in the country, however, remains unclear.

The duration of compulsory education in Libya is 10 years—from ages six to 15 years. Secondary school in Libya accommodates students from 15 to 18 years old and prepares them mostly for higher education. At about 83 percent, Libya has one of the highest literacy rates in North Africa and on the continent as a whole. Due to more educational opportunities for girls and women, the literacy rate of females has increased twofold since the 1970s. Nevertheless, the literacy of females lags behind that of males by nearly 20 percentage points.

In Libya there are 48 institutions of higher education, of which 28 are universities. Education reform in Libya occurred in 2004 with the establishment of the General People's Committee for Higher Education. This committee promotes further education not only for recent Libyan secondary school students but also to maintain a strong workforce through vocational training that emphasizes the needs of supply and demand for the twenty-first century.

Teacher Education

Primary school teacher preparation in Libya occurs after successful completion of primary school. Most programs consist of either a two-year postsecondary certificate or a five-year postprimary certificate. Secondary school teacher preparation in Libya requires that students complete a bachelor's degree in education at one of the country's universities.

System Economics

The total expenditures on education in Libya were 2.7 percent of the gross domestic product in 2008. This amounts to almost $2.3 billion, or $860 per student. In addition to Libya, only Liberia and Peru have the same percentage of GDP devoted to education.

Future Prospects

One of the main future goals of the educational system in Libya is to rid the schools of the nearly half century influence of Qadhafi. The so-called Green Book, which outlined the former leader's philosophy

---

Libya Education at a Glance

General Information

Capital	Tripoli
Population	6.4 million
Languages	Arabic, Italian, English
Literacy rate	83%
GDP per capita	US$12,300
People below poverty line	7%
Number of phones per 100 people	16
Number of Internet users per 100 people	5
Number of Internet hosts	12,432
Life expectancy at birth (years)	77

Formal Educational Information

Primary school age population	684,000
Secondary school age population	663,000
Primary school age population	11%
Number of years of education (primary/secondary)	6/6
Student/teacher ratio (primary)	5
Student/teacher ratio (secondary)	5
Primary school gross enrollment ratio	104%
Primary school entrants reaching grade 5	no data
Secondary school gross enrollment ratio	110%
Child labor (ages 5–14)	no data

Note: Unless otherwise indicated, all data are based on sources from 2011.

of rule, was used in schools as a means to inculcate children and adolescents in becoming staunch adherents of the regime. The current focus is to rid schools of the Green Book, and eventually invite educational curriculum specialists to assist in reforming the system of education throughout the country. In addition, there is some indication that the modified curriculum will become secularized; although classes on Islam will still be offered.

Daniel Ness and Chia-ling Lin

REFERENCES

Central Intelligence Agency. *The CIA World Factbook*. New York: Skyhorse, 2011. https://www.cia.gov/library/publications/the-world-factbook/index.html.

Duncan, Don. *Education in Libya After Gaddafi. The World: Public Radio International*, 2011. www.theworld.org/2011/11/education-in-libya-after-gaddafi/.

Nation Master. 2011. www.nationmaster.com.

UNESCO. *Global Education Digest 2012: Comparing Education Statistics Across the World*. Montreal: UNESCO Institute for Statistics, 2012.

———. "Strong Foundations: Early Childhood Care and Education." *Education for All Global Monitoring Report*. France: UNESCO, 2006.

UNESCO–IBE. www.ibe.unesco.org/en/worldwide/unesco-regions/africa/libyan-arab-jamahiriya.html.

UNESCO–UIS. www.uis.unesco.org.

United Nations Development Programme. *Human Development Report 2011*. http://hdr.undp.org/en.

World Bank Education Statistics. 2011. www.worldbank.org.

MADAGASCAR

Madagascar is an island nation of Africa located east of Mozambique in the Indian Ocean. Ethnic groups in Mozambique are Malayo-Indonesian, Cotiers (i.e., African, Malayo-Indonesian, and Arab ancestry), French, Indian, and Creole. At 52 percent, people with indigenous beliefs make up the largest religious group, followed by Christianity at 41 percent and Islam at 7 percent.

Madagascar was a kingdom for centuries. By 1896 the French colonized the island. The country regained independence as a republic in 1960. Single-party rule ended in 1993.

Educational System

Education in Malagasy society was always considered a central part of everyone's daily activity. Nevertheless, educational practice from a historical vantage point emphasized the status quo—in other words, education was not intended to be a means of advancement; it was to help in maintaining one's place in a hierarchical system. Moreover, educational practice focused on the training of ritual practice and also respect for the tradition of elders. By the early 1800s, David Jones, a missionary from Great Britain, established a school in Antananarivo. By the 1830s, over 20,000 Malagasy people knew how to read and write.

During the colonial period, which began in 1896 when Madagascar became a colony of France, there were two forms of schooling for children: elite schools for children of French citizens and vocational schools for children of indigenous Malagasy families. Clearly, this system inculcated glass-ceiling status for Malagasy children, who were unable to continue schooling for leadership positions. Greater opportunity for Malagasy students appeared after the end of World War II, when reforms in schooling made it more accommodating for students to engage in a greater variety of curriculum. By 1960 when Madagascar became independent, Malagasy children had similar opportunities that their French peers had earlier.

Precompulsory and Compulsory Education, Curriculum, Assessment, and Instruction

According to UNESCO (2006), by 1998, there were over 1,762 schools in Madagascar that accommodated preschools. These preschools are not autonomous entities. More than half of them were in the private sector. According to Law 2004–004, preschools have played a major role in the educational process in Madagascar since 2004. However, at present, only a bit more than 8 percent of children between the ages of three and five years attends preschool.

Compulsory education in Madagascar takes place for eight years, when children are between six and 14 years of age. Primary school years are between six and 11 years old, junior secondary school years last from 12 to 15, and senior secondary school, which is not compulsory, lasts from 16 to 18 years. Graduates of junior secondary school receive a certificate and graduates of senior secondary school receive the equivalent of a high school diploma, which can enable them to continue to the university level. There are also vocational degrees that are awarded for students entering these schools at the junior secondary or senior secondary levels.

Tertiary Education

The largest and most well-known university in Madagascar is the University of Madagascar, which was established in 1955. Originally, it was called Institute for Advanced Studies and located in Antananarivo, the country's capital. By 1961, under its present title, it branched out into six locations throughout the country. At present, these six locations serve in effect as the primary infrastructure of Malagasy higher education. The central administrative location, however, has remained in Antananarivo. The remaining five locations are in Antsiranana, Fianarantsoa, Toamasina, Toliara, and Mahajanga. Although the university maintains a generally high reputation with numerous separate colleges (i.e., arts and sciences, law and economics, business and administration, social science, and agronomy), the university at present graduates only 10 percent of its students. Moreover, students take, on average, eight to 10 years to complete a program (compared to approximately five years in other African nations). Reforms are currently under way to rectify these problems.

Teacher Education

Teacher training institutes act as an alternative to university education in Madagascar. The country went through a number of educational reforms between 1975 and 1990. Within this 15-year period, laws calling for the decentralization and democratization of schooling were ratified. One result of these laws was the establishment within the education sector of the government of numerous institutions of education and teacher training. This outcome positively affected the economy of the country by putting to work numerous people in many communities whose job it was to construct school buildings and teacher training centers.

The problems of Malagasy teacher training insti-

Madagascar Education at a Glance

General Information

Capital	Antananarivo
Population	21.2 million
Languages	French, Malagasy
Literacy rate	69%
GDP per capita	US$900
People below poverty line	50%
Number of phones per 100 people	<1
Number of Internet users per 100 people	1.5
Number of Internet hosts	27,606
Life expectancy at birth (years)	62

Formal Educational Information

Primary school age population	2.6 million
Secondary school age population	3 million
Primary school age population	12.5%
Secondary school age population	14.5%
Number of years of education (primary/secondary)	5/7
Student/teacher ratio (primary)	54
Student/teacher ratio (secondary)	17
Primary school gross enrollment ratio	139%
Primary school entrants reaching grade 5	43%
Secondary school gross enrollment ratio	14%
Child labor (ages 5–14)	32%

Note: Unless otherwise indicated, all data are based on sources from 2011.

---

tutions, however, are numerous. First, they tend to emulate secondary school practices. As a result, they suffer from lack of resources, neglect and isolation from the community, and erratic attendance rates. One positive aspect of graduates of these institutions, unlike those of universities, is the likelihood that they remain in remote rural regions. One possible positive alternative in Madagascar would be to streamline senior secondary teacher education institutions and reopen more junior secondary education regional teacher training centers in order to accommodate the student population.

Informal Education

Although informal education has been marginalized and considered insignificant in Madagascar, it is nevertheless presently part of the national education policy that is managed and controlled under the Ministry of Education. Given its importance in contributing to the elimination of illiteracy and innumeracy as well as racial stratification, success and realization of informal education in the country will be contingent on public awareness and participation in order to rectify the challenges, which include lack of financial investment, lack of qualified teachers and staff, and the generally erroneous belief that informal education is insignificant. The Madagascar Ministry of Education also needs to implement long-distance learning if it plans to reach remote areas.

System Economics

According to the United Nations Development Programme (2011), along with the total public expenditure on education in Albania, Bahrain, Cameroon, Georgia, Pakistan, Turkey, and Uruguay, that of Madagascar represented 2.9 percent of the gross domestic product in 2008. Madagascar ranks 152 of 186 in government expenditures on education. This amounts to a per capita expenditure on education of $102.

Future Prospects

The Madagascar Ministry of Education is focusing its efforts on improving the overall educational infrastructure of the country. This will involve support from international organizations like UNESCO and the World Bank and from private donors as well, who can supply Madagascar's students with up-to-date technologies and work skills that will allow the country to compete in the global economy. In addition, more needs to be done to improve the high rates of illiteracy throughout the country, gender inequality, and education for rural citizens, most of who rely on agriculture for income.

Daniel Ness and Chia-ling Lin

REFERENCES

Central Intelligence Agency. *The CIA World Factbook*. New York: Skyhorse, 2011. https://www.cia.gov/library/publications/the-world-factbook/index.html.

Nation Master. 2011. www.nationmaster.com.

UNESCO. *Global Education Digest 2012: Comparing Education Statistics Across the World*. Montreal: UNESCO Institute for Statistics, 2012.

————. *Madagascar Early Childhood Care and Education (ECCE) Programmes*. Geneva: UNESCO International Bureau of Education, 2006.

————. "Strong Foundations: Early Childhood Care and Education." *Education for All Global Monitoring Report*. Paris: UNESCO, 2006.

UNESCO–IBE. www.ibe.unesco.org/countries/Madagascar.htm.

UNESCO–UIS. www.uis.unesco.org.

United Nations Development Programme. *Human Development Report 2011*. http://hdr.undp.org/en.

World Bank Education Statistics. 2011. www.worldbank.org.

MALAWI

The Republic of Malawi is a land-locked country located in southeastern Africa. Malawi was a British colony between 1891 and 1964 under the names of British Central African Protectorate and Nyasaland. Malawi gained independence from the British in 1964 and has since been ruled by a one-party system of government.

Currently, the annual population growth rate in Malawi is 2 percent, with 12 percent of the total population living in the Northern Region, 42 percent in the Central Region and the remaining 46 percent in the Southern Region. Over 60 percent of the population lives below the poverty line.

History of Educational Development in Malawi

In 1860 the British colonial government first built schools in Malawi to Christianize primitive Africans through English education. The Dutch came to Malawi in 1889 with a similar mission because literacy was key to reading the Bible, and this became the foundation of the educational philosophy in Malawi. In fact, there was neither an act nor a policy for human resource development during the eighteenth century. In 1927 missionary agencies invested ten times more in education than the colonial government. The government did not see education as a profitable investment. Even in 1980, almost seventy years later, Malawi had the same proportion of its total population in elementary schools as in 1911. Secondary schooling in Nyasaland, as Malawi was known then, started in 1940. The first Education Act was enacted in 1962. After independence in 1964, the government first invited low salaried non-Malawians to teach in both primary and secondary schools. As a result, the gross enrollment rate at the primary level rose from 30 percent in 1962 to 57 percent in 1978. Nevertheless, significant achievements were made in the availability of classrooms, schools, and teacher salary increases during this time. In 1994, when the democratic government of Malawi came into power, Free Primary Education was introduced. As a result, primary school enrollment skyrocketed from 1.2 million in 1994 to 3 million in 1997. This sharp increase in enrollment brought an unprecedented stress on existing educational facilities, such as the availability of educational materials, schools, and teachers. To meet the immediate demand, the Ministry of Education recruited about 20,000 temporary teachers and gave them a two-week orientation course before sending them to the schools. As more Malawians gained access to schooling, the nation began to benefit from sound socioeconomic policies exemplified by freedom of speech and association. It is clear that the benefits of increased basic education are realized with the appreciation of global issues and respect for peoples' property among other things.

Educational System

The Ministry of Education is mainly responsible for the development and implementation of educational policies and strategies in the country. The objective of the ministry is to build a strong and capable organization, which can efficiently deliver education services to Malawians for the purpose of socio-economic development. The Government introduced a new curriculum in January 2007, aimed at making learners become productive citizens by addressing positive social change, and helping them to appreciate economic importance and positive political changes for the rapid development of the country. The Government has also developed Poverty Reduction Strategic Papers (PRSP) and recently the Malawi Growth and Development Strategy Paper (MGDSP) as well as addressed the issue of HIV/AIDS in its education policy to direct and support its Free Primary Education efforts, in order to attain Education For All (EFA) goals. Malawi is divided into six Education Divisions, namely, South West Division, South East Division, Shire Highlands Division, Central West Division, North Division, and Central East Division. Each Education Division comprises of 4 to 6 Education Districts. These districts are further divided into zones and each zone has six to 10 primary schools. In general, a single primary school may have student enrollments from 300 to 7,000 with two to 100 teachers. The educational system of Malawi consists of eight years primary school, four years secondary school, and four years university education, including opportunities for pre-school.

Primary education is free of charge to the citizens of Malawi since 1994. The official primary school starting age in Standard 1 is six years old. Students

Figure 1:   **The Structure of Public Education in Malawi**

PSLCE – Primary School Leaving Certificate Education

JCE – Junior Certificate Examination

MSCE – Malawi School Certificate Examination

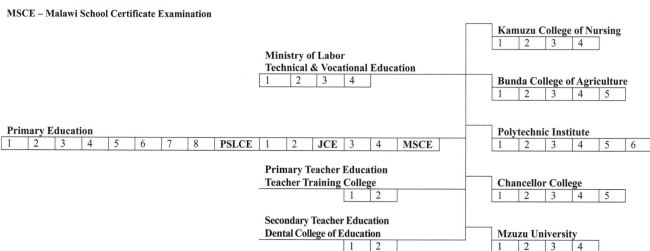

generally take eight years to reach standard 8. In standard 8, students sit for the Primary School Leaving Certificate examinations. If they should pass the examinations, they may continue their education in a government secondary school. However, due to space limitations in government secondary schools, not everyone who passes the examinations will get selected to continue their education. Those who can afford to do so go on to private secondary schools. Secondary school education, from Form 1 to Form 4, takes about four years to complete. Students in secondary schools sit for two examinations, a Junior Certificate Examination (JCE) in Form 2 after 2 years and a Malawi School Certificate Examination (MSCE) in Form 4 after two years following the JCE. The University offers a wide range of four to six years bachelor's degree courses and higher degrees, mainly two-year master's degree courses. In general, a Diploma certificate is awarded after three years of study in a professional course following secondary education. A doctor's degree is awarded after three to five years of study following the master's degree.

Beginning in January of 2008, the primary education section will have a new curriculum with a slight change to the structure. The first class is now designated the preprimary (only fist term) class and this will be followed by seven years of schooling before students sit for the Malawi Primary School Leaving Certificate Examinations.

The nonformal education section includes technical and vocational education lasting between six months and four years. Under the leadership of the Ministry of Labor and Vocational Training, courses in Forestry, Marine Science, Social Welfare and Hotel Management as well as in various trades are offered in this category. The Malawi National Examination Board (MANEB) is responsible for setting, administering, grading, and certifying all public examinations, such as the Malawi School Certificate of Education (MSCE), Junior Certificate of Education (JCE), Primary School Leaving Certificate of Education (PSLCE), including artisan examinations. Private schools in Malawi, also offer secondary education and some are registered with the "Private School Association of Malawi" (PRISAM), which is aimed at ensuring quality education to students in private schools.

Formal education in Malawi is managed by the Ministry of Education, which is primarily responsible for primary, secondary and teacher training, while the Ministry of Labor is responsible for technical and vocational training and the Ministry of Gender is responsible for preschool and child care.

Preprimary Education

The objective of preschool education is to promote the most favorable conditions for the well-being and holistic development of children in Malawi. The majority of preschool children below five years of age are found in rural areas, whereas preschools are established mainly in urban areas. In 2006 there were about 135,000 children in nearly 3,200 early childhood centers run by communities, private groups and nongovernmental organizations (NGOs). Communities in rural areas with the help of NGOs are increasingly getting organized to establish community based childcare centers (CBCC) to provide health care and education to children below five years. The curriculum for preschools, which are also called play groups, consists mainly of pictorial books and visual aids.

Primary Education

Malawi introduced Free Primary Education (FPE) in 1994, which is open to all children. All primary school fees were abolished as of the beginning of the new school year in October of 1994. The objectives of primary education are to instill basic literacy, numeracy, and life skills to over 90 percent of school going age population by the end of 2012. This effort can be achieved by the Universal Primary Education program through the abolition of school fees and school uniform costs, and the establishment of schools within reasonable walking distance for every community in the country. Many of these changes were triggered by the introduction of Free Primary Education as a result of which primary school enrollments rose dramatically. In 2006 there were 5,159 primary schools with an enrollment of about 3.2 million students. The new primary curriculum introduced in 2007 will continue to have an eight-year cycle with three phases:

1. Infant (Standards 1 and 2);
2. Junior (Standards 3 and 4); and
3. Senior (Standards 5 to 8).

Figure 2:   **Organizational Structure of Malawi Ministry of Education**

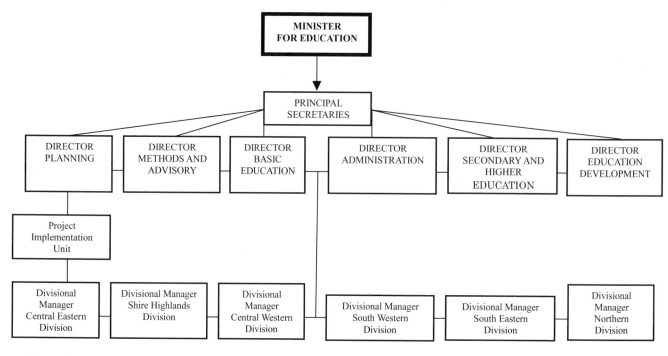

Source: Support to Secondary Education (Education V) Project, African Development Fund, Annex III.

It is mandated that students are required to study twelve subjects in Standard 1, seven at the Infant phase and nine at the Senior phase. The new curriculum is outcome-based with an emphasis on literacy, numeracy, expressive arts and continuous assessment.

Secondary Education

In Malawi secondary school is considered to be the crossroad whereby people either enter the labor force or continue with their higher education. Presently, secondary education is considered a gateway to higher paying jobs; as a result, the demand for secondary education has been increasing rapidly. As a part of the government strategy, the former Distance Education Centers (DECs) were changed to Community Day Secondary Schools.

Students can choose to attend either public or private schools based on their level of performance or choice. The quality of secondary education varies widely in both public and private schools. In general, fees in private schools are very high. Due to lack of sufficient government secondary schools, many students leave school after finishing primary education. However, this situation is changing for the better due to the rapid expansion of private schools and an increasing number of government-run community day secondary schools. There were approximately 978 secondary schools in Malawi, wherein 183,854 students were enrolled in 2006.

Vocational/Technical Education

Vocational/technical education was introduced with the objective of training students for professional roles, such as skilled personnel and technologists in various production areas, and servicing the formal and informal sectors. The government has been reviewing the current curriculum of the technical vocational education to make it more relevant, with an emphasis on entrepreneurship education at primary, secondary and postsecondary levels. There are four government technical colleges for craft, construction, engineering, and business studies with a capacity of around 1,500 students per year.

Tertiary Education

Tertiary education includes university education, primary and secondary school teacher training, technical education and other postsecondary professional courses in Malawi. The objective of the tertiary education is to optimize the use of available physical and human resources. The government policy on tertiary education is to increase access from 3,300 students in 1997 to 12,000 students by the year 2012.

University Education

The government of Malawi has taken many steps to restructure university systems in the country. One of their efforts has been to remove obstacles which hindered access even to successful candidates. Now the universities accept students in parallel programs and on a nonresidential basis, which has led to increased enrollment in the universities. Some universities remain open during the weekends and holidays to maximize the use of available facilities. At Mzuzu University and University of Malawi, distance education programs cater to at least 15 percent of the total tertiary student population. The government has been running a student loan scheme to distribute loans among needy students in the university. Further, it encourages private investors to establish and build universities of higher education. Currently, the University of Malawi and the Mzuzu University have the capacity for about 5,500 students together.

Teacher Education

The teacher training college offers a two-year program, which combines both residential and distance mode of training for its students. Currently, six Teacher Training Colleges (TTCs) with a capacity of 2,700 students are involved to produce teachers for primary education. Secondary school teachers are trained at Chancellor College, the Polytechnic, Domasi College of Education and Mzuzu University. Approximately 2,700 students can be enrolled in the six national primary teacher-training colleges altogether. Secondary school teacher colleges produce about 300 teachers annually. In both primary and secondary teacher training colleges, the number of trained teachers produced annually falls far short of the demand and this has created large teacher shortages in schools.

Informal Education

The government of Malawi introduced an Adult Literacy program in 1986, with the objectives to enhance the literacy of Malawians and to meet market demand related to the changing socio-economic situation. The primary goal of this program is to meet the demand of smallholder farmers. The government has instituted the National Literacy Program (NALP) alongside the free primary education program. The Ministry of Gender and Child Development is responsible for this program.

Education and Employment in Malawi

Malawi has 4.5 million people in its labor force but out of this, only 35 percent are female. The economy of Malawi is mainly based on agriculture, employing 80 percent of the work force and contributing 35.4 percent of the GDP. About 17.6 percent of the GDP comes from industry while 47 percent from services. About 60 percent of the total population lives below the poverty line and this has an enormous impact on the country's education system. Additionally, lower life expectancy (43 years) and high percentages of people living with AIDS/HIV affects both the education and employment sectors. These factors notwithstanding, the age composition of Malawi also has an impact on both the education and employment sectors. The working aged (15–64 years) population in Malawi is 51.2 percent with an inactive age group (65+) comprising only 2.7 percent. Forty-six percent of the population is within the child or youth age group (0–14 years), which means that a large proportion of the population consists of children of primary school-going age. This huge proportion of young people is a potential resource for growth and social development if they were gainfully and productively engaged. Due to high poverty rates in the country, the majority of children do not complete primary education as they prefer to work in the agricultural field rather than learning in school.

Eighty-three percent of children aged between seven and 14 prefer to attend school while at the same time are engaged in piecemeal work for a living during their primary level education and this tends to result in low academic performance. In the same age group, 10.6 percent are fully involved in the labor market instead of going to school. In the age group between 15 and 24, 7.9 percent are engaged in the labor force; however, 44.2 percent of females and 17.4 percent of males neither go to 1school nor work in the labor market. The unemployment rates in urban and rural areas are 21 percent and 5.5 percent, respectively, in the same age group. Only 30 percent of children who start primary education complete the primary school cycle. Only 18 percent and 0.3 percent of the cohort students complete secondary education and university, respectively. These percentages are among the lowest ranked in sub-Saharan Africa and they tend to cause a huge negative effect on the labor market in Malawi, namely, a shortage of qualified professionals in every sector of the economy.

International Support for Education Development

The government has a strong partnership with donor organizations for the development of education. All development partners have their own strategies for the betterment of the education sectors. The United States Agency for International Development (USAID) has been working on the development of Community Day Secondary Schools (CDSSs) in the country to increase access and improve quality with gender parity in postprimary education. The German Agency for Technical Cooperation (GTZ) has helped to set up teacher training programs designed to produce teachers as quickly as possible. The De-

partment for International Development (DFID) trained Primary Education Advisors and constructed Teacher Development Centers and classrooms blocks. The Canadian International Development Agency (CIDA) provided textbooks to meet the demand of a new curriculum. The European Union (EU) and the World Bank (WB) built schools in both urban and rural areas, while the Japan International Cooperation Agency (JICA) and Danish International Development Agency (DANIDA) assisted in various and significant ways to help the Government of Malawi meet its EFA goals by 2015.

Future Prospects

Malawi was one of the first developing countries to respond to the Jomtien declaration by making a bold decision to remove fees from primary education. Since then, Malawi has made remarkable progress in providing basic education to both children and adults as a key strategy in eradicating poverty and promoting development. The introduction of the Free Primary Education (UPE) policy and the rapid increase in enrollment that followed has brought along new challenges to the provision of quality education. The government of Malawi, together with its development partners, formulated effective policies and plans for effective implementation to achieve sustainable educational development, which in turn, will help to ensure the achievement of EFA goals by 2015.

Keiichi Ogawa

Malawi Education at a Glance

General Information

Capital	Lilongwe
Population	13.9 million
Language	Chichewa
Literacy rate	64%
GDP per capita	US$800
People below poverty line (2004)	60%
Number of phones per 100 people	7
Number of Internet users per 100 people	4
Number of Internet hosts	5,200
Life expectancy at birth (years)	43

Formal Educational Information

Primary school age population	2.3 million
Primary school age population	19%
Number of years of primary education	8 (ages 6–13)
Student/teacher ratio (primary/secondary)	70
Primary school gross enrollment ratio	122%
Primary school entrants reaching grade 5	58%
Secondary school gross enrollment ratio	37%
Child labor (ages 5–14)	10.6%

Note: Unless otherwise indicated, all data are based on sources from 2011.

REFERENCES

Central Intelligence Agency. *The CIA World Factbook*. New York. Skyhorse, 2012. https://www.cia.gov/library/publications/the-world-factbook/index.html.

Claussen, J., et. al. *Evaluation of General Budget Support: Malawi Country Report*. Edgbaston: University of Birmingham, 2006.

Government of Malawi. *Malawi Growth and Development Strategy, 2006–2011*.

Kadzamira, E.C. *Where Has All The Education Gone In Malawi?* Brighton, UK: Institute of Development Studies at the University of Sussex, 2003.

Ministry of Education. *Ministry of Education and Vocational Training*. www.malawi.gov.mw/Education/Home%20%20Education.htm.

Ministry of Foreign Affairs of Japan. *The Primary Education Expansion Program in Malawi Project/Program Summer*. www.mofa.go.jp.

UNICEF. *Malawi*. www.unicef.org.

United Nations Development Programme. *Human Development Report 2012*. New York. Palgrave Macmillan, 2012.

US Department of State. *Malawi*. www.state.gov/p/af/ci/mi.

Younis, A. *Support to Secondary Education (Education V) Project*. Malawi: Education Development Division, Social Development Department, 2006.

MALI

Mali is a large landlocked country in the Sahel region of northwestern Africa. In the late nineteenth century, Mali was controlled by the French, but gained its independence as a country in 1960. Mali was then under authoritarian rule for nearly 30 years. In 1991 the government was overthrown and a democratic republic took its place. Approximately 90 percent of the country's population is Muslim. The remaining 10 percent of the population is either Christian or members of indigenous beliefs. Ethnic groups include Mande (50 percent), Peul (17 percent), Voltaic (12 percent), Songhai (6 percent), and Tuareg and Moor (10 percent). With more than one-third of its people living in poverty, Mali ranks as one of the 25 poorest nations in the world.

Educational System

According to the United Nations Development Programme (UNESCO), Mali has the lowest literacy rate in the world—26.2 percent (this figure, however, differs from that given in the *CIA World Factbook*, which shows Mali's literacy rate as 46.4 percent). Education is compulsory for children between the ages of seven and 16. Although compulsory education is free, families must pay nominal fees for books and other school supplies. Like Niger, its neighbor to the east, Mali has extremely low gross enrollment rates. The primary school gross enrollment rate is 77 percent, while the secondary school gross enrollment is 27 percent. Roughly 87 percent of the school-age population reaches the fifth grade. French is typically the language of instruction, particularly at the primary level. Students who pass an exit examination at the end of primary school have the opportunity to continue to secondary school. Despite a growing number of students passing this exit examination, the Malian education system discriminates against girls by denying most of them an opportunity to attain secondary education. The Malian government is currently attempting to reach universal primary education by 2015, as well as attempting to increase secondary school attendance through the creation of more technical and vocational programs.

Although Mali ranks poorly in terms of educational advancement, the country has one of the oldest institutions of higher education on the African continent—the University of Timbuktu. The university, consisting of three mosques, was considered one of the most demanding institutions of higher education in medieval times. At its peak in the Twelfth and Thirteenth Centuries, it reached an enrollment of 25,000 and offered subjects as diverse as mathematics, science, astronomy, medicine, and law. The Sankoré, one of the three mosques of the early university, still functions as a teaching institution. Aside from this historical institution, the University of Bamako (also known as the University of Mali) is presently the premier tertiary institution in the country.

System Economics and Future Prospects

According to the United Nations Development Programme (2011), along with Egypt, Sierra Leone, Panama, Nepal, Kuwait, Honduras, and Gabon, total public expenditures on education in Mali represented 3.8 percent of the gross domestic product in 2008. Given the GDP of Mali at $18.26 billion, educational expenditure in the country amounts to slightly over $694 million, or about $191 per student (total amount equivalent to US dollars divided by 3,644,000, the approximate number of primary and secondary students in the country). Mali ranks 117 of 124 countries in percentage of educational expenditure.

In order to improve its standing in the world, the Malian government, like that of Niger, must invest its resources in improving the extremely low literacy rate. This can be done through both formal and informal education programs. Families must be committed to move beyond a solely agricultural and industrial society to an information-based society that can compete internationally. School attendance is extremely low, and teachers are often poorly educated. Schools in Mali often lack adequate facilities and resources. Also, Mali's rural populations are

---

Mali Education at a Glance

General Information

Capital	Bamako
Population	13.7 million
Languages	French (official), Bambara (80%), other indigenous languages
Literacy rate	46.5%
GDP per capita	US$1,300
People below poverty line	64%
Number of phones per 100 people	<1
Number of Internet users per 100 people	1.5
Number of Internet hosts	524
Life expectancy at birth (years)	50

Formal Educational Information

Primary school age population	2 million
Secondary school age population	1.6 million
Primary school age population	14.5%
Secondary school age population	12%
Number of years of education (primary/secondary)	6/6
Student/teacher ratio (primary)	54
Student/teacher ratio (secondary)	29
Primary school gross enrollment ratio	77%
Primary school entrants reaching grade 5	87%
Secondary school gross enrollment ratio	27%
Child labor (ages 5–14)	34%

Note: Unless otherwise indicated, all data are based on sources from 2011.

---

large, widespread, and often disinclined to change. Like families in neighboring countries, those in Mali are unable to afford the fees that are associated with a child's education. Families must pay for books and supplies as well as travel to and from school. With all of its social, financial, and infrastructural problems, Mali, like Niger, is lagging behind many developing countries of Africa.

Daniel Ness and Chia-ling Lin

REFERENCES

Central Intelligence Agency. *The CIA World Factbook.* New York: Skyhorse, 2011. https://www.cia.gov/library/publications/the-world-factbook/index.html.

Nation Master. 2011. www.nationmaster.com.

UNESCO. *Global Education Digest 2012: Comparing Education Statistics Across the World.* Montreal: UNESCO Institute for Statistics, 2012.

———. "Strong Foundations: Early Childhood Care and Education." *Education for All Global Monitoring Report.* Paris: UNESCO, 2006.

UNESCO–IBE. www.ibe.unesco.org/countries/Mali.htm.

United Nations Development Programme. *Human Development Report 2011.* http://hdr.undp.org/en.

World Bank Education Statistics. 2011. www.worldbank.org.

MAURITANIA

Mauritania is a rather large country in size, yet a rather small country in population. It became independent from France in 1960. The country also annexed the southern third of Spanish Sahara, which is presently Western Sahara. In 1976 Mauritanian soldiers left its annexed territory, at which time the Moroccan government took control of the entire Western Sahara. Despite relative peace in the country, there tend to be tensions between the Arab-Berbers and the blacks in the south and east. The country is almost entirely Muslim with ethnic groups split between Moor and Black populations.

Educational System

When educational practice reached Mauritania during the French colonial period (prior to 1960), native populations were generally reluctant to engage in formal schooling, due in part to conflicts between the French model of schooling and the Muslim tradition (given the predominance of Islam). However, by the late 1970s and early 1980s, families began to send their children to formal schools for economic benefit. Despite the growing rate of school attendance, illiteracy in Mauritania is high.

In Mauritania education is compulsory for students between the ages of six and 14. In general, nearly all four- and five-year-old children attend Quranic school, which provides them with a very basic knowledge of reading Arabic. The duration of primary school is seven years—ages six through 12, at which time students learn reading and writing in Arabic and mathematics and the natural sciences in French. Although students need not continue their education beyond 14 years of age—and most, as a result of abject poverty, are unable to do so—there is a secondary school option, which lasts for an initial four years (ages 13 to 16) and a subsequent level which lasts for three years (ages 17 to 19).

There are problems with enrollment, however. Although the gross enrollment rate for primary school is 99 percent, only slightly more than half of these children reach grade 5. The gross enrollment rate for secondary school is only 21 percent. The literacy rate of people 15 years and older is 51 percent. Moreover, a large gap exists between genders, with males having a nearly 17 percent edge (60 percent of males are literate compared to 43 percent of females). In addition, although Mauritanian families are more inclined than before to send their children to formal schooling, the educational outcomes of students do not adequately translate to the workings of a productive workforce. To be sure, the country suffers from a lack of skilled labor.

Mauritanian students who complete secondary school and have the physical and financial means to continue their education have the option to apply to the university or technical school. The predominant university in Mauritania is the University of Nouakchott. In addition to the its College of Arts and Letters, College of Natural Sciences and Technology, and College of Economics and Law, the university houses seven specialized schools in the areas of business administration, international business, Scientific Institute of Islamic Studies and Research, National School of Public Health, Higher Institute of Medical Specialization, Center for Advanced Technical Education, and the Institute for Teacher Training, which serves as the country's principle center for the education of future teachers.

System Economics and Future Prospects

Mauritania ranks 95 of 186 countries in percentage of educational expenditure, which, along with the percentages of Portugal and neighboring Mali, was 4.4 percent of the country's GDP. With a GDP of $7.242 billion, educational expenditure in the country amounts to nearly $319 million, or $348 per student (total amount equivalent to US dollars divided by 915,000, the approximate number of primary and secondary students in the country).

School attendance is hampered as a result of poor education for teachers, a lack of adequate facilities at schools, and difficulty in reaching large rural populations. Another major problem is that families are unable to afford the fees that are associated with a child's education. Although education is free, families must pay for books and supplies as well as travel to and from school. For families in rural communities, this is especially burdensome. Nevertheless, the country's government is attempting to institute universal primary education within the next five to 10 years. Therefore, the major initiative of the Mauritanian government is to lessen the burdens for children and families in order to keep students in school through the secondary level.

Daniel Ness and Chia-ling Lin

Mauritania Education at a Glance

General Information

Capital	Nouakchott
Population	3.2 million
Languages	Arabic, Pulaar, Soninke, French, Hassaniya, Wolof
Literacy rate	51%
GDP per capita	US$2,600
People below poverty line	40%
Number of phones per 100 people	2.5
Number of Internet users per 100 people	1.5
Number of Internet hosts	23
Life expectancy at birth (years)	54

Formal Educational Information

Primary school age population	458,000
Secondary school age population	457,000
Primary school age population	14%
Secondary school age population	14%
Number of years of education (primary/secondary)	6/7
Student/teacher ratio (primary)	40
Student/teacher ratio (secondary)	31
Primary school gross enrollment ratio	99%
Primary school entrants reaching grade 5	53%
Secondary school gross enrollment ratio	21%
Child labor (ages 5–14)	16%

Note: Unless otherwise indicated, all data are based on sources from 2011.

REFERENCES

Central Intelligence Agency. *The CIA World Factbook*. New York: Skyhorse, 2011. https://www.cia.gov/library/publications/the-world-factbook/index.html.

Nation Master. 2011. www.nationmaster.com.

UNESCO. "Strong Foundations: Early Childhood Care and Education." *Education for All Global Monitoring Report*. Paris: UNESCO, 2006.

———. *Global Education Digest 2012: Comparing Education Statistics Across the World*. Montreal: UNESCO Institute for Statistics, 2012.

UNESCO–IBE. www.ibe.unesco.org/countries/Mauritania.htm.

United Nations Development Programme. *Human Development Report 2011.* http://hdr.undp.org/en.

World Bank Education Statistics. 2011. www.worldbank.org.

MAURITIUS

Mauritius is an island nation of Africa located east of Madagascar in the Indian Ocean. The official language of the country is English, which is spoken by less than 1 percent of the population. Creole is spoken by more than 80 percent of the population, followed by Bhojpuri (12 percent) and French (about 4 percent). The United Nations population estimate of Mauritius for 2011 was 1.3 million. Ethnic groups in Mauritius include Indo-Mauritian, Creole, Sino-Mauritian, and Franco-Mauritian. The most common religion is Hinduism (48 percent), followed by Roman Catholicism (24 percent), Islam (17 percent), and other Christian or unspecified groups (11 percent).

Mauritius is an island that was controlled by several countries. The island was a naval destination for Arab sailors since the tenth century. Mauritius was under Portuguese control in the sixteenth century followed by Dutch control in the seventeenth century. The Dutch named the island after Prince Mauritz van Nassau—"Mauritz" eventually becoming Mauritius. In the eighteenth century, the French seized control and developed the island into a major center for sugar cane production. The island was under British control from 1810 to 1968. Mauritius has developed into one of the leading economies in all of Africa.

Educational System

Despite its independence from the United Kingdom, the Mauritian educational system is based on the British international model, which is common in numerous countries throughout the world. The educational system in Mauritius consists of three levels: six years of compulsory education at the primary level; five years of secondary education, which leads to the earning of the Cambridge School Certificate; and two years of higher secondary education, which leads to the Cambridge Higher School Certificate. The Cambridge Certificates are based on University of Cambridge International Examinations, which are offered in more than 150 countries. These examina-tions attempt to serve as a benchmark for a variety of academic subjects.

Compulsory education in Mauritius is controlled by the government's Ministry of Education. Mauritius consists of five educational regions. The ministry provides regional directorates to lead each of the five regions. These directorates are charged with managing school buildings, identifying the number of teachers per school, and obtaining materials and resources. Teachers with advanced experience in the field can be asked to serve as inspectors for primary and secondary schools.

Precompulsory and Compulsory Education, Curriculum, Assessment, and Instruction

Precompulsory education in Mauritius consists pri-marily of preschool education and caters to families of children between three and five years of age. Although attendance at the preschool level is not compulsory, the Mauritian government subsidizes preschool edu-cation for families of four- and five-year-old children. Most preschools in the country (approximately 83 percent) are privately owned. Managed by the Mauritian government, the Preschool Trust Fund controls the remaining 17 percent of preschools on the island. Most of these preschools are attached to primary schools. The Preschool Trust Fund partially subsidizes preschool education for families who send their children to private preschools.

Compulsory education in Mauritius lasts for six years, when children are between six and 11 years of age. Nearly every village in the island nation has one primary school. Large towns and urban areas, however, have much higher concentrations of pri-mary schools. In comparison to other nations of Africa, Mauritius has the highest gross enrollment rates (101.4) and net enrollment rates (95.4) at the primary level.

In the past, secondary schools were managed by private organizations. These schools accommodated nearly 75 percent of the Mauritian secondary-level population. However, secondary school in Mauritius today is public, controlled by the Ministry of Educa-tion. Since 2007 the number of secondary schools in the country has nearly doubled, due in part to the Mauritian government's massive investment in sec-ondary education. Not surprisingly, the enrollment rates of secondary education in Mauritius are somewhat lower than the rates of primary education. The secondary gross enrollment rate is nearly 88 percent while the net enrollment rate for secondary education is about 73 percent. Compulsory subjects at the secondary level include English, French, mathematics, the natural sciences, geography, and history.

Tertiary Education

The tertiary education system in Mauritius developed rapidly in a relatively short period of time. Given the country's overwhelming farming economy, the system began in the 1920s with a primary focus on agricultural sciences. After World War II, the Mauritian tertiary system branched out into a wellspring of institutions with emphases in numerous fields. The system is now divided into public, private, regional, and online and distance learning (also known as "open") institutions.

The Tertiary Education Commission oversees public and private institutions in the country. The largest public university in the country is the University of Mauritius. Founded in 1965, the university enrolls nearly 14,000 students annually. The university's focus is on agricultural sciences, engineering, law, management and marketing, the natural sciences, and social sciences and the humanities. Other large institutions in the country include the so-called polytechnic institutions (Swami Dayan and Institute of Management and Institut Supérieur de Téchnologie); University of Technology, Mauritius; Open University of Mauritius; Mauritius Institute of Education; Mahatma Gandhi Institute; Mauritius College of the Air; Rabindranath Tagore Institute; and 35 private colleges with specific areas of focus. These areas, also referred to as "niches," include business and management, medical science, and information technologies. These institutions include colleges of particular medical professions (overseen by the Mauritius Institute of Health), numerous business institutes, and technical colleges (overseen by the Industrial and Vocational Training Board). It is important to note that a large number of private tertiary institutions in Mauritius are affiliated with other colleges and universities overseas. For example, the Charles Telfair Institute in Port Louis, the capital of Mauritius, maintains strong ties with the Perth-based Curtin University of Technology in Australia.

Teacher Education

The chief tertiary-level institution in Mauritius that focuses on teacher education is the Mauritius Institute of Education. In addition, several schools of education are incorporated as part of other colleges and universities in the country. Preservice teachers who wish to teach in preprimary education schools must earn a Cambridge School Certificate (the secondary education certificate described above). They must also complete a teacher training course at one of the teacher training institutes in Mauritius. Preservice teachers who wish to teach at the primary education levels are required to complete a two-year teacher education program. Those wishing to teach at the secondary level have two options: they can earn a baccalaureate at the college or university level or a teaching diploma after completion of three years of part-time teacher training. These teachers are required to reach the level of "education officer," which means that they can engage in administrative duties in addition to teaching.

Informal Education

Through the use of technical institutes, adults who do not possess formal education degrees, diplomas, or certificates have the option of attending one of the many private schools that help retool skills for the changing employment market. Due to poor economic returns, many sugarcane farmers in Mauritius are finding it difficult to continue employment in agriculture. As a result, these farmers must find alternative employment opportunities. Informal skills training is one possible opportunity for these individuals. In addition to employment and skills retooling, informal education in the country also includes language instruction and communication skills in numerous languages and dialects. Training in these skills improves the overall literacy of both adult and youth populations and contributes to the country's commitment to lifelong learning skills.

System Economics

According to the United Nations Development Programme (2011), along with the total public expenditures on education in Andorra, Uganda, Chad, Guatemala, the British Virgin Islands, and Georgia,

Mauritius Education at a Glance

General Information

Capital	Port Louis
Population	1.2 million
Languages	Creole (80.5%), Bhojpuri (12%), French (3.5%), English (official)
Literacy rate	84.5%
GDP per capita	US$13,700
People below poverty line	10%
Number of phones per 100 people	29
Number of Internet users per 100 people	30
Number of Internet hosts	36,653
Life expectancy at birth (years)	73

Formal Educational Information

Primary school age population	119,000
Secondary school age population	146,000
Secondary school age population	14%
Number of years of education (primary/secondary)	6/7
Student/teacher ratio (primary)	22
Student/teacher ratio (secondary)	17
Primary school gross enrollment ratio	102%
Primary school entrants reaching grade 5	97%
Secondary school gross enrollment ratio	88%
Child labor (ages 5–14)	no data

Note: Unless otherwise indicated, all data are based on sources from 2011.

that of Mauritius represented 3.2 percent of the gross domestic product in 2009. Mauritius ranks 127 of 186 in terms of government expenditures on education. This amounts to a per capita expenditure on education of $2,181.

Future Prospects

Education in Mauritius is undergoing significant change. This is due in large part to the changing economic climate of the island nation as well as transition from an agricultural and industrial economy to a service economy. Both natural and economic events have adversely affected the nation's farming industry, particularly in sugarcane export. As a result, the economy of Mauritius is based on manufacturing, production, services, and tourism. Accordingly, the educational system of the country must accommodate these changes in order to meet the needs of the changing society. Despite encouraging educational progress in Mauritius, many students still do not have adequate resources for successful completion of primary and secondary education. Sauba and Lutchmiah (2011) have shown that approximately 14 percent of the

student population does not have basic learning materials needed for effective learning in the classroom. Moreover, one in ten students does not have sole use of a mathematics textbook. In certain urban areas, many students are required to share resources. It is necessary for the Ministry of Education to address these problems in order to accommodate employment and growth in emerging economic sectors.

Daniel Ness and Chia-ling Lin

REFERENCES

Central Intelligence Agency. *The CIA World Factbook.* New York: Skyhorse, 2011. https://www.cia.gov/library/publications/the-world-factbook/index.html.

EFA. "Strong Foundations: Early Childhood Care and Education." *Education for All Global Monitoring Report.* France: UNESCO, 2006.

GED. *Global Education Digest 2012: Comparing Education Statistics Across the World.* Montreal: UNESCO Institute for Statistics, 2012.

Nation Master. 2011. www.nationmaster.com.

Sauba, D., and B. Lutchmiah. *Quality of Primary School Inputs in Mauritius.* Cape Town: Southern and Eastern Africa Consortium for Monitoring Educational Quality, 2011.

UNESCO–IBE. www.ibe.unesco.org/countries/Mauritius.htm.

UNESCO–UIS. www.uis.unesco.org.

United Nations Development Programme. *Human Development Report 2011.* http://hdr.undp.org/en.

World Bank Education Statistics. 2011. www.worldbank.org.

MOROCCO

Morocco is the northwestern-most country in Africa. The official language is Arabic although French is also used for commerce and in some colleges and universities. Berber dialects are quite common, especially in rural communities. Roughly 99 percent of the population is Arab-Berber. The remaining 0.7 percent includes Sephardic Jewish populations and other groups. Approximately 99 percent of the population is Muslim. The remaining 1 percent consists of Christians and Jews.

Morocco has a rich history that dates back to the early Middle Ages. Before that time, the Phoenicians established the trading posts in the region that enabled them to trade with communities along the Atlantic coast of Europe. Morocco was ruled by a succession of Moorish dynasties approximately a century after the Arab conquest of northern Africa. Under the leadership of Ahmad Al-Mansur in the late sixteenth century, the region became self-sufficient, and it resisted foreign invasion for nearly two and a half centuries. By 1860 Spain occupied most of the northern part of the country. France occupied the region for nearly 45 years—from 1912 to 1956. About a decade after independence in 1956, Morocco annexed what is presently the Western Sahara.

Educational System

The Moroccan government has been instrumental in the last decade in improving its people's access to primary, secondary, and tertiary education. The Ministry of National Education and Ministry of Higher Education and Executive Training are the two governmental agencies that oversee education in Morocco. Primary education in Morocco is a period of six years. This is followed by an intermediate school period of three years, and then an upper secondary period for an additional three years. During the "education decade" in Morocco, between 1999 and 2009, the Ministry of National Education decentralized education oversight to a degree and allowed the country's districts and regions some autonomy in making educational decisions. The Ministry of National Education, however, still plays a crucial part in transitioning the country's education standing from a colonial system to a postcolonial, information-based system.

Precompulsory and Compulsory Education, Curriculum, Assessment, and Instruction

Preschool education in Morocco attempts to accommodate children less than six years of age. Families have the option to send their preschoolers to kindergartens or to Quranic schools. Kindergartens are private schools based primarily in urban areas. Given their private status, they seem to cater only to families who can afford them. Students in kindergartens learn how to read and learn basic mathematical skills. Quranic schools have been instrumental because they tend to be more accessible for most families. These schools also help children read and write. As a result

of Quranic schools, enrollment rates at the preschool level have exceeded the 60 percent mark.

Primary school, which lasts for six years, provides basic compulsory education for children. Those who pass a Certificate of Study can continue to the secondary level. Although the gross enrollment rate for primary school in Morocco is over 100 percent, there is a major gap between genders in terms of primary school education attainment, with males succeeding to secondary school at higher numbers than females. Although primary education attainment is improving, the percentage of students reaching grade 5 is still lower than in most Arab nations.

The lower secondary school level is essentially a continuation of basic education after primary school. In Morocco it typically lasts for three years. Upon successful completion of middle school, students continue to upper secondary school where they take more advanced courses, particularly in mathematics and the physical, life, and earth sciences, as well as technical and vocational courses. Unfortunately, school attendance drops precipitously from primary school to secondary school. The gross enrollment ratio for primary school is 107 percent while the ratio for secondary school is 49 percent, less than half the enrollment ratio for primary school.

Tertiary Education

During the Middle Ages, Morocco was a leading center of Islamic thought. Kairouyine University, a relatively unknown university in Fez, was established in 862. The development of educational institutions thrived for centuries. In the fourteenth century, the Ali ben Youssef Medersa University in Marrakech was established in order to promote Islamic religion and philosophy. Since independence in 1956, higher education enrollment in Morocco has grown more than 11 percent, and, despite gender disparity, a growing number of female students are entering higher education institutions. Currently, there are 14 public research universities in the country. Acceptance to these institutions is competitive and requires a baccalaureate degree, while acceptance to polytechnic institutions and other higher education schools requires students to pass an entry examination.

Among all the North African institutions of higher education, Moroccan universities have been leading centers in the areas of engineering, medicine, business, and law. Although Moroccan primary and secondary schools have progressed slowly, colleges and universities are more successful due to greater financial resources. Information and communication technologies and software and hardware development are becoming increasingly relevant at the university level as more students are majoring in these areas.

Teacher Education

Part of the tertiary education sector provides education for teachers—namely, teacher training institutes. As stated above, information and communication technologies have grown tremendously as areas of interest for many tertiary students, so much so that teacher training colleges emphasize the use of these technologies for the purpose of preparing future primary and secondary school teachers. Educational philanthropists and organizations in the United States and Europe, particularly the US Agency for International Development, have funded the Computer-Assisted Teacher Training (CATT) project to help preserve and in-service teachers in Moroccan teacher training schools, as well as teachers in other

developing nations, provide education in the most impoverished and hard-to-reach locations in the country (Coupe and Haichour 2002).

Informal Education

Informal education in Morocco primarily takes the form of literacy programs. These programs have become more successful in recent years. Data from the Ministry of National Education's Literacy Department suggest that the number of students in literacy programs rose from 655,000 students in 2003 to more than 705,000 in 2007. Literacy programs in Morocco have remained at the 700,000 enrollment levels in subsequent years. Nearly two-thirds of these students were adults, and 80 percent of these adults were women. Moreover, half of all women enrolled in literacy programs are from Morocco's rural areas. Although informal education in the form of the improvement of general and vocational skills is slowly on the rise, most instruction in these areas is provided through the media and the Internet. Mosques and other similar meeting places also provide informal education settings.

System Economics

According to the United Nations Development Programme (2011), total public expenditures on education in Morocco represented 5.7 percent of the gross domestic product in 2008. This amounts to over $8.778 billion, or $1,148 per student (total amount equivalent to US dollars divided by 7,650,000, the approximate number of students in the country). Other countries whose educational expenditures are 5.7 percent of their GDP include Cape Verde and Saudi Arabia. Morocco ranks 40 of 186 countries in percentage of educational expenditure.

Future Prospects

Like other countries throughout Africa, the largest educational concern in Morocco is the old school infrastructure from colonial times. Another major step that the ministry must take is to promote gender equality and political neutrality. Education access remains unequally distributed in Morocco. With a literacy rate of almost 52 percent, Morocco still faces difficulties with illiteracy. Further, there is an

---

Morocco Education at a Glance

General Information

Capital	Rabat
Population	31.6 million
Languages	Arabic, Berber, French
Literacy rate	52%
GDP per capita	US$4,600
People below poverty line	19%
Number of phones per 100 people	9.5
Number of Internet users per 100 people	32.5
Number of Internet hosts	277,793
Life expectancy at birth (years)	71

Formal Educational Information

Primary school age population	3.7 million
Secondary school age population	3.9 million
Primary school age population	12%
Number of years of education (primary/secondary)	6/6
Student/teacher ratio (primary)	27
Student/teacher ratio (secondary)	19
Primary school gross enrollment ratio	107%
Primary school entrants reaching grade 5	79%
Secondary school gross enrollment ratio	49%
Child labor (ages 5–14)	8%

Note: Unless otherwise indicated, all data are based on sources from 2011.

approximate gap of 26 percent between males (66 percent) and females (40 percent) in terms of the ability to read and write. Despite indices showing more students graduating from secondary schools, the Moroccan education ministries must continue to work on reducing the dropout rates throughout the country. At the same time, several educational initiatives are attempting to improve conditions for students through the use of information and communication technologies.

Daniel Ness and Chia-ling Lin

REFERENCES

Central Intelligence Agency. *The CIA World Factbook*. New York: Skyhorse, 2011. https://www.cia.gov/library/publications/the-world-factbook/index.html.

Coupe, J., and E. Haichour. "Rethinking Technology Pathways: Morocco's CATT-PILOTE Teacher Training Project." *Techknologia* 16 (2002).

Nation Master. 2011. www.nationmaster.com.

UNESCO. *Global Education Digest 2012: Comparing Education Statistics Across the World*. Montreal: UNESCO Institute for Statistics, 2012.

———. "Strong Foundations: Early Childhood Care and Education." *Education for All Global Monitoring Report*. Paris: UNESCO, 2006.

UNESCO–IBE. www.ibe.unesco.org/countries/Morocco.htm.

United Nations Development Programme. *Human Development Report 2011*. http://hdr.undp.org/en.

World Bank Education Statistics. 2011. www.worldbank.org.

MOZAMBIQUE

Mozambique is located on the southeastern coast of Africa, along the Indian Ocean. The official language is Portuguese, which is spoken by approximately one-third of the population, but mostly as a second language. Native languages include Emakhuwa, Xichangana, Elomwe, Cisena, and Echuwabo, as well as a large number of regional Mozambican languages. Ethnic groups in Mozambique are 99.66 percent African, with only 0.06 from Europe, 0.2 percent European and African, and 0.08 percent Indian. Religion in Mozambique is diverse, with 40 percent of the population Christian (23 percent Catholic), 18 percent Muslim, 18 percent practicing other religions, and 23 percent following none.

A Portuguese colony for nearly five centuries, Mozambique achieved independence in June 1975, about five months before Angola, another Portuguese colony, became independent. Mozambique, a republic with a unicameral legislative branch, consists of 10 provinces. Although the country was ravaged by civil war between the Marxist ruling Front for the Liberation of Mozambique and the rebel Mozambique National Resistance, during which development of infrastructure and education was stagnant for nearly two decades, a UN peace treaty formally ended fighting in 1992. Since then, Mozambique's development has steadily, but slowly, improved.

Educational System

In Mozambique the beginning of educational reform after independence from Portugal occurred in 1983 with the National System of Education (SNE). Prior to 1975, the year of independence, the colony's schools were primarily public schools in which content was taught in Portuguese, missionary schools, and private elite schools. At this time, public schools, which were located primarily in Maputo and other urban areas, functioned as institutions that educated the Portuguese population as well as those who planned to assimilate into Portuguese society. The missionary schools served primarily agrarian families who populated the rural regions of Mozambique and thus were unable to travel long distances to schools in urban areas. Although not considered missionary schools, private schools were owned by the church and functioned primarily to serve wealthy families who also lived in the cities. The major problem with the schools before independence was that the better schools were highly selective and served only a very small segment of the school-age population. This paradigm had become a staple of schooling in Mozambique even after the country became independent from Portugal.

The SNE comprises five subsystems, namely general education, adult education, technical training/vocational education, teacher training, and higher education. The education system is organized into three levels, namely, primary (lower primary and upper primary), secondary (junior secondary and senior secondary), and higher education.

Precompulsory and Compulsory Education, Curriculum, Assessment, and Instruction

Nearly all children in Mozambique have been affected by the AIDS epidemic. Many have lost parents and other relatives, while others have known friends who have died from the disease. To improve preschool education and the well-being of young Mozambican children, many of whom are orphans, the organization Save the Children has helped develop early childhood programs in both urban and rural areas. Their most innovative program to date is a visual arts curriculum that is intended to help children connect their own lives and experiences with those of others.

Since 1992 education in Mozambique has been free and compulsory for a period of 12 years. Despite free schooling, families, many of whom live below the international poverty line, are required to pay low, but at the same time burdensome, matriculation fees. It is, however, difficult to enforce compulsory schooling, particularly in the secondary grades, because the country lacks numerous resources for its formal schools. Moreover, schooling in rural areas makes it all the more difficult for administrators to enforce school attendance. Like many new African republics, school attendance remains a significant problem. During the 1990s, slightly over 50 percent of primary-school-age children were attending school. In the first decade of this century, slightly below 50 percent of Mozambican children who started primary school were expected to reach the fifth grade.

Education remains problematic for children and adults for several reasons; the most egregious are inadequate medical and healthcare, lack of financial and physical resources, and a poor communication system. As a case in point, in 2004 there were nearly 400,000 children in Mozambique who were orphans because their parents had died of AIDS. In other words, one in 10 school-age children was an orphan as a result of the deadly disease. HIV/AIDS infection has also contributed to a decline in the Mozambican teacher population. In 2007 one in four Mozambican children still did not attend school. The majority of these children live in rural regions, many of which are hundreds of miles from the nearest school. In addition, teacher training is in stark need of improvement; most teachers in rural schools are poorly trained. Although the education of girls has increased, the level of female student attrition far exceeds completion.

Primary education in Mozambique is a two-level system—lower primary (grades 1 to 5) and upper primary (grades 6 and 7). Due to either a paucity of schools in a given region or an excess of schools in an urban area, the ministry developed a shift system (i.e., one, two, or three shifts) whereby a greater number of students can be accommodated. Upon completion of seven years of primary school, students may be able to enroll in secondary schools, depending on family budget and school resources. Secondary education consists of two stages: junior secondary (grades 8 to 10) and senior secondary (grades 11 and 12).

Tertiary Education

Compared with the United States, which has in excess of 16.4 million students attending higher education institutions, a rate of over 5,000 per 100,000, Mozambique has a total higher education population of a little more than 11,000 students (about 50 in 100,000). Staff and students are still overwhelmingly European. When Mozambique reached independence, the staff and student population of Eduardo Mondlane University (formerly the University of Lourenço Marquez during Portuguese colonization) dropped precipitously—a nearly 70 percent decline. Eduardo Mondlane University officials have undergone reforms to increase the student population by instituting a Faculty of Education. With the establishment of a few other tertiary institutions (one for training diplomats and another for training teachers), Eduardo Mondlane University remains the premier institution in Mozambique, with over 8,000 students. Technical and vocational training takes place at the secondary level.

Teacher Education

The education of incoming teachers is headed by a branch of the Mozambican Education Ministry called the National Directorate for Teacher Training. Formal teacher education in Mozambique takes place primarily in two higher education institutions: Eduardo Mondlane University and the Higher Pedagogical Institute. The School of Education at

Eduardo Mondlane University maintains its focus on the theoretical and practical connections of education and the transmission of knowledge. It is one of the country's primary teacher education institutions that coordinate with the Education Ministry in terms of teaching curriculum and educational policy. The school attempts to implement strategies from education research as a means of improving teacher education and pedagogical skills throughout the country. Therefore, the education school at Eduardo Mondlane University bases its educational and research activities on the notion that the effectiveness and quality of teachers can be improved by increasing the level of teacher content knowledge and pedagogical knowledge. Although the school has collaborated with the Ministry of Education in obtaining new technology and attempting to educate and update the scientific knowledge and professionalism of secondary school teachers and other professionals, the country still remains deficient in financial and physical resources. One or two teacher training institutions is not sufficient in graduating teachers for a country whose student population is in excess of 6.3 million (nearly one-third of the country's total population). Other teacher training institutions are often found in secondary schools, particularly for students who completed grade 7 and wish to pursue teacher training for primary school. This characteristic of Mozambican teacher education for primary school teachers is in dire need of reform due to the very young ages, limited content knowledge, and lack of experience of primary school teacher candidates.

Informal Education

One of the most significant aspects of informal education in Mozambique is the ministry's growing commitment to eradicate illiteracy of both children and adults. Some organizations, most significantly UNESCO, have contributed resources toward this effort; however, due to lack of funding and poor infrastructure, this agenda remains of a challenge. Nevertheless, one major initiative that has been successful is secondary school for adults who wish to finish their secondary education. This service helps adults achieve strong literacy and numeracy skills and also allows them to pursue technical and vocational training in several areas.

Mozambique Education at a Glance

General Information

Capital	Maputo
Population	22 million
Languages	Emakhuwa, Xichangana, Portuguese (official), Elomwe, Echuwabo, other indigenous languages (32%)
Literacy rate	48%
GDP per capita	US$1,500
People below poverty line	70%
Number of phones per 100 people	<1
Number of Internet users per 100 people	1.5
Number of Internet hosts	21,172
Life expectancy at birth (years)	41

Formal Educational Information

Primary school age population	3.9 million
Secondary school age population	2.3 million
Primary school age population*	18%
Secondary school age population*	11%
Number of years of education (primary/secondary)	7/5
Student/teacher ratio (primary)	66
Student/teacher ratio (secondary)	32
Primary school gross enrollment ratio	102%
Primary school entrants reaching grade 5	62.5%
Secondary school gross enrollment ratio	13%
Child labor (ages 5–14)	22%

Notes: *Nearly 30 percent of Mozambique's population (close to one-third) is of school age (five to 18 years old).

Unless otherwise indicated, all data are based on sources from 2011.

System Economics

According to the United Nations Development Programme (2011), along with the total public expenditures on education in Costa Rica, Latvia, Estonia, and Seychelles, that of Mozambique represented 5 percent of the gross domestic product in 2008. Mozambique ranks 70 of 186 in government expenditures on education. The problem, however, is that per capita expenditure on education amounts to only $158. Despite this meager amount, children in Mozambique tend to stay in school for at least two to three years longer than in other developing countries.

Future Prospects

The Mozambican Ministry of Education is focusing its efforts on improving the overall educational infrastructure of the country. This will involve support from international organizations like UNESCO and the World Bank and from private donors as well, who can supply Mozambican students with up-to-date technologies and work skills that will allow the country to compete in the global economy. In addition, more needs to be done to improve the high rates of illiteracy throughout the country, lessen gender inequality, and provide education for rural citizens, most of who rely on agriculture for income.

Daniel Ness and Chia-ling Lin

REFERENCES

Central Intelligence Agency. *The CIA World Factbook.* New York: Skyhorse, 2011. https://www.cia.gov/library/publications/the-world-factbook/index.html.

Nation Master. 2011. www.nationmaster.com.

UNESCO. *Global Education Digest 2012: Comparing Education Statistics Across the World.* Montreal: UNESCO Institute for Statistics, 2012.

———. "Strong Foundations: Early Childhood Care and Education." *Education for All Global Monitoring Report.* Paris: UNESCO, 2006.

UNESCO–IBE. www.ibe.unesco.org/countries/Mozambique.htm.

UNESCO–UIS. www.uis.unesco.org.

United Nations Development Programme. *Human Development Report 2011.* http://hdr.undp.org/en.

World Bank Education Statistics. 2011. www.worldbank.org.

NAMIBIA

Namibia, located in southwestern Africa, is a country with many diverse languages. The official languages during the period of apartheid were Afrikaans, German, and English. Today, English is the sole official language of the country even though it represents only 1 percent of the country's native speakers. Afrikaans and German are widely spoken, particularly among the white population. Outside of the Indo-European languages, nearly half of the population of Namibia speaks one of the Oshiwambo dialects (part of the Bantu language family) and numerous dialects within the Khoisan language family (the so-called click language group). Given the diversity of languages in a country with slightly more than 2 million people, formal education practice in Namibia has struggled to unite all students, while, at the same time, preserving indigenous languages and the cultural backgrounds and heritage of individual students. Namibia gained independence from a South African mandate in 1990 and has a republican government system.

Educational System

Education in the Kalahari region of southwestern Africa has been notoriously unstable. This has been partly due to nineteenth- and twentieth-century colonization, the effects of apartheid, and overall political and economic instability. From the late sixteenth century to the early nineteenth century, Namibians represented part of the population that was exported to Brazil and other ports in South America during the slave trade. Thus, efforts in formalizing education in the area were futile. European colonization after this time only complicated the situation.

With a literacy rate of approximately 85 percent, Namibia has devoted much of its resources to education. The country's educational ministry has attempted to achieve several goals since its independence in 1990—schooling for all, high quality in terms of teaching and learning, internal efficiency of the education system through the implementation of an egalitarian system of participation for all stakeholders, and lifelong learning. All the efforts are directed toward the establishment of a unified, nonracial, nonethnic, and nonsexist national education system.

Precompulsory and Compulsory Education, Curriculum, Assessment, and Instruction

The Ministry of Health—not the Ministry of Education—controls precompulsory education in Namibia. Day-care and early childhood programs are severely underfunded and lack both human and physical resources. Compulsory education in Namibia consists of seven years of schooling (i.e., grades 1 through 7). On completion of seven years of primary education, students are expected to have adequate language skills in English or Afrikaans and have acquired an understanding of various vocations and skills (such as machine use in industry, manual labor practices, and agricultural science).

Despite mandatory secondary school attendance, schools in Namibia have rather high rates of attrition. The net enrollment ratio for primary school in

Namibia is 76.5 percent, and that of secondary school is essentially half this amount (38.7 percent). The economy of Namibia has a major agrarian and industrial component, which makes it all the more difficult for children and adolescents of school age to receive a formal education. A large part of the population is dependent on subsistence farming. Also, former primary school students who do not engage in agrarian labor attempt to find employment in industry.

Tertiary Education

Tertiary education is not compulsory at any level. There are few colleges and universities in Namibia. One important tertiary intuition of note is the University of Namibia, which was established in 1991. The university emphasizes curricula in the areas of agrology, various engineering disciplines, and information technology. Lack of financial resources, however, has prevented most tertiary institutions from diversifying their curriculum. Most of the tertiary student population in Namibia attends vocational institutes that specialize in agriculture and some forms of industry. However, there is increased interest and research in promoting sustainability education—that is, education that promotes the fostering of essential skills, critical thinking, systemic thinking skills for problem solving, partnerships, and environmental (or "green") studies—in Namibia.

Teacher Education

Despite its dire need of improvement, teacher training practice in Namibia is slightly more structured than it is in neighboring Angola. In Namibia, the Ministry of Higher Education, Vocational Training, Science and Technology (established in 1995) is responsible for the administration of four teacher education colleges, while the Ministry of Basic Education, Sport and Culture controls curriculum development and additional teacher training programs.

Informal Education

Informal education practices in Namibia are needed to provide educational resources for individuals engaged in manual labor, particularly farmers, artisans, laborers, and other nonformally educated citizens so that they can retool their skills as a means of finding more productive work opportunities. In doing so, the educational ministries need to allocate both public and private funding resources and to find solutions to eradicate student attrition. Current trends in the country show implementation of programs focusing on sustainability education in teacher training.

System Economics

According to the United Nations Development Programme (2011), public expenditure on education in Namibia represents a surprising 7.2 percent of the gross domestic product. Namibia ranks 23 out of 186 in public expenditure on education. It is important to note that the literacy rate in Namibia is the highest among its neighbors.

Future Prospects

The Education Ministry in Namibia is faced with problems of attrition. Nearly three-fourths of all chil-

---

Namibia Education at a Glance

General Information

Capital	Windhoek
Population	2.1 million
Languages	English (official, 7%), Afrikaans (60%), German (32%)
Literacy rate	85%
GDP per capita	US$7,600
People below poverty line	35% ($1 per day) 56% ($2 per day)
Number of phones per 100 people	6.5
Number of Internet users per 100 people	5.3
Number of Internet hosts	76,020
Life expectancy at birth (years)	43

Formal Educational Information

Primary school age population	376,000
Secondary school age population	268,000
Primary school age population*	17.5%
Secondary school age population*	12.5%
Number of years of education (primary/secondary)	7/5
Student/teacher ratio (primary)	31
Student/teacher ratio (secondary)	25
Primary school gross enrollment ratio	106%
Primary school entrants reaching grade 5	86%
Secondary school gross enrollment ratio	56%
Child labor (ages 5–14)	13%

Notes: *Over 30 percent of Namibia's population (close to one-third) is of school age (five to 18 years).

Unless otherwise indicated, all data are based on sources from 2011.

dren of primary school age attend school. However, about half of those students either do not finish this level or do not enter or enroll in secondary school. This problem poses potentially adverse outcomes in future literacy and, perhaps more important, workforce competition within a global economy. The educational system in Namibia is still developing, given the relatively poor quality of schools and the need to educate children of large rural populations for an information society. At present, education is a privilege for the few who can afford it. In addition, the quality of education depends on the price a family is willing to give. Finally, over 13 percent of the adult population of Namibia is infected by the HIV/AIDS virus, an indication that both directly and indirectly may adversely affect children's school attendance. The Education and Training Sector Improvement Program is being developed by the Namibian Ministry of Education in order to accommodate school attendance and a strong workforce.

Daniel Ness and Chia-ling Lin

REFERENCES

Central Intelligence Agency. *The CIA World Factbook*. New York: Skyhorse, 2011. https://www.cia.gov/library/publications/the-world-factbook/index.html.

Nation Master. 2011. www.nationmaster.com.

UNESCO. *Global Education Digest 2012: Comparing Education Statistics Across the World*. Montreal: UNESCO Institute for Statistics, 2012.

———. "Strong Foundations: Early Childhood Care and Education." *Education for All Global Monitoring Report*. Paris: UNESCO, 2006.

UNESCO–IBE. www.ibe.unesco.org/countries/Namibia.htm.

United Nations Development Programme. *Human Development Report 2011*. http://hdr.undp.org/en.

World Bank Education Statistics. 2011. www.worldbank.org.

NIGER

Niger is a rather large landlocked country in the Sahel region of north-central Africa. Like most French African colonies, Niger became independent from France in 1960. As a developing nation, it was ruled by a single party for more than three decades. A democratic government was created in 1993, but this was short-lived. A coup in 1996 was led by a military dictator, Ibrahim Bare, who was killed three years later. The democratic republic was restored in 1999. Although, politically, Niger is currently stable to a degree, the country's people remain some of the poorest in the world. Approximately 80 percent of the population is Muslim. The remaining 20 percent of the population is Christian or members of indigenous beliefs. Ethnic groups include Haoussa (55.4 percent), Djerma Sonrai (21 percent), Touareg (9.3 percent), Peuhl (8.5 percent), and Kanouri Manga (4.7 percent).

Educational System

At 28.7 percent, Niger has the second lowest literacy rate in the world; only Mali has a lower literacy rate. Niger, then, is in desperate need of strong educational reform to drastically improve the rate of literacy in the country. Primary education is compulsory in Niger. Students attend primary school between the ages of seven and 15. Like its neighbors, Niger suffers from rampant gender disparities. Boys are much more likely to attend school than girls. Gross enrollment rates are some of the lowest in the world. The primary school gross enrollment rate is 50 percent, and the secondary school gross enrollment rate is 10 percent. In addition to high levels of poverty and illiteracy, child labor in Niger contributes to a rather high primary school dropout rate. Only 60 percent of children reach the fifth grade. Cultural factors as well contribute to low levels of school attendance. Further, parents and families are reluctant to send their children off to school when agricultural duties seem more pressing to them. Families often attempt to avoid the compulsory school mandate by changing the birth records of their children. Also, rural, nomadic families in the northern and eastern regions avoid sending their children to school altogether. These situations make it difficult for teachers to travel to remote areas because they are often intimidated by reluctant families. Secondary schools are almost entirely near Niamey and other small cities in the south and west. There are only two universities in Niger: the Abdou Moumouni University (formerly the University of Niamey), founded in 1974, and the Islamic University of Niger in Say, Niger.

```
┌─────────────────────────────────────────────────┐
│           Niger Education at a Glance            │
│                                                  │
│ General Information                              │
│ Capital                              Niamey      │
│ Population                       15.8 million    │
│ Languages      French (official), Hausa, Djerma  │
│ Literacy rate                        29%         │
│ GDP per capita                    US$1,000       │
│ People below poverty line            63%         │
│ Number of phones per 100 people     <.05         │
│ Number of Internet users per 100 people  <1      │
│ Number of Internet hosts             172         │
│ Life expectancy at birth (years)      44         │
│                                                  │
│ Formal Educational Information                   │
│ Primary school age population     2.2 million    │
│ Secondary school age population   1.9 million    │
│ Primary school age population        14%         │
│ Number of years of education                     │
│    (primary/secondary)               6/7         │
│ Student/teacher ratio (primary)      44          │
│ Student/teacher ratio (secondary)    31          │
│ Primary school gross enrollment ratio 50%        │
│ Primary school entrants reaching grade 5  60%    │
│ Secondary school gross enrollment ratio  10%     │
│ Child labor (ages 5–14)              43%         │
│                                                  │
│ Note: Unless otherwise indicated, all data are   │
│ based on sources from 2011.                      │
└─────────────────────────────────────────────────┘
```

System Economics and Future Prospects

According to the United Nations Development Programme (2011), along with Brunei, Venezuela, Togo, Luxembourg, and Japan, total public expenditures on education in Niger represented 3.7 percent of the gross domestic product in 2008. Given the GDP of Niger at $11.93 billion, educational expenditure in the country amounts to nearly $441 million, or $106 per student (total amount equivalent to US dollars divided by 4,165,000, the approximate number of primary and secondary students in the country). Niger ranks 95 of 124 countries in percentage of educational expenditure.

In order to improve its standing in the world, the Niger government must invest its resources in improving the extremely low literacy rate. This can be done through both formal and informal education programs. Moreover, families must be committed to move beyond a solely agricultural and industrial society to an information-based society that can compete internationally. School attendance is extremely low, and teachers are often poorly educated. Schools in Niger often lack adequate facilities and

resources. Also, Niger's rural populations are large, widespread, and often disinclined to change. Like families in neighboring countries, those in Niger are unable to afford the fees that are associated with a child's education. Families must pay for books and supplies as well as travel to and from school. Many countries in Africa are witnessing clear positive changes in higher literacy rates and graduation rates. Unfortunately, Niger is lagging behind many countries of Africa in this regard.

Daniel Ness and Chia-ling Lin

REFERENCES

Central Intelligence Agency. *The CIA World Factbook.* New York: Skyhorse, 2011. https://www.cia.gov/library/publications/the-world-factbook/index.html.

Nation Master. 2011. www.nationmaster.com.

UNESCO. *Global Education Digest 2012: Comparing Education Statistics Across the World.* Montreal: UNESCO Institute for Statistics, 2012.

———. "Strong Foundations: Early Childhood Care and Education." *Education for All Global Monitoring Report.* Paris: UNESCO, 2006.

UNESCO–IBE. www.ibe.unesco.org/countries/Niger.htm.

United Nations Development Programme. *Human Development Report 2011.* http://hdr.undp.org/en.

World Bank Education Statistics. 2011. www.worldbank.org.

NIGERIA

The Federal Republic of Nigeria is one of the largest countries in Africa, with a land area of 364,000 square miles (910,000 square kilometers) and an additional 5,200 square miles (13,000 square kilometers) of water. It is Africa's most populous country, with over 146 million inhabitants and 250 diverse ethnic groups. The three largest groups, the northern Hausa/Fulani, the western Yoruba, and the southern Igbo, hold the most political and economic authority. For many Nigerians, basic needs such as sanitary drinking water, proper nutrition, and adequate healthcare are unmet. English is the official language of Nigeria, but Hausa, Yoruba, Igbo, and Fulani are also commonly spoken. Half of the national population identifies as Muslim, 40 percent as Christian, and 10 percent as practicing indigenous beliefs.

Educational System

Prior to Western influences in the late fifteenth century, traditional forms of education often included imitation, storytelling, initiation, ceremonies, apprenticeships, and play. Until about 1850, precolonial informal education was gender-dependent; social expectations for boys included farming, trading, and community leadership, while girls' roles were more family-oriented. Children were traditionally raised by the community and learned to appreciate and maintain ethnic affiliations, histories, languages, customs, and values. Early societies in Nigeria excelled in agricultural practices, pottery, leatherworking, ironworking, and trading.

Islam appeared in Nigeria in the late eleventh century with the conversion of the king of Kanem. By the fourteenth century, Muslim traders and scholars were migrating into northern Nigeria, bringing with them religious devotion, trans-Saharan trading opportunities, and Quranic schools of Islamic learning for elite male students. By the sixteenth century, these Quranic schools had advanced and begun training a select class of Islamic magistrates, scribes, and theologians. Islamic religious ideas and books also concurrently fostered literacy practices throughout the Hausa states and Borno.

British merchants interested in slave trading appeared in southern Nigeria in the late fifteenth century. By the mid-nineteenth century, Christian missionaries had entered Nigeria with imported forms of literacy focused on speaking, reading and writing in English. Christianized schools expanded rapidly. In addition, local missionaries were trained to encapsulate indigenous languages and histories in written forms.

At the Berlin Conference of 1884–1885, European nations instituted rules for territorial acquisition in Africa. Britain's Royal Niger Company was given control over many of the "Niger territories," and the British government began to politically and economically unify the region's diverse states and kingdoms. Within this system, a newly created caste of Nigerian men were European-educated and encouraged to develop basic primary literacy skills. By 1921, 32,000 southern Nigerians had been trained for low-level civil service positions in the colonial government, and this increase in literacy and paid work opportunities created a middle-class and a cash economy.

In 1920 the Phelps-Stokes Commission on Education in Africa was established in partnership with the American Baptist Foreign Missionary Society. Several years later, a 1926 report by domestic and foreign leaders led to new forms of rural community education and localized curricula. These efforts helped to unify existing schools in Nigeria and eventually led to the construction of a national education system. This transformation included the founding of Nigeria's first institution of higher learning, the Higher College at Yaba, in 1934.

In 1970, after the end of a three-year civil war, the new federal military government began a process of modernizing the Nigerian education system. Primary education became free in 1976, and six years of basic education became compulsory in 1979. The Nigerian government also formulated the National Policy on Education in 1977, thereby strengthening a federal commitment and responsibility toward public schooling. Policy proposals included the implementation of six years of secondary school, tuition-free federal universities, a nationwide mass literacy campaign, special education programs, teacher education mandates, and national education grants. Many of these programs have continued to receive federal attention under the present administration. Additional resources and initiatives have been allotted for current teacher training programs, curricula improvements, accountability measures, infrastructure demands, and information and communication technology (ICT) development.

Currently, both primary and secondary education is managed by local and state governments under the centralized authority of the Federal Ministry of Education (FME). Higher education is under the direction of both federal and state governments. According to the FME (2009), the purpose of public education in Nigeria is to "nurture the mind, create a good society, and compete globally." Under Nigeria's National Policy on Education, the FME is responsible for formulating national policies, collecting education data, maintaining high standards in all schools, developing curricula, and coordinating international collaborations.

Leadership roles in education are shared between the federal and state ministries of education. Although national policies and procedures must be followed throughout the educational system, individual states are encouraged to modify federal mandates in response to local needs. The highest policy-making body is the National Council of Education, which includes all state commissioners of education and is chaired by the federal minister of education. This council is then advised by the Joint Consultative Committee of Education, comprised of all federal and state directors of education, chief executives of education statutory bodies, and directors of university institutes of education.

Preschool, Primary, and Secondary Education

In 2004 Nigeria's Universal Basic Education Law was established, requiring all public primary schools to develop state-funded preschool programs for children ages three to five. The Federal Ministry of Education then developed a policy integrating early education and child healthcare in 2006 and became responsible for the implementation and oversight of a preschool curriculum and nationalized standards. The formal education system now includes six years of compulsory primary school beginning at age six, three years of compulsory junior secondary school, and three years of noncompulsory senior secondary school.

The school calendar runs from January to December and is divided into quarters, each separated by a month of vacation. Primary school education starts in the native language and transitions into English in the third year. Nearly one-half of these primary school graduates transition into secondary school. According to a recent survey conducted in Lagos, unregistered private schools have also become prominent in Nigeria, particularly in urban centers, where they serve the needs of poor households. In 2003 it was estimated that 33 percent of schoolchildren were enrolled in private unregistered schools (Tooley, Dixon, and Olaniyan 2005).

Although public education in Nigeria is free, secondary students are expected to pay various school-related fees (e.g., school uniforms and books). After three years of compulsory junior secondary school, remaining students are assessed and tracked into one of four streams: senior secondary schools (60 percent); technical colleges (20 percent); vocational training centers (10 percent); or apprenticeships (10 percent). In 2008 about 200 public and private secondary schools existed in Nigeria. Academically

gifted students may also apply to one of Nigeria's 102 Unity Schools. These government-run schools, established after the Biafran Civil War in 1970, were intended to reunite the nation by bringing together top students from Nigeria's diverse ethnic and religious groups. Upon the completion of secondary school, most students are then required to complete one year of civil duty in the National Youth Service Corps (NYSC).

Postsecondary Education

The Nigerian education plan has been called the "6-3-3-4 system" because students are expected to complete six years of primary school, three years of junior secondary school, three years of senior secondary school, and four years of higher education. Although college enrollment grew dramatically from 3,646 in 1962–63 to 216,200 in 1992–93, the participation rate in higher education was only 5 percent in 1999 and has remained the same percentage to 2012. However, public universities in Nigeria are tuition-free for those students who pass the national Joint Admissions and Matriculation Board entrance exam. In 2008 the FME list of higher education institutions included 30 federal universities, 29 state universities, and 23 private universities.

Curriculum, Instruction, and Assessment

The Federal Ministry of Education is responsible for the standardization of a national curriculum. In 2007 the FME's new basic education curriculum for primary and junior secondary schools established 12 core subjects: English, French, mathematics, science, social studies, civic education, computer studies, health, physical education, religious studies, culture, and art. This revised national curriculum also emphasizes value reorientation, poverty eradication, critical thinking, entrepreneurship, life skills, and wealth generation.

Within the FME, the Examination Group was established in 2007 to supervise national compulsory exams at the secondary and tertiary levels. In addition, the Education Resource Group and the Mathematical and Science Group share responsibility for maintaining relevant curricula and strengthening professional development goals. The FME also created a 10-year strategic plan in 2007 to improve infrastructural needs and learning outcomes in Nigeria. One of the plan's objectives is to place Nigeria within the top 20 world economies by 2020. However, constraints on policy implementation and chronic underfunding issues continue to present challenges.

Teacher Education

Since 1998 a National Certificate in Education obtained from a college of education has been the minimum requirement for teachers at the primary school level. In addition to three years of study at a teachers college, secondary teachers must earn a bachelor's degree from an accredited university. Furthermore, teachers of all levels are required to complete basic ICT training courses. Microsoft, in collaboration with the FME, has provided professional development workshops in ICT training since 2007. However, these types of in-service programs have yet to become widely available.

Although teachers are officially required to obtain national certification, the implementation of universal primary schooling and an increase in population growth have presented logistical challenges and created a teacher shortage. In 2004 the federal government responded with intermediary benchmarks requiring 80 percent of primary teachers to be qualified, 90 percent of secondary teachers to be qualified, and 80 percent of tertiary teachers to acquire pedagogical training. The FME, however, continues to support fully qualified teacher accreditation at all levels of education.

Nonformal Education

In Nigeria, nonformal education for youths and adults includes state-supported functional literacy programs and remedial and vocational education. The National Committee for Mass Literacy, Adult, and Non-Formal Education (NMEC) was established in 1990 and oversees the following programs: basic literacy; postliteracy; women's education; nomadic education; Arabic-integrated education; workers' education; functional literacy; vocational education; prison education; literacy for the blind; and literacy for the disabled. In 1996 over 1.1 million citizens were served by federal nonformal education programs. However, as of 2009, 10 million school-age children remain out of the formal school system, and 55 million Nigerians are classified as illiterate.

Programs have recently been developed to meet the needs of children in Quranic schools, particularly those in northern Nigeria, who do not attend public schools. Flexible education programs have also been started for girls engaged in petty trading and street hawking during regular school hours, and in eastern Nigeria, for boys who leave primary school to become shop apprentices. UNESCO, UNICEF, and the Cuban government have additionally partnered with NMEC to implement the Radio for Literacy Project. Supplemented by written materials, this venture is specifically designed to reach Nigerian adults who are illiterate. Although literacy rates continue to improve, mass literacy goals have been compromised by funding shortages, inadequate resources, ineffective monitoring, a lack of qualified personnel, and unmet transportation needs.

System Economics

In 2008 Nigeria's gross domestic product (GDP) was estimated at US$220.3 billion, with a real growth rate of 6.2 percent and an inflation rate of 10.6 percent. The national budget included US$29.49 billion in revenues (80 percent from the oil sector) and US$30.61 billion in expenditures. Public debt was 12.2 percent of GDP. In 2004 the federal government spent 11 percent (893.3 billion naira or US$6.86 billion) on education expenditures in Nigeria.

Nigeria's Federation Account holds all federally collected revenues. These funds are then distributed based on national value-added tax (VAT) revenues and adjustable formulae derived from states' contributions, with remaining funds divided between the federal government (57.7 percent), state governments (24.7 percent), and local governments (20.6 percent). States' revenue contributions rely heavily on petroleum reserves; consequently, oil-rich states that pay more revenue also receive more funding. This provides regions such as Anambra and Ondo with greater financial support for education, thereby helping to create better schools; keep poverty levels relatively low, around 20 percent; and raise primary school attendance rates to 85 percent. In contrast, poorer states such as Jugawa report a poverty rate of 95 percent, dilapidated classrooms, and a primary net attendance rate of only 30 percent.

Special Education

The Federal Ministry of Education has a four-unit Special Education Division that collectively supports Nigeria's goal of inclusive education for all students. The first unit is Language Projects, whose responsibilities include translating and interpreting for students, as well as teaching French at the federal and state levels. The second unit is Adult and Non-Formal Education, which coordinates learning activities for nomadic populations, out-of-school children, and adults. The third division is the Gender Education unit, which addresses gender inequities in education settings. Lastly, the Special Needs Education Branch provides support for students with special needs.

Special education sites are located throughout the country. The city of Suleja hosts the Federal Government Academy for the Gifted and Talented, and the University of Ilorin in the western Kwara state is home to the Centre for Supportive Services for the Deaf. The state of Oyo features a Federal College of Special Education, and additional courses in special education are offered elsewhere through the Universities of Ibadan, Jos, and Calabar. The National Braille Council of Nigeria has also collaborated with the Nigerian Educational Research and Development Council to establish a computerized Braille Press in Nigeria.

Special needs education is provided by the Federal Ministry of Education to those with visual or hearing impairments; communication or developmental disorders; intellectual, learning, physical, or multiple disabilities; and those categorized as intellectually gifted. A pilot project for classrooms of students with mixed abilities is currently under way through the Federal Ministry of Education; part of this initiative requires all teachers to be trained in working with special needs students. Other measures in support of an inclusive educational system involve the ongoing development of a sign-language curriculum, the production of Braille and large-print texts, collaborations between state ministries of education and health to build assessment centers, and support systems for families of students with special needs.

Gender and Education

Nigeria officially adopted its National Policy on Education in 1981, yet successful implementation of the policy's goals has been repeatedly challenged by rapid population growth, periods of political instability, and a scarcity of resources. A disproportionate number of Nigerians affected by these circumstances have been women and girls. In an attempt to address these inequalities and encourage more female enrollment in primary and secondary schools, Nigeria participated in UNICEF's 25 by 2005 initiative. Although the nation did not reach its goal of gender equality in student enrollment rates by 2005, the Federal Ministry of Education has continued to strive for male/female parity in schools through several national and international projects. These include the Nigeria Girls' Education Initiative (NGEI), the Girls Education Project (GEP), and the Education for All (EFA) plan associated with the United Nations' Millennium Development Goals.

The objective of NGEI is to foster support for girls' education through partnerships with state governments, the Nigerian federal government, and civil society organizations. In 2005 the Girls' Education Project was developed under this initiative to increase school participation for girls in northern Nigeria, where educational access has been traditionally limited for females. GEP targets six states in particular in northern Nigeria: Bauchi, Sokoto, Jigawa, Katsina, Borno, and Niger. Beyond increasing classroom access for girls, GEP has also worked to improve sanitation in schools, as unhygienic conditions are frequently cited by girls as being a deterrent to their attendance. From 2005 to 2007, gender gap enrollment rates in these six northern states were reduced by 13 percent. Female enrollment increased by 73 percent, and regular school attendance for females increased by 39 percent.

The Education for All initiative was also launched in 1990 to provide basic education for all children, youth, and adults by 2015. As a member of this international mission, Nigeria is expected to achieve gender equality by the project's end date. The EFA initiative has also focused upon meeting the Millennium Development Goals of the 2000 United Nations Summit, which include the general empowerment of women.

Technology and Education

In 2007 the Federal Ministry of Education created the first information and communication technology

(ICT) education department. By 2020 Nigeria hopes to reach 100 percent computer literacy in all secondary and tertiary schools and to establish a comprehensive network of ICT capacity in all public schools. At this time, constraining factors include the absence of electric power grids in specific regions, limited access to computer equipment, a weak telecommunications infrastructure, restricted government budgets, and a lack of consistent coordination at the ministerial levels.

Currently, Nigeria is participating in several ICT education projects. The FME recently ordered one million US$100 laptops from the Massachusetts Institute of Technology through the One Laptop per Child (OLPC) initiative. These computers are powered through cranking and do not require an external energy supply. Implementation began in October 2008 in the state of Sokoto with a partnership between the State Ministry of Education and the Federal Ministry of ICT. Other ICT ventures are currently under way at the secondary school level. Nonprofit organizations such as SchoolNet Nigeria, private companies such as Zinox (in collaboration with Microsoft), and additional groups such as Zenith Bank and its ICT project for Youth Empowerment are partnering with the FME to implement, support, and coordinate ICT development projects in education.

Dilemmas and Challenges

Nigeria continues to strive to meet its goal of universal primary education, but as the nation's school-age population grows, infrastructural vulnerabilities are becoming more prominent. Nigeria's largest city, Lagos, is experiencing an ongoing urban population crisis worsened by severe infrastructural decay, growing slums, and critical overcrowding. Public schools cannot keep pace with growing enrollment rates, particularly since many Nigerian schools still lack reliable access to basic amenities such as safe drinking water, toilets, electricity, and space. As 70 percent of Nigerians live in poverty and rely on subsistence farming for their livelihoods, issues related to population growth and limited economic opportunities have challenged sustainable improvements to education.

Low student achievement scores have also proven problematic. In 1997 national achievement tests for Nigerian fourth-graders reported competency levels of 32 percent in mathematics, 25 percent in literacy,

and 37 percent in life skills. Although the FME continues to set high standards, the implementation of these standards has been challenging. Possible remedies include improved infrastructures, incentives and professional development programs for teachers, greater supervision of programs, enhanced ICT development, and increased funding for education.

Struggling teachers in Nigeria generally report a lack of workplace motivation and job satisfaction. This has been attributed to low wages, irregular pay, insufficient benefits (e.g., the availability of house, car, motorcycle and bicycle loans, free medical services, and early payment of pension gratuities), mass promotion of teachers, lack of career advancement opportunities, low social status, high student/teacher ratios, and poor working conditions. Although improvements have occurred in the last several years, key concerns include inadequate opportunities for administrative promotion and decision making, the mass promotion of teachers without an evaluative mechanism, and low salaries in comparison to other professional workers, such as nurses and engineers.

Nigeria Education at a Glance

General Information

Capital	Abuja
Population	152.2 million
Languages	English, Hausa, Yoruba, Igbo, Fulani
Literacy rate	68%
GDP per capita	US$1,500
People below poverty line	60%
Number of phones per 100 people	<1
Number of Internet users per 100 people	7
Number of Internet hosts	1,378
Life expectancy at birth (years)	47

Formal Educational Information

Primary school age population	23.6 million
Secondary school age population	20.2 million
Primary school age population*	15.5%
Secondary school age population*	13.3%
Number of years of education (primary/secondary)	6/6
Student/teacher ratio (primary)	37
Student/teacher ratio (secondary)	40
Primary school gross enrollment ratio	96%
Primary school entrants reaching grade 5	73%
Secondary school gross enrollment ratio	32%
Child labor (ages 5–14)	13%

Notes: *Nearly 30 percent of Nigeria's population (close to one-third) is of school age (five to 18 years).

Unless otherwise indicated, all data are based on sources from 2011.

Future Prospects

Nigeria has recognized that it must become more globally interconnected if the country is to be in the world's top 20 economies by 2020. Accordingly, in 2006, the federal government partnered with private companies to invest US$8 billion in Nigeria's telecommunications sector. Furthermore, in May 2007, Nigeria launched Africa's first geosynchronous communications satellite, NIGCOMSAT-1, which was primarily designed to provide telecommunications coverage, direct broadcasting systems, digital broadband, and television.

In an effort to support globalization in the workforce, the Federal Ministry of Education has expanded higher education services and opportunities. Approximately 60 percent of the federal education budget is currently used to support tertiary education, with the remaining 40 percent allocated for primary and secondary education. However, the FME recognizes that low student achievement scores in elementary and secondary schools generally result in lower test scores at the university level. Consequently, attention has been given to strengthening and globalizing the entire education system.

Cheri Scripter and Jessica Phillips

REFERENCES

Adelabu, Modupe A. *Teacher Motivation and Incentives in Nigeria*. 2005. www.eldis.org.

Central Intelligence Agency. *The CIA World Factbook*. New York: Skyhorse, 2011. https://www.cia.gov/library/publications/the-world-factbook/index.html.

Educational Trust Fund. www.edtrustfun.org.

Fafunwa, Aliu Babatunde. *History of Education in Nigeria*. Ibadan, Nigeria: NPS Educational, 1974.

Falola, Toyin, and Matthew M. Heaton. *A History of Nigeria*. New York: Cambridge University Press, 2008.

Federal Ministry of Education. www.fme.gov.ng.

Measure DHS, Demographic and Health Surveys. www.measuredhs.com.

Moja, Teboho. *Nigeria Education Sector Analysis: An Analytical Synthesis of Performance and Main Issues*. 2000. www.worldbankorg.

National Information Technology Development Agency. "Nigerian National Policy for Information Technology." www.nitda.gov.ng.

Research Triangle Institute. *Understanding Public Financing of Primary Education in Nigeria*. 2010. www.rti.org.

Tooley, James, Pauline Dixon, and Olanrewaju Olaniyan. "Private and Public Schooling in Low-Income Areas of Lagos State, Nigeria: A Census and Comparative Survey." *International Journal of Educational Research* 43 (2005): 125–146.

UNESCO United Nations Educational, Scientific and Cultural Organization. www.unesco.org.

UNICEF. http://unicef.org.

———. *Educational Statistics*. www.unesco.org.

United Nations Girls' Initiative. www.ungei.org.

Women's Consortium of Nigeria. www.wocononline.org.

World Bank. GenderStats—Database of gender statistics. www.worldbank.org.

RWANDA

Rwanda is a relatively small landlocked country in south-central Africa. Approximately 56.5 percent of the country's population is Roman Catholic and 37 percent is Protestant. Four percent of the population is Muslim and the remaining people have indigenous beliefs or no beliefs. Ethnic groups include the Hutu (84 percent), Tutsi (15 percent), and Twa (1 percent).

Rwanda became independent from Belgium in 1962. The Hutus, the predominant ethnic group in the country, had overthrown the Tutsi king three years earlier and waged all-out persecution against non-Hutu peoples, particularly the Tutsis. As a result, the Tutsi minority fled to neighboring countries. By 1990 the Tutsi Rwandan Patriotic Front waged war against the Hutu regime, which eventually led to the genocide of over 800,000 Tutsis in the spring of 1994. The Tutsis eventually defeated the Hutu-led government in July 1994. However, despite international efforts to control the region and attempts by various nongovernmental agencies to broker peace between the two groups, Rwanda remains an unstable country, with inevitable adverse repercussions on its system of education.

Educational System

The system of education in Rwanda is unstable due to the volatile political situation that was brought on by decades of infighting and all-out war between Hutu and Tutsi ethnic groups. Ongoing belligerency between these two groups led to the deaths of well over 1 million people and the displacement of several million more who were forced to move to neighboring countries. In the first several decades of the twentieth century, education in Rwanda, which was under Belgian authority, began as an elitist institution. The Tutsi minority was in power and therefore controlled educational practice. Tutsi children, most of whom were male, were able to receive an education while Hutu children were forced into labor. After civil war in 1959, the Hutus finally took over. Many Tutsis were either killed or exiled.

Despite present-day efforts to eliminate illiteracy and to increase the country's potential in competing in the global market, problems with the educational system in Rwanda remain. Nevertheless, various cabinet departments in the Rwandan government have increased efforts to promote the education system. The Rwandan Division of Construction is responsible for the development of infrastructure and school construction. The National Examination Council is charged with setting the standards for curriculum in schools. And the General Inspectorate of Education is responsible for overseeing the entire education system.

The primary school system in Rwanda lasts for six years (roughly ages six through 11). In the first three years of schooling, the language of instruction is primarily Kinyarwanda. Students who are able to continue for the remaining three years are instructed in either French or English. It is difficult to determine a single reason why, despite efforts of reform, less than half of all primary school students are able to complete the fifth grade. Changes in language instruction in grade three, diversion of educational finances away from primary school, poverty, and tribal conflict may all contribute to this unfortunate phenomenon.

A small percentage of Rwandan students are fortunate enough to afford and have the abilities to enter secondary school. Those who do are instructed in either French or English. Despite the drawbacks of secondary education enrollment based on family finance and socioeconomic class, there are encouraging data that show little, if any, gap between males and females. However, the gap widens in higher education, where only 40 percent of female students enroll in universities. The oldest and largest university in the country is the National University of Rwanda, which was established in 1963—one year after independence. Another major institution is the Kigali Institute of Science and Technology, which caters to students preparing for the engineering professions. In addition, there are five public universities and fourteen private universities, mostly affiliated with a religious denomination. As a means of increasing access to higher education, the government is increasing its efforts in providing evening and night courses for students pursuing higher education degrees.

System Economics and Future Prospects

Despite the civil war and genocide that took place in 1994, total public educational spending in Rwanda grew from approximately 3 percent in 1995 to 5.5 percent in 2001. One major obstacle, however, was the fact that most of the expenditure was funneled away from primary school—the compulsory period—and into secondary education and higher education. According to the United Nations Development Programme (2011), along with Bulgaria, total public expenditures on education in Rwanda represented 4.1 percent of the gross domestic product in 2008. Given

---

Rwanda Education at a Glance

General Information

Capital	Kigali
Population	11 million
Languages	Kinyarwanda, French, English, Kiswahili
Literacy rate	70%
GDP per capita	US$1,600
People below poverty line	60%
Number of phones per 100 people	<0.5
Number of Internet users per 100 people	2.5
Number of Internet hosts	815
Life expectancy at birth (years)	49

Formal Educational Information

Primary school age population	1.4 million
Secondary school age population	1.5 million
Primary school age population	13%
Secondary school age population	13.5%
Number of years of education (primary/secondary)	6/6
Student/teacher ratio (primary)	62
Student/teacher ratio (secondary)	26
Primary school gross enrollment ratio	119%
Primary school entrants reaching grade 5	46%
Secondary school gross enrollment ratio	13%
Child labor (ages 5–14)	35%

Note: Unless otherwise indicated, all data are based on sources from 2011.

the GDP of Rwanda at $13.46 billion, educational expenditure in the country amounts to nearly $552 million, or $187 per student (total amount equivalent to US dollars divided by 2,945,000, the approximate number of primary and secondary students in the country). Rwanda ranks 104 of 186 countries in percentage of educational expenditure.

In order to improve its standing in the world, the Rwanda government must invest its resources in improving the extremely low literacy rate, which presently stands at 70.5 percent, with a disparity of 10 percent between males and females. Informal education programs can alleviate the illiteracy rate among adults. Moreover, families must be committed to move beyond a solely agricultural and industrial society to an information-based society that can compete internationally. School attendance is extremely low, and teachers are often poorly educated. Primary and secondary schools in Rwanda often lack adequate facilities and resources. From a demographic standpoint, the centralization of Kigali, the country's capital, is causing a great deal of rural poverty and lack of inclination on the part of rural families for change or reform. Like families in neighboring countries, those in Rwanda are unable to afford the fees that are associated with a child's education. Families must pay for books and supplies as well as travel to and from school, especially within the last five years as money for education in general has been completely diverted to secondary and higher education. Despite its war-ravaged history, there is evidence that the government of Rwanda is attempting to reform the education system to meet present-day standards. In doing so, the government and the private sector have initiated the country's information and communication technology programs to support educational efforts throughout the country. Their primary goal at the present time is to make information and communication technology more comprehensive by allowing such technologies to be shared with primary schools and secondary schools and not solely higher education institutions. The two universities that are spearheading efforts in spreading information and communication technology throughout the country's schools are the Kigali Institute of Technology and the Kigali Institute of Education.

Daniel Ness and Chia-ling Lin

REFERENCES

Central Intelligence Agency. *The CIA World Factbook.* New York: Skyhorse, 2011. https://www.cia.gov/library/publications/the-world-factbook/index.html.

Nation Master. 2011. www.nationmaster.com.

UNESCO. *Global Education Digest 2012: Comparing Education Statistics Across the World.* Montreal: UNESCO Institute for Statistics, 2012.

———. "Strong Foundations: Early Childhood Care and Education." *Education for All Global Monitoring Report.* Paris: UNESCO, 2006.

UNESCO–IBE. www.ibe.unesco.org/countries/Rwanda.htm.

United Nations Development Programme. *Human Development Report 2011.* http://hdr.undp.org/en.

World Bank Education Statistics. 2011. www.worldbank.org.

SENEGAL

Senegal, in western Africa, was originally granted independence from France as part of the Mali Federation in 1960. Senegal's government had been socialist for about four decades when, in 2000, the country officially became the Republic of Senegal. Senegal was to merge with The Gambia in 1982 to form a united republic, but this union never materialized. To this day, Senegal's government is one of the most stable governments in Africa, and, through its efforts in peacekeeping, it has set an example for neighboring countries. About 95 percent of all Senegalese are Muslim. Most of the remaining population is Christian, predominantly Roman Catholic.

Educational System

Compulsory education in Senegal became law in 2001 with the adoption of the constitution, which states that education is a right for all children throughout the country. The Senegalese government kept most of the structure and curriculum of the French model of education. Compulsory education is free and lasts for 10 to 11 years—from six to 16 years of age. Primary school lasts for six years. Secondary school is divided into two parts: lower secondary school and upper secondary school. Lower secondary school is a continuation of basic education that successful primary school students would be familiar with. The upper-level secondary school curriculum is more rigorous and meant to prepare successful students for the university or polytechnic institute. Despite the country's commitment to free public education, Quranic schools are more attractive and prevalent in certain regions of the country, especially in rural areas where traditional religious beliefs are strongest and where the education of females is often not encouraged. The country's primary gross enrollment rate is 80 percent, and only three-quarters of those who do start school reach the fifth grade. The secondary school gross enrollment rate is 22 percent, lower than the rate in some neighboring countries.

In Senegal, as in most other African nations, schools lack the necessary resources to function in a successful manner. Wealthy families in Dakar, the Senegalese capital, often send their children to private schools that are generally fully equipped to cover a thorough curriculum and prepare students for higher education. Given the very low attendance rate in secondary school, most students who do finish primary school learn a vocational skill or trade or work in agriculture. Few work in mining because natural resources are limited.

Higher education in Senegal is limited. There are only three public universities and three private universities in the country. The public universities are the Cheikh Anta Diop University, also known as the University of Dakar, Gaston Berger University in Saint-Louis, and Ziguinchor University. The private universities are the Suffolk University in Dakar, Dakar Bourguiba University, and the University of the Sahel in Dakar. The Suffolk University in Dakar is a satellite campus of Suffolk University in Boston, Massachusetts, and its focus is on economic development. The Cheikh Anta Diop University is considered the premier higher education institution by the Senegalese government. It offers courses in philosophy, religion, natural science, mathematics, and languages, as well as professional curricula, such as engineering, medicine, and law.

System Economics and Future Prospects

According to the United Nations Development Programme (2011), along with Belize, Bhutan, and Mongolia, total public expenditures on education in Senegal represented 5.8 percent of the gross domestic product in 2009. Given the GDP of Senegal

Senegal Education at a Glance

General Information

Capital	Dakar
Population	12.3 million
Languages	French, Wolof, Pulaar, Jola, Mandinka
Literacy rate	40%
GDP per capita	US$1,800
People below poverty line	54%
Number of phones per 100 people	2
Number of Internet users per 100 people	8
Number of Internet hosts	241
Life expectancy at birth (years)	57

Formal Educational Information

Primary school age population	1.8 million
Secondary school age population	1.8 million
Primary school age population*	15%
Secondary school age population*	15%
Number of years of education (primary/secondary)	6/7
Student/teacher ratio (primary)	42
Student/teacher ratio (secondary)	26
Primary school gross enrollment ratio	80%
Primary school entrants reaching grade 5	73%
Secondary school gross enrollment ratio	22%
Child labor (ages 5–14)	22%

Notes: *Over 30 percent of Senegal's population (close to one-third) is of school age (five to 18 years).

Unless otherwise indicated, all data are based on sources from 2011.

at $25.4 billion, educational expenditure in the country amounts to nearly $1.473 billion, or $395 per student (total amount equivalent to US dollars divided by 3,728,000, the approximate number of primary and secondary students in the country). Senegal ranks 64 of 186 countries in percentage of educational expenditure.

Education is compulsory at the primary and the first of the two secondary school levels in Senegal. But a large percentage of students do not complete school beyond the fifth-grade level, and even fewer continue to secondary school. As in neighboring countries, school attendance is hampered as a result of poor education for teachers, a lack of adequate facilities at schools, and difficulty in reaching large rural populations. Many families are also unable to afford the fees that are associated with a child's education. Although public education in Senegal is free, families must pay for books and supplies as well as travel to and from school. Rural families find it extremely difficult to send their children to schools because fees are expensive and children are needed by their families for agricultural labor, particularly in the rural north and east. In addition, families find educational alternatives; given that the overwhelming majority of Senegalese are Muslim, many families send their children to Quranic schools rather than free public schools. Therefore, the major initiative of the Senegalese government is to invest in services that will make it affordable and motivating for families to send their children to schools. One way to do this is to develop and foster information and communications technology that will lessen the burdens for children and families and will most likely keep students in school through the secondary level.

Daniel Ness and Chia-ling Lin

REFERENCES

Central Intelligence Agency. *The CIA World Factbook.* New York: Skyhorse, 2011. https://www.cia.gov/library/publications/the-world-factbook/index.html.

Nation Master. 2011. www.nationmaster.com.

UNESCO. *Global Education Digest 2012: Comparing Education Statistics Across the World.* Montreal: UNESCO Institute for Statistics, 2012.

———. "Strong Foundations: Early Childhood Care and Education." *Education for All Global Monitoring Report.* Paris: UNESCO, 2006.

UNESCO–IBE. www.ibe.unesco.org/countries/Senegal.htm.

United Nations Development Programme. *Human Development Report 2011.* http://hdr.undp.org/en.

US Department of Labor. *2001 Findings on the Worst Forms of Child Labor.* Washington, DC: Bureau of International Labor Affairs, US Department of Labor, 2002.

World Bank Education Statistics. 2011. www.worldbank.org.

SIERRA LEONE

Sierra Leone is a relatively small West African nation. The region of Sierra Leone served as a slave trafficking territory in the fifteenth and sixteenth centuries. Many slaves from this region were shipped off to both the North American and South American coasts as well as islands in the Caribbean where slavery was enforced. The country became independent from the United Kingdom in 1961. After independence, Sierra Leone witnessed one-party rule, which more or less lasted for three decades. Civil war broke out in 1991 and lasted for nearly eleven years until, in 2002, UN forces disarmed most of the rebel forces. Casualties of the war included more than 50,000 deaths and more than 2 million people displaced from their homes—approximately one-third of the country's population. Political insecurity is one of the most pressing issues facing the country today. The prospect of long-term peace is tenuous since rebel groups often attempt to seize control of the government or gold, diamond, and other gemstone mines.

About 60 percent of all Sierra Leoneans are Muslim and 10 percent are Christian. Approximately 30 percent of the population has indigenous religious beliefs.

Educational System

Compulsory education in Sierra Leone lasts for nine years. Sierra Leonean children are expected to attend primary school for six years (ages six to 11) and lower secondary school for three years (ages 12 to 15). There is also a noncompulsory upper secondary school period that lasts for three years. Despite a nine-year compulsory education period, the country is unable to enforce school attendance. According to the Bureau of International Labor Affairs, 1,270 primary schools were destroyed during the decade-long civil war. As a result, at one point during this time, more than two-thirds of all Sierra Leonean students were unable to attend school. To make matters worse, rebel groups drafted children as soldiers. At 48 percent, the percentage of children involved in labor is one of the highest in Africa and the world. In the early 1990s, government reforms and initiatives were proposed to reduce the illiteracy rate and increase the population's technical and vocational skills in order to create a stronger workforce. The civil war, however, put this goal on hold until only recently. Within the last five years, the government has allocated resources to the rebuilding of schools and accommodating primary education for most of the country's children.

The Sierra Leonean government enacted an education act that eliminated school and assessment fees for families of primary school children. Also, in a country that has discriminated in terms of gender, the act went as far as to promote the education of girls, particularly in rural regions in the north. This proved to be a successful law that helped to reinvigorate the educational system. At present, close to 100,000 schoolchildren reach the end of primary school, as opposed to one-quarter of this number in 2001. Although many students continue to secondary school, most enter a low-level vocation after sixth grade. Despite promising education results since the civil war, much needs to be done. Education statistics show that the primary school gross enrollment rate is 79 percent, and the gross enrollment rate for secondary school is only 26 percent. Further, nearly one-quarter of 1 million children do not attend school, either due to their families' inability to afford the travel to and from school or to religious beliefs that downplay the importance of public school.

Despite the turmoil in Sierra Leone as a result of postindependence skirmishes and a decade-long civil war, it is interesting to note that the region was considered a center for education in Africa during the nineteenth century. Founded in 1827, Fourah Bay College was probably the first higher education institution in West Africa that was based on the British education system. The college, however, was restricted to those who could afford it. Therefore, the majority of the population did not have access. Fourah Bay College became the University of Sierra Leone after independence. Njala University, which was established in 1910 as the Njala Agricultural Experimental Station, became the second university in Sierra Leone in 2005. Although the Sierra Leonean government is making efforts to improve the educational process, access to education for all children is far from reality. Part of the reason is that the country is slowly emerging from the devastation of a civil war. It also must grapple with resistance to change from rebel groups and communities that oppose formal education training. The literacy rate for individuals 15 years and older is only 35 percent and is indeed in dire need of improvement.

System Economics and Future Prospects

According to the United Nations Development Programme (2011), along with Egypt, Panama, Nepal, Mali, Kuwait, Honduras, and Gabon, total public expenditures on education in Sierra Leone represented 4.3 percent of the gross domestic product in 2009. Given the GDP of Sierra Leone at $5.1 billion, educational expenditure in the country amounts to nearly $220 million, or $136 per student (total amount equivalent to US dollars divided by 1,609,000, the approximate number of primary and secondary students in the country). Sierra Leone ranks 93 of 186 countries in percentage of educational expenditure.

Sierra Leone is a country whose government is attempting to make progress in education and improving the country's economic status by encouraging universal access to primary and lower-level secondary school. Although these attempts have been fruitful to some extent, they were severely hampered between 1991 and 2002 as a result of the devastating civil war. School life expectancy is on average six years—about eight years for boys and four years for girls. So gender disparity in education is another major problem. Few Sierra Leonean students continue to secondary school. As in neighboring countries, school attendance is hampered by poor education for teachers, a lack of adequate facilities at schools, and difficulty in reaching large rural populations, particularly in the northern and eastern parts of the country. The government has attempted to alleviate family burden with regard to school fees that pay for

---

Sierra Leone Education at a Glance

General Information

Capital	Freetown
Population	5.2 million
Languages	English (minority use), Mende, Temne, Krio (English-based Creole)
Literacy rate	35%
GDP per capita	US$900
People below poverty line	68%
Number of phones per 100 people	<1
Number of Internet users per 100 people	<0.5
Number of Internet hosts	281
Life expectancy at birth (years)	41

Formal Educational Information

Primary school age population	871,000
Secondary school age population	738,000
Primary school age population	16%
Secondary school age population	14%
Number of years of education (primary/secondary)	6/6
Student/teacher ratio (primary)	37
Student/teacher ratio (secondary)	27
Primary school gross enrollment ratio	79%
School life expectancy (years)	6.3%
Secondary school gross enrollment ratio	26%
Child labor (ages 5–14)	48%

Notes: Over 30 percent of Sierra Leone's population (close to one-third) is of school age (five to 18 years).

Unless otherwise indicated, all data are based on sources from 2011.

supplies. Nevertheless, many families are reluctant to send their children to school due to religion, lifestyle, or resistance to change and government policy. The Sierra Leonean government must search for alternative methods that motivate families to realize the importance of education and access for both boys and girls in order to create a productive workforce and a successful, growing economy.

Daniel Ness and Chia-ling Lin

REFERENCES

Central Intelligence Agency. *The CIA World Factbook.* New York: Skyhorse, 2011. https://www.cia.gov/library/publications/the-world-factbook/index.html.

Nation Master. 2011. www.nationmaster.com.

UNESCO. Global Education Digest 2012: *Comparing Education Statistics Across the World.* Montreal: UNESCO Institute for Statistics, 2012.

———. "Strong Foundations: Early Childhood Care and Education." *Education for All Global Monitoring Report.* Paris: UNESCO, 2006.

UNESCO-IBE. www.ibe.unesco.org/en/worldwide/unesco-regions/africa/sierra-leone.html.

United Nations Development Programme. *Human Development Report 2011.* http://hdr.undp.org/en.

US Department of Labor. *2001 Findings on the Worst Forms of Child Labor.* Washington, DC: Bureau of International Labor Affairs, US Department of Labor, 2002.

World Bank Education Statistics. 2011. www.worldbank.org.

SOMALIA

Somalia is a country on the Horn of Africa, a large peninsula in East Africa. The Somali Republic became independent in the spring and summer of 1960 after the merger of British Somaliland and Italian Somaliland. Ethnic fighting continued through the decade, however. After a coup in 1969, led by Mohamed Siad Barre, Somalia achieved relative peace until 1991, when various clans, particularly in the north, took up arms against the government. As a result, during the 1990s, the country became factionalized with a government whose importance in national unity diminished over time. By 2006 the Supreme Council of Islamic Courts, a group consisting of business leaders and Islamic clerics, overthrew warlords who were controlling the country's capital. Believing that the Supreme Council of Islamic Courts had close ties with al-Qaida, the Transitional Federal Government of Somalia drove out the Supreme Council and is currently in the process of developing an emergent government. At present, the political system in Somalia is unstable, and many Somalis live in an anarchic system. In recent years, the country has been the center of attention regarding frequent acts of piracy along its shores.

The religion in Somalia is almost entirely Sunni Muslim. The country is 85 percent Somali and 15 percent Bantu or of non-Somali ethnicity. The most commonly spoken languages are Somali, Arabic, Italian, and English.

Educational System

Given that the southern region of the country is controlled for the most part by a collection of Islamic militias, it is difficult to ascertain formal education practices in this region. The remaining parts of the country consist of Puntland, which makes up Africa's so-called horn, Somaliland in the northwest, and Galmudug, which is controlled by the Transitional Federal Government. Of these regions, Puntland has the most progressive educational program. Given great gender disparity in the country as a whole, the Ministry of Education in Puntland, in accordance with the Convention on the Rights of the Child, is attempting to close the gender gap so that more females will be able to attend school. The other regions are following Puntland's lead in this regard. The ministry is also attempting to emphasize the importance of early childhood education in terms of intellectual development and school success in later years.

Early childhood education is not uncommon in Somalia, particularly in the Puntland and Galmudug regions. Although not compulsory, early childhood education consists of early literacy. One primary method of literacy acquisition at this stage concerns the introduction to the Quran. Preschool in Somalia enrolls children between the ages of three and six years.

Primary school in Somalia is an eight-year period—when children are between the ages of six and 13 years. Given the numerous ethnic factions in the country, the various ministries of education have found it difficult to make education compulsory—at any level. Accordingly, it should not be surprising that the primary school gross enrollment rate is only 33 percent. The curriculum at the primary school level is basic and focuses primarily on Islamic traditions. Most families must pay for their children's education. The language of school instruction is mostly Arabic. Students study religion, Somali, mathematics, various natural, social, and professional sciences (such as engineering and medicine), history, geography, government, English, art, and physical education.

Secondary education in Somalia lasts for four years. Secondary students are mostly between the ages of 13 and 18 years. The secondary school gross attendance rate in the country is extremely bleak—approximately 13 percent of all children in the secondary school age range. The language of instruction at the secondary school level is English. However, English is not spoken when students learn Arabic or Somali. Students generally enroll in courses that are a continuation of the basic primary education curriculum. In addition, they take physics, biology, and other secondary-level natural science courses.

Most Somali students who graduate from secondary school enroll in one of the country's universities, almost all of which are private. The largest university in Somalia is Mogadishu University, which contains satellite branches in Puntland and other northern regions. Despite the country's political turmoil, tertiary education in Somalia has maintained academic rigor. Mogadishu University has been rated highly among universities in sub-Saharan Africa. Other tertiary institutions in Somalia are East Africa University, Puntland State University, Benadir University, Somalia National University, Kismayo University, and the University of Gedo. Teacher training institutions in Somalia are slow to emerge. This is evident given the poor quality of education for all Somali children. Most teachers are foreign-born from neighboring countries or from the Arabian Peninsula.

The tertiary system in Somalia, particularly in the areas of Puntland and Galmudug, also caters to students who wish to advance their skills in vocational and technical subjects. These students are more likely than students who drop out of secondary school to find employment in services or industry. Students who enter this particular educational sector have the best chance for improving the economic conditions of Somali citizens because it is most closely associated with technological advancement and the emergence of an information-based economy. Informal

---

Somalia Education at a Glance

General Information

Capital	Mogadishu
Population	10.1 million
Languages	Somali, Arabic, Italian, English
Literacy rate	38%
GDP per capita	US$600
People below poverty line	no data
Number of phones per 100 people	1
Number of Internet users per 100 people	1
Number of Internet hosts	3
Life expectancy at birth (years)	49

Formal Educational Information

Primary school age population	1.5 million
Secondary school age population	876,000
Primary school age population	15%
Number of years of education (primary/secondary)	8/4
Student/teacher ratio (primary)*	19
Student/teacher ratio (secondary)	16
Primary school gross enrollment ratio	33%
Primary school entrants reaching grade 5	92%
Secondary school gross enrollment ratio	13%
Child labor (ages 5–14)	49%

Notes: *Pupil/teacher ratio is based on UNICEF data from 1986.

Unless otherwise indicated, all data are based on sources from 2011.

---

education is available for Somali adults who wish to improve their literacy as well as those who wish to acquire new workforce skills. These programs are mostly found in annexed parts of school buildings or religious centers.

System Economics and Future Prospects

According to the United Nations Development Programme (2011), no data are available regarding total public expenditures on education in Somalia. For the most part, education in Somalia is either private or run by Quranic schools. Regional governments have most of the authority when it comes to the country's education systems. For example, Puntland, Somaliland, and Galmudug each has its own individualized Ministry of Education.

As described above, the overall system of education in Somalia is extremely poor and unorganized. Approximately 15 percent of Somalia's population is within the primary school age range. But only about one-third of this population (about 500,000 children) actually attends school. Of this group, only about 400,000 finish the fifth grade, and roughly 100,000 make it to secondary school. While tertiary education in Somalia is satisfactory, it is attended by an extremely small fraction of the Somali tertiary-age population. It is difficult to determine what the future of the educational system holds because Somalia is essentially a collection of four major autonomous regions, which themselves comprise a total of eighteen smaller regions divide into even smaller municipalities called divisions. Each of the four large autonomous regions has its own educational ministry and seems to function without the assistance of any centralized government.

Daniel Ness and Chia-ling Lin

REFERENCES

Central Intelligence Agency. *The CIA World Factbook.* New York: Skyhorse, 2011. https://www.cia.gov/library/publications/the-world-factbook/index.html.

Nation Master. 2011. www.nationmaster.com.

UNESCO. *Global Education Digest 2012: Comparing Education Statistics Across the World.* Montreal: UNESCO Institute for Statistics, 2012.

———. "Strong Foundations: Early Childhood Care and Education." *Education for All Global Monitoring Report.* Paris: UNESCO, 2006.

UNESCO–IBE. www.ibe.unesco.org/countries/Somalia.htm.

United Nations Development Programme. *Human Development Report 2011.* http://hdr.undp.org/en.

World Bank Education Statistics. 2011. www.worldbank.org.

SOUTH AFRICA

South Africa is the southernmost country in Africa. Roughly 80 percent of the population is black African, 10 percent is white, and the remaining 10 percent is Indian and other Asian groups. Approximately 80 percent of the country is Christian (7 percent Catholic) and 1.5 percent are Muslim. About 15 percent declare themselves as nonreligious while nearly 4 percent consist of members of regional religions or those whose religions are unspecified. One of the first groups of European settlers in the region came from The Netherlands. These settlers, known as Boers, were forced northward after the British colonized the Cape of Good Hope in 1806. During the late

nineteenth century, the region that is South Africa became famous for the discovery of diamonds and gold. Both the Boers and the British colonists believed that they had the sole access to the mining of gold and diamonds in the region. Antagonism between the two groups led to the Boer War in 1899. The Boers were eventually defeated. The government, which at this time was ruled by the British, instituted apartheid, a racist policy that separated whites from blacks in schooling and other public facilities. This policy gave preferential treatment to whites. The apartheid regime ended in the mid-1990s, with black majority governance.

Educational System

Prior to the 1980s, education in South Africa was simply perceived as one part of apartheid, a racist system that subjugated and segregated the black population, which was much larger than the population of ruling Whites. Black South Africans worked mostly as laborers and servants. Their children either did not receive a formal education or were not provided a full-scale, 12-year education as were white children. At present, thanks to the end of apartheid, all South Africans are able to receive an education. The country's Bill of Rights in its constitution (revised in 1997) makes education accessible to all populations regardless of ethnic background or gender. According to South Africa's National Qualifications Framework, there are three so-called bands of education: general education and training, further education and training, and higher education and training.

Precompulsory and Compulsory Education, Curriculum, Assessment, and Instruction

In 2009 the National Department of Education split into two ministries: the Ministry of Basic Education and the Ministry of Higher Education and Training. These ministries oversee education in South Africa as a whole, while each of the nine districts of South Africa has its own Department of Education. The ministries provide overall supervision of curriculum and policy. Administrative duties are the responsibility of the each of the districts. Private schools have more autonomy than public schools; however, these schools must adhere to laws regarding the acceptance of all children regardless of ethnicity or religious beliefs.

Schooling in South Africa begins with a year of kindergarten, or what the government refers to as a "reception school year." General education, the first of the three grade bands, consists of ten years of schooling—from grade 0 to grade 9. Compulsory education, however, is a nine-year period from grade 1 through grade 9 (age 15). Primary education consists of the first seven years of the nine-year compulsory education period. Perhaps more than any other educational system in sub-Saharan Africa, both Ministries of Education in South Africa have managed to provide the most access for educational opportunities for both black and white populations. For example, 82 percent of all students entering primary school are able to reach grade 5. The second set of three grades is what is known as further education, which is equivalent to the upper secondary school years in most Western high schools. Further education and training consists of grades 10, 11, and 12. Students at this level decide if they are capable to continue to the university or enter career-oriented fields. These fields are available through technical training institutions and community colleges. Students completing grades 10 and 11 receive certificates, which enable students to enter technical and vocational occupations. Students who successfully complete grade 12 receive a diploma. It is important to note the high secondary school gross enrollment rate of 95 percent—the highest rate among all sub-Saharan countries. Although lower than in most countries in Europe, the United States, Canada, Japan, Taiwan, South Korea, Singapore, Israel, parts of China, Australia, and New Zealand, the secondary net enrollment ratio of 62 percent is the highest in Africa. The further education and training division of the Ministry of Basic Education in South Africa manages the integration of mathematics, science, technology, and engineering. Its focus is to engage students in academic and technological disciplines that many educators are projecting will affect future world populations.

Higher education and training, the third grade band, consists of several years of college or university or trade school education, where students initially continue toward a baccalaureate. Those who do not complete the baccalaureate usually train for vocational occupations. Those who do complete the baccalaureate often continue for several years toward a master's degree and possibly a doctorate.

Tertiary Education

The Ministry of Higher Education and Training controls all levels of tertiary education from the first year of college or university to the qualification of doctoral degree, which can take as few as ten years after the diploma earned after the exit from secondary education. The Higher Education Ministry is also responsible for technical and vocational training. Unlike colleges and universities in the United States and certain European countries, those of South Africa require students to pass or excel in at least three academic disciplines. Some universities have exceptions to this rule. Technical and vocational schools of higher education require that students receive a senior-level certificate from their secondary-level institution.

Originally, there were 36 universities in South Africa, each having its own area (or areas) of specialization. Given great overlap in specialization, the Ministry of Higher Education agreed to merge several institutions and so-called technikons, which are technical institutes. At present, there are 24 publicly funded tertiary-level institutions in South Africa. These include 11 universities, five polytechnic universities, and six comprehensive colleges. In total, more than 1 million students attend these institutions—far exceeding the numbers of tertiary-level students in other sub-Saharan countries. Private universities in South Africa also make up a significant part of the country's tertiary education sector.

Several universities in South Africa are among the most competitive in Africa and comparable to those in other parts of the world. The oldest university in the country is the University of Cape Town, which has more than 23,000 matriculated students. Other extremely competitive state-funded institutions in South Africa are the University of Stellenbosch in Stellenbosch, University of the Witwatersrand in Johannesburg, University of the Free State in Bloemfontein, Rhodes University in Grahamstown, University of Fort Hare in Alice and East London, and the University of Pretoria. Established in 1873, the University of South Africa is the oldest comprehensive university in the country; it enrolls more than 300,000 students in any academic year, which makes it one of the largest institutions in the world in terms of enrollment. Well-known polytechnic institutes that merged from former technikons include Vaal University of Technology, Tshwane University of Technology, Mangosuthu University of Technology, Durban University of Technology, Central University of Technology, and Cape Peninsula University of Technology.

Teacher Education

During all of the nineteenth century and most of the twentieth century, management and organization of teacher training in South Africa was relatively weak. By the 1980s the Ministries of Education initiated efforts to improve the organization of the curriculum of teacher education programs and to step up resources in improving the overall process for becoming a pre-primary, primary, or secondary school teacher. During the early 1990s, the teacher education system in South Africa was patchy, consisting of a hodgepodge of courses in various tertiary institutions throughout the country. For nearly a decade, the Ministries of Education collaborated in instituting widespread reform in the training of future teachers. Teacher training programs improved the curriculum structure and the process to achieve the status of a teacher. At present, all teacher training must be carried out through university-level programs. In general, students with a three-year education qualification may apply for an initial Advanced Certificate in Education—the initial certification document that entitles students to engage in student teaching. Students who have earned the baccalaureate in education (BEd) at any university that offers education programs are automatically qualified for the Advanced Certificate in Education.

Informal Education

The Ministry of Education in South Africa is becoming more committed to eradicate illiteracy in both children and adults. United Nations–affiliated organizations have contributed resources toward this effort. However, this initiative is more successful in some states than in others. The areas of South Africa that have not been very successful lack funding and adequate infrastructure, and as a result, increasing the level of literacy remains a challenge. Similar to an agenda taking place in neighboring Mozambique,

South African educational policy makers have made it possible to provide secondary school for adults who wish to earn a secondary education certificate. This initiative has been successful in educating adults who need additional skills to compete in high-paying occupations.

System Economics

According to the United Nations Development Programme (2011), total public expenditures on education in South Africa represented 5.4 percent of the gross domestic product in 2009. This amounts to nearly $30 billion, or $2,495 per student (total amount equivalent to US dollars divided by 12,002,000, the approximate number of students in the country). Other countries whose educational expenditures are 5.4 percent of their GDP include Austria, Hungary, Samoa, Finland, and Ghana. South Africa ranks 49 of 186 countries in percentage of educational expenditure.

Future Prospects

South Africa is the most gender equitable country in Africa. Neighboring countries (such as Mozambique, Botswana, and Namibia) that do have gender disparity both in literacy and education access have followed the South African model in recent years.

Despite the promising future for education in South Africa, the Ministries of Education must grapple with the remnants of the racist apartheid system of education. Although education access has become more leveled in recent decades, there is more to be done with regard to improving the quality of education for Black students. One important goal in this regard is to transition poor, ethnically based communities into a more integrated environment in which all students, regardless of ethnicity, receive the same free, quality education. Certain provinces where the population is mostly black, such as the Eastern Cape and KwaZulu Natal, are extremely poor, while others, which have mostly white residents, such as Gauteng and the Western Cape, are much more affluent. These social and environmental issues impact educational problems in South Africa. To be sure, although the gap between ethnic groups is closing, White students have more access to educational opportunity than do other groups. Approximately 65 percent of White students complete secondary school or higher levels, compared to about 40 percent of Indian students and about 15 percent of black students. In addition, although South Africa has one of the highest levels of literacy in Africa, there are still 8 to 9 million South Africans who are unable to read and write. Moreover, these populations tend to be in poor communities located in poor provinces. These areas tend to have the poorest level of schooling and teacher qualifications.

The current government and the Ministry of Education in South Africa have established initiatives to correct these educational disparities. One initiative has been the creation of so-called fee-free schools in economically disadvantaged areas. In past decades, tuition-driven primary and secondary schools were prevalent throughout Africa, particularly in sub-Saharan Africa. As a result, only children of privileged families were able to attend school; the overwhelming majority of children were not. With the help of nongovernmental organizations, the South African government has been instituting fee-free schooling as a means of closing the educational access gap so that by 2015, half of all schools in the country will be fee-free. A second initiative is the promotion of HIV/AIDS awareness at the school level. In 2003 the HIV/AIDS prevalence rate was 21.5 percent. AIDS awareness programs have been instituted in order to lower or curb current prevalence rates.

The government has also instituted the National Schools Nutrition Program. Prior to 2005, schools in South Africa were unable to provide meals for students, again, mostly in economically disadvantaged areas. Results of the program show that nearly 8 million primary and secondary school students have benefited from the program in any given year since 2007. All these children live in poor urban neighborhoods or poor rural districts. The South African Department of Agriculture has played a crucial part in this effort through the establishment of school gardens throughout these low-income areas.

Daniel Ness and Chia-ling Lin

REFERENCES

Central Intelligence Agency. *The CIA World Factbook.* New York: Skyhorse, 2011. https://www.cia.gov/library/publications/the-world-factbook/index.html.

Nation Master. 2011. www.nationmaster.com.

UNESCO. *Global Education Digest 2012: Comparing Education Statistics Across the World.* Montreal: UNESCO Institute for Statistics, 2012.

———. "Strong Foundations: Early Childhood Care and Education." *Education for All Global Monitoring Report.* Paris: UNESCO, 2006.

UNESCO–IBE. www.ibe.unesco.org/countries/SouthAfrica.htm.

United Nations Development Programme. *Human Development Report 2011.* http://hdr.undp.org/en.

World Bank Education Statistics. 2011. www.worldbank.org.

South Africa Education at a Glance

General Information

Capitals	Pretoria (administrative), Cape Town (legislative), Bloemfontein (judicial)
Population	49.1 million
Languages	IsiZulu (24%), IsiXhosa (17.5%), Afrikaans (13%), Sepedi (9.5%), English (8%), Setswana (8%), Sesotho (8%), Xitsonga (4.5%), other languages (7.5%)
Literacy rate	86.5%
GDP per capita	US$13,300
People below poverty line	50%
Number of phones per 100 people	9
Number of Internet users per 100 people	8.5
Number of Internet hosts	3.7 million
Life expectancy at birth (years)	43

Formal Educational Information

Primary school age population	7.1 million
Secondary school age population	4.8 million
Primary school age population	14.5%
Number of years of education (primary/secondary)	7/5
Student/teacher ratio (primary)	36
Student/teacher ratio (secondary)	31
Primary school gross enrollment ratio	106%
Primary school entrants reaching grade 5	82%
Secondary school gross enrollment ratio	95%
Child labor (ages 5–14)	3%

Note: Unless otherwise indicated, all data are based on sources from 2011.

SOUTH SUDAN

On July 9, 2011, the Republic of South Sudan became the 193rd member state of the United Nations, making it the newest independent nation in the world. Its independence came after two long periods of war (1955 to 1972 and 1983 to 2005) between the government of Sudan and the Sudan People's Liberation Army (which fought on behalf of the southern Sudanese provinces) and starvation in which more than 2.5 million people died; a comprehensive peace treaty between the central Sudanese government, which controls present-day Sudan (the northern two-thirds of the former Sudan and is predominantly Muslim), and the Sudanese southern provinces (predominantly Christian) was signed in 2005 that granted the southern portion of Sudan political autonomy with the possibility of independence. South Sudan finally seceded s in July 2011. The Nile River supports a great deal of the new country's agricultural output.

The official languages of South Sudan are English and Arabic. However, there are numerous Sudanic languages, such as Dinka, Nuer, Bari, Zande, and Shilluk. Ethnic groups in South Sudan include the Dinka, Kakwa, Bari, Azande, Shilluk, Kuku, Murle, Mandari, Didinga, Ndogo, Bviri, Lndi, Anuak, Bongo, Lango, Dungotona, and Acholi. Most people in South Sudan are Christian.

Educational System

The major difference in schooling and education in South Sudan and Sudan is that schools in South Sudan are run primarily by Christian organizations and those of Sudan are run primarily through Muslim groups. Given the new country's fledgling status, the education system of South Sudan is in dire need of development and reform. The new country has one of the lowest rates of literacy in the world. About 27 percent of all individuals 15 years or older can read or write. More disconcerting is the large gap between the literacy rates of males (40 percent) and females (16 percent)—a nearly 24 percent difference.

Most schools in South Sudan are makeshift structures that were built outside under large trees. These schools are extremely limited in resources and barely have enough funding for essentials—chalkboards, writing tools, tables and chairs, and the like. Moreover, students must miss months of schooling as a result of a long rainy season. Recent efforts have been made through organizations, like South Sudan Education, to fund the construction of schools in various regions of the country.

Future Prospects

South Sudan faces a great deal of poverty, unequal distribution of income, and an extremely poor school-

---

South Sudan Education at a Glance

General Information

Capital	Juba
Population	8.2 million
Languages	English and Arabic (official), Dinka, Nuer, Bari, Zande, Shilluk
Literacy rate	27%
GDP per capita	US$1,546
People below poverty line	50%
Number of phones per 100 people	no data
Number of Internet users per 100 people	no data
Number of Internet hosts	no data
Life expectancy at birth (years)	49 (Sudan estimate)

Formal Educational Information

Primary school age population	2.4 million
Secondary school age population	approx. 2 million
Primary school age population	29%
Number of years of education (primary/secondary)	6/5 (same as Sudan)
Student/teacher ratio (primary)	29
Student/teacher ratio (secondary)	22
Primary school gross enrollment ratio	46%
Primary school entrants reaching grade 5	approx. 10%
Secondary school gross enrollment ratio	4%
Child labor (ages 5–14)*	0%

Notes: *The Child Act of 2008 prohibits any form of child labor in the South Sudan region. However, child labor in Sudan and South Sudan combined is approximately 13 percent of children between the ages of five and 14 years.

Unless otherwise indicated, all data are based on sources from 2011.

---

ing infrastructure. Moreover, there is a great deal of gender disparity. Educational opportunities are severely lacking for males, but even more so for females. International organizations and local groups have helped in improving these problems. The country needs more educational initiatives that will reduce the high rates of illiteracy throughout South Sudan, especially among South Sudanese girls and women, whose abilities to read and write are far lower than those of South Sudanese boys and men. There has been some indication that radio instruction is having a positive impact on student learning in the country, particularly for students who live in remote regions of South Sudan. This initiative, called the Learning Village, was promoted by the country's Ministry of Education, Science, and Technology.

Daniel Ness and Chia-ling Lin

REFERENCES

Brown, Tim. "South Sudan Education Emergency." *Forced Migration Review,* Supplement, 20–21 (2006).

Central Intelligence Agency. *The CIA World Factbook.* New York: Skyhorse, 2011. https://www.cia.gov/library/publications/the-world-factbook/index.html.

Education Development Center. 2010. "dot-EDU Southern Sudan Interactive Radio Instruction (SSIRI) Program." www.edc.org.

Nation Master. 2011. www.nationmaster.com.

UNESCO. *Global Education Digest 2012: Comparing Education Statistics Across the World.* Montreal: UNESCO Institute for Statistics, 2012.

————. "Strong Foundations: Early Childhood Care and Education." *Education for All Global Monitoring Report.* Paris UNESCO, 2006.

UNESCO–IBE. www.ibe.unesco.org/countries/south-sudan.htm.

UNESCO–UIS. www.uis.unesco.org.

United Nations Development Programme. *Human Development Report 2011.* http://hdr.undp.org/en.

World Bank Education Statistics. 2011. www.worldbank.org.

SUDAN

Sudan is a country in the northeastern part of Africa. The official language is Arabic but numerous Sudanic languages are spoken, as well as Nubian, Ta Bedawie, Nilo-Hamitic, and some English for business and international communications. Ethnic groups in Sudan are 52 percent black, 39 percent Arab, 6 percent Beja, and a remaining 3 percent who are from other countries. Most people in Sudan are Sunni Muslim—nearly 70 percent. Christians make up about 5 percent of the population. Followers of indigenous beliefs make up the remaining 25 percent of the population.

As a former British and Egyptian colony, Sudan achieved independence on January 1, 1956. Since independence, Sudan was largely ruled by Islamic-based military regimes. Civil war was a major factor for the remaining half of the twentieth century. The most adversarial disputes were between the largely Islamic north and the non-Muslim South. Rampant famine and displacement of the population occurred throughout the Sudanese civil wars. Repercussions of a second civil war that erupted in 1983 included 4 million displaced citizens and nearly 2 million deaths from war and starvation. Eruption broke out yet another time in 2003 in the Darfur region near the border with Chad, a conflict that has so far displaced nearly 2 million people and was responsible for nearly 500,000 deaths. Sudan, then, has serious problems that it must control—war, influx of refugees, poor infrastructure—before educational progress can be considered a national goal. The most recent event affecting the country was the secession of South Sudan as an independent nation in July 2011.

Educational System

Compulsory education in Sudan lasts from age six to 13 years and is tuition-free. Primary education is either six years or eight years, depending on region. It is followed by three to five years of secondary education. Despite the diversity of the country's citizens, Arabic is the official language that must be used as the primary language in the classroom. The Sudanese education system suffers like the systems of other African nations in that rural populations are shortchanged due to the poor educational facilities in remote regions. Despite the vastness of rural regions in Sudan and in other large African countries, rural populations tend to be large and, at the same time, underfunded in terms of resources. Moreover, schools in the rural regions of the south and west were consistently damaged as a result of ongoing wars. Both child and adult populations have been stricken with famine and illness. Given the abject poverty in the region, school enrollment in these areas also tends to be low because children and adolescents see agricultural labor as more necessary than a formal education. Given the dismal living conditions in the country, the literacy rate of Sudanese adults aged 15 years and older is 61 percent. To make matters worse, the literacy gap between males and females is huge; male literacy is 72 percent while just over half of all Sudanese females can read or write.

Precompulsory and Compulsory Education, Curriculum, Assessment, and Instruction

After independence in 1956, the school system in Sudan was restructured. Preschools began to enroll students in the 1970s. However, these schools were, and still are to a great extent, located in urban areas. Daycare or kindergarten usually begins when children are three years of age and lasts for two to three years.

Curriculum in the Sudanese primary school—which lasts for a six-year period—is considered "basic" in that it emphasizes the Arabic language and rudimentary mathematics skills. Students can then continue in one of three tracks: three years of secondary education, which prepares students for the tertiary level; three to five years of technical schools (which primarily focus on agriculture); or teacher training centers for students who wish to teach at the primary level.

Sudan faces a seminal dilemma that school systems in most developing countries must face: to determine if it is better to educate all children and run the risk of mediocre education at best, or to educate a few who can become educational leaders so that the economic system can possibly begin to flourish. Although thousands of primary and secondary schools as well as teacher training institutions were established in the 1980s, little headway was made in achieving positive educational outcomes or a better standard of living. The universal compulsory education has not seemed to work. Again, this is possibly due to the widespread deleterious effects of war and famine that have affected populations in the south and west.

Tertiary Education

There are forty-seven colleges and universities in Sudan. As in primary and secondary school, instruction is in Arabic. Secondary education and tertiary education in Sudan have been fraught with problems because females are often dissuaded from continuing to secondary school or possibly higher education. In addition, males must perform a regimen of military service before they can consider completing a degree at the college level. The most well-known university in the country is perhaps the University of Khartoum, which was established in 1902 as Gordon Memorial College (under British authority and named after Charles George Gordon, a well-known British army officer). The name of the college was changed in 1956. The University of Juba is also important in that it stands as one of the few universities that accommodate students in the southern areas of the country.

Teacher Education

As stated above, students in Sudan who wish to become teachers at the primary level must attend teacher training secondary schools that commence after the end of primary school. Students who wish to teach specific subject-related content areas in secondary school must enter the secondary school track after primary school and continue to study the specific subject or discipline at the college or university level. There are also postsecondary teacher training institutions for students who wish to teach at the junior and senior secondary levels.

Informal Education

Although small, the Almassar Charity Organization has requested funds for 2011 to build classrooms and help nomadic children and adults in the impoverished and war-stricken Darfur region of Sudan. This is one promising indication of continuing interest in promoting literacy in rural Sudanese communities.

Another organization that is assisting in efforts to motivate informal education throughout Sudan is the Southern Sudan Interactive Radio Instruction (SSIRI). The SSIRI, in collaboration with the Southern Sudan Ministry of Education, Science and Technology, has a funded project by the US Agency for International Development that enables both foreign and local teachers to provide learning opportunities for disadvantaged populations in southern Sudan. The project is divided into four areas: The Learning Village, RABEA, Professional Studies for Teachers, and Alternative Learning Technologies. The Learning Village enables students to engage in activities that promote literacy in Arabic and English, mathematics, and general life skills. RABEA is an acronym for Radio-Based Education for All. Professional Studies for Teachers is a distance-learning course that enables students in remote regions to become teachers. Finally, given that some classes in remote regions are unable to benefit from RABEA due to broadcast times, the project funds Alternative Learning Technologies, whereby students learn digitally through the Internet and other electronic modes of communication.

System Economics

According to the United Nations Development Programme (2011), expenditures on education in Sudan represented 6 percent of the gross domestic product in 2008. This amounts to over $5.83 billion. Per capita expenditure, however, only amounts to

Sudan Education at a Glance

General Information

Capital	Khartoum
Population	43.9 million
Languages	Arabic, Nubian, Ta Bedawie, dialects from Nilo-Hamitic, Sudanic languages, English
Literacy rate	61%
GDP per capita	US$2,400
People below poverty line	40%
Number of phones per 100 people	<1
Number of Internet users per 100 people	10
Number of Internet hosts	70
Life expectancy at birth (years)	49

Formal Educational Information

Primary school age population	5.8 million
Secondary school age population	4.2 million
Primary school age population	13%
Number of years of education (primary/secondary)	6/5
Student/teacher ratio (primary)	29
Student/teacher ratio (secondary)	22
Primary school gross enrollment ratio	57%
Primary school entrants reaching grade 5	79%
Secondary school gross enrollment ratio	33%
Child labor (ages 5–14)	13%

Note: Unless otherwise indicated, all data are based on sources from 2011.

REFERENCES

Brown, Tim. "South Sudan Education Emergency." *Forced Migration Review*, Supplement, 20–21 (2006).

Central Intelligence Agency. *The CIA World Factbook.* New York: Skyhorse, 2011. https://www.cia.gov/library/publications/the-world-factbook/index.html.

Education Development Center. 2010. "dot-EDU Southern Sudan Interactive Radio Instruction (SSIRI) Program." www.edc.org.

Nation Master. 2011. www.nationmaster.com.

UNESCO. *Global Education Digest 2012: Comparing Education Statistics Across the World.* Montreal: UNESCO Institute for Statistics, 2012.

———. "Strong Foundations: Early Childhood Care and Education." *Education for All Global Monitoring Report.* Paris: UNESCO, 2006.

UNESCO–IBE. www.ibe.unesco.org/countries/Sudan.htm.

UNESCO–UIS. www.uis.unesco.org.

United Nations Development Programme. *Human Development Report 2011.* http://hdr.undp.org/en/.

World Bank Education Statistics. 2011. www.worldbank.org.

$542. Sudan ranks 38 of 186 countries in government expenditures on education. This is despite the fact that the average school life expectancy is four years.

Future Prospects

Sudan faces similar problems that most Saharan and sub-Saharan African nations do: rabid poverty, chronic war, unequal distribution of income, and poor infrastructure. International organizations are just beginning to have a slight impact on the education of Sudanese youth. However, with ongoing war from one interval of years to the next, the rebuilding of the educational infrastructure will be a slow process. Only when the infrastructure is improved and resources are equally distributed among its citizens will Sudan be able to educate its youth to compete in the global economy. In addition, more needs to be done to reduce the high rates of illiteracy throughout Sudan, especially among Sudanese girls and women.

Daniel Ness and Chia-ling Lin

SWAZILAND

Swaziland is a landlocked kingdom that is bordered to the east by Mozambique and to the north, west, south, and southeast by South Africa. During the nineteenth century, British forces ensured some latitude of autonomy for the Swazis. It became independent from the United Kingdom in 1968. Civil unrest during the 1990s led King Mswati III to allow a certain level of democratic governance. Perhaps the most serious problem in recent years is the country's extremely high rate of HIV/AIDS infection (nearly 40 percent among adults) and death from the diseases associated with it. As a result, with an average life expectancy of 48, Swaziland has the lowest life expectancy in the world.

Educational System

Education in Swaziland is centralized: the National Ministry of Education controls curriculum, assessment, and teacher recruitment. Teachers are often recruited from teacher training centers and universities in South Africa. Swazi education is neither free nor compulsory. However, in 2005 the Swazi government mandated free public primary education for all its citizens by 2008. However, free primary education in Swaziland has not come to reality.

Schooling in Swaziland is divided into four types: preprimary education, basic education, secondary education, and nonformal education. In principle, the Ministry of Education would like to accommodate all children from birth through six years of age for preprimary education. However, the country's lack of financial resources prevents access to preprimary education. Basic education is analogous to primary education. Basic education schooling is a 10-year period that is based on practices of the Southern Africa Development Community Protocol on Education. Again, lack of resources makes it difficult for the Swazi government to institute compulsory basic education. Swazi children suffer from similar problems as most southern African schoolchildren in that although primary attendance is high, secondary school attendance is low. Only 77 percent of primary school children reach grade 5. After this point, attendance in school drops precipitously. The Swazi fledgling education system is investigating alternatives that will allow student attendance to continue beyond primary education so that Swazi citizens would be able to gain skills that will allow them to compete internationally. The ministry established a pilot project that directs primary students toward practical and vocational occupations for the purpose of helping the country's rather poor economy.

Similar to Basotho (Lasotho) students, Swazi students who are eligible and wish to pursue a university education, or who wish to study at universities abroad, often enroll in international schools in Mbabane, the country's capital. Classes are taught in SiSwati in the primary schools. Toward the end of primary school and in many secondary schools, English is also used for instruction. Nonformal education is run by nongovernmental organizations. Most nonformal education programs are in the business of increasing rates of literacy and numeracy.

System Economics and Future Prospects

Swaziland ranks 13 of 186 countries in terms of education expenditure. According to the United Nations Development Programme (2010), total public expenditures on education in Swaziland represented 7.9 percent of the gross domestic product in 2008.

Given the GDP of Swaziland at $6.055 billion, educational expenditure in the country amounts to nearly $478.35 million, or $1,329 per student (total amount equivalent to US dollars divided by 360,000, the approximate number of primary and secondary students in the country).

Although the gross enrollment rate for primary school is 102 percent, slightly more than three-quarters of these children reach grade 5. The gross enrollment rate for secondary school is only 45 percent. School attendance in Swaziland suffers from poor education for teachers, a lack of adequate facilities at schools, teacher bribery (given that teachers are paid by the government but do not earn very much), and difficulty in reaching rural populations. In addition, like families in other nearby countries, many Swazi families are unable to afford the fees that are associated with their children's schooling. Like the Basotho system, education in Swaziland is neither compulsory nor free, and families must pay for books and supplies as well as travel to and from school. Therefore, one major initiative of the Swazi National Ministry of Education is to

---

Swaziland Education at a Glance

General Information

Capitals	Mbabane (administrative), Lobamba (legislative)
Population	1.3 million
Languages	English, SiSwati
Literacy rate	82%
GDP per capita	US$5,200
People below poverty line	69%
Number of phones per 100 people	3.5
Number of Internet users per 100 people	3.5
Number of Internet hosts	2,335
Life expectancy at birth (years)	48 (32)*

Formal Educational Information

Primary school age population	207,000
Secondary school age population	153,000
Primary school age population	15%
Number of years of education (primary/secondary)	7/5
Student/teacher ratio (primary)	32
Student/teacher ratio (secondary)	18
Primary school gross enrollment ratio	102%
Primary school entrants reaching grade 5	77%
Secondary school gross enrollment ratio	45%
Child labor (ages 5–14)	9%

Notes: *Swaziland's life expectancy is 32 years when considering the number of fatalities as a result of HIV/AIDS infection.

Unless otherwise indicated, all data are based on sources from 2011.

lessen the burdens for children and families in order to keep students in school through the secondary level. Nonformal and informal education programs must diversify their offerings not only in promoting the worthy task of increasing literacy and numeracy, but in overcoming health obstacles, such as rampant HIV/AIDS cases that have notoriously made Swaziland the country with the highest rate of AIDS in the world.

Daniel Ness and Chia-ling Lin

REFERENCES

Central Intelligence Agency. *The CIA World Factbook.* New York: Skyhorse, 2011. https://www.cia.gov/library/publications/the-world-factbook/index.html.

EFA. "Strong Foundations: Early Childhood Care and Education." *Education for All Global Monitoring Report.* Paris: UNESCO, 2006.

GED. *Global Education Digest 2012: Comparing Education Statistics Across the World.* Montreal: UNESCO Institute for Statistics, 2012.

Nationmaster. 2011. www.nationmaster.com.

UNESCO–IBE.www.ibe.unesco.org/countries/Swaziland.htm.

United Nations Development Programme. *Human Development Report 2011.* http://hdr.undp.org/en.

World Bank Education Statistics. 2011. www.worldbank.org.

TANZANIA

Tanzania is located on the eastern coast of Africa, along the Indian Ocean. The official language is Swahili. However, English is used officially for commerce, administration, and within the tertiary education system. Arabic is spoken in Zanzibar. Ethnic groups in Tanzania are 99 percent African, with only 1 percent from Europe, Asia, or the Arabian Peninsula. Religion in Tanzania is diverse, with 30 percent of the population Christian, 35 percent Muslim, and the remaining 35 percent whose religions are indigenous.

As a former British colony, Tanzania achieved independence in June 1964, when the former colony of Tanganyika united with the island of Zanzibar.

Educational System

Formal education and training in Tanzania consists of the following: two years of preprimary education, seven years of primary education, four years of junior secondary education (which still falls under the heading of "general" education), two years of senior secondary education (or advanced education), and three or more years of tertiary education. Basic education is provided in preprimary, primary, and nonformal adult education school settings. Upper-level basic education curricula, followed by advanced education curricula, which consists of typical high school subjects, are instructed in secondary education school settings. Tertiary-level programs in Tanzania are those that can be found in higher education institutions, as well as institutions that accommodate informal or adult education settings. There are currently 507 public and private primary and secondary schools in Tanzania.

Precompulsory and Compulsory Education, Curriculum, Assessment, and Instruction

Government-run schools in Tanzania are taught mostly in Swahili. Many private primary schools are taught in English. Prior to 2002, primary school in Tanzania was not free. This caused a burden for millions of Tanzanian families to send their children to school. Fortunately, tuition was eliminated in 2002. Families of schoolchildren still had to pay for school uniforms and other school fees associated with supplies and assessment. Tanzania's literacy rate in 2002 was 69.4 percent—77.5 for males and 62.2 for females. However, with the elimination of tuition, schools have seen sweeping increases in primary school enrollment. In one sense, this is a positive trend toward the eradication of illiteracy. In another, it has caused the depletion of books, supplies, and resources in a number of schools. In addition, some teachers demand payment from families because they are not paid well by the school system. There are signs of hope when considering student academic performance in Tanzania. For example, in a standardized national exam that all students must pass in order to receive a certificate from primary school, approximately 80 percent of all students in grade 6 performed at or above the reading level for that grade. Students tend to do well in language and reading, but not so well in mathematics and science instruction. For example, in the national exams, only 21 percent of all students passed the mathematics portion. In 2010 nearly 90 percent of those who passed the national exam were accepted into secondary schools.

Although secondary school education is not free for Tanzanian families, they pay the equivalent of US$15 per year. This amount may seem small, but to the average Tanzanian family, it is another major expense. Moreover, families are charged for additional fees that contribute to school supplies, assessment measures books, and the upkeep of school furniture. As stated above, the Standard 7 Examination, which is given in grade 6, allows students to continue for secondary education. However, this exam is not a requirement for entry. There has been a large growth in the private school market that accommodates students who may not do well on the national test, but whose families can afford the tuition, which is upward of US$200 (and may even exceed US$20,000). It is required of all secondary school students, public or private, to be taught subjects in English. However, students still must continue enrolling in Swahili courses. Most secondary school students, therefore, particularly those in rural regions, are multilingual in that they speak their native language, which is most often not Swahili or English. Secondary school students who pass the national examination can receive a diploma. Their scores on the test will determine how they proceed in tertiary education.

Tertiary Education

There are 21 colleges and universities in Tanzania. These institutions vary in focus. They can safely be divided into four categories: institutions of arts and sciences, medical academies, agricultural institutions, and technological institutions. Some universities are hybrids, such as the International Medical and Technological University in Dar es Salaam. Some universities, like the Open University of Tanzania, have introduced distance learning courses, especially for students in rural parts of the country. The most well-known is perhaps the University of Dar es Salaam, which was established in 1970, after the division of the colonial University of East Africa.

Teacher Education

Teacher education in Tanzania is controlled by three ministries of education. The Ministry of Education and Culture manages 48 teacher training institutions; 34 of these institutions are public teachers colleges and 14 other institutions are private. The second is the Ministry of Science, Technology and Higher Education, which controls teacher training within the universities. Finally, the Ministry of Labor, Youth Development and Sports controls teacher education for vocational schools.

The Teacher Education Department is responsible for provision of teacher education in the Ministry of Education and Culture. It deals with preparation of grade A and diploma teachers to satisfy teachers' needs for preschool, primary, and secondary education.

Informal Education

One of the most significant aspects of informal education in Tanzania is the country's commitment to eliminate illiteracy among its citizens. Some organizations, most significantly UNESCO, have contributed resources toward this effort; however, due to lack of funding and poor infrastructure, this agenda remains a challenge. Nevertheless, one major initiative that has been successful is secondary school for adults who wish to finish their secondary education. As stated above, this service helps adults achieve strong literacy and numeracy skills and also allows them to pursue technical and vocational training in several areas. There is also an effort on the part of both religious and secular organizations to promote informal schooling on the topic of healthcare and the control of deadly diseases, most notably HIV/AIDS.

System Economics

According to the United Nations Development Programme (2011), expenditures on education in Tanzania represented 6.8 percent of the gross domestic product in 2008. This amounts to over $4.313 billion. Despite this promising figure, per capita expenditure only amounts to $346. In contrast, per capita expenditure on education in the United States amounts to $15,258. Tanzania ranks 25 of 186 countries in terms of government expenditures on education. This is despite the fact that the average school life expectancy is five years.

Tanzania Education at a Glance

General Information

Capital	Dar es Salaam
Population	41.8 million
Languages	Swahili (Kiunguja), English, Arabic, other indigenous languages
Literacy rate	70%
GDP per capita	US$800
People below poverty line	36%
Number of phones per 100 people	<0.5
Number of Internet users per 100 people	1
Number of Internet hosts	24,182
Life expectancy at birth (years)	51

Formal Educational Information

Primary school age population	7.2 million
Secondary school age population	5.2 million
Primary school age population*	17%
Secondary school age population*	12.5%
Number of years of education (primary/secondary)	7/6
Student/teacher ratio (primary)	52
Student/teacher ratio (secondary)	19
Primary school gross enrollment ratio	110%
Primary school entrants reaching grade 5	85%
Secondary school gross enrollment ratio	6%
Child labor (ages 5–14)	36%

Notes: *Data indicate that nearly 30 percent (close to one-third) of the population of Tanzania are between the ages of five and 17 years.

Unless otherwise indicated, all data are based on sources from 2011.

Future Prospects

As in other sub-Saharan African nations, the main goal of the Tanzanian Ministry of Education is to improve the country's overall educational infrastructure. With help and support from international organizations and private donors, children and adults in Tanzania need to be familiarized with current technologies and highly skilled professions so that the country can compete in the global economy. In addition, more needs to be done to reduce the high rates of illiteracy throughout Tanzania, eliminate gender inequality, educate orphaned children whose parents died of AIDS, and provide education for rural citizens, most of who rely on agriculture for income.

Daniel Ness

REFERENCES

Central Intelligence Agency. *The CIA World Factbook.* New York: Skyhorse, 2011. https://www.cia.gov/library/publications/the-world-factbook/index.html.

Nation Master. 2011. www.nationmaster.com.

UNESCO. *Global Education Digest 2012: Comparing Education Statistics Across the World.* Montreal: UNESCO Institute for Statistics, 2012.

———. "Strong Foundations: Early Childhood Care and Education." *Education for All Global Monitoring Report.* Paris: UNESCO, 2006.

UNESCO–IBE. www.ibe.unesco.org/countries/Tanzania.htm.

UNESCO–UIS. www.uis.unesco.org.

United Nations Development Programme. *Human Development Report 2011.* http://hdr.undp.org/en.

World Bank Education Statistics. 2011. www.worldbank.org.

TOGO

Togo is a small country in West Africa. French Togoland achieved independence from France in 1960. At that point, the country became the Togolese Republic, or Togo in short. Despite its status as a democratic republic with multiparty elections, the country was ruled by Gnassingbe Eyadema, a former general, for nearly forty years. After years of protest and sanctions by foreign countries and international organizations for not allowing political opposition and a free democracy, in 2005, the Togolese government deposed Eyadema's son from power and restored the multiparty election system.

More than half of Togo's population has indigenous beliefs. Approximately 30 percent of the population is Christian and 20 percent is Muslim. There are 37 ethnic groups in Togo, making up 99 percent of the country's population. The most prominent are the Ewe, Kabre, and Mina. The remaining 1 percent of the population includes Europeans and Syrians.

Educational System

Like its neighbor, Benin, Togo has a fledgling system of education that until only recently has shown signs of development and improvement. Although the adult literacy rate in Togo is higher than that of Benin, its 30 percent gender gap in literacy is 10 percent larger, making it one of the most unbalanced countries in sub-Saharan Africa in terms of gender disparity between the education and literacy rate of males (75.5 percent) compared to that of females (47 percent). Togo is no different than most other countries in Western Africa in terms of education. The Togolese schooling system suffers from lack of adequately trained teachers, poor educational infrastructure, lack of books and other educational resources, a lack of computer networks and other technological resources, and poor education in rural regions. Another similarity to other countries is the disparity in educational attainment of urban children when compared to that of rural children. Families in rural areas to the north are poorer and yet are more likely to pay extra fees to teachers, who are paid very poorly when compared to teachers in Lomé and other urban areas in the country.

The only compulsory education period in Togo is primary school, which lasts for six years. Children are required to attend school between the ages of six and 11 years. Togolese primary school children are instructed in French, the official language of education and commerce. They also learn Ewe and Mina, the two most commonly spoken African languages in the country. Children are also expected to learn basic arithmetic, religion, and physical education. Similar to that of its neighboring countries, the primary school enrollment rate is 90 percent, an indication that all students who are eligible for primary education are not attending school. In addition, of those who do enroll in primary school, only three-quarters finish the fifth grade. Another factor related to low enrollment is the lack of child labor laws. According to UNICEF, nearly 30 percent of children between the ages of five and 14 years are engaged in some form of labor. The secondary education period lasts for seven years. Its structure is similar to the Beninese system, whereby students who complete their primary education can continue for four years in junior high school, and, if they are able to pass an exit examination from junior high school, another three years in senior high school. Senior high school is intended to prepare Togolese students for a university education. Some senior high school graduates are eligible to enroll in the University of Lomé, located in the capital. However, many students eligible for university education study abroad if they have the funds to do so.

System Economics and Future Prospects

According to the United Nations Development Programme (2011), total public expenditures on education in Togo represented 4.6 percent of the gross domestic product in 2009. Given the GDP of Togo at $6.324 billion, educational expenditure in the country amounts to nearly $291 million, or $143 per student (total amount equivalent to US dollars divided by 2,041,000, the approximate number of primary and secondary students in the country). Togo ranks 123 of 186 countries in percentage of educational expenditure.

The problems of education in Togo are similar to those of other countries in the region. Poor financial and physical resources and a lack of public transportation hamper students' ability to attend school. Competent, trained teachers are difficult to attract because few teacher training institutes are available in the country. The Togolese government and education officials need to attract teachers from neighboring countries or must depend on external organizations for assistance in finding qualified teachers. Many poor Togolese families cannot afford to send their children to school or do not realize the significance of education as a potentially economic benefit. Child

---

Togo Education at a Glance

General Information

Capital	Lomé
Population	6.5 million
Languages	French, Ewe and Mina, Kabye, Dagomba
Literacy rate	61%
GDP per capita	US$1,700
People below poverty line	32%
Number of phones per 100 people	2
Number of Internet users per 100 people	5
Number of Internet hosts	860
Life expectancy at birth (years)	58

Formal Educational Information

Primary school age population	1 million
Secondary school age population	1 million
Combined primary/secondary population*	31%
Number of years of education (primary/secondary)	6/7
Student/teacher ratio (primary)	34
Student/teacher ratio (secondary)	30
Primary school gross enrollment ratio	90%
Primary school entrants reaching grade 5	75%
Secondary school gross enrollment ratio	40%
Child labor (ages 5–14)	29%

Notes: *Slightly over 31 percent of Togo's population falls between the ages five and 14 years (schoolage children).

Unless otherwise indicated, all data are based on sources from 2011.

labor is not uncommon in the country. Accordingly, many children and adolescents do not see the need for an education. Also, rural families do not have the type of technology that might be available to those who live in urban settings. This might also result in the lack of willingness on the part of rural families to seek education for their children. Therefore, it would be imperative for the Togolese government to find ways of educating all students who are eligible for both primary and secondary education. The institutionalization of information and communication technologies may enable more educational possibilities for rural children.

Daniel Ness and Chia-ling Lin

REFERENCES

Central Intelligence Agency. *The CIA World Factbook.* New York: Skyhorse, 2010. https://www.cia.gov/library/publications/the-world-factbook/index.html.

Nation Master. 2011. www.nationmaster.com.

UNESCO. *Global Education Digest 2006: Comparing Education Statistics Across the World.* Montreal: UNESCO Institute for Statistics, 2006.

———. "Strong Foundations: Early Childhood Care and Education." *Education for All Global Monitoring Report 2007.* Paris: UNESCO, 2006.

UNESCO–IBE. www.ibe.unesco.org/countries/Togo.htm.

United Nations Development Programme. *Human Development Report 2010.* New York: Palgrave Macmillan, 2010.

World Bank Education Statistics. 2011. www.worldbank.org.

TUNISIA

Tunisia is the northernmost country in Africa. The official language is Arabic, although French is also used for commerce and in some colleges and universities. Roughly 98 percent of the population is Tunisian. The remaining 2 percent includes Berbers and Europeans. Approximately 98 percent of the population is Muslim. The remaining 2 percent consists of Christians and Jews.

The country has a rich history that dates back to ancient Roman times. Earliest evidence of Tunisian society dates to the tenth century BCE, when Phoenicians settled on the coast. Within one century, the Phoenicians established the city of Carthage, which,

after the Second Punic War with Rome, became a central hub of trade and transportation during the growth of the Roman Empire. Berber tribes, however, always inhabited the region. By 1881 France had created a protectorate in present-day Tunisia. Tunisia finally became independent from France in 1956. Habib Bourguiba, the country's first president, took a hard-line stance against Muslim fundamentalists, allowing Tunisia to develop into a somewhat moderate political state. Tunisia has the most egalitarian system for women of all Arab nations. It has one of the most open political systems as well.

Educational System

Tunisia's education system improved greatly after gaining independence from France in 1956. Reform efforts at every educational level indicate that the Tunisian government has emphasized education from the perspective of economic growth and stability, as well as the changing needs of its population. Since independence, the Tunisian educational system followed the French model (see section on France on page 528) and slowly emerged in the 1960s and 1970s with an emphasis on Arabic. Tunisia's position among developing countries ranks high in terms of academic performance. Among the Arab nations, Tunisia's students rank the highest in the Trends in International Mathematics and Science Study (TIMSS). Moreover, education is one of the Tunisian government's main concerns.

Precompulsory and Compulsory Education, Curriculum, Assessment, and Instruction

In Tunisia preschool education accommodates children between three and six years old. There are three general types of preschools in the country: kindergartens, *kouttabs*, and preparatory-years institutions. Kindergartens prepare children to become socially responsible and, to some extent, infuse some academic content into the curriculum. They are funded by private donors and local public districts. Kindergartens are under the auspices of the Ministry of Women, Family and Childhood. *Kouttabs* are religious preschools that train young children in the study of the Quran. To some extent, these institutions provide a slightly greater emphasis on academic education, such as mathematical skills, at the preschool level. The *kouttabs*, which are one of the few institutions in the Arab world that promotes gender equality, are under the Ministry of Religious Affairs. Preparatory-year institutions are under the auspices of the Ministry of Education and Training. They are mostly public but not compulsory.

Tunisian primary education is six years in duration. Students must pass an exam for exiting the primary education level. Unfortunately, due to a high cut-off point for passing the examination, many students must repeat grade levels. This can pose problems later, given that many students who fail the examination cannot find employment. Government initiatives in recent years have rectified the problem to an extent since more students are passing the examination. It is not clear whether the content on the examination was simplified, the bar was lowered, or students were learning more.

Upon completion of primary education, students continue for three years in the lower secondary level, which is known as preparatory education. After this nine-year point, students must take a national examination of basic education. Those who pass are awarded a diploma. The Tunisian Ministry of Education emphasizes curriculum for gifted students as a means of increasing potential of academically able students to enter scientific, artistic, and literary disciplines at the university level.

After the nine-year basic education period, students who pass an examination have the opportunity to continue for four years in secondary education—a stepping-stone to the university. There are two stages at the secondary level. The first two-year stage stresses advanced general education. In the second two years of the program, students select from five specializations: language, mathematics, economics, practical sciences, and experimental or theoretical sciences. Students who do not pursue a university education have the opportunity to enter professional and vocational programs. These programs are under the auspices of the Ministry of Employment. In addition, students who complete the first two years of secondary school can enroll in two-year vocational programs. Professional and vocational programs include the areas of tourism, agriculture, business and management, and numerous technical skill careers.

Tertiary Education

The Higher Education Law, enacted in 1969, streamlined higher education programs in that any government-recognized higher education or university-level program must be under the direction of the University of Tunis. Established in 1960, the University of Tunis is the oldest university in the country. There are approximately 180 higher education institutions in the country, but they are under the auspices of the University of Tunis. Among these institutions, there are 13 universities, 24 technical colleges, and six teacher training institutions. The remaining 137 institutions are two-year technical or professional training centers. Higher education in Tunisia expanded from approximately 105,000 students in the mid-1990s to 365,000 in 2005. The student population increased 50 percent in 2010. These data are encouraging. However, if student growth in higher education continues and education infrastructure and curriculum content are not redesigned, the country's graduates run the risk of being unemployed upon graduation.

Teacher Education

As stated above, there are six teacher training institutions in Tunisia. Other than these institutions, individuals who wish to prepare for teaching licenses in Tunisia must contact the Ministry of Education and Training. In addition, those who specialize in a particular academic discipline may be qualified to teach in secondary schools in Tunisia.

Informal Education

Informal education in Tunisia is fairly uncommon and is something that the ministry might wish to address. Although public education institutions in Tunisia may have the financial resources to provide both children and adults with the opportunities of informal education, the Tunisian government does not seem to believe that informal education is a necessary component of learning at the present time. This is despite knowledge showing that informal education programs can contribute to the elimination of illiteracy, a problem with which Tunisia must contend, given a literacy rate of 75 percent of the population.

```
┌──────────────────────────────────────────────────┐
│           Tunisia Education at a Glance            │
│                                                    │
│  General Information                               │
│  Capital                                    Tunis  │
│  Population                           10.5 million │
│  Languages              Arabic (official), French  │
│  Literacy rate                                74%  │
│  GDP per capita                         US$8,800   │
│  People below poverty line                     7%  │
│  Number of phones per 100 people               12  │
│  Number of Internet users per 100 people     26.5  │
│  Number of Internet hosts                     490  │
│  Life expectancy at birth (years)              75  │
│                                                    │
│  Formal Educational Information                    │
│  Primary school age population          1 million  │
│  Secondary school age population      1.4 million  │
│  Primary school age population               10%   │
│  Number of years of education                      │
│     (primary/secondary)                       6/7  │
│  Student/teacher ratio (primary)               20  │
│  Student/teacher ratio (secondary)             17  │
│  Primary school gross enrollment ratio       110%  │
│  Primary school entrants reaching grade 5     97%  │
│  Secondary school gross enrollment ratio      83%  │
│  Child labor (ages 5–14)                  no data  │
│                                                    │
│  Note: Unless otherwise indicated, all data are    │
│  based on sources from 2011.                       │
└──────────────────────────────────────────────────┘
```

System Economics

According to the United Nations Development Programme (2011), total public expenditures on education in Tunisia represented 7.2 percent of the gross domestic product in 2008. This amounts to over $7.3 billion, or $2,909 per student (total amount equivalent to US dollars divided by 2,517,000, the approximate number of students in the country). The only other country spending 7.2 percent of its GDP on education is Burundi.

Future Prospects

The largest educational concern in Tunisia is to determine how to fix a somewhat old school infrastructure. In addition, despite promising trends in promoting gender equality and political neutrality, education access remains unequally distributed in Tunisia. There have also been several other reforms since independence to further improve the education system at all levels. First, part of the reform efforts in Tunisia since 1958 was to emphasize the Arabic language, literature, and history of North Africa in the schools at all levels. Second, by 1991, the New Education Act lengthened the number of primary and secondary years by one year (from 12 to 13). In addition, compulsory education included all children from six to 16 years of age. Third, by 2000, the Tunisia Ministry of Education focused on competency-based learning for improving examination scores. Finally, in 2002, a law was enacted that integrated information and communication technologies (ICT) into the curriculum. Despite these promising trends, however, with a literacy rate of almost 75 percent, Tunisia still faces difficulties with illiteracy.

Daniel Ness and Chia-ling Lin

REFERENCES

Central Intelligence Agency. *The CIA World Factbook.* New York: Skyhorse, 2011. https://www.cia.gov/library/publications/the-world-factbook/index.html.

Nation Master. 2011. www.nationmaster.com.

UNESCO. *Global Education Digest 2012: Comparing Education Statistics Across the World.* Montreal: UNESCO Institute for Statistics, 2012.

———. "Strong Foundations: Early Childhood Care and Education." *Education for All Global Monitoring Report.* Paris: UNESCO, 2006.

UNESCO–IBE. www.ibe.unesco.org/countries/Tunisia.htm.

UNESCO–UIS. www.uis.unesco.org.

UNICEF. www.unicef.org/infobycountry/Tunisia.html.

United Nations Development Programme. *Human Development Report 2011.* http://hdr.undp.org/en.

UGANDA

Uganda is a landlocked country in south-central Africa. Uganda was a former colony of the United Kingdom, consisting of numerous tribes with different cultures and languages. Even after independence in 1962, the country had difficulty in maintaining peace among the various groups. Under the dictatorial leadership of Idi Amin in the 1970s, nearly 300,000 opponents of Amin died as a result of antigovernment speech. The next ruler, Milton Obote, was responsible for additional uprisings that claimed another 100,000 lives. From 1986 to the present, the Ugandan government has been more or less stable. However, given the new, highly controversial antigay laws that have been proposed by the Ugandan parliament, social and political unrest still remains. Natural resources in the country include copper, cobalt, hydropower, limestone, and salt. The country is quite fertile, particularly within several miles on both sides of the Nile River. Approximately 42 percent of the country's population is Roman Catholic. The same percentage of Uganda's population is Protestant (mostly Anglican). More than 12 percent of the population is Muslim. Making up 70 percent of the population, the largest ethnic groups in Uganda include Baganda, Banyakole, Basoga, Bakiga, Iteso, Langi, Acholi, Bagisu, Lugbara, and Bunyoro tribes.

Educational System

Although education in Uganda consists of seven years of primary education and six years of secondary education, few students have the opportunity to enter secondary school. The number of students receiving primary education increased more than threefold since the 1980s—from 2 million in 1986 to approximately 6.3 million today. Since 1997 families with four or more children have been eligible to receive free education. Regardless of this seemingly positive outcome, less than half of all primary school students complete the fifth grade. Moreover, there is a disparity between males and females in the rate of literacy, with 77 percent of all males knowing how to read and write compared to only 58 percent of all females. Another possible dilemma is the fact that the majority of teachers in the schools throughout the country conduct their lessons in English. This poses problems for children of different ethnic backgrounds whose families speak different languages altogether. Also, classrooms are often filled to capacity, so much so that additional students who are enrolled in a particular school cannot find a place to sit.

Education for children and older students in northern districts of the country is particularly in dire need of aid. There are some 200 primary schools in northern Uganda, particularly the districts to the north and east of the Nile River. Of these schools, many of them are held outdoors because few facilities are able to accommodate large numbers of students. In some instances, the student/teacher ratio is as high as 200 to 1. Further, families who live in these regions have limited service for Internet capability, electricity, and continuous running water. As a result, students remain in poverty as adults because many

of them cannot complete primary school and others cannot travel long distances to attend secondary school even if they do have the skills to continue their education.

Nearly half of all students who graduate from primary school have the opportunity or skills to enter secondary school. Secondary schools in Uganda are divided into lower and upper levels—both levels are three years each for a total of six years. Students who do not have the ability to enter lower secondary school may have an option to enter a three-year technical school as an alternative. Students who are able to complete the lower secondary school but who are not accepted to upper secondary school may have the option of entering two-year institutes. These institutes prepare students for occupations that demand high-level skills and abilities as well as occupations related to education, such as teacher training centers and school administration. Upper-level secondary schools prepare students who are seeking university education. Many secondary schools throughout the country are single-gender schools, and most of these schools are funded by the Roman Catholic Church or various Protestant denominations.

The secondary school gross enrollment rate in Uganda is only 18 percent. This means that only 70,000 upper-level secondary school students are eligible to attend universities. Unfortunately, even with this small number of students graduating from upper secondary school, only 20,000 to 30,000 of these students actually attend universities. Otherwise, students must travel abroad to attend higher education institutions if their families can afford to send them. There are approximately 25 public and private universities in Uganda. More than half of these universities, which enroll only a small fraction of those eligible for university education, are religiously affiliated institutions. Of these institutions, Makerere University in Kampala is the largest and oldest university in the country.

System Economics and Future Prospects

According to the United Nations Development Programme (2011), along with Hong Kong, Montserrat, and Qatar, public expenditures on education in Uganda represented 3.3 percent of the gross domestic product in 2009. Given the GDP of Uganda at

$45.9 billion, educational expenditure in the country amounts to nearly $1.5 billion, or $142 per student (total amount equivalent to US dollars divided by 10,603,000, the approximate number of primary and secondary students in the country). Uganda ranks 139 of 186 countries in percentage of educational expenditure.

In order to improve its standing in the world, the Ugandan government must invest its resources in improving the extremely low literacy rate. This can be done through both formal and informal education programs. Moreover, families must be committed to move beyond a solely agricultural and industrial society to an information-based society that can compete internationally. School attendance is extremely low, and like teachers in neighboring countries, teachers in Uganda are often poorly educated. Schools in Uganda are in dire need of infrastructural repair as well as financial resources for books and supplies and for curriculum development. Also, Uganda's rural populations, like those of its neighbors, are large, widespread, and often disinclined to change. Moreover, families in Uganda are unable to afford

the fees that are associated with a child's education. Families must pay for books and supplies as well as travel to and from school. Uganda is lagging behind many developing countries of Africa in this regard. Further, Uganda has one of the highest populations of people between five and 17 (nearly one-third of the total population). So, although the country's GDP is average to above average for a population of more than 30 million people, more than 30 percent must share a relatively meager amount of school funding (i.e., slightly over the equivalent of $1 billion for more than 10 million primary and secondary school students. It is also important to note that virulent homophobia is severe throughout the country. The Ugandan Parliament has been considering a measure that, at its most heinous, extreme level, would allow officials to execute men and women who are gay. If passed, the infamous bill would be considered one of the most flagrant violations of human rights to be instituted in modern times, certainly in the twenty-first century.

Daniel Ness and Chia-ling Lin

REFERENCES

Central Intelligence Agency. *The CIA World Factbook*. New York: Skyhorse, 2011. https://www.cia.gov/library/publications/the-world-factbook/index.html.

Nation Master. 2011. www.nationmaster.com.

UNESCO. *Global Education Digest 2012: Comparing Education Statistics Across the World*. Montreal: UNESCO Institute for Statistics, 2012.

———. "Strong Foundations: Early Childhood Care and Education." *Education for All Global Monitoring Report*. Paris: UNESCO, 2006.

UNESCO–IBE. www.ibe.unesco.org/countries/Uganda.htm.

United Nations Development Programme. *Human Development Report 2011*. http://hdr.undp.org/en.

World Bank Education Statistics. 2011. www.worldbank.org.

WESTERN SAHARA

Western Sahara is a territory that had been fully annexed by Morocco when the Mauritanian army withdrew from the region in 1976. Despite its fairly large land area and relatively small population, the territory has a population growth rate of 3.72, ranking fourth in the world, behind Liberia, Burundi,

---

Uganda Education at a Glance

General Information

Capital	Kampala
Population	33.3 million
Languages	English, Ganda, Niger-Congo languages, Nilo-Saharan languages, Swahili, Arabic
Literacy rate	67%
GDP per capita	US$1,900
People below poverty line	35%
Number of phones per 100 people	<0.1
Number of Internet users per 100 people	7.5
Number of Internet hosts	19,927
Life expectancy at birth (years)	52

Formal Educational Information

Primary school age population	6.3 million
Secondary school age population	4.2 million
Primary/secondary school age population*	32%
Number of years of education (primary/secondary)	7/6
Student/teacher ratio (primary)	52
Student/teacher ratio (secondary)	21
Primary school gross enrollment ratio	118%
Primary school entrants reaching grade 5	49%
Secondary school gross enrollment ratio	18%
Child labor (ages 5–14)	36%

Notes: *Nearly one-third of Uganda's population (32 percent) consists of individuals between five and 18 years (school age).

Unless otherwise indicated, all data are based on sources from 2011.

Western Sahara Education at a Glance

General Information

Capital	none (El Aaiún is considered a regional capital)
Population	507,160
Languages	Berber, Hassaniya Arabic, Spanish, French
Literacy rate	no data
GDP per capita	US$2,500
People below poverty line	no data
Number of phones per 100 people	no data
Number of Internet users per 100 people	no data
Number of Internet hosts	no data
Life expectancy at birth (years)	61

Formal Educational Information

Primary school age population	approx. 130,000
Secondary school age population	approx. 130,000
Primary school age population	approx. 25%
Secondary school age population	approx. 25%
Number of years of education (primary/secondary)	6/6
Student/teacher ratio (primary)	approx. 25
Student/teacher ratio (secondary)	approx. 20
Primary school gross enrollment ratio	no data
Primary school entrants reaching grade 5	no data
Secondary school gross enrollment ratio	no data
Child labor (ages 5–14)*	approx. 8%

Notes: *Data based on the estimated child labor percentage of Morocco.

Unless otherwise indicated, all data are based on sources from 2011.

and Afghanistan. Education in the region is generally controlled by the Kingdom of Morocco, which has imposed its own form of curriculum on the territory's people. Arabic is the common language in schools in Western Sahara. In the third-grade level, students begin to learn French. Many families have the opportunity to send their young children to preschool for a two-year period. Primary school is six years in duration. This is followed by three years of preparatory school and another three years of high school. Students who successfully complete high school receive a baccalaureate degree and may continue to the university, most often in Morocco, since Western Sahara does not have a university.

Daniel Ness and Chia-ling Lin

REFERENCES

Central Intelligence Agency. *The CIA World Factbook.* New York: Skyhorse, 2011. https://www.cia.gov/library/publications/the-world-factbook/index.html.

UNESCO. *Global Education Digest 2012: Comparing Education Statistics Across the World.* Montreal: UNESCO Institute for Statistics, 2012.

————. "Strong Foundations: Early Childhood Care and Education." *Education for All Global Monitoring Report.* Paris: UNESCO, 2006.

United Nations Development Programme. *Human Development Report 2011.* http://hdr.undp.org/en.

ZAMBIA

Zambia is a landlocked country located in the southern region of Africa. The official language of Zambia is English, but numerous indigenous languages, such as Bemba, are spoken by various groups depending on region. One problem, then, is to reconcile formal education practice in a common language with the preservation and survival of indigenous languages.

The population estimate for the region in 2011 was 13.8 million. Ethnic groups in Zambia are African (98.7 percent), European (1.1 percent), and other (0.2 percent). The dominant religion is Christian. However, there are numerous syncretic adherents—namely, those who have a mixture of Christian and indigenous beliefs. In addition, approximately 25 percent of the population in Zambia is Hindu or Muslim. Zambia gained independence from Great Britain in 1964.

Educational System

Based on statutes set forth by the Zambian government that are initially suggested by the country's Ministry of Education, Zambia has a system of education that institutes compulsory schooling. Nevertheless, education laws and regulations are often ineffective and lack clarity. Moreover, individual schools and preparation programs do not always follow these laws.

Precompulsory and Compulsory Education, Curriculum, Assessment, and Instruction

In Zambia, there are three general levels of education: primary school, junior secondary school, and upper secondary school. Primary school lasts from grades 1 through 7, lower secondary school from grades 8 to 9, and upper secondary school from grades 10 to 12. The notion of "basic school" includes both primary and junior secondary levels, which are also the compulsory education years. However, only primary school is free for families. As a result, most students do not reach upper secondary school levels. The Zambian education system has been more successful than those in neighboring countries in terms of the percentage of students who complete primary education. Approximately 94 percent of students in the primary level complete the fifth grade. This rate is high when compared to that of Democratic Republic of the Congo, which is at 55 percent, Mozambique at 62.5 percent, Malawi at 58 percent, or Angola at 75 percent. The Zambian education system controls the curriculum of both public, government-funded schools and private schools. The private schools in Zambia are run mostly by various Christian denominations, whose curricula tend to be more diverse (e.g., classes in religion) than those in public schools. Both the United States and the United Kingdom systems of education strongly influence the curriculum in Zambian schools. English is the official language, particularly toward the end of primary school and in lower and upper secondary schools.

Tertiary Education

College and university education in Zambia is restricted in the sense that students have few institutions from which to select. Many students who are eligible for university education enroll in foreign universities if they can afford to do so. Nevertheless, there are at least six university-level institutions in the country: Cavendish University, Copperbelt University, Northrise University, University of Zambia, Zambia Adventist University (a religiously affiliated institution), and Zambia Open University. Located near Lusaka and established in 1966, the University of Zambia is the largest and oldest higher education institution in the country.

Teacher Education

Zambia has extemporized teacher training programs that are desperately lacking in both physical and financial resources. Teacher training does not generally take place in colleges, universities, or specialized teacher training institutions. Instead, teacher training often takes place in informal, makeshift environments that the Education Ministry develops for preservice teachers. Few universities in Zambia have annexed portions that serve as teacher training and pedagogical institutes. Students who graduate from these institutions most often become secondary education teachers in the most elite schools in the country. For example, the Nkrumah College of Education, affiliated with the University of Zambia, was established in 1967 to prepare teachers for the lower secondary school period, while those who prepared for the upper secondary level enrolled in courses at both Nkrumah and the University of Zambia.

At the same time, educational intervention initiatives by the Commonwealth of Learning, a British-based intergovernmental organization that is under the auspices of the Commonwealth Heads of Government, have assisted developing countries, such as Zambia, to overhaul their educational infrastructures by encouraging the implementation of learning technologies and distance education and improving these countries' access to better education and vocational training. Nevertheless, Zambia still faces many challenges. The country has severe problems with HIV/AIDS among adults and children who were born to parents with HIV. Schoolteachers have difficulty grappling with the extent of pain and suffering caused by HIV. In addition, little is being done in providing teachers with the resources to help families combat the epidemic. Zambia has a record of political instability that has both directly and indirectly thwarted efforts to meet basic needs of its citizens in ways that will positively influence educational endeavors.

Informal Education

One of the most important educational initiatives of Zambia is to maintain or increase the adult literacy rate. With the help of outside agencies and philanthropic organizations, the Zambian education system has initiated programs that enable adults to learn how to read and write. Other important informal education venues in Zambia are centers that emphasize the importance of health education, especially given the rather high prevalence rate of HIV/AIDS in the country. Some of these philanthropic organizations have collaborated with local agencies in promoting healthy living habits and lifestyles that will in the end prevent children from becoming orphans at young ages.

Zambia Education at a Glance

General Information

Capital	Lusaka
Population	13.4 million
Languages*	English (official), Bemba, Kaonda, Lozi, Lunda, Luvale, Nyanja, Tonga
Literacy rate	81%
GDP per capita	US$1,000
People below poverty line	86%
Number of phones per 100 people	<1
Number of Internet users per 100 people	5
Number of Internet hosts	14,771
Life expectancy at birth (years)	39

Formal Educational Information

Primary school age population	2.2 million
Secondary school age population	1.3 million
Primary/secondary school age population	27%
Number of years of education (primary/secondary)	7/5
Student/teacher ratio (primary)	51
Student/teacher ratio (secondary)	34
Primary school gross enrollment ratio	115%
Primary school entrants reaching grade 5	94%
Secondary school gross enrollment ratio	30%
Child labor (ages 5–14)	12%

Notes: *In addition to the languages mentioned, there are over 70 indigenous languages in Zambia, many of which cannot be used for correspondence or written communication.

Unless otherwise indicated, all data are based on sources from 2011.

System Economics

Based on 2008 estimates, according to the United Nations Development Programme (2011), along with the total public expenditures on education in Haiti, that of Zambia represented 1.4 percent of the gross domestic product. These countries rank 178 of 186 in terms of government expenditures on education. Most of the expenditure is allocated for the primary level. Nevertheless, this amounts to a mere $70 per student in Zambia.

Future Prospects

Two major problems in education in Zambia are the attrition rates of students and low per capita government educational expenditures. These problems alone are the result of poor infrastructure and reliance on outside sources for educational opportunity. In Zambia, one important source is the Cecily Eastwood Zambian AIDS Orphans Appeal, or Cecily's Fund.

As a 501(c)(3) nonprofit organization in the United States, the charity is called the American Friends of Cecily's Fund. This source provides more than 11,000 students, particularly those whose parents or guardians are HIV-positive or have died of AIDS, with funds so they can obtain an education. Although Zambia has a relatively high rate of literacy, perhaps due to strong influences from colonial schooling practices, the country needs to improve the overall educational infrastructure, especially by emphasizing up-to-date modes of technology and communication for training the workforce in service-related professions. It is also worthwhile noting that although Zambia invests a medium to high percentage of its labor sectors to services, the overwhelming majority of the labor force remains in agriculture. This indicates that more needs to be done in terms of Zambia's growth and development in education as well as technology and communication improvements.

Daniel Ness and Chia-ling Lin

REFERENCES

Central Intelligence Agency. *The CIA World Factbook.* New York: Skyhorse, 2011. https://www.cia.gov/library/publications/the-world-factbook/index.html.

EFA. "Strong Foundations: Early Childhood Care and Education." *Education for All Global Monitoring Report.* Paris: UNESCO, 2006.

GED. *Global Education Digest 2012: Comparing Education Statistics Across the World.* Montreal: UNESCO Institute for Statistics, 2012.

Nation Master. 2011. www.nationmaster.com.

UNESCO–IBE. www.ibe.unesco.org/countries/Zambia.htm.

United Nations Development Programme. *Human Development Report 2011.* http://hdr.undp.org/en.

World Bank Education Statistics. 2011. www.worldbank.org.

ZIMBABWE

Zimbabwe is a landlocked country located in the southern region of Africa. The official language of the country is English. However, numerous regional languages are spoken in Zimbabwe, Shona being one of the most common. There are also other indigenous languages spoken by various smaller cultural groups. Educational improvement in the country depends on the ability of Zimbabwean schools to provide literacy for all citizens while accommodating students whose spoken languages differ in particular communities. The population estimate for Zimbabwe in 2011 was 12 million. Ethnic groups in Zimbabwe are African (98 percent), Asian (1 percent), and European (1 percent). The dominant religion is Christian. However, there are numerous syncretic adherents who have a mixture of Christian and indigenous beliefs.

Educational System

The Zimbabwean government mandates compulsory schooling for primary and secondary children. However, education laws and school requirements are often ignored by children and their families. As in neighboring countries, individual schools in various parts of Zimbabwe do not always follow governmental laws and school requirements.

Precompulsory and Compulsory Education, Curriculum, Assessment, and Instruction

In Zimbabwe there are three general levels of education: primary school, lower secondary school, and upper secondary school. Primary school consists of seven years of education—ages six to 13—devoted to a basic primary school curriculum that emphasizes literacy and some arithmetic. Lower secondary school consists of a four-year period that continues the basic education that students cover in primary school. Most students at this level are between the ages of 13 and 17. Successful completion of the lower secondary school level is needed in order for students to enroll in upper secondary school, which lasts for two years. This period prepares students, mostly between 17 and 19 years of age, who are college- or university-bound. Zimbabwe's dropout rate is higher than those of neighboring countries. This is clearly evident when examining attrition rates of students from one grade level to the next. For example, compared to the percentage of students who complete fifth grade in Zambia, only 70 percent of primary students in Zimbabwe complete fifth grade. On the other hand, the literacy rates of both countries are approximately the same. In fact, Zimbabwe's literacy rate is slightly higher and is more equal in terms of gender.

Tertiary Education

There are at least sixteen institutions of higher education in Zimbabwe. The most well-known is the University of Zimbabwe in Harare. Established in 1952, it is the oldest university in the country and, with approximately 12,000 students, has the largest enrollment. As an outgrowth of the University of London, the University of Zimbabwe is modeled after the British higher education system. Excluding several universities in South Africa and the American University of Cairo, the University of Zimbabwe, according to the Quacquarelli Symonds World University Rankings, ranks second among all universities in Africa. Only the University of Tanzania in Dar es Salaam ranks higher.

Teacher Education

Zimbabwe has makeshift teacher training programs that lack both physical and financial resources. Teacher training practices often occur in informal, provisional environments that the Education Ministry of the country has developed for teacher preparation—primarily for primary-level schooling. Few universities in Zimbabwe have departments or pedagogical institutes for the purpose of teacher training. Graduates from these institutions often prepare for certification as secondary education teachers, particularly in schools that are unaffordable for most of the population.

The Commonwealth of Learning, a British-based intergovernmental organization, has assisted Zimbabwe in improving its educational infrastructure by fostering development of learning technologies and distance education and increasing Zimbabweans' access to better education and vocational training. The Commonwealth of Learning has also established initiatives to counteract the adverse effects of HIV/AIDS on students in Zimbabwe, a country where international health agencies have estimated that more than 120,000 children are HIV-positive. These initiatives have helped schoolteachers' efforts to control the extent of the epidemic. Teachers are more and more on the frontlines of the AIDs epidemic, yet they rarely receive education about the epidemic that will help them serve dual roles as teachers on the one hand and as support and health counselors to both children and adolescent populations who are dealing in various ways with HIV and AIDS. In addition, from a political perspective, little is being done to provide teachers with the resources to help families combat the epidemic. Zimbabwe, although a republic, nevertheless has a record of political instability that has both directly and indirectly thwarted efforts to meet the basic needs of its citizens in ways that will positively influence educational endeavors.

Informal Education

Promotion of literacy and the eradication of illiteracy, particularly among females, are two important factors in the informal education practice of Zimbabwe. With the help of outside agencies and philanthropic organizations, the Zimbabwe education system has enabled many adults to learn how to read and write for the purpose of retooling skills for a changing job market. Other important informal education venues in Zimbabwe are centers that emphasize the importance of health education as well as those that promote healthy living habits and lifestyles. The purpose of these centers is to prevent children from becoming orphans at young ages.

System Economics

Ranked at 87 of 186, Zimbabwe spends approximately 4.6 percent of its gross domestic product on education. Other countries with the same percentage of GDP devoted to education are Burkina Faso, Côte D'Ivoire, and the Czech Republic. However, in Zimbabwe, per capita educational expenditure amounts to less than $43 annually.

Future Prospects

Two major problems in education in Zimbabwe are high attrition rates of students and low per capita government educational expenditures. These problems alone are the result of poor infrastructure and reliance on outside sources for educational opportunity. Although Zimbabwe has a relatively high rate of literacy, probably as a result of strong influences from colonial schooling practices, there is a need for the government and Ministry of Education to improve the overall educational infrastructure. The country is in dire need of more current modes of technology and communication for training the workforce in service-related professions. It is also worthwhile noting that although Zimbabwe invests a medium to high percentage of its labor sector to services, the overwhelming majority of its labor force remains in agriculture. Given the high rate of subsistence farming in Zimbabwe, many families will find it difficult to transform from an agricultural economy into an industrial or service economy. In addition, despite the transition from a colony of the United Kingdom to a republic in 1979, the country has been governed by a single autocratic ruler for decades. This factor stymied economic and political progress and adversely affected the educational system.

Daniel Ness and Chia-ling Lin

REFERENCES

Central Intelligence Agency. *The CIA World Factbook.* New York: Skyhorse, 2011. https://www.cia.gov/library/publications/the-world-factbook/index.html.

Zimbabwe Education at a Glance

General Information

Capital	Harare (formerly Salisbury)
Population	11.6 million
Languages	English (official), Shona, Sindebele; numerous indigenous languages
Literacy rate	91%
GDP per capita	US$2,100
People below poverty line	80%
Number of phones per 100 people	3
Number of Internet users per 100 people	12
Number of Internet hosts	29,866
Life expectancy at birth (years)	40

Formal Educational Information

Primary school age population	2.4 million
Secondary school age population	2 million
Primary/secondary school age population*	38.5%
Number of years of education (primary/secondary)	7/6
Student/teacher ratio (primary)	39
Student/teacher ratio (secondary)	22
Primary school gross enrollment ratio	96%
Primary school entrants reaching grade 5	70%
Secondary school gross enrollment ratio	37%
Child labor (ages 5–14)	13%

Notes: *With approximately 40 percent of its population between the ages of five and 18, Zimbabwe ranks among the highest countries in population of school-age persons.

Unless otherwise indicated, all data are based on sources from 2011.

Nation Master. 2011. www.nationmaster.com.

Quacquarelli Symonds World University Rankings. 2012. www.topuniversities.com/university-rankings/world-university-rankings.

UNESCO. *Global Education Digest 2012: Comparing Education Statistics Across the World.* Montreal: UNESCO Institute for Statistics, 2012.

———. "Strong Foundations: Early Childhood Care and Education." *Education for All Global Monitoring Report.* Paris: UNESCO, 2006.

UNESCO–IBE. www.ibe.unesco.org/countries/Zimbabwe.htm.

United Nations Development Programme. *Human Development Report 2011.* http://hdr.undp.org/en.

World Bank Education Statistics. 2011. www.worldbank.org.

REFERENCE